CANADIAN CRIMINAL JUSTICE

Curt T. Griffiths
and
Simon N. Verdun-Jones

School of Criminology
Simon Fraser University

Butterworths
Toronto and Vancouver

Canadian Criminal Justice
© 1989 Butterworths Canada Ltd.

Printed and bound in Canada

The Butterworth Group of Companies

Canada
Butterworths Canada Ltd., 75 Clegg Road, MARKHAM, ONT. L6G 1A1 and 409 Granville St., Suite 1455, VANCOUVER, B.C. V6C 1T2
Australia
Butterworths Pty Ltd., SYDNEY, MELBOURNE, BRISBANE, ADELAIDE, PERTH, CANBERRA and HOBART
Ireland
Butterworth (Ireland) Ltd., DUBLIN
New Zealand
Butterworths of New Zealand Ltd., WELLINGTON and AUCKLAND
Puerto Rico
Equity de Puerto Rico, Inc., HATO REY
Singapore
Malayan Law Journal Pte Ltd., SINGAPORE
United Kingdom
Butterworth & Co. (Publishers) Ltd., LONDON and EDINBURGH
United States
Butterworth Legal Publishers, AUSTIN, Texas; BOSTON, Massachusetts; CLEARWATER, Florida (D. & S. Publishers); ORFORD, New Hampshire (Equity Publishing); ST. PAUL, Minnesota; and SEATTLE, Washington

Canadian Cataloguing in Publication Data

Griffiths, Curt T. (Curt Taylor), 1948-
    Canadian criminal justice

Bibliography: p.
Includes index.
ISBN 0-409-83453-X

1. Criminal justice, Administration of – Canada.
I. Verdun-Jones, Simon N. (Simon Nicholas),
1947-   .   II. Title.

KE8813.G74 1989   345.71'05   C89-094311-7
KF9223.G74 1989

Sponsoring Editor: Gloria Vitale
Editor: Anne Butler
Cover Design: Julian Cleva
Production: Nancy Harding

For

Karen, Collin and Lacey
and to
the memory of Lance Cpl. L.R. Crase (U.S.M.C.)

Curt Taylor Griffiths

For

Carmen and Maritza

Simon N. Verdun-Jones

PREFACE

Among the most critical components of any society are the arrangements for identifying and responding to criminal offenders. This is no less true in Canada, although historically our close proximity to the United States has tended to obscure the unique attributes of the Canadian criminal justice system. Scholars and students on both sides of the border have often assumed that the Canadian criminal justice system was a mirror image of its southern counterpart.

Prior to the 1970s, there were few critical analyses of the criminal justice process in this country. Of the published literature, most was descriptive in nature. The past decade, however, has witnessed a veritable explosion of empirical research on all phases of the criminal justice process. This research has included field studies, historical analyses, and national surveys conducted by scholars from a variety of disciplines, psychology, criminology, sociology, law, political science, history and public administration. As well, there has been an expanded capacity for criminal justice agencies and ministries to conduct research.

The findings of this interdisciplinary effort have confirmed the uniqueness of the Canadian criminal justice system while challenging much of the "common wisdom" and many of the "myths" that have surrounded the origins, development and operation of criminal justice.

A primary objective of this text is to capture the "spirit" of this new era of study of the Canadian criminal justice system. Throughout the following chapters, we attempt to provide the broad outlines of the structure and operation of the criminal justice process, while at the same time identifying many of the critical issues confronting the criminal justice system. A major theme of the book is that the structure and operation of the criminal justice system is strongly influenced by the social, political, geographical and economic attributes of Canadian society. In Canada, these factors have combined to produce unique settings in which the system operates. These include the one- and two-officer RCMP detachments in remote areas of the country and the fly-in or circuit courts that deliver justice services to native Indian and Inuit communities in northern and rural areas.

During the 1980s, there have been several major developments that have had and will likely continue to have a significant impact on the administration of Canadian criminal justice. These include the legislative provisions of the *Canadian Charter of Rights and Freedoms* and the *Young Offenders Act*. These developments have been accompanied by an unprecedented growth in the quantity and quality of empirical research on all aspects of the criminal justice system, from the attitudes of Canadians toward the law and legal system to studies of the effectiveness of policing strategies and correctional programs. Surely, this decade has been the most exciting to date in the ongoing "voyage of discovery," and it is the authors' hope that this book will assist Canadians in this quest.

A great many persons, too numerous to mention, played direct or indirect roles in the production of this text, which has taken much longer than originally anticipated to complete. Particular mention, however, should be made of the sterling research assistance provided by Maureen Ashworth, Karen Lyons, Garth Davies and Jay Solomon. The authors would also like to acknowledge the valuable contribution of the graduate and undergraduate students in the School of Criminology, past and present. It is from the classroom that many of our perspectives on criminal justice originated. So too have our colleagues in the School of Criminology contributed to an environment of interdisciplinary inquiry in which Canadian crime and criminal justice can be explored. Bill Glackman, Associate Director of the Criminology Research Centre at Simon Fraser University and Donna Robertson, Research Technician in the Criminology Research Centre, were always available to lend assistance in the preparation of the manuscript.

A particular debt of gratitude is owed to Alison Hatch, who not only co-authored the chapter on young offenders and the law, but also provided ongoing assistance in the preparation of the manuscript. Acknowledgement is also due to the Canadian scholars, criminal justice researchers and practitioners, from Halifax to Victoria, whose work is cited throughout the text. As this is the first edition of the text, the authors would like to solicit comments and criticisms of the materials produced, in the hope that the next edition of the book will be even a more valuable tool for students, instructors and criminal justice personnel.

The production of this book has taxed both the authors and the publishers. At Butterworths, Gloria Vitale, Linda Kee, Marie Graham and Joan Chaplin assisted in the race to the deadline, while Anne Butler provided incisive editorial expertise. The authors would also like to thank Richard Ericson, who reviewed the manuscript prior to production and provided many valuable comments and suggestions.

Curt Taylor Griffiths
Simon N. Verdun-Jones
Burnaby, British Columbia
1989

CONTENTS

4. THE POWERS AND DECISION MAKING OF THE POLICE 81

5. CRITICAL ISSUES IN CANADIAN POLICING 143

FIGURES

TABLES

1 CANADIAN CRIMINAL JUSTICE: AN INTRODUCTION

The Canadian criminal justice system includes a series of key stages ranging from the decision of citizens to telephone the police through the supervision of offenders released from correctional institutions (see Figures 1.1 and 1.2). However, the justice process is much more than criminal statutes, organizatonal structures, and formally stated objectives. It is a human process, one characterized by discretion and inconsistency rather than machine-like precision and predictability. The processing of criminal cases takes place within the social, economic, and political backdrop of Canadian society, which may significantly influence the operation of the criminal justice process, as well as the outcome of individual cases.

The Legislative and Political Bases of Criminal Justice

There are several pieces of legislation that provide the foundation and general framework within which the criminal justice system operates. Under the *Constitution Act, 1867*, the federal Parliament is given exclusive authority to enact criminal laws and the procedures to be followed in criminal matters. Jurisdiction over the administration of justice is given to the provinces, as is the responsibilty for establishing and maintaining a system of provincial courts. As we shall see, however, the federal government is also involved in the provision of justice services, the most notable example being the Royal Canadian Mounted Police, which acts as a federal, provincial, and municipal police force in many areas of the country.

The criminal law in Canada is primarily set forth in the *Criminal Code,* which was first enacted by Parliament in 1892 and has been continually revised. There are over 770 sections in the *Criminal Code,* covering substantive offences and the procedures to be followed in the administration of justice. There are other federal statutes that create criminal offences. Among the more significant of such statutes are the *Food and Drugs Act* and the *Narcotic Control Act.* The *Young Offenders Act* (1980-81-82-83) provides the legislative framework for the administration of youth justice in Canada and represents a philosophical shift in the response to youth in

1

FIGURE 1.1
THE CANADIAN CRIMINAL JUSTICE SYSTEM
Jurisdictions and Responsibilities

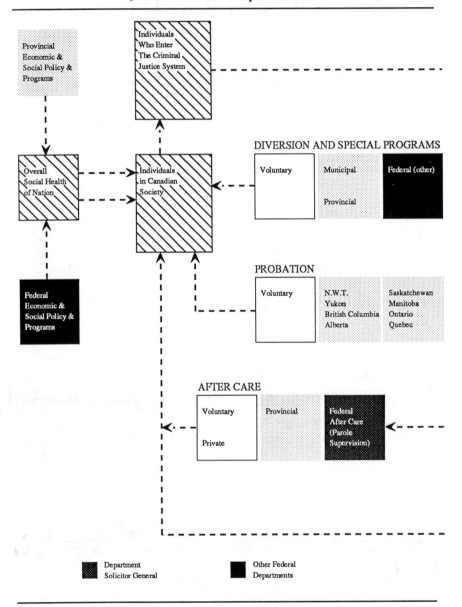

FIGURE 1.1
THE CANADIAN CRIMINAL JUSTICE SYSTEM
Jurisdictions and Responsibilities[1]

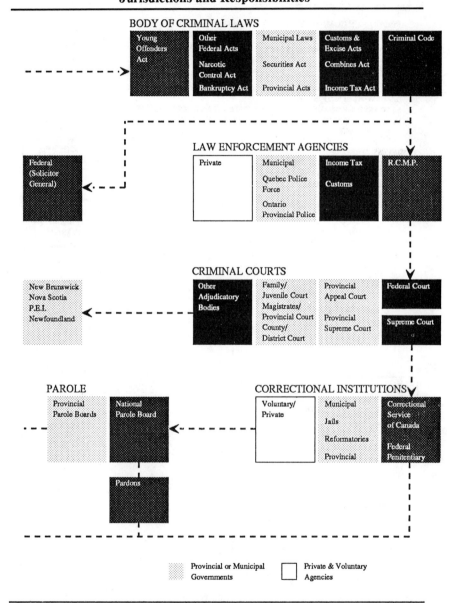

[1] Since this chart was published responsibility for the Young Offenders Act has been shifted to the Department of Justice.

Source: *Beyond the Walls* (Ottawa: Communications Branch of Correctional Service of Canada, Ministry of the Solicitor General of Canada, 1983), pp. 4 & 5.

FIGURE 1.2
FLOW OF CASES THROUGH THE CANADIAN
CRIMINAL JUSTICE SYSTEM

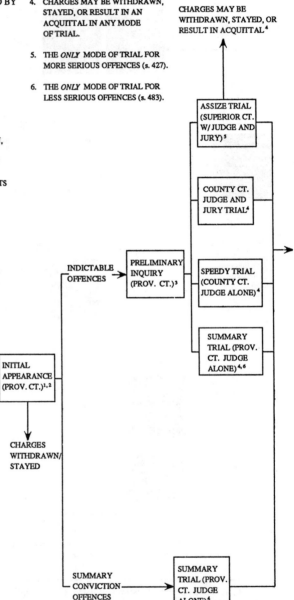

1. APPEARANCE COMPELLED BY SUMMONS, ARREST, OR APPEARANCE NOTICE.

2. INITIAL SORTING AND JUDICIAL INTERIM RELEASE (BAIL) ARE DEALT WITH. ELECTION AS TO MODE OF TRIAL MAY OCCUR HERE OR AT A LATER HEARING.

3. BYPASSED RE DIRECT INDICTMENT BY THE CROWN, FOR OFFENCES WITHIN THE ABSOLUTE JURISDICTION OF THE PROV. CT. (s. 483), AND WHERE ACCUSED ELECTS A SUMMARY TRIAL.

4. CHARGES MAY BE WITHDRAWN, STAYED, OR RESULT IN AN ACQUITTAL IN ANY MODE OF TRIAL.

5. THE *ONLY* MODE OF TRIAL FOR MORE SERIOUS OFFENCES (s. 427).

6. THE *ONLY* MODE OF TRIAL FOR LESS SERIOUS OFFENCES (s. 483).

CHARGES MAY BE WITHDRAWN, STAYED, OR RESULT IN ACQUITTAL [4]

ASSIZE TRIAL (SUPERIOR CT. W/ JUDGE AND JURY) [5]

COUNTY CT. JUDGE AND JURY TRIAL [4]

SPEEDY TRIAL (COUNTY CT. JUDGE ALONE) [4]

SUMMARY TRIAL (PROV. CT. JUDGE ALONE) [4,6]

INDICTABLE OFFENCES

PRELIMINARY INQUIRY (PROV. CT.) [3]

OFFENCES REPORTED TO POLICE

INFORMATION SWORN (CHARGE LAID)

INITIAL APPEARANCE (PROV. CT.) [1,2]

UNSOLVED

UNOFFICIAL RESOLUTION

CHARGES WITHDRAWN/ STAYED

SUMMARY CONVICTION OFFENCES

SUMMARY TRIAL (PROV. CT. JUDGE ALONE) [4]

FIGURE 1.2
FLOW OF CASES THROUGH THE CANADIAN
CRIMINAL JUSTICE SYSTEM

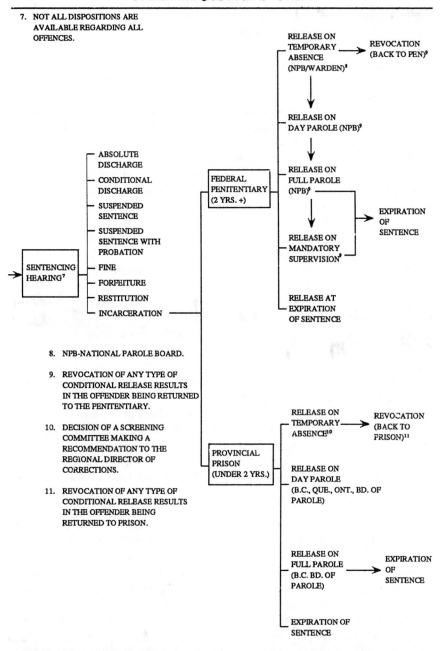

7. NOT ALL DISPOSITIONS ARE AVAILABLE REGARDING ALL OFFENCES.

8. NPB-NATIONAL PAROLE BOARD.

9. REVOCATION OF ANY TYPE OF CONDITIONAL RELEASE RESULTS IN THE OFFENDER BEING RETURNED TO THE PENITENTIARY.

10. DECISION OF A SCREENING COMMITTEE MAKING A RECOMMENDATION TO THE REGIONAL DIRECTOR OF CORRECTIONS.

11. REVOCATION OF ANY TYPE OF CONDITIONAL RELEASE RESULTS IN THE OFFENDER BEING RETURNED TO PRISON.

conflict with the law from the *Juvenile Delinquents Act*, which it replaced.

It is important to bear in mind that all legislation, both at the federal and provincial levels, is subject to the *Canadian Charter of Rights and Freedoms*, enacted in 1982. As the fundamental law of the land, the Charter guarantees basic rights and freedoms that may, in certain circumstances, be enforced by the courts in the face of legislative provisions that infringe upon them. The courts' recently acquired power to strike down legislation as unconstitutional, in light of the Charter, has effected a dramatic change in the Canadian constitutional landscape.

Politicians and legislators exert considerable influence over the operation of the criminal justice system, and through their decision making affect both the policy and line-level operations of the process (see Stolz, 1985). At the federal level, Parliament is involved in making additions or modifications to the *Criminal Code* and other federal legislation such as the *Parole Act* and the *Penitentiary Act*. Through its decision making, Parliament determines not only the types of behaviour that will be considered criminal, but the provisions for responding to accused persons. Federal legislators also control the budgets of the federal agencies involved in the delivery of justice services.

The political influence over the operation of the criminal justice process extends to the federal and provincial ministries charged with justice-related functions. At the federal level, the Ministry of the Solicitor General has responsibility for policing, corrections, and parole, as well as specialized activities such as the missing children's program and National Crime Prevention Week. Components of the Ministry of the Solicitor General include the Royal Canadian Mounted Police, the Correctional Service of Canada, a Secretariat, the National Parole Board, and the Canadian Security Intelligence Service.

The federal Department of Justice assumes a primary role in the area of criminal justice policy and has responsibility for the *Criminal Code,* the *Young Offenders Act,* the administration of justice at the federal level, and for criminal prosecution not assigned by statute to the provincial governments. The mandate of the Department of Justice also includes the areas of victims of crime, women and native Indians and the criminal justice system, and international criminal justice.

The provincial legislatures are also responsible for creating a form of criminal law, described as "quasi-criminal" law. Briefly, the *Constitution Act, 1867* provides that a number of matters fall within the exclusive jurisdiction of the provinces, including municipal institutions, health, education, highways, and liquor control. The province may enforce this legislation by the imposition of fines, imprisonment and other penalties.

The offences that may be created by provincial legislation are generally far less serious than the offences contained in the *Criminal Code* or other federal legislation such as the *Narcotic Control Act*. While the maximum penalties that may be imposed for violation of provincial statutes are generally no more than a fine or a maximum term of imprisonment of six months, or both, the penalties under the *Criminal Code* and the *Narcotic Control Act* may be as severe as life imprisonment.

The "System" of Criminal Justice

Among observers of the criminal justice process, there has been an ongoing debate about whether the various agencies and departments involved in the administration of justice function as a unified "system." While this text makes no attempt to resolve this (perhaps irresolvable) dispute, it is incumbent upon us to consider each perspective of the system/ non-system debate. There are some attributes of the Canadian criminal justice process that would seem to qualify it as a system, although there are others that operate to lessen the unity of action of the various agencies involved in the administration of justice.

All criminal justice agencies in Canada operate under the *Constitution Act, 1867* and process offenders under the provisions of the *Criminal Code* and in accordance with established rules of procedure and evidence and the tenets of the *Canadian Charter of Rights and Freedoms.* Further, there is an interdependence among criminal justice agencies, such that the activities of one component are likely to have an impact upon the others. The selective enforcement practices of the police, for example, may significantly affect the number and types of cases presented to Crown counsel for prosecution, while the sentencing practices of the courts will have a direct impact on the population of correctional institutions, as well as on the use of alternative programs and services.

These interdependencies are even greater in rural and remote areas of the country, where justice services are delivered by small RCMP detachments and via circut courts. The demography of Canada, then, including its large land areas and sparse population, may serve to increase the interdependency of the criminal justice system. As we shall see, however, this also results in a wide variety of settings in which the administration of justice occurs, from the southern, urban centres such as Montreal, Calgary and Vancouver, to the remote communities in the northern portions of the provinces and the communities of the Yukon and Northwest Territories. These environments present different challenges to the justice system and its personnel, who must adapt the requirements of legislation to the needs of victims, communities, and offenders.

The legislative and jurisdictional arrangements for the criminal justice process in Canada also serve to provide some degree of uniformity across the country. First, all criminal justice agencies and organizations carry out their tasks under a national *Criminal Code.* This is in contrast to the United States and Australia, where each state government is responsible for enacting criminal statutes and establishing systems of criminal justice.

Federal criminal statutes in the United States and Australia cover only a narrow range of offences.

The involvement of the RCMP in policing at the municipal, provincial, and federal levels in Canada makes it a truly national police force. There is no counterpart in the United States, where policing is organized primarily at the municipal and county levels, or in Australia with its state police. In the United States, the activities of the state police (or state patrol) are confined to the control of highway traffic, and federal forces such as the FBI and the Secret Service are involved in enforcing federal statutes.

In Canada, correctional services are divided between the provincial and federal governments on the basis of the length of sentence received by the offender. This has resulted in the creation of an extensive system of custodial and non-custodial facilities and programs operated by the federal Correctional Service of Canada for offenders who receive a sentence or sentences totalling more than two years. For the federal female offender, there is one custodial facility for the entire country. In the United States and Australia, on the other hand, state governments are responsible for operating correctional systems for offenders convicted of violating state criminal statutes, and only those offenders convicted of federal offences are sent to the federal correctional system.

A unique attribute of the United States system of criminal justice is the election of criminal justice officials, including county sheriffs, county prosecutors, and district and state judges. No such provision for the election of criminal justice personnel exists in Canada. The prosecution function in Canada is performed by Crown counsel, who are appointed by provincial and federal governments, as are criminal court judges.

The structure of Canadian criminal justice may, then, serve to increase its functioning as a system, although there are other forces at work to counter the ability of criminal justice agencies and personnel to act in concert with one another. First, each of the major components of the criminal justice system has a different mandate. The police, courts, and corrections system are charged with different tasks, and in the adversarial system, the courts are supposed to serve as a check and balance against the potential excesses of the other components.

Secondly, as our discussions throughout the following chapters reveal, the activities and decision making of criminal justice personnel in all components of the system are characterized by considerable diversity and by variability rather than uniformity. This variability exists not only between jurisdictions, but within individual agencies in the same jurisdiction. Among judges in the provincial court, for example, there may be a wide range of individual philosophies and "styles," resulting in disparity in sentencing practices. Similar disparities exist among police officers and other decision makers in the criminal justice system who are given considerable professional autonomy and discretion to carry out their tasks.

Third, despite the extensive involvement of the federal government in formulating criminal legislation and in the policing and corrections areas, there is no single coordinating agency or authority with the mandate to establish uniform operating guidelines and procedures for criminal justice agencies and personnel. And, even where guidelines do exist, such as the criteria listed in the *Parole Act* relating to a grant of parole by members of the National Parole Board, they do not, in practice, operate to control or confine the discretion exercised by members in their decision making.

This diversity in objectives and mandates, as well as the broad discretionary powers exercised by criminal justice personnel, has led observers such as Sheley (1985: 259) to depict the United States criminal justice system as "a collection of interrelated, semi-autonomous bureaucracies," while Cox and Wade (1985: 4) have spoken of a "criminal justice 'network' consisting of a web of constantly changing relationships among individuals, some of whom are directly involved in criminal justice pursuits, others of whom are not" (see also Moore, 1981).

These characterizations are valid for the Canadian criminal justice system as well. While there is an established structure through which criminal cases flow, the actual dynamics of the criminal justice process are quite varied and cannot be understood solely through an examination of a case-flow chart. Agencies and personnel throughout the Canadian criminal justice system often pursue conflicting goals, are influenced by external agencies and publics and have broad discretionary powers in carrying out their tasks.

Perhaps the most succinct characterization of the criminal justice process in terms of the system/non-system debate is provided by Cox and Wade (1985: 5):

> ... the best way to view the criminal justice system is as a network of interrelated, but independent individuals who are subject to many internal and external pressures, and who work under (and are at the same time developing) a set of operating procedures in pursuit of similar, but not always identical, goals. While public and political influence, legal requirements, and discretionary justice pervade the entire network, each party in the network has goals and problems not shared by other parties.

The Application of the Criminal Law

A significant contribution to understanding the operation of the criminal justice process was made by the late Herbert Packer (1968), who identified two competing value systems underlying the administration of criminal justice: the *crime control model* and the *due process model.* The crime control model views the primary purpose of the criminal justice system as the protection of the public through the deterrence and incapacitation of offenders. Criminal offenders are responsible for their actions, and the administration of justice should be swift, sure, and efficient. There is a strong presumption of guilt, and confidence that an efficient justice system will screen out innocent persons at the police or prosecutorial stages. There is also an emphasis on compensation for victims of crime.

The due process model, on the other hand, emphasizes procedural fairness and a presumption of innocence. The onus is on the criminal justice process to prove guilt, and there is a requirement that agencies and decision makers follow proper procedures in making such a determination. The possibilty exists that an accused person may be factually guilty, but legally innocent, if the proper procedures and rights of the accused have been violated. The due process model evidences a concern with structuring and confining the discretionary power of criminal justice decision makers.

Because of their location in the process, different components of the criminal justice system may tend toward one perspective or the other. The police, for example, have long been identified with the crime control perspective, while the courts have traditionally been viewed as operating within a due process approach. In fact, different components of the criminal justice system may be operating under different models, or be in pursuit of different, often conflicting, goals, decreasing the unity of the system and raising the spectre of organizational conflict between the various components.

Several observers, however, have noted that there is often a degree of organizational cooperation betweeen criminal justice agencies that undermines the adversarial nature of the criminal justice system and increases its interdependency. Feeley (1979) and others have argued that, in practice, the criminal courts often fail to approximate a due process model and Eisenstein and Jacob (1977) used the term *courtroom workgroup* to depict the extent of cooperation between judges, defence and prosecution lawyers, a process in which the defendant is an outsider.

Ericson and Baranek (1982) argue that accused persons have little power in the hierarchy of the criminal court and are largely excluded from the construction of the "reality" surrounding their case. In such instances, the activities of the court may serve more crime-control-oriented goals (see also Hagan and Zatz, 1985). Noting that researchers have long ignored the bureaucratic and organizational dimensions of criminal justice in favour of a nearly exclusive focus on the offender, Blumberg (1967: 19) argues that the criminal court is a "closed community" in which the defendant assumes secondary importance to the needs and priorities of the court organization and the professionals who practice within it:

> Organizational goals and discipline impose a set of demands and conditions of practice on the respective professions in the criminal court, to which they respond by abandoning their ideological and professional commitments to the accused client, in the service of these higher claims of the court organization.

A Critical Perspective of Canadian Criminal Justice

There are two explanations offered for the formulation and implementation of the criminal law that must also be considered in any study of the criminal justice system: the *value consensus model* and the *conflict model.* The value-consensus perspective views legislation as reflecting the needs and values of society and the application of the law as serving to reaffirm these consensual interests. The work of the Canadian Law Reform Commission has been characterized by Goode (1976; 1978) as representing a value-consensus approach.

In recent years, however, this view has been challenged by the emergence of a *critical perspective,* which considers legislation a consequence of specific group interests and the criminal justice system a "state-initiated and state-supported effort to rationalize mechanisms of social control" (Taylor, Walton and Young, 1975: 24; see also Pfohl, 1985). Advocates of the consensus model view the criminal law as expressing the values held by the majority of society, while proponents of the conflict model contend that law is an instrument of social control used by the powerful to protect their vested interests (see Chambliss and Seidman, 1982).

From the critical perspective, discussions about whether the process meets the criteria of an integrated system are less important than discussions about the role played by the criminal justice system as a key element of social control in the maintenance of the dominant economic and political order (see Johnston and Ornstein, 1985; McMullan and Ratner, 1983; Ratner and McMullan, 1983). And Hastings and Saunders (1987: 127) contend that the process of legal reform, as carried out by agencies such as the Law Reform Commission of Canada, "can only be adequately understood in the context of the wider role of the state in general and of the issues of ideology and social control in particular."

There have, in fact, been few substantive empirical inquiries into the operation of the Canadian criminal justice system that employ a critical perspective, although the emerging historical record, as well as contemporary events, would seem to provide the opportunity for such analyses (see Boyle et al., 1985; Ratner and McMullan, 1987). As the discussions in the following chapters will reveal, all segments of the criminal justice system have, at one time or another, been the subject of controversy. The early RCMP, for example, experienced numerous internal difficulties, despite the popular notions and myths that surround the creation and emergence of what has become a national "institution" (Morgan, 1972; Walden, 1982). And, more recently, the reports of a commission of inquiry found that over a two-decade period, the RCMP Intelligence Service engaged in illegal activities and cover-ups (McDonald, 1981).

In the criminal courts, plea bargaining, while not recognized or sanctioned under the *Criminal Code,* plays a key role in the processing of cases. And Canadian judges exhibit considerable disparity in their patterns of sentencing (Hogarth, 1971; Palys and Divorsky, 1986). Canadian prisons have often been the scene of brutality and violence, both historically and during contemporary times (Jayewardene and Doherty, 1985; Schoom, 1966). The negative consequences of unchecked discretion surrounding the decision making of parole boards and the supervision of offenders in the community have also been documented (Solicitor General of Canada, 1981). In recent years, many previously "invisible" problems have been brought to the fore, chief among them the "third world" status of many of Canada's native peoples and the impact of their socio-structural and political position on their victimization and involvement in the criminal justice system (Griffiths, Yerbury and Weafer, 1987).

In his treatise, *The Rich Get Richer and the Poor Get Prison,* Reiman (1979: 97) argues that the poor and members of ethnic minorities are more likely to be arrested, convicted, and sentenced to a period of confinement than their more wealthy counterparts: "There can be little doubt that the criminal justice process is distorted by racism as well as by economic bias." The high rates of native Indian victimization, arrests, guilty pleas and incarceration in many Canadian jurisdictions are closely related to the deprived socio-economic and socio-political position of native Indians in Canadian society. Reiman (1979) further argues that the criminal justice system perpetuates the view that the real threat to order and stability comes from the poor, a perception that led to the construction of the first Canadian penitentiary at Kingston, Ontario in 1835 (Ekstedt and Griffiths, 1988).

While it is not the intent of this volume to provide an analysis of the operation of the Canadian criminal justice system from only one perspective, there is considerable potential for the use of a critical analytical perspective in examining and understanding the events and activities of the criminal justice process, both historically and in contemporary times. Such a perspective requires a re-examination of much of the folk wisdom surrounding the criminal justice system and the adoption of a critical eye in interpreting historical and contemporary events. The materials presented in this volume are designed to provide readers with materials of a descriptive and analytical nature that can be used as a foundation for further study and research on the Canadian criminal justice system.

Criminal Justice Themes

The enormous complexity of the criminal justice system in Canada precludes definitive discussions in the space of one volume. There are, however, several themes that will emerge throughout the following chapters, and it is hoped they will provide the reader with a more thorough understanding of the criminal justice process, as well as of the forces that shape its day-to-day operation.

First, an effort has been made to construct the historical basis of the criminal justice process, noting the key events, and in some instances personalities, that shaped the development of the Canadian criminal justice system. Second, the operation of each component of the criminal justice system is tied to the larger Canadian context, and the influences from the social, cultural, political, and economic spheres are noted. Third, the role of the public as a key component of the criminal justice process, from the stage of victimization, to calling the police, to participation in the courts, and to involvement in the correctional process is discussed. Fourth, the findings of research on the criminal justice process are utilized to construct a composite picture of the operations of the system. And fifth, the human dimension of the criminal justice process, and all it entails, is illustrated.

The reader should be forewarned, however, that the Canadian criminal justice system is encountering serious difficulties in carrying out its mandate, and concerns are increasingly being voiced not only about the costs of the enterprise, but also its effectiveness. Historically, the development and expansion of the formal agents of social control have been accompanied by a shift of responsibility for addressing problems in the community from the public to these agents and by increasing community demands on criminal justice organizations. A parallel development is the increasing dissatisfaction with the performance of criminal justice agencies and increasing isolation of the public from the criminal justice system. As the twentieth century draws to a close, the search for alternative social control mechanisms that are not only less expensive, but more effective and more closely aligned with the community, is underway. The final destination of this search is still unclear.

REFERENCES

Blumberg, A. 1967. "The Practice of Law as a Confidence Game: Organizational Cooptation of a Profession." 1 *Law and Society Review* 15–39.

Boyle, C. L. M., M.-A. Betrand, C. Lacerte-Lamontagne, and R. Shamai. 1985. *A Feminist Review of Criminal Law*. Ottawa: Supply and Services Canada.

Chambliss, W., and R. Seidman. 1982. *Law, Order, and Power,* 2nd ed. Reading, Mass.: Addison-Wesley Publishing Co.

Cox, S. M., and J. E. Wade. 1985. *The Criminal Justice Network: An Introduction*. Dubuque, Iowa: W. C. Brown Publishers.

Eisenstein, J., and H. Jacob. 1977. *Felony Justice*. Boston: Little, Brown and Co.

Ekstedt, J. W., and C. T. Griffiths. 1988. *Corrections in Canada: Policy and Practice,* 2nd ed. Toronto: Butterworths.

Ericson, R. V., and P. M. Baranek. 1982. *The Ordering of Justice: A Study of Accused Persons as Dependants in the Criminal Process.* Toronto: University of Toronto Press.

Feeley, Malcolm M. 1979. *The Process Is the Punishment: Handling Cases in a Lower Criminal Court.* New York: Russell Sage Foundation.

Goode, M. R. 1976. "Law Reform Commission of Canada — Political Ideology of Criminal Justice Reform." 54 *Canadian Bar Review* 653–74.

———. 1978. "The Law Reform Commission of Canada, Barnes and the Value-Consensus Model: More About Ideology." 4 *Dalhousie Law Journal* 793–812.

Griffiths, C. T., J. C. Yerbury, and L. F. Weafer. 1987. "Canada's Natives: Victims of Socio-Structural Deprivation?" 46 *Human Organization* 277–82.

Hagan, J., and M. S. Zatz. 1985. "The Social Organization of Criminal Justice Processing: An Event History Analysis." 14 *Social Science Research* 103–25.

Hastings, R., and R. P. Saunders. 1987. "Social Control, State Autonomy and Legal Reform: The Law Reform Commission of Canada." In *State Control: Criminal Justice Politics in Canada,* edited by R. S. Ratner and J. L. McMullan, 126–48. Vancouver: University of British Columbia Press.

Hogarth, J. 1971. *Sentencing as a Human Process.* Toronto: University of Toronto Press.

Jayewardene, C. H. S., and P. Doherty. 1985. "Individual Violence in Canadian Penitentiaries." 27 *Canadian Journal of Criminology* 429–39.

Johnston, W., and M. Ornstein. 1985. "Social Class and Political Ideology in Canada." 22 *Canadian Review of Sociology and Anthropology* 369-93.

McDonald, Mr. Justice D. C. (Chairman). 1981. *Commission of Inquiry Concerning Certain Activities of the Royal Canadian Mounted Police. Third Report. Certain R.C.M.P. Activities and the Question of Governmental Knowledge.* Ottawa: Minister of Supply and Services.

McMullan, J. L., and R. S. Ratner. 1983. "State, Labour, and Justice in British Columbia." In *Deviant Designations,* edited by T. Fleming, 5–36. Toronto: Butterworths.

Moore, R. 1981. "The Criminal Justice Non-System." In *Order under Law,* edited by B. Culbertson and M. Tezak, 40–48. Prospect Heights, Ill. Waveland Press.

Morgan, E. C. 1972. "The Northwest Mounted Police: Internal Problems and Public Criticism, 1874–1883." 26 *Saskatchewan History* 41–62.

Packer, H. L. 1968. *The Limits of the Criminal Sanction.* Stanford: Stanford University Press.

Palys, T. S. and S. Divorsky. 1986. "Explaining Sentence Disparity." 23 *Canadian Journal of Criminology* 347–62.

Pfohl, S. J. 1985. *Images of Deviance and Social Control: A Sociological History.* New York: McGraw-Hill.

Ratner, R. S., and J. L. McMullan. 1983. "Social Control and the Rise of the 'Exceptional State' in Britain, The United States, and Canada." 19 *Crime and Social Justice* 31–43.

_____. 1987. *State Control: Criminal Justice Politics in Canada.* Vancouver: University of British Columbia Press.

Reiman, J. H. 1979. *The Rich Get Richer and the Poor Get Prison: Ideology, Class, and Criminal Justice.* New York: John Wiley and Sons.

Schoom, S. 1966. "Kingston Penitentiary: The Early Decades." 8 *Canadian Journal of Corrections* 215–20.

Sheley, J. F. 1985. *America's "Crime Problem": An Introduction to Criminology.* Belmont, Calif.: Wadsworth Publishing Co.

Solicitor General of Canada. 1981. *Solicitor General's Study of Conditional Release: Report of the Working Group.* Ottawa: Supply and Services Canada.

Stolz, B. A. 1985. "Congress and Criminal Justice Policy Making: The Impact of Interest Groups and Symbolic Politics." 13 *Journal of Criminal Justice* 307–19.

Taylor, I., P. Walton, and J. Young. 1975. *Critical Criminology.* London: Routledge and Kegan Paul.

Walden, K. 1982. *Visions of Order — The Canadian Mounties in Symbol and Myth.* Toronto: Butterworths.

LEGISLATION

Constitution Act, 1867, 1867 (U.K.), c. 3
Criminal Code, R.S.C. 1985, c. C-46
Food and Drugs Act, R.S.C. 1985, c. F-27
Juvenile Delinquents Act, R.S.C. 1970, c. J-3
Narcotic Control Act, R.S.C. 1985, c. N-1
Parole Act, R.S.C. 1985, c. P-2
Penitentiary Act, R.S.C. 1985, c. P-5
Young Offenders Act, S.C. 1980-81-82-83, c. 110 (see now R.S.C. 1985, c. Y-1)

2 CRIME, CRIMINAL JUSTICE AND THE CANADIAN PUBLIC

Canadian Crime Rates

Any discussion of crime rates is limited by the particular period of time chosen, and in this chapter we can provide no more than a "snapshot" of the nature and extent of criminal activity in Canada. There have been few inquiries into the patterns of crime at the provincial/territorial and municipal levels or into how the patterns of criminality in the various jurisdictions have fluctuated over time. Brantingham and Brantingham (1984: 192) note that, historically, crime rates in Canada have shown a steady increase from the early 1800s to the mid-1970s and are more similar to those in France than to those in England or the United States.

In discussing Canadian crime rates, it is important to remember that official statistics have many limitations and should be utilized only as general indicators of criminal activity. Differences in crime statistics that emerge between jurisdictions and regions in Canada may be a function of many factors, including: (1) environmental attributes, such as the size and composition of the population; (2) characteristics of the community, including public attitudes toward the police and citizen involvement in crime prevention initiatives; (3) characteristics of the police force, including the manner in which departments deploy officers and allocate resources, and the methods of collecting and recording criminal offences; and (4) the particular attributes of the criminal justice system in the various jurisdictions, including the charging practices of Crown counsel.[1]

In Canada, the primary method by which statistics on crime rates are gathered is through the Uniform Crime Reporting system, which was established in 1962. Information is gathered and reported on those crimes that come to the attention of the police either through citizen reporting or through proactive police activities. Policing agencies participating in the Uniform Crime Reporting system include municipal police forces, the Quebec and Ontario provincial police, the RCMP, the Canadian National and Canadian Pacific Railways Police, Ports Canada police, the New Brunswick Highway Patrol, and the Royal Newfoundland Constabulary. The Uniform Crime Reports are comprised of "actual" offences — those reported or detected offences that have been found, upon preliminary investigation, to have actually occurred, as opposed to being unfounded.[2]

Statistics from the Uniform Crime Reporting system (Canadian Centre for Justice Statistics, 1988) indicate that the total number of actual offences in Canada (*Criminal Code,* federal statutes, provincial statutes, and municipal by-laws) increased steadily between 1978 and 1981. During the period 1982–1984, there were consecutive declines in the total number of offences, although a slight increase was recorded between 1984 and 1985. During 1986, the total number of offences increased 4.9%, and this figure rose by 3.4% again in 1987 (Figure 2.1). Among the factors associated with these increases were an increase in population size and a shift in the age structure of the country. Further, Lee (1984: 37) has reported that while the involvement of males in criminality did not change significantly during the period 1949–1968, there has been an increase in female criminality. More than 50% of the offences committed by women in 1985 involved fraud and theft, and women are heavily involved in non-violent property offences (see also Johnson, 1986; 1987; Maxim and Jocklin, 1980).

FIGURE 2.1
TOTAL OFFENCES 1978-1987 AND PERCENTAGE
DISTRIBUTION OF 1987 DATA, CANADA

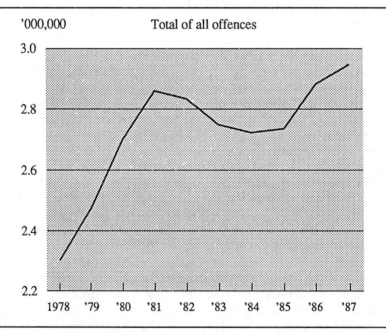

Source: Canadian Centre for Justice Statistics. *Canadian Crime Statistics, 1987* (Ottawa: Statistics Canada, 1988), p. 27. Catalogue No. 85-205. Reproduced with permission of the Minister of Supply and Services Canada, 1989.

In 1987, nearly 3 million offences were committed in Canada (Figure 2.1). These offences were distributed as follows: *Criminal Code* offences (80.0%), federal statute offences (3.5%), provincial statute offences (12.9%), and municipal by-laws (3.6%) (Figure 2.1). Drug offences accounted for nearly 60% of the total federal statute offences in 1987, and *Liquor Act* offences accounted for almost 70% of the total provincial statute offences.

The national rate of offences per 100,000 population increased steadily during the period 1978–1981, recorded consecutive decreases for the years 1982–1985, and then increased 4.1% during 1986 and 2.3% between 1986 and 1987 (Figure 2.2). For the period 1978–1987, the national offence rate increased 17.6%. Figure 2.3 depicts rates of *Criminal Code* offences per 100,000 population, by offence category, for the years 1978–1987. During this period, the property crime rate increased 22.8%, the violent crime rate increased 44.8%, and the rate per 100,000 population for "Other Crimes" (all *Criminal Code* offences except violent crimes and property crimes) increased 29.7%. During this period, property crimes accounted for approximately two-thirds of all *Criminal Code* offences.[3]

Statistics from the Uniform Crime Reporting system also suggest considerable regional variability in the rates of *Criminal Code* offences per 100,000 population, as well as in the rates of violent crimes and property offences (Figures 2.4, 2.5, and 2.6). These figures indicate that the rates per 100,000 for all three of these categories increase as one moves from east to west. However, there are exceptions to this general rule. Elie and Normandeau (1984) note that the rates of robbery in Quebec are similar to those reported in United States cities. This is illustrated by the annual armed robbery rate in Montreal, which is three times that of Vancouver, four times that of Calgary and Edmonton, and eight times that of Toronto (see Gabor and Normandeau, 1987). Also, the Province of Quebec recorded the highest rate of bank robberies in the country, and in 1985, this rate was above that for New York City.[4] However, the 1987 homicide rate per 100,000 population in the United States was still more than three times higher than the rate in Canada.

There is a substantial price tag attached to crime. A portion of the overall costs is illustrated by Himelfarb (1984: 39), utilizing data collected by the Canadian Urban Victimization Survey from seven major Canadians cities:

Unrecovered Property and Cash: $211.5 million
Damage to Property: $41.9 million
Medical Expenses and Lost Wages: $7 million
Private Insurance Payments to Victims: $170 million
Criminal Injuries Compensation to Victims: $20 million

The total real cost of crime in the seven cities surveyed was in excess of $431 million annually. This figure, however, does not include the emo-

FIGURE 2.2
RATE PER 100,000 POPULATION OF TOTAL OFFENCES 1978-1987

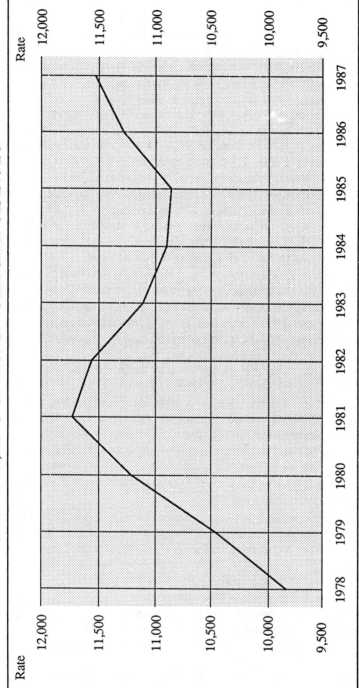

Source: Canadian Centre for Justice Statistics. *Canadian Crime Statistics, 1987* (Ottawa: Statistics Canada, 1988), p. 28. Catalogue No. 85-205. Reproduced with permission of the Minister of Supply and Services Canada, 1989.

FIGURE 2.3

RATE PER 100,000 POPULATION OF CRIMINAL CODE OFFENCES, BY CATEGORY, 1978-1987

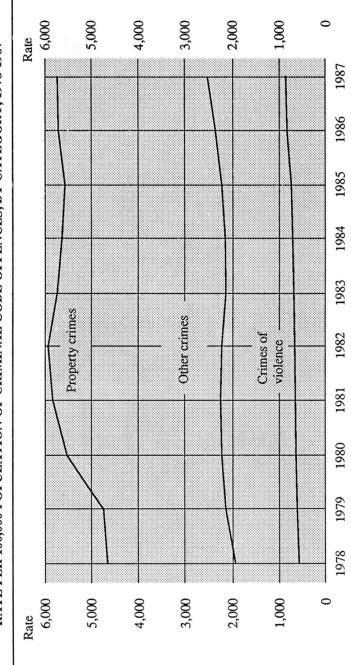

Source: Canadian Centre for Justice Statistics. *Canadian Crime Statistics, 1987* (Ottawa: Statistics Canada, 1988), p. 29. Catalogue No. 85-205. Reproduced with permission of the Minister of Supply and Services Canada, 1989.

FIGURE 2.4

RATE PER 100,000 POPULATION OF CRIMINAL CODE OFFENCES, CANADA AND THE PROVINCES/TERRITORIES, 1978 AND 1987

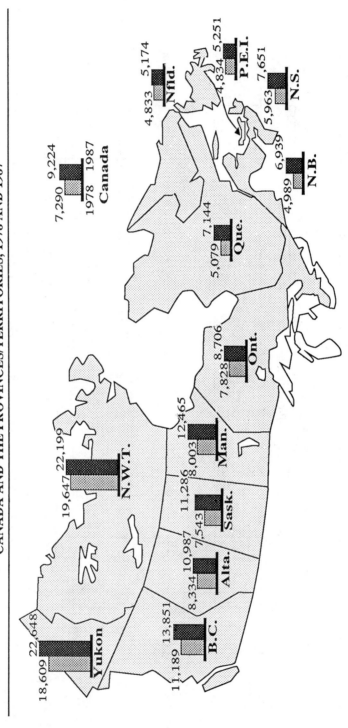

Source: Canadian Centre for Justice Statistics. *Canadian Crime Statistics, 1987* (Ottawa: Statistics Canada, 1988). p. 30. Catalogue No. 85-205. Reproduced with permission of the Minister of Supply and Services Canada, 1989.

FIGURE 2.5

RATE PER 100,000 POPULATION OF VIOLENT CRIME OFFENCES, CANADA AND THE PROVINCES/TERRITORIES, 1978 AND 1987

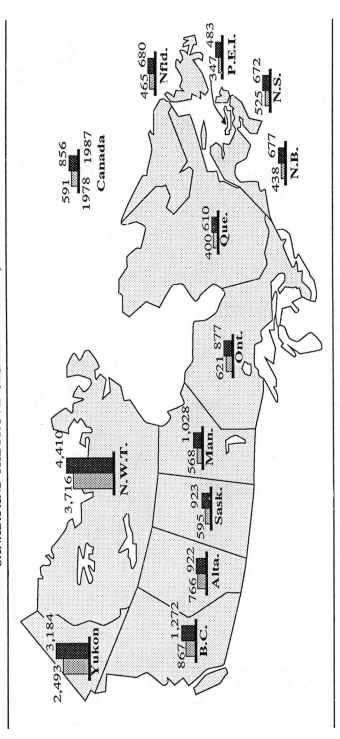

Source: Canadian Centre for Justice Statistics. *Canadian Crime Statistics, 1987* (Ottawa: Statistics Canada, 1988), p. 33. Catalogue No. 85-205. Reproduced with permission of the Minister of Supply and Services Canada, 1989.

FIGURE 2.6

RATE PER 100,000 POPULATION OF PROPERTY CRIME OFFENCES, CANADA AND THE PROVINCES/TERRITORIES, 1978 AND 1987

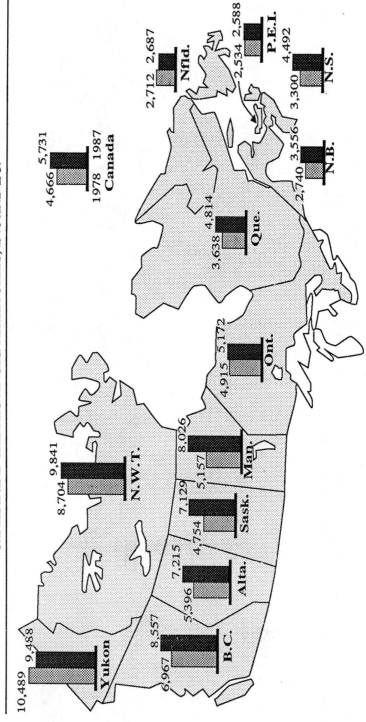

Source: Canadian Centre for Justice Statistics. *Canadian Crime Statistics, 1987* (Ottawa: Statistics Canada, 1988), p. 41. Catalogue No. 85-205. Reproduced with permission of the Minister of Supply and Services Canada, 1989.

tional costs to victims of crime, Himelfarb (1984: 48) noting that in the victimization study, "about one quarter of the victims said that victims of their type of crime should have emotional or psychological counselling available to them." Neither do these figures include the costs of private security for corporations and other costs associated with crime prevention and detection.

Public Perceptions of Crime

There have been several attempts to determine the perceptions of crime held by the Canadian public, and recent studies suggest that an increasing number of citizens are concerned with both the amount and seriousness of criminal behaviour. While Courtis reported in a 1970 study that fewer than one in ten Canadians mentioned crime as an important social problem, in 1984 Brillon, Louis-Guerin, and Lamarche (p. 68) found that 19.3% of those surveyed (nearly one in five) ranked crime as the most important social problem in Canada today (see also Sacco, Glackman, and Roesch, 1984).

Canadians, however, have misperceptions of the true nature and extent of criminal behaviour in this country. Among the findings of a 1982 Gallup Poll, reported by Doob and Roberts (1982: 2), was that Canadians overestimated both the extent and seriousness of crime, viewing crime as more serious than it actually is and perceiving that the levels of violence in Canada were similar to those in the United States, when in fact they are much lower. While nearly 75% of the respondents felt that at least 30% of all crimes committed in Canada involved violence, police statistics indicate that violent offences represent only about 5.8% of the total crimes reported to the police. As Brillon et al. (1984: 145–46) note: "People's perceptions of crime in Canada have little connection with the surrounding criminal reality . . ."

Brillon et al. (1984: 257) also found that Canadians tend to think of crime in terms of stereotypes: ". . . the images that emerged were cut and dried, without distinction, and . . . were like the stereotypes portrayed in mystery novels, on police programmes on television, or in the criminal cases that make the headlines in the newspapers." The persistence of such images among the general public is due in large measure to the public's reliance on the media for information on crime and criminals.

A major contributor to the perceptions (and misperceptions) that Canadians have of crime appears to be the media (see Ericson, Baranek, and Chan, 1987; Gebotys, Roberts, and DasGupta, 1988). Waller and Okihiro (1976) concluded that crime reporting on television from the United States influenced the perceptions of crime held by Torontonians. Possibly due to the type of criminal activity that television focuses on, Brillon et al. (1984: 71) note that it is the crimes of violence that cause the greatest fear among Canadians. In his Canadian research, however, Gomme (1986) found no relationship between exposure to media and fear of crime, indicating that the role of the media in creating public perceptions of crime is a complex one.[5]

The impact of the media appears to be limited to citizens' perceptions of crime at the national level, Brillon et al. (1984: 78) noting that no such relation appears to exist between media exposure and perceptions of crime at the local level. Rather, a person's view of crime in his or her immediate locale is based on actual victimization experiences and local crime rates. Brillon et al. (1984: 89) found that Canadians are not overly concerned with crime at the local level, with only one person in ten listing crime as an important personal problem. As the authors (1984: 146) note: ". . . the perceptions people have of crime in their immediate environment and of their risks of victimization seem to be relatively realistic and show an awareness of the objective risks."[6]

Fear of Crime and the Risks of Victimization

Brillon et al. (1984: 106) found that 41% of those surveyed made adjustments to their daily life due to the fear of victimization, with the chief pattern of avoidance being that of not going out at night. Women and the elderly in the sample were the most likely to feel the greatest vulnerability and to engage in patterns of avoidance. The *Canadian Urban Victimization Survey* (Solicitor General of Canada, 1985a) found that the fear of crime was strongly related to perceived vulnerability, with the greatest fear being expressed by women and the elderly (see also Atkinson, 1981; Brantingham, Brantingham, and Butcher, 1986; Hylton and Matonovich, 1980; Krahn and Kennedy, 1985; Sacco et al., 1984; Sacco, 1988). Similarly, Gomme (1986) found from interviews with residents of three Canadian urban centres that the fear of crime was highest among women, the less affluent, those persons who lived alone, and individuals who had been previously victimized.

Despite the greater feelings of vulnerability among women and the elderly in Canada, the actual patterns of victimization are quite different. The *Canadian Urban Victimization Survey* (Solicitor General of Canada, 1984: 5) reported an inverse relation between age and rates of victimization: as age increases, the risks of victimization decrease for all age categories. Those under the age of 25, who express the least concern with crime, are most likely to be the victims of personal offences (see also Stuebing, 1984).

The increased risk for Canadians under the age of 25 is partially explained by the additional findings from the national survey (Solicitor General of Canada, 1984) and Stuebing (1984) that there are higher rates of victimization among the unmarried and those who spend a number of evenings outside the home each month. While the elderly are less likely to be victimized, the physical, emotional, and economic consequences of victimization may be much more severe than for younger persons (see Jayewardene, Juliani, and Talbot, 1983; McLaughlin, 1984; Solicitor General of Canada, 1985a). For the elderly, the fear of crime is as significant as the consequences of actual victimization (see Brillon, 1987).

Similarly, while women are more likely than men to be the victims of sexual assault and to be the victims of property crimes, men are twice as likely to be the victims of robbery or assault. From a study of crime victims in Red Deer, Alberta, however, Stuebing (1984: 6) reported that males were more likely to be the victims of property offences, while the victims of crimes against the person were more likely to be female.

While it might be assumed that citizen fear of crime and perceptions of vulnerability would lead to increased participation in police-sponsored crime prevention programs, the results of the *Canadian Urban Victimization Survey* (Solicitor General of Canada, 1984: 8) reveal that Canadians are not likely to take advantage of the opportunity to participate in programs that are designed to reduce their chances of being victimized. Similarly, Brantingham et al. (1986) reported from a study in Vancouver that while residents in the high density West End area perceived crime as a problem in their area, few took security precautions. Crime was viewed by residents as a problem, but not as a personal problem. The extent to which the public participates in police-initiated crime prevention programs will be considered further in Chapter 5.

The Victims and Witnesses of Crime

Over the past decade there has been an increased concern with the needs of the victims and witnesses of crime and the impact of victimization on both individuals and communities (see Karmen, 1984).[7] At least part of the impetus for these developments has come from the view that the criminal justice system has traditionally given more attention to the perpetrators of crime than to the victims of criminal offences. This concern has resulted in the creation of a wide range of services for the victims of crime operated by government and private, non-profit agencies, a large number of which rely heavily on voluntary support for their operation.[8] Further, it has been recognized that the victims and witnesses of crime require specialized attention, not only to address the physical and emotional consequences of crime, but to ensure their active involvement in the criminal justice process (Department of Justice, 1986b; Daubney, 1988).

Indicative of the increasing attention being given to the victims of crime was the passage of the *Justice for Victims of Crime Act* in Manitoba in 1987. This Act, the first of its type in Canada, outlines a set of principles for providing justice for the victims of crime, and includes sections on victim assistance, the treatment of victims, the provision of information to the victims of crime, and consideration of victim's needs during the criminal justice process.

In a survey of crime victims conducted in the city of Red Deer, Alberta, Stuebing (1984: 9) found that the needs most frequently mentioned were for "someone to talk to after the police left; someone to stay and provide security or protection; and advice on how to get help for problems which arose as a result of the crime." As a consequence of their experiences, victims expressed a general distrust of people and a fear of being alone. One-third of the victims were unable to find assistance for their needs.

The witnesses of crime in the survey experienced difficulties caused by a lack of information about the criminal justice process and uncertainty about the resources that were available to provide assistance. These difficulties were compounded by the lack of attention given to witness needs by the criminal justice system, particularly by the courts and prosecutors.

Among the recommendations offered by Stuebing (1984: 28–31) were that the police give more attention to the needs of victims and witnesses by providing in-service training for officers, that a victims' services program be developed in the community, and that the court and Crown counsel become more sensitive to victim and witness needs. Similar recommendations were made in a report of victim and witness needs in the Yukon Territory (see McLaughlin, 1984).

Norquay and Weiler (1981: 3–9) note that the services for victims of crime in Canada can be divided into five broad categories:

1. crisis intervention services operated by community-based agencies, the police, and for specific types of victims such as the elderly, children, and women;
2. programs designed to protect the rights of victims and witnesses and ensure their participation in the criminal justice process by providing information on the status of the case and on court procedures;
3. criminal injuries compensation programs which provide financial remuneration to the victims of crime;
4. restitution and victim-offender reconciliation programs; and
5. information and referral services for victims and witnesses of crime.

The Victim Assistance Program operated by the Winnipeg Police Department is illustrative of the programs developed by many municipal, provincial, and RCMP detachments. The program provides information to victims on the progress of case investigations, facilitates the return of property to victims, and refers victims to other services in the community. In addition, the Victim Assistance Program sponsors training sessions for officers to sensitize them to the needs of victims and to inform them of the various resources that are available in the community.

The Victim Services Unit in the Edmonton Police Department provides similar services to crime victims (see Brickey and Guest, 1984). An evaluation of this program conducted by Pullyblank (1986) found that the Victim Services Unit was favourably viewed by crime victims, members of the police department, and the volunteer victim advocates who staffed the program. In Ottawa, the Salvation Army operates a victim assistance program in collaboration with the Ottawa Police Department, and in Montreal, the Integrated Victim Assistance Program is run by the University of Montreal in close cooperation with the Montreal police (see also Canyltec Social Research Corporation, 1987; Meredith, 1984a).

Recognition of the needs of witnesses of crime has led to the development of witness assistance programs such as the Ottawa Witness Coordinator Project, which operates within the Crown Attorney's office in Ottawa. Similar witness assistance programs have been established across the country from St. John and Campbellton, New Brunswick to Vancouver. These programs are most often affiliated with Crown Prosecutor's offices, utilize both paid staff and volunteers and provide information to witnesses on court procedures and case details (see Abt. Associates, 1985).

There has also been an exponential growth in services for specific groups of victims, including battered and sexually abused women and children, native Indians, and the elderly (see Norquay and Weiler, 1981). This has included the establishment of transition and "safe" houses, sexual assault centres, various crisis intervention services including 24-hour "hotlines," and counselling and information on alternative shelters (see City of Ottawa Task Force on Wife Assault, 1984; McLeod, 1987).

The increased focus on the victims of crime by the provincial and federal levels of government in the early 1980s was reflected in the creation of the Federal-Provincial Task Force on Justice for the Victims of Crime (Canada, 1983). Included in the mandate of the Task Force was an examination of victim needs, as well as of the requirements for effective victim services. In its final report, the Task Force (Canada, 1983: 155–67) made 79 recommendations, including several proposed amendments to the *Criminal Code,* which would facilitate the return of property to victims, increase the use of restitution, insure criminal injuries compensation, and provide for the participation of victims at the sentencing stage of the criminal court.

Criminal Injuries Compensation

One method by which the needs of crime victims are met is through criminal injuries compensation. The first criminal injuries compensation plan was created in Saskatchewan in 1967, and since that time all provinces and territories, with the exception of Prince Edward Island, have enacted legislation that provides financial compensation for injuries or death in-curred from a crime committed by another person or from efforts to prevent a crime or arrest an offender, with or without the assistance of a police officer.[9] Compensation may also be provided for the surviving dependants of victims of crime and to those responsible for the maintenance of the victim. Compensation is generally limited to instances of violent crime, with private insurance companies providing recompense for the victims of property offences. Crime victims may also seek compensation through civil suits.

In some jurisdictions, applications for compensation are made to the Worker's Compensation Board, while in others an administrative tribunal known as the Criminal Injuries Compensation Board receives and adjudicates requests for compensation. In the Northwest Territories applications are filed with the Department of Justice and Public Services. These compensation programs are operated on a cost-sharing basis between the provincial/territorial and federal governments. Monies awarded to applicants may be made in a lump sum or in periodic payments. In 1985–86, $22.9 million was paid out in compensation to victims, an increase of 76.6% from 1980, when awards totalled almost $13 million (Department of Justice, 1988).

An evaluation of the Service d'indemnisation des victimes d'actes criminels du Québec (Quebec crime victims compensation scheme, or IVAC) (Baril et al., 1984a) provides some insights into the operation of criminal compensation programs, as well as the limitations of such programs. Among the findings of the evaluation was that, while victims were generally satisfied with the IVAC in terms of its provision of financial compensation, there was less enthusiasm among those who had expectations that IVAC could assist them in dealing with the psychological effects caused by the victimization experience. The psychological and support needs of victims were often viewed as paramount to financial compensation, a situation that often resulted in conflict between the IVAC program and its clients.

In late 1987, the federal government proposed several amendments to the *Criminal Code* that would significantly alter the way in which the courts handle crime victims. Bill C-89, enacted in 1988, requires convicted offenders to pay restitution to their victims, as well as forcing all offenders convicted of *Criminal Code* or narcotic offences to contribute up to 15% of any fine to a fund to be used by the provincial victim compensation programs. The legislation also allows criminal courts to accept victim-impact statements, both in written form and, in certain circumstances, in person from the victim in court.

Victim Involvement in Sentencing

The extent to which crime victims should be involved in the criminal justice process, particularly at the sentencing stage, is the focus of considerable discussion in Canada (see Daubney, 1988). In the United States, several states have enacted legislation requiring input from the victim at various stages of the criminal justice system. Since 1982 in California, for example, victims or their next of kin have had the right to present their views on the crime and its impact during sentencing hearings and to appear before the state board of parole when the offender is being considered for release (see Ranish and Shichor, 1985). In 1987, pilot projects under which crime victims speak to the court at the sentencing stage were being carried out in six Canadian cities.

In a consideration of the issues surrounding victim participation at the sentencing stage in Canada, Rubel (1986: 249) argues that efforts to address the concerns of victims should not be "foisted upon the courts," which already consider the public interest in their procedures and decision making. In support of this position, Rubel (1986: 239) cites the findings of Hagan (1982), who found few differences between victims who attended court and those who did not in terms of demands for severity of sentence. In addition, Hagan found that contacts between the victim and defence counsel, prosecutors and police served only to aggravate tensions between the victim and the accused (see also Davis, Kunreuther, and Connick, 1984). Further, Hagan (1982) and others have pointed out that a high percentage of criminal activity is directed toward corporations, raising additional issues relating to victim input into the criminal justice process.

Victim-Offender Reconciliation

Several provinces have developed victim-offender reconciliation programs (VORP's), which are designed to increase community participation and to "personalize and humanize" the criminal justice process (Ekstedt and Jackson, 1986: 31). While generally limited to minor offences, these programs operate at the post-charge, pre-trial stage and involve the voluntary participation of the victim and the offender. In many jurisdictions, mediation programs form the basis of victim-offender reconciliation efforts and involve the use of mediation between the two parties (Daubney, 1988).[10] Private agencies such as the John Howard Society and local organizations such as the St. Leonard's Society in North Vancouver, British Columbia, are extensively involved in operating VORP's across the country on a contract basis.

In Quebec, the provincial Department of Justice operates a VORP in several communities that involves the use of conciliators who attempt to resolve summary conviction matters outside of court between the victims and the offender. Ekstedt and Jackson (1986: 73) note that during 1984–85, there were 317 referrals to the program, the majority of which involved store owners and business people who were the victims of theft. In nearly 80% of the cases, conciliation agreements were reached whereby the offender performed a specified number of community service hours for non-profit organizations.

VORP's have also been operating in Ontario for over a decade and involve programs for adult and juvenile offenders at the pre-sentence and post-plea stages. The conciliation agreement that is mediated between the offender and the victim is reached prior to the passing of sentence in court and is included in the probation order. One of the better-known programs is operated under contract in Kitchener by the Mennonite Central Committee. In the Yukon Territory, the focus of the VORP is on family mediation, particularly the resolution of issues surrounding child custody and support.

Preliminary evaluations of VORP's suggest that they may be a viable alternative to the formal criminal justice process and increase the participation of both the victim and the offender in the resolution of conflicts (see Gibson, 1986). Among the issues requiring further research are the under-use of VORP's by the courts, the impact of participation in VORP's on recidivism, and the cost of VORP's as compared to other alternatives (Dittenhoffer and Ericson, 1983). Further, criminal justice agencies and communities must explore the potential for expanding the use of mediation as an alternative to the formal criminal justice process.

Canadian Attitudes Toward the Law and the Criminal Justice System

In one of the most thorough examinations of Canadian attitudes toward the law and legal system, conducted in 1980, Robert J. Moore (1985) interviewed citizens in Montreal, Toronto, and Winnipeg. The information gathered from 640 respondents provides critical insights into not only the attitudes held by Canadians, but also the determinants of these perceptions.

Moore (1985: 48) reports that while the majority of citizens surveyed felt that the laws represent a consensus of the majority and stated that they would obey the law, even in those instances where they disagreed with a specific law:

> ... many were critical of the way in which justice was currently being dispensed: a majority of respondents indicated that something needs to be done to improve the way the legal system operates and the laws it produces; that the legal system favours the rich and powerful, and that it takes too long to get anything done through the legal process.

Moore (1985: 48) also discovered a relation between perceptions of the law and the legal system and the respondents' political affiliation, gender, marital status, education level, and age. Those respondents with higher levels of education, for example, tended to be satisfied with the operation of the legal system and to feel that the law gave too much protection to criminal offenders, although these respondents indicated less willingness to adhere to the law at all times and tended to view the abuses of authority by government as serious. With respect to the gender of the respondent, Moore (1985: 48–49) reported that, in comparison with men, women "were less satisfied with the current operation of the legal system and did not see the law as representing a consensus; they tended to advocate law reform and tougher laws." Respondents who were supporters of the New Democratic Party viewed law reform rather than law enforcement as a priority and perceived abuses of authority by government agencies as serious.

In his survey, Moore (1985) also attempted to determine the perceptions of Canadians toward specific components of the Canadian criminal justice system. Respondents gave local police high marks on performance, although Moore (1985: 52) reports that "concern was shown about the unnecessary use of physical force, the use of illegal methods in getting information, the keeping of suspects in jail for excessive periods of time, and, to a lesser extent, the covering up of illegal police activity."

While evidencing high levels of support for the police, the public is less sympathetic toward and less trustful of the courts. Many Canadians blame the judiciary for being too lenient with criminal offenders (Moore, 1985: 55). Sixty-seven per cent of the respondents surveyed by Brillon et al. (1984: 226) felt that the courts hindered the effectiveness of the police. There is also a widely-shared view that the courts tend to favour certain groups over others. Many of the respondents interviewed by Moore (1985: 53–54), for example, felt that the courts tended to favour the wealthy, while the poor received less favourable treatment. Seventy-four per cent of the respondents felt that guilty persons could go free if they had a good lawyer. Ericson, Baranek, and Chan (1989) suggest that the high levels of public support for the police, in comparison to other components of the criminal justice system, are due in large measure to police control over media communications, which facilitates the creation of positive images of police activity.

With respect to public perceptions of the correctional system, Moore (1985: 55) reported that respondents tended to view prisons as doing only a "fair to good job" of protecting society and punishing offenders. Fifty-eight per cent of those interviewed by Brillon et al. (1984: 214–15) believed that prisons were "veritable hotels," these respondents also perceiving that sentences meted out by the courts were generally not harsh enough.

An important finding of the Moore (1985) study was the considerable variability between respondents in the three cities in their perceptions of the law and the legal system. For example, respondents in Montreal — as opposed to their counterparts in Toronto and Winnipeg — were more likely to be strongly oriented toward law enforcement, to feel that the legal system was inefficient, and to perceive that laws were often enacted to benefit certain groups of people. These findings suggest that there may be considerable differences between regions of the country in perceptions of the criminal justice system (see Brillon et al., 1984; Ribordy and Barnett, 1979).[11]

Costs of the Criminal Justice System

During the twenty-year period 1961–1980, expenditures for criminal justice services in Canada rose dramatically. In 1961, overall expenditures were $293 million, increasing to $1,066 million in 1971 and to $3,824 million in 1980 (Solicitor General of Canada, 1985b: 25). Total federal spending on police, courts, and corrections in 1961 was $4.38 per Canadian, while in 1980, it was $16.85 per Canadian (adjusted to Implicit Price Index). According to Demers (1984: 7-9), the increase of expenditures to nearly $4 billion can be attributed to the expansion of policing responsibilities by the RCMP, a rapid growth in the Correctional Service of Canada, including the construction of new correctional facilities, and "the pronounced effect of inflationary forces on a labour-intensive delivery system."

In reviewing the expenditures for criminal justice services during the period 1961–1984, Demers (1984: 4–5) notes that at the federal level, 60% of the financial resources allocated for criminal justice services were expended on the RCMP, 30% on correctional services and the National Parole Board, and 10% on the courts. In contrast, provincial and territorial governments allocated roughly one-third of their budgets to policing, courts, and corrections, while municipal governments allocated nearly all of their budgets to policing. The costs and expenditures of the various components of the Canadian criminal justice system will be considered in greater detail throughout the text.

NOTES

1. For a discussion of the difficulties surrounding the use of official statistics in criminal justice research, see Connidis (1979).

2. For a more detailed discussion of the various operational attributes of the Uniform Crime Reporting system, as well as the limitations of using data collected by this system, see the annual report produced by the Canadian Centre for Justice Statistics, a division of Statistics Canada, entitled *Canadian Crime Statistics.*

3. Violent crime includes homicide, attempted murder, sexual assault and robbery. Property crime includes break and enter, motor vehicle theft, possession of stolen goods, and fraud. Recent years have witnessed an increased concern with several types of offence that, traditionally, received very little attention from the public, politicians and legislators. Among these are domestic violence and impaired driving (Donelson, 1985; Donelson and Beirness, 1985; McLeod, 1987).

4. For statistical summaries of general crime patterns in Canada, as well as for specific types of offence, e.g., homicide, see the *Juristat Service Bulletins* and the annual reports *Canadian Crime Statistics* and *Homicide in Canada* published by the Canadian Centre for Justice Statistics, a division of Statistics Canada.

5. There has also been an attempt to discover the role of other factors that may influence the perceptions that Canadians hold toward crime. For example, see Sacco (1985) for an examination of the relation between city size and perceptions of crime.

6. For a discussion of the interrelationship between Canadians' perceptions of crime and their attitudes toward society and change, see Brillon et al. (1984); see also Moore (1985).

7. For an overview of victim needs and an annotated bibliography of Canadian and United States materials addressing these issues, see Norquay and Weiler (1981); Weiler and Desgagne (1984); Meredith (1984b). Bradley and Delisle (1983) provide insights into the impact of case management practices on the victims and witnesses of crime in British Columbia, while Baril et al. (1984b) have conducted an analysis of victim needs in the courts in Montreal.

8. For a description of the victim/witness programs operating in the provinces and territories, see Weiler and Desgagne (1984). See Brown and Peachy (1984) for an evaluation of the victim services program in Waterloo, Ontario, and Department of Justice (1986a) for a review of witness programs operating across Canada.

9. For a detailed report on the structure and operation of criminal injuries compensation programs across Canada, see the report *Criminal Injuries Compensation in Canada, 1986* (1988) produced by the Department of Justice. See also Hastings (1983) for an in-depth examination of the rationale, structure and operation, and evaluation of criminal injuries compensation programs operating in Canada.

10. For programmatic descriptions and evaluation outcomes of community-based conciliation and mediation programs in Canada, see Dube-Ouellet and Belanger (1984).

11. For a discussion of the impact of the media on public opinion about the law, see Kent (1985). There does appear to be, among the Canadian public, a general lack of knowledge of the law and how the criminal justice system operates. Seventy-five per cent of the respondents interviewed by Brillon et al. (1984: 226) felt that "justice is so complicated that no one can understand it." One attempt to increase public knowledge is the Public Legal Education programs sponsored by the federal Department of Justice (see Ribordy, Laflamme, and Cazabon, 1986).

REFERENCES

Abt. Associates. 1985. *Access to Justice — Review of Court-Based Victim/ Witness Projects.* Ottawa: Supply and Services Canada.

Atkinson, T. 1981. *Perceptions of Crime in Metropolitan Toronto.* Downsview, Ont.: Institute for Behavioural Research, York University.

Baril, M., S. Laflamme-Cusson, and S. Beauchemin. 1984a. *Crime Victims. Working Paper No. 12. Crime Victims Compensation: An Assessment of the Quebec IVAC Program.* Ottawa: Policy Planning and Development Branch, Department of Justice.

Baril, M., S. Durand, M.-M. Cousineau, and S. Gravel. 1984b. *Victimes d'Actes Criminels. Document de travail no. 10. Mais Nous, Les Temoins . . .: Une etude exploratoire des besoins des temoins au Palais de Justice de Montreal.* Ottawa: Direction de la planification et de l'elaboration de la politique, Ministere de la Justice.

Bradley, H. J., and D. M. A. Delisle. 1983. *Crime Victims. Working Paper No. 7. Evaluation of Case Management Procedures in the British Columbia Justice System and Their Impact on Victim/Witnesses.* Ottawa: Policy Planning and Development Branch, Department of Justice.

Brantingham, P. J., and P. L. Brantingham. 1984. *Patterns in Crime.* New York: Macmillan.

Brantingham, P. J., P. L. Brantingham, and D. Butcher. 1986. "Perceived and Actual Crime Risks." In *Metropolitan Crime Patterns,* edited by R. M. Figlio, S. Hakin, and G. F. Renget, 139–59. Monsey, N.Y.: Criminal Justice Press.

Brickey, S., and A. Guest. 1984. *Crime Victims. Working Paper No. 8. The Evaluation of the Winnipeg Victim/Witness Assistance Program.* Ottawa: Policy Planning and Development Branch, Department of Justice.

Brillon, Y. 1987. *Victimization and Fear of Crime Among the Elderly.* Toronto: Butterworths.

Brillon, Y., C. Louis-Guerin, and M.-C. Lamarche. 1984. *Attitudes of the Canadian Public Toward Crime Policies.* Montreal: International Centre for Comparative Criminology, University of Montreal.

Brown, S. D., and D. Peachy. 1984. *Evaluation of the Victim Services Program in the Region of Waterloo, Ontario.* Ottawa: Solicitor General of Canada.

Canada. Federal-Provincial Task Force on Justice for Victims of Crime. 1983. *Report.* Ottawa: Supply and Services Canada.

Canadian Centre for Justice Statistics. 1986. *Criminal Injuries Compensation.* Ottawa: Supply and Services Canada.

———. 1988. *Canadian Crime Statistics, 1987.* (Catalogue No. 85-205.) Ottawa: Supply and Services Canada.

Canyltec Social Research Corporation. 1987. *An Evaluation of Two Approaches to Delivery of Police-Based Victim Assistance: Neighborhood-Focussed vs. Headquarters-Based.* Ottawa: Solicitor General of Canada.

Connidis, I. 1979. "Problems in the Use of Official Statistics for Criminal Justice System Research." 21 *Canadian Journal of Criminology* 397–415.

Courtis, M. C. 1970. *Attitudes to Crime and the Police in Toronto.* Toronto: Centre of Criminology, University of Toronto.

Daubney, D. (Chairman). 1988. *Taking Responsibility. Report of the Standing Committee on Justice and Solicitor General on Its Review of Sentencing, Conditional Release and Related Aspects of Corrections.* Ottawa: Supply and Services Canada.

Davis, R. C., F. Kunreuther, and E. Connick. 1984. "Expanding the Victim's Role in the Criminal Court Dispositional Process: The Results of an Experiment." 75 *Journal of Criminal Law and Criminology* 491–505.

Demers, D. J. 1984. "Criminal Justice Spending in Canada: Recent Trends." In Solicitor General of Canada, *IMPACT — Costs of Criminal Justice*, 4–12. Ottawa: Supply and Services Canada.

Department of Justice. 1986a. *Access to Justice — Review of Court-Based Victim/Witness Projects.* Ottawa: Supply and Services Canada.

_____. 1986b. *Access to Justice — Survey of Victims' Legal Information Needs.* Ottawa: Supply and Services Canada.

_____. 1988. *Criminal Injuries Compensation in Canada, 1986.* Ottawa: Supply and Services Canada.

Dittenhoffer, T., and R. V. Ericson. 1983. "The Victim-Offender Reconciliation Program: A Message to Correctional Reformers." 33 *University of Toronto Law Journal* 315–47.

Donelson, A. C. 1985. *Impaired Driving. Report No. 4. Alcohol and Road Accidents in Canada: Issues Related to Future Strategies and Priorities.* Ottawa: Department of Justice.

Donelson, A. C., and D. J. Beirness. 1985. *Impaired Driving. Report No. 2. Legislative Issues Related to Drinking and Driving.* Ottawa: Department of Justice.

Doob, A. N., and J. V. Roberts. 1982. "Crime: Some Views of the Canadian Public." Unpublished paper. Toronto: Centre of Criminology, University of Toronto.

Dube-Ouellet, F., and L. Belanger. 1984. *Crime Victims. Conciliation in the Community. Evaluation of a Conciliation Program of the Delinquent with the Victm.* Ottawa: Policy and Planning Development Branch, Department of Justice.

Ekstedt, J. W., and M. A. Jackson. 1986. *A Profile of Canadian Alternative Sentencing Programmes: A National Review of Policy Issues.* Burnaby, B.C.: School of Criminology, Simon Fraser University.

Elie, D., and A. Normandeau. 1984. *Armed Robbery in North America: Current Trends.* Montreal: International Centre for Comparative Criminology, University of Montreal.

Ericson, R. V., P. M. Baranek, and J. B. L. Chan. 1987. *Visualizing Deviance: A Study of News Organization.* Toronto: University of Toronto Press.

———. 1989. *Negotiating Control: A Study of News Sources.* Toronto and Milton Keyes, U.K.: University of Toronto Press and Open University Press.

Gabor, T., and A. Normandeau. 1987. *Armed Robbery: Cops, Robbers, and Victims.* Springfield, Ill.: Charles C. Thomas Publishers.

Gebotys, R. J., J. V. Roberts, and B. DasGupta. 1988. "News Media Use and Public Perceptions of Crime Seriousness." 30 *Canadian Journal of Criminology* 3–16.

Gibson, A. 1986. *Victim-Offender Reconciliation Program: Research Project.* Vancouver: Consultation Centre, Solicitor General of Canada.

Gomme, I. M. 1986. "Fear of Crime Among Canadians: A Multi-Variate Analysis." 14 *Journal of Criminal Justice* 249–58.

Hagan, J. 1982. "Victims Before the Law: A Study of Victim Involvement in the Criminal Justice Process." 73 *Journal of Criminal Law and Criminology* 317–30.

Hastings, R. 1983. *Crime Victims. Working Paper No. 6. A Theoretical Assessment of Criminal Injuries Compensation in Canada: Policy, Programs and Evaluation.* Ottawa: Policy Planning and Development Branch, Department of Justice.

Himelfarb, A. 1984. "Cost of Crime to Victims: Preliminary Findings of the Canadian Urban Victimization Survey." In Solicitor General of Canada, *IMPACT: Costs of Criminal Justice,* 36–49. Ottawa: Supply and Services Canada.

Hylton, J. H., and R. Matonovich. 1980. *Public Attitudes About Crime and the Police in Moose Jaw.* Regina: School of Human Justice, University of Regina.

Jayewardene, C. H. S., T. J. Juliani, and C. K. Talbot. 1983. *Crime Victims. Working Paper No. 5. The Elderly as Victims of Crime.* Ottawa: Policy Planning and Development Branch, Department of Justice.

Johnson, H. 1986. *Women and Crime in Canada.* Ottawa: Solicitor General of Canada.

———. 1987. "Getting the Facts Straight: A Statistical Overview." In *Too Few To Count: Canadian Women in Conflict with the Law,* edited by E. Adelberg and C. Currie, 23–46. Vancouver: Press Gang Publishers.

Karmen, A. 1984. *Crime Victims: An Introduction to Victimology.* Monterey, Calif.: Brooks-Cole.

Kennedy, L. W., and H. Krahn. 1984. "Rural-Urban Origin and Fear of Crime: The Case for 'Rural Baggage'." 49 *Rural Sociology* 247–60.

Kent, T. 1985. "Media Influence on Opinion and Policy." In *Law in a*

Cynical Society? Opinion and Law in the 1980's, edited by D. Gibson and J. K. Baldwin, 341-49. Calgary and Vancouver: Carswell Legal Publications, Western Division.

Krahn, H., and L. W. Kennedy. 1985. *Producing Personal Safety: Parallel Production, Police, Fear and Crime.* Edmonton: Centre for Criminological Research, University of Alberta.

Lee, G. W. 1984. "Are Crime Rates Increasing? A Study of the Impact of Demographic Shifts on Crime Rates in Canada." 26 *Canadian Journal of Criminology* 29–41.

Maxim, P. S., and A. Jocklin. 1980. "Population Size, Age Structure, and Sex Composition Effects on Official Crime in Canada." 4 *International Journal of Comparative and Applied Criminal Justice* 147–63.

McLaughlin, A. 1984. *Crime Victims. Working Paper No. 11. An Analysis of Victims/Victim Witness Needs in Yukon.* Ottawa: Policy Planning and Development Branch, Department of Justice.

McLeod, L. 1987. *Battered But Not Beaten . . . Preventing Wife Battering in Canada.* Ottawa: Canadian Advisory Council on the Status of Women.

Meredith, C. 1984a. *Access to Justice — Evaluation of the Ottawa Witness Co-ordinator Project.* Ottawa: Supply and Services Canada.

———. 1984b. *Overview and Annotated Bibliography of the Needs of Crime Victims.* Ottawa: Solicitor General of Canada.

Moore, R. J. 1985. "Reflections of Canadians on the Law and the Legal System: Legal Research Institute Survey of Respondents in Montreal, Toronto and Winnipeg." In *Law in a Cynical Society? Opinion and Law in the 1980's,* edited by D. Gibson and J. K. Baldwin, 41–87. Calgary and Vancouver: Carswell Legal Publications, Western Division.

Norquay, G., and R. Weiler. 1981. *Services to Victims and Witnesses of Crime in Canada.* Ottawa: Solicitor General of Canada.

Ottawa (City of) Task Force on Wife Assault. 1984. *Report of the City of Ottawa Task Force on Wife Assault.* Ottawa.

Pullyblank, J. 1986. *The Victim Services Unit of the Edmonton Police Department: An Evaluation.* Ottawa: Solicitor General of Canada.

Ranish, D. R., and D Shichor. 1985. "The Victim's Role in the Penal Process: Recent Developments in California." 49 *Federal Probation* 50–57.

Ribordy, F. X., and A. N. Barnett. 1979. "La conscience du droit chez les etudiants anglo et franco ontariens." 21 *Canadian Journal of Criminology* 184–96.

Ribordy, F. X., S. Laflamme and B. Cazabon. 1986. *Legal Education and Information: Exploratory Study.* Ottawa: Supply and Services Canada.

Rubel, H. C. 1986. "Victim Participation in Sentencing Proceedings." 28 *Criminal Law Quarterly* 226-50.

Sacco, V. F. 1985. "City Size and Perceptions of Crime." 10 *Canadian Journal of Sociology* 277-93.

―――. 1988. "Public Definitions of Crime Problems and Functionalist Processes: A Reassessment." 25 *Canadian Review of Sociology and Anthropology* 84-97.

Sacco, V. F., W. Glackman, and R. Roesch. 1984. *Factors Associated with Public Perceptions of Crime.* Burnaby, B.C.: Criminology Research Centre, Simon Fraser University.

Solicitor General of Canada. 1984. *Canadian Urban Victimization Survey. Bulletin 3. Crime Prevention: Awareness and Practice.* Ottawa: Research and Statistics Group, Programs Branch.

―――. 1985a. *Canadian Urban Victimization Survey. Bulletin 6. Criminal Victimization of Elderly Canadians.* Ottawa: Research and Statistics Group, Programs Branch.

―――. 1985b. *Ministry Facts.* Ottawa: Supply and Services Canada.

Stuebing, W. K. 1984. *Crime Victims. Working Paper No. 9. Victims and Witnesses: Experiences, Needs, and Community/Criminal Justice Response.* Ottawa: Policy Planning and Development Branch, Department of Justice.

Waller, I., and N. R. Okihiro. 1976. *Burglary and the Public.* Toronto: Centre of Criminology, University of Toronto.

Weiler, D., and J.-G. Desgagne. 1984. *Victims and Witnesses of Crime in Canada.* Ottawa: Department of Justice.

LEGISLATION

Criminal Code, R.S.C. 1985, c. C-46
Justice for Victims of Crime Act, S.M. 1986-87, c. 28 (C.C.S.M., c. J40)

3 THE STRUCTURE AND OPERATION OF CANADIAN POLICING

Our consideration of policing in Canada will reveal that the emergence of designated officials and organizations charged with a law enforcement function was closely intertwined with changes that were occurring in the socio-political milieu of early Canada. In fact, numerous observers have documented the relation between the identification and response to criminal behaviour and the social, political, religious and philosophical attributes of society (see Ekstedt and Griffiths, 1988; Robinson and Scaglion, 1987).

Policing in Early Canada

The development of policing in Canada was strongly influenced by the system of policing that emerged in England, although as the following discussion will reveal, Canadian policing has its own unique history and was to evolve into a structure quite distinct from its counterparts in England and the United States.[1] While a detailed examination of the factors — social, political, geographical, and cultural — that combined to influence the development of Canadian policing is beyond the scope of this text, it is incumbent upon us to consider the major events that served to shape the course of Canadian policing from the days of the early settlers to the present.[2]

Early Municipal Policing

Chapman (1977: 496) notes that prior to Confederation in 1867, each area of the country had its own particular policing arrangements, depending upon the pattern of settlement and the origin of the settlers. Areas such as Newfoundland, which very early attracted fishermen on a seasonal basis, and French Canada, which was settled early, encountered pressures to make some provision for law enforcement much earlier than did the West, which remained sparsely settled well into the late 1800s.[3]

The development of structures for maintaining order in Newfoundland are instructive and provide an illustration not only of the types of problem that emerged, but the remedies that were put forth for maintaining order.

Fox (1971: 4) notes that considerable disorder existed among the fishermen who came ashore during the fishing season. In an attempt to establish order, English authorities established the institution of the "Fishing Admirals," captains of fishing vessels who were empowered to settle disputes among the fishermen. However, as Fox (1971: 4) points out, these untrained men were largely ineffective in securing order, being "ill-fitted to carry out the functions of the law properly, and they abused their power by a particularly corrupt administration of the laws." In 1729, a royal proclamation authorized the governor of Newfoundland to appoint justices of the peace and constables, although no regulations governing their supervision were established until 1825 (Stenning, 1981a: 38).

While these developments were occurring on the East Coast, settlers in French Canada instituted a French system of policing (Dickinson, 1987). In 1651, what are considered by Canadian historians to have been the first Canadian policemen, appeared on the streets of Quebec City. However, Juliani, Talbot, and Jayewardene (1984: 321) argue that "real police work was apparently assigned to the police in Quebec City only in 1673" with the imposition of British laws and justices of the peace, and with increased commerce on the St. Lawrence River, which brought large numbers of immigrants and seamen into the community. The duties of these first police officers in Quebec City centred on watching for fires and ensuring the safety of citizens after dark. A system of policing was also introduced in the city of Montreal, although its primary purpose was the protection of the residents from the Iroquois Indians.

The conquest of New France by the British in 1759 radically altered the system of policing that had been developing in French Canada, and in 1787 an ordinance was passed that authorized justices of the peace to appoint persons to assist in carrying out the orders of the court and to maintain order in the cities of Montreal and Quebec. This legislation served to introduce the position of constable, which was to provide the model of policing throughout the province.

In Upper Canada (now the Province of Ontario), the English settlers implemented a system of laws and a legal system that directly mirrored that of England. Sheriffs, constables, and justices of the peace formed the basis of the peacekeeping function. In 1792, the English common law was installed as the law of Upper Canada, and in 1793, the *Parish and Town Officers Act* was enacted and provided for the appointment of high constables for each provincial district, who in turn, were to appoint citizens to act as unpaid constables in each parish and township in the district.

While this legislation was designed to expand the system of policing throughout Upper Canada, there is considerable evidence to suggest that community officials and citizens did not regard crime as a serious problem, nor the development of crime control structures such as the police and jails as a high priority (see Baehre, 1977; Ekstedt and Griffiths, 1988). During this time, citizens were often reluctant to serve in the position of constable, and while many of the charters establishing towns required the creation of systems of law enforcement, "a truly functional police force was established only when there was a felt need that had become compelling" (Juliani et al., 1984: 326).

The early 1800s, however, produced a major shift in the approach toward policing in Canada, precipitated by many of the same factors that had occurred previously in England. During this time, there emerged a growing concern with crime and the "criminal classes." Whether this shift in Canadian attitudes toward crime and criminality was due to an actual increase in the amount and seriousness of crime or merely to citizens' perceptions that crime was increasing has been the subject of considerable debate (see Baehre, 1977; Beattie, 1977; Bellomo, 1972; Ekstedt and Griffiths, 1988). What is clear is that Canadians became more interested in developing systems for the control of crime, including police forces.

Again, Newfoundland provides a good illustration of the changes that were occurring. The police force in St. John's at the beginning of the nineteenth century consisted of tavern-keepers who performed police duties in return for being granted licences to operate their businesses. In 1848, the first night-watch system was established in the city and consisted of 16 special constables and 4 constables under the supervision of a high constable. These officers were the predecessors of the Royal Newfoundland Constabulary, which was formed in 1872.

Similar developments were occurring in Upper Canada, with a full-time police force of six men replacing the night-watch system in the city of Toronto in 1835. In 1858, the *Municipal Institutions of Upper Canada Act* authorized towns and cities to form police forces and to create boards of commissioners to oversee the activities of the police.

Given the patterns of settlement in Canada, municipalities in the areas west of Upper Canada did not have organized policing and municipal police forces until the late 1800s. Calgary hired its first constable in 1885, and the city of Lethbridge appointed its first officer in 1891. In the absence of police forces, most communities maintained order on a self-policing basis similar to that employed by the villages in England prior to the Industrial Revolution.[4] A major role in law enforcement during these times was played by the Hudson's Bay Company, Skinner, Driedger, and Grainger (1981: 16) noting that as late as 1861, "the Hudson's Bay Company presiding judicial officer held the positions of sheriff, coroner, jailor, and chief medical officer." As settlements grew in size, provisions were made for the appointment of constables, who were paid a small sum of money for carrying out peacekeeping duties (see Stenning, 1981a).

A unique development at this time was the creation in 1858 (in what is now the Province of British Columbia) of the first organized "provincial" police force, based on the Royal Irish Constabulary. This force was created in response to the increasing violence and disorder that had occurred with the discovery of gold deposits in the area. There was also concern by the governor and British authorities that the United States had territorial ambitions in the area. This police force was the predecessor of the provincial police force that was formed in 1871 when British Columbia joined Confederation. Chapman (1977: 497) notes that the constables in the force "came to act as revenue officers, claims officers, excise officers and providers of emergency services, as well as law enforcement officers."[5]

The lack of serious crime was also a reason for the late development of policing systems in the West. With the exception of the disorder caused by fortune-seekers in the far West, the Canadian West was, compared to its American counterpart, relatively violence-free. Gray (1971: 2) notes, for example, that "Aside from sex-and-whiskey-based enterprises, frontier Canada was almost unbelievably law-abiding. Nobody held up trains or stages, or robbed banks, or shot up towns or even saloons."

While municipal police forces were the first structures of organized policing to appear in Canada, their development was not without controversy. Considerable documentary evidence exists to indicate that corruption and criminal activity were widespread (and even accepted) practices among many municipal forces, both in Eastern Canada and on the Prairies. Further, when corrupt police officers were removed from office, Juliani et al. (1984: 337) note that having engaged in corrupt activities was rarely given as the reason for the dismissal: "When the boozing, brawling chief of the Winnipeg police was caught 'in flagrante delicto' in a Colony Creek whorehouse, he was fired because he was stupid enough to get caught."[6]

In tracing the development of municipal police forces in Canada into the twentieth century, Juliani et al. (1984: 340) found that municipal police were required to perform three broad categories of tasks: (1) preventing conflicts between ethnic groups and between labour groups and industry; (2) maintaining the moral order through the enforcement of puritanical laws, particularly in the areas of prostitution and drinking; and (3) the apprehension of individuals involved in criminal activity. According to these authors, there is considerable evidence that municipal police carried out these tasks with considerable tolerance, which was reflected in a policy of non-intervention, officers often electing not to intervene in labour disputes out of sympathy with the workers, and exhibiting considerable tolerance for prostitution and alcohol use.

This approach to policing led to conflict with the RCMP, the federal police force, Juliani et al. (1984: 340) noting that: "Whenever possible, the local police did not hesitate to impede the federal police in their law enforcement and peacekeeping functions; nor did the federal police hesitate to impede the local municipal police." This conflict often resulted in members of each force being arrested by the other. In fact, these conflicts, along with the difficulties afflicting municipal forces previously mentioned, facilitated the increased involvement of the federal police at the local level, providing the basis for the policing arrangements that exist in Canada today.

Early Provincial Policing and the Birth of the RCMP

The emergence of provincial police forces following Confederation in 1867 was closely intertwined with the origins and growth of the federal police force, now called the Royal Canadian Mounted Police. Under the provisions of the *Constitution Act, 1867,* the federal government was given the authority to enact criminal law and procedure, while the enforcement of laws and the administration of justice were delegated to the provinces. Provincial governments, through the office of the Attorney General, were required to establish law enforcement agencies, courts and correctional institutions.

While the *Constitution Act, 1867,* appeared to establish clearly that the enforcement of the criminal law was under the jurisdiction of provincial governments, Stenning (1981a: 40) notes that "both the federal and provincial levels of government considered that it entitled them to establish police forces." In 1868, Parliament passed the *Police of Canada Act,* which authorized the federal government to establish the Dominion Police Force. This federal police force, with Canada-wide jurisdiction, had as its primary duty the protection of federal buildings, including Parliament, although it later became involved in enforcing laws in the area of counterfeiting, as well as guarding naval shipyards and other government properties. The Dominion Police were absorbed by the RCMP in 1920 (see Kelly and Kelly, 1976). Stenning (1981a: 41) makes the important observation that the *Police of Canada Act* was the first major departure from the English model of policing, as it provided for the creation of a police force that had jurisdiction outside of one specific locale.

Under the terms of the *Constitution Act, 1867,* upon entry into Confederation, provinces enacted legislation providing for the creation of provincial police forces. Legislation authorizing the creation of provincial police forces was passed in Manitoba and Quebec in 1870, British Columbia in 1871, Ontario in 1909, New Brunswick in 1927, Nova Scotia in 1928, and Prince Edward Island in 1930. In Newfoundland, where the Royal Newfoundland Constabulary had been operating since 1872, a second provincial police force, the Newfoundland Company of Rangers, was formed in 1935. Chapman (1977) notes that, similar to their municipal counterparts, provincial police forces, particularly in Quebec, Ontario, and British Columbia, experienced considerable difficulties, including being subjected to political pressures.

The emerging pattern of provincial policing was disrupted, however, by the governments of Alberta and Saskatchewan. Following their entry into Confederation in 1905, the provincial governments in Alberta and Saskatchewan enacted legislation providing for provincial police forces. But, unlike the other provinces, these governments entered into negotiations with the federal government for the services of the Royal North-West Mounted Police. Under contracts signed between the federal and provincial governments, the RNWMP would act as the provincial police under a cost-sharing agreement.

The North-West Mounted Police had been created under the *Act of 23, May, 1873* to police the vast area known as Rupert's Land, which had been purchased from the Hudson's Bay Company in 1869. The reasons for the creation of this federal force have been the subject of considerable debate. Most observers contend that the NWMP were established to maintain law and order among the settlers and to protect the indigenous Indian population from unscrupulous traders and whiskey runners. However, others, including Brown and Brown (1973: 10) argue that the NWMP were created to "facilitate the transfer of most of the territory of the region from the Indian tribes to the federal government with a minimum of expense and bloodshed." These authors (1973: 23) further contend that the NWMP did not work to protect the rights and interests of the indigenous population, but rather collaborated closely with business interests such as the Canadian Pacific Railway, that were involved in the economic development of the Prairies and the West (see also Horrall, 1972).

While there is disagreement over the origins of the force, the Mounted Police were to become a national symbol, Walden (1982: 2) noting that, "To attack the force, which embodied everything that was valuable in the Canadian tradition, was tantamount to attacking the country itself." The exploits and daring of the Mounties were immortalized by Canadian, American, and European authors in such books as *Clancy of Mounted* (1923), *Tales of the Mounted* (1949), *Yukon Patrol* (1936) and *Arctic Patrols* (1937).[7]

While the stature and popularity of the Mounted Police are well documented, it is not generally known that the force was beset with considerable internal difficulties in the early days of its existence and that there was, in fact, hostility toward the force by both the settlers and federal legislators. Walden (1982: 5) notes that there were many reasons for citizens to dislike the Mounties, including the fact that officers were given the authority under law to act as magistrates and justices of the peace, meaning that "in some cases police officers could arrest, try, and sentence an accused who had no means of appeal." There is also evidence that the Mounties experienced high rates of desertion, resignations and improper conduct, including drunkenness and illicit sexual alliances with Indian women. Morgan (1973: 41) ascribes these and other problems to the isolation and harsh conditions of the frontier, inadequate housing and medical attention, and the failure to pay officers, often for months at a time. Morgan (1973: 56) argues that these internal difficulties made the force controversial "both in the House of Commons and in the public press."

While the difficulties experienced by the RCMP have been documented by historians, it appears that much of the criticism against the Mounties was politically motivated, a consequence of the previously noted conflicts that occurred between the Mounties and the municipal police forces. Illustrative of one community's sentiment toward the Mounties is an editorial, cited by Morgan (1973: 60) which appeared in the Regina *Leader,* charging that "many a scalawag and scroundrel, many an idle loafer, many a brainless young blood, has worn its uniform and fed at its trough" (see also Gray, 1971).

In 1904, the name of the federal force was changed to the Royal North-West Mounted Police. The following year, with the assumption of provincial policing responsibilities in Alberta and Saskatchewan, a major expansion of the force's policing activities occurred. In these provinces, members of the force acted as both federal and provincial law enforcement officers. Alberta and Saskatchewan were policed by the Mounties until 1916, when the services of the force were withdrawn by mutual agreement of the provinces and the federal government. Both provinces then created provincial police forces in 1917. Robertson (1978: 2) notes that while the official reason for the withdrawal of the RNWMP from provincial policing was that "the federal force should be used for federal purposes only", it was precipitated by factors such as the onset of World War I, and, it is speculated, the desire of politicians for a police force more amenable to the political interests of the provincial government.

Provincial police forces in Alberta and Saskatchewan, however, were to be short-lived. The Saskatchewan Provincial Police, in particular, experienced numerous difficulties and, according to Robertson (1978: 7), became "a source of embarrassment to the politicians in power." Anderson (1972: 18) notes that while many of the men recruited for the SPP were capable and experienced, "there were many who were merely 'filling the gap'. Some barely understood the words of their oath, while others would have been stumped to spell some of them." The lack of qualified manpower, inadequate physicial facilities, poor equipment, and a reluctance on the part of many municipalities in the province to contract for the services of the SPP, contributed to its dissolution in 1928. The Alberta Provincial Police remained in operation until 1932. The Royal Canadian Mounted Police (the name having been changed in 1920) resumed provincial policing duties in both provinces.

The RCMP continued to expand into provincial policing, absorbing provincial police forces in New Brunswick, Nova Scotia, and Prince Edward Island in 1932, and in Newfoundland and British Columbia in 1950 (see Cooper, 1981). In the 1930s, under legislation which allowed municipalities to contract with the provincial police for policing services, the federal force also began policing at that level. With these developments, only three provincial police forces remained — the Ontario Provincial Police, the Quebec Police Force, and the Newfoundland Constabulary, which today polices only in the city of St. John's.[8]

Contemporary Canadian Policing

Policing in Canada today is carried out at three levels: municipal, provincial, and federal.[9] In 1986, there were 54,604 full-time police officers in the country, distributed as follows. Of these officers, 59.6% were involved in municipal policing, 26.2% in provincial policing, and 12.8% in federal policing. The remaining 1.4% included the National Harbours Board Police, the Canadian National Railways Police, the Canadian Pacific Investigation Service, and the New Brunswick Highway Patrol (Canadian Centre for Justice Statistics, 1986; 1987).[10]

During the 25-year period 1962–1986, the number of police personnel increased steadily, although during the 12-year period from 1975–1986, the increase was 11.8% as compared to the 91.3% increase registered during the period from 1962–1975. There is considerable variation across Canada in the ratio of population per police, ranging from 221:1 in the Northwest Territories and 191:1 in the Yukon to 610:1 in Nova Scotia and 696:1 in Prince Edward Island (Canadian Centre for Justice Statistics, 1986).

In addition to the police forces operating at the municipal, provincial, and federal levels, there are several other police services in Canada. These include the National Harbours Board Police, who have as their primary objective the protection of property owned by the National Harbours Board, and the Canadian Pacific Railways Police and the Canadian Pacific Investigation Service, which fulfil a similar role for their organizations.

Recent years have also witnessed the emergence of several "autonomous" native Indian police forces that are involved in policing native Indian reserves and communities. The largest Indian police force is the Amerindian Police Service, which in 1986 was policing 20 reserves in Quebec. Founded in 1978, the headquarters for the Amerindian Police is in Lac St. Jean, and the force employs approximately 70 constables. The Dakota-Ojibway Tribal Council police force is the other large band constable program operating in Canada. In 1986, 24 constables were involved in providing policing services to eight reserves in southwest Manitoba. Other, smaller autonomous band constable programs are operating on the Kahnawake reserve near Montreal and on several reserves in Alberta, and many reserves across the country have hired constables to enforce by-laws of a civil nature on the reserve. The authority of band constables is limited to the reserve, and they are under the supervision of the band council.[11]

Municipal Police Forces

There are approximately 450 municipal police forces operating in Canada today, and municipal police officers constitute the largest body of police personnel in the country. Municipal forces range in size from units of one or two officers to the over 6,000 members of the Montreal Urban Community Police Force. Municipal police officers enforce all laws relating to their area of jurisdiction, including the *Criminal Code,* provincial statutes, municipal by-laws and, in recent years, certain federal statutes such as the *Narcotic Control Act.* Municipalities that operate their own policing services generally assume the majority of the policing costs, with some assistance provided by the provincial governments.

Many municipalities, rather than establishing and maintaining their own police forces, have chosen to contract with the provincial police force for municipal policing services. In all provinces except Quebec, provincial police forces are involved in municipal policing. In Ontario, municipal policing is carried out under contracts between the Ontario Provincial Police and the municipalities, while in the remaining provinces, the RCMP, acting as the provincial police force, contracts to provide municipal policing services. This *contract policing* is authorized by the *Royal Canadian Mounted Police Act* and by provisions in provincial police legislation (see Grant, 1980; Talbot, Jayewardene, and Juliani, 1984). The contracts set out the cost-sharing arrangement between the municipality and the federal government, authorize RCMP officers to undertake municipal policing duties, and require officers in charge of the RCMP detachment to report to the chief executive of the municipality.[12] In 1987, the RCMP provided municipal policing services under contract to 192 communities in all provinces and territories except Ontario and Quebec.

While municipal forces remain a dominant feature of contemporary Canadian policing, there are two trends that are discernible and that could, in the long term, have a significant impact on policing arrangements: (1) the increasing provincial control over municipal policing, and (2) the regionalization of municipal police forces. Stenning (1981a: 58) notes that through the passage of legislation, the provinces "have significantly asserted provincial control over the provision and regulation of local policing services." Provincial police acts often set uniform policing standards for municipalities; provide for the creation of provincial police commissions, which become involved in monitoring the performance of municipal forces; and authorize provincial subsidization of municipal policing services. Such developments, Stenning (1981a: 60) argues, have contributed "to the erosion of the traditional view that policing is primarily a local responsibility . . . a local service, and that the constable is essentially a local officer serving parochial interests."

Several provinces have established police academies to standardize the training of municipal police officers. The Atlantic Police Academy, located in Charlottetown, Prince Edward Island, serves the provinces of Prince Edward Island, Nova Scotia, and New Brunswick and is funded by the provinces and the federal government. The training program, which began in 1971, includes a basic recruit training course and specialized courses. In British Columbia, the British Columbia Police Academy, which is situated at the Justice Institute of British Columbia in Vancouver, operates a municipal recruit training program — a series of five courses spread over three years. Under the *Police Act* of British Columbia, successful completion of this training course is a prerequisite for admission to a municipal police force. L'Institut de police du Québec provides basic training, in-service training, and specialized training for both provincial and municipal police officers in Quebec, while the Ontario Police College provides a similar training facility for police forces in Ontario.

Another trend that is reshaping the structure of municipal policing in Canada is regionalization. During 1962–1977, 150 municipal police forces in Ontario were involved in amalgamation, the largest force created being the Peel Regional Police Force, involving several municipalities immediately to the west of Toronto. Ten regional police forces in Ontario now provide policing services to more than 50% of Ontario's population. A similar regional police force, the Montreal Urban Community Police Force, was formed in 1972 to police Montreal and surrounding areas.

While regionalization was designed to increase cost-effectiveness and police efficiency, considerable concern and dissatisfaction have been expressed regarding the level and quality of policing provided to the municipalities. Critics have argued that regionalization has increased the costs of policing to taxpayers in many communities and, further, that regionalization has resulted in less personalized relations between the police and the public.[13] Despite these and other criticisms, the Ontario Police Commission (1978: 2), in a review of regionalized policing in Ontario, concluded that: "*Regionalized policing is more economically and operationally viable than any other form of policing. Furthermore, it offers the best long-term capability to cope with, and contain the law enforcement challenges and problems of the future*" (emphasis in original).

Provincial Police Forces

While nearly all the provinces at some point in their history have operated provincial police forces under the authority of the *Constitution Act, 1867* and under the provisions of various provincial police acts, only three provincial forces are operating in Canada today: the Ontario Provincial Police, the Quebec Police Force (Sûreté du Québec) and the Newfoundland Constabulary. Provincial police forces are responsible for policing those areas outside municipalities and for the enforcement of provincial laws and the *Criminal Code*.

As noted earlier, provincial police forces may also be involved in policing municipalities under contract. In all provinces except Quebec and Ontario, this is done by the RCMP. Under the Ontario *Police Act,* the Ontario Provincial Police contract to provide municipal policing services, and in 1988 were policing in 13 communities. There is, however, no provision under law for the Quebec Police Force to contract to provide municipal policing services.[14] The Ontario and Quebec provincial police also operate Native Special Constable programs, which involve the recruitment and training of native Indians to police on reserves in these two provinces.

The Royal Canadian Mounted Police

Canada's federal police force, the RCMP, is organized under the authority of the *Royal Canadian Mounted Police Act* and is headed by a Commissioner under the direction of the Solicitor General of Canada. The RCMP operates in all provinces and territories to enforce those federal statutes for which it is responsible, such as the *Narcotic Control Act*, the *Food and Drugs Act*, and the *Indian Act*. The RCMP also provides provincial and municipal policing services under contract. The RCMP is the only police force in the Yukon Territory and the Northwest Territories and operates under agreements signed between the federal government and the Territorial governments.[15]

In 1985–86, the RCMP had 15,206 personnel, which was approximately 28% of all police personnel in Canada. Forty-six per cent of these officers were involved in federal policing, including the enforcement of federal statutes, Canadian policing services and departmental and divisional administration; 35% in provincial policing and 19% in municipal policing (Canadian Centre for Justice Statistics, 1987).

The force is organized into 16 divisions (Figure 3.1). There are 13 operational divisions, with headquarters usually located in the provincial and territorial capitals. When acting in the capacity of a federal police force, the RCMP does not normally enforce the *Criminal Code,* unless it receives a request from a federal government department to investigate allegations of fraud connected with the use of public funds or when it lays a conspiracy charge in relation to a drug offence under the *Narcotic Control Act* or the *Food and Drugs Act.*

The RCMP provides a 12-month training program for its recruits. Basic recruit training is a 25-week course at the Training Depot in Regina, Saskatchewan, where recruits undergo a rigorous course structured around both physical and academic activities. Based on the British Cavalry model, the recruits train in groups of 32 and the training course stresses peer pressure and peer accountability. Academic courses range from the technical aspects of the police role, including report writing, identification processes and the study of federal statutes, to courses in human relations. Following successful completion of the training course in Regina, the recruits enter a six-month practical component in a field training detachment.

It should be noted that the RCMP does not act in isolation, even when

FIGURE 3.1
ORGANIZATION OF THE ROYAL CANADIAN MOUNTED POLICE

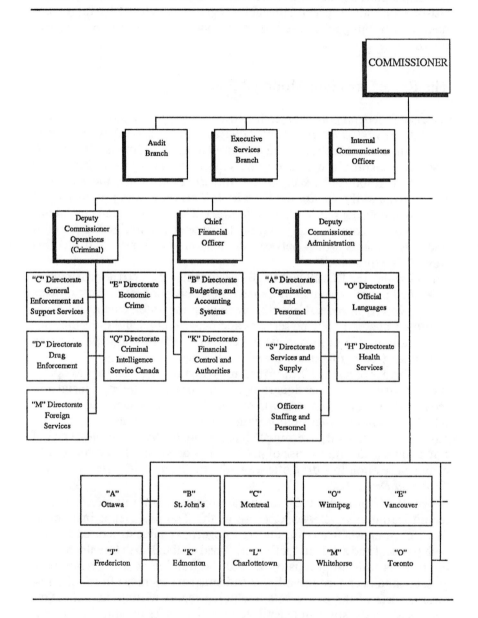

FIGURE 3.1
ORGANIZATION OF THE ROYAL CANADIAN MOUNTED POLICE

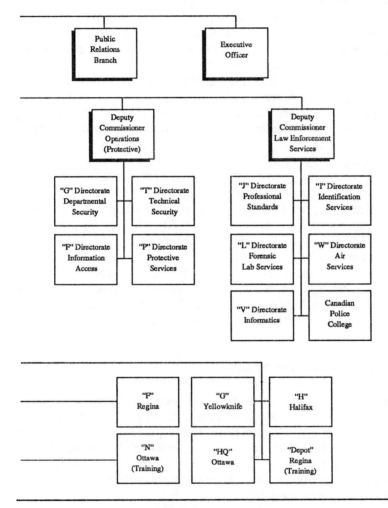

Source: Solicitor General of Canada. *Annual Report, 1985-86* (Ottawa: Supply and Services Canada, 1987), p. 22. Catalogue No. JS1-1986. Reproduced with permission of the Minister of Supply and Services Canada.

operating as a federal police force. The force operates several different branches that serve as an information resource for all police departments in the country. These include the Economic Crime Branch, which provides assistance in the investigation of economic crimes, and the National Crime Intelligence Branch, which combats organized crime and cooperates with special units in municipal and provincial police forces. Through its "L" Directorate, the RCMP provides the services of its Crime Detection Laboratories, which are located across the country, and Identification Services (fingerprints, criminal history files, etc.). "V" Directorate includes CPIC (Canadian Police Information Centre), a computerized information system providing police forces with instant information on criminal records, vehicles, wanted or missing persons, stolen property, and persons for whom there is an outstanding warrant.[16]

The RCMP also operates the Canadian Police College, a training facility that is funded by the Solicitor General of Canada. The programs at the Canadian Police College are intended to be national in scope and purpose, and include education and training courses designed to provide Canadian police forces with upgrading and development programs, research and information, and advisory services (see Muir, 1986).

One of the more unique programs sponsored by the RCMP is the Native Special Constable program, which was initiated in 1973. Known as Option 3(b), the Native Special Constable program was designed and implemented in response to concerns with native-police relations, particularly in northern and rural areas of the country, and was an attempt to increase the involvement of native Indians in policing Indian people. The Native Special Constable program currently operates in all provinces in which the RCMP acts as the provincial police force, as well as in the Yukon and Northwest Territories. In Chapter 14 we consider the operation and impact of the Native Special Constable program in greater detail.

Police Boards and Commissions

Prior to concluding our discussion of the structure of Canadian policing, it is important to consider the role of municipal police boards and provincial police commissions in the supervision and regulation of municipal and provincial police forces. Our task is made easier by the recent work of Stenning (1981a; 1981b; 1981c), who has examined the emergence of police boards and commissions and the role they have played historically and in contemporary Canadian policing.[17]

From the discussion of municipal policing earlier in this chapter, it will be recalled that one of the most significant pieces of legislation in the development of policing in Canada was the *Municipal Institutions of Upper Canada Act* (1858), which not only authorized cities and towns to establish police forces, but also required that police boards be created to supervise the operation of municipal police services. Stenning (1981b: 168) notes that these early police boards were involved in the selection of officers who "held office at the pleasure of the board." The boards also assisted in determining the size of municipal police departments and in ensuring that officers discharged their duties in a proper fashion. The early police boards were independent of the municipal councils, an arrangement that Stenning (1981b: 168) points out is "one of the major characteristics of many of the modern, as well as of the original, police boards in Canada." However, the exact nature and extent of police board control over the local forces were dependent upon the provincial legislature, which had full authority over policing under the provisions of the *Constitution Act, 1867.*

Following the creation of police boards in the 1850s in what is now the Province of Ontario, cities in other provinces moved to establish similar supervisory bodies, although the pattern of development was not uniform. Stenning (1981b: 174–75) notes, for example, that in Manitoba, only the cities of Brandon and Winnipeg created police boards, while in British Columbia, all municipalities with their own police forces were required to create a board. In many provinces, police boards were not created until the 1970s, while such boards have never existed in Quebec and Newfoundland.

Today, although there are approximately 130 police boards in operation across the country, Stenning (1981b: 176) makes the important observation that: "The majority of municipal police forces in Canada are not now, nor have they ever been, governed by police boards. Rather, they are subject to the direct control of their local municipal councils, or committees thereof." Further, there is considerable variation in the size and composition of boards, in the selection and role of the chairperson, and in the statutory mandate of the boards. For example, while some boards are extensively involved in the preparation and control of the municipal police budget, others are relegated to more limited activities. Stenning (1981b: 193) has also noted that police boards have been the focus of continuing controversy, and in several instances, review commissions have recommended their abolition and the return of control over municipal forces to the municipal councils (see Hann et al., 1985).

At the same time that police boards were developing in many jurisdictions, the provinces were becoming increasingly involved in the control of municipal policing. One of the trends in municipal policing noted earlier is the increasing provincial interest in municipal policing, facilitated by the provisions of the various provincial police acts. The precedent-setting legislation was the Ontario *Police Act* of 1946, which standardized provincial regulations for policing, established uniform discipline codes and procedures for handling complaints against the police, and set out a system for monitoring the performance of municipal police forces.

In 1962, Ontario created the first provincial police commission, which now has counterparts in seven provinces. While the specific activities of the provincial police commissions vary, their roles generally centre around the establishment of policing standards, promoting research into police issues, and exercising appellate jurisdiction over internal disciplinary matters and over complaints against municipal police officers. Provincial police commissions are also involved in training programs for provincial and municipal police officers, with the Ontario Police Commission operating the Ontario Police College at Aylmer, Ontario, and the British Columbia Police Commission overseeing the programs of the British Columbia Police Academy in Vancouver.[18] In Quebec and Ontario, provincial police commissions monitor activities of both the provincial police forces and municipal police services, while in the remaining provinces, police commission activities are directed only toward non-RCMP municipal forces.[19]

The Role of the Police in Canadian Society

In tracing the origins of policing and the emergence of organized police forces in England and Canada, it was revealed that, as societies increased in diversity and complexity, systems of peacekeeping and order maintenance premised on self-policing and individual responsibility deteriorated. The development of state-operated policing services has involved not only the transfer of law enforcement duties to the police, but a wide range of other functions as well. These developments have had profound implications for both the structure and operation of policing and the community's perceptions of the police role. Thomas and Hepburn (1983: 338) note that "the public has gradually abdicated its right to manage its daily affairs and has increasingly relinquished the civic duty to become involved in the affairs of others, thereby creating greater opportunities and pressures for the police to intervene officially in many extralegal, civil matters." The following discussion will reveal, however, that there is considerable uncertainty and confusion on the part of both the police and the community about the role of the police in Canadian society.

The broadening of the goals of Canadian police forces is reflected in the *Report of the Canadian Committee on Corrections* (Ouimet, 1969), which listed the following functions of the police: (1) prevention of crime, (2) detection and apprehension of criminal offenders, (3) maintenance of order in the community, and (4) control of highway traffic. Several years later, the report of the Task Force on Policing in Ontario (1974) proposed the additional functions of public education and referral. Public education involves the development of programs and services that provide citizens with information on crime prevention and protection, while referral denotes police involvement in the development of alternative dispositions and programs for individuals who come into contact with the criminal justice system, such as diversion.[20] These six functions were reiterated by the Hickling-Johnston (1982: 4) report in its evaluation of the Metropolitan Toronto Police Force.

Crime Control versus Order Maintenance and Service

While there has been an expansion of the police role, the activities of police forces are generally discussed in terms of the following three categories:

1. crime control: responding to and investigating crimes and patrolling the streets to prevent offences from occurring;
2. order maintenance: preventing and controlling behaviour that disturbs the public peace, including quieting loud parties, settling domestic disputes, and intervening in conflicts that arise between citizens;
3. service: the provision of a wide range of services to the community, often as a consequence of the 24-hour availability of the police, including assisting in the search for missing persons and acting as an information/referral agency.

In addition to carrying out these functions, the police play a role in the larger societal context. Weiner (1976: 14) notes that the police act as a "buffer" between the social and political structure of the community and potentially disruptive elements: "The police do all the 'dirty work,' take the blows, absorb the hostility." Further, through their enforcement patterns and the exercise of discretion, the police function as a mechanism for testing the limits of social tolerance, particularly in relation to moral issues.[21]

While the police perform a wide range of functions, it is the crime control role that assumes primacy in the minds of both the police and the public. As Thomas and Hepburn (1983: 345) state: "Both the public and the police define the mission of policing in terms of excitement, danger, and the importance of crime control to the community." And Ericson (1982: 5) notes that, in Canada, "the image is constantly reinforced that crime is almost everything the police are about . . . (and that) real police work is crime work."

Despite the widely held perception that the police spend the majority of their time detecting and apprehending offenders, a considerable amount of research conducted in Canada and the United States indicates that crime control activities generally occupy less than 25% of police officers' time, and for most officers, this percentage is considerably lower. In one of the first investigations of public requests for police assistance, Wilson (1968: 18) found that 38% of the telephone calls to the Syracuse, New York police were for service, 30% were for order maintenance, 22% were requests for information, and only 10.3% were related to crime control. These initial findings received support from Webster (1970), who reported that 39% of all assignments and 50% of all time spent by police officers involved administrative activities, such as attending court, serving warrants, and participating in community relations. Similarly, Reiss (1971), in a study of Chicago police, found that more than 80% of the incidents responded to by officers were non-criminal in nature and that only 3% of patrol officers' time was spent on criminal matters (see also Cumming, Cumming, and Edell, 1965; Lab, 1984; Pepinsky, 1975).

Research on the activities of Canadian police has also revealed that the police spend only a small percentage of their time on law enforcement. In an examination of the telephone calls received by the Vancouver City Police Department over a six-month period, Levens (1976) found that 49% of the calls were for service, and Ericson (1982: 206) concluded from extensive observations of patrol officers in an Eastern Canadian city that:

> The bulk of the patrol officer's time was spent doing nothing other than consuming the petrochemical energy required to run an automobile and the psychic energy required to deal with the boredom of it all . . . [E]ven in their "crime work," patrol officers are most often ordering petty disturbances, regulating driving, and sorting out property relations.

Ericson (1982: 6) also found, similar to Reiss' (1971) Chicago study, that patrol officers had little contact with citizens, noting that "the vast majority of their time is spent alone in their patrol cars without any direct contact with citizens."

In a recent study of citizen mobilization of the police in an Eastern Canadian city, Shearing (1984: 20–22) found that calls to the police broke down into the following categories:

Internal Police Business: 23.6%
Response of Fire Department and/or Ambulance Service: 3.4%
Suspicious Circumstances: 8.9%
Reports of Thefts: 6.7%
Robbery or Hold-Up: 0.3%
Report of Injury or Damage to Person or Property: 2.5%
Disputes: 5.5%
Accidents, Collapses, Illness: 16.3%
Public Nuisance: 7.4%
Traffic Problems: 8.7%
Services: 7.2%
Return Calls: 2.2%
Other types of calls: 7.3%

Of particular interest in Shearing's (1984) findings is the high percentage of calls that were related to internal police business and the fact that, although the department studied was situated in a large metropolitan area, only a small percentage of calls related to law enforcement or order maintenance. However, a cautionary note in interpreting the results of these inquiries is raised by Shearing (1984: 29), who points out that studies that utilize telephone request data to determine the extent to which the police are engaged in law enforcement versus order maintenance and other activities may present a misleading picture: "It is necessary to distinguish between troubles where law enforcement is seen by the attending police officer as possible and troubles where the officer actually decides to enforce the law as a means of coping with the trouble." Given this, Shearing (1984: 31) concludes that, while police officers may seldom use law enforcement as a method for dealing with trouble, the possibility for such use exists in most citizen requests.[22] In Chapter 4, we will consider further the mobilization of the police by the community, as well as the police response to citizen requests for assistance.

The discrepancy between the traditional perception of the police as "crime fighters" and the reality of police activities has given rise to debate among police administrators and scholars on whether the organization of policing services should be altered to reflect more accurately the tasks that officers perform, or whether the police should maintain their current organizational arrangements and focus solely on crime control. Many observers argue that there may be dysfunctional consequences should the police focus only on law enforcement activities. Ericson (1982: 10) notes that such a position would serve to make the police responsible for crime control, "even though the causes of crime (social, economic, cultural, and political) are clearly beyond their control." The police would then be unable to meet the expectations of the community, and this would, in turn, result in frustration on the part of both the police and the public.

Another difficulty in maintaining a crime control orientation, while being asked to perform other duties by the public, is the creation of considerable confusion and uncertainty among police officers about their proper role. Ericson (1982: 63) found that officers in an Eastern Canadian department had considerable difficulty responding to a survey question about their role: "38 per cent did not define any particular role in their work, while 12 per cent said their role is primarily public relations (social service) work, and 9 per cent defined it mainly in terms of traffic law enforcement. Only 41 per cent said their prime role is law enforcement under the Criminal Code."

Two Canadian observers, Murphy and Muir (1985: 79-80), have also raised the important point that the crime control model of policing may be inappropriate for the Canadian context:

> ... the bulk of criminal activity in most communities is of a less serious nature and has not yet created the levels of crime fear characteristic of the American situation. The majority of police departments in Canada are located in small cities, towns or rural areas with relatively low crime rates. An exclusive emphasis on crime fighting in these settings may be entirely inconsistent with community policing needs and priorities.

Murphy and Muir (1985: 80) further contend that the crime control model of policing is "a particular product of the 'American' historical and cultural experience in which an aggressive law enforcement role for the police has traditionally been accepted." These and other criticisms of the crime control model of policing are utilized by Murphy and Muir (1985) as the basis for considering an alternative model of policing — community-based policing — which will be discussed in Chapter 5.

In fact, police involvement in activities other than crime control may serve to produce numerous benefits. Thomas and Hepburn (1983: 344) note that "an alert police officer can use the opportunity of providing a public service to gain the kind of information about people, places and situations that will be of value in performing the crime control function", and Johnson, Misner, and Brown (1981: 26) point out that "police involvement in the noncriminal aspects of their task gives them an opportunity to meet citizens in essentially a nonadversary relationship." In Chapter 5, we will consider the consequences of the continued adherence by the police to a crime control model of policing and the impact of this on the strategies employed by police forces, as well as the criteria utilized to evaluate the success of police initiatives and to assess the performance of officers.

In concluding our discussion, we should take note of Radelet's (1986: 38) observation that the question is not whether the police should relinquish the law enforcement function in favour of a community service function, but rather what the emphasis of policing should be: "If . . . the police spend most of their time in keeping peace . . . why should a police agency be organized as if this were not so? And why should police officers be trained as if most of their time were spent catching crooks, when most of their time is not spent catching crooks?" In our discussion of the police occupation, it will become apparent that the discrepancy between the traditional conception of the police role and the realities of police work is a primary source of conflict and stress for police officers.

The Police Occupation

In addition to the uncertainty surrounding the role of the police that is enhanced by the discrepancy between the traditional perception of the police role and the actual tasks that police officers perform, police observers have identified several sources of conflict surrounding the police occupation that may have a significant impact on police officers, and on their relation to the communities they serve.

Role Conflicts and Consequences

As we have seen in the preceding discussion, a major source of conflict and frustration for police officers is the discrepancy between the traditional conception of the police role and the actual requests that are made of the police by the community, "between what the police actually do and what they think they should be doing" (Weiner, 1976: 17).[23]

A second source of conflict for police officers is the uncertain and often conflicting expectations that communities have of the police. The relation between the police and the community is vitally important, for as we will see in our discussion in Chapter 4, the police rely extensively upon the public for mobilization. Radelet (1986: 30) notes that any consideration of police-community relations requires an understanding of the mutual expectations of each. Unfortunately, the police often feel that the community is not clear and consistent in its expectations. Weiner (1976: 16) characterizes the resulting conflict as follows:

> On the one hand, the public expects the police to be the symbol of authority, to enforce the law, and to prevent crime. On the other hand, the public also expects the police to provide services and to maintain public order. At the same time, they resent the policeman's presence when he uses his authority, or when he inconveniences them, or when his response is not quick enough. And, they resent the policeman when he intrudes upon them, at which point they often ask, "Why are you bothering honest people? Why don't you do something useful, like catch a crook?"

A third factor that often causes conflict is the problems associated with policing in a democratic society, which require that officers balance the need to assert authority and maintain order while respecting the rights and freedoms of citizens (Broderick, 1987). In our discussion of police decision making in Chapter 4, it will be revealed that while police officers have considerable powers at their disposal, the full force of the law is invoked infrequently, requiring officers to develop a wide variety of strategies for managing the conflicts and contingencies they encounter.

As a consequence of these and other conflicts surrounding the police occupation, many police observers have argued that police officers develop a "working personality," "a unique set of attitudinal and behavioral expectations or working norms that differentiate police officers from the public" (Bennett, 1984: 47). In his classic work, *Justice Without Trial,* Jerome Skolnick (1966: 42) proposed the existence of a working personality of police officers, arguing that "the police, as a result of the combined features of their social situation, tend to develop ways of looking at the world distinctive to themselves, cognitive lenses through which to see situations and events. The strength of the lenses may be weaker or stronger depending upon certain conditions, but they are ground on a similar axis."[24]

Skolnick (1966) and Niederhoffer (1967), among others, have identified several components of the working personality of the police, including (1) a preoccupation with danger, (2) excessive suspiciousness of people and situations, (3) a protective cynicism, and (4) the difficulties associated with the exercise of authority. For example, while policing is less hazardous than many other occupations in society, officers come to be preoccupied with danger largely because of the unpredictable nature of many of the people and events they encounter.[25] This also results in police officers developing a suspicious view of the community and the people they police. The concern with the exercise of authority arises from the fact that the police are charged with enforcing many statutes that are unpopular with the community. An additional component of the police personality is cynicism toward the community, which develops largely as a defense mechanism. The police find themselves doing society's "dirty work" and tend to see only certain sides of the human condition — the unpleasant side, "when they are dirty, angry, rowdy, obscene, dazed, savage or bloody" (Wilson, 1968: 36).[26]

An attempt to refine the concept of the working personality of the police has been made by Broderick (1987), who categorized patrol officers in his study on the basis of the emphasis that they placed upon (1) the need for social order, or (2) due process and the constitutional rights of citizens. We have previously noted that one of the contingencies encountered in police work in a democratic society is the balance between the maintenance of social order and the need to recognize the rights of citizens. From his inquiry, Broderick (1987) identified four types of working personality among police officers: idealists (high emphasis on social order, high emphasis on due process), enforcers (high emphasis on social order, low emphasis on due process), optimists (low emphasis on social order, high emphasis on due process), and realists (low emphasis on social order, low emphasis on due process). While Broderick cautions that these are only ideal types — that officers may only approximate one type of personality or another — nevertheless his work represents an important contribution to the policing literature and provides the basis for additional research on the concept of the working personality.

The working personality of police officers is a component of the larger occupational subculture of the police that has been widely reported and discussed in the policing literature (see Manning, 1977; Neiderhoffer, 1967; Skolnick, 1966; Westley, 1953; 1970). Strecher (cited in Radelet, 1986: 96): defines the police subculture as "the organized sum of police perspectives relevant to the police role." Two of the major attributes of the occupational subculture of the police are: (1) the social isolation of police officers from the community, with a resulting solidarity among officers which includes a "blue shield" of secrecy and in-group support, and (2) police perceptions that the public is hostile and nonsupportive of their efforts.

A widely held view in the policing literature is that police officers are isolated from the communities they serve. In his early work on the police, Westley (1953) used the term "pariah" to describe officers' feelings of social estrangement from the community, and more recent observers have characterized police-community relations as follows:

> Because police officers are, by occupational prescription, inclined to be suspicious, they tend to isolate themselves from an unsympathetic, critical, untrustworthy, and

uncomprehending community, and to form their own in-group alliances with fellow officers. [Radalet, 1986: 95].

Even during off-duty hours, he is rarely allowed to forget that he is a policeman — even if by nothing more than the joking remarks of his friends. [Wilson, 1968: 192]

Although the working personality and occupational subculture of the police are discussed throughout the policing literature, an emerging body of research in Canada and the United States has called these concepts into question. Research suggests that there may be considerable diversity in the extent to which officers exhibit the attributes of a working personality or adhere to a subcultural position that creates social isolation and perceptions of an unsympathetic public. For example, in a close examination of the working personality of the police, with its attendant attitudes of suspicion, authoritarianism, and a preoccupation with danger, Balch (1972: 119) concluded that there was "simply not enough good evidence to support or refute any side of the controversy," arguing that the extensive focus on the personality of individual officers "has obscured the important role that organizational factors play in shaping police behavior." In their research, Bennett and Greenstein (1975) found that police officers were no more authoritarian in their attitudes or value systems than the general public, further calling into question the existence of a distinct police personality.

Similiar questions have been raised about the extent of social isolation of officers from the community. Griffiths and Hall (1973) found in a study of rural peace officers in the United States that the majority of the officers interviewed did not feel isolated socially from the communities they policed, nor did they perceive the public to be hostile and non-supportive of their efforts. Rather, most participated in a wide range of community activities with non-police. These findings led Griffiths and Hall (1973) to conclude that a critical determinant of the extent to which the members of a police department will experience isolation from the public and perceive the public as hostile and non-supportive is the nature of the community and area policed — the policing or "task" environment.

In a more recent United States study, Hageman (1979) found that the police officers surveyed did not have high social-isolation scores, and concluded that the police are a "new Breed," who have a desire to work with the public and become involved in the community (see also Wilt and Bannon, 1976). Sterling (1969) has also argued that the solidarity evidenced among police officers is no greater than that among individuals whose occupations centre around shift work. Yarmey and Rashid (1983: 94) found, however, that a group of Canadian police officers rated other police officers more favourably on a number of performance criteria than did a sample of lawyers, community residents, and probation officers, leading these authors to conclude that in-group solidarity did exist among the police in their study.

Further questions about the uniform characterization of police officers as social isolates are raised by Canadian research. In a study of an Ontario police department, Vincent (1979: 81) found that while those officers who had been in police work for a long period of time and had higher rank in the organization tended to socialize with other officers, this was not the case with the younger, more educated officers who had a wider circle of friends. While one high-ranking officer stated that he did not "feel at home with outsiders," a younger officer in the same department commented: "No, I don't go out a lot with other cops . . . I'm getting tired of cop talk. I want a fuller life. I want to be accepted, not because I'm a cop, but because I am me" (Vincent, 1979: 84).

Poel (1985: 10), in a study of the Cape Breton Police Force, reported that only 36% of the officers in the force expressed feelings of isolation from both the public and other professionals in the criminal justice system and concluded (1985: 20): "isolation is experienced or expressed more by those least socialized to the policing role — the youngest, less senior, and part-time constables." These findings are in a direction opposite to that reported by Vincent (1979) and suggest that there may be considerable variability between police departments in the extent of officer isolation from the community. The risk of officer isolation may be particularly acute in small RCMP detachments situated in remote and rural areas of the country. However, such an environment may also provide a unique opportunity for the development of positive police-community relations that is generally absent in urban areas.

Several observers have also argued that this diversity may exist within police departments. Johnson et al. (1981: 270), for example, assert that patrol officers represent a distinct subculture. According to these authors, officers on the line level share certain attitudinal and behavioural norms and values that distinguish them from other levels of the police organization, including the administration and other specialized units, such as the detectives.

Among the shared attributes of patrol officers are (1) the relegation of patrol officers to the lowest levels of the police organization, often with little opportunity for upward mobility; (2) the fact that the discretionary powers of patrol officers are subject to greater scrutiny than are those exercised by police administrators, making line-level officers more vulnerable to public criticism; and (3) the fact that patrol officers are often the recipients of a one-way flow of communication from the administrative levels. In fact, Shearing (1981: 292) has argued that line-level officers may view their interests as distinct from those of the police administrators, reporting from his inquiry that "the brass were accorded an explicitly ideological role and this role was seen as not only different from, but often opposed to, the demands of 'real' police work" (see also Reuss-Ianni and Ianni, 1983).

Our consideration of the police occupation, the subculture of the police, and of the research findings from Canada and the United States suggests that, rather than being a monolithic phenomenon, attributes of the police subculture may appear to varying degrees both within the same policing organization and between police departments, or as Poel (1985: 3) has argued, "one can expect varying degrees of suspicion, cynicism, or low esteem and in some officers these characteristics may not be found at all."

Another key tenet of the concept of the police as an occupational subculture is that officers perceive the public to be hostile and non-supportive. Canadian research, however, has consistently revealed that police officers perceive the public to be generally supportive. A study by the Calgary Police Service (1977) found that 80% of the police constables surveyed felt that the public was supportive, and in a survey of the police in British Columbia, Koenig (1975a) found that the police had an accurate perception of the high levels of public support for them.

Rather than viewing relations with the public in an "us versus them" perspective, it appears that police officers make a distinction between the general public, which is viewed as holding supportive (or at least neutral) attitudes toward the police, and a smaller segment of the population that has high rates of conflict with the police and is viewed as presenting difficulties for both the police and the public. Shearing (1981: 286) found, for example, that officers made a distinction between the general public, whom they did things for, and the "dregs" or "scum" in the community, whom they did things to: "The public consisted of those the police believed they should serve and protect. The scum . . . were the people whom police prosecuted in the course of helping the public."

Among the officers interviewed by McGahan (1984: 165) in St. John's, there was the perception that public respect for and cooperation with the police varied across the various districts of the city:

> Mount Pearl is excellent. Really good. No problem there. Mostly because it is residential and there's nothing much there to pose any problems really. So people are fairly cooperative because you are not in there all the time . . . It's the type of people you are dealing with. These types that you have here and in Buckmaster Circle and Chalker Place, where the problems are, that's where you'll have no cooperation. They just go hand in hand.

In Chapter 4, we will examine how police officers categorize situations and people, and the consequences of these categorizations for the exercise of discretion and decision making by police officers.

In addition to the sources of diversity within and between police departments in the extent to which the subcultural attributes of the police are evident, the conflicting findings reported in the policing literature may be due, in large measure, to the different socio-political context within which the police operate. As our discussion earlier in the chapter revealed, there were critical historical differences in the emergence of the police in the two countries. In addition, much of the policing literature is premised on research conducted on urban police forces operating in large urban settings in the United States, where there has traditionally been conflict between the police and racial minorities, as well as high rates of violent crime and arrests.

However, we must not assume that police officers in Canada do not experience conflict with certain segments of the public or have feelings of isolation from the communities they serve. In our discussion of the relations between the police and native Indians in Chapter 15, for example, we will see that in some jursidictions there is conflict between the police and the public.

Public Perceptions of the Police

In the preceding discussion, it was revealed that in contrast to the arguments of many police observers, police officers in many parts of Canada do not feel that the public is hostile and non-supportive of their efforts. To date, however, there has not been a Canada-wide investigation of the attitudes held by adults and adolescents toward the police, and much of the research that has been undertaken has been confined to urban areas of the country.

Prior to presenting an overview of the materials that have been produced, it is important to keep in mind that the attitudes toward the police held by adults may differ from those of adolescents and that similar differences may exist between rural and urban populations, as well as among the different minority and ethnic groups across the country. In Chapter 5, we will consider in greater detail the topic of police-community relations. It is also important to note that there may be differences in public perceptions of the various police forces operating in the country (municipal, provincial, and RCMP) and that the findings of studies in one particular jurisdiction may not be applicable to other areas of the country.

The research on adult and adolescent attitudes toward the police that has been conducted to date in Canada suggests high levels of support for the police and generally high levels of satisfaction with police services. Koenig (1975b) found high levels of support for both municipal police forces and the RCMP in British Columbia, and in a 1976 survey of 859 residents in the city of Edmonton (Alberta Bureau of Statistics and Edmonton Police Commission, 1976: 1), 49.0% of those surveyed reported "very favourable" attitudes toward the police, with 37.0% indicating they held "moderately favourable" attitudes. Similarly, 31.3% of the respondents reported that relations between the police and the public were "very good," while 52.5% characterized relations as "moderately good."

A study of public perceptions of the police in Calgary by Klein, Webb, and DiSanto (1978) found that 76% of those questioned felt that the police were doing a good job in a wide range of tasks, from handling personal assaults to investigating break-ins. In addition, 86% of the respondents rated the police highly on measures of fairness, honesty, and job knowledge. Similar findings were reported by Hylton et al. (1979) in a study of public attitudes about crime and the police in Regina, and by Hylton and Matonovich (1980) in Moose Jaw. Citizens surveyed reported generally positive views about the range of services provided by the police and the manner in which police officers exercised their authority. And Yarmey and Rashid (1983) found that similar views were held among a small sample of residents in Guelph.

In a wide-ranging survey of attitudes of the Canadian public toward crime and the criminal justice system, Brillon, Louis-Guerin, and Lamarche (1984: 174) surveyed residents in rural and urban areas in Quebec, Ontario, and Manitoba and found that 86% of those surveyed reported high levels of satisfaction with the police. The highest levels of citizen satisfaction were with the activities of traffic control, protection of life and property, and detecting and apprehending criminal offenders, while lower levels of satisfaction were reported for police handling of automobile drivers, information and leisure programs for youths, and crime prevention programs.

These findings of Brillon et al. (1984) suggest that within the generally high levels of support for the police by the general public, there are areas in which difficulties exist. In the Regina police study, Hylton et al. (1979: 55) discovered concern among citizens about the quality of communication between the public and the police. Further, they found (1979: 87) that while there was general agreement that the public was not well informed and lacked understanding about the role of the police, neither were the police successful in rectifying this situation. A similar lack of knowledge among the general public about police work was reported by Yarmey and Rashid (1983: 94). In a survey of the perceptions of the public toward the police in southern Ontario, the authors found that "most persons, including police officers, indicated that their subjective understanding of police is relatively poor." And Amoroso and Ware (1981: 330) found that the students in their sample rated the police the lowest among five groups, which included teachers, and mothers and fathers, in terms of understandability: "(the police) are seen as less relaxed and more difficult to understand than other parental and nonparental authority figures" (see also Moore, 1985).

Of considerable significance is the additional finding of the Hylton et al. (1979: 87) study that while the police felt that they were treated differently in social situations, the public did not share this view, with only one in six respondents stating that they were inclined to treat police officers differently in social situations. This finding led the authors (1979: 87) to conclude that "the police tend to exaggerate the extent to which the public views them as 'different'." This finding not only raises additional questions about a key tenet of the occupational subculture of the police — social isolation — but has considerable significance for our discussion of police-community relations in Chapter 5.

In both Canada and the United States, the attitudes that adults hold toward the police have received considerably more attention than those of juveniles. While many observers have expressed concern about the negative attitudes of juveniles toward the police, the research findings that are available in Canada suggest that, similar to their adult counterparts, juveniles hold generally positive perceptions of police officers. Amoroso and Ware (1981: 330–31) reported that students in their sample ranked police officers second to doctors among 12 professionals in order of importance, while Griffiths and Winfree (1983), in a study of the attitudes held by students in grades 9 to 12 in seven Vancouver schools, found that students held positive attitudes toward the police.

While research in both Canada and the United States has revealed high levels of public support for the police, Griffiths, Klein, and Verdun-Jones (1980: 68) caution that "in discussing attitudes towards the police, one should avoid making generalizations and should be sensitive to both the particular community in which the survey is being conducted as well as the group of citizens being questioned." Of more importance than the general community view of the police are the perceptions held by specific groups, such as blacks and native Indians. In our discussion of native Indians and the criminal justice system in Chapter 14, we will see that in many jurisdictions there is conflict between native Indians and the police, resulting in high arrest rates, and suspicion and animosity toward the police.

The Determinants of Attitudes Toward the Police

Much of the research into attitudes toward the police has focused on the role of (1) the socio-biographical attributes of the individual, including ethnicity, gender, and socio-economic status, and (2) experiential or contact variables, including the impact of victimization and positive and negative encounters with enforcement officers (see Decker, 1981).

With respect to the socio-biographical attributes of citizens, concern has been expressed that blacks, native Indians, young persons, and citizens of low socio-economic status have a greater likelihood of experiencing negative contacts with the police, which, in turn, produces negative perceptions of the police. This view is reflected by observers such as Radelet (1986: 121–22), who concluded that "young people are generally more negative than older persons in their attitudes toward the police. Similarly, the poor have generally less favorable attitudes toward the police than the affluent." In a review of studies of attitudes toward the police, Decker (1981) notes, however, that the research is inconsistent with respect to the impact of socio-biographical attributes on the formulation of perceptions of the police, and this is illustrated by two Canadian studies.

From a survey of attitudes toward the police among a random sample of adults in British Columbia, Thornton found (1975: 338) a "definite link between the number and kinds of contacts with the police and attitudes toward, and support for, the police." Thornton (1975: 333) further reported that the frequency and types of contact with the police were not randomly distributed, but varied among age groups, between sexes, and between socio-economic groups, with young males in the sample tending to have the greatest number of experiences with crime, violence and the police. However, in a survey of Calgary residents, Klein et al. (1978) found that those respondents of lower socio-economic status were the most favourable in their attitudes toward the police and, further, that socio-economic status was not related to either the frequency or the purpose of contact with the police. Respondents' perceptions of the police, however, were strongly influenced by the quality of previous encounters with police officers.

Mixed results regarding the role of socio-biographical attributes in determining attitudes toward the police have also been reported in studies that have surveyed adolescents. While Winfree and Griffiths (1977) found that the ethnicity (black, white, and native Indian) of a large sample of rural and urban high school students in the western United States was not related to attitudes toward the police or to the types of contacts (positive and negative) with the police, Rusinko, Johnson, and Hornung (1978) reported that ethnicity was a significant determinant of perceptions of the police, with black youths holding less favourable perceptions than their white counterparts.

In a comparative analysis of the attitudes of a sample of Canadian and United States adolescents toward the police, Griffiths and Winfree (1983) reported that socio-biographical variables such as age, sex, and socio-economic status were not related either to the likelihood of positive or negative contacts with the police, or to overall attitudes toward the police. These findings, however, are in contrast to those of Amoroso and Ware (1981: 333), who found that grade level was related to evaluation of the police, as were the socio-economic status of the youth, and gender, albeit to a lesser degree. More specifically, these authors reported (1981: 333) that the generally positive perceptions of the police tended to decrease among older youths, with the positive evaluations of female students, which were generally higher than those of their male counterparts, also decreasing at the higher age levels.

Studies that have examined the impact of experiential or contact variables have produced more consistent findings. Research in both Canada and the United States suggests that the type of contact (positive or negative) that citizens have or have had with the police is a major determinant of the perceptions that both adults and adolescents hold toward the police. From their comparative study, Griffiths and Winfree (1983) reported that those juveniles who reported negative experiences with the police were negative in their views of police officers, while the converse was true for youths who had had positive encounters with the police.

With respect to the impact of victimization on attitudes toward the police, the results are less clear. While Thomas and Hyman (1977) reported in a United States study that no relation existed between victimization and attitudes toward the police, Koenig (1980: 246) found that public evaluation of the police in British Columbia was less favourable among respondents living in households that had experienced victimization in the previous 12 months. These findings are supported by those of Brillon et al. (1984: 176), who reported that among those respondents dissatisfied with the police, a large percentage were persons who had been victims of crime.

Contrasting findings are provided by the results of the *Canadian Urban Victimization Survey* (Solicitor General of Canada, 1983a: 10), which reported that both the victims and non-victims of crime gave the police high ratings, although the victims of violent crime were less positive in their attitudes toward the police. In studies of victim's attitudes toward the police in the Yukon Territory, McLaughlin (1984: ix), nearly 91% of the victims surveyed stated they were satisfied with the help they received from the police, and in a similar investigation in Red Deer, Alberta, Stuebing (1984: 8) reported that 80% of those surveyed perceived the investigating officer to be understanding and sympathetic to their plight. In a recent examination of the effects of victimization on attitudes toward the police in the United States, Homant, Kennedy, and Fleming (1984) reported that victimization increased negative perceptions of the police, but that such attitudes could be offset by the implementation of follow-up procedures that gave attention to victim needs.

The inconsistent findings of the research to date on adult and juvenile perceptions of the police are not surprising. First, there is wide variation in communities across the country and considerable diversity in the settings in which police and citizens interact. Secondly, the concept of "attitude" is very complex, and there are difficulties surrounding its definition and measurement. Thirdly, there is considerable evidence to suggest that attitudes toward the police do not exist in isolation from other attitudes and larger value systems or separate from the larger socio-political context. Amoroso and Ware (1983) reported, for example, that attitudes toward the police were in part a function of youths' attitudes toward parents, teachers, and self, and Brillon et al. (1984: 184) found that the public's attitudes toward the police were related to their image of the larger criminal justice system. These researchers (1984: 175–76) also found evidence that satisfaction with the police was in part a function of lifestyle and the socio-cultural context within which people lived, noting that French Canadians were less satisfied with the police than English Canadians and that dissatisfaction with the police was high among those persons who did not like the area of the city and neighbourhood in which they lived.

And, finally, perceptions of the police may also be related to changes in the larger socio-political context. The Royal Commission Inquiry into Metropolitan Toronto Police Practices observed (Morand, 1976: 158) that during the "permissive" decades of the 1960s and early 1970s, "people involved in the administration of justice, and particularly the police, were faced with the difficult task of reconciling the liberal views of the public with the need for an orderly and peaceful society," but that the pendulum had swung to the support of law and order, with the result that "there are now complaints that the police and the courts are not sufficiently strict." Such a perspective is supported by the findings of Koenig (1980: 247), who found a perception among respondents that the police were "too lenient rather than too harsh."

In summary, it can be stated that, contrary to the statements made by many observers in the policing literature, the large majority of adults and juveniles in Canada appear to hold favourable attitudes toward the police. This has led Koenig (1980: 248) to argue that: "Any lingering police perceptions of widespread public hostility are unwarranted, even in the case of traffic violators and those who have been arrested or convicted. Such hostility is minimal." We must, however, remember that levels of support may vary among different groups and communities across the country and that further research is required on the relations between police and specific groups, including native Indians, Inuit and blacks.

NOTES

1. For historical materials on the origins and development of policing, see Critchley (1975; 1978); McDougall (1988).

2. For a concise overview of the emergence of policing in Canada, see Talbot, Jayewardene, and Juliani (1983; 1984).

3. Talbot et al. (1984: 274–75), while acknowledging Chapman's point that the emergence of policing arrangements in early Canada was to some extent influenced by an English or French heritage, nevertheless caution that, "the establishment of police forces in this country was definitely not the result of a nostalgia that prompted the immigrants to re-create, in their new home, a replica of the society that they had left behind. The establishment of police forces was the natural reaction to a felt need. . . . In some places it was for a reactive control system while in other places it was for a proactive one."

4. While there were not organized "white" systems of policing in the early West, native Indian bands did have in place systems of social control and order maintenance, as had native bands throughout the country prior to the arrival of the English and French settlers. See Griffiths and Yerbury (1983); Carswell (1984).

5. In the early days, many municipal police constables performed a wide range of duties other than law enforcement. Among the tasks assigned to the municipal police constable in Sudbury, Ontario, for example, were jailer, engineer of the fire department, caretaker of the firehall, tax collector, sanitary inspector, truant officer, bailiff, chimney inspector, and animal caretaker (Juliani et al., 1984: 326).

6. Gray (1981) presents a thorough historical analysis of the role of municipal police forces in early Prairie towns, particularly in relation to the control of prostitution. McGahan's (1988) work, *Crime and Policing in Maritime Canada* also provides fascinating insights into policing in this region of the country from the 1830s to the 1930s.

7. For an in-depth examination of the emergence of the image of the Mounted Police and the societal factors that contributed to the mass appeal and popular culture that grew up around the force, see Walden (1982), and Thacker (1980). See also Morrison (1985) for a historical analysis of the role of the RCMP in the northern and western areas of Canada.

8. For a discussion of the development of provincial police forces and the RCMP, see Talbot et al. (1984).

9. For a general consideration of the advantages and disadvantages of current policing arrangements in Canada, see Grant (1980).

10. The New Brunswick Highway Patrol was disbanded on February 1, 1989. It had been established in 1980 and operated 16 detachments throughout the province, servicing cities that did not have a RCMP detachment and outlying areas that were not under RCMP contracts. The RCMP have now assumed the policing responsibilities of the New Brunswick Highway Patrol.

11. For a discussion of other agencies and individuals who play a policing role in Canada, see Kelly and Kelly (1976) and Cooper (1981). See also *Policing in Canada,* the annual report published by the Canadian Centre for Justice Statistics.

12. For a review of the operant legislation relating to the legal status of municipal police forces, as well as the difficulties that may arise with the RCMP acting in the role of municipal police, see Stenning (1981a).

13. An illustration of the regional delivery of police services and policing costs is presented in *Task Force on Municipal Policing Costs in British Columbia* (British Columbia, 1978). See also Commission de police du Québec (n.d.) for a discussion of regional policing in Quebec.

14. For a general overview of the organization and operation of provincial police forces, see Kelly and Kelly (1976) and Talbot et al. (1984).

15. There are several potential difficulties relating to the accountability of the RCMP to provincial authorities under contract policing and to the legal status of RCMP personnel as both federal and provincial officers. See Stenning (1981a: 69–77).

16. While the RCMP traditionally were also responsible for internal security matters, this function has been taken over by the Canadian Intelligence Service, a civilian agency, which was created in 1984.

17. For an exhaustive examination of the origins, development, and role of police boards and commissions in Canada, see Stenning (1981c).

18. For a descriptive profile of provincial police commissions, see Implementation Work Group on Criminal Justice Information and Statistics (1982).

19. RCMP officers policing municipalities and provinces under contract are outside the control of police commissions, with complaints against RCMP officers being handled through the provincial Attorney General's office.

20. Observers such as Johnson et al. (1981: 20) contend, however, that merely listing the responsibilities of the police is misleading and uninformative:

> What is meant . . . by the responsibility for "prevention of criminality"? The police role in crime prevention is clouded with uncertainties, with differences of opinion even within police ranks. Most observers would admit that the police have some role in crime prevention activities, but there would be lengthy discussion about the precise character of that role, about the relationship of the police in this matter to other social institutions.

21. For a discussion of the changing role of the police and of the political role of the police in society, see Rumbaut and Bittner (1979); Quinney (1977); Goldstein (1977). For a critical discussion of the police role in Canada, see Taylor (1986). See also Ericson and Shearing (1986).

22. It should be noted that there may be considerable variation between police departments in the activities of patrol officers. This may be due to the particular organizational priorities of the department and the demands placed upon the police by the task environment. The task environment is comprised of the community and the areas that are being policed, and the demographic characteristics, including the size and composition of the population and the nature and extent of criminal activity. It might be expected, for example, that officers working in urban police departments would be involved in law enforcement activities to a greater degree than their rural counterparts, although the findings of both Canadian and United States studies demonstrate quite conclusively that this is not the case.

23. A major attribute of the police role that may significantly influence the performance of officers, but that is generally not discussed in the policing literature, is boredom. As Weiner (1976: 17) notes, "Many people enter the police service expecting to be active crime fighters, but end up spending most of their time on patrol. . . . This lack of action serves to aggravate the frustration that arises from the police role." See also Ericson (1982).

24. In the policing literature, there are two competing explanations for the emergence of the police "working personality." One focuses on the demands of the police occupation, which, it is argued, produce attitudinal and behavioural differences between the police and the public (Skolnick, 1966). An alternative explanation maintains that the occupation of policing tends to attract individuals with certain personality traits, such as authoritarianism, which are subsequently enhanced by the police occupation (Bennett and Greenstein, 1975).

25. While police officers encounter a wide variety of situations and circumstances in their work, some of which may involve the potential of danger or violence, many other occupations in Canadian society have higher risks. Whittingham (1984) notes that the fatality risk for Canadian police officers is lower than that for those individuals employed in construction, in transportation, and in work associated with natural resources, such as mining. In fact, Whittingham (1984) points out that the rate of homicide victimization for the four-year period 1975–1979 (per 100,000 population) is higher for the general public than for the police. These findings suggest that the actual amount of danger experienced by police officers in carrying out their tasks should be the subject of further inquiry.

26. A major role in the socialization of new recruits into the police occupation is played by officers in the department, Van Maanen (1973: 413) pointing out that: "A whole folklore of tales, myths, and legends surrounding the department is communicated to the recruit by his fellow officers — conspicuously by his FTO (Field Training Officer). Through these anecdotes — dealing largely with mistakes or ('flubs') made by policemen — the recruit begins to adopt the perspectives of his more experienced colleagues."

REFERENCES

Alberta Bureau of Statistics and Edmonton Police Commission. 1976. *Residents' Attitudes Towards the Police.* Edmonton.

Amoroso, D. M., and E. E. Ware. 1981. "Adolescents' Perceptions and Evaluation of Police." 13 *Canadian Journal of Behavioural Science* 326–35.

———. 1983. "Youth's Perception of Police as a Function of Attitudes Towards Parents, Teachers and Self." 25 *Canadian Journal of Criminology* 191–99.

Anderson, F. W. 1972. *Saskatchewan's Provincial Police.* Calgary: Frontier Publishing Co.

Baehre, R. 1977. "Origins of the Penitentiary System in Upper Canada." 69 *Ontario History* 185–207.

Balch, R. W. 1972. "The Police Personality: Fact or Fiction?" 63 *Journal of Criminal Law, Criminology, and Police Science* 106–19.

Beattie, J. M. 1977. *Attitudes Towards Crime and Punishment in Upper Canada, 1830–1850: A Documentary Study.* Toronto: Centre of Criminology, University of Toronto.

Bellomo, J. J. 1972. "Upper Canadians' Attitudes Towards Crime and Punishment, 1832–1851." 64 *Ontario History* 11–26.

Bennett, R. R. 1984. "Becoming Blue: A Longitudinal Study of Police Recruit Occupational Socialization." 12 *Journal of Police Science and Administration* 47–58.

Bennett, R. R., and T. Greenstein. 1975. "The Police Personality: A Test of the Predispositional Model." 3 *Journal of Police Science and Administration* 439–45.

Brillon, Y., C. Louis-Guerin, and M.-C. Lamarche. 1984. *Attitudes of the Canadian Public Toward Crime Policies.* Montreal: International Centre for Comparative Criminology, University of Montreal.

British Columbia. 1978. *Task Force on Municipal Policing Costs in British Columbia.* Victoria: Ministry of the Attorney General.

Broderick, J. J. 1987. *Police in a Time of Change.* 2nd ed. Prospect Heights, Ill.: Waveland Press.

Brown, L., and C. Brown. 1973. *An Unauthorized History of the RCMP.* Toronto: James Lorimer.

Calgary Police Service. 1977. *A Report on Zone Policing.* Calgary: Planning Branch, Calgary Police Service.

Canadian Centre for Justice Statistics. 1986. *Policing in Canada.* Ottawa: Supply and Services Canada.

———. 1987. 7 *Juristat Bulletin.* Ottawa: Supply and Services Canada.

———. 1988. 8 *Juristat Bulletin.* Ottawa: Supply and Services Canada.

Carswell, M. 1984. "Social Controls Among the Native Peoples of the N.W.T. in the Pre-Contact Period." 22 *Alberta Law Review* 303–308.

Chapman, B. 1977. "The Canadian Police: A Survey." 12 *Government and Opposition* 496-516.

Commission de police du Québec. n.d. *Regional Policing in Quebec.* Quebec.

Cooper, H. S. 1981. "The Evolution of Canadian Police." In *The Police Function in Canada,* edited by W. T. McGrath and M. P. Mitchell, 37–52. Toronto: Methuen.

Critchley, T. A. 1975. "The New Police in London, 1750–1830." In *Police in America,* edited by J. K. Skolnick and T. C. Grey, 6–15. Boston: Little, Brown, and Co.

———. 1978. *A History of Police in England and Wales.* London: Constable.

Cumming, E., I. Cumming, and L. Edell. 1965. "The Policeman as Philosopher, Guide, and Friend." 12 *Social Problems* 276–86.

Decker, S. H. 1981. "Citizen Attitudes Toward the Police: A Review of Past Findings and Suggestions for Future Policy." 9 *Journal of Police Science and Administration* 80–87.

Dickson, J. A. 1987. "Réflexions sur la police en Nouvelle-France." 32 *McGill Law Journal* 497–522.

Ekstedt, J. W., and C. T. Griffiths. 1988. *Corrections in Canada: Policy and Practice.* 2nd ed. Toronto: Butterworths.

Ericson, R. V. 1982. *Reproducing Order: A Study of Police Patrol Work.* Toronto: University of Toronto Press.

Ericson, R. V., and C. D. Shearing. 1986. "The Scientification of Police Work." In *The Knowledge Society: The Growing Impact of Scientific Knowledge on Social Relations,* edited by G. Bohme and N. Stehr, 129–59. Dordrecht: D. Reidel Publishing Co.

Fox, A. 1971. *The Newfoundland Constabulary.* St. John's: Robinson, Blackmore Printing and Publishing, Ltd.

Goldstein, H. 1977. *Policing a Free Society.* Cambridge, Mass.: Ballinger Publishing Co.

Grant, A. 1980. *The Police — A Policy Paper.* Ottawa: Law Reform Commission of Canada.

Gray, J. H. 1971. *Red Lights on the Prairies.* Toronto: Macmillan.

Griffiths, C. T., and E. L. Hall. 1973. "Social Isolation Among Rural Sheriffs Deputies." Unpublished paper. Missoula, Mont.: Department of Sociology, University of Montana.

Griffiths, C. T., J. F. Klein, and S. N. Verdun-Jones. 1980. *Criminal Justice in Canada: An Introductory Text.* Toronto: Butterworths.

Griffiths, C. T., and L. T. Winfree. 1983. "Attitudes Toward the Police: A Comparison of Canadian and American Adolescents." 6 *International Journal of Comparative and Applied Criminal Justice* 127–41.

Griffiths, C. T., and J. C. Yerbury. 1983. "Conflict and Compromise: Canadian Indigenous Peoples and the Law." In *Papers of the Symposia on Folk Law and Legal Pluralism, XIth International Congress of Anthropological and Ethnological Sciences,* edited by H. W. Finkler, 975–1002.

Hageman, M. J. C. 1979. "Who Joins the Force for What Reasons: An Argument for 'The New Breed.' " 7 *Journal of Police Science and Administration* 206–10.

Hann, R., et al. 1985. "Municipal Police Governance and Accountability in Canada: An Empirical Study." 9 *Canadian Police College Journal* 1–85.

Hickling-Johnston, Ltd. 1982. *Metropolitan Toronto Police Management Study: Productivity Improvements — Delivery of Cost Efficient Police Services to Metropolitan Toronto Citizens.* Toronto: Hickling-Johnston, Ltd.

Homant, R. J., D. B. Kennedy, and R. M. Fleming. 1984. "The Effect of Victimization and the Police Response on Citizens' Attitudes Toward Police." 12 *Journal of Police Science and Administration* 323–32.

Horrall, S. W. 1972. "Sir John A. Macdonald and the Mounted Police Force for the Northwest Territories." 53 *Canadian Historical Review* 179–200.

Hylton, J. H., and R. Matonovich. 1980. *Public Attitudes About Crime and the Police in Moose Jaw.* Regina: School of Human Justice, University of Regina.

Hylton, J. H., R. Matonovich, J. Varro, and D. Broad. 1979. *Public Attitudes About Crime and the Police in Regina*. Regina: Regina Police Department.

Implementation Work Group on Criminal Justice Information and Statistics. 1982. *Justice Information Report — Police Services in Canada, 1978/79; 1979/80*. Ottawa: Department of Justice.

Johnson, T. A., G. E. Misner, and L. P. Brown. 1981. *The Police and Society: An Environment for Collaboration and Confrontation*. Englewood Cliffs, N.J.: Prentice-Hall.

Juliani, T. J., C. K. Talbot, and C. H. S. Jayewardene. 1984. "Municipal Policing in Canada: A Developmental Perspective." 8 *Canadian Police College Journal* 315–85.

Kelly, W., and N. Kelly. 1976. *Policing in Canada*. Toronto: Macmillan.

Klein, J. F., J. R. Webb, and J. E. DiSanto. 1978. "Experience with the Police and Attitude Towards the Police." 3 *Canadian Journal of Sociology* 441–56.

Koenig, D. J. 1975a. *RCMP Views of Themselves, Their Jobs and the Public*. Victoria: Ministry of the Attorney General, British Columbia.

———. 1975b. "Police Perceptions of Public Respect and Extra-Legal Use of Force: A Reconsideration of Folk Wisdom and Pluralistic Ignorance." 3 *Canadian Journal of Sociology* 313–24.

———. 1980. "The Effects of Criminal Victimization and Judicial or Police Contacts on Public Attitudes Toward Local Police." 8 *Journal of Criminal Justice* 243–49.

Lab, S. P. 1984. "Police Productivity: The Other Eighty Percent." 12 *Journal of Police Science and Administration* 297–314.

Levens, Bruce R. 1976. *The Social Service Role of the Police: Domestic Crisis Intervention — Citizen Requests for Service and Vancouver Police Response*. Vancouver: Lower Mainland United Way.

Manning, P. K. 1977. *Police Work: The Social Organization of Policing*. Cambridge: MIT Press.

McDougall, A. K. 1988. *Policing: The Evolution of a Mandate*. Ottawa: Supply and Services Canada.

McGahan, P. 1984. *Police Images of a City*. New York: Peter Lang.

———. 1988. *Crime and Policing in Maritime Canada*. Fredericton, N.B.: Goose Lane Editions, Ltd.

McLaughlin, A. 1984. *Crime Victims. An Analysis of Victims/Victim Witness Needs in Yukon. Working Paper No. 11*. Ottawa: Policy Planning and Development Branch, Department of Justice.

Moore, R. J. 1985. "Reflections of Canadians on the Law and the Legal System: Legal Research Institute Survey of Respondents in Montreal, Toronto, and Winnipeg." In *Law in a Cynical Society? Opinion and the Law in the 1980's*, edited by D. Gibson and J. K. Baldwin, 41–87. Calgary and Vancouver: Carswell Legal Publications, Western Division.

Morand, D. (Chairman). 1976. *Royal Commission Inquiry into Metropolitan Toronto Police Practices.* Toronto: Government of Ontario.

Morgan, E. C. 1973. "The North-West Mounted Police: Internal Problems and Public Criticism, 1874-1883." 26 *Saskatchewan History* 41-62.

Morrison, W. R. 1985. *Showing the Flag: The Mounted Police and Canadian Sovereignty in the North, 1894-1925.* Vancouver: University of British Columbia Press.

Muir, R. G. 1986. "The Canadian Police College: A Decade of Service." 10 *Canadian Police College Journal* 169-88.

Murphy, C., and G. Muir. 1985. *Community-Based Policing: A Review of the Critical Issues.* Ottawa: Royal Canadian Mounted Police and Solicitor General of Canada.

Niederhoffer, A. 1967. *Behind the Shield: The Police in Urban Society.* Garden City, N.Y.: Anchor Books.

Ontario Police Commission. 1978. *A Review of Regionalized Policing in Ontario.* Toronto.

Ouimet, R. (Chairman). 1969. *Report of the Canadian Committee on Corrections — Toward Unity: Criminal Justice and Corrections.* (Catalogue No. JS52-1-1968.) Ottawa: Information Canada.

Pepinsky, H. 1975. "Police Decision Making." In *Decision Making in the Criminal Justice System: Reviews and Essays,* edited by D. Gottfredson, 21-52. Rockville, Maryland: National Institute of Mental Health.

Poel, D. H. 1985. "Dimensions of 'Hard' Policing: Competing Notions of Applied Justice within Local Police Cultures." Unpublished paper. Halifax: Department of Political Science, Dalhousie University.

Quinney, R. 1977. *Class, State and Crime.* New York: David McKay.

Radelet, L. A. 1986. *The Police and the Community.* 3rd ed. New York: Macmillan.

Reiss, A. J. 1971. *The Police and the Public.* New Haven: Yale University Press.

Reuss-Ianni, E., and F.A.J. Ianni. 1983. "Street Cops and Management Cops: The Two Cultures of Policing." In *Control in the Police Organization,* edited by M. Punch, 251-74. Cambridge, Mass.: MIT Press.

Robertson, D. F. 1978. "The Saskatchewan Provincial Police, 1917-1928." 31 *Saskatchewan History* 1-11.

Robinson, C. D., and R. Scaglion. 1987. "The Origin and Evolution of the Police Function in Society: Notes Toward a Theory." 21 *Law and Society Review* 109-53.

Rumbaut, R., and E. Bittner. 1979. "Changing Conceptions of the Police Role: A Sociological Review." In *Crime and Justice: An Annual Review of Research. Vol. 1,* edited by N. Morris and M. Tonry, 239-88. Chicago: University of Chicago Press.

Rusinko, W. T., K. W. Johnson, and C. A. Hornung. 1978. "The Importance of Police Contact in the Formulation of Youths' Attitudes Toward Police." 6 *Journal of Criminal Justice* 53-67.

Shearing, C. D. 1981. "Subterranean Processes in the Maintenance of Power: An Examination of the Mechanisms Coordinating Police Action." 18 *Canadian Review of Sociology and Anthropology* 283–98.

———. 1984. *Dial-A-Cop: A Study of Police Mobilisation.* Toronto: Centre of Criminology, University of Toronto.

Skinner, S., O. Driedger, and B. Grainger. 1981. *Corrections: An Historical Perspective of the Saskatchewan Experience.* Regina: Canadian Plains Research Centre, University of Regina.

Skolnick, J. K. 1966. *Justice Without Trial: Law Enforcement in a Democratic Society.* New York: John Wiley and Sons.

Solicitor General of Canada. 1983. *Canadian Urban Victimization Survey. Bulletin No. 1. Reported and Unreported Crimes.* Ottawa: Research and Statistics Group, Programs Branch.

Stenning, P. C. 1981a. *Legal Status of the Police.* Ottawa: Law Reform Commission of Canada.

———. 1981b. "The Role of Police Boards and Commissions as Institutions of Municipal Police Governance." In *Organizational Police Deviance: Its Structure and Control,* edited by C. D. Shearing, 161–208. Toronto: Butterworths.

———. 1981c. *Police Commissions and Boards in Canada.* Toronto: Centre of Criminology, University of Toronto.

Sterling, J. W. 1969. *Changes in Role Concepts of Police Officers During Recruit Training.* Washington, D.C., International Association of Chiefs of Police.

Stuebing, W. K. 1984. *Crime Victims. Victims and Witnesses: Experiences, Needs, and Community/Criminal Justice Response.* Ottawa: Policy Planning and Development Branch, Department of Justice.

Talbot, C. K., C. H. S. Jayewardene, and T. J. Juliani. 1983. *The Thin Blue Line: An Historical Perspective of Policing in Canada.* Ottawa: CRIM-CARE, Inc.

———. 1984. *Policing in Canada: A Developmental Perspective.* 8 *Canadian Police College Journal* 218–88.

Task Force on Policing in Ontario. 1974. *Report to the Solicitor General.* Toronto: Government of Ontario.

Taylor, I. 1986. "Martyrdom and Surveillance: Ideological and Social Practices of Police in Canada in the 1980s." 26 *Crime and Social Justice* 60–78.

Thacker, R. 1980. "Canada's Mounted: The Evolution of a Legend." 4 *Journal of Popular Culture* 298–312.

Thomas, C. W., and J. R. Hepburn. 1983. *Crime, Criminal Law, and Criminology.* Dubuque, Iowa: Wm. C. Brown Co. Publishers.

Thomas, C., and J. Hyman. 1977. "Perceptions of Crime, Fear of Victimization and Public Perceptions of Police Performance." 5 *Journal of Police Science and Administration* 305–17.

Thornton, L. M. 1975. " People and the Police: An Analysis of Factors

Associated with Police Evaluation and Support." 1 *Canadian Journal of Sociology* 325–42.

Van Maanen, J. 1973. "Observations on the Making of Policemen." 32 *Human Organization* 407-18.

Vincent, C. L. 1979. *Policeman.* Toronto: Gage Publishing, Ltd.

Walden, K. 1982. *Visions of Order: The Canadian Mounties in Symbol and Myth.* Toronto: Butterworths.

Webster, J. 1970. "Police Task and Time Study." 61 *Journal of Criminal Law, Criminology, and Police Science* 94–100.

Weiner, N. L. 1976. *The Role of the Police in Urban Society: Conflicts and Consequences.* Indianapolis: Bobbs-Merrill.

Westley, W. A. 1953. "Violence and the Police." 59 *American Journal of Sociology* 34–41.

––––––. 1970. *Violence and the Police: A Sociological Study of Law, Custom, and Morality.* Cambridge: MIT Press.

Whittingham, M. D. 1984. "Police/Public Homicide and Fatality Risks in Canada: A Current Assessment." 3 *Canadian Police Chief* 4–8.

Wilson, J. Q. 1968. *Varieties of Police Behavior: The Management of Law and Order in Eight Communities.* Cambridge: Harvard University Press.

Wilt, G. Marie, and J. D. Bannon. 1976. "Cynicism or Realism: A Critique of Niederhoffer's Research into Police Attitudes." 4 *Journal of Police Science and Administration* 38–45.

Winfree, L. T., and C. T. Griffiths. 1977. "The Determinants of Adolescent Attitudes Toward the Police: A Survey of High School Students." In *Juvenile Delinquency: Little Brother Grows Up,* edited by T. N. Ferdinand, 79–99. Beverly Hills: Sage Publications.

Yarmey, A. D., and S. Rashid. 1983. "Perceptions of the Public and Legal Professionals Toward Police Officers." 7 *Canadian Police College Journal* 89-95.

LEGISLATION

Constitution Act, 1867, 1867 (U.K.), c. 3
Criminal Code, R.S.C. 1985, c. C-46
Food and Drugs Act, R.S.C. 1985, c. F-27
Indian Act, R.S.C. 1985, c. I-5
Municipal Institutions of Upper Canada Act, S.C. 1858, c. 99
Narcotic Control Act, R.S.C. 1985, c. N-1
Parish and Town Officers Act, S.U.C. 1793, c. 2
Police Act, R.S.B.C. 1979, c. 331
Police Act, S.O. 1946, c. 72
Police Act, R.S.O. 1980, c. 381
Police of Canada Act, S.C. 1868, c. 73
Royal Canadian Mounted Police Act, R.S.C. 1985, c. R-10

4 THE POWERS AND DECISION MAKING OF THE POLICE

In this chapter, we will consider the powers of the Canadian police, the police exercise of discretion, and the factors that appear to influence the decision making of police officers in encounter situations with citizens and suspects. However, prior to this, it is important to examine the often overlooked role of the public as a key decision maker in the criminal justice system and as a primary determinant of the actions of the police.

The activities of line-level police officers can be generally grouped into those that are reactive and those that are proactive.[1] *Reactive policing* results from spontaneous or planned requests by citizens or groups for police intervention, while *proactive policing* has been defined as "spontaneous decisions by individual patrol officers to stop citizens for investigative checks ... to pursue particular types of people and the trouble associated with them" (Ericson, 1982: 73).[2] A high percentage of crimes are brought to the attention of the police by the general public, who, through their decision either to report or not report crimes, act as the gatekeepers of the criminal justice system. However, the police also engage in a considerable amount of proactive policing during their routine activities, including traffic stops, questioning suspicious persons and investigating suspicious circumstances.

Calling the Police

Recognizing the importance of the general public in bringing criminal offences to the attention of the police, a considerable amount of research has focused on the extent to which criminal behaviour is reported (and underreported) by the victims and witnesses of crime. Victimization studies in both Canada and the United States have attempted to ascertain the extent to which various types of criminal offences occur in communities and the reasons why citizens choose to call or not to call the police. This research has uncovered a "dark figure" of crime — a wide range of criminal offences that are not reported to the police.

In 1982, the federal government undertook an extensive victimization survey in seven major urban centres in Canada. The results of this study (Solicitor General of Canada, 1983a; 1983b) provide us with valuable insights into the reporting patterns of victims of crime across the country.[3] Among the findings of the survey was that more than half (58%) of the estimated incidents involving victims were never brought to the attention of the police, and only 3% were discovered as a consequence of proactive policing. Further, more than 80% of the reports made to the police came from victims or from members of the victims' households. Data from the survey also revealed considerable underreporting of incidents across the major offence categories, with theft or attempted theft of a motor vehicle being the crime most likely to be reported to the police (70% report rate) and theft of personal property being the crime least likely to be reported to the police (29% reported) (see Table 4.1).

Not only was there massive underreporting of criminal victimization across the country, but the survey discovered differences in reporting rates between Canadian cities (see Table 4.2). More specifically, there was a 7% difference between the city with the highest reporting rate (Montreal) and the city with the lowest reporting rate (Vancouver). The reporting differences between Canadian cities were much larger, however, for specific offence categories, suggesting regional differences in attitudes about particular crimes and differences in the perceived benefits to be gained from reporting.

An attempt was also made to ascertain the reasons why citizens who had been the victims of crime had failed to report the incident. The reasons for the failure to report an incident were grouped under the categories "No Perceived Benefit," "Costs Outweigh Benefits," "Personal Reasons" and "Reported to Another Official." The findings presented in Table 4.3 reveal that the most common reason (66%) given by victims for failing to report was that the victimization was not serious enough to warrant contacting the police. The second most commonly given reason (61%) for the failure to report was the victims' belief that the police would have been unable to do anything about the victimization. Other commonly cited reasons were that the victim felt that the inconvenience resulting from the reporting would outweigh the benefits (24%) and that nothing had been taken or the items that had been taken had been returned (19%). In Figure 4.1 and Figure 4.2, the reasons for the failure to report personal violent offences and property offences are presented (see also Hylton and Matonovich, 1980).

Of particular interest is the opinion of many citizens that "the police couldn't do anything," given as a reason for failing to report in 61% of the incidents. While this may be interpreted as indicating suspicion or distrust of the police, it may be that citizens have a fairly accurate perception of the abilities of the police: "Clearly for such crimes as petty theft, purse snatching, vandalism and even assault, there is often very little the police can do — through traditional law enforcement techniques — and victims perceive no real benefits in reporting" (Solicitor General of Canada, 1983b: 3). The decisions by victims of crime to report or not report an incident to the police may thus serve to filter out a large number of relatively minor

TABLE 4.1

NUMBER OF INCIDENTS OF SELECTED TYPES AND PROPORTION NOT REPORTED TO POLICE IN SEVEN CITIES

Type of Incident	Estimated Incidents	Percent of Estimated Incidents	Percent Unreported	Percent Reported
Sexual Assault	17,200	1	62	38
Robbery	49,300	3	55	45
Assault	285,700	18	66	34
Break & Enter	227,400	14	36	64
Motor Vehicle Theft	40,600	3	30	70
Household Theft	417,300	26	56	44
Personal Theft	349,900	22	71	29
Vandalism	213,100	13	65	35
TOTAL	1,600,500	100	58	42

Source: *Bulletin No. 1. Canadian Urban Victimization Survey: Victims of Crime* (Ottawa: Programs Branch, Research and Statistics Group, 1983), p. 3.

TABLE 4.2
PER CENT OF INCIDENTS COMING TO ATTENTION OF THE POLICE, BY CITY

	Per cent Reported in Seven Cities	Vancouver	Edmonton	Winnipeg	Toronto	Montreal	Halifax Dartmouth	St. John's	Reported Range
Sexual Assault	38	32 (5)*	15 (7)	33 (4)	40 (2)	50 (1)	29 (6)	40 (3)	(15 – 50)
Robbery	45	43 (6)	46 (1)	42 (7)	46 (2)	45 (3)	45 (4)	44 (5)	(42 – 46)
Assault	34	34 (4)	32 (6)	23 (7)	36 (2)	39 (1)	35 (3)	33 (5)	(23 – 39)
Break & Enter	64	61 (7)	62 (5)	62 (4)	65 (3)	66 (2)	61 (6)	68 (1)	(61 – 68)
Motor Vehicle Theft	70	71 (6)	77 (1)	73 (4)	72 (5)	67 (7)	74 (3)	74 (2)	(67 – 77)
Household Theft	44	39 (7)	46 (4)	47 (3)	46 (5)	46 (6)	48 (1)	48 (2)	(39 – 48)
Personal Theft	29	29 (4)	30 (3)	25 (7)	30 (2)	31 (1)	28 (5)	26 (6)	(25 – 31)
Vandalism	35	29 (6)	39 (2)	38 (3)	37 (4)	36 (5)	40 (1)	27 (7)	(27 – 40)
Overall Percentage Reported	42	38 (7)	42 (4)	40 (5)	42 (3)	45 (1)	42 (2)	39 (6)	(38 – 45)
Over Percentage Not Reported	58	62	57	60	58	55	58	61	

* Numbers in brackets indicate the rank-ordering of cites within offence categories. A "1" indicates the city with the highest percentage reported, and a "7" indicates the city with the lowest percentage of reported incidents.

Source: *Bulletin No. 2. Canadian Urban Victimization Survey: Reported and Unreported Crime* (Ottawa: Programs Branch, Research and Statistics Group, 1983), p. 5.

TABLE 4.3
REASONS GIVEN BY VICTIMS FOR FAILURE TO REPORT INCIDENTS TO THE POLICE

Reasons	Per Cent of All Unreported Incidents
No Perceived Benefit	
Too Minor	66
Police Couldn't Do Anything	61
Nothing Taken/Items Recovered	19
Costs Outweigh Benefits	
Inconvenience	24
Fear of Revenge	4
Concern with Attitude of Police or Courts	8
Personal Reasons	
Protect Offender	6
Personal Matter	13
Reported to Another Official	12
Overall % Unreported	58

Percentages do not add to 100% since respondents could indicate more than one reason for failure to report any one incident.

Source: *Bulletin No. 2. Canadian Urban Victimization Survey: Reported and Unreported Crime* (Ottawa: Programs Branch, Research and Statistics Group, 1983), p. 3.

FIGURE 4.1
GROUPED REASONS FOR FAILURE TO REPORT

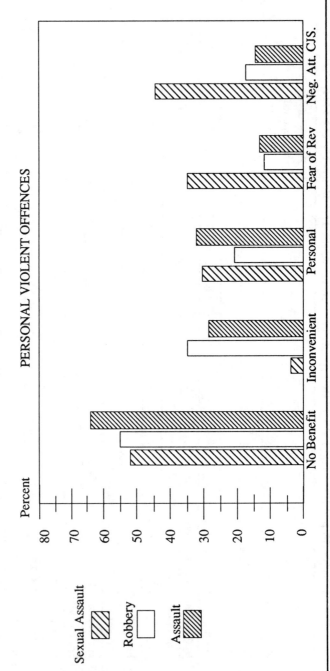

PERSONAL VIOLENT OFFENCES

Source: *Bulletin No. 2. Canadian Urban Victimization Survey: Reported and Unreported Crime* (Ottawa: Programs Branch, Research and Statistics Group, 1983), p. 5.

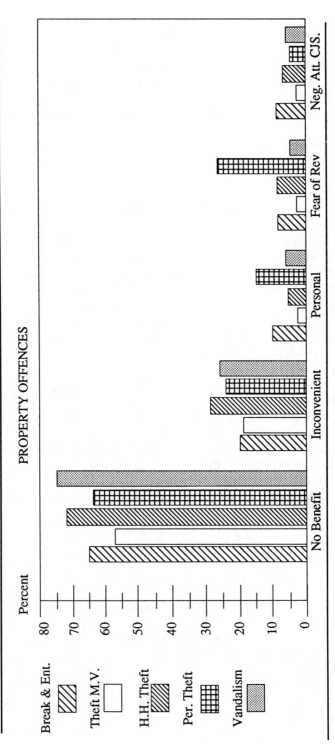

FIGURE 4.2
GROUPED REASONS FOR FAILURE TO REPORT

PROPERTY OFFENCES

No Perceived Benefit includes: "Nothing taken or items recovered"; "Police couldn't do anything"; and "Too minor".
Personal reasons includes: "Protect offender"; and "Personal matter".

Source: *Bulletin No. 2. Canadian Urban Victimization Survey: Reported and Unreported Crime* (Ottawa: Programs Branch, Research and Statistics Group, 1983), p. 5.

offences that may be more effectively resolved without police intervention. However, the results of the Canadian victimization survey revealed that many serious victimizations, incuding violent personal offences, were not reported to the police because the victim perceived no real benefit in doing so. This finding has significant implications for police-community relations and particularly for the victim-assistance initiatives discussed in Chapter 2.

The findings of the Canadian Urban Victimization Survey are generally consistent with victimization surveys that have been conducted in the United States. In the United States, the U.S. Bureau of the Census gathers data on victimization in a program called the National Crime Panel. Data gathered from a large number of jurisdictions suggest that there is massive underreporting of even serious criminal offences. For example, only one-third of the rapes, two-fifths of the robberies, and one-half of the burglaries experienced by respondents were reported to the police. Among the most commonly cited reasons for not calling the police were that "nothing could be done" and the "victimization was not important enough" (cited in Gottfredson and Gottfredson, 1980: 30-31). As Gottfredson and Gottfredson (1980: 29) note: "Many victims apparently believed that the crime was not worthy of official state action, either because it was seen by the victim as not being important or because the victim perceived the police as being uninterested."

Victimization research has also revealed the factors that appear to be associated with a decision by the victims of criminal offences to call the police. Attention has focused on the role of the seriousness of the offence, the characteristics of the victim, the relationship between the offender and the victim, and the attitudes of the victim toward the police. With respect to the seriousness of the offence, it has been found that the greater the severity of the crime, either in terms of physical harm to the victim or amount of financial loss, the more likely the offence will be brought to the attention of the police (see Gottfredson and Hindelang, 1979; Hindelang, 1976; McGahan, 1984).

Hindelang (1976) found that for crimes against the person, younger persons were less likely to call the police than were older persons and males were generally less likely to call the police than were females. The Canadian Urban Victimization Survey (Solicitor General of Canada, 1983b: 4-7) also reported that females were more likely than males to telephone the police for both personal and property offences. While it is generally felt that the relationship of the victim to the offender is a primary determinant of the decision to report, the Canadian survey (1983b: 8) found that the reporting rates were unaffected by the relationship between the offender and the victim: "37% of the incidents involving strangers were reported; 36% of incidents involving acquaintances; and 38% of those involving relatives." Similarly, Gottfredson and Hindelang (1976) reported only a slight difference between reporting of those offences in which the victim was victimized by a stranger and those in which it was by someone known to the victim (see also Blum-West, 1983).

In our consideration of attitudes toward the police in Chapter 3, we saw that having been a victim of a crime may affect a person's attitudes toward the police. Perceptions of the police also appear to affect citizen reporting patterns. The Canadian Urban Victimization Study (Solicitor General of Canada, 1983b: 10) found that citizens who rated police performance favourably were more likely to report victimizations. These findings contrast with those reported in the United States, Gottfredson and Gottfredson (1980: 41) concluding from a survey of the research literature that ratings of the police were not related to victim reporting. A general conclusion that can be drawn from this brief review is that while there are inconsistent findings with respect to the impact of the characteristics of the victim on the decision to call the police, the severity of the offence or the gravity of the harm (physical or financial) suffered is highly related to the decision to call the police.[4]

Police Response to Citizen Requests

While research generally focuses on police decision making in the encounter situation with the victim and/or suspects of crime, there is an additional stage of discretionary decision making involving police telephone operators, complaint officers, and dispatch officers who receive citizen requests and assess whether police intervention is warranted. In Chapter 3, it was noted that the public requests a wide range of services from the police, only a fraction of which are directly related to the enforcement of the law or crime control. Given limited organizational resources, the police must determine the priority of the requests they receive and this involves discretionary decision making by police personnel even before an officer is sent to the scene.

Perhaps the most extensive Canadian analysis of citizens' requests for police service and the police response to such requests has been undertaken by Shearing (1984) (see also Chappell, Jessup, and Moore, 1984; Manning, 1988). In a study of the Metropolitan Toronto Police Department, Shearing (1984: 104) found that police complaint officers employed a system for determining the priority of calls, with those related to serious property damage and bodily injury being rated first, followed by alarms, fires, domestic disputes and traffic parking violations. Shearing also discovered that the decision of the complaint officer was strongly influenced by the officer's perception of the amount of trouble represented by the call, the degree of deference shown to the police by the caller, and the manner in which the "trouble" was presented by the caller. Those callers, for example, who exhibited deference toward the police in their telephone conversation with the complaint officer were more likely to receive a sympathetic consideration of their request for police intervention (see also Jorgensen, 1981).

In those instances in which the complaint officer decided that the dispatch of a patrol unit was warranted, the request was forwarded to the dispatch officers in the department, who then engaged in additional discretionary decision making. The dispatch officers attempted to reconcile the "demands for police service with the resources available" (Shearing, 1984: 161). Utilizing two indicators, the number of units dispatched and the elapsed response time for the dispatch of a unit, Shearing (1984: 166) found that dispatcher decisions were also affected by a priority system that was premised on the perceived probability that a suspect could be apprehended. The screening of citizen requests is also illustrated by the findings of Levens (1976), who in an examination of the telephone requests made to the Vancouver City Police Department over a six-month period, found that a patrol car was dispatched in 43.8% of the cases in which it was requested, with the remaining calls from citizens being handled by referral or the provision of information over the telephone.

These research findings indicate that the discretionary decision making of the police begins long before the police officer arrives at the scene. However, it is important to note that there may be considerable variability between police departments in the criteria utilized in assessing citizen requests for intervention and in determining that the dispatch of a patrol car is warranted. From their study of police telephone operators in the United States, Antunes and Scott (1981: 177) concluded: "The criteria used to judge whether a call merits a dispatch of a patrol officer will vary from department to department as a matter of official policy and as a result of informal decision rules developed by phone operators."

Police Discretion

While the patrol officer occupies the lowest level in the hierarchy of the police organization, this is the position in which the most discretion is exercised. Ericson (1982: 25) points out that while in most organizations policies are established by the senior administrative level and implemented by the managerial level who supervise line-level personnel, "In the police organization, the administration can establish general production guidelines, but it is much more heavily dependent on the decisions taken and information produced by line members." Police discretion, then, can be broadly viewed as the autonomy that individual police officers have in carrying out their tasks and it permeates all police activities.

In Canada, there is no specific legislation that addresses the exercise of discretion by police officers. The *Criminal Code* appears to encourage the exercise of discretion by police officers, providing that a police officer may make an arrest in those instances in which there are reasonable and probable grounds to believe that an offence has been committed. The *Report of the Canadian Committee on Corrections* (Ouimet, 1969: 45-46) stated that the exercise of discretion by police officers was a critical ingredient in ensuring justice: "We think that a decision not to prosecute and merely to give a warning may best advance the ends of justice in some circumstances." However, the Law Reform Commission of Canada (1975) has argued that there is a need for published guidelines to structure the broad discretionary powers of Canadian police officers.

Throughout the policing literature, there is a considerable diversity of opinion regarding the exercise of discretion by the police and the extent to which such discretionary power should be structured and controlled. There are differing perspectives on how much discretion police officers actually have and whether such discretion is exercised in a fair and equitable manner.

In an early treatise on police discretion, Goldstein (1960) noted that not only were the decisions of police patrol officers of extremely "low visibility," not subject to judicial review, and generally immune from supervisory control, but also that through their discretionary decision making, patrol officers established enforcement policy for the police organization. Further, many observers have argued that unchecked police discretion results in discrimination, particularly towards members of ethnic minorities and those citizens of lower socioeconomic status (cf. Chambliss, 1969; Quinney, 1970; Reiman, 1979; Taylor, 1983; Turk, 1969). The possibility that discrimination will occur is enhanced by the fact that officers rely upon their personal judgment and experience in dealing with situations, which may require the legitimate exercise of discretion, yet be interpreted as having been unfair and discriminatory by the suspect or members of the general public.

One of the most significant and influential contributions to the debate on police discretion has been made by Kenneth Culp Davis (1978: 123-24). Noting that much of the discretionary power exercised by the police is of doubtful legality and exempt from judicial review, Davis argues that police discretion should be structured, confined, and checked. Davis (1975: 34) and other police observers contend that one of the most damaging aspects of police discretion is the myth of full enforcement of the law, an impossibility given the limited resources of the police and the resistance of the general community to such a policy. Accordingly to Davis (1975: 54), this pretence is caused by "the combination of full enforcement legislation (statutes and ordinances) with the lack of resources for full enforcement and the common sense of some nonenforcement." While there is in Canada no legislative stipulation for full enforcement, the pretence of full enforcement is pervasive.

Cooley (1981: 194) reports the results of a 1971 survey of police discretion that found general agreement among police officers and citizens that the exercise of discretion should vary with the circumstances of the case: ". . . 82 percent of the public and 83 percent of the police disagreed with the statement that the police should charge everyone who commits an offence, regardless of the nature of the offence and other circumstances surrounding it."

The same group of police and citizen respondents agreed that offenders should always be charged in serious offences, while in minor offences discretion should be exercised. Cooley (1981: 195) also reported that the public was more in favour of the exercise of discretion than the police and that both the police and public felt that the total circumstances surrounding a particular offence should be examined by the police in their decision making.

While it is generally acknowledged that the elimination of police discretion is impossible, Davis (1975: 139) and others have argued that there should be complete disclosure by police forces of their policy of selective enforcement and that there should be an appropriate mix of procedural guidelines and discretion.[5]

Although there is widespread concern with the exercise of discretion by police officers, considerable evidence exists to suggest that officers may not have as wide discretionary powers as is generally thought. Sykes, Fox, and Clark (1976: 179), for example, found that due to the constraints of legal statutes and departmental policies, patrol officers had little, if any, discretion regarding whether to arrest or release a suspect in nearly half of the encounter situations observed. Lundman (1980: 125) has also pointed out that the discretionary powers of police officers are often constrained by the actions of the general public, including the initial decision to call the police and whether the witness or victim chooses to remain at the scene: ". . . for every encounter in which it appears possible for a police officer to exercise discretion, there is at least one other that never took place because a citizen chose not to call the police or decided not to interact even though a call had been made."

Despite the controversy that continues to surround the exercise of discretion by police officers, most observers agree that discretion is a necessary element in policing and is likely to remain a vital part of the police officer's role. However, there continues to be concern that the police not abuse their discretionary powers or misuse their authority in carrying out their tasks. To understand more fully the consequences of police discretion, we must consider the powers and decision making of the police in greater detail.

Police Powers

Introduction: The Significance of the *Canadian Charter of Rights and Freedoms*

As the Law Reform Commission of Canada (1984b: 6) has noted:

> The balance between law enforcement and effective protection of individual interests is, ultimately, a working definition of justice, and the prospect of agreement on this aspect of social policy is always elusive.

Historically, in Canada the police have been given broad powers to carry out their function of law enforcement, and it is fair to say that the courts have generally leaned toward support of "crime control" rather than "due process" values in performing their immensely difficult task of balancing the rights of individual citizens and the perceived needs of law enforcement (Cohen, 1984b: 267). However, it may be contended that the balance between police powers and individual rights has shifted since the enactment of the *Canadian Charter of Rights and Freedoms* in 1982[6] (Luther, 1987). In this section concerning the powers of the police in Canada, we shall examine the nature and extent of these powers in light of the impact of the *Charter* and analyze the current state of the balance between the powers of the police and the rights of the individual citizen.

The *Charter* entrenches a number of constitutional rights on behalf of an accused person in the criminal justice process and provides various remedies for the infringement of those rights. Section 24(1) provides that a court may grant "such remedy as the court considers appropriate and just in the circumstances" (see Roach, 1987). It has been suggested that possible remedies under this provision may include a notice to quash a search warrant, a stay of proceedings, an action for damages, a prosecution for an offence or for an infringement of the *Charter,* or a petition for an injunction or a declaration (for example, a declaration that certain criminal legislation is void because it infringes the guarantees of the *Charter*).[7] Any of these remedies may be sought in the situation where it is alleged that a police officer has infringed rights guaranteed by the *Charter*. In addition, section 24(2) of the *Charter* provides the courts with a totally new power; namely, the *discretion* to exclude evidence from the trial of an accused person where such evidence was obtained in a manner that infringed or denied any of the rights and freedoms protected by the *Charter*. However, the discretion to exclude such evidence will be exercised only where it is established that its admission "would bring the administration of justice into disrepute." This particular provision of the *Charter* created a considerable degree of concern among the police, who feared that the courts would be willing to release dangerous criminals back onto the streets because there had been a mere "technical violation" of the law. However, as we shall see, this fear is unjustified since the *Charter* clearly does not establish a rule that automatically excludes illegally obtained evidence, and in practice, the courts have been very reluctant to exercise their discretion to exclude evidence (Luther, 1987).

Furthermore, one important point that should be made about the rights and freedoms guaranteed by the *Charter* is that they are by no means absolute in nature. Indeed, section 1 states that such rights can be subject to "such reasonable limits prescribed by law as can be demonstrably justified in a free and democratic society."

There is little doubt that the advent of the *Charter* has injected a totally new dimension into the debate over the extent of police powers vis-à-vis the individual citizen (Stewart, 1987). As we shall see, it is clear that there have been some important decisions by the courts that have resulted in additional restrictions being placed on the police. However, there is a debate concerning exactly how effective the *Charter* is likely to be in altering the balance of power between the police and a suspect in a criminal case. At one end of the spectrum, there have been claims that the *Charter* has tilted the balance in favour of criminals. Certainly, at the time of its enactment, there was no shortage of police officers in Canada who were prepared to express the view that the *Charter* had left them to fight crime "with one hand tied behind their backs." On the other hand, there have been criminologists who have suggested that the *Charter* will have very little impact on criminal justice practices. Indeed, Ericson (1983: 53) has contended that judicial decisions, in general, have relatively little effect on police practices. In his view, it is the actions of the police rather than the decisions of judges that are most likely to affect the average citizen in his or her day-to-day affairs:

> In sum, it is the law of arrest, the law of search and seizure, and the prison rules, more than the [*Charter*]; and, the police more than the judiciary; that make evident that the law is there more to restrict than liberate, more to regulate than to provide relief, more to deny the rights of many and grant privileges to a few.

Indeed, Ericson (1983: 25) has dismissed as "fiction" the belief that the *Charter* will "profoundly alter" criminal procedure. He contends (1983: 53-54) that the *Charter* has little direct impact in protecting the rights and freedoms of individual citizens and that its major function is to "guarantee a framework of official discretion" for the police and for "legitimating decisions about the restriction of rights in any given conflict." Instead, the *Charter* provides a "protective symbolic canopy for a statutory and common law scheme" that permits the police to "get on with their routine social control tasks."

Clearly, there are a number of sharply conflicting views on the potential efficacy of the *Charter* as a means of setting boundaries to the exercise of police powers within the criminal justice system. However, the initial experience with the *Charter* suggests that there, probably, has been a slight shift in the balance between police powers and individual rights and freedoms and that this shift has favoured the private citizen. On the other hand, the shift has not been as marked as any of the *Charter's* proponents would have wished. As Russell (1985: 368) noted in 1985:

> After three years of living with a constitutional charter of fundamental rights and freedoms, the only safe thing to say is that it has turned out to be not nearly as bad as its opponents feared it might be nor nearly as great as its promoters promised it would be.

Similarly, with specific reference to criminal justice, it is interesting to read the comments of McMahon (1984: 145), who states:

> In sum, neither the extreme view that criminals are enjoying a "golden age", or the opposite one that the Charter offers accused people no protection would appear to be substantiated by the limited data available. Nor is it clear that the provisions of the Charter are impeding the police in their work.

It is hoped that the following discussion of police powers will put readers in a position in which they can form their own views on the significance of the *Charter* in this area.

Arrest

Perhaps the police power that first springs to most people's minds is that of arrest. The Law Reform Commission of Canada (1985: 27-28) has contended that the purposes of arrest or detention can be classified as being "either protective or repressive." Protective (or preventive) purposes include the use of the power to arrest or detain in order to prevent the commission of an offence or to terminate a breach of the peace. Repressive purposes include the utilization of the power to compel an individual's attendance in court or to collect evidence in relation to a criminal offence.

As the Law Reform Commission of Canada (1985: 7) has stated, "the principles governing arrest are a fundamental aspect of any legal system which give practical shape to relations between the state and individual citizens." Arrest represents one of the most far-reaching of the encroachments that the state makes upon the lives of citizens (Cohen, 1981; Pavlich, 1981), and therefore it is scarcely surprising that the exercise of the police power to make an arrest is hedged around with numerous legal restrictions. These restrictions are not only contained in the *Criminal Code* and in case law, but are also enshrined in the *Charter* (Friedland, 1982).

What is an "arrest"? Unfortunately, the definition of *arrest* has created a considerable amount of difficulty for Canadian courts. The common sense definition would appear to revolve around the *physical* taking into custody of a suspect against his or her will (Pavlich, 1981: III-56-60). However, it appears that Canadian courts are prone to adopt a somewhat more expansive definition. Indeed, the Law Reform Commission of Canada (1985: 31) has suggested that judicial authority has ruled that an arrest may be carried out in one of two ways: "(i) touching with a view to detention, even where the suspect may not submit voluntarily; or (ii) stating that the suspect is under arrest where the suspect submits." As we shall see, an arrest may take place either with or without the authority of a judicial warrant.

It is also important to bear in mind that there are a number of statutory provisions, both federal and provincial, that authorize the police to exercise a power of *detention* that falls short of amounting to a full arrest in the sense outlined above. One striking example of such a power is the demand that a citizen blow into a breathalyzer. Individuals who are asked to carry out this request clearly suffer some restriction upon their liberty, but the degree of this restriction falls considerably short of that which would apply were they subjected to arrest. It is necessary to pay close attention to the power to *detain* because the *Charter* (section 10) contains specific guarantees of the legal rights of those who have experienced "arrest or detention." In several critical decisions, the Supreme Court of Canada appears to have adopted a very broad definition of *detention* for the purpose of the *Charter*.[8] It was suggested that there is a "detention" whenever a police officer "assumes control over the movement of person by a demand or direction which may have significant legal consequence and which prevents or impedes access to [legal] counsel."[9] There must be an element of compulsion, the court ruled, but *psychological* compulsion, in the form of a "reasonable perception of suspension of freedom of choice"[10] is sufficient for this purpose. Most individuals do not have a working knowledge of the precise scope of police powers, and if they submit to a police demand because they believe they have no real choice but to do so, then there has been a detention and their rights are protected by section 10 of the *Charter*.

The power of a police officer to effect an arrest is derived from legislation, both federal and provincial (Law Reform Commission of Canada, 1985: 15-26). The most significant federal statute for this purpose is, of course, the *Criminal Code*. At the provincial level, powers of arrest are frequently specified by, for example, motor vehicle and liquor licensing and control legislation.

The primary pupose of arrest, in the Canadian system of criminal procedure, is to compel an accused person's attendance at trial (Law Reform Commission of Canada, 1985: 28; 1988). It is important, therefore, to underscore that arrest is only one of a number of alternative mechanisms for effecting this purpose. Indeed, the *Criminal Code,* as we shall see shortly, provides the police officer with the options of arresting an individual, issuing an appearance notice, or seeking a summons.

A police officer may arrest *without a warrant* any individual:

(a) who has committed an indictable offence or whom the officer believes, on reasonable and probable grounds, has committed or is about to commit an indictable offence; or

(b) whom the officer finds actually committing any criminal offence (whether it be an indictable or a summary conviction offence); or

(c) for whom the officer has reasonable and probable grounds to believe that a warrant of arrest or committal is in force within the jurisdiction in which he or she is found.[11]

The *Criminal Code* grants police officers additional powers of arrest without a warrant in relation to such *Code* offences as breach of the peace[12] and being found in a common gaming or betting house.[13]

It is important to recognize that there are some significant restrictions upon the power of a police officer to arrest a suspect without a warrant. The most important of these restrictions were imposed as a consequence of certain recommendations made by the Ouimet Committee (1969) and acted upon by Parliament in the form of the *Bail Reform Act*, which came into force in January, 1972.[14] The Act amended the *Criminal Code* so as to require that for the less serious criminal offences, police officers *not* use their discretion to make an arrest unless they have reasonable grounds to believe that the "public interest" can be satisfied only by adopting such a course or they have reasonable grounds to believe that if an arrest is not made, the suspect will not show up in court.[15] The term *public interest* is given concrete hands and feet by requiring the police officer to have "regard to all the circumstances including the need to (i) establish the identity of the person, (ii) secure or preserve evidence of or relating to the offence, or (iii) prevent the continuation or repetition of the offence or the commission of another offence." Even where the officer has decided to utilize the option of arrest without a warrant, the *Code* requires that he or she release the suspect "as soon as practicable" with the intention of compelling the suspect's later attendance in court by means of a summons or appearance notice, provided, of course, that such a release would be in the public interest and that there are no reasonable grounds for believing that the suspect will fail to show up in court in the absence of an arrest.[16] The *Bail Reform Act* further strengthened the presumption in favour of releasing an arrested suspect from custody by permitting the officer in charge of a police lock-up to release the suspect and to ensure his or her attendance by means of a summons or appearance notice.[17]

The *Criminal Code* also contains provisions for the arrest of suspects under the authority of a judicial warrant (see Salhany, 1984: 64-70). More specifically, a justice of the peace may issue a warrant for the arrest of an individual suspected of having committed either an indictable or a summary conviction offence.[18] A warrant may be issued only after someone (usually a police officer) lays an information before a justice, alleging that he or she has reasonable grounds to believe that an offence has been committed.[19] Except insofar as the most serious offences are concerned, the justice is required to issue a summons, rather than an arrest warrant, unless the evidence available to him or her discloses reasonable grounds for believing that the "public interest" requires that an arrest be made.[20] Significantly, in relation to all but the most serious offences, the justice may endorse the arrest warrant so as to provide for the subsequent release of the suspect by the officer in charge of a lock-up.[21]

In order to ensure that a suspect is not detained in custody unnecessarily after arrest (whether or not this has been brought about by virtue of a warrant), the *Criminal Code* places the arresting police officer under a duty to bring the suspect before a justice "without unreasonable delay" and, in any event, within 24 hours (unless a justice is not available within this period; in which case, the suspect must be brought before a justice "as soon as possible").[22] The justice may decide to release the suspect to the community, pending his or her later appearance in court, either unconditionally or upon conditions. Failure, on the part of the police, to bring a suspect before a justice as soon as possible will not only infringe the relevant provision of the *Code,* but may also represent a breach of the *Charter,* since section 9 of the latter protects the citizen from arbitrary detention or imprisonment.[23]

Alternatives to Arrest

As we noted earlier, instead of making an arrest, the police officer has the option of releasing suspects with the intention of securing their appearance in court by means of a summons or an appearance notice (Pavlich, 1981: III-41). A summons is issued by a justice of the peace after an information has been laid before him or her, alleging that the accused has committed an offence. The summons has been described as a "formal document which is directed to the accused and which sets out the charge as well as the time and place at which the accused is to appear in court" (Law Reform Commission of Canada, 1985: 43). It might also require the accused person to go to a designated place for fingerprinting and photographing (assuming the offence charged is indictable in nature).[24] An appearance notice is similar to a summons, insofar as it is a mechanism that is geared toward compelling the attendance of a suspect without the necessity of an arrest (Pavlich, 1981: 46-50). However, it differs from the summons, since it does not require the intervention of a justice; in other words, the police officer can issue it "on the spot."[25] As is the case with a summons, an appearance notice may require the accused person to go to a designated place for fingerprinting, and so forth. Once an appearance notice has been issued, the police officer must "as soon as practicable" ensure that an information is laid before a justice of the peace.[26] In order to be effective, the notice must be confirmed by the justice. The latter may confirm the notice or cancel it outright (giving the suspect notice that this has been done); alternatively, the justice may decide to cancel the notice and issue a summons or an arrest warrant instead.[27]

With the advent of the *Charter,* the police have been placed under a duty to provide certain critical information to a suspect who has been arrested or detained. Indeed, section 10 of the *Charter* provides that everyone who has been arrested or detained has the right (a) "to be informed promptly of the reasons therefor"; and (b) "to retain and instruct counsel without delay *and to be informed of that right* (emphasis added)" (Conway, 1985). The first of these duties has existed for many years under the common law, and failure to adhere to it may render an arrest unlawful (Law Reform Commission of Canada, 1985: 51). It is also enshrined in the *Criminal Code*, which states that it is the duty of an arresting officer, where it is feasible to do so, to give notice of the process or warrant under the authority of which he or she is acting or the reason for the arrest.[28] The second duty has been added by the *Charter* and failure to perform it may result in charges being dismissed or evidence being excluded from the suspect's trial.[29] The significance of this duty was dramatically illustrated in the *Therens* case,[30] where the accused, who had lost control of his vehicle and driven into a tree, was required by a police officer to take a breathalyzer test and to accompany the latter to the police station for that purpose. The accused duly supplied samples of his breath. However, the police never informed Therens of his right to retain and instruct counsel. At his trial, the charge of driving with an excessive level of alcohol was dismissed because Therens's right, under the *Charter,* to be informed of his right to counsel had been violated by the police. The Supreme Court of Canada upheld the dismissal of the charge, noting that although he had not been "arrested," Therens had certainly been "detained" within the meaning of section 10 of the *Charter*, and that evidence obtained as a result of the violation of the accused's constitutional rights in this manner should be excluded from consideration by the courts because its admission would bring the administration of justice into disrepute within the meaning of section 24(2) of the *Charter*.[31]

Police officers' powers of arrest have also been circumscribed by other provisions of the *Charter*. Section 7 guarantees the "right to life, liberty and security of the person and the right not to be deprived thereof except in accordance with the principles of fundamental justice." This provision clearly affects the exercise of a variety of police powers (Law Reform Commission of Canada, 1985: 9-12). In addition, section 9 protects citizens from arbitrary detention or imprisonment, a provision that is also likely to serve as the basis for constitutional challenges to the use of the power of arrest by the police. For example, in one case,[32] the Court stayed the proceedings against a woman who had been arrested and charged with the summary conviction offence of soliciting for the purposes of prostitution. She had been held overnight in the police cells because of a departmental policy that all such persons should be held in custody overnight and taken to a justice in the morning. However, as we have seen, the *Criminal Code* provides that a police officer who is considering whether to make an arrest for a less serious offence must first consider whether the "public interest" or the possibility that the accused will not appear in court requires that an arrest be made or, even after an arrest has been made, whether the accused should be released from custody. Here the police have not even considered whether the accused should be given an appearance notice or be summonsed as an alternative to arrest and continuing custody. For these reasons, the conduct of the police was considered to be a clear breach of section 9 of the *Charter* as well as of their duties under the *Criminal Code*.

Before leaving the issue of police powers of arrest, it is important to note that the police have the power to take photographs and fingerprints from suspects who have been charged with an indictable offence. This particular power arises under the terms of the *Identification of Criminals Act*. The police may take photographs and fingerprints while the accused is in custody, or the latter may be ordered to attend at the police station at a particular time, specified in an appearance notice or a summons. This power may be exercised against even those accused persons who are charged with what are known as "mixed offences" (offences that may be tried either on indictment or by summary conviction procedures), despite the fact that the prosecution may ultimately decide to proceed by way of summary conviction procedures rather than by indictment. This means that the intrusive powers granted to the police under the *Identification of Criminals Act* apply to a broad range of criminal charges.[32a]

Police Use of Force

One controversial aspect of police powers in Canada concerns the use of force, particularly when the making of an arrest is concerned (Pavlich, 1981: III-176-80). Section 25(1) of the *Code* permits police officers to use "as much force as is necessary" for the purpose of carrying out what they are required or authorized to do in the administration or enforcement of the law, provided that they act on "reasonable grounds." Subsections (3) and (4) permit the use of deadly force in certain circumstances. Subsection (3) is unobjectionable and, indeed, clearly necessary, since it permits police officers to use force that is intended to inflict death or grievous bodily harm, where they believe, on reasonable grounds, that it is necessary to do so for the purpose of preserving themselves from death or grievous bodily harm. Subsection (4), however, is much more problematic, since it provides that where a suspect is bent on escape by fleeing from the police, then an officer who is seeking to make an arrest may use "as much force as is necessary to prevent the escape by flight, unless the escape can be prevented by reasonable means in a less violent manner."[33] The problem with this subsection is that it is not limited in its operation to suspects who pose a danger either to the police themselves or to the community at large.

Therefore, the subsection permits the use of firearms by the police to prevent an escape even if the suspect is not really "dangerous." Although the police in Canada do not resort to the use of firearms nearly as frequently as do many of their counterparts south of the border, some 119 citizens were shot to death by police officers in Canada between 1970 and 1981, and it has been suggested that perhaps three times as many individuals were injured as a result of the use of firearms by the police (Chappell and Graham, 1985: 10, 33). According to Solomon (1985: 333), an unpublished study by the Ministry of the Solicitor General of Canada "revealed that the police in Canada had used their guns mainly against unarmed fleeing suspects (some of whom turned out to be innocent) and that the guns did not usually help in their apprehension." Unfortunately, there is still a relative dearth of information concerning the nature of the use of deadly force by the police in Canada; however, a recent study in the area has recommended that it be limited to situations where it is necessary for the defence of life (Chappell and Graham, 1985: 194).

What happens if the police wish to arrest someone who is in private premises, particularly their own home? Is a person's home really their castle? Where the officers have a warrant for the arrest of a suspect, then they may forcibly enter private premises, even the suspect's home, in order to make the arrest, provided they have reasonable grounds to believe that the person named in the warrant is in those premises and provided that they have announced their presence, demanded entry and have been refused (Law Reform Commission of Canada, 1985: 55). What is the situation where the police do not have an arrest warrant in their pockets? It seems that where officers believe on reasonable grounds that a suspect has or is about to commit an indictable offence and seek to make an arrest, then they may enter private premises, without the consent of the occupier, in order to carry out that arrest. However, there must be reasonable grounds for believing that the suspect is actually on the premises, and the police must have properly announced their presence and purpose before being refused entry.[34]

Can a citizen resist an unlawful arrest? In theory, this is certainly the case. However, in practice, resisting a police officer is a course of action that is fraught with pitfalls and dangers (Law Reform Commission of Canada, 1984a: 56). Even where the citizen is, in fact, innocent of committing an offence, an arrest may still be lawful because a police officer has reasonable grounds to believe to the contrary. Furthermore, the Supreme Court of Canada has ruled that where, for example, the *Criminal Code* permits the arrest of someone found "committing a criminal offence," this phraseology should be interpreted as meaning "*apparently*" committing an offence.[35] Clearly, both the *Code* and the courts give the police officer considerable leeway to make honest errors of judgment, and it would be a foolhardy citizen who decided to resist arrest, except in the most blatant cases of abuse of police power (Pavlich, 1981: III-205). In addition, as

Ericson and Baranek (1982: 45) point out, the police have the ability to "worsen a situation through more charges (e.g. 'obstruct police,' 'assault police,' 'cause a disturbance')."

What remedies are available to a citizen who has been wrongfully arrested or detained? We have seen that a violation of a suspect's constitutional rights under the *Charter* may result in the staying of a prosecution or the exclusion of evidence from the suspect's trial. These are important remedies, from the citizen's point of view. However, it is important to bear in mind that, in theory, criminal charges could be laid against an errant police officer (Law Reform Commission of Canada, 1985: 57). Section 26 of the *Criminal Code* states that a person authorized to use force may be held criminally responsible for "any excess thereof according to the nature and quality of the act that constitutes the excess." Therefore, depending on the circumstances, a number of criminal charges (such as assault) may be laid against a police officer. However, as the Law Reform Commission (1985: 57) points out, a criminal proceeding may not be the most practical course for a wronged individual to pursue, unless the provincial authorities are willing to prosecute, and it is widely believed that there is considerable reluctance on their part to publicize police wrongdoing. A citizen could lay an information him/herself; however, the cost of pursuing a "private" prosecution might well be beyond the citizen's means, and there is always the danger that the Crown may terminate such a prosecution by staying it. An unlawful arrest could also be the subject of a civil action for damages (Law Reform Commission of Canada, 1985: 58), although such an action is clearly out of the question for many individuals because they lack the means to pursue a potentially expensive case in the courts. Finally, there is always the possibility of launching a complaint by using the particular procedures prescribed in the various provincial police Acts or by approaching the Royal Canadian Mounted Police Public Complaints Commission.

Search and Seizure

The police powers of search and seizure have been aptly described as "exceptional powers" because they permit the police to do "what an individual is, in ordinary circumstances, forbidden to do" (Law Reform Commission of Canada, 1983a: 10). The Commission goes on to state that

> The ambit of these exceptional powers is of equally grave concern to society as a whole. For the interests with which these powers conflict are among the most critical accorded to individuals in a liberal democracy: interests involving the inviolability and dignity of the person, the concept of privacy, the security of possessions and self-expression. [p. 11]

The general rule is that the police powers of search and seizure are derived from specific legislative authority. There is, however, one major exception to this rule; namely, the power of the police to search an individual as part of the process of effecting an arrest (Law Reform Commission of Canada, 1983a: 48). For this purpose, a suspect may be searched with a view both to discovering evidence that may be relevant to any charge(s) that might be laid and to seizing any weapon(s) that might be carried on his or her person. The question of just how intrusive a personal search may be is one that has acquired critical importance, given the guarantee, enshrined in section 8 of the *Charter*, against unreasonable search and seizure. For example, it has been held by the British Columbia Court of Appeal that grabbing an individual by the throat as a means of conducting a search for concealed drugs is "unreasonable,"[36] although it has been ruled that forcing a suspect, with medical assistance, to drink a substance that induces vomiting in order to cause him to bring up a narcotic was reasonable as a means of gathering evidence and protecting the "health of the accused."[37]

It remains to be seen how, in the future, the Supreme Court of Canada will establish principles that will guide the use of section 8 as a means of preventing excessively intrusive search techniques by the police. Early indications are that the court will exercise strict control over such techniques. Indeed, in *Pohoretsky v. R.*,[37a] the Supreme Court of Canada ruled that taking a blood sample from an "incoherent and delirious" accused person, lying in a hospital bed, constituted an unreasonable search in violation of section 8 of the *Charter*. Significantly, the Court declared that the admission of the evidence of intoxication, gained from the blood sample, could not be admitted at the accused's trial on a charge of driving a car while having a blood alcohol level of more than 90 mg. The Court stated that to admit such evidence would bring the administration of justice into disrepute (within the meaning of section 24(2) of the *Charter*). As Justice Lamer said,[37b] the police had taken "advantage of the [accused's] unconsciousness to obtain evidence which they had no right to obtain from him without his consent had he been conscious."

In addition to the powers of search and seizure, which have been considered to be incidental to the process of arrest, it should also be remembered that the police may conduct a search, without any specific legislative authority, if a citizen *consents* to such an intrusion. Of course, the issue of consent is a difficult one, since individuals may feel compelled to cooperate with the police and may, in fact, be unaware of their right to refuse.[37c] As Ericson and Baranek (1982: 47) noted in their observational study of the processing of defendants:

> ... accused people frequently explained compliance in terms of a belief that resistance would incur further assertions of police power. Police power is taken for granted by the accused so that its exercise becomes routine.

Apparently, some police forces (including the RCMP) have devised special procedures for handling "consent" searches, and some require the use of written consent forms, which, in addition to offering subsequent evidence of an individual's consent, notify him or her of the right to refuse (Law Reform Commission of Canada, 1983a: 52-53).

In general, however, the police have no powers of search and seizure, except insofar as statute law clearly grants them such authority. Traditionally, such legislation gave the police these powers within the framework of a system of prior authorization by judicial warrants. However, the more recent legislative trend has been toward granting the police considerably greater powers to conduct searches without previously obtaining a warrant (Law Reform Commission of Canada, 1984b: 4). Such a trend raises major concerns about the protection of individual privacy, since the increase of warrantless searches represents, in theory at least, a major reduction in the degree of formal legal control over the search power of the police (Law Reform Commission of Canada, 1983a: 35). Instead of an independent justice deciding whether there are adequate grounds for a search, the system of permitting warrantless searches leaves that decision to the police themselves; this is a troublesome situation, since the police clearly have a stake in the outcome of such a decision (Law Reform Commission of Canada, 1983a: 35).

The most important *general* source of statutory powers of search and seizure is section 487 of the *Criminal Code,* which authorizes a justice to issue a search warrant in certain clearly specified circumstances (Salhany, 1984: 74). Basically, before a search warrant may be issued, an information must be sworn on oath before the justice, who may issue a warrant if he or she is satisfied (on the basis of the information sworn) that there are "reasonable grounds to believe that there is in a building, receptacle or place":

(i) anything upon or in respect of which an offence has been, or is suspected to have been, committed against the *Criminal Code*;
(ii) anything that it might reasonably be considered will furnish evidence in relation to such an offence; or
(iii) anything that it is reasonably believed is intended to be used to commit any offence against the person for which an individual may be arrested without a warrant.

The intention underlying the *Code* procedures is to prevent the police from undertaking speculative "fishing expeditions" in the vague hope that they may turn up something illegal. Normally, a warrant must be "executed" during daytime hours, although the justice can authorize a nighttime search, if it is necessary to do so.[38] The warrant must state, with a reasonable degree of particularity, the articles to be searched for and must also indicate the alleged offence(s) involved (Salhany, 1984: 79). Significantly, the *Criminal Code* provides that the police may seize not only the items specified in the warrant, but also "anything that on reasonable grounds" they believe has been "obtained by or has been used in the commission of an offence."[39] The police officer named in the warrant must carry the warrant with him or her and is required to produce it, if requested to do so.[40] Should the occupants of the premises concerned refuse to let an officer in, after he or she has made a formal request to enter, then the officer may make a forcible entrance in order to execute the warrant (Salhany, 1984: 80). If police officers seize anything that is not required for the purposes of investigation or in connection with any court hearing and are satisfied that there is no dispute as to their ownership, then they must normally return them to the person lawfully entitled to them.[41] If the officers do not return the items seized, then they are required to bring them physically before a justice or to make a report to the justice that they have seized the items and are holding them pending the justice's decision on what should be done with them.[42]

Although the procedures for obtaining a search warrant may appear to establish a formidable barrier of protective mechanisms, it is important to bear in mind that the "law in the books" might not always match the "law in action." The Law Reform Commission of Canada (1983b: 83) conducted a survey of search warrant procedures and concluded that almost 60% of the warrants sampled were invalidly issued as they stood. This did not mean that the warrants could not have been issued legally, but rather that the strict legal procedures were not followed to the letter (*ibid.*: 85). The Commission, in fact, found that there were considerable differences across Canada in the extent to which warrant procedures were followed to the letter of the law. The Commission states (*ibid.*: 87) that

> The more common apprehension, however, remains the suspicion that the justice treats search warrant issuances as a "formality". While obtaining a warrant was by no means a formality in all of the cities surveyed, there were some instances in which the detail presented in the publication to the issuer was so sketchy as to call into question whether the issuer really bothered to evaluate the documents he was given.

Ericson (1981) conducted an observational study of the activities of police detectives in one Ontario jurisdiction and demonstrated that detectives tended to develop long-term, cooperative relationships with individual justices and "relied on their routine cooperation to ease their tasks":

> Occasionally, this co-operation went well beyond the point of signing warrants without question. On one occasion, two detectives went to five addresses, mainly for the purpose of locating a suspect. Anticipating resistance from the various occupants, they took along unsigned search warrants and "left handed" them (signed a J.P.'s name). These warrants were later logged in the divisional records, and the two Justices of the Peace whose names were used were subsequently contacted and their collaboration gained. [*Ibid.*, 153-54]

There are other provisions in the *Criminal Code* that deal with the power of the police to conduct searches and to seize property in particular circumstances. For example, special provisions exist concerning searches conducted under the authority of a warrant in relation to offences involving gaming houses, bookmaking, and common bawdy-houses.[43] These provisions generally grant slightly expanded powers of search and seizure to the police. Other provisions of the *Code*, however, go much further and permit searches *without a warrant* in certain circumstances; for example, a police officer may conduct a warrantless search of a person, a vehicle or any premises other than a dwelling house for prohibited or restricted weapons, firearms or ammunition.[44]

Very broad powers of search and seizure may be granted to the police under other federal legislation. For example, both the *Narcotic Control Act* and the *Food and Drugs* Act permit warrantless searches to be made in places other than dwelling houses.[45] The legislative trend toward granting the police greater powers to conduct searches *without* warrants is, as we have seen, quite troublesome. As the Law Reform Commission (1984b: 4) pointed out, in a report to the Minister of Justice,

> . . . warranted searches remain relatively constrained compared to warrantless ones. In addition, the warrant procedure with its reliance on documentary authority facilitates review of the legality of the search or seizure.
>
> By way of contrast, a warrantless power of search and seizure represents a relatively discretionary mode of authorization, in respect of which accountability is impeded by the lack of any kind of documentary record.

However, as we shall see, the trend toward warrantless powers of search and seizure may well be dramatically reversed as a consequence of the enactment of section 8 of the *Charter*.

Telewarrants

One important change to the powers of the police in the areas of search and seizure was made by Parliament in 1985,[46] when the *Code* was amended so as to permit police officers to obtain search warrants, in certain circumstances, without the need for the officers to appear personally in front of a justice when they are making an application (Brodsky, 1987; Law Reform Commission of Canada, 1983b; McCalla, 1984). The availability of so-called telewarrants may be of particular advantage to police officers in drug cases, where there may be an urgent need to conduct a search before the suspects concerned take advantage of an opportunity to destroy any relevant evidence (Brodsky, 1987: 345). There is no space to deal with the details of the relevant procedures connected with telewarrants. However, suffice it to say that a telewarrant may be issued only in respect of an indictable offence, and there must be reasonable grounds for dispensing with the police officer's personal attendance. The officer will swear an information over the telephone. The statement will be recorded by the justice, and if it is decided that a warrant should be issued, the justice fills one out and signs it. The officer must then fill out a facsimile warrant, which he or she is required to produce at the scene of the search. The advent of telewarrants has rendered it relatively simple for the police to obtain *prior* judicial authorization for a search, even in most situations of an emergency nature, and therefore it could be argued that the justification for searches without warrant has been greatly reduced. It will be interesting to see to what extent the courts will be prepared to declare invalid statutory provisions that permit warrantless searches. Such a development may well occur in light of the requirement of section 8 of the *Charter* that searches be "reasonable," since it could be contended that prior judicial authorization may readily be sought under the new telewarrant procedure (Brodsky, 1987).

Search and Seizure and the *Charter*

Prior to the coming into effect of the *Charter,* relatively little attention needed to be paid, as a matter of practice, to the question of whether a search was illegal, because the fruits of an illegal search could be admitted as evidence in a criminal trial regardless of their tainted origins. The *Charter* has dramatically altered this unsatisfactory situation. Section 8 guarantees "the right to be secure against unreasonable search or seizure" (Connelly, 1985). There are two major consequences stemming from this development. First, evidence that has been obtained as a result of an "unreasonable" search may be excluded from any subsequent trial if the court believes that to admit it would bring the administration of justice into disrepute (according to the provisions of section 24(2) of the *Charter*). For example, in one case[47] evidence was not admitted at the accused's trial on a charge of simple possession of *cannabis* resin because the search of the accused by the police officer had been illegal and unreasonable (given that the latter was acting solely on mere suspicion). On the other hand, it should be emphasized that the exclusion of evidence is considered to be a course of action that is not to be taken lightly by the courts.[48] Evidence will not be automatically excluded merely because the officer has blundered (see Jull, 1988; Mitchell, 1988). Indeed, in *Collins v. R.*,[49] the Supreme Court of Canada emphasized that the accused is placed under the burden of establishing that the admission of illegally obtained evidence at his or her trial would bring the administration of justice into disrepute. Justice Lamer suggested that the real question was whether the admission of the evidence would " 'bring the administration of justice into disrepute in the eyes of the reasonable man, dispassionate and fully apprised of the circumstances of the case' "[50] Among the factors that the Supreme Court thought were important to take into account when deciding whether or not to exclude evidence are the following:

— what kind of evidence was obtained?
— what Charter right was infringed?
— was the Charter violation serious or was it of a merely technical nature?
— was it deliberate, wilful or flagrant, or was it inadvertent or committed in good faith?
— did it occur in circumstances of urgency or necessity?
— were there other investigatory techniques available?
— would the evidence have been obtained in any event?
— is the offence serious?
— is the evidence essential to substantiate the charge?
— are other remedies available?[50a]

In a recent case[51] in the Province of Quebec, the Court of Appeal indicated just how restrictively the power to exclude evidence should be exercised by the courts. In the view of the Court, section 24(2) should not be used as a means of "deterring" police officers from infringing the constitutional rights of citizens. Instead, the task of controlling, deterring, or punishing police officers should be undertaken by resorting to section 24(1) of the *Charter,* which permits the Court to grant such remedy as it deems appropriate and just in the circumstances of the case:

> In this traditional manner the remedies are exercised against the parties alleged to be responsible who are given a full opportunity to defend themselves. In the event of a condemnation the sanctions are imposed on the offending officers and not on the community. If evidence is excluded it means, in certain cases, that truth is suppressed and it is society that suffers rather than those who have infringed the rights of the individual.[52]

Section 24(1) of the *Charter,* as we have already seen, provides that anyone whose rights or freedoms under the *Charter* have been infringed may apply to a court to obtain "such remedy as the court considers appropriate and just in the circumstances."

Second, the guarantee enshrined in section 8 may be used to strike down statutory provisions that are deemed to give the police unreasonable powers of search or seizure. This development is of critical importance given the trend over the past few decades to grant the police increasing powers to conduct warrantless searches: indeed, section 8 could well reverse this trend, particularly since the advent of the telewarrant has greatly weakened the rationale for such warrantless searches. Indeed, in a seminally important case, the Supreme Court of Canada unanimously ruled that, provided it is feasible to require it, prior authorization (viz., the granting of a warrant) is a *precondition* for a valid search or seizure,[53] and the Court struck down certain powers of search and seizure under the *Combines Investigation Act,* on the basis that they infringed section 8 (Rosenberg, 1985). Dickson J. stated that

> A requirement of prior authorization, usually in the form of a valid warrant, has been a consistent prerequisite for a valid search and seizure both at common law and under

most statutes. Such a requirement puts the onus on the State to demonstrate the superiority of its interests to that of the individual. As such it accords with the apparent intention of the Charter to prefer, where feasible, the right of the individual to be free from State interference to the interests of the State in advancing its purposes through such interference.[54]

Powers of Interrogation

The police may well wish to question suspects in order to obtain information that may lead to the discovery of evidence that is relevant to their investigations, and they may also seek to elicit an incriminating statement that may later be used in court against the suspect concerned. In general, the police do not have any formal powers to compel a suspect to answer their questions (Coughlan, 1985; Ratushny, 1983: 182). In this sense, the accused person has a "right to silence."[55] Of course, in practice it may be very difficult for an accused person to resist answering police questions. A failure to provide an explanation when the accused is found in suspicious circumstances may well precipitate an arrest. It would be a foolhardy person who, when found with stolen goods in his or her possession, refused to give a reasonable explanation of how the goods came to be there. Furthermore, it is important to bear in mind that a right to remain silent does not extend so far as to permit a citizen to obstruct the police in the execution of their duties. For example, in *Moore v. The Queen*[56] the Supreme Court of Canada demonstrated that it believes that the right to remain silent has some very definite limitations. Moore had ridden his bicycle through a red light, and this infraction was witnessed by a police officer. The latter asked Moore to identify himself so that a highway traffic ticket could be written out. Moore ignored the request and continued his journey. He was subsequently stopped forcibly. After a bitter argument, Moore was arrested and charged with the *Criminal Code* offence of obstructing a police officer in the execution of his duty. Moore was not required by any statute to identify himself; however, the Supreme Court ruled that the police officer was required to issue an appearance notice rather than make an arrest whenever this was possible, and therefore, in requesting Moore to give his name, the officer was acting in the execution of his duty. This decision has been strongly criticized (Cohen, 1981: 554), insofar as it weakens the right to remain silent:

> Due to this judgment social cooperation has been transformed into social coercion. The right to silence, long believed to be an inviolate cornerstone of just criminal procedure, has peripherally suffered an assault.

Depending on the nature of the circumstances of any particular case, the police may need to engage in interrogation in order to obtain a confession. In many cases, as where there is independent evidence establishing the guilt of the accused, a confession is superfluous. However, in cases where there is no other available evidence to "clinch a conviction," then a confession may be the only means of making a charge stick in court. In their observational study, Ericson and Baranek (1982: 50-52) noted that a clear majority of defendants (nearly 60%) gave verbal statements to the police "in field settings" during preliminary questioning and prior to their questioning in police custody. Furthermore, of those who were asked to give written statements to the police while in custody, nearly 70% did so. The authors (1982: 52) concluded that "most suspects do not successfully resist giving a confession."

It is clear that there is a great potential for abuse in the ability of the police to obtain confessions from accused persons who are in their custody. In Canada, judicial scrutiny of the questioning process is exercised in a rather indirect manner. There is a special rule of evidence that operates to place confessions given to the police under close scrutiny before they may be introduced in evidence against the accused. The rule is that "no statement made out of Court by an accused to a person in authority can be admitted into evidence against him unless the prosecution shows, to the satisfaction of the trial Judge, that the statement was made freely and voluntarily."[57] Where the prosecution seeks to rely upon a confession, the Court must hold a *voir dire* (or a trial-within-a-trial) in order to determine whether the confession is admissible (McWilliams, 1984: 504). If there is a jury, then the *voir dire* will, of course, be held in their absence. It is up to the prosecution to prove that the confession was made voluntarily. The critical issue in this process is the manner in which the courts have fashioned a test for determining whether a statement has been made voluntarily.

For many years, the exclusive test was derived from a case decided by the English Law Lords in 1914,[58] in which it was stated that a statement would be considered voluntary if it was not obtained from the accused "either by fear of prejudice or hope of advantage exercised or held out by a person in authority." In other words, the court is limited to investigating whether the confession was obtained by threats or inducements (or, of course, actual violence). In recent years, this formulation of the test of voluntariness has been considered to be excessively technical, and the Supreme Court of Canada has indicated a willingness to expand the scope of the test (Conway, 1984). For example, it has been held that the accused must have an "operating mind" before a confession will be considered admissible at the accused's trial.[59] Therefore, it has been held that a confession will not be admissible where a police interrogator unwittingly placed the accused in a light hypnotic trance.[60] However, while the Supreme Court has been willing to exclude confessions that have been induced by threats or promises or obtained when the accused is lacking an "operating mind," it has not been prepared to exclude confessions merely because they have been induced by police trickery (McLachlin and Miller, 1982). For example, in the critical case of *Rothman*,[61] the accused indicated that he did not want to make a statement to the police. A police officer then disguised himself as a person who had returned from a fishing expedition, and had himself placed in the accused's cell. The police officer pretended that he was being held on a drugs charge and denied that he was a narcotics officer. The accused then made a statement to this officer, and the prosecution later sought to introduce it as evidence. Ultimately, the Supreme Court of Canada ruled that the statement was admissible because the confessions rule applies only when the accused believes that the person to whom he makes a statement is a "person in authority." Here, Rothman did not believe that the person to whom he confessed was a police officer (of course, a police officer is the classic example of a "person in authority"). As McLachlin and Miller (1982: 130) point out, "public confidence in the system of justice may be eroded if that system accepts evidence obtained by trickery and deception, thereby implicitly condoning such conduct."

The Law Reform Commission of Canada (1984a) has expressed considerable dissatisfaction with the existing rule relating to confessions and has suggested that the courts should exercise a much greater degree of control over the process of police questioning of suspects. One of its recommendations to the Minister of Justice would represent a major shift in the balance of power between the police and the accused (Solomon, 1985); more specifically, the Commission has recommended that a general rule be introduced to the effect that no confession may be admitted in evidence "unless the prosecution establishes that the admission of evidence would not bring the administration of justice into disrepute" (1984a: 13). This rule would clearly furnish the trial courts with considerable freedom to control police interrogation and would free them from the confines of the existing rule, which focuses on only a few of the ways in which a statement may be obtained unfairly.

One technique that is increasingly being used by the police during the course of questioning a suspect is the videotaping of the whole process (Grant, 1987). The playing of the relevant videotape in court permits the trial judge to gain a much more complete understanding of the circumstances surrounding the making of a confession than is possible from the reading of a written statement alone. It is certainly possible that while the use of videotaping may benefit the police in terms of their ability to contradict claims that they obtained a statement unfairly, it may also serve to reduce the possibility that the police will resort to illegal behaviour in order to extract a confession.

We noted earlier that the police are now placed under a number of significant duties as a consequence of section 10 of the *Charter*. Indeed, section 10(a) provides that the police must inform an accused promptly of the reasons for an arrest or detention. Furthermore, section 10(b) establishes that an accused person who has been arrested or detained has the right to "retain and instruct counsel without delay and to be informed of that right." This particular provision may well have an important part to play in regulating the questioning process (Cohen, 1984a: 113; Conway, 1985). If a confession is obtained and the accused has not been informed of his or her right to counsel, or worse still, the right to counsel has been ignored, then it is possible that the confession may be excluded from consideration at the trial. This result would be possible as a consequence of the discretion under section 24(2) of the *Charter* to exclude evidence obtained in violation of an accused's rights under the *Charter* where the court considers that to admit the evidence would bring the administration of justice into disrepute.[62] Such protection of the accused may well be necessary in light of the findings of Ericson and Baranek (1982: 55), whose subjects suggested that their requests to see third parties (such as friends, relatives or lawyers), during questioning in custody were frequently refused by the police.

It appears that the courts are concerned to ensure that the accused actually comprehends his or her right to counsel. In one case,[63] an accused, who had been drinking and was possibly mentally unstable, was given a "potted version" of his rights (Conway, 1985: 50), and the accused said that he understood these rights. The police immediately proceeded to ask questions about the incident that led to a charge of murder being laid against the accused. The trial court ruled that the accused's rights had been infringed, and the statement was excluded. The Court held that an accused person should have a "fair opportunity" to consider whether he or she wishes to take advantage of the right to counsel. The police should not read a "potted version" of the accused's rights and then launch right into questioning. Given the accused's mental condition at the time and his limited educational background, it was held that the provisions of section 10(b) had not been properly complied with.

While section 10 of the *Charter* guarantees that the police will inform the accused of their right to retain and instruct counsel, there is no similar constitutional requirement that accused be informed of the right to remain silent. However, it seems that the police in Canada almost invariably do inform the accused of such right (Conway, 1985: 41). At present, the absence of a caution (bringing the right to silence to the attention of the accused) is not, in itself, a reason to exclude a confession. However, it is considered to be a very important factor in determining whether a confession was given "freely and voluntarily" (McWilliams, 1984: 499; see also Paciocco, 1987).

Ericson and Baranek (1982: 56–59) discovered that many defendants have difficulty understanding the right-to-silence caution. The authors also suggest (1982: 59) that the existence of a rule requiring a police caution prior to questioning has little impact in practice:

> The accused left us with the impression that the right-to-silence caution is a legal formalism that they see as largely irrelevant to their circumstances, or is simply not mentioned at all. The accused certainly did not see it as a possible resource to be used to justify silence.

Electronic Surveillance

The inexorable march of modern technology has afforded police officers with a formidable array of electronic devices for monitoring the activities of criminal suspects. Electronic surveillance and the interception of private conversations have become standard weapons in the police armoury and have created considerable concern about the implications of such technology for the civil liberties of those who may be subjected to such electronic monitoring (see Burtch, 1979; Cohen, 1983; Frankel, 1981).

The Canadian Committee on Corrections pointed out in their 1969 report (Ouimet, 1969: 85) that electronic surveillance was taking place on a widespread scale and that there was an urgent need to regulate it. The response of the Canadian Government to this challenge was embodied in the *Protection of Privacy Act,* 1973-74.[64] The Act was designed to meet two major objectives: (1) to criminalize unauthorized electronic surveillance with a view to protecting the privacy of individual citizens, and (2) to provide a formal set of procedures for authorizing the legitimate use of electronic surveillance by the police (see Law Reform Commission of Canada, 1986: 2–5). In fact, very few prosecutions have ever been launched against individuals for infringing upon the privacy of other citizens, whereas there have been literally thousands of authorizations for "wire taps" since the legislation came into force in 1974 (Law Reform Commission of Canada, 1986: 7). In this sense, the legislation has, in practice, had much more to do with authorizing the use of police powers of surveillance than with the protection of individual freedoms (see MacDonald, 1987; MacLean, 1987).

The *Protection of Privacy Act* provides safeguards in relation to private communications. According to the Act, *private communication* "means any oral communication or any telecommunication made under circumstances in which it is reasonable for the originator thereof to expect that it will not be intercepted by any person other than the person intended by the originator thereof to receive it."[65] The Act renders it a criminal offence to intercept a private communication, although no offence is committed where either the originator of the message or its intended recipient consents to the interception.[66] Most important from the police point of view are the provisions of the Act that permit them to intercept private communications if they have obtained prior judicial authorization to do so. The *Criminal Code*[67] states that such authorization may be obtained only in relation to a select list of criminal offences, although this list is quite extensive. In most circumstances, the police must ask either the Solicitor General of Canada (for offences falling within the federal jurisdiction to prosecute), the Attorney General of the particular province concerned (for any other offences) or specially designated agents of these officials to seek authorization from a judge of the Supreme or County Court of the province in question.[68] Police investigators may ask a designated agent to seek authorization for a wire tap only if they have received written approval of a senior officer in their respective police forces (Solicitor General of Canada, 1987: 4).

A judge may give the "go ahead" to electronic surveillance in a particular case if he or she is satisfied that "it would be in the best interests of justice to do so" and that other investigative procedures have been tried and have failed, other methods of investigation are unlikely to succeed or the urgency of the matter is such that it would be impractical to carry out the investigation of the offence concerned by using only other types of investigative procedures.[69] The judge may impose conditions on the conduct of the surveillance; indeed, during 1986, 57% of the judicial authorizations included such conditions (Solicitor General of Canada, 1987: 9). The authority for such surveillance is valid for up to 60 days,[70] although it is possible for a renewal of the authorization to be granted for a further period of up to 60 days. A significant feature of the legislation is the requirement that the person who is the object of police surveillance be notified within 90 days that this has taken place,[71] although it is possible, if the police claim that their investigations are still going on, to extend this period up to a maximum of three years.

An important component of the *Protection of Privacy Act* is the provision that the contents of a wire tap that has been illegally made may not be used as evidence in a trial unless either the originator or the intended recipient of the private communication give their consent.[72] However, what is the situation where the prosecution wish to introduce not the communication itself but evidence derived from it (what would, in the United States, be referred to as the "fruit of the poisonous tree")? The original legislation excluded such evidence on the same basis as the communication itself. However, in 1977, a number of amendments were made and, among these, was the provision that rendered such *derivative* evidence admissible as evidence *unless* the trial judge is "of the opinion that the admission thereof would bring the administration of justice into disrepute." In effect, such evidence is now generally admissible, whereas before 1977 it had been completely excluded from consideration by the court (Burns, 1979; Law Reform Commission of Canada, 1986: 84–86). Certainly, this view has been supported by judicial authority, which emphasizes that the mere fact that a communication has been intercepted unlawfully does not mean the admission of evidence derived from it will bring the administration of justice into disrepute.[73] In other words, there have to be other "aggravating factors" before such derivative evidence is excluded. Of course, under section 24(2) of the *Charter*, the courts now have a similar power to exclude all illegally obtained evidence, in the situation where it would bring the administration of justice into disrepute to admit it.

The Solicitor General of Canada is required[74] to prepare an annual report concerning requests for authorization to carry out electronic surveillance that have been made by him or her or by his or her designated agents in relation to alleged offences *falling within federal prosecutorial jurisdiction*. This report, therefore, provides only a partial picture of the use of electronic surveillance by the police in Canada. The number of applications for authorizations or renewals in 1986 was 435. Significantly, only one of these requests was rejected by the judge concerned. The amazingly low number of refusals is attributable, in the view of the Solicitor General, to two factors. First, the strict procedural regime that must be followed before an application is made minimizes the possibility that a request for an authorization will be unwarranted. Secondly, it is argued that judges may "turn back" applications until the police can provide further information so as to convince them that an authorization should be granted (Solicitor General of Canada, 1987: 9). Despite these explanations, the impression is clearly left that requests for authorization to wire tap are almost always granted by the judges concerned. The number of authorizations or renewals requested appears to have been decreasing, quite significantly, over the past five years (Solicitor General of Canada, 1988: 8):

Year	Requests
1982	770
1983	728
1984	736
1985	604
1986	434
1987	408

The vast majority of the authorizations were granted in connection with "serious drug related offences" and were in relation to alleged criminal conspiracies. Indeed, some 96.5% of the authorizations, in 1986, concerned conspiracies to commit serious drug offences. On this basis, the Solicitor General of Canada (1987: 15) claims that the use of electronic surveillance is focusing on the more serious federal drug offences, and organized conspiracies to commit these offences.

It is claimed by the proponents of electronic surveillance that such surveillance is a vital tool for the control of organized crime and the illicit drug trade in Canada. For example, it has been pointed out (Solicitor General of Canada, 1987: 31) that although, as previously noted, most crimes that come to the attention of the police do so as the result of a complaint by a citizen, many drug-related offences would never come to their attention if it were not for their power to conduct electronic surveillance. Of those persons charged by federal authorities during 1982–86, 63.5% had their criminal activities come to the attention of the police as a result of electronic surveillance, while 75.1% of these individuals were charged with an offence specified in the authorization for surveillance. Critics of the existing powers of the police to conduct electronic surveillance suggest that such powers may be easily exceeded and extend to the control of relatively petty crimes, and that the efficacy of electronic eavesdropping in actually securing convictions has not been unequivocally established (Burtch, 1979: 9). In the latter respect, although the statistics are notoriously difficult to interpret, it appears that from 1982–86, 54% of federally laid charges, based on evidence derived from electronic surveillance, resulted in convictions; the remainder were disposed of by way of a dismissal, a withdrawal, or a stay or proceedings (Solicitor General of Canada, 1987: 37).

The Law Reform Commission of Canada (1986) has strongly recommended that substantial reform of the existing *Protection of Privacy Act* be undertaken with some celerity. The Commission notes that there is an apparent "reticence on the part of the judiciary, at the application stage, to see their role as one of supervising the exercise of police discretion" (p. 12). However, the Commission suggests that the *Charter* clearly implies that judicial control of police discretion is entirely appropriate and recommends that Parliament spell out the circumstances in which the judiciary should and should not grant authorizations, as well as clarify what the contents of such authorizations should be:

> The legislation must recognize that it is essentially unfair to expect a judge, who is used to being the impartial arbiter, in effect to accept a supervisory role over the prosecution, without some very clear guidelines as to the limits of his authority. We feel that it is primarily up to Parliament, rather than the judiciary, to strike the balance between a justifiable intrusion and an unwarranted invasion of privacy, although obviously in the particular case the ultimate decision mut be for the judge to make. [*ibid.*]

The Police and Entrapment

A highly controversial matter relating to the exercise of police powers concerns the problem of entrapment (France, 1988; Stober, 1985). The police may well decide to use informers, *agents provocateurs*, or decoys in an attempt to enforce the law, particularly when victimless offences (such as drug-related crimes) are concerned. The police are unlikely to receive a citizen complaint in such cases and can rarely expect to catch a drug-dealer "red-handed" unless they adopt the proactive techniques of employing informers, and so forth. It is, of course, difficult to decide when such techniques cross the borderline between legitimate law enforcement techniques that must be considered necessary in all the circumstances, and unsavoury police misconduct that should be soundly deprecated (Wool, 1985–86). In the United States, the issue of entrapment has assumed a high profile in recent years, as the police have engaged in various "sting" operations in an attempt, for example, to suppress alleged corruption among high-placed officials. Indeed, one prominent ex-automobile manufacturing executive in the United States made headline news in many parts of the world, when he was acquitted of drug-dealing charges on the basis that he had been entrapped by the police.

Essentially, entrapment occurs when the police (usually in the form of an undercover agent of some kind) persistently harass an individual into committing an offence that he or she would not have committed, had it not been for the persistent inveigling by the police. More specifically, in the *Mack* case,[75] the Supreme Court of Canada stated that entrapment exists when

> (a) the authorities provide a person with an opportunity to commit an offence without acting on a reasonable suspicion that this person is already engaged in criminal activity or pursuant to a *bona fide* inquiry;
> (b) although having such a reasonable suspicion or acting in the course of a *bona fide* inquiry, they go beyond providing an opportunity and induce the commission of an offence.[76]

The Supreme Court also said that when asking the question whether entrapment has actually occurred, it is "useful to consider whether the conduct of the police would have induced the average person in the position of the accused." The Court emphasized that the rationale underpinning the defence of entrapment was the need for the courts to preserve the "purity of the administration of justice." In this sense, entrapment must be regarded as an aspect of the doctrine of abuse of process, whereby the courts have an inherent power to stay (or terminate) the proceedings where it is believed that the police or the prosecution have been using the judicial process for unfair purposes. In the words of the Supreme Court of Canada,

> The court is, in effect, saying it cannot condone or be seen to lend a stamp of approval to behaviour which transcends what our society perceives to be acceptable of the part of the state. The stay of the prosecution of the accused is the manifestation of the court's disapproval of the state's conduct. The issuance of the stay obviously benefits the accused but the court is primarily concerned with a larger issue: the maintenance of public confidence in the legal and judicial process.[76a]

In the *Mack* case itself, the Supreme Court of Canada ordered that a stay of proceedings be entered in relation to a charge of possession of narcotics for the purpose of trafficking. Mack had been a drug user and had been convicted of several drug charges in the past. However, he had given up the use of drugs for quite a long period. Nevertheless, he was approached by a police informer and was *repeatedly* asked to supply the informer with narcotics. This suggested that the police were trying to make the accused "take up his former life-style." The Court said that

> The length of time, approximately six months, and the repetition of requests it took before [Mack] agreed to commit the offence also demonstrate that the police had to go further than merely providing [Mack] with the opportunity once it became evident that he was unwilling to join the alleged drug syndicate.
> Perhaps the most important and determinative factor . . . is [Mack's] testimony that the informer acted in a threatening manner. . . . I believe this conduct was unaccept-

able.... I have come to the conclusion that the average person in the position of the appellant might also have committed the offence, if only to satisfy this threatening informer and to end all further contact.[76b]

Since the Mack case was the first in which the Supreme Court of Canada actually applied the defence of entrapment, it remains to be seen just how restrictively it will be applied by other courts in everyday practice. Most Canadians would agree that the individual citizen must be protected from overzealous (or even corrupt) law enforcement; however, the problem lies in deciding exactly where the courts should draw the line in any individual case. This is certain to be a hard task for the Canadian courts to shoulder in the future.

Police Decision Making

In the policing literature, there is a considerable amount of research on the decision making of the police — far more than we are able to consider within the space limitations of this text. Nevertheless, we will endeavour to identify the potential sources of influence on the exercise of discretion by line-level patrol officers, as well as the findings of specific research studies that have examined the decision making of the police. Our discussion of police decision making is confined to the exercise of discretion by uniformed patrol officers in encounter situations where either the suspect or the victim or complainant, or both, are present. In future editions of the text, we will attempt to bring together materials on police decision making in other circumstances, including detective work, policing union strike actions, and surveillance.

It was noted earlier that the majority of police activity does not involve crime control, but rather the response to requests for service or order maintenance. Further, the exercise of discretion by police officers in encounter situations may occur only after previous decisions by the general public, police complaint and/or dispatch officers. Gottfredson and Gottfredson (1980: 63) remind us that the information available to patrol officers, as well as the alternative courses of action, are "influenced strongly by the cases made available by others for their decisions."

It is also important to remember that the decision to arrest a suspect is only one of the many alternatives available to patrol officers, and in the majority of instances, the situation is resolved through mediation between the disputing parties, by issuing a warning, or by some other mechanism that serves to restore order. Black and Reiss (1970), in their United States study of police-juvenile encounters, and Lundman, Sykes, and Clark (1978), in a replication of the Black and Reiss (1970) investigation, reported that most encounters involved relatively minor offences, resulting in low arrest rates. Sykes, Fox, and Clark (1976) found that police officers made an arrest in less than one-third of the encounters in which an arrest could actually have been made.

These findings suggest that in a large number of encounter situations police officers do not invoke their arrest powers. Research in Canada also suggests that even in situations where an arrest is made, the suspect may not be formally charged. Doob and Chan (1978: 1) found, for example, that only 13% of the youths apprehended by Youth Bureau officers in Peel County were ultimately charged after having been arrested.

While the actions of police officers in carrying out their tasks are constrained by such factors as the provisions of the *Criminal Code* and the protections of the *Canadian Charter of Rights and Freedoms*, officers do have considerable discretion and there are a myriad of factors that may influence their behaviour (see Sherman, 1980; Albanese, 1984). For purposes of our discussion, we will group the potential sources of influence on police decision making into three major categories, recognizing that there may well be others in any specific encounter situation:[77]

1. the task or policing environment in which the encounter occurs;
2. the organizational policies and "style" of the police department or detachment of which the officer is a member;
3. the participants in the encounter situation, including the individual police officer, the complainant and the suspect.

Our discussion will reveal that a number of factors, other than the alleged offence committed by the suspect, may determine the actions taken by the police.[78]

The Task or Policing Environment

There is a considerable amount of evidence to suggest that the particular environment in which police officers carry out their tasks will influence the decisions they make in encounter situations. The task or policing environment of a police department includes the physical environment (the geographic boundaries that establish the size and shape of the area policed), the demographic features of the area policed, including population size and the ethnicity and socio-economic status of the population policed, and man-made characteristics, such as the presence of industry, farms, parks, and waterfront. The attributes of the policing environment play a role in determining the nature and extent of criminal activity, the demands that are placed on policing services by the community, and the ability of the police to address adequately community concerns and expectations.[79]

It is important to note that not only is there a wide variety of policing environments across Canada, as illustrated by policing in the Inuit village of Arctic Bay on Baffin Island as opposed to policing in Montreal, but there may be differing environments within a particular urban area as well. In the City of Vancouver, for example, members of the Vancouver City Police Department are involved in policing the area known as Chinatown; the fashionable Point Grey district near the University of British Columbia; the Skid Row area of the city, and the West End, an area of high density apartment blocks near English Bay. Each of these areas produces different demands upon the police, as well as variety of police-citizen encounter situations.[80]

The particular attributes of the community or area within the community being policed may also have a substantive impact on the nature of police-community relations, the willingness of the citizens to telephone the police, and the extent to which citizens cooperate with the police. It is well known, for example, that ethnic minorities, such as the Chinese, are often reluctant to involve the police in difficulties that arise, and it can be assumed that such a hesitancy may also exist on the part of many native Indians across the country.[81]

One of the major sources of influence on patrol officer decision making that arises from the policing environment is community expectations. Reid (1985: 382) has argued that "the police decide whom to arrest not in terms of legal prescriptions or even departmental orders but in terms of their perceptions of community expectations," and in an early study of police handling of juvenile offenders in four United States communities, Goldman (1963) found that the enforcement and arrest patterns of the police reflected community attitudes and standards. Given that police forces, by necessity, engage in selective enforcement of the law, it is unlikely that any police department or detachment in Canada is free from community pressures or able to remain unaffected by them in terms of either official or unofficial department policy or actual patrol officer practice.

The role of community expectations, however, is often confounded by the mixed signals that the police receive, Trojanowicz and Dixon (1974: 129) noting that many communities are unable to make up their collective minds about what kind of policing they want and often expect only "symbolic" enforcement of the law in relation to many types of activity. What is apparent is that the police are sensitive to the desires of those groups in the community that are successful in making their concerns known. An increased level of enforcement in any given area — commonly known as a crackdown — may come about as a consequence of a media exposé, the protests of an organized group of citizens about the activities of street prostitutes or drug addicts in a particular area of the community, or a petition from residents in a given neighbourhood regarding the problems they are having with vehicles exceeding the posted speed limits, the traffic and noise created by a concentration of street prostitutes, or similar concerns.[82]

The Police Organization

Another potential source of influence on the decision making of patrol officers in encounter situations is the organization in which the officer works and the goals and policies of the department or detachment (see Lundman, 1979; Swanson, 1979; Talarico and Swanson, 1979). Grant, Grant, and Toch (1982: 56) note: "There are differences among police professionals, and thus among police departments, in their use of arrest authority and in their view of arrests as a measure of good police work." From his study of police patrol work in a Canadian city, Ericson (1982: 21) concluded:

> ... what happens inside a police organization influences the initiation of encounters with citizens and what happens in those encounters. Available manpower, organizational priorities, production expectations, "recipe" rules for "targeting" segments of the population, and many other elements influence transactions and the production of case outcomes.

One area that has received considerable attention is the administrative leadership of departments, with observers such as Holten and Jones (1978: 136) noting that police administrators play a major role in the setting of departmental goals and policies: "Decisions from leadership may result in policies of selective enforcement, organizational change, or specifications for operating procedures." Pursley (1974) has also attempted to determine the role played by departmental administrators, categorizing police administrators as either traditional or non-traditional, on the basis of criteria that included level of education and length of police service.

In his inquiry, Pursley (1974: 419) found differences between the two groups of police administrators in the manner in which they carried out their roles. While traditional administrators attempted to control and structure the work and activities of subordinates, including those of line-level patrol officers, the non-traditional administrators, who as a group evidenced higher levels of education and greater involvement in innovative policing strategies, tended to delegate decision making authority to officers lower in the organizational hierarchy and to encourage the exercise of discretion in carrying out policing tasks.

Similar results were reported by Grosman (1975) in a study of Canadian police chiefs. It should not be forgotten, however, that the particular actions of police administrators, such as the formulation and implementation of specific policies, may be a consequence of pressure from the community or legislative enactments and that the demands and contingencies presented by the policing environment in which the administrator operates may constrain their actions.

In what has become a classic study in the policing literature, Wilson (1968a) attempted to determine the impact of the police organization on the decision making of patrol officers. From extensive observations of eight departments in the United States, Wilson (1968a) identified three "ideal types" of police organization: watchman, legalistic, and service.[83] In the watchman departments, police officers were very much part of the community they served, having been recruited locally. With low salaries and minimum training, officers in watchman-style departments attempted to avoid work as much as possible, and in carrying out their duties, officers exhibited a considerable amount of personal judgment rather than strict adherence to the law and departmental policies. Order maintenance was preferred to law enforcement, and there was considerable tolerance of illegal activities, such as gambling, in the community.

In the legalistic departments, on the other hand, there was a strong professional orientation among the officers, who had high levels of education and training. Cases were handled "by the book," and the informal resolution of disputes was not encouraged. In carrying out their daily tasks, officers adhered to the formal policies of the department, and enforcement was the dominant characteristic of the officers' work. A service style of policing was evident in departments operating in affluent suburbs — in areas with homogeneous populations where clear standards of behaviour existed. Officers in the service departments were less likely to use arrest as a formal sanction, and they were oriented toward community relations. Leniency characterized the decision making of officers in encounter situations, and officers engaged in a considerable amount of counselling and referral.

Subsequent to the identification of these three styles of police organization, Wilson (1968b) undertook to examine the impact of departmental style on decision making. In contrasting the decision making of officers in a legalistic department with that of officers in a watchman-style policing organization, Wilson (1968b) discovered that the officers in the legalistic department arrested and sent to the juvenile court a much larger number of youths. In the watchman department, on the other hand, difficulties with juveniles tended to be resolved on an informal basis, often through the use of "rough" justice.

In discussing the results of the study, Wilson (1968b) concluded that the professional orientation of the officers in the legalistic department exerted pressure for formal action, while in the less professional watchman department, no such pressures existed. Further, among the officers in the legalistic organization, there was the perception that youths could be helped by being sent to court, while officers in the watchman department felt youths were best dealt with on the street. Wilson's (1968a; 1968b) findings that "style" of a police organization may have a significant impact on the decision making of its officers are supported by Conly (1978), who found variations in the rates of charging, warning, and referring juveniles between 12 metropolitan police departments across Canada.

While several researchers have attempted to ascertain the impact of the police organization on the decision making of individual patrol officers and have uncovered variability in the decision making of officers from different police departments, Sherman (1980: 87) notes that it is difficult to establish the cause of these differences: "A central problem is the confusion between the behavior itself, the organizational sources of the behavior differences, and the community sources of the differences." In fact, the relationships that exist between a police department and other agencies in the criminal justice system in a particular jurisdiction may have a significant influence on the decision making of patrol officers. Ericson (1982: 22) notes, for example, that "Judicial practices in sentencing can influence police practices in charging ... The unwillingness of the courts to grant sentences other than discharges for certain types of offences and offenders may encourage the police to handle them without charge."

The Encounter

The Police Officer

In our discussion of the police role in Canadian society, we noted that, given limited resources, police departments determine the priority of requests from the community. Lundman (1980: 104), however, argues that the greatest pressure to handle cases efficiently is borne by patrol officers, as they are involved in responding to calls from the public:

> It is virtually impossible for patrol officers to practice a style of policing emphasizing responsiveness to particular people and their unique problems. If individual responses were attempted, officers would be "off the air" talking, writing reports, and going through booking procedures almost from the moment they began their shift. Individualizing policing is a luxury most patrol officers cannot afford.

Lundman (1980) argues that in response to external community and internal organizational pressure to handle cases efficiently, police officers employ two methods of conceptual shorthand — typifications and recipes for action — which enable them to classify situations and to decide upon the proper course of action to be taken.

Typifications are constructs or formulations of events based on experience and involve what is typical or common about routinely encountered events, and according to Lundman (1980: 110), officers utilize their experience to classify or typify situations into one of two general categories: those that require "real" police work, and those that are "bullshit." Lundman (p. 111) notes that police officers classify as real police work those situations that involve "a substantial threat of injury to person or damage to property," or as one patrol officer stated to Van Maanen (1973: 413), those situations "where you figure you may have to use the tools of the trade."

Most requests made of the police, however, are not classified as requiring real police work, a patrol officer confiding to Van Maanen (1973: 414):

"You could give most of what we do around here to any idiot who could put up with the insanity that passes for civilized conduct." Domestic disputes, minor traffic accidents, and noisy parties are examples of situations that many officers feel have little to do with real police work. As we will see in our consideration of the police-citizen encounter, police officers not only typify events, but also the people involved in them.[84]

Recipes for action are the second phase of the conceptual shorthand utilized by patrol officers and constitute the actions taken and decisions that are normally made in certain instances. In a study of police patrol in a major Canadian city, Ericson (1982: 100) found that officers employed the techniques of typification and recipes for action described by Lundman (1980). Rather than accept citizen definitions that a criminal offence had occurred, officers translated requests "within the framework of the police organization, employing 'recipe' rules, legal rules, and/or community rules to decide whether the matter could or should be transformed into police property." Typifications and recipes for action, then, are two methods by which patrol officers classify events and formulate a response to them.

A further observation made by Lundman (1980: 107–108) is that typifications and recipes for action are generally non-negotiable and may be based on stereotypes and discriminatory views of people and circumstances. While a portion of the information that officers use to formulate typifications and recipes for action may be learned during initial training in the police academy, most is learned "on the street" from fellow officers and through personal experience.

Discussing the role of officers as a primary source of socialization into the police role, Van Maanen (1973: 412) notes that the new recruit "quickly is bombarded with 'street wise' patrolmen assuring him that the police academy was simply an exercise all officers endure and has little, if anything, to do with real police work." The Field Training Officer plays a major role in introducing the new recruit to the intricacies and complexities of real police work: "By watching, listening, and mimicking, the neophyte policeman learns how to deal with the objects of his occupation — the traffic violator, the hippie, the drunk, the brass, and the criminal justice complex itself" (Van Maanen, 1973: 412–13; see also Shearing and Leon, 1978).

There is considerable evidence to suggest that police officers, utilizing typifications and recipes for action, tailor their decision making to the particular area and population they are policing. For example, in a study of police practices in the Skid Row area of a United States city, Bittner (1967: 715) found that officers viewed their role as one of keeping the peace rather than one of crime control, and had developed their own strategies and procedures for carrying out their policing tasks. Similarly, Ericson (1982: 86) has argued that "Patrol officers develop and use cues concerning 1) individuals out of place, 2) individuals in particular places, 3) individuals of particular types regardless of place, and 4) unusual circumstances regarding property." Thus, a poorly dressed, disshevelled individual in a fashionable residential district would draw police attention, as would a well-dressed person loitering in a Skid Row area.

Similarly, in a study of policing in St. John's, Newfoundland, McGahan (1984: 43) found that officers held specific mental images of different sections of the city, which influenced the manner in which they carried out their tasks: "Distinctiveness is derived especially from the types of crime and calls characteristic of each district, and whether it contains residents presenting problems for the police."

Given the great amount of discretion that individual patrol officers have, it is likely that various "styles" of policing, such as those identified by Broderick (1987) and discussed in Chapter 3, will develop and have an impact on the decisions officers make (see Grant et al., 1982). Gandy (1970), for example, found considerable variability in decision making among officers of the Metropolitan Toronto Police force in their handling of juvenile offenders, both in terms of the assessment of juvenile misbehaviour and in the decisons made. The disposition received by juveniles was largely a function of the particular officer making the decision and the administrative sub-unit of the department to which the officer was assigned. In discussing patrol officer decision making, Ericson (1982: 101) succinctly notes that "He takes into account who the citizens are, their claims within the context in which they are made, expectations within the police organization, and the resources (legal and otherwise) available . . ."

Research studies have also examined the potential influence of officer attributes including age, length of service, gender, ethnicity, and level of education on the exercise of discretion. While the age of the officer has not been found to be related to either the quality or the quantity of arrests, those officers with less experience made more arrests and the arrests made by more experienced officers were more likely to result in convictions (see Sherman, 1980).

Sherman (1980: 75) notes that research studies examining the influence of education on police officer performance have found that college-educated officers were more active in detecting offences, made more arrests, suffered fewer injuries from assaults, and were the subject of fewer citizen complaints than their less educated colleagues.

There also appear to be differences between male and female patrol officers both in the detection of offences and in the decision to arrest. Bloch and Anderson (1974), in one of the first studies of policewomen, reported that female officers initiated fewer citizen encounters and made fewer arrests in situations involving both serious and minor offences than did male officers, although these data cannot be taken as conclusive. The issues surrounding women in policing and the role of education in policing are discussed in greater detail in Chapter 5.

The Complainant

A consistent finding from studies of police decision making is that the preferences of the complainant have a substantial impact on the decision making of police officers in encounter situations (see Black and Reiss, 1970; Black, 1971; Lundman et al., 1978; Doob and Chan, 1978). The role played by citizens is thus not confined to the decision to mobilize the police. Gottfredson and Gottfredson (1980: 73) note that the major role played by complainants in police decision making "undoubtedly derives from the requirements of subsequent processing; police are aware that successful prosecution of suspects requires the active participation of complaining witnesses. There is little to be gained by an arrest for an offense when the complainant prefers to drop the matter, because prosecution will be futile."

In his study of patrol officers in an eastern Canadian city, Ericson (1982: 103) found that the socio-economic status, age, gender, demeanour, and ethnicity of the complainant influenced decision making and, further, that the impact of the attributes of the complainant varied between encounters involving minor incidents and those in which a serious offence was alleged to have occurred. In minor complaint situations, the police were more likely to provide advice and assistance to lower status persons and to complainants who were cooperative. Higher status and uncooperative complainants, on the other hand, were less likely to receive assistance from the police.

In encounters involving major incidents, Ericson (1982: 106) found that complainants who were older, male, and non-white were more likely to receive assistance and advice from the police. Ericson (p. 111) also found that the police officer was more likely to write a formal report on the incident if the complainant were of a high socio-economic status or male, but less likely to prepare such a report if the situation involved an interpersonal dispute.

In a United States study, Smith, Visher, and Davidson (1984) found that in encounter situations in which both the complainant and the suspect were present, the police decision to arrest was strongly influenced by the ethnicity of the victim, rather than the race of the offender. In those encounters without complainants present, the ethnicity of the suspect did not directly influence the police officer's decision to arrest. More specifically, police officers in the study appeared more willing to comply with requests for arrests from white victims, leading Smith et al. (1984: 248) to conclude that black complainants were denied equal protection under the law.[85]

The Suspect

A primary target of police officer typifications is suspects. Van Maanen (1978: 223) has identified three types of people who comprise the "occupational world" of the police officer: "(1) 'suspicious persons' — those whom the police have reason to believe may have committed a serious offense; (2) 'assholes' — those who do not accept the police definition of the situation; and (3) 'know-nothings' — those who are not either of the first two categories but are not police and therefore, according to the police, cannot know what the police are about." Similarly, Shearing (1981: 286), as we noted in Chapter 3, argues that police officers make a distinction between the general public, who are to be protected, and the "dregs" or "scum," who are to receive considerable police attention.

Research has examined the impact of the characteristics of the suspect on the decision making of the police in encounter situations, focusing on the role of both the seriousness of the alleged offence and the socio-biographical attributes of the suspect, including ethnicity, age, relationship to the victim, and attitude or demeanour exhibited toward the officer.

Of particular concern to police researchers has been whether the socio-biographical attributes of the suspect such as age, gender, socio-economic status, and ethnicity have an impact upon the patrol officer's decision. Research findings to date have provided an inconsistent picture with respect to the role of suspect ethnicity. Black and Reiss (1970) reported higher arrest rates for blacks in their United States study, a finding replicated several years later by Lundman et al. (1978). However, upon closer analysis, it was found that the higher arrest rates were due to the preferences of black complainants, who more often than their white counterparts wanted the police to arrest black youths.

While there is no consistent evidence that police officers in Canadian jurisdictions discriminate in their arrest practices on the basis of the ethnicity of the suspect, the high arrest rates of native Indians in many areas of the country warrant close examination, and we will address this further in Chapter 15. In his Canadian study, Ericson (1982: 152, 159) found that male suspects, those in the age group 16–24, and suspects of lower socio-economic status were more likely to be checked by patrol officers through CPIC, the national Canadian Police Information Centre, as well as to be searched by police officers. In addition, formal action was more likely to be taken against suspects of lower socio-economic status who were non-white and in those instances where property loss or damage had occurred.

Research studies have consistently reported a relation between the attitude or demeanour of the suspect and police decision making. Those suspects who are disrespectful toward the police or who are uncooperative are more likely to be arrested than those who behave in a deferential and civil manner. One interesting finding of several studies is that those juveniles who were unusually respectful or extremely deferential toward the police were also more likely to be arrested (Lundman et al., 1978; Doob and Chan, 1978). Another important factor in the decision making of the police appears to be the relational distance between the suspect and the victim/complainant. The more distant the relationship, the more likely police officers are to arrest (Black, 1971).

Police research has also revealed that the seriousness of the offence is strongly related to the action taken by police officers in encounter situations, with those suspects who are alleged to have committed serious offences being more likely to be arrested than those alleged to have committed a minor offence (Doob and Chan, 1978; Lundman et al., 1978; Sykes et al., 1976). In addition, Doob and Chan (1978) found that those youths who had prior contact with the police, either in terms of previous charges or cautions, were more likely to be arrested by Youth Bureau officers.

It appears that in more serious cases, the discretion of the police officer is reduced, as is the role of the preferences of the complainant and extra-legal variables, such as the ethnicity and demeanour of the suspect. Gottfredson and Gottfredson (1980: 93, n. 58) summarize the findings of the research to date: "For major crimes, whenever the rule is transgressed, there will be an arrest for that reason alone. For less serious events . . . an arrest might be made but is not determined by the law — these arrests are made within the law but for other reasons." In discussing the relative importance of extra-legal factors in police decision making relative to organizational and legal factors, Sykes et al. (1976: 179) concluded that the latter played a more important role in the decision to arrest: "Legal and organizational policy criteria generally had to be taken into account before extralegal variables had a chance to affect arrest decisions. But once these criteria were taken into account, the chances of arrest fell rather heavily on those who showed disrespect for the officers' role or threatened his safety."

The discussion in this chapter, while limited by space considerations, has attempted to present the more significant materials on police powers and the exercise of discretion. In Chapter 5, we will consider in further detail many of the issues raised in this chapter and Chapter 3, including the effectiveness of the police, police-community relations, women and policing, and the role of education in policing.

NOTES

1. For additional materials on police operations and activities including detective work and the decision to investigate criminal offences, see Banks (1984); Chappell, Gordon, and Moore (1982); Ericson (1981).

2. In his study of police patrol work in Peel County, Ericson (1982: 74) found, contrary to previous investigations, that 47.4% of police-citizen encounters were the result of proactive police mobilization. This finding may be a consequence of organizational policies and priorities of the department studied or may suggest that social and cultural differences between Canada and the United States, where most police research has been undertaken, might result in a more assertive approach to policing by

Canadian officers than by those in the United States. Ericson's findings may also be due to the fact that a full range of police activities were monitored, in comparison to the field sample taken by Black and Reiss (1970) in their original study.

3. Most victimization surveys, including the national study in Canada, suffer from severe methodological shortcomings, which preclude the results from being considered on any more than a general level. The Canadian Urban Victimization Survey (Solicitor General of Canada, 1983a; 1983b), for example, utilized telephone interviews to gather data, a technique that severely limits the reliability and validity of the data collected, particularly in jurisdictions with minority populations that may not speak English or have telephones. For a discussion of the methodological limitations of victimization surveys, see Gottfredson and Gottfredson (1980).

4. While the Canadian Urban Victimization Survey (Solicitor General of Canada, 1983a; 1983b) represents the first nation-wide attempt to survey victims of crime and to ascertain the extent of "hidden crime," as well as the patterns of offence reporting, no data were gathered on the patterns of victimization or reporting among ethnic minorities across the country. It is highly likely that the patterns of victimization and levels of reporting for native Indians, for example, are considerably different from those of white English or French Canadians, although the nature and extent of these differences remain to be determined. Similarly, as the survey was confined to selected urban areas of the country, no data are available on reporting practices or victimization in rural jurisdictions.

5. Several observers, albeit representing a minority view, have argued for the total abolition of police discretion. See Goldstein (1960); American Friends Service Committee (1971).

6. Hereinafter referred to as the *Charter*.

7. See *R. v. Genest* (1986), 32 C.C.C. (3d) 8, 54 C.R. (3d) 246 (Que. C.A.).

8. *R. v. Therens et al.* (1985), 45 C.R. (3d) 97, [1985] 1 S.C.R. 613, [1985] 4 W.W.R. 286.

9. Le Dain J., *supra*, at 124.

10. *Ibid.*, at 125–26. See, also, *R. v. Keats* (1987), 39 C.C.C. (3d) 358, 48 D.L.R. (4th) 87, 206 Nfld. & P.E.I.R. 116 (Nfld. C.A.). In this case, the Court ruled that there was a "detention" because there was an element of *psychological compulsion* in the accused's mind, even though a police officer had told her she was "free to leave" the police station. Since her original detention continued, in spite of her being told she could leave, the Court ruled that she should have been informed of her right to counsel.

On the other hand, in *R. v. Nelson* (1987), 35 C.C.C. (3d) 347, 29 C.R.R. 80, [1987] 3 W.W.R. 144, the Manitoba Court of Appeal ruled that a routine stopping of a motorist (as part of a general program of checking licences, etc.) did not constitute a "detention" within the meaning of section 9 of the *Charter* (which protects the citizen against "arbitrary detention").

11. Section 495(1) of the *Criminal Code*.

12. Section 31(1).

13. Section 199(2).

14. *Bail Reform Act*, R.S.C. 1970 (2nd Supp.), c. 2.

15. Section 495(2).

16. Section 497. It has been held that, under the provisions of section 497(1)(f), a police officer may continue to detain a motorist, arrested for impaired driving, until he or she has sobered up. Such a continuing detention does not infringe the *Charter*'s guarantee against arbitrary detention (section 9): See *R. v. Williamson* (1986), 25 C.C.C. (3d) 139, 40 M.V.R. 15 (Alta. Q.B.) and *R. v. Pashovitz* (1987), 59 C.R. (3d) 396, 59 Sask. R. 165, 1 M.V.R. (2d) 32 (Sask. C.A.).

17. Section 498.

18. Sections 507, 512 and 795.

19. Sections 504 and 795.

20. Section 507(4).

21. Sections 507(6) and 499.

22. Section 503.

23. It was held to be an arbitrary detention, under section 9, where a suspect was kept in custody for 8 hours for the purpose of interrogation, despite the fact that a justice was readily available; *R. v. Reeves* (1985), 70 N.S.R. (2d) 165 (N.S. Prov. Ct.).

24. Section 509.

25. Sections 496 and 501.

26. Section 505.

27. Section 508.

28. Section 29(2).

29. Section 24 of the *Charter*.

30. *R. v. Therens et al.* (1985), 45 C.R. (3d) 97, [1985] 1 S.C.R. 613, [1985] 4 W.W.R. 286.

31. In *R. v. Mohl* (1987), 34 C.C.C. (3d) 435, 30 C.R.R. 28, 50 M.V.R. 237, the Saskatchewan Court of Appeal ruled that evidence obtained from a breathalyzer test should be excluded (under section 24(2) of the *Charter*), where the accused had been required to blow at a time when he was too intoxicated to comprehend his right to counsel (as guaranteed by section 10(b) of the *Charter*). In exercising its discretion to exclude the evidence, the Court placed great emphasis on the fact that the police were well aware of the accused's extreme state of intoxication. On the other hand, in *R. v. McAvena* (1987), 34 C.C.C. (3d) 461, 34 C.R.R. 130, 49 M.V.R. 243, the same Court of Appeal ruled that where the accused might not have understood his right to counsel because of a concussion, the evidence obtained from a breathalyzer test should be admitted even though it had been obtained in violation of section 10(b) of the *Charter*. Chief Justice Bayda said that the police officer concerned had "made an honest, dedicated and diligent attempt to comply with the requirements of the Charter" (at p. 472).

The issue of when evidence obtained in violation of the accused's rights under section 10(b) should be declared inadmissible at the trial was also considered by the Supreme Court of Canada in *Jacoy v. R.* (1988), 45 C.C.C. (3d) 46, [1988] 2 S.C.R. 548, [1989] 1 W.W.R. 354. Here the accused had not been informed of his right to counsel during a customs search that revealed the presence of cocaine on his person. Although the Court ruled that the accused's right to counsel had been infringed, it refused to exclude the evidence of narcotics. Chief Justice Dickson pointed out that the customs officers had acted in good faith (since they were acting on a policy directive based on a decision of the Ontario Court of Appeal) and they held no malice to Jacoy himself. Furthermore, Jacoy was not mistreated. In short, the violation of the accused's right to counsel was not "deliberate or flagrant."

32. *R. v. Pithart* (1987), 34 C.C.C. (3d) 150, 57 C.R. (3d) 144, 29 C.R.R. 301 (B.C. Co. Ct.).

32a. In *R. v. Beare; R. v. Higgins* (1988), 45 C.C.C. (3d) 57, [1988] 2 S.C.R. 387, 33 C.R.R. 382, the Supreme Court of Canada held that compulsory fingerprinting under the *Identification of Criminals Act* did not infringe sections 7, 8, 9, 10, and 11 of the *Charter*. Justice La Forest said:

> It seems to me that a person who is arrested on reasonable and probable grounds that he has committed a serious crime, or a person against whom a case for issuing a summons or warrant, or confirming an appearance notice has been made out, must expect a significant loss of personal privacy. He must expect that incidental to his being taken in custody he will be subjected to observation, to physical measurement and the like. Fingerprinting is of that nature. While some may find it distasteful, it is insubstantial, of very short duration, and leaves no lasting impression. There is no penetration into the body and no substance is removed from it. [P. 77 C.C.C.]

33. The offence, in connection with which the officer seeks to make an arrest, must be one for which the suspect can be arrested without a warrant.

34. *R. v. Landry* (1986), 25 C.C.C. (3d) 1, [1986] 1 S.C.R. 145, 26 D.L.R. (4th) 368.

35. *R. v. Biron* (1975), 23 C.C.C. (2d) 513, [1976] 2 S.C.R. 56, 30 C.R.N.S. 109.

36. *R. v. Cohen* (1983), 5 C.C.C. (3d) 156, 148 D.L.R. (3d) 78, 33 C.R. (3d) 151 (B.C. C.A.). Subsequently, in *Collins v. R.* (1987), 33 C.C.C. (3d) 1, [1987] 1 S.C.R. 265, 28 C.R.R. 122, the Supreme Court of Canada held that a throat hold would be unreasonable only if the police were not searching a person whom they believed on reasonable grounds to be a drug handler.

37. *R. v. Meickle*, unreported, April 29, 1983, Ont. Co. Ct., Matlow, Co. Ct. J. In another case, *R. v. McCready* (November 25, 1982), 9 W.C.B. 109 (B.C. Prov. Ct., Smith, Prov. Ct. J.), it was held that a search, performed by medical personnel, of the accused's bodily orifices for cocaine was reasonable in the circumstances.

37a. (1987), 33 C.C.C. (3d) 398, [1987] 1 S.C.R. 945, 29 C.R.R. 238. Note that a sample of blood taken for legitimate *medical* purposes could be the subject of a "reasonable" (and, therefore, valid) search and seizure within the meaning of section 8 of the *Charter*. *R. v. Katsigiorgis* (1987), 39 C.C.C. (3d) 256, 62 O.R. (2d) 441, 4 M.V.R. (2d) 102 (Ont. C.A.).

37b. 33 C.C.C. (3d) 398 at 402. In *R. v. Racette* (1988), 39 C.C.C. (3d) 289, [1988] 2 W.W.R. 318, 6 M.V.R. (2d) 55, the Saskatchewan Court of Appeal ruled that provincial legislation giving the police the right to demand blood samples or the taking of such samples without consent where the subject is unconscious, was in violation of sections 7 and 8 of the *Charter*, it was also held that the legislation could not be rescued as a "reasonable limitation" within the meaning of section 1.

37c. In *R. v. Nielsen* (1988), 43 C.C.C. (3d) 548, [1988] 6 W.W.R. 1, 66 Sask. R. 293, the Saskatchewan Court of Appeal indicated that the Crown is under a duty to establish that any consent to a search by law enforcement officers is valid and effective. It is not enough for the Crown merely to show that the accused did not object to a search. It would have to establish that the accused had full knowledge of both his right to be protected from an unreasonable search and the impact that a waiver of that right would have in his particular case.

38. Section 488.

39. Section 489.

40. Section 29(1).

41. Section 489.1.

42. The ultimate disposition of the seized items, by the justice, is governed by section 490.

43. See section 199.

44. Section 101.

45. Section 10 of the *Narcotic Control Act* and section 42 of the *Food and Drugs Act*. Searches of dwelling houses require the issue of a warrant, obtained under the authority of the respective statutes.

46. The new section 487.1 of the *Code* was proclaimed in force in December, 1985.

47. *R. v. Stevens* (1983), 7 C.C.C. (3d) 260, 1 D.L.R. (4th) 465, 35 C.R. (3d) 1 (N.S. C.A.).

48. *R. v. Hamill* (1984), 14 C.C.C. (3d) 338, 13 D.L.R. (4th) 275, 41 C.R. (3d) 123 (B.C.C.A.); affirmed [1987] 1 S.C.R. 301, 38 D.L.R. (4th) 611, 56 C.R. (3d) 220.

49. (1987), 33 C.C.C. (3d) 1, [1987] S.C.R. 265, 28 C.R.R. 122.

50. 33 C.C.C. (3d) 1 at 18, quoting Morissette (1984: 538).

50a. 33 C.C.C. (3d) 1 at 18–19.

51. *R. v. Genest* (1986), 32 C.C.C. (3d) 8, 54 C.R. (3d) 246 (Que. C.A.).

52. *Ibid.* at 22 (*per* Owen, J.A.).

53. *Hunter et al. v. Southam Inc.* (1984), 14 C.C.C. (3d) 97, [1984] 2 S.C.R. 145, 11 D.L.R. (4th) 641.

54. *Ibid.*, 109.

55. It should be noted that the right to refuse to answer police questions is not derived from any general right against self-incrimination. The accused's right against self-incrimination refers only to the right of the accused to refuse to enter the witness box in the course of his or her trial (see section 11(c) of the *Charter*).

56. [1979] 1 S.C.R. 195, [1978] 6 W.W.R. 462.

57. *Per* Dickson, J. in *Erven v. The Queen* (1978), 44 C.C.C. (2d) 76 at 87, [1979] 1 S.C.R. 926, 6 C.R. (3d) 97.

58. *Ibrahim v. The Queen*, [1914] A.C. 599 (P.C.).

59. *Ward v. The Queen*, [1979] 2 S.C.R. 30, 7 C.R. (3d) 153, 44 C.C.C. (2d) 498.

60. *Horvath v.The Queen*, [1979] 2 S.C.R. 376, 7 C.R. (3d) 97, 44 C.C.C. (2d) 385.

61. *Rothman v. The Queen* (1981), 20 C.R. (3d) 97, [1981] 1 S.C.R. 640, 59 C.C.C. (2d) 30.

62. This was the course approved by the Supreme Court of Canada in *R. v. Manninen* (1987), 34 C.C.C. (3d) 385, [1987] 1 S.C.R. 1233, 58 C.R. (3d) 97. In this case, a police officer questioned the accused and elicited a statement from him even after the accused had stated that he did not want to say anything until he saw his lawyer. In light of the flagrant violation of the accused's right to counsel (guaranteed by section 10(b) of the *Charter*), the Court upheld the view that the incriminating statement should not be admitted in evidence on the basis that, if this were permitted, the administration of justice would be brought into disrepute. See, also, the similar case of *R. v. R. (P. L.)* (1988), 44 C.C.C. (3d) 174 (N.S.C.A.).

A confession may also be excluded if it was obtained during a period of "arbitrary detention" (contrary to section 9 of the *Charter*); see *R. v. Spence* (1988), 41 C.C.C. (3d) 354, [1988] 3 W.W.R. 180, 62 C.R. (3d) 293 (Man. C.A.).

63. *R. v. Nelson* (1982), 3 C.C.C. (3d) 147, 32 C.R. (3d) 256, 4 C.R.R. 88 (Man. Q.B.).

64. S.C. 1973-74, c. 50. Note that there were some major changes to this Act in 1977 (Bill C-51). The legislation is contained in the *Criminal Code*, Part VI.

65. Section 183 of the *Criminal Code*.

66. Section 184.

67. Section 183.

68. Section 185. The precise name of the court concerned will vary from province to province; however, the judge from whom the authorization is sought will be a federally appointed judge.

69. Section 186(1).

70. Section 186(4). Note that section 188 of the *Code* contains provisions for an "emergency" authorization, which is valid for up to 36 hours only.

71. Section 196.

72. Section 189(1). In an important decision, the Supreme Court of Canada has ruled that surreptitious entry by the police in order to install a listening device did not render the evidence inadmissible because authorization had been duly obtained for the "interception"; *Lyons et al. v. The Queen* (1984), 15 C.C.C. (3d) 417, [1984] 2 S.C.R. 633, 43 C.R. (3d) 97. This particular section of the *Code* refers only to the requirement that the "interception" be lawfully made before it may be admissible as evidence.

In *R. v. Thompson* (1986), 29 C.C.C. (3d) 516, the British Columbia Court of Appeal refused to hold that such surreptitious entry violated section 8 of the *Charter*, although the Court did indicate (at 528) that "a reconsideration of this issue as a constitutional one ought to be left to the Supreme Court (of Canada)."

In an important case, *R. v. Paterson et al.* (1985), 18 C.C.C. (3d) 137, 44 C.R. (3d) 150, 7 O.A.C. 105, the Ontario Court of Appeal held that the use of so-called "basket clauses" in wiretap authorizations was invalid. Such clauses purported to give the police the authority not only to eavesdrop on parties who were specifically named in the judicial authorization, but also any other persons (unspecified) for whom there are "reasonable and probable grounds to believe that the interception of such private communications may assist the investigation." The Court held that such clauses were invalid because they, in effect, delegated the judge's responsibility, to determine who should be the object of surveillance, to the police themselves. This judgment was later affirmed by the Supreme Court of Canada, in *R. v. Paterson et al.* (1987), 39 C.C.C. (3d) 575, 60 C.R. (3d) 107, 79 N.R. 316.

73. *R. v. Dennison* (1984), 15 C.C.C. (3d) 510, 6 O.A.C. 235 (Ont. C.A.).

74. Section 195.

75. *Mack v. R.* (1988), 44 C.C.C. (3d) 513, [1989] 1 W.W.R. 577, 90 N.R. 173.

76. 44 C.C.C. (3d) 513 at 559.

76a. 44 C.C.C. (3d) 513 at 542.

76b. 44 C.C.C. (3d) 513 at 570.

77. As we noted in Chapter 3, an overlooked and underresearched dimension of police work is the role of boredom and its contribution to the overreaction of police officers in encounter situations. One officer in Ericson's (1982: 70) study described officer overreaction as a "tendency to create a new scene rather than to patch up an old one," and on these occasions, Ericson (1982: 70) notes, "officers may produce disorder rather than reproduce order."

78. Most of the studies in Canada and the United States have focused on police decisions about juveniles. It is important to note that the factors influencing decison making involving youths may be different than those operating in encounter situations with adults.

79. While acknowledging that the particular community in which a police department operates will result in some variability in police functions, Meagher (1985: 44) discovered in a study of police tasks in 249 municipal police departments in the United States that there was a core of tasks that were common to small, medium and large municipal police departments: (1) general patrol tasks, (2) offender processing, (3) traffic accident tasks, and (4) driving tasks. These findings led Meagher (1984: 42) to conclude that the activities of patrol officers in municipal departments are quite similar. It must be remembered, however, that while the types of tasks performed by officers may be similar across departments in different jurisdictions, the level of demand for these tasks may vary considerably, as may the settings in which the encounters between police and citizens take place.

80. One of the more unique attributes of Canadian policing is the frequent transfer (often every two years) of officers in the RCMP. During their policing careers, RCMP officers are likely to be exposed to a variety of policing environments, with the concurrent requirement that adjustments be made in policing style. One rationale offered by the RCMP for the transfer policy is to prevent officers from becoming involved in the community to the extent that it adversely affects their ability to perform their duties. Ironically, as we will see in our discussion of native Indians and the police in Chapter 15, one of the major complaints of many communities in Northern Canada is that the frequent transfer of officers prevents the development of police-community relations that would improve the delivery of policing services.

81. A critical issue in policing is the extent to which the police, in their enforcement patterns and decision making, should take into account the customs, practices, and standards of conduct of different groups in the community or of communities in certain geographical locations. Should, for example, the Chinese community be policed in the same fashion as other districts of an urban area? Similarly, to what extent should policing and enforcement practices vary in Inuit communities in the Arctic, where many of the laws appropriate to "southern," urban areas, may be inappropriate or even irrelevant?

82. In the United States, County Sheriffs, who are responsible for policing areas of a county that lie outside of incorporated cities and towns, are elected by popular vote. This may increase the likelihood that enforcement and arrest patterns are reflective of community expectations and standards, or at least the needs of certain groups in the community. In Canada, there are no elected policing officials.

83. Similar to Broderick's (1987) identification of "ideal types" of police officers discussed in Chapter 3, it is unlikely that a police department will evidence all the attributes of a specific style. Rather, a police organization will approximate one style or another.

84. While a large percentage of situations to which police officers respond on a reactive basis are not classified as "real" police work, Lundman (1980: 115) points out that most police initiated encounters are of the "real police work" variety.

85. In addition to examining the factors associated with the decision by police officers to arrest in encounter situations, researchers have focused on the factors that influence police decision making in follow-up investigations. Bynum, Cordner, and Greene (1982), for example, have reported that the characteristics of the victim may play a major role in the decision to investigate a complaint and in the extent to which complaints are followed up by detectives.

REFERENCES

Albanese, J. S. 1984. "The Outer Limits of Law Enforcement." 12 *Journal of Police Science and Administration* 27–31.

American Friends Service Committee. 1971. *Struggle for Justice.* New York: Hill and Wang.

Antunes, G., and E. J. Scott. 1981. "Calling the Cops: Police Telephone Operators and Citizen Calls for Service." 9 *Journal of Criminal Justice* 165–79.

Banks, L. K. 1984. "Case Screening: A Study of Police Decision Making." M.A. thesis. Burnaby, B.C.: School of Criminology, Simon Fraser University.

Bittner, E. 1967. "The Police on Skid Row: A Study of Peace Keeping." 32 *American Sociological Review* 699–715.

Black, D. 1971. "The Social Organization of Arrest." 23 *Stanford Law Review* 1087–1111.

Black, D., and A. J. Reiss, Jr. 1970. "Police Control of Juveniles." 35 *American Sociological Review* 63–77.

Bloch, P., and D. Anderson. 1974. *Policewomen on Patrol: Final Report.* Washington, D.C.: Police Foundation.

Blum-West, S. 1983. "Calling the Cops: A Study of Why People Report Crimes." 11 *Journal of Police Science and Administration* 8–15.

Broderick, J. J. 1987. *Police in a Time of Change.* 2nd ed. Prospect Heights, Ill.: Waveland Press.

Brodsky, D. J. 1987. "Telewarrants." 29 *Criminal Law Quarterly* 345–67.

Burns, P. T. 1979. "A Retrospective View of the Protection of Privacy Act; A Fragile Rede is Recked." 13 *U.B.C. Law Review* 123–57.

Burtch, B. E. 1979. "Electronic Eavesdropping and Legal Civil Liberties." 1 *Canadian Criminology Forum* 1–12.

Bynum, T. S., G. W. Cordner, and J. R. Greene. 1982. "Victim and Offense Characteristics: The Impact on Police Investigative Decision Making." 20 *Criminology* 301–18.

Chambliss, W. 1969. *Crime and Legal Process.* New York: McGraw-Hill.

Chappell, D., R. Gordon, and R. Moore. 1982. "Criminal Investigation: A Selective Literature Review and Bibliography." 6 *Canadian Police College Journal* 13–64.

Chappell, D., and L. P. Graham. 1985. *Police Use of Deadly Force: Canadian Perspectives.* Toronto: Centre of Criminology, University of Toronto.

Chappell, D., J. Jessup, and R. D. Moore. 1984. *An Examination of Criminal Investigation Process at Vancouver Police Department.* Burnaby, B.C.: Criminology Research Centre, Simon Fraser University.

Cohen, S. A. 1981. "The Investigation of Offences and Police Powers." 13 *Ottawa Law Review* 549–70.

————. 1983. *Invasion of Privacy: Police and Electronic Surveillance in Canada.* Toronto: Carswell Co.

————. 1984a. "Controversies in Need of Resolution: Some Threshold Questions Affecting Individual Rights and Police Powers under the Charter." 16 *Ottawa Law Review* 97–116.

————. 1984b. "The Impact of the Charter Decisions on Police Behaviour." 39 *Criminal Reports* (3d) 264–80.

Conly, J. 1978. *Patterns of Delinquency and Police Action in the Major Metro Areas of Canada during the Month of December, 1976: Final Report.* Ottawa: Solicitor General of Canada.

Connelly, P. 1985. "The Fourth Amendment and Section 8 of the Canadian Charter of Rights and Freedoms. What Has Been Done? What Has to Be Done?" 27 *Criminal Law Quarterly* 182–211.

Conway, R. 1984. "No Man's Land: Confessions Not Induced by Fear of Prejudice or Hope of Advantage." 42 *University of Toronto Faculty Law Review* 26–49.

————. 1985. "The Right to Counsel and the Admissibility of Evidence." 28 *Criminal Law Quarterly* 28–63.

Cooley, J. W. 1981. "Police Discretion and Public Attitudes." In *The Police Function in Canada*, edited by W. T. McGrath and W. T. Mitchell, 186–96. Toronto: Methuen.

Coughlan, S. 1985. "Police Detention for Questioning: A Proposal." 28 *Criminal Law Quarterly* 64–90 and 170–202.

Davis, K. C. 1975. *Police Discretion.* Minneapolis: West Publishing Co.

————. 1978. "An Approach to the Legal Control of the Police." In *The Invisible Justice System: Discretion and the Law*, edited by B. Atkins and M. Pogrebin, 123–36. Cincinnati: Anderson Publishing Co.

Doob, A. N., and J. B. L. Chan. 1978. *The Exercise of Discretion with Juveniles: A Study of the Youth Bureau of the Peel Regional Police.* Toronto: Centre of Criminology, University of Toronto.

Ericson, R. V. 1981. *Making Crime: A Study of Detective Work*. Toronto: Butterworths.

————. 1982. *Reproducing Order: A Study of Police Patrol Work*. Toronto: University of Toronto Press.

————. 1983. *The Constitution of Legal Inequality*. Ottawa: Carleton Universtiy Press.

Ericson, R. V., and P. M. Baranek. 1982. *The Ordering of Justice: A Study of Accused Persons as Dependants in the Criminal Process*. Toronto: University of Toronto Press.

France, S. 1988. "Problems in the Defence of Entrapment." 22 *University of British Columbia Law Review* 1–20.

Frankel, S. D. 1981. "Interception of Private Communications." In *Criminal Procedure: Canadian Law and Practices*, edited by J. Atrens, P. T. Burns, and J. P. Taylor, VIII-i to VIII-81. Vancouver: Butterworths.

Friedland, M. L. 1982. "Legal Rights under the Charter." 24 *Criminal Law Quarterly* 430–54.

Gandy, J. M. 1970. "The Exercise of Discretion by Police as a Decision Making Process." 8 *Osgoode Hall Law Journal* 329–44.

Goldman, N. 1963. "The Differential Selection of Juvenile Offenders for Court Appearance." In *Crime and Legal Process*, edited by W. J. Chambliss, 264–90. New York: McGraw-Hill.

Goldstein, J. 1960. "Police Discretion Not to Invoke the Criminal Process." 69 *Yale Law Journal* 543–94.

Gottfredson, M. R., and D. M. Gottfredson. 1980. *Decision Making in Criminal Justice: Toward the Rational Exercise of Discretion*. Cambridge, Mass.: Ballinger Publishing Co.

Gottfredson, M. R., and M. J. Hindelang. 1979. "A Study of the Behavior of Law." 44 *American Sociological Review* 3–18.

Grant, A. 1987. "Videotaping Police Questioning: A Canadian Experiment." (June) *Criminal Law Review* 375–83.

Grant, J. D., J. Grant, and H. H. Toch. 1982. "Police-Citizen Conflict and Decisions to Arrest." In *The Criminal Justice System — A Social-Psychological Analysis*, edited by V. J. Konecni and E. B. Ebbesen, 133–58. San Francisco: W. H. Freeman and Co.

Grosman, B. 1975. *Police Command: Decisions and Discretion*. Toronto: Methuen.

Hindelang, M. J. 1976. *Criminal Victimization in Eight American Cities: A Descriptive Analysis of Common Theft and Assault*. Cambridge, Mass.: Ballinger Publishing Co.

Holten, N. G., and M. E. Jones. 1978. *The System of Criminal Justice*. Boston: Little, Brown, and Co.

Hylton, J. H., and R. Matonovich. 1980. *Public Attitudes about Crime and the Police in Moose Jaw*. Regina: School of Human Justice, University of Regina.

Jorgensen, B. 1981. "Transferring Trouble — The Initiation of Reactive Policing." 23 *Canadian Journal of Criminology* 257–78.

Jull, K. 1988. "Exclusion of Evidence and the Beast of Burden." 30 *Criminal Law Quarterly* 178–89.

Law Reform Commission of Canada. 1975. *Studies on Diversion.* Ottawa: Information Canada.

———. 1983a. *Police Powers — Search and Seizure in Criminal Law Enforcement. Working Paper No. 30.* Ottawa: Supply and Services Canada.

———. 1983b. *Writs of Assistance and Telewarrants. Report No. 19.* Ottawa: Supply and Services Canada.

———. 1984a. *Questioning Suspects. Report No. 23.* Ottawa: Supply and Services Canada.

———. 1984b. *Search and Seizure. Report No. 24.* Ottawa: Supply and Services Canada.

———. 1985. *Arrest. Working Paper No. 41.* Ottawa: Supply and Services Canada.

———. 1986. *Electronic Surveillance. Working Paper No. 47.* Ottawa: Supply and Services Canada.

———. 1988. *Compelling Appearance, Interim Release and Pre-Trial Detention. Working Paper No. 57.* Ottawa: Supply and Services Canada.

Levens, B. R. 1976. *The Social Service Role of the Police: Domestic Crisis Intervention — Citizens Requests for Service and Vancouver Police Response. Monograph One.* Vancouver: United Way.

Lundman, R. J. 1979. "Organizational Norms and Police Discretion: An Observational Study of Police Work with Traffic Law Violators." 17 *Criminology* 159–71.

———. 1980. *Police and Policing — An Introduction.* New York: Holt, Rinehart, and Winston.

Lundman, R. J., R. E. Sykes, and J. P. Clark. 1978. "Police Control of Juveniles: A Replication." 15 *Journal of Research in Crime and Delinquency* 74–91.

Luther, G. 1987. "Police Power and the Charter of Rights and Freedoms: Creation or Control?" 51 *Saskatchewan Law Review* 217–27.

MacDonald, N. 1987. "Electronic Surveillance in Crime Detection: An Analysis of Canadian Wiretapping Law." 10 *Dalhousie Law Journal* 141–66.

MacLean, S. C. 1987. "Video Surveillance and the Charter of Rights." 30 *Criminal Law Quarterly* 88–123.

Manning, P. 1988. *Symbiotic Communication: Signifying Calls and Police Response.* Cambridge, Mass.: MIT Press.

McCalla, W. 1984. "Telewarrants." 16 *Ottawa Law Review* 425–30.

McGahan, P. 1984. *Police Images of a City.* New York: Peter Lang.

McLachlin, B. M., and A. Miller. 1982. "Rothman: Police Trickery: Is the Game Worth the Candle?" 16 *U.B.C. Law Review* 115–30.

McMahon, M. 1984. "The Canadian Charter of Rights and Freedoms: A Study of the Creation and Use of Legal Authority." 6 *Canadian Criminology Forum* 131–50.

McWilliams, P. K. 1984. *Canadian Criminal Evidence.* 2nd ed. Aurora, Ont.: Canada Law Book Ltd.

Meagher, M. S. 1985. "Police Patrol Styles: How Pervasive Is Community Variation?" 13 *Journal of Police Science and Administration* 36–45.

Mitchell, G. E. 1988. "The Supreme Court of Canada on the Exclusion of Evidence in Criminal Cases under Section 24 of the Charter." 30 *Criminal Law Quarterly* 165–77.

Morrissette, Y-M. 1984. "The Exclusion of Evidence under the Canadian Charter of Rights and Freedoms: What to Do and What Not to Do." 29 McGill Law Journal 521.

Ouimet, R. (Chairman). 1969. *Report of the Canadian Committee on Corrections — Toward Unity: Criminal Justice and Corrections.* (Catalogue No. JS52-1-1968.) Ottawa: Information Canada.

Paciocco, D. M. 1987. "The Development of Miranda-like Doctrines under the Charter." 19 *Ottawa Law Review* 49–70.

Pavlich, D. J. 1981. "Law and Arrest." In *Criminal Procedure: Canadian Law and Practice,* edited by J. Atrens, P. T. Burns, and J. P. Taylor, III-1 to III-211. Vancouver: Butterworths.

Pursley, R. D. 1974. "Leadership and Community Identification Attitudes among Two Categories of Police Chiefs." 2 *Journal of Police Science and Administration* 414–22.

Quinney, R. 1970. *The Social Reality of Crime.* Boston: Little, Brown, and Co.

Ratushny, E. 1983. "Emerging Issues in Relation to the Legal Rights of a Suspect under the Canadian Charter of Rights and Freedoms." 61 *Canadian Bar Review* 177–89.

Reid, S. T. 1985. *Crime and Criminology.* 4th ed. New York: Holt, Rinehart, and Winston.

Reiman, J. H. 1979. *The Rich Get Richer and The Poor Get Prison — Ideology, Class and Criminal Justice.* New York: John Wiley and Sons.

Roach, K. 1987. "Section 24(1) of the Charter: Strategy and Structure." 29 *Criminal Law Quarterly* 222–72.

Rosenberg, M. 1985. "Unreasonable Search and Seizure: *Hunter v. Southam Inc.*" 19 *U.B.C. Law Review* 217–95.

Russell, P. H. 1985. "The First Three Years in Charterland." 28 *Canadian Public Administration* 367–96.

Salhany, R. E. 1984. *Canadian Criminal Procedure.* 4th ed. Aurora, Ont.: Canada Law Book.

Shearing, C. D. 1981. "Subterranean Processes in the Maintenance of Power: An Examination of the Mechanisms Coordinating Police Action." 18 *Canadian Review of Sociology and Anthropology* 283–98.

————. 1984. *Dial-A-Cop: A Study of Police Mobilisation.* Toronto: Centre of Criminology, University of Toronto.

Shearing, C., and J. Leon. 1978. "Reconsidering the Police Role: A Challenge to a Challenge of a Popular Conception." 19 *Canadian Journal of Criminology and Corrections* 331–45.

Sherman, L. W. 1980. "Causes of Police Behavior: The Current State of Quantitative Research." 17 *Journal of Research in Crime and Delinquency* 69–100.

Smith, D. A., C. A. Visher, and L. A. Davidson. 1984. "Equity and Discretionary Justice: The Influence of Race on Police Arrest Decisions." 75 *Journal of Criminal Law and Criminology* 234–49.

Solicitor General of Canada. 1983a. *Canadian Urban Victimization Survey. Bulletin No. 1 — Victims of Crime.* Ottawa: Programs Branch, Research and Statistics Group.

————. 1983b. *Canadian Urban Victimization Survey. Bulletin No. 2 — Reported and Unreported Crimes.* Ottawa: Programs Branch, Research and Statistics Group.

————. 1987. *Annual Report on Electronic Surveillance (Section 178.22 of the Criminal Code); 1986.* Ottawa: Solicitor General of Canada.

————. 1988. *Annual Report on Electronic Surveillance (Section 178.22 of the Criminal Code); 1987.* Ottawa: Solicitor General of Canada.

Solomon, P. H. 1985. "The Law Reform Commission of Canada's Proposals for Reform of Police Powers: An Assessment." 27 *Criminal Law Quarterly* 321–51.

Stewart, D. 1987. "Four Springboards from the Supreme Court of Canada: *Hunter, Therens, Motor Vehicle Reference* and *Oakes* — Asserting the Basic Values of our Criminal Justice System." 12 *Queen's Law Journal* 131–54.

Stober, M. I. 1985. *Entrapment in Canadian Law.* Toronto: Carswell Legal Publications.

Swanson, C. 1979. "A Comparison of Organizational and Environmental Influences in Arrest Policies." In *Determinants of Law-Enforcement Policies,* edited by F. A. Meyer and R. Baker, 15–33. Lexington, Mass.: D. C. Heath.

Sykes, R. E., J. C. Fox, and J. P. Clark. 1976. "A Socio-Legal Theory of Police Discretion." In *The Ambivalent Force: Perspectives on the Police,* edited by A. Niederhoffer and A. S. Blumberg, 171–83. Hinsdale, Ill.: The Dryden Press.

Talarico, S. M., and C. R. Swanson. 1979. "Styles of Policing: An Exploration of Compatability and Conflict." In *Determinants of Law-Enforcement Policies,* edited by F. A. Meyer and R. Baker, 35–44. Lexington, Mass.: D. C. Heath.

Taylor, I. 1983. *Crime, Capitalism and Community — Three Essays in Socialist Criminology.* Toronto: Butterworths.

Trojanowicz, R. C., and S. L. Dixon. 1974. *Criminal Justice and the Community.* Englewood Cliffs, N.J.: Prentice-Hall.

Turk, A. 1969. *Criminality and Legal Order.* Chicago: Rand McNally.

Van Maanen, J. 1973. "Observations on the Making of Policemen." Reproduced by permission of Society for Applied Anthropology from *Human Organization* 32 (1973) pp. 407–18.

————. 1978. "The Asshole." In *Policing: A View from the Street,* edited by P. K. Manning and J. Van Maanen, 221–38. Santa Monica, Calif.: Goodyear Publishing Co.

Wilson, J. Q. 1968a. *Varieties of Police Behavior: The Management of Law and Order in Eight Communities.* Cambridge, Mass.: Harvard University Press.

————. 1968b. "The Police and the Delinquent in Two Cities." In *Controlling Delinquents,* edited by S. Wheeler, 9–30. New York: John Wiley and Sons.

Wool, G. J. 1985–86. "Police Informants in Canada: The Law and Reality." 50 *Saskatchewan Law Review* 249–70.

LEGISLATION

Bail Reform Act, R.S.C. 1970 (2nd Supp.), c. 2; see now *Criminal Code,* Part XVI

Combines Investigation Act, R.S.C. 1970, c. C-23; see now R.S.C. 1985, c. C-34

Criminal Code, R.S.C. 1985, c. C-46

Food and Drugs Act, R.S.C. 1985, c. F-27

Identification of Criminals Act, R.S.C. 1985, c. I-1

Narcotic Control Act, R.S.C. 1985, c. N-1

Protection of Privacy Act, S.C. 1973-74, c. 50; see now *Criminal Code,* Part VI

5 CRITICAL ISSUES IN CANADIAN POLICING

The Effectiveness of the Police

In our discussion of the role of the police in Canadian society in Chapter 3, it was noted that police organizations are structured as though crime control were the primary activity, although as we have seen, service and order maintenance tasks constitute the largest percentage of citizen requests for police service. This crime control emphasis has a profound effect on the allocation of police resources and deployment of manpower, as well as on the criteria utilized to assess police effectiveness and productivity.[1]

Traditional Policing: The Watch System

Within the crime control model, the primary strategy for deploying manpower is the *watch system*, or preventive patrol. In watch policing, officers are assigned to patrol large districts on a rotating basis under the supervision of higher level officers, who also rotate. On patrol, officers are allowed to move at will within the district. Szynkowski (1981: 167) notes that the basic premise of watch, or preventive, policing is that "visible police presence deters potential offenders and allays citizens' fear of crime." Research, however, has raised serious questions about the effectiveness of the watch system, Moore and Kelling (1983: 57) arguing that it "provides neither general deterrence, nor successful apprehension of individual offenders."

In what is considered a landmark study, the effectiveness of preventive patrol was empirically examined in Kansas City (Kelling et al., 1974). Fifteen police beats in the city were divided into five groups of three precincts each. Each group included beats that were as similar as possible in population, crime level and calls for police service. Within each group, three different patrol strategies were used for one year. One beat was patrolled in the customary fashion by a single patrol car, a second beat received patrol activity two to three times the normal level, and in the third beat, preventive patrol was eliminated and service was provided only in response to specific citizen requests. Prior to and following the experiment, citizens in the beat areas were interviewed regarding their perceptions of police service, whether they had been victimized, and their level of fear of becoming a victim of crime.

Among the findings of the investigation were that preventive patrol had no real effect upon the incidence or the type of crime that occurred in the three types of beat, on police response time, the rates of victimization and of fear of victimization, or upon public perceptions of police performance. The Kansas City study also produced data on the activities of officers on preventive patrol, the investigators reporting that 60% of patrol time was uncommitted. Of considerable significance was that 25% of this uncommitted time was spent on non-police-related tasks.

The findings of the Kansas City study led many observers to conclude that major alterations in policing strategy were required to make police organizations more effective and efficient. While the methodology and conclusions of the Kansas City study have been criticized, Koenig, DeBeck, and Laxton (1983a: 118) point out that the importance of the study is "the fact that it was the first widely disseminated and discussed systematic external research of a police department, supported by management, which was intended not merely to monitor police tasks or behaviours, but to monitor the effectiveness of traditional police practices." The findings of the Kansas City study also provided the impetus for a consideration of an alternative model of policing known as zone, or team, policing.

Concurrent with the focus on the watch system has been an increased concern with mobile patrol, the primary mechanism through which policing services are delivered to communities. From a review of the evaluative literature, Woods (1981: 9) concluded that patrol cars staffed by one officer were more productive, less expensive and safer than two-officer patrols.

In a study of the San Diego Police Department, Boydstun, Sherry, and Moelter (1977) found that two one-officer cars responded to an incident faster than one two-officer car. This research was subsequently replicated and corroborated by Kessler (1985), using data from the Kansas City response time analysis study. Kessler identified peer pressure as a primary reason for this finding, noting: "When two officers in separate cars are assigned to a call, they each have a responsibility to arrive as quickly as possible for their mutual protection . . . each officer has an incentive to observe who is reliable and who is not . . ." (p. 61). The "two-officer car" issue has recently been raised in Canada, with the Hickling-Johnston (1982) report on the Metropolitan Toronto Police Department recommending that increased attention be given to the use of one-officer cars.

There has also been a renewed interest in foot patrol, due in part to concern with the effectiveness of mobile patrols and an increased focus on methods to improve police-community relations. In an evaluation of the Foot Patrol program in Newark, New Jersey, Kelling et al. (1981) reported that while foot patrol did not have a significant effect on the crime rate, it did reduce citizen fear of crime and increase feelings of personal safety among citizens in the community. A similar evaluation by Trojanowicz (1983) of the Neighborhood Foot Patrol program in Flint, Michigan also revealed that there were increased feelings of safety among citizens and, further, that foot patrol officers handled a large number of complaints informally on the street, reducing calls for service to the Flint Police Department by 43%. Research by Trojanowicz and Banas (1985) in Michigan has also found that foot patrol officers have higher levels of familiarity with the neighbourhoods in which they work, feel safer in their work, and perceive higher levels of community support than do their motor patrol counterparts (see also Bowers and Hirsch, 1987; Esbensen, 1987).

In arguing that Canadian police departments should consider similar experiments with foot patrol, Murphy and Muir (1985: 265) state: "The findings . . . seem to suggest that foot patrol has a beneficial effect on police-community relations, heightens cooperation between the public and the police, while not compromising the traditional role of the police in terms of patrol methods."[2]

Zone, or Team, Policing

Zone, or team, policing, which was first introduced into North America in the 1960s and in Canada in 1970, differs considerably from preventive, or watch, policing. Hylton et al. (1979: 2) identified the two primary objectives of zone policing as the improvement of police services and job satisfaction among police personnel. These authors (1979: 2) also noted that zone policing was designed to restructure the organization and delivery of policing services, shifting the focus from the traditional "call-oriented enforcement" orientation to crime prevention and community service.[3]

The major operational attributes of team policing, as outlined by Johnson, Misner, and Brown (1981: 137) are:

1. geographic stability of patrol through permanent assignment of police teams to small areas or neighborhoods
2. maximum communication, interaction, coordination, and cooperation among team members, fostered through the practice of working together to solve common problems
3. better communication and interaction between team members and residents of the community or neighborhood in which they work
4. different styles of management, supervision, and decision making, which emphasize the involvement and participation of individual team members in making decisions that affect the operations of the team
5. de-emphasis of specialists' skills in favor of a generalist approach in which team members are given wider latitude in dealing with day-to-day problems.

Team policing was designed to improve effectiveness through increasing contact with the community and having officers concentrate their efforts in well-defined neighbourhood areas on a permanent basis. Through an increased focus on the community, another objective was to lessen the insularity of the police and improve police-community relations. Talarico and Swanson (1980: 22) note that team policing "was partially envisioned as a way to balance the need for efficiency with the community's preference for decentralized and more responsive policing."

Despite the initial enthusiasm with which the concept of team policing was implemented in Canada and the United States, it met with mixed success and has been largely discarded, and Szynkowski (1981: 168) concludes that "traditional preventive patrol is yet considered the backbone of the police agency." Woods (1981: 11) notes that during the first year in which team policing was adopted in the City of Cincinnati, Ohio, there was a significant increase in citizen satisfaction with the police, a lowering of crime rates and evidence of an improvement in the attitudes and outlook of police personnel. In the second year, however, there was a recentralization of authority and a shift back to earlier organizational arrangements and team policing "expired."

Many of the difficulties encountered by team policing are similar to those that have hindered police-community relations initiatives. Organizationally, team policing involved a decentralization of authority and decision making in the police force, with an accompanying reduction in the power of many mid-management officers. As Woods (1981: 11) points out: "Team Policing represents a threat to both formal and informal distribution of authority. Although officers may be enthusiastic about the concept, organizational decentralization threatens established interest groups which often have considerable power inside the organization."[4]

There was also substantial evidence that line-level officers, who despite being given added responsibility and authority under team policing schemes, believed the crime control mandate was being compromised. This is poignantly illustrated by an exchange that occurred between Superintendent Bob Heywood, Officer in Command of the RCMP detachment in North Vancouver, who introduced team policing to Canada in 1970, and an officer in the detachment:

> "When we first started in the schools," observes Heywood, "a senior NCO complained, 'We have eight cars on duty and five a,e out at the schools. What if there's a bank robbery?' "
> "What if there is?" Heywood queried. "How many robberies have there been in the last two years?"
> "Three."
> "How many were solved by police getting to the scene quickly?"
> "None."
> "Well, then, how important is it if we don't get there right away?"
> "Bank robberies are the *real* police work," his NCO declared. "We have to respond and be there."
> [Solicitor General of Canada, 1983: 12–13]

Many police administrators complained that team policing placed financial and resource burdens on their organizations that were difficult to meet.

The experience of the Calgary Police Department, however, was that the additional financial burden was related primarily to the process of conversion to team policing and that once this had taken place, team policing was no more expensive to operate than the traditional watch system (Calgary Police Service, 1977).[5]

Further insights into the difficulties encountered by team policing are provided by Revitt (1984), who traced the introduction and subsequent abandonment of team policing in Vancouver, as well as the perceptions of police officers toward the concept. Team policing was adopted in Vancouver in 1976, but was operationally terminated in 1981, when the size of the team areas was increased and responsibility for community relations was returned to the police-community relations section. The introduction of a ten-hour day, a shift in managerial responsibility, opposition from detectives to the generalist concept, and a lack of manpower were several of the factors that precipitated these changes.

The officers interviewed were generally favourable in their perceptions of team policing. Revitt (1984: 32–33) found that the department had attempted to retain some of the basic concepts of team policing, even though the structure for the delivery of policing services had been altered: "Organizationally and operationally there have been changes [which] have left the department somewhere between the idealistic concept of team policing and the traditional style of policing . . . "[6]

While team policing has been discarded and resistance to the adoption of or experimentation with new strategies such as foot patrols and the use of one-man patrol units continues, there are likely to be increased pressures on police organizations to alter their administration and operations to become more effective and efficient. The impetus for change will come from evaluations, such as the Hickling-Johnston report (1982) on the Metropolitan Toronto Police Department. This inquiry resulted in a series of reports and recommendations on how the effectiveness, efficiency, and accountability of the Toronto police could be enhanced. Among the initiatives that the authors (1982: iv–xi) believed would improve the delivery of policing services to the community were:

1. a stronger emphasis on community-based policing;
2. an expansion of the role and duties of the constable to that of a "generalist";
3. increased use of technology and computerization, including the installation of Mobile Digital Terminals in patrol cars;
4. renewed efforts to increase police-community cooperation;
5. adoption of a strategy of "high profile policing," involving high levels of moving vehicle violation stops, of street stops for interrogation, and increased community involvement through crime prevention programming.

A detailed consideration of these and other recommendations of the Hickling-Johnston (1982) report are beyond the scope of this discussion. However, perhaps a word of caution might be raised about the recommendation relating to the increased use of computerization in policing and, more specifically, the installation of Mobile Digital Terminals in patrol cars. While such innovations are viewed as increasing the effectiveness and efficiency of the police, research by Palys, Boyanowsky, and Dutton (1983; 1984) in Vancouver suggests that such technology may have unanticipated consequences.

The research focused on the attitudes of users toward the system, an assessment of how the system was used by police officers, and an assessment of the implications of the system for policing. While both administrative personnel and line-level officers in the department were generally favourable in their evaluations of the Mobile Radio Data System (MRDS), there was considerable variability among the officers in their perceptions of the utilization of the system. Although many officers viewed the system as providing them with access to greater amounts of information, which increased their efficiency and effectiveness on patrol, there was concern that younger officers, in particular, would come to rely too extensively on the MRDS for primary rather than supportive information: "They feared that their colleagues would let the system make decisions for them, ultimately allowing it to become a buffer between officers and the community (Palys et al., 1983: 88).

A similar note of caution regarding the limits of technology in policing has been raised by Moore and Kelling (1983: 62):

> The enormous investment in telephones, radios, and cars that now allow the police to respond to crime calls in under five minutes (often with more than one car) has brought little crime control, no greater sense of security, and has prevented the police from taking order maintenance and service functions seriously.

The concept of *community-based policing* was defined by Murphy and Muir (1985: 81) as "an 'umbrella term' used to describe any approach to policing that encourages involvement with the community." Among the key principles of community-based policing as outlined by Murphy and Muir (1985: 81–95) are:

1. The community has a key role to play in the development of the philosophy, management, and delivery of police services.
2. The objectives of policing should be community-defined and include service and order maintenance as well as crime control.
3. The diverse functions that the police perform in the community are legitimate elements of the police role.
4. The police are but one component of the informal and formal network of social control in the community and must share with

    the community the responsibility for solving community policing problems.

5.   The police, in assuming a proactive stance toward community problems, must place greater emphasis on prevention, referral, and eduation.

Murphy and Muir (1985) note that there are many unresolved issues surrounding the concept of community-based policing and its implementation (see also Loree and Murphy, 1987). A particularly critical view of the concept is held by Manning (1984: 212–13), who argues that the assumptions behind the concept are "largely untested and untestable." Manning further cautions that "if a community police scheme is to be successful, it will require: structural and legal change, changes in the habits of dispute settlement and definition, in organization structure, performance evaluation and in reward structures within the police" (p. 224). It remains to be seen whether attempts to implement a community-based model of policing in municipal and provincial forces and the RCMP will encounter the same obstacles (and meet the same fate) as its predecessor, team policing.[7]

A Note on Police Productivity

Swanson (1983: 329) states that increased police productivity occurs when (1) the level of output rises while the level of resources remains constant, or (2) the level of output remains constant while the level of resources decreases. Among police administrators and observers, however, there is a lack of consensus on the most appropriate manner by which to measure police productivity. As George Kelling (1978: 199), who directed both the Kansas City Preventive Patrol study and the Newark Foot Patrol Experiment, stated in a workshop on police productivity held at the Canadian Police College: ". . . police productivity is a very mixed and confusing issue. It is not clear what it is to be productive or, beyond that, how to measure it. . . . The issue in policing is not simply one of 'productivity' but what kind of productivity."

The most common method of measuring police effectiveness is by clearance rates, which are the proportion of offences known to the police that are cleared by a charge or other means. Similarly, performance may be measured by the number of arrests made or appearance notices issued. Those officers who issue a higher number of appearance notices or make a large number of arrests are often seen as performing their duties more effectively than those who do not.

Figure 5.1 reveals the clearance rates for major categories of *Criminal Code* offences during 1987. The data, drawn from the Uniform Crime Reporting system (Canadian Centre for Justice Statistics, 1988: 31) indicate, as would be expected, that the clearance rates for violent crimes are higher (74.7%) than those for property offences (26.9%), a trend that has existed historically in Canada.

Rossum (1978) and others, however, have argued that while these measures provide some indication of quantity of police performance, they tell us little about the *quality* of police service. Clearance rates are in part a function of the willingness of the public to report crimes to the police, and tend to vary by the type and seriousness of offences. While nearly all categories of offence have clearance rates of less than 50%, some categories, such as homicides, typically have high rates of clearance, while others, such as break and enter, tend to have low clearance rates. Clearance rates may also depend upon the resources a department or detachment has at its disposal. In fact, the police, as a reactive agent in the criminal justice system, may have little control over, or impact on, the nature and extent of crime in their jurisdiction (see Elie and Kapetanaki-Barake, 1985; Wilson, 1978).

Similarly, arrests may be a poor indicator of officer performance. As Hatry (1975: 102) points out, "The mere fact that an arrest was made . . . does not mean that the person committing the crime was successfully brought to justice, nor that the person arrested was actually the guilty party." In addition, Hatry notes that many arrests may be of poor quality, reflecting "poor judgement, insufficient diligence in collecting evidence, mishandling of evidence, (and) misunderstanding of the law" (p. 103).

Current indicators of police productivity do not measure either the organization's or individual officer's performance in carrying out the service or order maintenance tasks. Lab (1984: 300) notes that the overwhelming amount of police activity does not result in either formal reports or arrests being made. Further, measures of performance premised on official action do not reveal the majority of instances in which officers intervene as mediators in disputes or the effectiveness of their techniques in reducing tensions and avoiding violence.[8]

There are, in fact, several levels at which productivity could be measured within individual police organizations — the individual line-level officer, police units, particular kinds of units, such as foot patrols and investigative units, and the police department as a whole (see Jobson and Schneck, 1982). Alternative measures of police productivity that would more accurately reflect the tasks the police are asked to perform in the community are surveys of community perceptions of the police, satisfaction with police services among those requesting assistance, and the number of complaints filed against police officers (see Hatry, 1975; Murphy, 1985).

Women in Policing

We have seen in our previous discussions that police organizations have often displayed considerable resistance to innovation and change. A sim-

FIGURE 5.1
CLEARANCE RATES FOR THE MAJOR CATEGORIES OF CRIMINAL CODE OFFENCES, CANADA, 1987

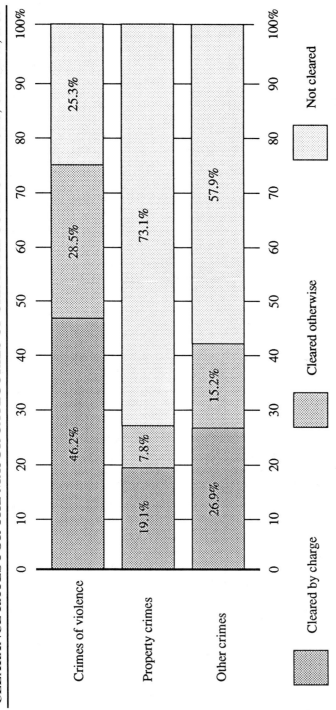

Note: Due to rounding procedure, percentages may not aggregate to 100%.

Source: Canadian Centre for Justice Statistics. *Canadian Crime Statistics, 1987* (Ottawa: Statistics Canada, 1988), p. 31. Catalogue No. 85-205. Reproduced with permission of the Minister of Supply and Services Canada, 1989.

ilar pattern of resistance is evident in the response of many police organizations and line-level officers to the recruitment and deployment of women police officers.

The following consideration of women in Canadian policing draws heavily from the work of Rick Linden, who has conducted empirical studies of women police officers in the Vancouver Police Department and in RCMP detachments in the Lower Mainland area of British Columbia. In his investigations, Linden utilized questionnaires, interviews with supervisory personnel, dispatchers, and male and female line officers. In addition, observations were conducted via ride-alongs with male and female officers, and dispatch records were examined to compare the assignment of male and female officers to incidents.

While women have been employed in Canadian police forces since the early 1900s, traditionally their duties were confined to specific areas, such as clerical work, handling juveniles and women and serving as jail matrons. According to the Canadian Centre for Justice Statistics (1984: 7), in 1983 there were 1,460 women police officers employed by municipal and provincial forces and the RCMP, representing 2.7% of the full-time police officers in Canada. Women, however, remain overrepresented in non-policing roles in police organizations, constituting 65.4% of "other full-time personnel." Many observers have argued that police departments have been reluctant to hire and promote female officers or to utilize them in the full range of policing tasks (Linden and Minch, 1982). In recent years, however, there has been increased pressure on police organizations to recruit women, and in 1983, females constituted 10.1% of the police cadets in training (Canadian Centre for Justice Statistics, 1984: 7; see also Ontario Ministry of the Solicitor General, 1986).

From an exhaustive review of the North American literature on women in policing, Linden and Minch (1982: 43–44) reported that the objections to women becoming involved in general-duty policing have been due to: (1) the perception of male police officers that the image of policing will suffer if women are hired, (2) concern by male police officers that women are less committed to policing as a career, (3) the threat that women would pose to the social world of male police officers, and (4) the perception that women are unable to cope with the violent and physical aspects of police work. Concerns have also been expressed about community acceptance of women police officers (Bell, 1982; Martin, 1979).

Despite these concerns, which appear to be widespread among officers at the line level, research findings reported in Canada by Linden (1980; 1983), as well as the results of numerous studies in the United States, suggest that the above-noted objections are largely unfounded. Linden (1980: 67) found no significant differences between male and female officers in their patterns of arrests and, further, that male and female officers tended to handle similar types of calls. There also appeared to be no difference between male and female officers in their abilities to carry out general police duties. These findings are consistent with those reported by the Ontario Provincial Police (1978) and by Bloch and Anderson (1974), who conducted an extensive study of women police officers in Washington, D.C. (see also Sichel et al., 1978).

From interviews with supervisory personnel in Vancouver and an examination of departmental records, Linden (1980: 16) found no significant differences in the job performance assessments of male and female officers, leading the author to conclude that "most of those who supervise female officers have a relatively favourable opinion of their work" (p. 55). A similar positive attitude toward female officers was recorded in the investigation of the Ontario Provincial Police (1978) and by Bloch and Anderson (1974) in their United States study.

Despite the favourable impression of women officers among supervisory personnel, male general-duty officers evidenced strong negative attitudes toward women, which Linden (1980: 30) noted could be aptly summed up in the comment of one respondent: "Eliminate females!" The majority of the male officers felt that the activities of female officers should be limited to handling juveniles, questioning rape victims, searching females and other traditionally "female" activities, although more positive attitudes were held by those male officers who had had the opportunity to work with women officers. Widespread negative attitudes on the part of male officers have been reported in Canadian and United States studies, although Hylton et al. (1979: 30) found male officers had relatively positive attitudes toward their female counterparts in Regina, with 70% of the officers interviewed stating that it made no difference whether they worked with a female or a male partner (see also Wexler and Logan, 1983).

An additional area examined by Linden (1980) in his study of the Vancouver Police Department was the extent of community acceptance of women police officers. From observations of police-citizen encounters, Linden reported that "more citizens are classified as 'Very Friendly' toward female officers" and further, that "citizens also tended to be somewhat more respectful to female officers" (p. 70). Linden also concluded that women officers were more effective in their interactions with the general public than were male officers (p. 74).

The finding that the general public was positively oriented toward women officers is consistent with the results obtained by Bloch and Anderson (1974) and Kerber, Nades, and Mittler (1977) in the United States, although Homant (1983: 22) found in a study of the impact of women officers on police-community relations in the Detroit area that "the community is not giving women police an unqualified welcome, and . . . the increase in women police in regular, traditionally male police roles is a factor detracting from the police image." While Homant attributed the negative public perceptions of women officers to the community's view of the police role as primarily one of crime-fighting, this study suggests that in some communities there may be resistance to the involvement of women in general-duty policing.

Linden (1983) also conducted an inquiry into women officers in RCMP detachments in the Lower Mainland area of British Columbia and reported findings similar to those obtained in the study of the Vancouver Police. While there were few differences in the performance assessments of male and female officers by RCMP supervisory personnel, who held generally favourable images of women officers, negative perceptions were widespread among male general-duty officers, the author noting that "a substantial proportion of male members does not look favourably upon female members and particularly object to women being assigned to general patrol duties" (p. 221).

However, while there were no differences in rates of attrition for male and female officers in Vancouver, women officers left the RCMP in greater numbers than did their male counterparts. Upon closer examination, Linden (1985: 97) found that this higher attrition rate for women officers was due to marriage-related reasons rather than to dissatisfaction with policing or difficulties in job performance. The transfer policy of the RCMP in particular, was identified by women as a major reason for their having left the force.

Our brief consideration of women in policing suggests that while the available evidence from both empirical studies of women police officers and performance evaluations by supervisory personnel suggest that women are more than capable of performing a wide range of policing duties as effectively as, and in some instances more effectively than, their male counterparts, there continue to be negative attitudes among a large number of male general-duty officers (see also Lord, 1986). This resistance exists despite the efforts of municipal and provincial police forces and the RCMP to recruit and deploy female officers. Perhaps the generally favourable assessments and impressions of supervisory personnel in policing organizations and the more positive perceptions of those male officers who have had the opportunity to work with women officers will function, over time, to break down the negative attitudes of male line-level officers.

Among the recommendations put forth by Linden (1980: 82) from his study of women officers in the Vancouver Police Department was the suggestion that a period of time be set aside during recruit training and in-service training for a discussion of the role of women officers within police organizations. A continued effort to address the difficulties encountered by women police officers is critical, for it is apparent that the general public supports the increased involvement of women in general-duty policing and also that women officers make a significant contribution to police-community relations and the overall image of the police.

Police-Community Relations Programs

Concern with the effectiveness of traditional policing strategies and with the quality of the relations between the police and various segments of the community provided increased pressure for the implementation of community relations and crime prevention programs. The following discussion is not intended to be an exhaustive consideration of the myriad of police-community and crime prevention programs that have been developed by Canadian police organizations at the federal, provincial, and municipal levels. The specific initiatives covered should be taken only as illustrative of the range of programs and their objectives and apparent success in achieving their stated goals. Because many community relations programs have as a major objective the prevention of crime, it is often difficult to separate strictly the two types of program.

Radelet (1986: 26) offers a definition of police-community relations that takes into account the reciprocal attitudes of both the public and the police and includes

> ... the sum total of activities by which it may be emphasized that the police are an important part of — not apart from — the communities they serve ... It is an attitude and an emphasis for all phases of police work, not merely for a specialized unit in the department. It is a way for a police officer to view his work in dealing with citizens. For citizens, it is a way for viewing the police officer. Ideally, it is a matter of striving to achieve mutual understanding and trust, as with any human relationship.

This definition identifies the organizational prerequisites for police-community relations programs, as well as the contributions required of police officers and citizens in the community.

The Toronto Mini-station Project

One of the more innovative community-based initiatives is the mini-station project operated by the Metropolitan Toronto Police Department. The project was modelled on the Detroit mini-station program, which was found to increase citizen reporting of offences and to improve public perceptions of the police (see Tornatzky et al., 1978). Among the goals of the Toronto mini-station, which opened in May, 1983, were: (1) to provide an opportunity for increased community participation in crime prevention programs, and (2) to provide greater public access to policing services.

An evaluation of the Toronto mini-station (A.R.A. Consultants, 1985) found that it facilitated community exposure to a broad range of policing services and the opportunity for police-community contact in a positive environment. This resulted in increased public awareness of crime prevention programs (although only a marginal increase in public participation in such programs), increased ability of the six officers staffing the mini-station to identify and respond to community needs and concerns, and a decrease in the crime rate in the vicinity of the mini-station during the period covered by the evaluation.[10]

Police School-Programs

The established link between the nature and types of contact between juveniles and the police and the formation of adolescent attitudes toward the police (see Chapter 3) has provided the impetus for the development of a wide range of police school-programs. These programs vary considerably in their structure and operation, but often include among their objectives both the improvement of relations with youths and the control of juvenile misbehaviour. Generally, the programs that have been developed by police departments in Canada and the United States can be categorized as either non-residential or residential.

Non-residential police programs often involve visits by police officers to schools on a regular basis to make class presentations, generally of an informational nature. In addition, youths may participate in sports activities with officers or accompany officers on patrol. The results of evaluations of non-residential police school-programs in Canada and the United States suggest that such initiatives increase positive police-adolescent interaction and create a more favourable view of the police among youths. It is unclear, however, whether non-residential school programs result in *behavioural* changes among the youths participating in them, nor is there any evidence to suggest that the positive adolescent perceptions of the police persist over time (see Griffiths, 1982).

Residential programs involve a police officer in residence in a school on a full-time basis during school hours. Illustrative of a residential program is the Police School Liaison Program operated by the Vancouver City Police Department. This program involves 10 officers, who are involved with approximately 44,000 of the city's 66,000 students. Similarly, the St. John, New Brunswick Police operate a School Liaison Program, in which officers not only patrol school property, but participate in extra-curricular activities and make formal class presentations on a variety of subject areas from drug abuse to the operation of the criminal justice system.[11]

The extent to which residential police programs are successful in achieving their objectives is unclear. While Radelet (1986: 468) concluded from a review of the evaluative literature on programs in the United States that "the statistical evidence of apparent success is persuasive," such statements regarding Canadian programs are hindered by the lack of published evaluations. Police forces across Canada also operate a variety of prevention, counselling and diversion programs for young offenders in conflict with the law. These will be considered in our discussion of the youth justice system in Chapter 14.[12]

Victim Services Programs

Municipal, provincial, and RCM Police departments have also developed victim services programs in an attempt to respond to the needs of crime victims. These programs are often located in the community relations units of the department, although there is considerable variability across the country in the organizational structure, services provided, and human and financial resources directed toward these efforts. The Victims Services Project, operated by the Winnipeg Police Department, provides information to crime victims on the progress of case investigations, attempts to facilitate the return of property to victims, and refers victims to other services in the community. In addition, the Victim Services Project sponsors training sessions to sensitize police officers to the needs of victims and to familiarize them with resources available in the community.

A Victim Services Unit (VSU) was created in the Edmonton Police Department in 1979. Among the objectives of the VSU are to lessen the impact of crime on victims by providing victims with information about their case, to increase the involvement of police officers in assisting crime victims, and to involve citizen volunteers in the provision of services to victims. An extensive evaluation of the activities of the VSU in Edmonton (Pullyblank, 1986) revealed that the program is perceived very positively by police officers, victims, and the volunteers involved in the program (see also Canyltec Social Research Corporation, 1987).

Police Resistance to Community Relations Programs

Many police observers, such as Heywood (Solicitor General of Canada, 1983: 13), argue that there is a need to return the responsibility for crime prevention and the maintenance of order back to the community: ". . . we've gone through 25 years of encouraging people to phone the police about everything. We've allowed them to abdicate all responsibility for themselves and for order in the community." Johnson et al. (1981: 269) contend that much of the police resistance to police-community relations stems from the feeling among many officers that the police should not have to undertake what are basic community responsibilities.

There are a variety of additional reasons why the police may resist developing and implementing community relations programs. These include dissatisfaction with the community, police opposition to a perceived change in the crime control mission, extreme in-group pressures among police officers for conformity to crime control objectives, and the failure of police administrators to recognize and reward officers' efforts in police-community relations (see Johnson et al., 1981: 73–82).

In many police organizations, there is no clear-cut conception of where the community relations unit "fits," and organizational support for its program initiatives is often lacking. As an officer in the Calgary Police Department (Solicitor General of Canada, 1984a: 17) stated: "No one's handing out kudos for visiting schools and community organizations, so there hasn't been much incentive to change." Similarly, in discussing police school-programs, Griffiths (1982: 338) has argued that retention of the crime control model has hindered the ability of police school-programs to have a significant impact on police relations with adolescents: "While individual officers in the department may establish rapport with juveniles in the community, the majority of officers in the organization may remain unappreciative of their efforts and may, through their treatment of youths in encounter situations, neutralize the positive gains made by the community relations officers."

The opposition encountered by officers involved in police-community relations units are aptly illustrated by the comments of an officer in St. John's, Newfoundland:

> It changed my attitude and my image toward the public . . . It changed what I think about people . . . But the only thing that saddens me is your own fellow police officers sometimes I won't say look down on you but they think you're running a bluff . . . It's not real police work (to them). They'll see you in the hallways, and say, "How many crimes did you prevent today?" [McGahan, 1984: 182]

Crime Prevention Programs

Normandeau and Hasenpusch (1980: 307) note that crime prevention programs include "up-to-date and understandable criminal legislation, efficient criminal justice services, education in the schools and through the media, specialized services from basic family and child welfare services to highly experimental programs to reduce delinquency, and social adaptation, i.e. redirecting criminal careers through legitimate opportunities." In Canada, the increased focus on crime prevention is highlighted by the annual Crime Prevention Week sponsored by the Solicitor General of Canada and the emergence of provincial crime prevention associations across the country.

The most common crime prevention programs are what Brantingham and Faust (1976) label *primary* crime prevention. These programs seek to identify opportunities for criminal offences and to alter these conditions so as to reduce the likelihood of crimes being committed. Among the primary crime prevention programs operated by Canadian police departments are Operation Identification, Operation Provident, Neighborhood Watch, and various Blockwatch programs. In addition, there has been increased police participation in Crime Prevention Through Environmental Design (CPTED) initiatives.[13]

As the majority of offences committed in Canada are property related, most crime prevention programs are oriented toward these crimes. The

Solicitor General of Canada (1984b: 38) notes that there are three types of community-based crime prevention programs operating across the country: (1) Operation Identification for residential communities, (2) Operation Provident for the business communities, and (3) Neighborhood Watch, in which neighbours assume collective responsibility for preventing crime in the neighbourhood.

Operation Identification and Operation Provident involve citizens and businessmen marking property with identification numbers to make the disposal of stolen goods difficult and to assist in the recovery of items by the police. While these programs have been implemented by the RCMP, provincial, and municipal forces, their impact in terms of increased community involvement in crime prevention and in reducing the rate of property crime is not clear.

In an evaluation of the Operation Identification program run by the RCMP in Burnaby, British Columbia, Meuser (1976) reported a decrease in the rate of residential and industrial break and enters during the 17-month period covered by the study. However, areas adjacent to Burnaby, which were not participating in the program, also experienced decreased break-and-enter rates during this period. Meuser (1976) was unable to credit the decline in property offences in Burnaby directly to the Operation Identification program.

An evaluation of Operation Identification and Operation Provident initiated by the RCMP in Portage La Prairie, Manitoba in 1979 revealed that seven months following the implementation of the programs, there had been a 68% decease in business break and enters and a 48% reduction in residential break and enters. Over the next two years, the rates of business break and enters continued to decline, while offences against residences increased slightly. As a report by the Solicitor General (1984b: 39) points out, "Most businesses and residences that had been broken into had not participated in the program."

Neighborhood Watch involves mobilizing the "eyes and ears" of citizens in the community in the crime prevention effort. While it has been adopted widely across the country, there are few evaluations of its effectiveness. An exploratory investigation by Turk (1987) found high resident turnover on Neighborhood Watch committees and raised concerns about the effectiveness of the Neighborhood Watch program. And Rosenbaum (1987) has offered a detailed critique of the operational assumptions of Neighborhood Watch programs operating in the United States, arguing that they may serve to reduce neither the actual amount of crime in communities nor the levels of crime fear.

The Future of Crime Prevention Programs

Not only is there a need for further evaluations of crime prevention programs such as Operation Identification, but it is apparent that the extent of public participation in such initiatives is a primary determinant of their success. Normandeau and Hasenpusch (1980: 309) argue that a major obstacle to the implementation of crime prevention programs is "the lack of demonstrable effects of prevention . . . we know very little about whether and how prevention programs do succeed . . ."[14]

Citizen participation is a critical ingredient for success. The evaluation (A.R.A. Consultants, 1985) of the Toronto mini-station program revealed that while citizens became more aware of the crime prevention activities of the police, there was no increase in the rate of participation in these initiatives by the public. Similarly, Silverman and Sacco (1981) found from an evaluation of a crime prevention information campaign in Alberta that although citizens recognized the major campaign slogan, the likelihood of citizens taking crime prevention measures was not significantly related to exposure to the information campaign.

From an experimental study of citizen involvement in crime prevention in the United States (recording bystander intervention in 16 incidences of simulated automobile break and enter), Formby and Smykla (1981: 401) concluded that, at least in the area in which they conducted their experimental research, "community awareness and involvement in crime prevention are nonexistent." These authors argue that for citizens to become more aware of crime prevention, the police "must change their conception of their role from that of a law enforcement agency dedicated to catching crooks to that of a public service agency devoted to close relationships with, and assistance to, the people and the communities being policed" (p. 403) (see also Boostrom and Henderson, 1983).

Moore and Kelling (1983: 64) offer two features of a new police strategy: (1) an increased role for private citizens in efforts to control crime and maintain order in the community, and (2) greater police participation in community activities, which would increase accessibility of the police to citizens (Sherman, 1986). While it is likely that police-community relations and crime prevention programs will remain a basic component of Canadian policing, the extent to which these initiatives are successful in achieving their goals will depend upon both the police and the citizens they serve.

Training and Education of the Police

In our discussion in Chapter 3, it was noted that provincial governments, through the development of police commissions, have become extensively involved in the training of police officers for municipal and provincial police forces. The increased concern with training is reflected in the establishment of various police colleges and central training facilities and the provision, in many jurisdictions, of university or college-based education programs.[15]

Professionalization of the Police

The education and training of police officers is closely related to the concept of the professionalization of the police, which has received considerable attention over the past decade.[16] Professionalization of the police has been viewed as a mechanism for increasing the effectiveness and efficiency of police organizations, as a way to gain public confidence and as the foundation for police reform (Smith, 1978). Baker, Meyer, and Rudoni (1979: 99), however, argue that the concept of "police professionalism" lacks clarity:

> To some analysts, police professionalism is seen as a primary way of upgrading police personnel and police operations. Others view professionalism as a political strategy used by the police to further their own occupational and economic ends.

Despite the extensive literature on the professionalization of the police, there is an ongoing debate concerning whether police work is a profession (see Vogel and Adams, 1983). While there is a great deal of variation in the occupations that are classified as professions and individuals who are labelled professionals, it is generally agreed that the minimum requirements for such designations include (1) an agreed upon body of knowledge, (2) an established standard for admission, (3) a period of training and education, (4) a process for certifying or licensing members, (5) a code of ethics, and (6) a shared identity among members of the occupation.

Policing in Canada has many of the above attributes, although many observers contend that policing cannot be considered a profession until several major issues are addressed and resolved. A major obstacle is the conflict over the role of the police in Canadian society, which was discussed in detail in Chapter 3. For example, if the role of the police is conceptualized as one of crime control, then those departments that utilize strategies aimed at fighting crime will be viewed as more professional. If, however, the role of the police is seen as primarily one of order maintenance and service, then emphasis will be placed on the extent to which the department or detachment successfully carries out these functions.

Neither have Canadian police forces developed uniform standards of admission, training, promotion, or transfer of certification and rank across jurisdictions. Rather, considerable variation exists in the standards for the recruitment and training of officers, and there is little opportunity for officers to move laterally between departments without a loss of rank. In addition, in most police organizations in Canada, officers are required to advance through the ranks of a paramilitary structure. There is little "lateral" entry of officers into police departments from the outside. On occasion, police chiefs may move from one department to another, and former high-ranking RCMP officers, provincial police officers in Ontario and Quebec, and municipal police officers have been hired to head municipal departments. These, however, are exceptions to the general rule that officers must work their way up the organizational hierarchy (see McGinnis, 1985a; 1985b).

The RCMP as a police force more closely approximates the criteria for a profession outlined above, as all officers are trained in a central location, are subject to the same requirements and receive similar certification. In addition, under the RCMP transfer policy, there is considerable mobility of officers between detachments situated across the country. As a career RCMP officer stated to one of your text authors (only partially tongue-in-cheek) in explaining the difference between RCMP and municipal police officers: "For them it's a job, for me it's a profession." Certainly the RCMP, with the *esprit de corps* that is fostered by training in small units in Regina, the red serge, traditions such as the musical ride, and the general "Mountie mystique," which remains an integral part of Canadian culture, would lend credence to this officer's observations, although not without strong exception being taken by members of municipal and provincial forces.

It would appear, then, that while the professionalization of the police has received a considerable amount of attention, defining what actually is meant by a "professional" police officer and a "professional" police organization is difficult. As Baker et al. (1979: 110) note: "For an 'idea whose time has come,' the concept of police professionalism is encumbered with a heavy gloss of uncertainty, ambivalence, and controversy." Perhaps one of the most insightful observations on the professionalization of the police in Canada has been made by Muir (1982: 23), who argues: "Professionalism is a conferred status which comes from the community and must be earned through public recognition of services rendered. The police must look to the community for confidence and approval and it is the community which will, in the end, bestow the earned status of 'professional'."

Police Training and Education

The confusion surrounding the discrepancy between the view of the police as crime fighters and the actual activities of the police, which centre on order maintenance and community service, has important implications for the training of police officers and the potential influence of education on police organizations and line-level officers.[17] Blake (1981: 78) asserts:

> Society has changed, but the police have not changed with it. Their training is not geared to meet the needs of today's society. Quite simply, policemen are not being trained to deal with people ... the majority of a recruit's time is spent learning law enforcement functions, with very little training provided for the major portion of his job — community service and order maintenance functions. Most policemen are offended if they are referred to as social workers, yet they are Canada's most visible front-line social workers.

Throughout the policing literature, education is viewed as the cornerstone of the professionalization of the police, or as Muir (1982: 21) notes, ". . . as a rite of passage to professionalization." Higher education is seen as necessary to assist the police officer not only in dealing with increasingly sophisticated crime and criminals, but also in better responding to the demands of the community in a time of rapid social change and high technology. Educated police officers are believed to have higher levels of job performance and job satisfaction.

Prior to providing an overview of the research to date, it is important to note that the majority of studies have been conducted in the United States and that most of these investigations took place during the 1970s. Few studies of the impact of higher education on policing have been conducted during the 1980s, and with the exception of the inquiry by Muir (1982), Canadian investigations are virtually non-existent.

Two of the areas that have been examined by numerous studies are the relation between higher education and the attitudes and job performance of police officers and the relation between higher education and job satisfaction. While several investigators have found little evidence that increased levels of education improve job performance, others have reported a strong correlation between education and the acceptance of members of minority groups, greater flexibility in carrying out policing tasks, less use of official sanctions and more positive assessments of officer performance and fewer complaints by citizens (see Vogel and Adams, 1983; and Fischer, Golden, and Heininger, 1985).

Similarly, several United States studies have reported that college-educated officers are less authoritarian and more flexible in the performance of their duties, and more likely to exercise leadership. However, from his review of the literature, Muir (1982: 116) concluded that the research findings "show only an inconsistent and tenuous relationship between education and an improved ability to deal with increasingly complex and ambiguous police tasks."

It has also been widely argued that higher education is positively correlated with job satisfaction among police officers, although Vogel and Adams (1983: 475) concluded that "overall, the literature does not indicate that education positively correlates with job satisfaction." In fact, there is some evidence to suggest that educated officers may experience conflict with senior administrative officers, as well as with their line-level colleagues. Muir (1982: 33) notes: "Policies towards educated personnel have artfully managed to produce the facade of 'better' personnel while requiring undying loyalty and compliance to traditional values and norms." And Fischer et al. (1985) reported from a study of police officers in the State of Illinois that education played a minimal role in promotion within the police force and that the majority of officers perceived that politics rather than merit continued to be the primary basis upon which advancement in the police force took place.

In what is perhaps the most extensive Canadian investigation into the impact of higher education on policing, Muir (1982) examined the empirical validity of three of the assertions made by the Canadian Police College regarding educated police officers in Canada: (1) they are better able to tolerate differences and ambiguity in carrying out their tasks, (2) they are less authoritarian, and (3) they are more willing to take the initiative and exercise leadership.

To test the validity of these assertions, Muir (1982) selected a sample of 202 officers from municipal and RCMP detachments. The officers represented a broad range of experience and operational capacities, from line-level officers to middle-management personnel and senior police administrators. In an analysis of the responses to a questionnaire, Muir (p. 118) found no statistical support for the assertion that education is positively related to the ability of police officers to tolerate ambiguity. Neither was there a statistically significant relation between higher education and levels of authoritarianism or between higher education and the assertion of initiative and leadership.

Muir (1982) and others have argued that changes in the structure and organization of Canadian policing are required if higher education is to have a significant impact on line-level officers and the departments and detachments in which they work. Police organizations have, in many instances, resisted the changes in structure and operating procedures that would facilitate professionalization, encourage a modification of training programs to reflect more accurately the tasks the police are asked to perform, and alter the organizational environment so as to enhance the benefits to be derived from increased levels of education among line-level officers. As Baker et al. (1979: 106) argue: "Officer education does not in itself change the conditions which most often appear to impede professionalization: these include para-military, hierarchical organization; political control, and institutional ambivalence toward education."

In considering training and education within the larger context of the professionalization of the police, we should heed Niederhoffer's (1967: 32–33) observations, made two decades ago: ". . . professionalization is a wonderful tonic for the police occupation because it brings to an institution in transition the enthusiasm, pride, and ideas it needs to build. But the erection of a new structure on old foundations necessarily produces strains and weak spots" (see also Sherman et al., 1978; Sherman, 1979).

Police Accountability

Closely related to police-community relations is the issue of police accountability. In recent years, there has been increased concern with the procedures for filing complaints against the police, the creation of "external" mechanisms for civilian review of the police, and police misconduct.

Citizen Complaints against the Police

Caiden and Hahn (1979: 169–70) note that "it is a premise of democratic society that citizens should have the right to complain against public officials in their official capacity in exercising the powers entrusted to them by the community." Citizen complaints against the police generally involve allegations of officer dereliction of duty, such as the excessive use of force or disrespectful behaviour. While provincial police commissions and municipal police boards have played a major role in establishing complaint procedures, considerable diversity exists in the systems that are in place across the country.

The complaint system in British Columbia, encompassing four stages, is illustrative of the review systems currently in operation in Canada. Initially, an attempt is made to resolve the complaint informally between the officer and the complainant. The majority of complaints against the police are resolved in this fashion. For those cases not resolved informally, a police investigation and disciplinary hearing may occur. The third and fourth stages involve the complaint being brought before the municipal police board and the British Columbia Police Commission. Figure 5.2 illustrates the disposition of the 1,122 complaints brought against RCMP and municipal police officers in the Province of British Columbia during 1985.[18]

There are also complaint systems that involve an ombudsman and external review boards. In Metropolitan Toronto, the Public Complaints Commissioner oversees the police handling of complaints and may intercede in the investigation at any time. Should a citizen be dissatisfied with the outcome of the police investigation into the complaint, a public inquiry may be held before a 24-person tribunal (civilian review board), comprised of judges, lawyers, police, and citizens. In cases of serious misconduct, the board may dismiss the officer from the force, while a finding of responsibility for lesser offences may result in a period of suspension. Legislation establishing the office of the Public Complaints Commissioner was enacted in 1981, and in 1986, a Bill was tabled in the Ontario Legislature to permit other municipalities in the province to create a similar review process (see Lewis, Linden, and Keene, 1986).

The creation of civilian review boards such as the Toronto tribunal is an attempt to provide for the external review of police activities, although Lundman (1980: 181), in assessing the impact of these structures on North American policing, argues, "Police . . . have long and successfully resisted attempts to create effective civilian review." Line-level officers and police administrators are generally opposed to civilian review on the grounds that the public does not understand the complexities of police work and is therefore not in a position to evaluate police conduct (see Jolin and Gibbons, 1984).

FIGURE 5.2
COMPLAINTS AGAINST THE ROYAL CANADIAN MOUNTED POLICE AND MUNICIPAL POLICE DEPARTMENTS — BRITISH COLUMBIA, 1985.

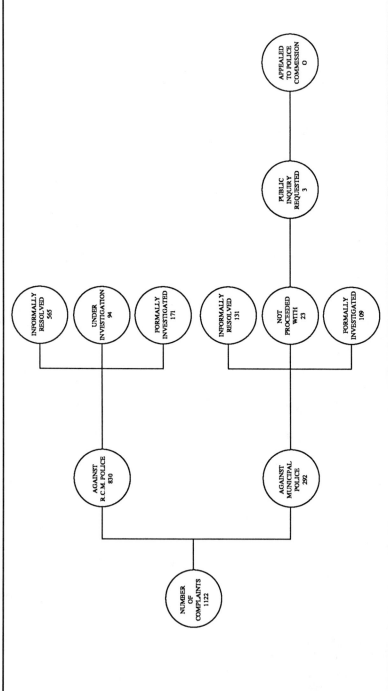

Source: British Columbia Police Commission. *Annual Report. 1985/86* (Victoria: Queen's Printer, 1986), p. 10.

This resistance and the difficulties encountered by "outside" reform groups are poignantly illustrated by the experience of a civilian review board in Metropolitan Toronto called the Citizens' Independent Review of Police Activities. CIRPA's formation was precipitated by allegations of police misconduct and was to provide a mechanism for community and minority groups to pressure the police and local government on issues related to alleged police misconduct.

In a unique and insightful study, McMahon and Ericson (1984: 34) trace the origins and operation of CIRPA as an "outside reform group," noting that, initially, the position of CIRPA vis-à-vis the policing authorities was "antagonistic and oppositional." Over time, however, the role of CIRPA became more characterized by cooperation and compromise. McMahon and Ericson argue that this transformation was due in large measure to the groups' search for legitimacy and credibility: "CIRPA changed its strategies in order to try and legitimate the existence of the organization itself and hence the status of its calls for reforming police. In the process CIRPA necessarily became co-opted by the state system for policing reform" (p. 91).

The RCMP has traditionally been even more resistant to external review of its internal policies and procedures than have municipal police agencies. In 1986, amendments to the *Royal Canadian Mounted Police Act* resulted in the creation of two external boards of review. The Public Complaints Commission will review complaints made by citizens against members of the RCMP who are policing under contract. The External Review Committee will hear appeals from regular members who have been disciplined for an infraction of force regulations. The creation of external review mechanisms for complaints and internal disciplinary decisions in the RCMP was first recommended by a commission of inquiry under the chairmanship of Judge Rene Marin (1976) ten years earlier.

Police Wrongdoing

While Canadians have long assumed that organizational police deviance and wrongdoing are confined to police departments in the United States, several inquiries into the activities of municipal police forces and the RCMP have challenged this perception. Without delving into an extensive discussion of police corruption, it is critical that we examine, albeit briefly, several of these inquiries and their major findings (see Ericson, 1981; Ellis, 1987).

In 1976, in response to increasing tensions between citizens and the police in Toronto, a Royal Commission was created under the direction of Mr. Justice Donald Morand to investigate police practices. More specifically, the commission was charged with investigating allegations of excessive use of force in the apprehension, arrest, and detention of several citizens in the community and determining whether the use of force was a widespread practice in the department. The commission also examined the complaint procedure and the manner in which citizen allegations arising from specific incidents were handled.

The Morand inquiry found evidence that excessive force was often used by Metropolitan Toronto Police officers. Further, police officers called to testify before the commission often gave false evidence in an attempt to protect fellow officers, Commissioner Morand (1976: 123) stating that "one of the most disturbing things which came out of the hearings was the extent to which I found the evidence of police officers mistaken, shaded, deliberately misleading, changing to suit the circumstances and sometimes entirely and deliberately false." Among the recommendations of the Morand report (1976: 266–72) were that a citizen complaint procedure, independent of the police, be created and that the use of force by officers be carefully monitored by the department.

In 1977, a Commission of Inquiry under Mr. Justice M. J. McQuaid, was appointed to investigate various allegations of misconduct among members of the Charlottetown, Prince Edward Island police department. The allegations had been made by police recruits in training, who had observed members on duty. The commission found many irregularities in the performance of officers in the department, including sleeping on duty, the practice of officers keeping confiscated liquor, drinking while on duty, as well as numerous internal difficulties within the force that resulted in low morale among the officers.

While the Morand report (1976) and the lesser known report of the McQuaid Commission (1977) provided key insights into police misconduct in two municipal departments, the three reports of the Commission of Inquiry Concerning Certain Activities of the Royal Canadian Mounted Police (McDonald, 1980, 1981a, 1981b) (more commonly known as the McDonald Commission) constitute the most significant materials on illegal police practices in Canada.

Created by an order-in-council, the mandate of the McDonald Commission was to investigate activities of the RCMP that were not authorized or provided for by law and to report on the policies and procedures that govern the activities of the RCMP in the discharge of their duties. In its reports, the commission examined in detail activities engaged in by the RCMP Security Service that were either contrary to the provisions of the *Royal Canadian Mounted Police Act* or illegal. As well, the commission examined the extent to which senior government officials and Ministers were aware of these activities. The reports also contained the commission's view of the factors to be considered by authorities in determining whether certain individuals should be prosecuted for their activities.

Areas investigated by the commission included surreptitious entry, the use of electronic surveillance, the opening of mail by the RCMP, activities of the RCMP during and after the October Crisis in Quebec during the years 1970–1972, and specific operations including "Operation Ham," the "Keller Mail Incident," the "Northstar Inn Incident," and "Checkmate."[19] From its investigation, the commission concluded that there were numerous instances in which members of the RCMP intentionally deceived those with constitutional or jurisdictional authority over them and engaged in activities that were illegal.[20]

The reports of the McDonald Commission provided the impetus for the passage of Bill C-9, which created the Canadian Security Intelligence Service (CSIS). This civilian agency, separate from the RCMP, is responsible for all foreign and domestic intelligence and security. It is noteworthy that 95% of the members of the RCMP Security Service chose to transfer to the new agency (Security Intelligence Review Committee, 1986: 19). The activities of the CSIS are overseen by the Security Intelligence Review Committee, which was created by the *Canadian Security Intelligence Act* (1984).

Three years after its creation, however, CSIS was experiencing considerable organizational and operational difficulties. In 1986, many of the CSIS officers returned to the RCMP under a special "bridge-back" provision, due to internal organizational difficulties and low morale. Further, the third report of the Security Intelligence Review Committee (1986) noted that there remained a considerable amount of professional jealousy and tension between the RCMP and CSIS, and concerns were raised about the counter-subversion activities of the agency.[21] In response to these concerns, the Solicitor General appointed an independent advisory team to examine in greater detail elements of the organizational structure and operation of CSIS. In its report (Solicitor General of Canada, 1987), the advisory team outlined a number of recommendations designed to correct deficiencies in the recruitment, training, and management of personnel and in the collection and utilization of intelligence information.

While the McDonald Commission inquiry provided an unprecedented examination of the activities of the RCMP and other agencies of government, Hogarth (1982: 113) has argued that Canadians are relatively unconcerned about police misconduct. Public opinion polls during the McDonald Commission inquiry revealed that a majority of Canadians did not view the allegations of wrongdoing in a serious light. This is due in large measure to the historical image of the RCMP, discussed in Chapter 3 (see also Mandel, 1982; Penner, 1979; Taylor, 1986).

Lee (1981) argues that the RCMP, in particular, have been successful in avoiding being labelled as having engaged in misconduct or deviance. Among the reasons for this avoidance are the traditional Canadian deference to authority and the trust that Canadians have in bureaucracies. Any unlawful actions of the police are believed to be justified to protect law, order, and national security (see also Brodeur, 1981). As Hogarth (1982:

113) notes: "... the majority of the Canadian public appear not only to support the police but to be unconcerned about what they believe to be isolated instances of overzealousness in the interest of a good cause."

In discussing the issue of police accountability in Canada, Hogarth (1982: 113) notes that the dilemma "is to try and ensure the accountability of the police and at the same time protect the police from unwarranted political interference in their day to day professional decisions and discharge of their duties." To accomplish this, Hogarth offers the following suggestion:

> We must set out, in the most precise and concrete terms possible, the lines of authority and responsibility for managing the police function in Canadian society. It should be a framework which gives the civilian authority all the workable controls that are necessary to ensure that police practice conforms to the social and political goals of the government ... At the same time, the day-to-day exercise of discretion of individual police officers must be safeguarded in situations where control is neither feasible nor desirable. [Pp. 120–21]

NOTES

1. For an overview of research on police effectiveness in North America, see Koenig et al. (1983a); Woods (1981).

2. Research in Canada and the United States has also focused on the investigative function carried out by detectives, and the results have raised serious questions about the efficacy of the methods employed in the process of criminal investigation. See Chappell, Gordon, and Moore (1982); Banks (1984); Greenwood and Petersillia (1975).

3. For a discussion of the theoretical, organizational and operational differences between watch policing and team policing, see Talarico and Swanson (1980). Radelet (1986: 483) has pointed out that the term *team policing* has been used to describe such a wide variety of policing patterns that "what is called team policing in one place is quite different from what is called by this name in another place."

4. Talarico and Swanson (1980: 21) take issue with those police observers who argue that the police are resistant to change, arguing that "police have exhibited a willingness to employ new programmatic responses to combat crime — particularly in the recent decade." However, from their comparative analysis of police departments operating on a traditional model with one organized around team policing, the authors conclude that "initially the implementation of team policing in large departments may produce short-run changes in organizational form, processes, and member perceptions of the agency. Over a period of years, however, the net result may ultimately be an altered organizational form which has been corrupted by the 'staying power' of traditional bureaucracy" (p. 28).

5. For an overview of community-based policing, including a discussion of team policing experiments in Canadian and United States police departments, the difficulties encountered in implementing team policing, and the potential for team policing in Canada, see Manning (1984); Murphy and Muir (1985); Wasson (1984).

6. Revett (1984: 84–85) notes that the Vancouver City Police Department retains many of the programs and training components that were developed under team policing, and concurs with the conclusion of Talarico and Swanson (1980) that the implementation of team policing may meet with greater success in smaller departments.

7. For an extensive discussion of the social changes in Canadian society that are likely to have an impact on crime and policing, as well as the intervention strategies that the police might develop to address these changes, see Koenig, DeBeck, and Laxton (1983); Koenig and DeBeck (1983).

8. For a discussion of organizational development and police productivity, see Souryal (1985).

9. Concern with the relations between the police and ethnic minorities, particularly blacks and native Indians, precipitated the creation of race relations committees and commissions of inquiry in cities such as Toronto and Regina. For a discussion of police-minority relations in Ontario, see Cryderman and O'Toole (1986).

10. In an evaluation of the community relations programs and public evaluations of the police in 14 United States cities, however, Decker, Smith, and Uhlman (1979) found no relation between such programs and public evaluations of the police, suggesting that such programs in themselves may not be sufficient to increase police-citizen interaction and cooperation.

11. The School Liaison Program is one component of the Saint John Youth Project, a preventive policing project initiated by the Saint John City Police in 1978. The police also operate a Diversion Program, which utilizes alternatives such as restitution and work agreements for youths in conflict with the law. The third component of the project is the Community Support Program, which recruits volunteers to increase community involvement in the project's activities. For a description of the Saint John Youth Project, see Lajeunesse (1982).

12. For a discussion of the issues surrounding non-residential and residential police school-programs, see Griffiths (1982).

13. For a discussion of CPTED, see Moffat (1983); Newman (1976); Stanley (1977).

14. See Normandeau and Hasenpusch (1980) for a discussion of possible criteria for measuring the success of crime prevention programs.

15. For a discussion of the selection and training of police officers in the Province of British Columbia, see Taylor (1983).

16. For concise discussions of the issues surrounding the professionalization of the police, see Baker et al. (1979); Muir (1982); Radelet (1986).

17. It is important at this juncture to distinguish between training and education. Blake (1981: 83) delineates the two by noting that "training is skill learning, whereas education is concerned not only with how, but also with why."

18. For an analysis and discussion of citizen complaints against the police in Metropolitan Toronto, see Henshel (1983).

19. For additional perspectives on the activities of the RCMP Security Service, see French and Beliveau (1979); Filder (1978).

20. A federal/provincial committee (McLeod, 1983) subsequently examined many of the recommendations of the McDonald inquiry. In considering whether legislation was required to avoid the instances of wrongdoing documented by the McDonald Commission, the committee (1983: 1) took strong issue with both the findings and the methodology of the McDonald report and concluded generally that either no formal legislative action was required to constrain the activities of the police or areas of concern could appropriately be addressed by new policy directives. Taylor (1986) and Mandel (1982) discuss the government's attempt to discredit the report and findings of the McDonald Commission (see also Way, 1985).

21. In a critique of the legislation establishing CSIS, Russell (1983) anticipated many of the difficulties that the new agency has encountered.

REFERENCES

A.R.A. Consultants. 1985. *Final Report on the Evaluation of the Toronto Mini-station Pilot Project*. Ottawa: Solicitor General of Canada.

Baker, R., F. A. Meyer, and D. Rudoni. 1979. "Police Professionalism: The Need for Clarity." In *Evaluating Alternative Law-Enforcement Policies*, edited by R. Baker and F. A. Meyer, 99–111. Lexington, Mass.: D. C. Heath.

Banks, L. W. 1984. "Case Screening: A Study of Police Decision Making." M.A. thesis. Burnaby, B.C.: School of Criminology, Simon Fraser University.

Bell, D. J. 1982. "Policewomen: Myths and Reality." 10 *Journal of Police Science and Administration* 112–20.

Blake, J. A. 1981. "The Role of Police in Society." In *The Police Function in Canada*, edited by W. T. McGrath and M. P. Mitchell, 77–84. Toronto: Methuen Publications.

Bloch, P., and D. Anderson. 1974. *Policewomen on Patrol: Final Report*. Washington, D.C.: Police Foundation.

Boostrom, R. L., and J. H. Henderson. 1983. "Community Action and

Crime Prevention: Some Unresolved Issues." 19 *Crime and Social Justice* 24–30.

Bowers, W. J., and J. H. Hirsch. 1987. "The Impact of Foot Patrol Staffing on Crime and Disorder in Boston: An Unmet Promise." 6 *American Journal of Police* 17–44.

Boydstun, J. E., M. E. Sherry, and N. P. Moelter. 1977. *Patrol Staffing in San Diego: One-or-Two Officer Units.* Washington, D.C.: Police Foundation.

Brantingham, P. J., and F. L. Faust. 1976. "A Conceptual Model of Crime Prevention." 22 *Crime and Delinquency* 284–96.

Brodeur, J.-P. 1981. "Legitimizing Police Deviance." In *Organizational Police Deviance*, edited by C. D. Shearing, 127–60. Toronto: Butterworths.

Caiden, G., and H. Hahn. 1979. "Public Complaints against the Police." In *Evaluating Alternative Law-Enforcement Policies*, edited by R. Baker and F. A. Meyer, 169–76. Lexington, Mass.: D. C. Heath.

Calgary Police Service. 1977. *A Report on Zone Policing.* Calgary: Planning Branch, Calgary Police Service.

Canadian Centre for Justice Statistics. 1984. 4 *Juristat Service Bulletin.* Ottawa: Supply and Services Canada.

_____. 1988. *Canadian Crime Statistics, 1987.* (Catalogue No. 85-205.) Ottawa: Supply and Services Canada.

Canyltec Social Research Corporation. 1987. *An Evaluation of Two Approaches to Delivery of Police-Based Victim Assistance: Neighborhood-Focussed vs. Headquarters-Based.* Ottawa: Solicitor General of Canada.

Chappell, D., R. Gordon, and R. Moore. 1982. "Criminal Investigation: A Selective Literature Review and Bibliography." 6 *Canadian Police College Journal* 13–64.

Cryderman, B. K., and C. N. O'Toole. 1986. *Police, Race and Ethnicity: A Guide for Law Enforcement Officers.* Toronto: Butterworths.

Decker, S. H., R. L. Smith, and T. M. Uhlman. 1979. "Does Anything Work? An Evaluation of Urban Police Innovations." In *Evaluating Alternative Law-Enforcement Policies*, edited by R. Baker and F. A. Meyer, 43–54. Lexington, Mass.: Lexington Books.

Elie, D., and A. Kapetanaki-Barake. 1985. "The Impact of the Police Response on the Evolution of Crimes of Violence." 18 *Criminologie* 47–61.

Ellis, D. 1987. *The Wrong Stuff — An Introduction to the Sociology of Deviance.* Don Mills, Ont.: Collier Macmillan.

Ericson, R. V. 1981. "Rules for Police Deviance." In *Organizational Police Deviance: Its Structure and Control*, edited by C. D. Shearing, 83–110. Toronto: Butterworths.

Esbensen, F.-A. 1987. "Foot Patrols: Of What Value?" 6 *American Journal of Police* 45–65.

Fidler, R. 1978. *RCMP — The Real Subversives.* Toronto: Vanguard Publications.

Fischer, R. J., Kathryn M. Golden, and Bruce L. Heininger. 1985. "Issues in Higher Education for Law Enforcement Officers: An Illinois Study." 13 *Journal of Criminal Justice* 329–38.

Formby, W. A., and J. O. Smykla. 1981. "Citizen Awareness in Crime Prevention: Do They Really Get Involved?" 9 *Journal of Police Science and Administration* 398–403.

French, R., and A. Beliveau. 1979. *The RCMP and the Management of National Security.* Toronto: Butterworths.

Greenwood, P. W., and J. Petersillia. 1975. *The Criminal Investigation Process.* New York: The Rand Corporation.

Griffiths, C. T. 1982. "Police School Programs: The Realities of the Remedy." 24 *Canadian Journal of Criminology* 329–40.

Hatry, H. P. 1975. "Wrestling with Police Crime Control Productivity Measurement." In *Readings on Police Productivity*, edited by J. L. Wolfle and J. F. Heaphy, 86–128. Washington, D.C.: Police Foundation.

Henshel, R. L. 1983. *Police Misconduct in Metropolitan Toronto: A Study of Formal Complaints.* Toronto: LaMarsh Research Programme on Violence, York University.

Hickling-Johnston. 1982. *Metropolitan Toronto Police Management Study: Productivity Improvements — Delivery of Cost Efficient Police Services to Metropolitan Toronto Citizens.* Toronto: Hickling-Johnston, Ltd.

Hogarth, J. 1982. "Police Accountability." In *The Maintenance of Order in Society*, edited by R. Donelan, 111–25. (Catalogue No. JS66-2/1982E.) Ottawa: Supply and Services Canada. Reproduced with permission of the Minister of Supply and Services Canada, 1989.

Homant, R. J. 1983. "The Impact of Policewomen on Community Attitudes toward the Police." 11 *Journal of Police Science and Administration* 16–22.

Hylton, J. H., Rae Matanovich, James Varro, and Bijal Thakker. 1979. *Job Satisfaction in the Regina Police Department.* Regina, Sask.: Regina Police Department.

Jobson, J. D., and R. Schneck. 1982. "Constituent Views of Organizational Effectiveness: Evidence from Police Organizations." 25 *Academy of Management Journal* 25–46.

Johnson, T. A., G. E. Misner, and L. P. Brown. 1981. *The Police and Society: An Environment for Collaboration and Confrontation.* Englewood Cliffs, N.J.: Prentice-Hall.

Jolin, A. I., and D. C. Gibbons. 1984. "Policing the Police: The Portland Experience." 12 *Journal of Police Science and Administration* 315-22.

Kelling, G. L. 1978. "The Role of Research in Maximizing Police Productivity." In *Report of the Proceedings-Workshop on Police Productivity and Performance*, edited by P. Engstad and M. Lioy, 196-207. Ottawa: Solicitor General of Canada.

Kelling, G. L., T. Pate, D. Dieckman, and C. E. Brown. 1974. *The Kansas City Preventive Patrol Experiment: A Summary Report.* Washington, D.C.: Police Foundation.

Kelling, G. L., et al. 1981. *The Newark Foot Patrol Experiment.* Washington, D.C.: Police Foundation.

Kerber, K. W., Steven M. Nades, and Michele D. Mittler. 1977. "Citizen Attitudes Regarding the Competence of Female Police Officers." 5 *Journal of Police Science and Administration* 337-47.

Kessler, D. A. 1985. "One- or Two Officer Cars? A Perspective from Kansas City." 13 *Journal of Criminal Justice* 49-64.

Koenig, D. J., E. P. DeBeck, and J. Laxton. 1983. "Routine Activities, Impending Social Change, and Policing." 7 *Canadian Police College Journal* 96-136.

Koenig, D. J., and E. P. DeBeck. 1983. "Proactive Police Intervention and Imminent Social Change." 7 *Canadian Police College Journal* 310-28.

Lab, S. P. 1984. "Police Productivity: The Other Eighty Percent." 12 *Journal of Police Science and Administration* 297-302.

Lajeunesse, T. 1982. *The Saint John Youth Project.* Ottawa: Minister of Supply and Services.

Lee, J. A. 1981. "The RCMP's Real Dilemma." 6 *Canadian Journal of Sociology* 33-52.

Lewis, C. E., S. B. Linden, and J. Kenne. 1986. "Public Complaints against Police in Metropolitan Toronto — This History and Operation of the Office of the Public Complaints Commissioner." 29 *Criminal Law Quarterly* 115-44.

Linden, R. 1980. *Women in Policing: A Study of the Vancouver Police Department.* Ottawa: Solicitor General of Canada.

————. 1983. "Women in Policing: A Study of Lower Mainland R.C.M.P. Detachments." 7 *Canadian Police College Journal* 217-29.

————. 1985. "Attrition among Male and Female Members of the RCMP." 9 *Canadian Police College Journal* 86-97.

Linden, R., and C. Minch. 1982. *Women in Policing: A Review.* Ottawa: Solicitor General of Canada.

Lord, L. K. 1986. "A Comparison of Male and Female Peace Officers' Stereotypic Perceptions of Women and Women Peace Officers." 14 *Journal of Police Science and Administration* 83-97.

Loree, D., and C. Murphy. 1987. *Community Policing in the 1980's: Recent Advances in Police Programs.* Ottawa: Supply and Services Canada.

Lundman, R. J. 1980. *The Police and Policing: An Introduction.* New York: Holt, Rinehart, and Winston.

Mandel, M. 1982. "Discrediting the McDonald Commission." 61 *Canadian Forum* 14-17.

Manning, P. K. 1984. "Community Policing." 3 *American Journal of Police* 205–27.

Marin, R. C. (Chairman). 1976. *Report of the Commission of Inquiry Relating to Public Complaints, Internal Discipline and Grievance Procedure within the Royal Canadian Mounted Police.* Ottawa: Information Canada.

Martin, S. E. 1979. *"Police* women and Police*women*: Occupational Role Dilemmas and Choices of Female Officers." 7 *Journal of Police Science and Administration* 314–23.

McDonald, Mr. Justice D. C. (Chairman). 1980. *Commission of Inquiry Concerning Certain Activities of the Royal Canadian Mounted Police. First Report. Security and Information.* Ottawa: Supply and Services Canada.

————. 1981a. *Commission of Inquiry Concerning Certain Activities of the Royal Canadian Mounted Police. Second Report. Freedom and Security under the Law.* Ottawa: Supply and Services Canada.

————. 1981b. *Commission of Inquiry Concerning Certain Activities of the Royal Canadian Mounted Police. Third Report. Certain R.C.M.P. Activities and the Question of Governmental Knowledge.* Ottawa: Supply and Services Canada.

McGahan, P. 1984. *Police Images of a City.* New York: Peter Lang.

McGinnis, J. H. 1985a. "Career Development in Municipal Policing: Part I." 9 *Canadian Police College Journal* 154–206.

————. 1985b. "Career Development in Municipal Policing: Part II." 9 *Canadian Police College Journal* 254–94.

McLeod, R. M. (Chairman). 1983. *Report of the Federal/Provincial Committee of Criminal Justice Officials with Respect to the McDonald Commission Report.* Ottawa: Solicitor General of Canada.

McMahon, M. W., and R. V. Ericson. 1984. *Policing Reform: A Study of the Reform Process and Police Institution in Toronto.* Toronto: Centre of Criminology, University of Toronto.

McQuaid, Mr. Justice M. J. (Commissioner). 1977. *Report of the Commission of Inquiry into Matters Pertaining to the Charlottetown Police Force.* Charlottetown, P.E.I.: Queen's Printer.

Meuser, P. 1976. *An Assessment of the Burnaby R.C.M.P. Project Operation Identification.* Vancouver: British Columbia Police Commission.

Moffatt, R. E. 1983. "Crime Prevention through Environmental Design — A Management Perspective." 25 *Canadian Journal of Criminology* 19–31.

Moore, M. H., and G. L. Kelling. 1983. " 'To Serve and Protect': Learning From Police History." 70 *The Public Interest* 49–65.

Morand, Mr. Justice D. R. (Commissioner). 1976. *The Royal Commission into Metropolitan Toronto Police Practices.* Toronto: Queen's Printer.

Muir, R. G. 1982. "Considerations in Educating the Police." M.A. thesis. Burnaby, B.C.: School of Criminology, Simon Fraser University.

Murphy, C. 1985. *Assessing Police Performance: Issues, Problems, and Alternatives.* Ottawa: Solicitor General of Canada.

Murphy, C., and R. G. Muir. 1985. *Community-Based Policing: A Review of the Critical Issues.* Ottawa: Solicitor General of Canada.

Niederhoffer, A. 1967. *Behind the Shield: The Police in Urban Society.* Garden City, N.Y.: Doubleday Books.

Newman, O. 1976. *Defensible Space: Crime Prevention through Urban Design.* New York: Macmillan Publishing Co.

Normandeau, A., and B. Hasenpusch. 1980. "Prevention Programs and Their Evaluation." 22 *Canadian Journal of Criminology* 307–19.

Ontario Ministry of the Solicitor General. 1986. *Report on the Study of Female Police Officers, Ontario Regional and Municipal Police Forces.* Toronto: Ontario Ministry of the Solicitor General.

Ontario Provincial Police. 1978. *Policewoman Program Report.* Toronto.

Palys, T. S., E. O. Boyanowsky, and D. G. Dutton. 1983. *A Behavioural Evaluation of the Vancouver Police Department's Mobile Radio Data System.* Burnaby, B.C.: Criminology Research Centre, Simon Fraser University.

———. 1984. "Mobile Data Access Terminals and Their Implications for Policing." 40 *Journal of Social Issues* 113-27.

Penner, N. 1979. "How the RCMP Got Where It Is." In *The R.C.M.P. vs. The People,* edited by W. Edward Mann and John Alan Lee, 107–21. Don Mills, Ontario: General Publishing Co.

Pullyblank, J. 1986. *The Victim Services Unit of the Edmonton Police Department: An Evaluation.* Ottawa: Solicitor General of Canada.

Radelet, L. A. 1986. *The Police and the Community.* 4th ed. New York: Macmillan.

Revitt, J. 1984. "A Study of Police Officer Attitudes towards Team Policing in Vancouver." Unpublished paper. Burnaby, B.C.: School of Criminology, Simon Fraser University.

Rosenbaum, D. P. 1987. "The Theory and Research behind Neighborhood Watch: Is It a Sound Fear and Crime Prevention Strategy?" 33 *Crime and Delinquency* 103–34.

Rossum, R. A. 1978. *The Politics of the Criminal Justice System: An Organizational Analysis.* New York: Marcel Dekker.

Russell, P. H. 1983. "The Proposed Charter for a Civilian Intelligence Agency: An Appraisal." 9 *Canadian Public Policy* 326–37.

Security Intelligence Review Committee. 1986. *Annual Report, 1985–86.* Ottawa: Supply and Services Canada.

Sherman, L. W. 1979. "College Education for Police: The Reform That Failed?" 1 *Police Studies* 32–38.

———. 1986. "Policing Communities: What Works?" In *Crime and Justice: A Review of Research.* Vol. 8, edited by A. J. Reiss and M. Tonry, 343–86. Chicago: University of Chicago Press.

Sherman, L. W., and The National Advisory Commission on Higher

Education for Police Officers. 1978. *The Quality of Police Education: A Critical Review with Recommendations for Improving Programs in Higher Education.* San Francisco: Jossey-Bass Publishers.

Sichel, J. L., L. N. Friedman, J. C. Quint, and M. E. Smith. 1978. *Women on Patrol: A Pilot Study of Police Performance in New York City.* Washington, D.C.: National Institute of Law Enforcement and Criminal Justice.

Silverman, R., and V. Sacco. 1981. "Selling Crime Prevention: The Evaluation of a Mass Media Campaign." 23 *Canadian Journal of Criminology* 191–202.

Smith, D. 1978. "Dangers of Police Professionalization: An Empirical Analysis." 6 *Journal of Criminal Justice* 199–216.

Solicitor General of Canada. 1983. "Sophistication and Support — Keys to Effective Policing." 8 *Liaison* 10–17.

――――. 1984a. "Liaison and Crime Analysis to Aid Zone Policing." 10 *Liaison* 15–19.

――――. 1984b. *Selected Trends in Canadian Justice.* Ottawa: Research and Statistics Group, Programs Branch.

――――. 1987. *People and Process in Transition. Report to the Solicitor General by the Independent Advisory Team on the Canadian Security Intelligence Service.* Ottawa: Supply and Services Canada.

Souryal, S. S. 1985. "Increasing Police Productivity through Organizational Development." 47 *RCMP Gazette* 1–11.

Stanley, P. R. A. 1977. *Crime Prevention through Environmental Design: A Review.* Ottawa: Solicitor General of Canada.

Swanson, C. R. 1983. "The Evolution, Practice, and Future of Productivity." 10 *Journal of Police Science and Administration* 326–34.

Szynkowski, L. J. 1981. "Preventive Patrol: Traditional versus Specialized." 9 *Journal of Police Science and Administration* 167–83.

Talarico, S. M., and C. R. Swanson. 1980. "The Limits of Team Policing?" 3 *Police Studies* 21–29.

Taylor, I. 1986. "Martrydom and Surveillance: Ideological and Social Practices of Police in Canada in the 1980s." 26 *Crime and Social Justice* 60–78.

Taylor, K. 1983. "The Selection and Training of Police Officers in British Columbia." 6 *Police Studies* 44–49.

Tornatzky, L. G., J. M. Wisenbaker, R. L. Green, G. W. Logan, H. P. Pachon, J. H. Schweitzer, and T. W. Tenbrunsel. 1978. "The Detroit Mini-station Program: An Evaluation." 6 *Journal of Police Science and Administration* 232–40.

Trojanowicz, R. C. 1983. "An Evaluation of a Neighborhood Foot Patrol Program." 11 *Journal of Police Science and Administration* 410–19.

Trojanowicz, R. C., and D. Banas. 1985. *Perceptions of Safety: A Comparison of Foot Patrol versus Motor Patrol Officers.* East Lansing,

Michigan: National Neighborhood Foot Patrol Center, Michigan State University.

Turk, A. 1987. "Popular Justice in Toronto: A Pilot Study." Unpublished paper. Toronto: Department of Sociology, University of Toronto.

Vogel, R., and R. Adams. 1983. "Police Professionalism: A Longitudinal Cohort Study." 11 *Journal of Police Science and Administration* 474–84.

Wasson, D. K. 1984. *Community-Based Preventive Policing: A Review.* Ottawa: Solicitor General of Canada.

Way, R. C. 1985. "The Law of Police Authority: The McDonald Commission and the McLeod Report." 9 *Dalhousie Law Journal* 683–723.

Wexler, J. G., and D. D. Logan. 1983. "Sources of Stress among Women Police Officers." 11 *Journal of Police Science and Administration* 46–53.

Wilson, J. Q. 1978. "Do the Police Prevent Crime?" In *Criminal Justice: Allies and Adversaries,* edited by John R. Snortum and Ilana Hadar. Pacific Palisades, Calif.: Palisades.

Woods, J. G. 1981. "The Implications of Recent Police Research." In *Ministry of the Solicitor General of Canada. Criminal Justice Research: A Selective Review,* 2–16. Ottawa: Supply and Services Canada.

LEGISLATION

Canadian Security Intelligence Service Act, S.C. 1984, c. 21; now R.S.C. 1985, c. C-23

Criminal Code, R.S.C. 1985, c. C-46

Royal Canadian Mounted Police Act, R.S.C. 1985, c. R-10

6 THE STRUCTURE AND OPERATION OF THE SYSTEM OF CRIMINAL COURTS IN CANADA

Introduction

The criminal courts occupy a special place at the heart of the criminal justice system.[1] The courts are responsible for determining the guilt or innocence of accused persons and are also charged with the task of imposing an appropriate sentence upon those who are convicted. In this sense, they are part of the vast criminal justice apparatus that plays a major part in maintaining social control in Canada. However, unlike the police or corrections components of the criminal justice system, the courts have a critical function to play in the protection of the rights of those individuals who become enmeshed in the criminal justice process. In this respect, the courts are responsible for monitoring the activities of the various agents of the criminal justice system with a view to enforcing the rights of accused persons. The courts are, therefore, responsible for protecting the rights of persons who may well be intensely unpopular in the arena of public opinion. As Friedenberg (1985: 417) notes:

> The law derives its moral authority, as distinct from its legal authority from its commitment to protect as well as to control or punish those who come before it and especially those whom public opinion would condemn.

The extent to which the courts should balance the competing demands of social control and protection of individual accused persons is a matter that will fuel continuing debate into the indefinite future. Suffice it to say that the advent of the *Charter* in 1982 has raised expectations that the courts will place considerably more emphasis on the protection of individual rights in the years immediately ahead (Friedenberg, 1985).

It is interesting to note that almost $424 million was expended by all levels of government in Canada for the operation of the court system in 1983–84. A further $91 million was expended on criminal prosecutions in the same fiscal year (Statistics Canada, 1985: 1). The provincial and territorial governments contributed some 81% of the cost of court operations, with the federal government contributing the remaining 19% (Statistics Canada, 1985: 2).[2] In spite of the central role of the courts in the system of criminal justice, it is significant that they receive a relatively small proportion of the total funds that are dedicated to criminal justice expenditures in Canada. For example, in 1980 court expenditures represented only 6% of federal expenditures on criminal justice; 27% of provincial and territorial expenditures; and only 2% of local government spending (Demers, 1984: 6–7). These percentages may be considered in light of the following total criminal justice spending figures for 1980: federal, $1,204 million; provincial, $1,353 million; and local, $1,267 million (Demers, 1984: 5). These figures raise some critical questions regarding whether enough priority is being given to the funding of Canada's court system.

The Structure of the System of Criminal Courts in Canada

The major objective of this chapter is to follow the progress of a criminal case through the various stages of the court process, from the laying of a charge right through to the final appeal that may be made. Before embarking on this particular journey, however, it is necessary to set the stage by outlining both the basic structure of the system of criminal courts and the nature of the classification of criminal offences in Canada.

In discussing the system of criminal courts that exists in Canada, it is always necessary to be aware of two important distinctions. First, there is a sharp distinction between the *trial* and the *appellate* functions of the courts. The trial function, as the name suggests, is concerned with the actual trial of criminal cases, while the appellate function is concerned with the hearing of appeals from the decisions of courts that are lower in the judicial hierarchy. It is important to recognize that, as we shall see shortly, some courts may exercise *both* trial and appellate functions in relation to criminal cases. The second distinction that should be noted is that between *provincial* and *federal* courts; in effect, there are two separate courts systems in Canada, with the Supreme Court of Canada serving as the tribunal of ultimate resort for both systems.

What is the nature of the system of *provincially* established courts in Canada? The *Constitution Act, 1867*[3] grants to the provinces the power to make laws in relation to "the Administration of Justice in the Province," and this power expressly includes the "Constitution, Maintenance, and Organization of Provincial Courts, both of Civil and of Criminal Jurisdiction."

Until recently, it was possible to identify a three-tiered court system in every province except Quebec[4] (Hogg, 1985: 134). This system consisted of (1) a *superior court*, which included a *court of appeal* as well as a *trial division*; (2) the *county* or *district courts*; and (3) the so-called inferior courts, which are now known as the *provincial courts*. However, beginning in the 1970s, there was a move in a number of provinces to amalgamate the county or district courts with the superior courts. The form that the amalgamation took was the abolition of the county or district courts and a consequent expansion of the jurisdiction of the superior courts (Hogg, 1985: 134). This process of amalgamation has occurred in five provinces (Alberta, Saskatchewan, Manitoba, New Brunswick, and Prince Edward Island). The county or district courts never existed in the Province of Quebec, so there are now only four provinces that maintain this intermediate tier in their court system; namely, British Columbia, Ontario, Nova Scotia, and Newfoundland. In other words, while these four provinces maintain a three-tiered system of courts, the majority of provinces now have only two tiers in their system of courts.

The precise name of the superior court varies from province to province (Waddams, 1987: 129). In Manitoba, Saskatchewan, Alberta, and New Brunswick, it is known as the *Court of Queen's Bench*, and in Quebec as the *Cour Superieur*. In Ontario, the superior court is technically known as the *High Court of Justice* (which, together with the Court of Appeal, constitutes the *Supreme Court*). In the other provinces, it is known as the *Supreme Court*, which, in some of these jurisdictions, is divided into a *trial division* and an *appellate division* (which would be called the Court of Appeal in the other provinces). The superior courts, as we shall soon see, try the more serious indictable offences and also hear appeals from the provincial courts in relation to summary conviction offences.

Where county or district courts exist, they try most of the more serious (indictable) offences, although the most serious offences of all (such as murder, treason, and piracy) may be tried only by the superior courts. The county or district courts may also hear most appeals from the provincial courts in relation to minor (summary conviction) offences.[5]

At the bottom of the hierarchy of courts in the provincial system are the so-called *Provincial Courts*. These courts deal with an enormous workload of criminal cases. In fact, all criminal cases enter the provincial courts, and the vast majority are tried and finally disposed of there. The most serious criminal cases, however, will be tried in the higher courts (the superior courts, or if they exist, the county or district courts). Where the nature of the case is such that it cannot be tried in the provincial court, a judge of this court will hold a *preliminary inquiry* to determine whether there is enough evidence to warrant sending the accused for trial in a higher court. The provincial courts are also responsible for holding the great majority of bail hearings. The provincial courts are usually organized in a number of separate divisions, or in some provinces, in separate courts. As far as criminal cases are concerned, it is necessary to be aware of the *Criminal Division* of the Provincial Court (which deals with offences committed by persons aged 18 or above), the *Family Division* (which, in addition to dealing with family issues, such as the maintenance and custody of children, deals with certain *Criminal Code* offences, such as assault of a spouse or of a child,[6] and the *Youth Court* (which deals with offences committed by young persons under the age of 18).

In each province, there is a court of appeal that sits above both the superior courts and the county or district courts in the judicial hierarchy. In British Columbia, Alberta, Saskatchewan, Manitoba, Ontario, Quebec and New Brunswick, it is known simply as the *Court of Appeal*. However, in Nova Scotia, Prince Edward Island, and Newfoundland, it is known as the *Appeal* or *Appellate Division* of the *Supreme Court* (Waddams, 1987: 129). Depending on the nature of the offence concerned, the courts of appeal may hear appeals from the superior courts, the county or district courts, and in some circumstances, from the provincial courts.

Under the Canadian Constitution (Hogg, 1985: 136–37), the federal government appoints and pays the judges of the "superior" courts (as well as the county or district courts, where these still exist).[7] On the other hand, the various provincial governments appoint and pay the judges of the "provincial" courts.[8]

Let us now turn our attention to the federal system of courts. The tribunal of last resort in Canada is the *Supreme Court of Canada*. Insofar as its criminal jurisdiction is concerned, the Supreme Court hears appeals from the provincial courts of appeal in relation to both indictable and summary conviction offences. Since the Supreme Court of Canada is a federal court, the justices are appointed by the federal government (albeit from lists prepared by the provinces), and the salaries of the justices and the operations of the court are paid for by the federal government.

There is another court in the federal system that should be mentioned at this point; this is the *Federal Court of Canada*, which is divided into a *Trial Division* and a *Court of Appeal*. The Federal Court is not involved in the trial of criminal cases, but it does deal with actions brought against the federal government and federal agencies and therefore may hear cases involving criminal justice agencies (such as the Correctional Service of Canada). In this respect, the Trial Division of the Federal Court of Canada may hear, for example, cases challenging the disciplinary practices of federal penitentiaries or the constitutionality of their regulations. Appeals from the decisions of the Trial Division may be made to the Federal Court of Appeal, from which the tribunal of last resort is the Supreme Court of Canada.

Before leaving our discussion of the basic structure of the criminal court system in Canada, there is one particularly important point that must be made; namely, that the *justices of the peace* play a critically important role in the criminal justice process in Canada. The office of justice of the peace has been in existence for more than 600 years in England (Stenning, 1986: 8). Indeed, justices of the peace originally tried most of the less serious criminal cases in England and still perform this function in that country to this day. In Canada, the major functions of the office of justice of the peace are to be found in the *pre-trial* process. All criminal charges are laid before a justice of the peace, who is also responsible for reviewing the status of those accused persons held in custody and, in most cases, has the power to release such persons on bail. The justice of the peace is also the official charged with the task of issuing search or arrest warrants to peace officers and may secure the attendance of an accused person at his or her trial by confirming the appearance notice issued by a peace officer or by issuing a summons. Furthermore, in many Canadian jurisdictions, the justices retain a judicial role in addition to their pre-trial functions. In some provinces and territories, they may try summary conviction offences in certain circumstances, although in order to do so they may be required to sit in groups of two or more.[9] In certain jurisdictions, they may also conduct the preliminary inquiries that are held in order to establish whether there is enough evidence to send an accused person to one of the higher courts (the superior or county/district courts) for trial on one of the more serious criminal charges. It is important to bear in mind the distinction between the jurisdiction of Provincial Court Judges and the jurisdiction of justices of the peace. Provincial Court Judges have all the powers of a justice of the peace *in addition* to those that flow from their appointment to the Provincial Court (such as the power to try all but the most serious criminal cases).[10] In other words, while Provincial Court Judges have all the powers of a justice of the peace, the converse is not true.

A rapid overview of the criminal court system in Canada may be gained by making reference to Figure 6.1.

The Classification of Offences

The classification of offences is a vital aspect of the procedure that dictates the manner in which cases flow through the criminal justice system in Canada (Atrens, 1985; Salhany, 1984; Shetreet, 1979: 71). The classification of offences determines, for example, the nature of the powers of arrest that the police may exercise in any specific case, the type of court before which the accused must be tried, whether the accused has any choice regarding the method of trial, the severity of the maximum penalty that may be imposed upon conviction, and the nature of the appeal process.

In 1892, the *Criminal Code* created three categories of criminal offence: (1) *summary conviction offences*; (2) *indictable offences*; and (3) so-called *"hybrid" offences*, which are both summary conviction and indictable offences. Summary conviction offences are the least serious and carry the most lenient penalties, while indictable offences are the most serious and carry the most severe penalties. The "dual" or "hybrid" offences lie somewhere between the other two categories of offence in terms of the scale of

FIGURE 6.1
THE CANADIAN CRIMINAL COURT SYSTEM

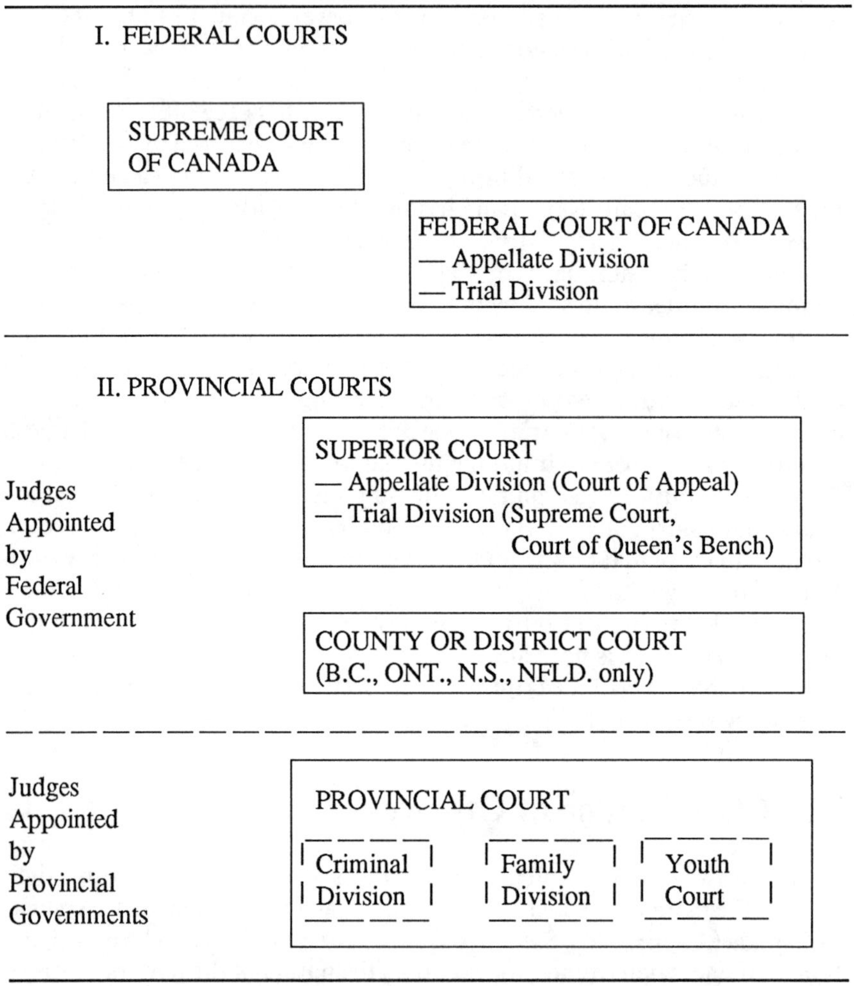

I. FEDERAL COURTS

> **SUPREME COURT OF CANADA**

> **FEDERAL COURT OF CANADA**
> — Appellate Division
> — Trial Division

II. PROVINCIAL COURTS

Judges
Appointed
by
Federal
Government

> **SUPERIOR COURT**
> — Appellate Division (Court of Appeal)
> — Trial Division (Supreme Court,
>   Court of Queen's Bench)

> **COUNTY OR DISTRICT COURT**
> (B.C., ONT., N.S., NFLD. only)

- -

Judges
Appointed
by
Provincial
Governments

> **PROVINCIAL COURT**
>
> | Criminal Division | Family Division | Youth Court |

Note: This chart presents a simplified overview of the criminal courts in Canada. As the text indicates, the precise names of the courts vary from province to province. The chart does not apply to the Province of Quebec.

seriousness (Atrens, 1985: I-6–8). Summary conviction offences may be tried only by a provincial court judge sitting alone. On the other hand, indictable offences may be tried in a number of different courts, depending on several factors, including the seriousness of the offence and the choice of the accused.

The category of "hybrid" offences has given rise to a considerable degree of concern because the prosecutor has the absolute discretion to decide whether a "hybrid" offence will be prosecuted by way of indictment or by way of summary conviction procedures. Cohen (1977: 140) has estimated that there are at least 30 sections in the *Criminal Code*, as well as provisions in some 40 other federal statutes, that create "hybrid" offences. Among the better known "hybrid" offences are theft and fraud under the value of $1,000, impaired driving or driving with more than 80 milligrams of alcohol per 100 millilitres of blood, assault, sexual assault, and assaulting a peace officer.

Until the prosecutor actually elects the method of trial that will be employed, a "hybrid" offence is *considered to be an indictable offence* (Salhany, 1984: 3). This is critical because it means that the police may exercise the expanded rights that exist in relation to indictable offences, and may require, for example, that suspects undergo fingerprinting and photographing in accordance with the *Identification of Criminals Act* (procedures that are not required for individuals charged with summary conviction offences).[11] Where the prosecutor fails to make an election and a trial proceeds in a court that has the jurisdiction to try summary conviction cases, then the general rule appears to be that the Crown will be deemed to have elected trial by summary conviction procedures.[12] The Crown may even change its mind and reverse its choice of procedure, as long as this is done before the trial actually commences.[13]

The right of the prosecutor to select the mode of trial in relation to "hybrid" offences represents a most powerful weapon in the prosecutor's armoury. The prosecutor's choice will effectively determine which set of procedural rules will apply to the case in question (Atrens, 1985: 1–17). Most dramatically, an election to proceed by way of indictment will expose the accused to the risk of a more severe penalty upon conviction. On the other hand, an election to proceed summarily may prevent the accused from choosing the method of trial (a right that exits in relation to a number of indictable offences).

Given the enormous degree of discretionary power vested in the prosecutor in relation to "hybrid" offences, it is somewhat surprising that the courts have shown an extreme reluctance to interfere with the exercise of that discretion. The courts have consistently held that it is not open to either the defence or the court to decide how a "hybrid" offence is to be dealt with (Stenning, 1986: 216). Indeed, it has been said in the Ontario Court of Appeal that:

The Crown Attorney, when exercising the discretion to prosecute by way of indictment, is acting as an officer of the Crown and performing a function inherent in the
office of the Attorney-General whose agent he is for that purpose. He is not acting
pursuant to a statutory power and is not exercising a statutory discretion and accordingly his decision is not subject to review by the Courts.[14]

Significantly, the advent of the *Charter* has apparently had little effect on
the courts' apparent unwillingness to interfere with the manner in which
the Crown exercises its power to choose the method of trial for "hybrid"
offences. Indeed, to date, the courts have rejected any *Charter* assaults
launched against the exercise of such discretion (see Ramsey, 1988; Vanek,
1988). In one case,[15] for example, the Ontario High Court ruled that the
accused's right, under section 11(a) of the *Charter*, to "be informed without
unreasonable delay of the specific offence," did not give him or her the
right to be informed in advance regarding how the Crown will elect to
proceed with a "hybrid" offence; indeed, it was ruled that the accused's
rights in this case were not infringed despite the fact that the Crown only
made its choice of procedure on the day of the trial. Similarly in another
case,[16] the Ontario Court of Appeal held that the accused's right to a trial by
jury where the maximum penalty is more than five years in prison (guaranteed by section 11(f) of the *Charter*) is not infringed by the Crown's power to
elect summary conviction procedures that do not permit the presence of a
jury. In this particular case, if the Crown had decided to proceed by
indictable procedures, then the accused would have had the option to select
trial by jury.

On the other hand, it appears that the courts are prepared to use the
doctrine of abuse of process to prevent the Crown from trying to change its
mind after a summary conviction trial has actually commenced solely in
order to avoid the effect of the limitation period that applies to summary
conviction cases. In an Ontario case,[17] the Crown had decided to proceed
on a charge of sexual assault by way of summary conviction procedures.
During the presentation of the Crown's evidence it became clear that the
events in question had occurred more than six months before the laying of
the information, and therefore the limitation period applicable to summary conviction offences barred prosecution in these circumstances. The
Crown withdrew the charge with the approval of the trial judge and
presented a new information with a view to proceeding by way of trial on
indictment (to which the limitation period would not apply). The Ontario
Court of Appeal held that the proceedings should be "stayed" (or terminated) on the basis that the Crown's actions constituted an abuse of the
court's process. The circumstances in this case were most unusual, given
that the trial had already started when the Crown sought to change its mind
regarding how to proceed in relation to a "hybrid" offence. However, it will
be interesting to see whether, in the future, the courts will be prepared to
exercise a greater degree of control over the Crown's discretion with respect

to the method of trial in "hybrid" offences, through use of the abuse of process doctrine.

This Ontario case demonstrates the important distinction to be drawn between summary conviction offences and indictable offences insofar as the question of imposing a time limit on the initiation of criminal proceedings is concerned. The *Criminal Code*[18] provides that summary conviction proceedings shall not be "instituted more than six months after the time when the subject-matter of the proceedings arose." There is no time limit, however, for the initiation of proceedings in relation to indictable offences. Of course, "hybrid" offences will be considered indictable offences for the purpose of this rule, although the Crown would be obliged to proceed by way of indictment should the six-month period have expired.

Setting the Ball Rolling: Bringing a Case to the Criminal Court

The essential first step in launching a prosecution against a suspect is the laying of an *information* before a justice of the peace (Atrens, 1986: IX-4).[19] The Supreme Court of Canada has referred to "the citizen's fundamental and historical right to inform under oath a justice of the peace of the commission of a crime,"[20] and it appears that the origins of this procedure may be traced back to early sixteenth century England (Stenning, 1986: 17). The *Criminal Code* provides that any one who "on reasonable grounds" believes that a person has committed an offence may lay an information in *writing and under oath* before a justice of the peace.[21] "Laying an information" basically means that an individual must present a formal, written accusation that an offence has been committed to a justice of the peace for the latter to sign (Salhany, 1984: 58). Of course, several different charges may well be contained in one information, although it is important to remember that each charge must be contained in a separate "count" (Atrens, 1986: IX-12). If insufficient details of the alleged offence appear in the information, it is possible that a court will rule that there has been a breach of section 11(a) of the *Charter*, which guarantees any person charged with an offence "the right to be informed without unreasonable delay of the specific offence."[22]

In practice, the informant is usually a peace officer, although there is nothing in the *Code* that requires that an information must be laid by someone acting in any sort of official capacity (Atrens, 1986: IX-7). In some jurisdictions, the police lay charges under the direct supervision of Crown counsel (the prosecutors), while in other jurisdictions, it appears that the police perform this function without much consultation with Crown counsel (except for the most serious cases).[23] Clearly, the choice of the specific charge(s) to lay is a critical one since it will determine how the particular case is dealt with in the criminal court system.

The justice of the peace is required to "receive" the sworn information, provided certain jurisdictional requirements are met; in other words, he or she has no discretion to refuse to receive it. However, once the information has actually been laid, then the justice of the peace does have the discretion to decide whether the accused will be required to appear in court for trial to answer the charge(s) laid against him or her. At this point, therefore, the justice of the peace is considered to be acting in a judicial capacity. The justice must hear the allegations of the informant and, if he or she thinks it is desirable or necessary to do so, may hear the evidence of witnesses.[24] However, this process is nothing like a criminal trial; indeed, the hearing is conducted *ex parte* or, in other words, in the absence of the accused person.

If the justice determines that the accused person should be required to attend court for a trial, then the question arises how the latter should be compelled to appear in court. In order to achieve this result, the justice may issues a *summons*, requiring that the accused attend for trial at a certain date and, if the offence is indictable, that he or she appear at a police station for photographing and fingerprinting under the *Identification of Criminals Act*. On the other hand, the justice may issue a warrant for the *arrest* of the accused, but this procedure is to be used only where there are "reasonable grounds to believe that it is necessary in the public interest to issue a warrant for the arrest of the accused."[25] Therefore, a justice is much more likely to compel the attendance of the accused by means of a summons than an arrest warrant.[26]

Now it may well be that the accused has already been given an appearance notice by a peace officer or has been arrested and then released by the officer in charge of the police lock-up. In the latter case, the officer in charge will have released the accused in one of two ways; either by obtaining the accused's *promise to appear* or by requiring that the accused enter into a *recognizance* (these terms are explained in the next section on bail). In these circumstances, once the information has been laid, the justice of the peace must decide whether to confirm the appearance notice, promise to appear, or recognizance or to cancel it and issue a summons or arrest warrant instead.[27]

The procedure for laying a charge and obtaining the accused person's attendance in court has been considerably simplified in the case of the vast number of traffic offences that arise under provincial motor vehicle legislation.[28] In place of the rather cumbersome procedure discussed above, a traffic ticket system has been instituted under which a traffic violator can be given a ticket and then given the opportunity to mail the penalty in to the court, unless he or she wishes to dispute liability. As Atrens (1986: IX-6) points out, the "traffic ticket fulfills the function of both information and summons" and, thus, significantly streamlines a system that might otherwise collapse under the strain of the flood of traffic violations that appear to be an inevitable consequence of a society that is dominated by the automobile.

Once the information has been laid, it may be that the accused person is still in police custody. At this point, the critical consideration is whether he or she should be granted bail. This is the subject of the next section. A general overview of the early stages of the criminal court process may be gained by referring to Figure 6.2.

The Bail Process

When the police have decided to arrest a suspect, or a justice of the peace has decided to issue a warrant for the arrest of a person who has been charged, the critical question arises whether the suspect or accused person should be detained in custody pending trial or whether he or she should be granted bail. The *Bail Reform Act*[29] has established a legal framework in which an accused person may be released from custody either by the officer in charge of a police lock-up, or by a justice of the peace or a judge at a formal bail hearing.

A lengthy period of pre-trial detention may well prove to be disastrous to accused persons, who may lose their jobs, thus rendering it impossible for them to fulfil their obligations to either their family or their community (Ouimet, 1969: 101–102). Furthermore, pre-trial incarceration may render it more difficult for accused persons to engage the services of a lawyer and to assist in the assembling of evidence for their defence (Hagan and Morden, 1981: 14). Particularly disturbing is the conclusion of a number of Canadian studies that the denial of bail to a suspect has a significant effect upon both the likelihood of a *conviction* and the *severity* of any sentence that is ultimately meted out (Friedland, 1965: 124; Hagan and Morden, 1981; Koza and Doob, 1975a; Doob and Cavoukian, 1977). For example, in a study conducted in Peel County, Ontario, Hagan and Morden (1981) found that being held for a bail hearing increased both the possibility of a conviction and the likelihood that, if convicted, the accused person would ultimately be incarcerated. It is not clear exactly how the suspect's bail status exerts such an impact upon the trial and sentencing processes; however, there is a strong possibility that an aura of suspicion may surround a defendant who appears in custody before the court and that this negative impression may well affect the outcome of the case (Koza and Doob, 1975a).

The *Bail Reform Act* was enacted primarily as a response to the recommendations of the Ouimet Committee (1969), which vigorously asserted that suspects should not be detained in custody unless it is necessary to do so as a means either of ensuring their appearance at trial or of protecting the public. In turn, the Ouimet Committee was strongly influenced by a major study conducted by Friedland (1965), who concluded that a considerable proportion of arrested suspects (40%) were being kept in custody pending their trial. It was therefore generally felt that reforms needed to be intro-

FIGURE 6.2
OVERVIEW OF THE LEGAL PROCESS

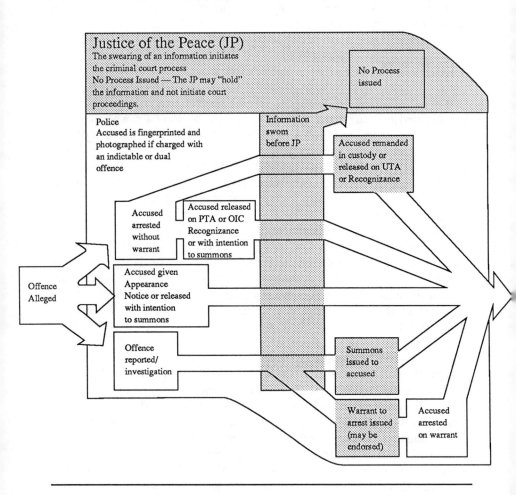

FIGURE 6.2
OVERVIEW OF THE LEGAL PROCESS

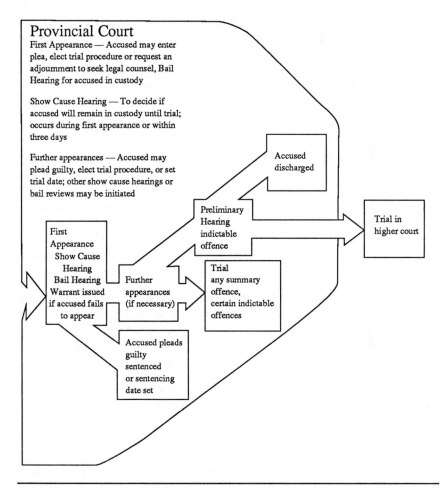

Provincial Court

First Appearance — Accused may enter plea, elect trial procedure or request an adjournment to seek legal counsel, Bail Hearing for accused in custody

Show Cause Hearing — To decide if accused will remain in custody until trial; occurs during first appearance or within three days

Further appearances — Accused may plead guilty, elect trial procedure, or set trial date; other show cause hearings or bail reviews may be initiated

First Appearance Show Cause Hearing Bail Hearing Warrant issued if accused fails to appear

Further appearances (if necessary)

Accused pleads guilty sentenced or sentencing date set

Accused discharged

Preliminary Hearing indictable offence

Trial any summary offence, certain indictable offences

Trial in higher court

Source: Legal Services Society of British Columbia, Ministry of the Attorney-General of British Columbia. Reprinted with permission.

duced in order to reduce the incidence of pre-trial detention in Canada, and hence the *Bail Reform Act* was explicitly conceived as a device for achieving this goal. Indeed, the very fact that the Act appeared to place stringent limitations on the power to detain suspects engendered a considerable degree of opposition among police officers at the time of its passage (Koza and Doob, 1977). Of course, since 1982 the application of the *Bail Reform Act* must be considered in light of the enactment of section 11(e) of the *Charter*, which guarantees the right of a person charged with an offence "not to be denied reasonable bail without just cause."

Release by the Officer in Charge of a Police Lock-up

As we saw in Chapter 4, the *Bail Reform Act* placed a police officer under a duty, in certain circumstances, to release a suspect whom he or she has arrested. However, if the police officer decides to keep the suspect in custody, then the officer in charge of the police lock-up is required to consider whether or not the suspect should be released. Indeed, as a general rule, where the offence with which the suspect is charged carries a penalty of imprisonment for five years or less,[30] then the officer in charge is under a duty to release the suspect "as soon as practicable" *unless*:

1. he or she has "reasonable grounds" to believe that it is necessary in the "public interest"[31] that the suspect be detained in custody, or
2. he or she has "reasonable grounds" to believe that if the suspect is released, the latter will fail to show up in court.[32]

There are four different methods by means of which the officer in charge may release a suspect from police custody. Indeed, the officer may

1. release the suspect with a view to compelling his or her attendance in court by way of a *summons*;
2. release the suspect upon the latter giving a *promise to appear* (which is accomplished by the suspect signing a formal document);
3. release the suspect upon the latter entering into a *recognizance* (or a formal acknowledgement of debt to the Crown) for any amount up to $500 without requiring any deposit;
4. release the suspect (if he or she does not ordinarily live in the province where the arrest occurred or within 200 kilometres of the place where he or she is being held in custody) upon the suspect's entering into a recognizance for any amount up to $500 and, if the officer in charge requires it, upon the suspect's depositing a sum of money or some other form of valuable security not exceeding $500 in value.[33]

Upon releasing the suspect, the officer in charge may require that he or she attend, at a subsequent date, to be fingerprinted or photographed in accordance with the provisions of the *Identification of Criminals Act*. If the suspect fails, without a lawful excuse, to attend for trial or to appear for the taking of fingerprints or photographs, then he or she may be guilty of an offence,[34] and any recognizance or security will be forfeited. In addition, a warrant may be issued for the arrest of the suspect.[35]

Hagan and Morden (1981) have pointed out that these provisions grant a considerable degree of discretionary power to the police. Indeed, they suggest that the *Bail Reform Act* "seems intentionally vague and ambiguous" (p. 10). In particular, the Act does not specify what types of circumstances may provide the officer in charge with "reasonable grounds" to conclude that the suspect would fail to attend for trial in the event of his or her release. These authors conducted research in Peel County, Ontario, in order to examine the variables that were associated with the refusal of the police to grant bail to a suspect. They found that prior convictions, prior incarceration, employment status, and the suspect's behaviour toward the police had a significant impact on the decision to release, as did the seriousness of the offence charged, the type of victim, whether a warrant had been issued and whether a statement had been taken. Hagan and Morden (p. 19) indicate that their finding that employment status affects the police decision to release a suspect gives rise to considerable concern. Indeed, taking account of this factor constitutes a significant way in which the criminal justice system may discriminate against the poor, even though there is little evidence to suggest that the unemployed are more likely to abuse the granting of bail. Furthermore, the impact of this form of discrimination may be compounded at a later stage of the criminal justice process because the accused's bail status appears to exert a significant impact upon the ultimate outcome of a criminal case (in terms of both verdict and sentence).

Another finding that is cause for concern is that suspects who were deemed to be "uncooperative" with the police were more likely to be retained in custody by the police. Hagan and Morden (1981: 19) consider this to be an example of "police deviance," insofar as the *Bail Reform Act* provides no legal basis for using the threat of detention as a means of making suspects more cooperative with the police or, alternatively, as a method of punishing those who are deemed to be uncooperative. This finding becomes even more troublesome in light of the observation by Ericson and Baranek (1982: 61) that the police may engage in so-called bail bargaining, in the course of which threats of continued detention or of police opposition to bail at a judicial hearing may be used as a device to extract confessions or information from a suspect in their custody.

Despite the philosophy of liberal release enshrined in the *Bail Reform Act*, it appears that the police nevertheless retain a considerable proportion of arrested suspects in their custody prior to their appearance before a justice or a provincial court judge. Indeed, Mackaay (1976: 8) conducted research immediately after the implementation of the *Bail Reform Act* in 1973, and found that some 53% of accused persons were in custody prior to their first appearance before the Montreal Municipal Court.

Release by a Justice or a Judge (Judicial Interim Release)

If the police decide not to release a suspect whom they have arrested, then the latter must, in normal circumstances, be brought before a justice or a provincial court judge within 24 hours of the arrest.[36] At this stage, the justice or judge may immediately consider the question of bail, although the proceedings may be adjourned for periods of up to three days, upon the application of the prosecutor or the accused.[37] Although the great majority of bail decisions are made by a justice or a provincial court judge, there are certain circumstances in which only a judge of the superior court of criminal jurisdiction may release an accused person on bail.[38] More specifically, only a superior court judge may release a suspect who has been charged with such serious offences as murder, treason, sedition, and piracy.[39]

Bail hearings are called show cause hearings because either the prosecutor or the accused must "show cause" why the latter should not, or should be, released, as the case may be.[40] In the vast majority of cases, the *Bail Reform Act*[41] clearly places the burden of justifying the continued detention of the accused squarely upon the shoulders of the prosecution (Hamilton, 1985: IV-6–10). Furthermore, if the suspect is ultimately released on bail, the onus is placed on the prosecution to justify the imposition of any conditions upon his or her release, the presumption being that a suspect should normally be released merely upon giving an undertaking to appear for trial.

In 1976, the *Bail Reform Act* was amended[42] so as to reverse the onus in certain situations and to require the accused to justify why he or she should be released by the justice or provincial court judge. In brief, the burden of justifying release is placed upon the accused's shoulders when he or she is charged with:

(a) an indictable offence alleged to have been committed while the accused was at large after having been released on bail in connection with another indictable offence;

(b) an indictable offence and the accused is not ordinarily resident in Canada;

(c) an offence connected with failing to show up in court or to fulfil the conditions attached to the accused's bail while he or she was waiting to be tried for another offence;

(d) trafficking in or exporting/importing narcotics or conspiring to commit these offences.

In addition, the *Bail Reform Act* specifies that a suspect charged with one of the offences in relation to which only a Superior Court Judge may grant bail must justify his or her release.[43] It is interesting that this "reverse onus" provision, which places the burden on the accused to justify his or her release, has been challenged under the *Charter* as constituting an infringement of the right "not to be denied reasonable bail without just cause." However, this constitutional challenge has generally been rejected by the courts (Salhany, 1984: 106). After all, the provision does not *prohibit* the granting of bail to suspects charged with these offences, but merely places the onus on the accused to justify his or her release.

Continued detention of the accused is justified only on the following grounds:

(i) on the primary ground that it is necessary to ensure the accused's attendance at trial; and

(ii) on the secondary ground that it is necessary in the public interest or safety of the public, "having regard to all the circumstances including any substantial likelihood that the accused will, if he is released from custody, commit a criminal offence or interfere with the administration of justice."[44]

The secondary ground may be considered only after the justice or judge has determined that detention is not justified on the basis of the need to ensure that the accused will show up at trial. In determining the likelihood that the accused will appear for trial, the justice or the judge will take into account a broad range of personal circumstances, including whether the accused has a fixed address, his or her employment and marital or family status, any prior record of criminal convictions, and his or her relationships with friends and relatives in the community (Hamilton, 1985: IV-25). As noted earlier, the attention paid to factors such as employment status raises a considerable degree of concern insofar as it almost inevitably results in discrimination against those of low socio-economic status. As far as the secondary ground is concerned, one Ontario Court[45] has indicated that

"Public interest" involves many considerations, not the least of which is the "public image" of the *Criminal Code*, the *Bail Reform Act* amendments, the apprehension and conviction of criminals, the attempts at deterrence of crime, and ultimately the protection of that overwhelming percentage of citizens of Canada who are not only socially conscious but law-abiding. This cannot be emphasized too strongly. . . .

One situation in which a court may decide to detain an accused for the "protection or safety of the public" arises where an accused is alleged to be a major trafficker in drugs (Hamilton, 1985: IV-31). Similarly, the courts have ruled that major drug traffickers may also be detained on the basis that there would be a "substantial likelihood of [their] committing a criminal offence" if they were to be released (Hamilton, 1985: IV-32–35).

If the justice or judge decides to release the accused, then he or she may do so according to one of five different methods. The accused may be released

(a) upon giving an undertaking to appear, together with such conditions (if any) as the justice or judge directs;

(b) upon entering into a recognizance in such amount and with such conditions as the justice or judge may direct;

(c) upon entering into a recognizance in such amount and with such conditions as the justice or judge may direct, together with the requirement of *sureties* (friends or relatives who assume responsibility for ensuring that the accused shows up for trial);

(d) (provided the prosecutor consents) upon entering into a recognizance in such amount and with such conditions as the justice or judge may direct, together with a deposit of cash or other valuable security;

(e) (if the accused is not ordinarily resident in the province or within 200 kilometres of the place in which he or she is in custody) upon entering into a recognizance either with or without sureties in such amount and upon such conditions as the justice or judge may direct together with the requirement of a deposit of cash or some other valuable security.[46]

It will be seen that the relevant *Criminal Code*[47] provisions set out these five methods according to a "ladder of increasing severity." The Crown is required to progress up the ladder of severity in recommending the specific form of release that should be made; in other words, the prosecutor must justify the imposition of a requirement of a recognizance as opposed to the requirement of a simple undertaking to appear, and so on "up the ladder" (Hamilton, 1985: IV-15; Salhany, 1984: 111).

Obviously, taking on the responsibility of being a surety is a serious matter. As Salhany (1984: 138) points out, it is a "fundamental principle of the law of bail that the surety's prime obligation is to ensure the appearance of the accused at the proper time and place." Therefore, if the accused fails to show for trial or breaches the conditions of bail, then the surety's recognizance may be forfeited, either in part or in whole, to the Crown. In determining whether the surety should forfeit his or her recognizance, the courts generally consider the extent to which the surety was personally responsible for the accused's failure to live up to his or her obligations (Salhany, 1984: 140). If the surety wishes to back out of his or her commitment, the *Code* establishes procedures that may accomplish this objective.[48] In some cases, the accused may have to be taken into custody once the surety has been released from his or her recognizance. However, it is possible for a justice or a judge simply to substitute another surety without the necessity of taking the accused into custody again.[49]

The conditions that may be imposed when an accused person is released on bail include regular reporting to a peace officer, remaining in a particular area, notifying the police of a change in address or employment, refraining from communicating with any witness or other person named in the release order, and depositing one's passport. The *Criminal Code* also contains a general provision that requires the released suspect to "comply with such other reasonable conditions specified in the order as the justice considers desirable."[50] This particular provision has been interpreted very broadly by the courts (Salhany, 1984: 112).[51] For example, it was held to be legitimate for a justice to impose a condition that an alleged prostitute stay away from that part of the city where the alleged offence had occurred, in order to prevent the commission of further offences while she was on bail.[52]

To what extent have the provisions of the *Bail Reform Act* encouraged the release of accused persons pending their trial? It is now clear that the great majority of accused persons are released on some form of bail once they have made an initial appearance in court. Indeed, a national survey (Canadian Centre for Justice Statistics, 1986) indicated that, on a *Canada-wide basis*, only about 1 out of every 15 persons (7%) charged with an offence is remanded in custody by a court pending his or her trial.

Is there any evidence that bail courts "rubber stamp" the recommendations of the police and prosecutors? A study of bail hearings in Toronto by Koza and Doob (1975b) suggests that the judges in the study were, apparently, quite willing to apply the philosophy of liberal release that underlies the *Bail Reform Act*, even in the face of opposition from the prosecutor. Indeed, in those cases where the prosecutor urged that the accused should remain in custody, the court nevertheless released 43% of the accused persons concerned. On the other hand, where the prosecutor made a positive recommendation for release, the court was much more likely to implement the recommendation (which it did in some 95% of cases). This study suggests that, in this jurisdiction at least, the judges did not simply endorse the restrictive recommendations of the prosecutor and the police, but rather appeared to apply the liberal spirit of the *Bail Reform Act*.

In recent years, a number of provinces have established programs to facilitate the granting of bail in urban areas. For example, Toronto established a bail program in 1979 (Morris, 1981). This program was designed to provide two types of service: bail verification and bail supervision. *Verification* is designed to prevent the unnecessary detention of accused persons who would be released if only fuller and more accurate information about their background were available to the courts earlier in the process. Bail verification interviewers ask accused persons who are in police custody a series of questions as soon as the police have completed their interrogation of them. The interviewers then make the information available to the appropriate bail court. *Bail supervision,* on the other hand, is designed to deal with those accused persons for whom bail has been set but who do not have a surety who will enter into a recognizance for them. Impecunious accused persons, who cannot come up with a surety who will stand bail for them, may stay in jail merely because of their lack of financial resources (Morris, 1981: 158). If an accused person is eligible for release with the requirement of a surety but is unable to find someone to take on this responsibility, then bail supervision may be proposed as an alternative. The accused may be released on his or her own recognizance, but would be required to report to and be subject to the supervision of the bail program. Similar programs exist not only elsewhere in Ontario[53] but also in a number of other provinces and territories.[54]

What happens if an accused person fails to live up to the conditions of his or her bail? The *Criminal Code* provides that where an accused person on bail has (a) violated or is about to violate the terms of his or her release or (b) committed an indictable offence while on bail, then he or she may be arrested either by the police on their own initiative or on the basis of a warrant signed by a justice.[55] In these circumstances, the suspect's bail will be cancelled unless he or she "shows cause" why he or she should not be detained.[56]

In general, a bail order remains in effect until the accused's trial has been completed, and if he or she is convicted, the trial court has the discretion to extend the order pending sentence.[57] However, the courts do have the power to order that the accused be detained in custody at any stage in the trial process or to make any variation in the order that they may deem to be appropriate.[58] There are also provisions giving courts the power to grant or continue bail pending an appeal of either a conviction or sentence.[59]

The *Criminal Code*[60] makes provision for either the accused or the prosecutor to apply for a review of the bail decision made by a justice or provincial court judge to a judge of the superior court of criminal jurisdiction. Similarly, a review of the bail decision made by a superior court judge may be undertaken by the Court of Appeal.[61]

Review of the Accused's Detention Where the Trial is Delayed

The *Criminal Code*[62] provides for an *automatic* review of the continuing detention of an accused person whose trial has been delayed.[63] The purpose of this provision is clearly to ensure that a detained suspect does not become "lost in the system." The review must generally be conducted within 90 days of the accused first coming before a justice in the case of an indictable offence, and within 30 days in the case of a summary conviction offence. The review is conducted by a judge of the superior court of criminal jurisdiction. In deciding whether or not to release an accused person, the judge may take into consideration whether the accused or the prosecutor has been responsible for "any unreasonable delay in the trial of the charge."[64] If the judge does not think that continued detention is necessary, then the accused may be released on bail. The *Code*[65] also provides that where such an automatic review takes place, the judge shall give directions for speeding up the accused's trial.

The Trial of Criminal Cases

Having examined the process by means of which bail may be granted, we shall now turn our attention to the manner in which criminal cases are tried in Canada. It is important to remember that the classification of offences determines how individual cases will be tried within the system of criminal courts. The *Criminal Code* provides for only one method of trial for summary conviction offences but as many as three alternative methods for indictable offences. Figure 6.3 provides a very general overview of the various methods of trial for both summary and indictable offences in the Province of British Columbia, which has the extra tier (the county court) in its system of criminal courts; it should be remembered that, as noted earlier, the majority of provinces do not have the extra tier (either the county or district court) in their criminal court system.

The Trial of Summary Conviction Offences

Part XXVII of the *Criminal Code* lays out the procedures for the trial of summary conviction offences arising either under the *Code* itself or under other federal statutes (Salhany, 1984: 359–78). Similar procedures exist to deal with the summary conviction offences created by provincial statutes.[66] Typical summary conviction offences in the *Criminal Code* are wilfully committing an indecent act, causing a disturbance in or near a public place, soliciting for the purpose of engaging in prostitution or obtaining sexual services from a prostitute, driving a motor vehicle without the consent of the owner, and fraudulently obtaining food from a restaurant. Of course, where the Crown has elected to proceed with a "hybrid" offence summarily, then that offence will be tried according to summary conviction procedures.

In general, summary conviction offences may be tried only before a *provincial court judge sitting without a jury*, although the *Criminal Code* does permit such offences to be tried, in certain circumstances, before a justice of the peace sitting alone, or before two or more justices sitting together.[67] Although accused persons, if they so wish, may appear in person at their trial for a summary conviction offence, they may also send their

FIGURE 6.3

OVERVIEW OF CRIMINAL TRIAL PROCEDURES IN THE PROVINCE OF BRITISH COLUMBIA[1]

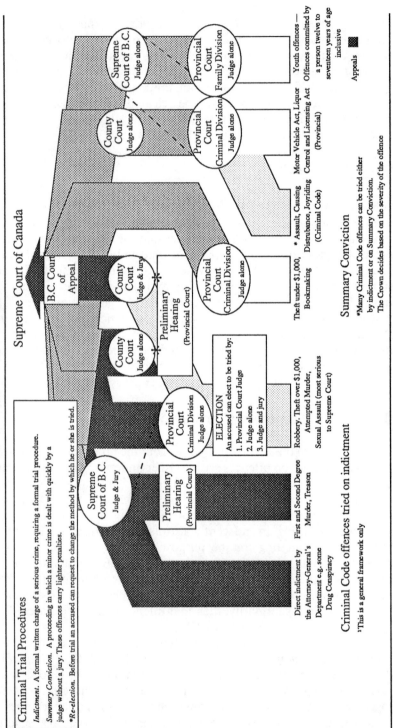

Source: Legal Services Society of British Columbia, Ministry of the Attorney-General of British Columbia. Reprinted with permission.

lawyer to represent them in their absence.[68] Nevertheless, the court does have the power to require their attendance and may issue an arrest warrant for that purpose. If an accused person who has been given an appearance notice or a summons fails to attend for trial in accordance with the written instructions provided, then the court may conduct a trial in his or her absence (an "*ex parte* trial") or may issue an arrest warrant and adjourn the trial until the accused appears.[69] Although, at first blush, a trial in the accused's absence may seem somewhat drastic, the courts have ruled that it does not infringe the accused's right to be treated in accordance with the fundamental principles of justice or the right to a fair trial, protected by sections 7 and 11(d) respectively of the *Charter*.[70] It is likely, of course, that a court would not conduct a trial in the accused's absence if the latter were prevented from attending by forces beyond his or her control.[71]

As the term suggests, *summary conviction* procedures were meant to provide "summary" justice, and there is some evidence that the provincial courts, whose workload consists to a large extent of summary conviction cases, do provide exactly that. In a study of the provincial courts in Toronto, for example, Hann (1973: Vol. 1) discovered that the courts devoted, on average, a mere five minutes to each appearance by an accused person and that more than 75% of all cases were dealt with in only three or less court appearances. This certainly suggests that, in this jurisdiction at least, justice was dispensed swiftly when summary conviction offences were involved. Perhaps, this swiftness is inevitable given both the heavy caseload faced by the provincial courts and the relatively minor nature of summary conviction cases. However, it is at least questionable whether due process is being served by what appears to be "assembly line justice."

The Trial of Indictable Offences

Historically, a trial on indictment meant that the accused would be tried before a judge and jury (Atrens, 1985: 1-29). Indeed, the *Criminal Code*[72] states that "except where otherwise expressly provided by law, every accused who is charged with an indictable offence shall be tried by a court composed of a judge and jury." In fact, the exceptions provided for in the *Code* itself have grown to be so numerous that, as Atrens (1985: 1-30) notes, "while any indictable offence *may* be tried by judge and jury, only a *few* must be so tried." Indeed, the *Code* provides for a number of different forms of trial depending upon the classification of the offence(s) concerned. For the purpose of determining the form of trial, there are three major categories of indictable offence:

Offences That May Be Tried Only by a Judge of the Superior Court Sitting with a Jury

In this category are the most serious offences, such as murder, treason and piracy.[73] However, the *Code*[74] provides that an accused person charged with one of these offences may be tried by a superior court judge *without* a jury, provided both the accused and the Attorney General of the province give their consent.

Offences That May Be Tried Only by a Provincial Court Judge

Into this category fall the least serious of the indictable offences. They are said to fall within the "absolute jurisdiction" of a provincial court judge.[75] They include such offences as theft (other than theft of cattle), obtaining money or property by false pretences, possession of stolen goods, and keeping a bawdy-house.[76]

Offences for Which the Accused May Elect the Method of Trial

If a person is charged with an offence falling within the two categories above, he or she has no choice with respect to the method of trial. However, if the accused is charged with an offence falling within this third category, then he or she has the right to "elect" the mode of trial. This category is a *residual* category in that it contains all those indictable offences not falling within the two categories above. Among the "electable" offences are robbery, dangerous driving, assault, sexual assault, breaking and entering, and attempted murder. The accused person may choose between three different methods of trial:

  (i) *trial by a provincial court judge*
 (ii) *trial by superior court judge and jury* (in the four provinces that maintain a second tier in their court system, the trial will instead be conducted before a *county or district court judge and jury*).
(iii) *trial by a superior court judge* (or, where applicable, by a *county or district court judge*) sitting alone without a jury.

If the accused fails to make an election, he or she will be deemed to have chosen to be tried by a court composed of a judge and jury.[77]

However, the right to elect the method of trial is not an absolute one (Salhany, 1984: 8), since the Attorney General of the province can override an accused's election to be tried by a provincial court judge or by a superior (or county or district court) judge sitting alone. Indeed, the *Criminal Code*[78] provides that the Attorney General may require that the accused be tried by a judge and jury, provided the offence charged carries a maximum penalty of more than five years' imprisonment.

The whole process of election is a complex one because the *Criminal Code* allows the accused to change his or her mind and to "re-elect" the mode of trial in certain circumstances (Taylor and Irvine, 1986: XIV-16). The right to re-elect is nevertheless subject to certain important restrictions.[79]

1. Re-election where the accused originally chose to be tried by either a judge alone or a judge and jury. Where the accused has elected to be tried in the higher courts by a judge sitting alone or by judge and jury, there is a right to re-elect the mode of trial, provided that no more than 14 days have passed since the preliminary inquiry (if there was one) was completed. The accused has an absolute right, in such circumstances, to re-elect a method of trial *other than trial by a provincial court judge.* If the accused wishes to re-elect in favour of trial by provincial court judge, then Crown counsel must give his or her written consent.[80] The *Code* also provides that on or after the 15th day following the completion of the preliminary inquiry, the accused can re-elect in favour of *any mode of trial,* but can only do so with the written consent of the prosecutor.[81]

2. Re-election where the accused originally chose trial before a provincial court judge. An accused person who initially chose to be tried by a provincial court judge has an absolute right to re-elect in favour of trial by a higher court, provided the re-election takes place not later than 14 days before the day first appointed for trial. After this period has elapsed, re-election is permitted only with the written consent of the prosecutor. There are certain other restrictions on the right to re-elect, but they are too complex to consider here (see Taylor and Irvine, 1986: XIV-16–XIV-17).

The fairly generous provisions permitting re-election are somewhat problematic given that they offer accused persons and their lawyers a golden opportunity to delay court proceedings (albeit not indefinitely). Amendments to the *Criminal Code* made in 1985 tightened up the preexisting re-election provisions quite considerably by imposing stricter time limits. In an interesting study conducted in Montreal before the 1985 amendments, Mackaay (1976) found that a very high proportion of accused persons who decided to plead not guilty took advantage of the re-election provisions. Significantly, some 86% of defendants initially chose trial by judge and jury, but the great majority of them later changed their minds and re-elected in favour of trial by judge alone. Indeed, it turned out that only some 4% of those defendants who pleaded not guilty were ultimately tried by a judge and jury, while 90% of them were tried by judge alone. In Mackaay's view (1976: 94), the generous system of re-election contributed directly to the problem of excessive delays in the court system. Whether the 1985 restrictions will improve the situation remains to be seen.

Picking One's Way through the Labyrinth: How Indictable Offences Travel through the Court Process

The various methods of trial that are available in the case of an indictable offence render the whole process an exceedingly tortuous one. Having identified the various methods of trial that are available for indictable offences, we shall now turn our attention to the more concrete issue of how individual cases travel through the court process.

The point has already been made that all accused persons make their first appearance in the provincial court. However, while some of the cases involving indictable offences will be finally disposed of in the provincial court, some cases will be moved on to the *higher courts* (the superior court or the county or district court, where it exists) for trial. If the accused is charged with an offence that falls within the so-called absolute jurisdiction of a provincial court judge, then the latter may proceed to try the accused immediately or set a later date for trial. The trial proceeds on the basis of the information that is before the provincial court judge (Salhany, 1984: 5). The same situation exists where the accused has elected to be tried by a provincial court judge (in relation to that category of offences which give the accused a right to elect). In such a case, the provincial court judge must endorse the election on the information and then try the accused immediately or fix a date for trial in the future.[82] Unlike cases tried in the higher courts, no indictment needs to be drawn up for the trial of indictable offences in the provincial court.

Where the accused is charged with an offence that may be tried only by the superior court or where he or she has elected trial by judge sitting alone or by judge and jury, then the trial will be conducted in the higher courts. However, before such a case may proceed to the higher courts, the provincial court judge must first conduct a *preliminary inquiry* to determine whether there is sufficient evidence to warrant committing the accused for trial.

The Preliminary Inquiry

The origins of the preliminary inquiry have been traced back to English legislation passed in 1554 (Taylor and Irvine, 1986: XIV-1). The preliminary inquiry may be conducted either by a provincial court judge or, in some circumstances, by a justice of the peace. It should be emphasized that a preliminary inquiry is not a trial. The provincial court judge or the justice is not concerned with establishing the guilt or innocence of the accused. Indeed, no plea to the charge may be taken at the preliminary inquiry. The Crown may call whatever witnesses it wishes, and the provincial court judge or the justice of the peace does not have any power to order the Crown to call any particular witnesses.[83] If witnesses are called by the Crown, the accused's counsel may cross-examine them. Those witnesses who are called must give their evidence on oath and may be cross-examined.[84] Accused persons may also call witnesses and give evidence themselves but there is no obligation on them to do so.[85] However, it would appear that witnesses are actually summoned in only a minority of the preliminary inquiries that are conducted across Canada. Indeed, a federal Department of Justice study of preliminary inquiries in 13 judicial districts across Canada (cited in Law Reform Commission of Canada, 1984: 11) found that witnesses were summoned and heard in only 46% of the cases in which preliminary inquiries were conducted. In 80% of the cases, moreover, the preliminary inquiry lasted for less than a day.

The provincial court judge or the justice of the peace may impose a ban on the publication of the evidence taken at a preliminary inquiry. This provision is clearly necessary for ensuring that the accused has a fair trial, because pre-trial publicity may prove to be very prejudicial, particularly in a jury trial. The ban will continue until either the accused is discharged or, if he or she is ordered to stand trial, the trial has been completed.[86]

When all the evidence has been taken at the preliminary inquiry, the provincial court judge or the justice of the peace has two options:

(a) if in his opinion there is sufficient evidence to put the accused on trial for the offence charged or any other indictable offence in respect of the same transaction, order the accused to stand trial; or

(b) discharge the accused, if in his opinion on the whole of the evidence no sufficient case is made out to put the accused on trial for the offence charged or any other indictable offence in respect of the same transaction.[87]

It will be noted that the provincial court judge or justice of the peace may commit the accused where there is sufficient evidence to warrant committal for trial. The Crown does not have to establish guilt or innocence at the preliminary inquiry; instead, the Crown must merely "make a prima facie case" (Holmes, 1982: 263).

To what extent does the preliminary inquiry serve as an "effective filter," in the sense of weeding out those cases that are not strong enough to warrant a trial? Empirical evidence would appear to suggest that relatively few accused persons are discharged after a preliminary inquiry. Mackaay (1976: 38), in his study of the Montreal court system, concluded that only one in nine cases resulted in a discharge as opposed to a committal for trial. Similarly, in a study of 13 judicial districts across Canada conducted by the federal Department of Justice in 1980, it was found that only ten per cent of those cases that went to a preliminary inquiry resulted in withdrawal of the charges or discharge of the accused (cited in Law Reform Commission of Canada, 1984: 11). The small percentage of cases in which the accused is discharged as the result of a preliminary inquiry would appear to suggest that the latter serves as a rather inadequate filter. On the other hand, the Department of Justice study did find that 71% of the cases that led to a committal for trial after a preliminary inquiry ultimately resulted in a plea of guilty; this would suggest that the Crown must have possessed reasonably strong evidence against the accused in the clear majority of cases where a committal for trial was ultimately made by the provincial judge or justice of the peace.

It should be noted that there are two circumstances in which a preliminary inquiry will *not* be held even though the accused is to be tried in the higher courts. First, the prosecutor and the accused may jointly agree to waive the preliminary inquiry.[88] In the Department of Justice study (cited in Law Reform Commission of Canada, 1984: 11), a preliminary inquiry was held in only 30% of the cases in which it was available, while Mackaay (1976) found in his study of the Montreal courts that an inquiry was held in only 37% of eligible cases at the Montreal Court House, and 50% at the Montreal Municipal Court; these studies would appear to suggest that a considerable proportion of defendants waive their right to a preliminary inquiry.

Second, it is possible for the Attorney General of the province or his or her deputy to by-pass the preliminary inquiry and prefer a so-called *direct indictment*.[89] This procedure is very rare (Taylor and Irvine, 1986: XIV-7), and it is contended that it is most likely to be employed in cases involving major drug conspiracies. Only the Attorney General or the Deputy Attorney General may exercise this power in a public prosecution,[90] and his or her actions may not be questioned by the courts. In other words, "ordinary" Crown counsel do not have the power to prefer a direct indictment (Atrens, 1986: IX-41). The use of the direct indictment procedure raises a considerable degree of concern, since it can deprive an accused of his or her right to a preliminary inquiry. Nevertheless, it has been held that the preferring of a direct indictment, where no preliminary inquiry has been held, does not infringe the accused's right to be treated in accordance with the principles of fundamental justice guaranteed by section 7 of the *Charter*.[91] On the other hand, it has been held that a remedy may be available under the *Charter* where the use of the direct indictment procedure results in *unfairness to the accused*.[92] A direct indictment may be preferred not only in the situation where there has not been a preliminary inquiry, but also in the situation where the accused has been *discharged* as a consequence of a preliminary inquiry, although the courts would be unlikely to permit this drastic step to be taken unless new evidence had been uncovered since the accused's discharge or different charges were concerned.[93]

The Preliminary Inquiry and the Issue of Discovery

Although the Supreme Court of Canada has stated that the sole purpose of the preliminary inquiry is to determine whether there is sufficient evidence to commit an accused person for trial,[94] it has been widely recognized that the preliminary inquiry also permits the accused to obtain "discovery" of the prosecution's case against the accused (Ferguson, 1985: XIII-112–14). The *Criminal Code* obliges the Crown to reveal relatively little of the evidence that it intends to bring against the accused at the latter's trial (Ferguson, 1985; Law Reform Commission of Canada, 1984), although provincial guidelines for Crown counsel, as well as ethical principles,[95] may well operate, in practice, to persuade prosecutors to reveal more than they are obliged to under the *Code*.[96] The preliminary inquiry does afford the accused the opportunity to gain a reasonable degree of knowledge concerning the Crown's case against him or her, although the prosecutor only has to introduce *sufficient* evidence to warrant a committal for trial (in other words, the prosecutor does not have to introduce *all* the evidence that he or she later intends to use at the accused's trial).

Ferguson (1985: XIII-6–10) has contended that discovery is essential to the "effective working of our adversarial system of justice." In his view,

> The adversary system is based on the assumption that a legally correct verdict is most likely to arise if opposing parties devote their full attention to marshalling and presenting all evidence favourable to their position before an impartial judge. However, this assumption is hardly realistic unless the evidence favourable to either side is accessible. Since the evidence most favourable to the accused may not be accessible to him because of his lesser opportunities, capacities and resources to conduct investigations, this assumption of the adversary system will not work unless the State at least discloses all the results of its investigation to the accused.

In 1974, the Law Reform Commission of Canada (1974: 35) recommended that a formal system of discovery be introduced on a uniform basis across the country. At that time, the Commission recommended that the system be based on a requirement of full disclosure of the Crown's case, coupled with a special pre-trial court hearing to ensure that the disclosure was adequate. Following this recommendation, there were a number of experimental projects designed to introduce a system of disclosure in certain Canadian cities (such as Montreal, Ottawa, Toronto, Winnipeg, Edmonton and Vancouver). The pilot project in Montreal conducted in the mid-1970s, which implemented the Commission's specific recommendations, was formally evaluated and was considered to be successful (Law Reform Commission of Canada, 1984: 7–9).

In its 1974 recommendation, the Law Reform Commission had suggested that the preliminary inquiry could be abolished if a formal system of discovery were introduced. The rationale for this approach was the Commission's belief that the most important function of the preliminary inquiry was to provide the accused with a form of discovery and that if this function were to be pre-empted by a formal system of discovery, then the preliminary inquiry would no longer have a *raison d'être*. However, in its more recent report on discovery, the Law Reform Commission (1984) recommends a less ambitious approach to the issue of discovery and no longer advocates the abolition of the preliminary inquiry. The Commission (1984: 13–15) proposes that the accused be entitled to specific rights of discovery and that these be enforced by the judicial officer concerned (a justice of the peace or a provincial court judge) adjourning the case until the rights had been duly granted to the accused. The Commission (1984: 11) contends that a system of full disclosure will reduce the length and number of preliminary inquiries and asserts that "if there is full disclosure, the preliminary inquiry will survive to perform its true function as a screen against an insufficient case."

Recent amendments to the *Criminal Code* (which have not yet been proclaimed in force) may lay the basis for a more formal system of obtaining discovery.[97] Indeed, the new provisions require that all jury trials be preceded by a pre-trial hearing before a judge of the court in which the trial is to take place. The hearing is to "consider such matters as will promote a fair and expeditious trial." It is most likely that one of the matters that could be raised at the hearing is discovery of the Crown's case against the accused. In non-jury trials, the pre-trial hearing would not be mandatory but would be held only with the consent of both the prosecutor and the accused.

Trial on Indictment

Once the preliminary inquiry has been completed and the accused committed for trial, the next step in the process is for the Crown to "prefer an indictment" (Atrens, 1986: IX-28). An *indictment* is merely a formal, written accusation of a crime made by either the Attorney General personally or by one of his or her agents (Crown counsel). An indictment may be preferred against an accused person either in relation to the charge on which he or she was committed for trial or any charge "founded on the facts disclosed by the evidence taken on the preliminary inquiry, in addition to or in substitution for any charge on which that person was ordered to stand trial."[98] As noted earlier, the normal procedure of committal for trial after a preliminary inquiry may be by-passed by the so-called direct indictment procedure. In this situation, the Attorney General may prefer an indictment either where there has been no preliminary inquiry or where the accused has been discharged after such an inquiry. The trial by judge or by judge and jury in the higher courts will then take place on the basis of the indictment.

The intricate details of the trial process in relation to indictable offences cannot be dealt with in this book. However, one or two comments are certainly in order. First it is interesting to note that unlike the situation that exists in relation to the trial of summary conviction offences, the accused is required to be present during his or her trial for an indictable offence[99] (Proulx, 1983).

Second, it is important to bear in mind that the realities of the trial process may be at considerable odds with the popular image of how serious criminal offences are dealt with in the courts. As Hagan (1984: 167) notes, the "media image of the court process is that of a trial by jury, with prosecution and defence attorneys assuming adversarial roles in a battle for justice." In reality, the great majority of cases involving indictable offences are dealt with in a very different manner. Jury trials are relatively rare in Canada, despite the fact that section 11(f) of the *Charter* guarantees the accused person's right to a jury trial for any offence that carries a maximum sentence of five years or more imprisonment. Indeed, according to Hagan (1984: 167), there are less than two thousand jury trials in Canada in any given year.[100] The reality is that the great majority of criminal cases are actually tried in the provincial courts. For example, in the Province of British Columbia during 1986, about 96% of all cases entering the provincial court system were finally disposed of within this system; in other words, only some 4% of criminal cases were subsequently sent on to the higher courts for trial.[101]

A significant proportion of defendants plead guilty to the charges laid against them rather than participate in an adversarial trial. The percentage of guilty pleas varies from jurisdiction to jurisdiction across Canada. However, it is difficult to make direct comparisons. A plea of guilty may be entered at different stages of the trial process, and published statistics do not always make it clear whether the percentage of guilty pleas quoted refers to guilty pleas entered at *any* stage of the trial process or only to guilty pleas entered at one particular stage of the process. In British Columbia, for example, during 1986 about 46% of all defendants before the provincial court entered a plea of guilty on their *very first appearance in court.*[102] Almost 70% of the defendants studied by Ericson and Baranek pleaded guilty at some stage in the trial process (Ericson and Baranek, 1982: 157). Mackaay (1976: 32) found that 63.5% of defendants pleaded guilty at the Montreal Municipal Court, and 31.4% at the Montreal Court House. No matter what the variation between jurisdictions may be, it is clear that a very considerable proportion of criminal cases are disposed of without a trial of the innocence or guilt of the accused person. This observation has important implications for the image of the criminal courts that is held by many Canadians.

The System of Appeals

Once the trial has been concluded, it is always possible that either the accused or the Crown may wish to appeal against the verdict or the sentence meted out. Until 1923, there was no formal appeal structure in existence in Canada (Salhany, 1984: 436). However, at the present time, there is a fairly elaborate system of appeals that operates in relation to criminal cases. There is a marked difference between the system of appeals available in relation to summary conviction offences and the system that operates in relation to indictable offences.

Appeals in Relation to Summary Conviction Offences

While the trial process in relation to summary conviction offences is relatively straightforward, the appeal process is quite complex (Atrens,

1985: I-40). This contrasts sharply with the situation applicable to indictable offences where, although the various trial options are almost labyrinthine in their complexity, the system of appeals is relatively simple in its basic structure.

There are basically two major forms of appeal available in relation to a summary conviction offence; in the words of the *Criminal Code*[103] they are (i) "Appeal to a Section 812 Appeal Court"; and (ii) "Summary Appeal on Transcript or Agreed Statement of the Facts."

Appeal to a Section 812 Appeal Court

In this appeal procedure, either the Crown or the accused may appeal from a decision of a provincial court to a court designated by section 812 of the *Code*. In the Provinces of New Brunswick, Manitoba, Alberta and Saskatchewan, this court will be the Court of Queen's Bench; in Newfoundland, a judge of the Supreme Court; in Prince Edward Island, the Trial Division of the Supreme Court; in Quebec, the Superior Court; and in Nova Scotia, Ontario and British Columbia, the District or County Court.

Until 1976, this form of appeal took the shape of a completely new trial, or trial *de novo* (Salhany, 1984: 484). One of the reasons for this rather costly form of appeal procedure was to remedy the possibility that there would not be a proper record of the original trial in the magistrates' courts (the predecessors of the modern provincial courts). Another reason for adopting this procedure was that many of the magistrates did not have any formal legal training. However, by the mid-1970s, magistrates were being appointed exclusively from the ranks of professional lawyers, and proper transcripts were being taken at all criminal trials. In light of these developments, it seemed unnecessary to require the expense of an entirely new trial, together with the concomitant inconvenience that such an appeal procedure thrust upon witnesses; therefore, in 1976 the *Code* was amended so as to require that this form of appeal be conducted on the basis of the transcript taken in the original trial. However, the *Code* does preserve the option of a full trial *de novo* in exceptional cases. The trial *de novo* will now be held only in the situation where, "because of the condition of the record" or for "any other reason," the appeal court "is of the opinion that the interests of justice would be better served" by staging a completely new trial.[104] Clearly, the trial *de novo* procedure is intended to be used only in rare situations.

Who may appeal and in what circumstances? Defendants may appeal either from a conviction or order made against them or against the sentence passed on them. On the other hand, the prosecutor may appeal either from an order that stays proceedings on an information or dismisses an information or, alternatively, against the sentence passed on the accused.[105]

What are the powers of the appeal court insofar as the disposition of the appeal is concerned? Very briefly, in the case of an *appeal by the accused against conviction*, the appeal court may allow the appeal, set aside the verdict and either direct a judgment or verdict of acquittal be entered or order a new trial.[106] If a new trial is to be held, then it will normally be held in a different court than the one that entered the original conviction.[107] On the other hand, of course, the appeal court could find that the appeal does not have sufficient merit and dismiss it. *Where the prosecutor is appealing against an "acquittal,"* the court may, of course, just dismiss the appeal if it does not believe that it has adequate merit. On the other hand, it may decide to allow the appeal and set aside the verdict of the trial court; in this case, the appeal court has two options: It may order a new trial or it may enter a verdict of guilty with respect to the offence of which the accused should have been found guilty by the trial court. In the latter situation, the appeal court may pass sentence itself or hand the case back to the trial court for sentencing.[108] *In the case of an appeal against sentence* (either by the accused or by the prosecution), the appeal court has the power to vary the sentence "within the limits prescribed by law" or it may just dismiss the appeal altogether.[109] It is critical to bear in mind that the court has the power either to decrease or to increase the sentence meted out at the trial level.

Summary Appeal on Transcript or Agreed Statement of Facts

This form of appeal is much more restricted in its scope than its companion form of appeal. It is concerned exclusively with *questions of law*; in other words, unlike the appeal to a section 812 appeal court, the summary appeal on transcript or agreed statement of facts cannot be concerned with the facts of a case. Either the accused or the prosecution may appeal to the superior court of criminal jurisdiction for the province concerned. Either party may appeal, as the case may be, "against a conviction, judgment or verdict of acquittal or other final order or determination of a summary conviction court" on the basis that

(a) it is erroneous in point of law;
(b) it is in excess of jurisdiction; or
(c) it constitutes a refusal or failure to exercise jurisdiction.[110]

An appeal launched in this way will be made on the basis of either a transcript of the trial court proceedings or, if both parties give their consent, an agreed "statement of facts." Since the issues raised are much more narrow than those that may be raised in an appeal to a section 812 court, the superior court has fewer options to summon in disposing of a case. The appeal court may either "affirm, reverse or modify the conviction, judgment or verdict of acquittal or other final order or determination," or alternatively, it may send the case back to the trial court with the appeal court's opinion on the matter of law raised and "may make any other order in relation to the matter . . . that it considers proper."[111] It is important to note that the appeal court does not have the power to order a new trial.[112]

Appeal to the Provincial Court of Appeal

Once an appeal has been dealt with either by a section 812 court or by the superior court of criminal jurisdiction in relation to an appeal on the transcript or agreed statement of facts, there is the possibility of a further appeal by either party to the provincial Court of Appeal.[113] However, such an appeal may be made only in relation to a matter of law (not a question of fact).[114] Since the appeal is limited to questions of law, there is no appeal against sentence, in the sense that neither party may raise the issue of the appropriateness of the sentence. However, a question regarding the legality of any particular sentence may be the subject of an appeal, on the basis that it constitutes a genuine question of law (Salhany, 1984: 515). Similarly, an appeal may be made on the question of whether a sentence infringed any of the provisions of the *Charter*.

Appeal to the Supreme Court of Canada

The *Criminal Code* does not make any provision for an appeal from the decision of a provincial court of appeal to the Supreme Court of Canada insofar as summary conviction offences are concerned. However, according to Salhany (1984: 518), "under section 41(1) and (3) of the Supreme Court of Canada Act, an appeal lies to the Supreme Court of Canada from the judgment of the highest court of final resort in the province acquitting or convicting an accused, or setting aside or affirming a conviction or acquittal on any question of law or jurisdiction."

The system of appeals in relation to summary conviction offences is summarized in Figure 6.4 for the purpose of easy reference.

Appeals in Relation to Indictable Offences

Appeal to the Provincial Court of Appeal

Unlike the situation that exists in relation to summary conviction offences, the *Criminal Code*[115] has established only one method of appeal insofar as indictable offences are concerned. *All appeals from the decisions of trial courts are to be taken to the provincial court of appeal.*[116] Both the accused and the prosecutor may appeal, but the prosecutor's rights of appeal are more limited than those of the accused.

The accused may appeal against *conviction* in the following circumstances:

  (i) (as a matter of right) on a question of law alone;
  (ii) on a question of fact or a question of mixed fact and law, provided

FIGURE 6.4
THE SYSTEM OF APPEALS: SUMMARY CONVICTION OFFENCES

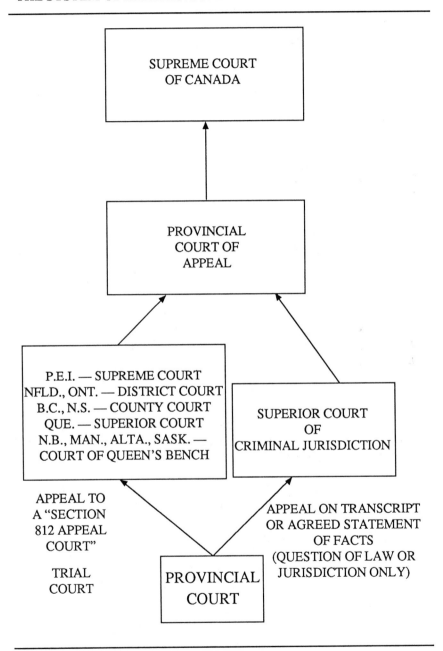

that he or she first obtains the permission ("leave") of the court of appeal or that the trial judge issues a certificate indicating that the case is a "proper case for appeal"; and

(iii) on any ground other than those mentioned in (i) and (ii) above, provided that the court of appeal considers it to be "a sufficient ground of appeal" and gives the accused leave to appeal.[117]

The accused may also appeal against *the sentence meted out*, provided he or she first obtains the leave of either the court of appeal or a single judge of that court (unless, of course, the sentence is fixed by law, such as is the case, for example, in first degree murder).[118]

The prosecutor (either the Attorney General or counsel appointed by him or her) may appeal in the following circumstances only:

(i) against acquittal on any ground that involves a question of law alone;

(ii) against an order of a superior court of criminal jurisdiction that quashes an indictment or in any manner refuses or fails to exercise jurisdiction on an indictment;

(iii) against an order of a trial court that stays proceedings on an indictment or quashes an indictment; and

(iv) against the sentence passed by the trial court, provided either the court of appeal or a single judge of that court give their leave (unless, of course, the sentence is one fixed by law).[119]

It will be readily seen that the major difference between the rights of appeal enjoyed by the accused and by the Crown lies in the fact that, in general, the prosecution may appeal against an acquittal only if it involves a question of law, whereas the accused may appeal against conviction not only on a question of law, but also on a question of fact (or mixed law and fact). It has been suggested, from time to time, that the Crown and the accused should be on the same footing when it comes to their rights of appeal. However, it should be pointed out that the Crown already has more extensive rights of appeal than exist in certain other countries. For example, in England, a country whose legal system has many affinities with the Canadian legal system, the Crown does not even have the right to appeal against an acquittal. To allow the Crown, in Canada, to appeal against an acquittal on a question of fact as well as a question of law would place a very considerable burden on the shoulders of *every* accused person who has been acquitted at trial. Such a person would be constantly subjected to the threat of prolonged uncertainty and continuing expense until the appeal process had run its protracted course. Perhaps limiting the Crown's right of appeal to questions of law is a more satisfactory compromise, always assuming that it is desirable for the Crown to be able to appeal against an acquittal in the first place.[120]

In an important provision, the *Criminal Code*[121] states that the court of appeal or a judge of that court may assign a lawyer to act on behalf of an accused person who has brought an appeal, where in their opinion "it appears desirable in the interests of justice that the accused should have legal aid and where it appears that the accused has not sufficient means to obtain that aid."

Where the accused is appealing against conviction, the court of appeal may decide to allow his or her appeal in the following situations: namely, where in its opinion,

   (i) The verdict should be set aside on the ground that it is unreasonable or cannot be supported by the evidence,

  (ii) The judgment of the trial court should be set aside on the ground that there was a wrong decision on a question of law, or

 (iii) On any ground there was a miscarriage of justice.[122]

On the other hand, of course, the court of appeal may dismiss the accused's appeal. It may take this course of action where:

   (i) The court is of the opinion that the accused, even though he or she was not properly convicted on one count or part of the indictment, was properly convicted on another count or part of the indictment;

  (ii) The appeal is not decided in the accused's favour on the basis of any of the three grounds for allowing an appeal that are set out above;

 (iii) Even though the court is of the opinion that there was a mistake of law made by the trial court, it is nevertheless of the opinion that no substantial wrong or miscarriage of justice has occurred; or

 (iv) Even though there was a procedural irregularity at the trial, the trial court had the necessary jurisdiction over the class of offences of which the accused was convicted, and the appeal court is of the opinion that the accused did not suffer any prejudice as a consequence of the irregularity.[123]

Where the court of appeal decides to allow the accused's appeal, it has two options; it may

  (a) direct that a judgment or verdict of acquittal be entered, or

  (b) order a new trial.[124]

On the other hand, where the court of appeal decides to dismiss the accused's appeal, it may substitute the verdict that in its opinion should have been found and

(a) affirm the sentence passed by the trial court; or
(b) impose a sentence itself or send the matter back to the trial court with a direction to impose the appropriate sentence.[125]

What is the situation *where the prosecution is appealing against acquittal?* Of course, the court of appeal may just dismiss the appeal. Or, alternatively, it may allow the appeal, set aside the verdict and

(i) order a new trial, or
(ii) except where the acquittal was made by a jury, enter a verdict of guilty with respect to the offence of which, in its opinion, the accused should have been found guilty but for the error in law, and either impose a sentence itself, or send the case back to the trial court for the imposition of an appropriate sentence.[126]

Where an appeal has been made against the sentence imposed by the trial court, then the court of appeal may (provided, of course, that the sentence is not fixed by law) either

(a) vary the sentence within the limits permitted by the law, or
(b) dismiss the appeal.[127]

It is important to bear in mind that the court may vary a sentence upwards (in terms of severity) as well as downwards, even in the situation where it is the accused who has appealed against his or her sentence.[128] However, as a matter of basic justice, the Crown must give reasonable notice that it wishes to seek an increased sentence, and the accused be given the opportunity to be heard on this issue. Nevertheless, the threat of the possibility that a sentence could be increased is likely to have something of a chilling impact upon an accused person contemplating an appeal against his or her sentence.

Appeal to the Supreme Court of Canada

The *Criminal Code*[129] makes provision for an appeal from the decision of the court of appeal to the Supreme Court of Canada. A person who has been convicted of an indictable offence and whose conviction has been upheld by the provincial court of appeal may appeal to the Supreme Court of Canada:

(a) (as a matter of right) on any question of law on which a judge of the court of appeal has dissented,[130] or
(b) on any question of law if the accused obtains the leave of the Supreme Court of Canada or a judge of that court.

In addition, a person who has been acquitted of an indictable offence at trial and whose acquittal has been set aside by the court of appeal may appeal (as a matter of right) to the Supreme Court of Canada on a question of law.[131]

The Crown may appeal against the decision of the court of appeal in the following circumstances:

(a) (as a matter of right) on a question of law on which a judge of the court of appeal has dissented, or

(b) on any question of law with the leave of the Supreme Court of Canada.[132]

The powers of the Supreme Court of Canada in relation to indictable offences are the same as those available to the provincial courts of appeal, as discussed earlier.

Power of the Minister of Justice to Refer a Case to the Court of Appeal

Even though the appeal process may have been exhausted, there is one provision of the *Criminal Code*[133] that may be used to "re-open" an accused person's case. This provision gives the federal Minister of Justice, upon receiving an application by or on behalf of the accused person "for the mercy of the Crown," the power to

(i) order a new trial;

(ii) refer the case to the court of appeal for a hearing (as though it were an appeal by the accused person);

(iii) refer to the court of appeal, at any time, for its opinion, any question upon which he or she desires the assistance of that court, and "the court shall furnish its opinion accordingly."

Where the Minister of Justice refers a case to the court of appeal, it is highly likely that the court will be presented with fresh evidence that was not available at the original trial and the associated appeals.[134] It appears that the court of appeal, dealing with a reference from the Minister of Justice, may be willing to be more flexible in receiving new evidence than it would be if it were dealing with an "ordinary" appeal.[135]

Perhaps the most famous exercise of the minister's power to order a new trial occurred in the case of Dr. Henry Morgentaler during the mid-1970s. Dr. Morgentaler was acquitted by a Quebec jury of the charge of unlawfully procuring a miscarriage (abortion). However, the Crown appealed, and the Court of Appeal allowed the appeal and substituted a verdict of guilty. This was the first occasion upon which a court of appeal had used its power to

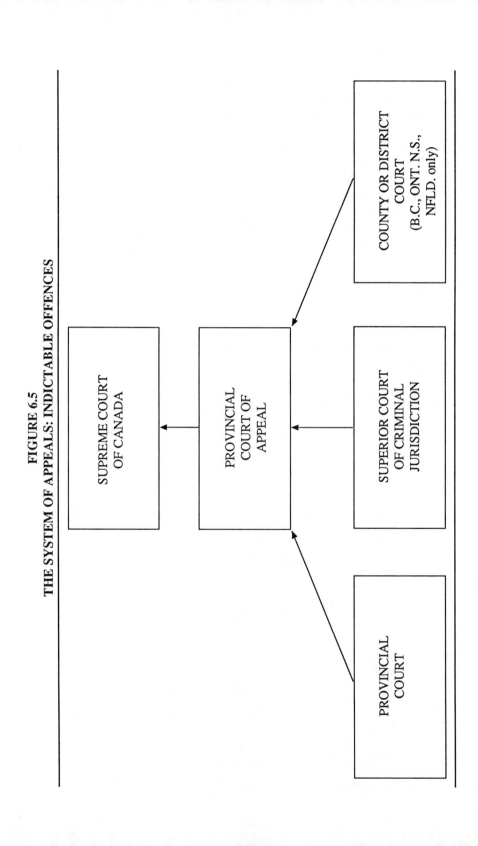

FIGURE 6.5
THE SYSTEM OF APPEALS: INDICTABLE OFFENCES

SUPREME COURT OF CANADA

PROVINCIAL COURT OF APPEAL

COUNTY OR DISTRICT COURT
(B.C., ONT. N.S., NFLD. only)

SUPERIOR COURT OF CRIMINAL JURISDICTION

PROVINCIAL COURT

substitute a verdict of guilty for an acquittal by a jury.[136] The Supreme Court of Canada ultimately upheld the Court of Appeal's decision.[137] The Minister of Justice subsequently ordered a new trial, at which Morgentaler was again acquitted by a jury (Dickens, 1976).

For easy reference, the process of appeals in relation to indictable offences has been summarized in Figure 6.5.

NOTES

1. The historical evolution of the criminal courts followed different paths in the various provinces and territories of Canada. The complexity of this process precludes an examination of the history of the criminal courts in this book. However, there is a rapidly burgeoning field of literature in this area, which may be usefully consulted. See, for example, Banks (1981); Bindon (1981); Flaherty (1981); Hett (1973); Knafla (1986); Knafla and Chapman (1983); Risk (1981); Williams, D. C. (1962, 1963); Williams, D.C. (1963, 1964, 1965, 1966); Williams, D. R. (1986).

2. Statistics from the Province of Alberta were not included in these figures.

3. Section 92(14).

4. For a detailed discussion of the court system in the Province of Quebec, see Giard and Proulx (1985). In Quebec, there is no intermediate court between the *Cour superieur* (Superior Court) and the *Cour provinciale* (Provincial Court). Above the Cour superieur is the appeal court, *la Cour d'appel.* There are two other courts, which have a similar jurisdiction to that of the Cour provinciale; namely, the *Cour des sessions de la paix* (Court of the Sessions of Peace) and the *cours municipals* (municipal courts). In practice, the judges of the municipal courts deal with relatively minor criminal cases. The Youth Court *(Tribunal de la jeunesse)* is a separate court in the Quebec judicial system.

5. Section 812 of the *Criminal Code.*

6. In some areas, so-called unified family courts have been established in order to try and bring all matters relating to the family (including youth offences) within one court building. This involves bringing together judges of the superior courts (who have jurisdiction to grant divorces, for example) as well as judges of the provincial courts (family division). For a discussion of a uniform family court project in British Columbia, see Waterhouse and Waterhouse (1983).

7. Sections 96 to 101 of the *Constitution Act, 1867.*

8. Section 92(4) of the *Constitution Act, 1867.*

9. Section 790 of the *Criminal Code.*

10. Section 2 of the *Code.*

11. See Pavlich (1985: III-172–75).

12. *R. v. Robert* (1973), 13 C.C.C. (2d) 43 (Ont. C.A.).

13. *R. v. German* (1947), 3 C.R. 516, [1947] O.R. 395 (C.A.).
14. *Re Abarca and The Queen* (1980), 57 C.C.C. (2d) 410, *per* Lacourciere J.A., at 416.
15. *Re Warren et al. and The Queen* (1983), 10 W.C.B. 146.
16. *R. v. Darbishire* (1983), 11 W.C.B. 5.
17. *Re Parkin and The Queen* (1986), 28 C.C.C. (3d) 252, 140 O.A.C. 150 (Ont. C.A.).
18. Section 786(2).
19. The exception to this general rule is the rarely used direct indictment procedure that is discussed later in this chapter.
20. *Per* Lamer, J., in *Dowson v. The Queen* (1983), 7 C.C.C. (3d) 527 at 536, [1983] 2 S.C.R. 144, 35 C.R. (3d) 289.
21. Section 504.
22. See, for example, *Myhren v. R.* (1985), 48 C.R. (3d) 270, [1986] N.W.T.R. 15 (S.C.). The Supreme Court of Canada has ruled that there must be a reasonable degree of specificity in an information; *R. v. WIS Development Corp. Ltd.* (1984), 12 C.C.C. (3d) 129, [1984] 1 S.C.R. 485, 40 C.R. (3d) 97.
23. It has been argued that in Toronto, for example, the police lay most of the routine criminal charges without consultation with Crown counsel (Wheeler, 1987).
24. Sections 507 and 508.
25. Section 507(4).
26. Even where an arrest warrant is issued, the *Code* gives the justice the discretion, in relation to most offences, to endorse the warrant so that the officer in charge of a police lock-up may later release the accused on bail (sections 510 and 499). The details of the bail procedure are discussed in the next section.
27. Section 508.
28. See, for example, section 14 of the *Offence Act*, RSBC 1979, c. 305, which sets out the traffic ticket scheme for the Province of British Columbia.
29. The *Bail Reform Act* is incorporated in the *Criminal Code.*
30. *Criminal Code*, section 498(1).
31. In deciding whether the "public interest" requires that the suspect be kept in custody, the officer in charge is required to have regard to "all the circumstances," including the need to (i) establish the identity of the suspect, (ii) secure or preserve evidence relating to the offence, or (iii) prevent the continuation or repetition of the offence or the commission of another offence (section 498(1)(i)).
32. Section 498(1)(i) and (j).
33. Where a police officer has arrested a suspect under a warrant, issued by a justice of the peace, then the officer in charge may release the suspect *provided the justice has endorsed the warrant so as to permit this course of action*: section 499. The suspect may be released upon giving a

promise to appear, a simple recognizance or (in the case of a non-resident) a recognizance and some form of security.

34. Section 145(5).

35. Section 502.

36. Section 503(1).

37. Section 516. Adjournments of more than three days may not take place without the consent of the accused.

38. Section 522.

39. Section 469.

40. It should be noted that upon the application of the accused, the justice or the judge will impose a press and media blackout on the evidence presented at a bail hearing (section 517). This provision is intended to protect the accused from the impact of publicity that may prejudice him or her at trial.

41. See section 515(1) of the *Criminal Code.*

42. S.C. 1974-75-76, c. 93.

43. Section 522(2).

44. Section 515(10).

45. *Re Powers and The Queen* (1972), 9 C.C.C. (2d) 533, 20 C.R.N.S. 23 (Ont. H.C.J.), *per* Lerner, J., at 544–45.

46. These five methods of release (and the conditions that may be imposed in connection with them) are also applicable to those cases involving the serious charges that may be dealt with only by a judge of a superior court of criminal jurisdiction: section 522(3).

47. Section 515(2).

48. Sections 766 and 767.

49. Section 767.1.

50. Section 515(4).

51. Insofar as the question of the imposition of conditions is concerned, it should be noted that an Ontario court decision has held that section 11(e) of the *Charter* requires that each bail application must be considered on an individual basis, in terms of the offence and the accused person, and that the *justice must inquire as to the ability of the accused person to meet the conditions that may be imposed: Re R. and Brooks et al.* (1982), 1 C.C.C. (3d) 506, 2 C.R.R. 246, 143 D.L.R. (3d) 482 (Ont. H.C.J.).

52. *R. v. Bielefeld* (1981), 64 C.C.C. (2d) 216 (B.C.S.C.).

53. In 1985, the various organizations providing bail verification and supervision services in Ontario formed the Association of Pre-Trial Services of Ontario.

54. Bail programs exist, for example, in British Columbia, the Yukon, Alberta, Saskatchewan and Ontario.

55. Section 524(1) and (2).

56. Section 524(4).

57. Section 523.

58. Section 523(2).

59. Section 679(1); sections 816 and 831.

60. Section 520.

61. Section 680.

62. Section 525.

63. This provision does not apply, however, to those accused persons whose offences are so serious that their bail status can be determined only by a judge of the superior court of criminal jurisdiction.

64. Section 525(3).

65. Section 525(9).

66. These procedures are normally contained in the applicable provincial *Summary Convictions Act.*

67. Section 785(1).

68. Section 800(2).

69. Section 803(2).

70. *R. v. Tarrant* (1984), 13 C.C.C. (3d) 219, 11 C.R.R. 368, 10 D.L.R. (4th) 751 (B.C.C.A.); *R. v. Rogers*, [1984] 6 W.W.R. 89, 13 C.R.R. 189, 34 Sask. R. 284 (Sask. C.A.).

71. *R. v. McLeod* (1983), 36 C.R. (3d) 378 (N.W.T.S.C.).

72. Section 471.

73. Section 469.

74. Section 473.

75. Technically, the term *absolute jurisdiction* is misleading because the superior court of criminal jurisdiction in each province has the jurisdiction "to try any indictable offence" (section 468). However, it would be very rare indeed for a superior court to try an offence falling within the so-called absolute jurisdiction of a provincial court judge.

76. Section 553.

77. Section 535(2).

78. Section 568. It has been held that this provision does not infringe either section 7 or section 11(f) of the *Charter: Re Hanneson and The Queen* (1987), 31 C.C.C. (3d) 560, 27 C.R.R. 278 (Ont. H.C.J.).

79. Section 561.

80. Section 561(1)(b).

81. Section 561(1)(c).

82. Section 536(3).

83. *Re R. and Brass* (1981), 64 C.C.C. (2d) 206 (Sask. Q.B.).

84. Section 540.

85. Section 541.

86. Section 539. It has been held that this section does not infringe the guarantee of freedom of the press contained in section 2(b) of the *Charter: R. v. Banville* (1983), 3 C.C.C. (3d) 312, 5 C.R.R. 142, 34 C.R. (3d) 20.

87. Section 548.

88. Section 549.

89. Section 577.

90. In the case of private prosecutions, the written consent of a judge is required for the direct indictment procedure. See section 577(d).

91. *Re R. and Arviv* (1985), 19 C.C.C. (3d) 395, 13 C.R.R. 358, 45 C.R. (3d) 354 (Ont. C.A.). This ruling was predicated on the assumption that the accused must be given a full disclosure of the Crown's case.

92. *R. v. Rosamond* (1983), 5 C.C.C. (3d) 523, 4 C.R.R. 311, 149 D.L.R. (3d) 716 (Sask. Q.B.).

93. In *Re Oshaweetok and The Queen* (1984), 16 C.C.C. (3d) 392, 12 C.R.R. 330, [1985] N.W.T.R. 47 (N.W.T.S.C.), for example, it was held that laying an identical charge after the accused has been discharged in the course of a preliminary inquiry constitutes an abuse of process and violates the fundamental principles of justice guaranteed by section 7 of the *Charter* *unless* there is some *new evidence* that has been uncovered since the preliminary inquiry.

94. *Patterson v. The Queen*, [1970] S.C.R. 409; *Caccamo v. The Queen*, [1976] 1 S.C.R. 786.

95. See, for example, *Cunliffe v. Law Society of B.C.; Bledsoe v. Law Society of B.C.,* [1984] 4 W.W.R. 451, 40 C.R. (3d) 67, 13 C.C.C. (3d) 560 (B.C.C.A.).

96. An important question that remains to be answered is whether courts will consider that the *Charter* requires that an adequate degree of discovery be given to the accused. There are at least two potentially relevant provisions. Section 7 states that a person may only be deprived of "life or liberty" in accordance with the "principles of fundamental justice." Section 11(d) preserves the accused's right to a "fair hearing." It is not yet clear how the courts are likely to decide this issue. See Ferguson, 1985: Supp. XIII-3.

97. Section 625.1. This provision was enacted in 1985 but has not yet come into force.

98. Section 574.

99. Section 650(1).

100. The Law Reform Commission of Canada (1980: 22) noted that there were 1,370 jury trials across Canada in 1976–77. Various issues concerning the jury are discussed in Law Reform Commission of Canada (1980 and 1982).

101. Unpublished statistics from "Disposition Report: Provincial Adult Criminal Court, Jan. 01, 1986 to Dec. 31, 1986," made available by Ministry of Attorney General, Policy Planning Branch. The percentage cited does not include the vast number of provincial motor vehicle offences.

102. *Ibid.*

103. Part XXVII.

104. Section 822(4).

105. Section 813.

106. Section 822, incorporating section 686.

107. Section 822(2).

108. Section 686.

109. Section 687.

110. Section 830.

111. Section 834(1).

112. *R. v. Giambalvo* (1982), 70 C.C.C. (2d) 324, 39 O.R. (2d) 588 (Ont. C.A.).

113. It should be noted, as a technical point, that for *some purposes* in *some* provinces, the superior court of criminal jurisdiction may well be the provincial court of appeal (see section 2). In this situation, there could be no appeal along the lines discussed in the text (see section 839(1)(b)) since there could not be an appeal from the court of appeal to itself.

114. Section 839.

115. Part XXI.

116. Section 673.

117. Section 675(1)(a).

118. Section 675(1)(b).

119. Section 676.

120. In *Morgentaler et al. v. The Queen* (1988), 37 C.C.C. (3d) 449, [1988] 1 S.C.R. 30, 31 C.R.R. 1, the majority of the justices of the Supreme Court of Canada who heard the case ruled that the right of the Crown to appeal against an acquittal, on a matter of law, does not offend the *Charter's* guarantee against double jeopardy (section 11(h) of the *Charter*).

121. Section 684.

122. Section 686(1)(a).

123. Section 686(1)(b).

124. Section 686(2).

125. Section 686(3).

126. Section 686(4).

127. Section 687.

128. *Hill v. The Queen*, [1977] 1 S.C.R. 827, 25 C.C.C. (2d) 6, 62 D.L.R. (3d) 193.

129. Sections 691–695.

130. A judge of the court of appeal dissents when he or she disagrees with the decision of the court in any particular case and provides his or her reasons in a separate opinion.

131. Section 691(2). This subsection also provides for an appeal (as a matter of right) on a question of law in the situation where the accused was tried jointly with another, was convicted and his or her conviction was upheld on appeal, while his or her co-accused, on the other hand, was acquitted at trial and his or her acquittal was set aside by the court of appeal.

132. Section 693.

133. Section 690.

134. *Reference Re R. v. Gorecki (No. 2)* (1976), 32 C.C.C. (2d) 135 (Ont. C.A.).

135. *R. v. Marshall* (1983), 57 N.S.R. (2d) 286 (N.S.C.A.).

136. This power has now been removed, and the court of appeal is now restricted to ordering a new trial where it allows an appeal against acquittal. See section 686(4)(b)(ii).

137. *Morgentaler v. The Queen*, [1976] 1 S.C.R. 616, 30 C.R.N.S. 209.

REFERENCES

Atrens, J. 1985. "The Classification of Offences." In *Criminal Procedure: Canadian Law and Practice*, edited by J. Atrens, P. T. Burns, and J. Taylor, I-1–I-42–44. Vancouver: Butterworths & Co. (Western Canada).

———. 1986. "The Charging Procedure." In *Criminal Procedure: Canadian Law and Practice,* edited by J. Atrens, P. T. Burns, and J. Taylor, IX-i–IX-51. Vancouver: Butterworths & Co. (Western Canada).

Banks, M. A. 1981. "The Evolution of the Ontario Courts 1788–1981." In *Essays in the History of Canadian Law*, Vol. II, edited by D. H. Flaherty, 492–572. Toronto: University of Toronto Press.

Bindon, K. M. 1981. "Hudson's Bay Company Law: Adam Thom and the Institution of Order in Rupert's Land 1839–54." In *Essays in the History of Canadian Law,* edited by D. H. Flaherty, 44–87. Toronto: University of Toronto Press.

Canadian Centre for Justice Statistics. 1986. *Custodial Remand in Canada — A National Survey.* Ottawa: Canadian Centre for Justice Statistics.

Cohen, S. A. 1977. *Due Process of Law: The Canadian System of Criminal Justice.* Toronto: Carswell.

Demers, D. J. 1984. "Criminal Justice Spending in Canada: Recent Trends." 2 *Impact* 4–12.

Dickens, B. 1976. "The *Morgentaler* Case: Criminal Process and Abortion Law." 14 *Osgoode Hall Law Journal* 229–73.

Doob, A. N., and A. Cavoukian. 1977. "The Effect of the Revoking of Bail: *R. v. Demeter.*" 19 *Criminal Law Quarterly* 196–202.

Ericson, R. V., and P. M. Baranek. 1982. *The Ordering of Justice: A Study of Accused Persons as Dependants in the Criminal Process.* Toronto: University of Toronto Press.

Ferguson, G. 1985. "Discovery in Criminal Cases." In *Criminal Procedure: Canadian Law and Practice*, edited by J. Atrens, P. T. Burns, and J. Taylor, XIII-i–XIII-195. Vancouver: Butterworths & Co. (Western Canada).

Flaherty, D. H. 1981. "Writing Canadian Legal History: An Introduction." In *Essays in the History of Canadian Law*, Vol. I, edited by D. H. Flaherty, 3–42. Toronto: University of Toronto Press.

Friedenberg, E. Z. 1985. "Law in a Cynical Society". In *Law in a Cynical Society: Opinion and Law in the 1980's*, edited by D. Gibson and J. K. Baldwin, 417–26. Vancouver: Carswell Legal Publications.

Friedland, M. 1965. *Detention before Trial.* Toronto: University of Toronto Press. XIII-i–XIII-195.

Gall, G. L. 1983. *The Canadian Legal System.* 2nd ed. Toronto: Carswell Legal Publications.

Giard, M., and M. Proulx. 1985. *Pour Comprendre l'Appareil Judiciaire Québécois.* Sillery, Que.: Presses de l'Université du Québec.

Hagan, J. 1984. *The Disreputable Pleasures: Crime and Deviance in Canada.* 2nd ed. Toronto: McGraw-Hill Ryerson Ltd.

Hagan, J., and C. P. Morden. 1981. "The Police Decision to Detain: A Study of Legal Labelling and Police Deviance." In *Organizational Police Deviance: Its Structure and Control,* edited by C. D. Shearing, 9–28. Toronto: Butterworths.

Hamilton, K. R. 1985. "Judicial Interim Release." In *Criminal Procedure: Canadian Law and Practice,* edited by J. Atrens, P. T. Burns, and J. Taylor, IV-i–IV-91. Vancouver: Butterworths & Co. (Western Canada).

Hann, R. 1973. *Decision-Making in a Canadian Criminal Court System: A Systems Approach.* 2 Vols. Toronto: Centre of Criminology, University of Toronto.

Hett, R. 1973. "Judge Willis and the Court of King's Bench in Upper Canada." 65 *Ontario History* 19–30.

Hogg, P. W. 1985. *Constitutional Law of Canada.* 2nd ed. Toronto: Carswell Co.

Holmes, R. D. 1982. "The Scope of Judicial Review of Preliminary Hearings and Committals for Trial." 16 *U.B.C. Law Review* 257–94.

Knafla, L. A. 1986. "From Oral to Written Memory: The Common Law Tradition in Western Canada". In *Law and Justice in a New Land. Essays in Western Canadian Legal History,* edited by L. A. Knafla, 31–77. Toronto: Carswell.

Knafla, L. A., and T. L. Chapman. 1983. "Criminal Justice in Canada: A Comparative Study of the Maritimes and Lower Canada 1760–1812." 21 *Osgoode Hall Law Journal* 245–74.

Koza, P., and A. N. Doob. 1975a. "The Relationship of Pre-trial Custody to the Outcome of a Trial." 17 *Criminal Law Quarterly* 391–400.

———. 1975b. "Some Empirical Evidence on Judicial Interim Release Proceedings." 17 *Criminal Law Quarterly* 258–72.

———. 1977. "Police Attitudes toward the Bail Reform Act." 19 *Criminal Law Quarterly* 405–14.

Law Reform Commission of Canada. 1974. *Working Paper No. 4: Criminal Procedure: Discovery.* Ottawa: Information Canada.

———. 1980. *Working Paper No. 27: The Jury in Criminal Trials.* Ottawa: Minister of Supply and Services Canada.

_____. 1982. *Report No. 16: The Jury.* Ottawa: Minister of Supply and Services Canada.

_____. 1984. *Report No. 22: Disclosure by the Prosecution.* Ottawa: Minister of Supply and Services Canada.

MacKaay, E. 1976. *The Paths of Justice: A Study of the Operation of the Criminal Courts in Montreal.* Montreal: Groupe de Recherche en Jurimetrie, Université de Montréal.

Morris, R. 1981. "Toronto Bail Program." 25 *International Journal of Offender Therapy and Comparative Criminology* 156–67.

Ouimet, R. (Chairman). 1969. *Report of the Canadian Committee on Corrections — Toward Unity: Criminal Justice and Corrections.* (Catalogue No. JS52-1-1968.) Ottawa: Information Canada.

Pavlich, D. J. 1985. "Law of Arrest." In *Criminal Procedure: Canadian Law and Practice,* edited by J. Atrens, P. T. Burns, and J. Taylor, III-1–III-211. Vancouver: Butterworths & Co. (Western Canada).

Proulx, M. 1983. "The Presence of the Accused at Trial." 25 *Criminal Law Quarterly* 179–205.

Ramsey, J. A. 1988. "Prosecutorial Discretion: A Reply to David Vanek." 30 *Criminal Law Quarterly* 378–83.

Risk, R. C. B. 1981. "The Law and the Economy in Mid-Nineteenth Century Ontario: A Perspective". In *Essays in the History of Canadian Law,* Vol. I, edited by D. H. Flaherty, 88–131. Toronto: University of Toronto Press.

Salhany, R. E. 1984. *Canadian Criminal Procedure.* 4th ed. Aurora, Ont.: Canada Law Book Inc.

Shetreet, S. 1979. "The Administration of Justice: Practical Problems, Value Conflicts and Changing Concepts." 13 *U.B.C. Law Review* 52–80.

Statistics Canada. 1985. "Manpower, Resources and Costs of Courts and Criminal Prosecutions in Canada 1983–84." 5(2) *Juristat Service Bulletin* 1–6.

Stenning, P. C. 1986. *Appearing for the Crown: A Legal and Historical Review of Criminal Prosecutorial Authority in Canada.* Cowansville, Que.: Brown Legal Publications.

Taylor, J. P., and F. M. Irvine. 1986. "The Preliminary Inquiry and the Election". In *Criminal Procedure: Canadian Law and Practice,* edited by J. Atrens, P. T. Burns, and J. Taylor, XIV-i–XIV-52. Vancouver: Butterworths & Co. (Western Canada).

Vanek, D. 1988. "Prosecutorial Discretion." 30 *Criminal Law Quarterly* 219–37.

Waddams, S. M. 1987. *Introduction to the Study of Law.* 3rd ed. Toronto: Carswell.

Waterhouse, J., and L. Waterhouse. 1983. "Implementing Unified Family Courts." 4 *Canadian Journal of Family Law* 153–71.

Wheeler, G. 1987. "The Police, the Crowns and the Courts: Who's Running the Show?" February 1987 *Canadian Lawyer* 27–31.

Williams, D. C. 1962 and 1963. "The Dawn of Law on the Prairies." 26 and 28 *Saskatchewan Bar Review* (vol. 26) 126–33; (vol. 28) 17–27, 63–69.

———. 1963, 1964, 1965 and 1966. "Law and Institutions in the North West Territories (1869–1905)." 28, 29, 30, and 31 *Saskatchewan Bar Review* (vol. 28) 109–18; (vol. 29) 83–101; (vol. 30) 51–66; (vol. 31) 1–26, 137–61.

Williams, D. R. 1986. "The Administration of Criminal and Civil Justice in the Mining Camps and Frontier Communities of British Columbia." In *Law and Justice in a New Land. Essays in Western Canadian Legal History*, edited by L. A. Knafla, 215–32. Toronto: Carswell.

LEGISLATION

Bail Reform Act, R.S.C. 1970 (2nd Supp.), c. 2; see now *Criminal Code*, Part XVI

Constitution Act, 1867, 1867 (U.K.), c. 3

Criminal Code, R.S.C. 1985, c. C-46

Identification of Criminals Act, R.S.C. 1985, c. I-1

Offence Act, R.S.B.C. 1979, c. 305

7 CURRENT ISSUES CONCERNING THE COURT PROCESS

This chapter addresses four of the current issues that are frequently raised in connection with the operation of the court process in Canada; namely, the right to counsel and legal representation in court; court delay; prosecutorial discretion; and plea bargaining. Each of these issues raises some fundamental questions about the degree to which the criminal courts are capable of ensuring that each accused person is treated in accordance with the rights enshrined in the *Canadian Charter of Rights and Freedoms.*

The Right to Counsel and Legal Representation in Court

The immensely complex structure of the court process, together with the intricate set of procedural and evidential rules that govern the conduct of a criminal trial, place the accused person at a considerable disadvantage vis-à-vis the professional lawyer who conducts the prosecution on behalf of the Crown. In these circumstances, it is not surprising that considerable emphasis has been placed upon the need to ensure that accused persons are treated with "due process of law" by providing them with legal representation when they appear in court. Indeed, Greenspan (1985: 207) has contended that the "due process without the right to counsel is as empty as democracy without free elections."

It has often been suggested that the right to counsel is an essential component of a criminal court system that is based on an adversarial approach to matters of justice. As a former Chief Justice of British Columbia remarked in a case before the Court of Appeal:

> Our criminal justice system is administered under the adversary system; that is to say, a system where when a conflict arises between a citizen and the state the two are to be regarded as adversaries. The conflict is to be resolved by fighting it out according to fixed, sometimes rather arbitrary, rules. The tribunal trying the matter settles the dispute on the basis of only such evidence as the contestants choose to present.[1]

The Chief Justice went on to point out that the rules of procedure and evidence that are employed in a criminal trial are so complex that they can be understood only after a long period of training and experience. It is for this reason, he said, that the Crown employs counsel who are well versed in the law and are knowledgeable about the techniques of advocacy. Prosecutors also have the resources of both the government and the police to support them in presenting their cases. It would be unrealistic, therefore, to expect the average defendant in a criminal case to be able to compete on an equal basis with Crown counsel if he or she is unrepresented by a lawyer (Griffiths, Cousineau and Verdun-Jones, 1980: 217).

The Right to Counsel

There are a number of provisions in both the *Charter* and the *Criminal Code* that have a direct bearing on the right to counsel. Section 10(b) of the *Charter*, as we have seen in our earlier discussion of police powers, guarantees to a person who has been arrested or detained the right to "retain and instruct counsel without delay and the right to be informed of that right." This particular provision, however, does not apply specifically to the representation of an accused person in the courtroom setting. Section 11(d) of the *Charter*, on the other hand, is of considerable relevance to the trial situation since it protects the right to a "fair and public hearing by an independent and impartial tribunal," and it can well be argued that a necessary component of a fair hearing is that an accused person should be represented by legal counsel of his or her choice[2] (Osborne, 1986).

The *Criminal Code*[3] provides that "an accused is entitled, after the close of the case for the prosecution, to make full answer and defence personally or by counsel." Thus the courts have ruled that a lawyer cannot be forced upon an unwilling defendant[4] and that a court cannot proceed with a trial where the accused's lawyer fails to show up in court.[5] Furthermore, it has been held that where the accused is unrepresented, the trial judge has a special duty to ensure that there is a fair hearing.[6] If an accused person is not granted his or her right to counsel at trial, then a new trial may be ordered by the appropriate appeal court (Ziskrout, 1985: XIX-32).

An important provision of the *Code*[7] empowers the provincial court of appeal, or a judge of that court, to assign counsel to act on behalf of a defendant who is involved in an appeal, "where, in the opinion of the court or judge, it appears desirable in the interests of justice that the accused should have legal aid and where it appears that the accused has not sufficient means to obtain that aid." This statutory provision applies only to appeals to the court of appeal. However, there has been some suggestion that other courts may have a residual power to assign counsel to act on behalf of an accused person who lacks the means to engage counsel.[8] In a significant case in Alberta,[9] a Supreme Court Judge ruled that there may be exceptional circumstances in which a trial court has the power to assign counsel to a defendant. According to this decision, the factors that would need to be taken into account in deciding whether counsel should be assigned might include the financial position and educational level of the accused, the complexity of the case, and the possibility that the accused may be imprisoned if convicted. In addition, it may be the case that the legal aid authority is willing to grant a legal aid certificate, in which case there should be an adjournment to permit the accused to apply to the authority in question. However, it is important to note that the court in this case did not go so far as to suggest that *all* indigent accused are entitled to have counsel appointed for them, nor did it express the view that there can never be a fair trial where the accused is unrepresented.

In a case decided before the enactment of the *Charter*,[10] the British Columbia Court of Appeal ruled that indigent accused were not entitled to have counsel appointed for them, *as a general rule*, but at least one of the judges suggested that the duty of the trial judge to ensure that there is a fair trial might require the appointment of counsel in special circumstances, such as where the case is exceedingly complex (Ziskrout, 1985: XIX-28). This approach was also embraced by Craig, J., of the Ontario Divisional Court in a case decided more recently under the provisions of the *Charter*.[11] Craig, J., clearly rejected the contention that the *Charter* had entrenched a "right to funded counsel." Indeed, he said:

> . . . the right to a funded counsel has not been entrenched by s. 7 and/or s. 11(*d*) of the Charter. With the exception of the language provisions, most of the rights guaranteed by the Charter are expressed in negative terms, in the sense that they require that the state refrain from certain activities. To impose a constitutionally entrenched positive duty on the government to expend public funds on the defence of persons accused of crimes would require a specific guarantee in express language [(1985), 48 C.R. at 172]

However, he also stated that there may be certain exceptional cases in which legal counsel must be appointed by the court if the accused is to be accorded a fair trial:

> Pursuant to s. 7 of the Charter, the accused has an entrenched right not to be deprived of his liberty except in accordance with the principles of fundamental justice. Also, pursuant to s. 11(*d*), he has an entrenched right to a "fair and public hearing". The right to fundamental justice and a fair and public hearing includes the right to a fair trial. There may be rare cases where legal aid is denied to an accused person facing trial, but, where the trial judge is satisfied that, because of the seriousness and complexity of the case, the accused cannot receive a fair trial without counsel, in such a case it seems to follow that there is an entrenched right to funded counsel under the Charter. [(1985), 48 C.R. at 173–74]

It remains to be seen whether, in the future, other courts (and, in particular, the appellate courts) will prove willing to give a broader interpretation of the right to a fair trial. Nevertheless, the present position is that, while accused have an absolute right to counsel, they do not have the absolute right to have counsel appointed for them and paid for with government funds.[11a]

Legal Aid in the Criminal Courts

In order to ensure that the poorest members of the community are not denied access to counsel because of lack of funds, legal aid programs have been established across Canada. The first comprehensive legal aid system was introduced in the Province of Ontario in 1967 (Wilkins, 1975: Zemans, 1986: 47). Today, most legal aid plans are based on provincial legislation and are administered independently of government departments.

In 1984–85, legal aid plans received $182.1 million to provide legal services across Canada. Ninety per cent of these moneys were provided by government, with the remaining funds coming from lawyers' trust accounts (5%; in four provinces only), and from clients (3%) (Canadian Centre for Justice Statistics, 1986: 13).

Legal aid agencies provide a range of services, including not only legal representation but also referral and information services. These services cover the criminal law and also various areas of civil law (such as family law). However, about 46% of the 460,412 applications for legal aid that were approved during 1984–85 related to criminal cases (Canadian Centre for Justice Statistics, 1986: 13).

As far as criminal cases are concerned, legal aid is generally provided for all indictable offences and for summary conviction offences where there is a reasonable chance that the accused will go to jail or will lose his or her livelihood (e.g., through the revocation of a driving licence).[12] However, it is important to emphasize that even if accused persons should qualify in terms of these general criteria of eligibility, they will not be granted legal aid unless they also meet certain financial requirements, designed to limit the award of legal aid to the most needy citizens. These requirements vary from province to province. However, an evaluation conducted in British Columbia suggests that, in that province at least, only the most impoverished members of the community were likely to qualify. For example, the average monthly income of those who qualified for legal aid, during 1982, was only $500 (Brantingham and Brantingham, 1984: 171).[13]

Legal aid services are not provided in a uniform manner across Canada. Indeed, there are three models for delivering such services across the country. In the Provinces of New Brunswick and Alberta (as well as in the two territories), legal aid services are provided by *private* lawyers on a fee-for-service basis, with the legal aid plan bearing all or most of the costs; this model, which gives each client the choice regarding which lawyer will represent him or her, is known as the *judicare model*. On the other hand, in Prince Edward Island, Nova Scotia and Saskatchewan, legal aid is provided through a *staff system* in which staff lawyers are employed directly by the legal aid plan.[14] In this system, the individual client does not have the opportunity to choose his or her lawyer.[15] This system is based on the so-called *public defender model*. In Newfoundland, Quebec, Ontario, Manitoba and British Columbia, the judicare and public defender models are combined in one system for the delivery of legal aid. In this *combined model*, legal services are provided by both staff lawyers and private lawyers on a fee-for-service basis (Canadian Centre for Justice Statistics, 1986: 13).

What are the comparative advantages of the judicare and public defender models for delivering legal aid services? According to Burns and Reid (1981: 412–14), the advantages claimed on behalf of the judicare system include the following: in the judicare system, the client has the choice of lawyer; the ordinary lawyer-client relationship that exists in non-legal aid cases is extended to the poor in the judicare system; the judicare lawyer is independent and owes a duty only to the client and the court; the judicare system is better equipped to deal with rural and remote areas because it is decentralized in nature; the judicare system is no more costly than the public defender system. On the other hand, the advantages claimed on behalf of the public defender system, according to Burns and Reid (1981: 414–16), include the following: public defenders are specialists in their particular area of law; they are less costly than judicare lawyers; the public defender system is more efficient because it is centralized; public defenders become spokespersons for the poor; since public defenders are salaried, they do not have any incentive to adopt tactics that are in their own financial interest rather than in the interests of their clients. Without the necessary research, it is not possible to evaluate all the relative claims made in support of one system or the other. However, there have been studies that have attempted to evaluate the two systems in order to determine their relative cost efficiency and whether there are any differences in the results achieved by lawyers in the two systems.

There have been two major studies of the costs of the public defender and judicare systems. An evaluation, over three years, of a relatively small public defender program in a suburb of Vancouver (Burnaby) found that there was very little difference between the costs of services provided by the public defender system and the costs of services delivered by private lawyers on a fee-for-service basis (Brantingham and Burns, 1981). However, an evaluation conducted in the Province of Quebec by the Commission des Services Juridiques (cited in Zemans, 1986: 54) indicated that the public defender model was more cost effective than the judicare system. The reason for the difference in the outcome of these studies seems to lie in the different nature of the public defender programs evaluated. The British Columbia study was based on a small public defender project employing only three lawyers and a paralegal, and it dealt almost exclusively with criminal cases. The Quebec study, on the other hand, was concerned with both civil and criminal legal aid cases and involved a greater number of lawyers, thereby permitting economies of scale.

While the research is equivocal about the relative cost efficiency of the two systems, it is interesting to note that insofar as criminal cases are concerned, the evaluation of the British Columbia public defender project did indicate that there were significant differences between the results obtained by public defenders and private lawyers operating on a fee-for-service basis. Brantingham (1985) found that there were no significant differences between public defenders and private lawyers insofar as findings of guilt or innocence were concerned. However, it was found that there were strong differences in the sentencing outcomes obtained by private lawyers and public defenders. Convicted clients of the public defenders were much less likely to be incarcerated (24.5%) than were the clients of the private lawyers (40.4%), although there were no major differences in the length of the jail terms or the size of the fines imposed on the two groups. The reason for the differences in the incarceration rates was to be found in "differences in discussion patterns between defence counsel and Crown counsel" (Brantingham, 1985: 76). Clients of the private lawyers received similar sentences whether or not discussions were held with the Crown (about 40% of the sentences involved imprisonment). On the other hand, when public defenders had discussions with the Crown, their clients were much less likely to be imprisoned (17%). However, when no such discussions occurred, the incarceration rates of clients of the public defenders were similar to those of the clients of the private lawyers (36% versus 40%, respectively). It seems that the public defenders found it relatively easy to discuss cases with Crown counsel because they were in daily contact with them. Although this study might well suggest that the public defender system may be more effective in terms of achieving a more satisfactory sentencing outcome, it also raises serious questions about the desirability of a system that appears to deny many of the benefits of plea bargaining to private lawyers while offering such benefits to the public defender lawyers who happened to interact frequently with Crown counsel.

In addition to appointing lawyers to represent individual accused persons, both the judicare and public defender systems generally provide *duty counsel* to assist in the representation of accused persons, particularly before they make their first appearance in court. Duty counsel are either private lawyers paid by the legal aid plan or staff lawyers (if the province concerned is based on the public defender model) who give summary advice primarily to those who are held in custody. They may ensure that the accused applies for legal aid and that bail is applied for where appropriate. They may also represent the accused at the sentencing hearing if the latter should plead guilty on his or her first appearance in court. The provision of duty counsel is an extremely cost-effective method of offering legal services to a large number of clients and is particularly useful as a means of bringing legal advice to those accused who are held in custody by the police prior to their first appearance in court. However, it is not a system that is able to provide close personal attention to the problems of individual clients. Indeed, in their interviews of 101 defendants in an Ontario municipal jurisdiction, Ericson and Baranek (1982: 85) found that most of their subjects talked negatively of duty counsel because of their being simultaneously involved in a large number of cases. However, Ericson and Baranek (1982: 201) also point out that duty counsel are so overburdened with cases that it is not surprising that they cannot gain a complete understanding of the client's circumstances.

As well as making the services of duty counsel available, most Canadian jurisdictions provide funding for various organizations to offer the services of courtworkers to accused persons caught up in the criminal court process (Brantingham and Brantingham, 1984: 65). Courtworkers provide valuable assistance to accused persons, largely in the form of helping them to understand the court process and ensuring that they are aware of their legal rights and their entitlement to apply for legal aid. Courtworkers may also be called upon to provide information to the court, particularly on matters relevant to sentencing. Among the organizations that may provide services primarily (but by no means exclusively) to clients from specific "minority groups" are the Elizabeth Fry Society and various native courtworker organizations (for example, the Native Courtworker and Counselling Association of B.C. and the Native Counselling Services of Alberta). One organization that may provide courtworker services on a more general basis in the provincial courts is the Salvation Army.

One of the most significant of the recent developments in the provision of legal aid services is the emergence of paralegals, non-lawyers who provide various legal services to low-income persons, under the supervision of lawyers (Zemans, 1986: 57). They may offer services directly to clients or may operate in a support role to lawyers in a community legal aid clinic setting. The emergence of paralegals as important contributors to the system for delivering legal services to the poor may well permit legal aid authorities to meet some of the ever-increasing demand for such services at a time when governments have implemented policies of financial restraint that have assigned a relatively low priority to spending on legal aid.[16] Indeed, paralegals not only provide a cost-effective service, but also tend to be particularly responsive to the needs of the local community (Zemans, 1986: 61).

Canadian Research into the Nature and Extent of Legal Representation in the Criminal Courts

What does Canadian research suggest about the nature and extent of legal representation in Canada? It would appear that most defendants in a criminal case obtain legal representation where the charge is indictable, but that a significant proportion are unrepresented when the charge relates to a summary conviction offence. For example, in a study of a Toronto provincial court, Taman (1975) found that only 48% of those persons charged with *summary* offences were represented, while 72% of those charged with *indictable* offences enjoyed the services of legal counsel. In a more comprehensive study, Renner and Warner (1981) studied defendants appearing before three magistrates' courts and two county courts in Halifax. They found (1981: 69) that 90% of the defendants charged with *indictable* offences were represented, while a majority of persons facing *summary* conviction charges were unrepresented (59%).

Renner and Warner also addressed the complex question of whether the presence or absence of legal representation had any impact on the outcome of a criminal case. They found that accused persons who pleaded guilty were *less* likely to have a lawyer (34%) than those who pleaded not guilty (61%). However, there were no significant differences in the *conviction* rates of those accused persons who pleaded not guilty. On the other hand, there were significant differences in the treatment of represented and unrepresented defendants *at the sentencing stage*. Even when the variables of plea and prior record were controlled, it was found that first offenders who were legally represented and pleaded guilty to summary charges were more likely to receive more lenient treatment, such as a discharge or a suspended sentence (64%), than persons who appeared in court without a lawyer (20%) (Renner and Warner, 1981: 69).

The researchers also investigated whether there were any differences in the outcome of cases in which the accused was represented by a private lawyer as opposed to a legal aid lawyer. They found that private lawyers were more successful in obtaining an acquittal for their clients than were legal aid lawyers. Privately represented defendants were found guilty in 54% of their trials, while the equivalent figure for defendants represented by legal aid lawyers was 72% (Renner and Warner, 1981: 70). As far as sentencing was concerned, defendants represented by legal aid lawyers were more likely to receive punitive sentences in relation to summary conviction offences (although this did not apply in the case of indictable offences). Privately represented first offenders were more likely to receive a discharge (50%) than legal-aid-represented first offenders (15%) (Renner and Warner, 1981: 71). In a separate article, Warner and Renner (1981: 84) note that 54% of all defendants in their study were unrepresented and state that "this observation alone calls into serious question the reality of the adversary model of justice." They conclude (1981: 91) that "most defendants, who are largely the poor and marginal, are not represented and do not experience the benefits of a legal adversary system."

Ericson and Baranek (1982) have presented some fascinating data on the reasons why defendants either do or do not decide to seek the assistance of legal counsel. According to Ericson and Baranek, from the point of view of an accused person,

> The potential benefits of engaging a lawyer include his or her superior specialist and "recipe" knowledge and his or her access to other criminal control agents to negotiate settlements. The potential costs include the obvious financial burden if a private lawyer is chosen and the loss of control over decision-making. [P. 76]

Three-quarters of the 101 accused whom Ericson and Baranek (1982) interviewed decided to engage a lawyer. Seventeen of the 25 persons who did not retain counsel said they had made this decision because they felt that a lawyer would be of no benefit in influencing the outcome of the case (p. 79). Such a decision is understandable when relatively minor charges are involved, since it will probably cost a defendant more to invoke his or her rights in such circumstances than it would to plead guilty at the earliest opportunity (p. 79). Eleven of the accused who were interviewed gave as their reason that they could not afford a lawyer (p. 80), a finding that raises serious questions about the extent to which legal aid was available to those who needed it.

Of those who were represented by lawyers, 32 retained private lawyers, 29 legal aid lawyers, and 12 duty counsel (Ericson and Baranek, 1982: 84). What were the reasons advanced for making the decision to retain a lawyer? Of the 75 interviewees who retained a lawyer, 54 felt that there was some "strategic advantage" in having a lawyer (e.g., that a lawyer could obtain a more lenient disposition of the case than the accused could on his or her own) (p. 81). According to the researchers, lawyers were considered to be in possession of two major assets that gave them a "strategic advantage" in the criminal court system: "superior knowledge" and "superior credibility" in the eyes of the judge and other criminal justice officials (p. 82).

Paradoxically, Ericson and Baranek (1982) suggest that obtaining the services of a lawyer does not put accused in a position where they have much of an opportunity to influence the course of events in the criminal trial process. In essence, accused are placed in a dependent position, and have little grasp of what is taking place around them. Most defendants, particularly those without extensive prior experience of the criminal justice system, find it very difficult to understand what is happening to them in the courtroom situation. As Ericson and Baranek suggest,

> The regular courtroom participants, who are well versed in the legal rhetoric used to orchestrate the rules, have a monopoly on use of them. The accused seldom acquires this knowledge in time. His inability to participate reaffirms his dependent status. As a result, his definitions and interpretations are given less acknowledgment. [P. 193]

Accused persons lack the specialist knowledge to evaluate the performance of their lawyer in court, and furthermore, they are excluded from the discussions that are frequently held between Crown and defence counsel that may result in the arrangement of a so-called plea bargain (Ericson and Baranek, 1982: 77). Indeed, according to Ericson and Baranek (1982: 99), the lawyer has a "godfather" quality to his or her role vis-à-vis the defendant in a criminal case. This quality is particularly marked when critical decisions must be made, because the lawyer often presents the "choices" open to the accused in terms of "an offer you can't refuse." Ericson and Baranek found, in this respect, that many accused persons felt that their lawyer was making the really critical decisions concerning the conduct of their case. For example, the majority of accused persons who had the option to elect the mode of their trial believed that this critical decision was made by their lawyer rather than by themselves (Ericson and Baranek, 1982: 101). Certainly, the perspective advanced by Ericson and Baranek raises some provocative questions about the real nature of the adversarial system that occupies such an important place in the traditional conceptualization of the criminal trial process.

Court Delay and the Impact of the *Charter*

Section 11(b) of the *Charter*

Solomon (1983: 51) states that in "Canada and the United States the past decade has witnessed growing public concern about the 'crisis of the courts,' as manifested by congestion, backlogs, and delays in the processing of criminal cases." Significantly, section 11(b) of the *Charter* now guarantees the right of an accused person to "be tried within a reasonable time." This important right, which was not previously recognized in Canadian jurisprudence, has brought an added urgency to the task of coping with court delays, congestions and backlogs. Indeed, section 11(b) has already had a considerable impact on the way in which the courts are conducting their work, and a number of charges against defendants in criminal cases have been dismissed owing to *unreasonable* delay on the part of the prosecution (Walker, 1984: 83).

The delay covered by this section of the *Charter* is the delay between *the laying of the charge* and *the time that a person is tried.*[17] The reason for this approach is that a person's liberty and security are not impinged upon until a charge is laid against him or her.[18]

What is considered a "reasonable time"? It is clear that the courts will decide this issue in light of the particular circumstances of each case; in other words, there is no arbitrary period for completion of all cases in the court process. Justice Lamer of the Supreme Court of Canada has expressed his views on the criteria that should be applied in answering the question of whether a delay in completing a trial should be considered reasonable in all the circumstances of the case:

> There are, in my view, four factors which must be considered under s. 11(*b*) in determining the reasonableness of any given delay. These are:
> 1. the growing impairment of the interests of the accused by the passage of time;
> 2. waiver of time periods;
> 3. the time requirements inherent in the nature of the case;
> 4. institutional resources.[19]

As far as the first criterion is concerned, it is apparent that an accused person's interest in liberty is severely impaired by pre-trial detention. However, it is clearly recognized that this interest is also impaired by the restrictions on freedom of movement that might be imposed as part of the conditions for obtaining bail. In the view of Lamer, J.,

> It is incumbent upon the government and the courts, in such cases, to accord a first priority to those persons whose interests in both liberty and security of the person have been impaired and particularly to those whose liberty is most severely limited, *i.e.*, those persons who remain in detention prior to and during the trial. Such persons are, in effect, purging a sentence before they have ever been found guilty; while detention may be required under the circumstances of the case it nevertheless represents the most serious transgression of the presumption of innocence and must be limited to the shortest possible time.[20]

Solomon (1983: 52) found, in a study of "Robert County" in Ontario, that priority in the scheduling of cases was indeed given to those defendants held in custody pending their trial; the average length of the case of a detained person was 81 days from the first appearance to the ultimate disposition, whereas the equivalent figure for those not in custody was 137 days.

The second criterion is concerned with whether or not accused persons have, in some way, waived their right to a speedy trial. If accused persons willingly acquiesce in the delay of their trial, then it should not be possible for them to turn around and claim that their right to a speedy trial has been violated. However, it has been stressed that waiver of the right to speedy trial cannot be inferred from mere silence on the part of the accused. In fact, the waiver of the right by the accused must be both "express and informed."[21] Furthermore, consent to one particular period of delay may, in no way, be interpreted as acquiescence to any previous or subsequent delay caused by the Crown.

The third criterion relates to the specific time requirements that are inherent in any particular case. Obviously, application of this criterion requires a close scrutiny of the elements of each case on an individual basis:

> ... the court must fix an objective and realistic time period for the preparation of the type of case which is at bar. It must determine the period which would normally be required, taking into account the number of charges, the number of accused, the complexity and volume of similar objective elements, for the preparation and completion of the case if fully adequate institutional resources and facilities were available.[22]

The fourth criterion concerns the institutional resources available within the court system. However, it is not entirely clear to what extent the prosecution can rely on inadequate resources as a justification for delay. While limited resources may well be highly relevant to determining whether a delay is reasonable, Lamer J. also stressed that this did not mean that the courts were limited to "affixing a constitutional seal of approval upon the *status quo*." In other words, courts are not required to accept the inevitability of what he called *systemic delay* ("delay attributable to the fault of no specific individual actor or actors within the criminal justice system"). Indeed, the courts must be responsible for ensuring that the system of justice adapts to the needs of section 11(b) of the *Charter* and not the other way around:

> There can be no assumption that the constitutional right to be tried within a reasonable time must conform to the *status quo*; rather it is the system for the administration of criminal justice which must conform to the constitutional requirements of the Charter. We cannot shrink from our task of interpreting the Charter in a full and fair manner, even when, and perhaps especially when, we are confronted with the possibility of resulting significant institutional adjustment.[23]

A good illustration of the practical application of these criteria occurred in a case that reached the Saskatchewan Court of Appeal in 1986.[24] After a three-day investigation, the accused had been charged, in April 1982, with a number of offences relating to drugs, as well as with counselling an individual to commit an offence of personal violence. He was committed for trial in October 1982, but there were three adjournments of the case, and the trial did not take place until March 1984. There were no explanations for these delays in commencing the trial. Pending his trial, the accused was free on bail, but was subject to relatively stringent conditions. In addition, he was suspended from practising medicine by the College of Physicians and Surgeons. At the trial, in March 1984, the jury could not agree on a verdict and the case was retained on the trial list. In November 1984, defence counsel sought relief under the *Charter*, but relief was refused. A trial took place, and the accused was convicted.

The accused appealed against his conviction to the Court of Appeal and raised the issue of whether his right to be tried within a reasonable time under section 11(b) of the *Charter* had been infringed. The Court of Appeal set aside the conviction and stayed the indictment.[25] Tallis J.A. said that he had "no hesitation in concluding that the delay following committal for trial which was unexplained is clearly unreasonable."[26] The Crown did not try to justify the delay in terms of institutional resources, so the Court of Appeal concentrated on the elements of "waiver of time periods" and the "time requirements inherent in the nature of the case." Since the investigation of the accused had taken only three days and the evidence was quite straightforward, it could not be said that this was a complex case that required elaborate preparation for trial; on the contrary, it was a "run-of-the-mill case." Furthermore, there was no evidence that the accused had, in any way, waived the extensive periods of delay preceding his trial. Therefore, the Court took the drastic step of quashing the accused's conviction.

Court Delay and the Canadian Literature

The introduction of a right to a speedy trial has prompted a significant degree of analysis of the issue of court delays in Canada. What does the Canadian literature suggest about the nature of court delays, and what strategies have been proposed as a means of implementing the right to a speedy trial?

Of course, an initial point that must be made is that justice delayed is not *necessarily* justice denied. Indeed, it has been contended that a certain degree of delay is necessary in order to permit both sides to prepare their cases adequately (Wilson, 1987: 117). It has also been suggested that a certain delay is necessary to permit the emotions aroused by a criminal offence to die down sufficiently for the accused to obtain a fair trial (Osborne, 1980: 6). Clearly, what needs to be avoided is *excessive* delay.

It is widely believed that court delay is caused primarily by the excessive use of postponements that are made at the request of the defence or the Crown (and, sometimes, the judge). These postponements are officially known as "adjournments, remands or continuances" and are made at the discretion of the judge[27] (Osborne, 1986: 32). In a study of provincial courts in the Province of Ontario, Hann (1973) suggested that the major cause of delay was the propensity of the courts to grant far too many remands. Indeed, Hann found that only one per cent of the requests for remands were ever refused by the courts. It is argued that while many of the remands may well be perfectly justifiable (e.g., because an essential witness has fallen sick), many postponements of a trial are not justifiable[28] and granting them merely results in excessive delays (Osborne, 1986: 32). Where an excessive number of postponements are granted, courtrooms may well be left standing empty with no other cases ready for trial. This results in a serious wastage of court resources.

Why do lawyers seek so many remands and thereby cause a significant proportion of court delay? Sometimes, the high number of requests for remands is prompted by the heavy caseloads of lawyers, which necessitate frequent adjournments in order to avoid conflicts between cases (Walker, 1984: 90). In particular, defence counsel may be forced to request remands frequently because of economic pressures that force them to take under their wing considerable numbers of poorly reimbursed legal aid cases simply in order to keep their legal practices going (Osborne, 1986: 32). It has also been argued that lawyers' requests for an excessive number of postponements may be connected with an abuse of the legal aid system; the argument is based on the premise that it is sometimes in the economic interests of defence counsel to request numerous postponements if they are paid on the basis of each appearance that they make in court (Walker, 1984: 91). However, Solomon (1983: 59) discounts this view, pointing out that in a study of an Ontario municipal jurisdiction, there was no evidence that defence counsel made a disproportionate number of requests for remands. In addition, there was no financial incentive for defence counsel to extend the lives of their cases; indeed, the lawyers charged a flat fee for cases going to the provincial court, regardless of the number of appearances they made. Furthermore, according to Solomon, there was no relation between the length of case and the type of legal representation. It has also been alleged that lawyers may seek an excessive number of remands as part of the technique known as "judge shopping," in which lawyers seek to manipulate the court process by seeking adjournments with a view to arranging that their clients appear before judges who may be considered more sympathetic to their cause (for example, by being more lenient sentencers). It has been contended that "judge shopping" is a major cause of excessive remands in Ontario (Walker, 1984: 89).

Another alleged cause of court delay is the shortage of resources allocated to the courts (Wilson, 1987: 118). For example, a Royal Commission in Ontario (Zuber, 1987) found that less than one per cent of total provincial government expenditures were being directed toward the court system. However, the relation between court resources and delay is by no means simple. Mackaay (1976) suggests that merely increasing resources (by, for example, providing more judges and more courts) will not *necessarily* reduce delay and congestion in the courts. Indeed, he suggested, as did Hann (1973), that *it is the seeking of adjournments and other time-wasting devices that are the primary causes of delay.*[29] In a similar vein, Solomon (1983) reviews two major American studies dealing with the issue of delay (Church, 1978: Nimmer, 1978). He suggests that these studies indicate that much of the traditional thinking about the causes of court delay is flawed. In particular, it appears that the size of the courts' workload (or caseload) does not have any clear relation to the phenomenon of delay. According to Solomon (1983: 58), the studies found that:

> The length of cases in the courts studied was unrelated to the size of the courts, to the frequency of trials held, to the type of scheduling . . . or *to the amount or the character of a court's case load.*

The particular finding is clearly of considerable policy significance for, if there is no clear relation between caseload and delay, then it would not be wise to try to fight delay by merely increasing the number of courts and judges (Solomon, 1983: 58). Indeed, it has even been suggested that increasing the number of judges may merely cause the judges to spend more time on each case, so that there would be no real increase in the total number of cases being processed by the courts in any given period (Wilson, 1987: 118). If the sheer number of cases being dealt with by the courts did *not* contribute significantly to delay, what factors *were* most associated with differences in the periods that it took the courts to process cases? According to

Solomon (1983: 58–59), the American studies, referred to above, concluded that:

> ... the variations in time were found to relate to the "established expectations, practices and informal rules of judges and attorneys" or "to the prevailing informal norms of the judicial process and ... the personal motivations of participating attorneys and judges," or put simply, to the local legal culture. How fast dispositions in criminal cases occur depends upon how the lawyers and judges do their work and what incentives they have to move cases quickly.

If the level of resources and the workload of the courts are not directly related to delay, it is quite plausible that delay may be caused, at least in part, by the *inefficient use of existing resources* (Wilson, 1987: 124). It has been suggested, for example, that not all judges handle their workload as efficiently as they might. Walker (1984: 88) quotes statistics that show that, on average, judges spent only 2.6 hours a day in court in the Ontario Provincial Court during 1981–82.[30] However, this situation may be caused by various factors unconnected with the trial judge. As we have seen, the inefficient use of resources may also be caused by the excessive number of requests for postponements that are made by lawyers. These requests, often made at the very last minute, may result in the courtroom standing empty because there are no cases ready for trial. Furthermore, it has been suggested that the police and prosecutors may use resources inefficiently, and thereby contribute to court delay by laying too many charges. This practice can result in a significant proportion of charges being withdrawn, thus wasting valuable court resources (Walker, 1984: 91; Wilson, 1987: 119–21).

In any event, it has been contended that steps should be taken to ensure court resources are utilized more efficiently. For example, it has been suggested that each province should introduce guidelines to determine when and how cases are dealt with, so that there is a greater degree of predictability and, therefore, more effective planning (Wilson, 1987: 125). In addition, it has been asserted that there should be better "caseflow management" by the judiciary, who should assume a greater degree of control over the use of court resources (Miller and Barr, 1979; Walker, 1984: 102).

Would judicial moves to reduce court delay have any real impact upon the problem? Solomon (1983: 61–64) refers to two attempts to reduce court delay in Ontario, both of which assigned a major role to the judiciary. In 1979, the Chief Justice, William Howland, directed an order to all judges in Ontario. The order was concerned with two issues. First, it sought to abolish the practice whereby judges allowed trial dates set for the higher courts to take precedence over dates set for the provincial courts. This practice meant that trials in the higher courts were being set without reference to the commitments of counsel in the provincial courts, thus causing an increased number of requests for postponements in the latter. Second, judges were asked to adopt a much stricter approach to requests for remands. Although success has been claimed for the Howland directive, no concrete evidence has been advanced in support of this claim (Solomon, 1983: 62).

The other experiment was the establishment of "90-day courts" at the College Park Courthouse. A *routing system* was used: one courtroom was dedicated to first appearances only; two courtrooms were set aside for long trials; and the five remaining courtrooms were intended to deal with the main bulk of the criminal trials. In these five courtrooms, each judge organized his or her own calendar and worked directly with a single Crown attorney, who was also committed to completing a group of cases within the 90-day period. According to Solomon (1983: 63), the 90-day court experiment was a "partial success." While the majority of cases in the five courtrooms were completed in 90 days, the two courts set aside for long trials encountered lengthy delays. Solomon (p. 64) concludes that both the Howland direction and the 90-day court experiments support the view that "judge-centred" reform is relatively effective, but the cost of such reforms may be unduly high; Crown counsel were forced to dismiss a significant number of cases, and defence counsel found it very difficult to meet their manifold obligations.

It has also been contended that a significant contributor to court delay is the traditional organization of the system of criminal courts in a number of Canadian provinces. For example, in Ontario it has been suggested that the three-fold division of the court system contributes to an inefficient use of resources (Wilson, 1987: 123). As we noted earlier, in Ontario there is a three-tiered court system consisting of the Provincial Court, the District Court and the Supreme Court. In a Royal Commission report (Zuber, 1987), it has been recommended that the District and Supreme Courts be amalgamated and the jurisdiction of the Provincial Court be expanded as a means of creating greater efficiency in the use of court resources. As we saw earlier, a number of other provinces have already amalgamated the jurisdiction of their superior and district or county courts as a means of enhancing efficiency.

It has also been argued that a major factor in the generation of delay in the courts is the manner in which governments are increasingly creating a veritable multitude of minor offences as a means of enforcing their regulatory legislation, while simultaneously failing to make additional resources available to the courts (Walker, 1984; Wilson, 1967). As an indicator of the extent to which minor criminal matters are dominating the workload of the provincial courts, Wilson (1987: 119) points out that 85 to 88% of all cases handled by the criminal justice system in Ontario related to traffic offences and other regulatory legislation such as municipal by-laws.

Solomon (1983: c. 5) also contends that there are far too many minor cases coming before the criminal courts. By minor offences, Solomon

(1983: 65) means "offences that present a relatively small degree of social danger and usually result in a mild punishment." He suggests that some 37% of the cases tried in the Ontario jurisdiction of "Robert County" were minor offences within the terms of this definition (Solomon, 1983: 66) and that the number of minor offences brought before the courts will, in all probability, continue to rise in the future. Since the penalty is usually a fine or a discharge and minor offenders usually plead guilty on their first appearance in court, Solomon questions whether it is really worth while to employ such an expensive method of prosecuting essentially trivial cases. Costs include the expense to the taxpayer; the burdens placed on the accused, witnesses and victims as a consequence of their being put through the "wringer" of the court process; and finally, the creation of heavy workloads in the courts. Indeed, insofar as the human costs of the criminal court process are concerned, Solomon refers to the work of Feeley (1979), who points out that the experience of being forced to go through the court process in the lower courts ultimately becomes a greater "punishment" for the accused than the relatively mild penalty that is ultimately imposed upon conviction of a minor offence; in this sense, Feeley contends that the court process itself becomes the real punishment. In light of this analysis, Solomon raises the question:

> Does one want to support the multifaceted expense of taking to court larger numbers of minor offenders who plead guilty? Would it not be worth while to seek out ways of dealing with some of these persons and their offences outside of court? [P. 67]

How can the tide of minor cases, which are currently flooding the provincial courts, be stemmed? Among the alternative methods recommended for the disposition of minor cases outside of the formal court system are *decriminalization* and *diversion* (Wilson, 1987: 119–21). *Decriminalization* refers to the removal of certain offences from the criminal law (either by legalization of the conduct or by controlling it through some device other than the criminal law, such as civil or administrative law), while *diversion* refers to the re-direction of offenders from the courts to some other agency for disposition (Solomon, 1983: 71).

According to Solomon (1983: 73), decriminalization involves the "transfer from criminal to civil or administrative sanctioning." A prominent example of this approach is the decriminalization of the possession of *cannabis* in the State of California in 1976. However, it has been contended (Ericson and Baranek, 1982: 226; Solomon, 1983: 73) that there is little public support for such a strategy in Canada.

Solomon (1983: 72) notes that diversion in Canada primarily takes the form of sending cases to mediation by agencies that are usually staffed by volunteers. Mediation programs are becoming increasingly popular in Canada (Anon., 1987: 4). Usually, the parties to a dispute are brought together by two mediators. At the conclusion of a two- or three-hour session, a written memorandum of agreement is drawn up and signed (Anon., 1987: 6). Solomon points out that the problem with diversion programs of the mediation type is that they apply only to a relatively limited number of offences — namely, those that have a victim — whereas many minor crimes are victimless in nature. Court diversion programs can assist in reducing the workload facing the judiciary, but they are problematic in the sense that there is no clear method available for enforcing agreements entered into by the offender (many diversion programs, for example, involve an element of community service on the part of the offender) (Walker, 1984: 95).[31] In addition, it has been suggested that diversion programs do not decrease the actual number of cases being dealt with by the courts but rather *increase the net of social control* (that is, they deal with cases that would previously have been left alone by the authorities) (see Blomberg, 1977; Elton, 1980; Ericson and Baranek, 1982: 228).

Another technique for dealing with the rising tide of minor offences is to devise alternative methods of processing them in the court system. For example, a number of provinces have introduced a ticketing system in relation to the minor offences that arise under their own regulatory legislation. For example, Wilson (1987: 120) refers to the Ontario *Provincial Offences Act*, which establishes a ticketing system that allows a defendant to plead guilty without having to go to court, although, of course, he or she always has the option of attending court and pleading not guilty. It was estimated that more than 60% of the summary conviction tickets issued in 1986 culminated in trials in the absence of the defendant (Wilson, 1987: 120). It has been suggested that the ticketing system be extended to certain of the summary and hybrid offences arising under the *Criminal Code* (Wilson, 1987: 120).

Solomon (1983: 74) believes that a more effective way of reducing the number of minor cases that come to court is the adoption of a penal order procedure (see also Wilson, 1987). He points out that penal orders are used in Germany with particular regularity in relation to driving offences and minor property matters. A penal order is a document that sets out the nature of the offence that the accused is alleged to have committed, indicates the evidence that is available to support the charge, cites the applicable provisions of the *Criminal Code*, and clearly states the punishment that will be imposed upon conviction. The accused may challenge the order and ask for a trial on the merits; however, if he or she does not do so within one week, then a conviction will be entered against the accused. Imprisonment is never available as a sentencing option when the penal order procedure is used; the most likely punishment is a fine. Solomon (p. 75) emphasizes that a penal order is not like a traffic ticket handed out by a peace officer. Indeed, the penal order must be prepared by a prosecutor and must be signed by a member of the judiciary. If there is any doubt concerning the guilt of the accused, the prosecutor or the judge must order that the accused stand trial. Similarly, if the accused has a prior criminal record or may be in need of psychiatric help, then a trial must be ordered. According to Solomon, there are a number of reasons why the introduction of a penal order procedure is more desirable than placing reliance upon diversion programs:

> To begin with, penal order procedure should prove attractive to accused persons; it reduces their costs and does not add to their punishments. Secondly, penal orders pose no problems of financing; instead of costing the government money, penal order procedure would save it money, for the execution of the orders would cost much less than even a short trial. Thirdly, penal orders can cover the full spectrum of crimes, with or without victims, and they do not depend upon the cooperation of volunteers. Fourthly, penal orders do not raise questions of due process that have troubled commentators on diversion. The accused is not required to submit to punishment without a formal admission of guilt and without the opportunity to dispute charges if he so desires . . . [P. 76]

What Are the Consequences of Delay?

What are the negative consequences that flow from court delay? As noted earlier, the human costs to defendants, victims and witnesses of extended delays and repeated court appearances can never be underestimated (Feeley, 1979). Among some of the more specific arguments made against excessive delay is that it renders it more difficult to obtain a conviction since it is more difficult for witnesses to recall events (Wilson, 1987: 118). It is also contended that excessive delay causes a loss of respect for the courts on the part of both witnesses and victims and that judges, prosecutors and court staff become demoralized by the overwhelming pressure of cases (Walker, 1984: 85). It has also been suggested that excessive delay causes accused persons on bail to be more likely to fail to turn up for trial or to commit another offence (Walker, 1984: 87). Finally, it has been asserted that excessive delay can result in increased costs that flow from keeping accused persons in custody for longer periods (Walker, 1984: 87).

It is widely supposed that delay necessarily works to the accused's advantage. In particular, it is believed that delay will cause a deterioration in the Crown's evidence against the accused (for example, witnesses will find it more difficult to remember evidence as time goes by). However, Solomon suggests that both the American and Canadian evidence does not support this thesis. In the study of "Robert County" in Ontario, he found that although cases that resulted in dismissals or acquittals lasted longer than other cases, the deterioration of evidence from witnesses did *not* account for any of these dismissals or acquittals (Solomon, 1983: 53). It is also argued that delay may result in accused persons obtaining more lenient sentences since they can obtain a job, and so forth, and claim that they are rehabilitated. However, once again, Solomon (1983: 53–54) asserts that the research findings have *not* established a relation between case length and lenience of sentence.

In a perceptive analysis of the issue, Solomon (1983: 56) suggests that perhaps delay *per se* is not really the major problem many analysts consider it to be. In his view, the major problems facing the courts are not so much those surrounding delay as those arising from the burdens imposed on participants in the court process by repeated court appearances and from the flooding of the courts by minor criminal cases. In his view, resources should be devoted not to eliminating delay but rather to reducing the number of appearances and to removing the large number of minor cases coming before the courts. According to Solomon:

> The evidence suggests that long cases consistently produce few, if any, harmful consequences. Delay does not help the accused by eroding the evidence against him, nor does it hurt him much as long as he is at liberty and does not have to make many appearances in court. Delay does not waste court time (it may even save it); it does not place burdens on witnesses (they derive from the number of appearances not the length of cases); and it does not weaken the effect of general deterrence. Delay may affect the public evaluation of the courts, but in all likelihood only marginally. [P. 56]

Solomon believes that it is most desirable to reduce the number of cases flowing into the system of criminal courts in Canada. If caseloads were decreased, it might facilitate a number of other beneficial changes to the court system; for example, if there were fewer cases flowing into the court system, it might permit the payment of witnesses and the provision of special services for them (Solomon, 1983: 69). It would also permit more rational scheduling of cases, thus reducing the burdens on witnesses, counsel, and the accused.

Solomon's approach, if implemented, would certainly result in substantial improvements to the system of criminal courts in Canada. However, it does seem to underestimate the costs to the accused of *unwanted* delay. The continuing uncertainty facing accused persons confronted by delay *caused by the Crown* may have a devastating impact on them. Persons who have the sword of Damocles hanging over their heads in the form of unresolved criminal charges may suffer severe social isolation and stigma; furthermore, they may be prevented from pursuing their livelihood as a consequence of the outstanding criminal proceedings. In these circumstances, it seems important to ensure that the guarantee of a speedy trial, enshrined in section 11(b) of the *Charter*, should continue to be enforced strictly by the courts and that efforts should continue to be directed toward the elimination of delay that is caused by the prosecution contrary to the wishes of the accused.

Prosecutorial Discretion

This section deals with a number of critical issues surrounding the exercise of prosecutorial discretion. As we have already seen, the Canadian prosecutor enjoys a formidable degree of discretion in carrying out his or her duties in the court process. For example, attention has already been drawn to the prosecutor's discretionary powers in relation to such important matters as selecting how to proceed on a dual or hybrid offence; restricting an accused person's right to elect the method of trial in relation to an indictable offence by laying a direct indictment or by insisting on a trial by judge and jury where an offence carrying a maximum penalty of more than five years' imprisonment is concerned; deciding whether or not to oppose bail; deciding to what extent he or she will grant discovery of the prosecution's case against the accused; and deciding whether or not to appeal against an acquittal. The present section focuses on a few specific discretionary powers of the prosecution that are generally considered to be of major importance and analyzes the extent to which there can be a degree of control over the exercise of prosecutorial discretion in Canada.

The Canadian Prosecutor

It is still theoretically possible for private citizens to conduct prosecutions of criminal cases in Canada, although this is rarely done at present (Burns, 1975 and 1986; Law Reform Commission of Canada, 1986; Stenning, 1986: c. 12). In the great majority of cases, prosecutions are conducted by public officials. Furthermore, even where a private citizen has laid an information alleging an offence, the Attorney General of the jurisdiction concerned can either take over the prosecution him or herself or bring it to an end; thus the so-called right of a private citizen to prosecute an offence is little more than the right to lay an information[32] (Burns, 1986: V-24; Stenning, 1986: 263).

Prosecutions under the *Criminal Code* are conducted by the Attorney General or Minister of Justice of the province concerned or by one of his or her agents, since under the *Constitution Act, 1867*, the provinces are responsible for the administration of justice.[33] The Minister of Justice of Canada or his or her agents are responsible for the conduct of prosecutions of offences arising under federal statutes *other than the Criminal Code* (for example, the *Narcotic Control Act* and the *Food and Drugs Act*), as well as conspiracies to commit such offences.[34] The precise degree of overlap between the federal and provincial prosecuting powers, however, is a matter of some uncertainty (see Burns, 1986: V-27; Stenning, 1986: c. 10).[35]

It has been contended in a good deal of the traditional literature that the prosecutor is not a partisan advocate but is rather a "minister of justice"

(Gourlie, 1982: 32; Stenning, 1986: 240). Indeed, in an often cited passage from a decision in the Supreme Court of Canada, Rand, J., said:

> It cannot be over-emphasized that the purpose of a criminal prosecution is not to obtain a conviction, it is to lay before a jury what the Crown considers to be credible evidence relevant to what is alleged to be a crime. Counsel have a duty to see that all available legal proof of the facts is presented: it should be done firmly and pressed to its legitimate strength but it must also be done fairly. The role of prosecutor excludes any notion of winning or losing; his function is a matter of public duty than which in civil life there can be none charged with greater personal responsibility. It is to be efficiently performed with an ingrained sense of the dignity, the seriousness and the justness of judicial proceedings.[36]

Stenning (1986: 241) points out that there may well be a sharp discrepancy between the theoretical role of the prosecutor as a minister of justice and the reality of everyday practice in the courts (see Grosman, 1969). However, regardless of the accuracy of the conception of the prosecutor as a "minister of justice," Stenning (1986: 241) suggests that this conception has, nevertheless, strongly influenced the Canadian judiciary in its "hands off" approach toward defining and supervising the exercise of prosecutorial discretion. What is the nature of the prosecutor's discretionary power?

The Discretionary Power to Lay Charges

The *Criminal Code* says nothing about the discretion of a prosecutor to lay criminal charges. However, as Stenning (1986: 243) points out, Canadian courts have long been willing to accept that prosecutorial powers are derived from the common law (or the law developed by judges in specific cases), as well as from statutory provisions. Furthermore, the courts have emphasized that, in general, they are not prepared to investigate the manner in which a prosecutor decides to exercise his or her discretion whether or not to lay charges in *specific cases* (Morgan, 1986: 24*ff.*).[37] Nevertheless, it appears that there are some restrictions that may be imposed on the exercise of this discretionary power in exceptional circumstances. For example, while the prosecutor is perfectly free to decide not to lay charges in individual cases, he or she cannot adopt a policy in which this discretion is exercised in such a manner as to preclude prosecution in relation to a whole category of offences or offenders without consideration of the specific facts in each case; if the prosecutor were permitted to adopt such a policy, it would be tantamount to permitting Crown counsel to override the will of the legislature (Stenning, 1986: 244). For example, in one case,[38] a native Indian was prosecuted for illegal hunting. The defendant claimed that the prosecution was an abuse of process and sought to have the prosecution stayed, since there was an explicit policy on the part of both the federal and provincial governments not to prosecute native Indians for such offences within the Province of Manitoba. The Court of Appeal ruled that there was no abuse of process because, while the prosecuting authorities have the power to refuse to prosecute *in light of the particular facts of an individual case*, they have no power to adopt a blanket policy of refusing to prosecute any of the members of a particular group. Indeed, the Court said that a blanket dispensation in favour of a particular group must always be considered invalid:

> Today the dispensing power may be exercised in favour of Indians. Tomorrow it may be exercised in favour of Protestants, and the next day in favour of Jews. Our laws cannot be so treated. The Crown may not by Executive action dispense with laws. The matter is as simple as that, and nearly three centuries of legal and constitutional history stand as the foundation for that principle.[39]

The Discretionary Power to Stay Proceedings

The prosecutor has the discretionary power to *stay* (or suspend) criminal proceedings in relation to both indictable and summary conviction offences (Cohen, 1977: 150; Sun, 1974; Salhany, 1984: 264).[40] According to Salhany (1984: 264):

> This right is based upon the principle that since all criminal prosecutions are carried out in the name of the Queen, the Queen may, through her Attorney-General, intimate to the officer of the court that proceedings are stayed by her direction.

A stay can be entered at any time after proceedings have been commenced[41] and before the judgment in the case is delivered (Salhany, 1984: 267). In order to stay proceedings, the prosecutor merely instructs the clerk of the court to enter the stay on the record; neither the clerk nor the judge have any discretion over the matter (Burns, 1986: V-5; Morgan, 1986: 29). An extreme example of the ability of the Crown to enter a stay at the last possible moment occurred in a case that came before the British Columbia Court of Appeal in 1967.[42] In this case, the Crown had entered a stay of proceedings *after* the trial judge had charged the jury and directed them to find the accused not guilty but *before* the jury had actually returned with their verdict. Despite the fact that the Crown was using the stay merely to avoid the impact of an adverse ruling that would have resulted in the accused being acquitted,[43] the appeal court nevertheless ruled that the Crown's entry of the stay of proceedings was perfectly valid. Bull J.A. said the "the entry of a stay is a statutory administrative discretion given to the Attorney General, and, if exercised, his direction is to the Clerk of the Court as such and is outside any control of the Judge."[44] The courts' unwillingness to exercise control over the power of the Crown to enter a stay of proceedings has clearly placed a powerful tactical weapon in the armoury of the prosecutor.

The effect of a stay of proceedings is to *suspend* the proceedings rather than to terminate them altogether (Stenning, 1986: 232). The *Code*[45] provides that insofar as indictable offences are concerned, the prosecutor can recommence the proceedings *within one year* of entering the stay merely by giving notice to the clerk of the court. As far as summary conviction offences are concerned, the *Code* states that the proceedings must be recommenced either within one year of the entry of the stay or "before the expiration of the time within which the proceedings could have been commenced, whichever is the earlier." The latter restriction apparently refers to the fact that a limitation period of six months normally applies in relation to summary conviction offences, and therefore, in most cases, a stay in relation to a summary conviction offence will suspend court proceedings only until the expiry of the limitation period (normally six months from the date on which criminal proceedings could first have been commenced). Once the specified periods have elapsed, the Crown cannot revive the proceedings; indeed, "the proceedings shall be deemed never to have been commenced." However, there is nothing to prevent the prosecutor from initiating fresh proceedings for the same offence, provided that (as far as summary conviction offences are concerned) this is done within the appropriate limitation period (Stenning, 1986: 233).

Sun (1974: 488) has noted that there is a marked disparity in the use of the stay in different provinces across Canada. In some provinces, such as British Columbia and Manitoba, she found that the stay was used with some degree of frequency, while in others it was rarely used (the withdrawal of charges mechanism was apparently used instead).

The Discretionary Power to Withdraw Charges

Although the *Code* does not expressly give prosecutors the right to withdraw charges, once an information has been laid or an indictment preferred, the courts have nevertheless recognized that this right does indeed exist (Burns, 1986: V-3; Salhany, 1984: 263; Stenning, 1986: 245).[46] Osborne (1983: 57) indicates that from 20 to 30% of criminal cases in Canada are terminated by a withdrawal or staying of charges.

It is important to distinguish between the staying and the withdrawal of charges. As we have seen, entering a stay of charges merely *suspends* them, whereas the withdrawal of charges results in their *termination*. In other words, after a withdrawal of charges, the Crown cannot continue the prosecution without laying completely new charges.

As Osborne (1983: 58) points out, "the withdrawal of charges does not put the stamp of finality on a case although such a disposition may reasonably give rise to an expectation in the mind of an accused that the matter is closed." Indeed, provided the court does not consider it an abuse of process, the prosecutor may always lay new charges and thereby reactivate a case in which charges had previously been withdrawn.[47]

To what extent does the power to withdraw charges fall within the discretion of the Crown? The generally accepted view (Burns, 1986: V-4; Osborne, 1983: 58) is that the Crown has an *absolute right* to withdraw a case before a plea is taken but that the trial judge has a *discretion* whether to grant the Crown's request to withdraw charges as soon as any evidence has been heard following the entry of the accused's plea.[48] In theory, it would appear that the necessity of obtaining judicial approval for the withdrawal of criminal charges renders the withdrawal a much more palatable device from the point of view of the civil liberties of the individual citizen (Cohen, 1977: 159). However, it appears that, in practice, judges very rarely withhold their consent to the withdrawal of charges (Osborne, 1983: 58).

In what sorts of circumstances is the Crown likely to withdraw charges? In an important study, Osborne (1983) discovered that charges were frequently withdrawn because the victim or other witnesses did not appear in court. Similarly, in certain cases that stemmed from so-called domestic disputes, the charges had to be withdrawn because the complainant was unwilling to proceed with the prosecution of a spouse. The researcher also found that charges were likely to be withdrawn where the police had laid charges before obtaining the necessary supporting evidence (for example, where analysis of a blood sample failed to indicate that the accused had the prohibited level of alcohol required in order to sustain the charge). Osborne (1983: 73–74) concluded that the reasons for withdrawing charges were varied and that, in most cases, these reasons were beyond the personal control of Crown counsel:

> His options are limited by the willingness of victims and witnesses to co-operate; the preferences of the police; the strategies of the accused and his counsel; the willingness of the judge to grant remands and the state of the day's court lists. These factors are above all unpredictable. The decision to withdraw is a heavily contingent one.

Limiting the Discretion of the Prosecutor

It is clear that the scope of prosecutorial discretion is very broad in Canada and that Canadian courts are generally highly reluctant to interfere with the exercise of that discretion. However, this does not mean that there are absolutely no limits to what prosecutors can or cannot do in the exercise of their discretionary powers. Indeed, the Attorney General or Minister of Justice of a province is ultimately accountable to the legislature for the conduct of prosecutions, the individual Crown counsel is accountable to the Attorney General or Minister of Justice for his or her decisions, and the courts are gradually developing a mechanism for controlling the most excessive abuses of prosecutorial powers.

The Accountability of the Attorney General to the Legislature

The Chief Law Officer of the Crown (the Attorney General or the Minister of Justice) is a member of his or her appropriate legislature and, therefore, is ultimately accountable to the members of that legislature for the exercise of prosecutorial discretion in criminal proceedings (Stenning, 1986: 301). This accountability is primarily exercised through the Attorney General's duty to answer questions about his or her department. However, he or she is liable to answer questions about the exercise of prosecutorial discretion only *after* a particular decision has been made (Stenning, 1986: 303). Furthermore, as Stenning (1986: 305) points out, since the Attorney General is a member both of the government and of the party with the largest number of seats in the legislature, it is unlikely that the Attorney General's responsibility to the legislature will represent a significant method of controlling his or her prosecutorial discretion.[49]

The Accountability of Crown Counsel to the Attorney General or Minister of Justice

Of course, the Attorney General or Minister of Justice does not conduct prosecutions him or herself, other than in the most exceptional cases. However, Crown counsel are accountable to the Attorney General or Minister of Justice for the conduct of individual prosecutions. Stenning (1986: 312) points out that since the Attorney General or Minister of Justice is not involved personally in the day-to-day administration of justice, the individual prosecutor has a considerable degree of autonomy *in practice*; however, this does not prevent the Attorney General or Minister of Justice from becoming involved in particular cases, if he or she thinks this course is desirable.[50] In addition to issuing directions to Crown counsel in specific cases, the Attorney General or his or her deputy may issue general guidelines indicating the broad principles that should be applied in exercising prosecutorial discretion in relation to particular types of offences or offenders or in relation to such matters as plea bargaining (Stenning, 1986: 316–17; Verdun-Jones and Cousineau, 1979: 239–40).

The Accountability of Crown Counsel to the Individual Citizen

In an important case,[51] the Ontario Court of Appeal ruled that a private citizen could not sue either the Attorney General or his or her agent for damages sustained as a result of the conduct of their prosecutorial functions. Indeed, the Attorney General and Crown counsel may be said to enjoy an "absolute immunity" from such law suits. In the view of the

Court, the need to maintain the independence of the Crown and to protect it from harassment outweighs the interests of the accused person who claims that he or she has been wrongly prosecuted.

The Accountability of the Prosecutor to the Courts

Historically, the Canadian courts have been most reluctant to exercise any control over the exercise of prosecutorial discretion (Morgan, 1986: 24). According to Morgan (1986: 31), the major reason for this approach is the courts' view of "how the criminal justice system best operates":

> It is apparently thought, for various reasons, to work most effectively through a very broad grant of prosecutorial discretion, and conversely, with a minimum of judicial interference. Courts have seemingly concluded that virtually any form of challenge could hamper the independence and fearlessness of the prosecutor, regarded as vital to the efficacy of the prosecutorial process generally.

However, in more recent years, the courts have begun to exercise a very limited degree of control over prosecutorial decision making in certain exceptional circumstances. This process commenced well before the advent of the *Charter* and was encapsulated within a legal doctrine known as *abuse of process*, which first came to prominence in Canada at the outset of the 1970s (Morgan, 1986; Salhany, 1984: 268; Taylor, 1985). Abuse of process refers to the courts' inherent jurisdiction to protect their process from abuse by the prosecution. The courts' powers in this respect may be enforced by the entry of a stay of proceedings in those cases where it is believed that there has been an exceptional abuse of the court process on the part of the prosecution and that this abuse has resulted in "an unacceptable degree of unfairness to an accused" (Morgan, 1986: 35). According to Taylor (1985: VI-21), the abuse of process doctrine has been applied in five distinct situations: (1) cases where the Crown has used the court process for some "collateral motive" that is considered to be improper (e.g., using the criminal courts as a means of collecting a civil debt); (2) cases where a delay in prosecuting the accused has created an abuse of the court process (although such cases are now more likely to be dealt with under section 11(b) of the *Charter*); (3) cases involving entrapment; (4) cases involving "multiple proceedings," where the prosecutor has attempted to circumvent an adverse judicial ruling or decision by staying or withdrawing charges (so that the existing judicial proceedings are halted) and then starting new proceedings on identical charges; (5) cases in which it is considered that the prosecution has brought the administration of justice into disrepute by acting unfairly (e.g., where the prosecutor breaks an undertaking to the accused, who has acted upon it in the belief that the prosecutor will keep his or her promise).

For many years, the extent to which the Supreme Court of Canada was prepared to embrace the doctrine of abuse of process was left in a considerable degree of doubt. That doubt was largely dispelled in the critical case of *Jewitt*,[52] decided in 1985. In this case, involving entrapment of the accused, the Supreme Court unequivocally endorsed the conclusion of the Ontario Court of Appeal in *R. v. Young* that a trial court has the residual jurisdiction to stay proceedings if forcing the accused to stand trial would violate "those fundamental principles of justice which underlie the community's sense of fair play and decency and to prevent the abuse of a court's process through oppressive or vexatious proceedings."[53] However, it was emphasized that this power may only be exercised in the "clearest of cases."

In a subsequent case,[53a] the Supreme Court unequivocally indicated just how reluctant the courts should be to use the abuse of process doctrine in the control of the prosecutor's discretionary powers. The accused had been subjected to two trials on a charge of criminal negligence causing death; however, both trials ended with the jury failing to agree on a verdict. The trial judge applied the abuse of process doctrine (as well as section 7 of the *Charter*) and stayed a third trial. The Saskatchewan Court of Appeal allowed the Crown's appeal and ordered that the accused be tried again. The Supreme Court of Canada upheld the Court of Appeal's decision. In delivering the judgment of the Supreme Court, Madam Justice Wilson said:

> ... [the accused] has, in my view, failed to demonstrate that this is one of those "clearest of cases" which would justify a stay. The charge is a serious one. The proceedings have not occupied an undue amount of time. The accused has not been held in custody, and, while he has undoubtedly suffered substantial trauma and stigma from the proceedings and the attendant publicity, he is probably not distinguishable in this respect from the vast majority of accused. A third trial may, indeed, stretch the limits of the community's sense of fair play but does not of itself exceed them. [40 C.C.C. (3d) at 483]

It is not entirely clear how the doctrine of abuse of process will develop in light of the availability of remedies under the *Charter* (Morgan, 1986: 43*ff.*). As noted elsewhere, section 24 of the *Charter* provides the courts with the power to invoke a number of alternative remedies whenever there has been a violation of an accused person's rights under the *Charter*. We have already seen, for example, that the courts have been prepared to enter a stay of proceedings where there has been a violation of the right to be tried within a reasonable time, as guaranteed by section 11(b) of the *Charter*. However, it is likely that section 7, which guarantees the right not to be deprived of "life, liberty and security of the person" except in accordance with "the principles of fundamental justice," will provide the basis for the courts to move beyond the narrow scope of the doctrine of abuse of process in controlling prosecutorial excesses. Indeed, the Ontario Court of Appeal[54] has already ruled that section 7 does, in fact, incorporate some degree of protection against "abuses of process" (Morgan, 1986: 52). In this sense, it is possible that section 7 may well be used to broaden most significantly the impact of the doctrine of abuse of process in Canada in the years ahead.

Plea Bargaining

Plea bargaining has, for some time, been one of the most controversial, and perhaps least understood, aspects of the Canadian criminal justice system (Cousineau and Verdun-Jones, 1979; Genova, 1981; Verdun-Jones and Cousineau, 1979; Verdun-Jones and Hatch, 1985 and 1987). At first blush, the idea of accused persons bargaining for lenience behind closed doors is a singularly unattractive one. However, the reality of the situation is much more complex than this popular image would lead one to believe.

The Law Reform Commission of Canada (1975b: 45) once defined *plea bargain* as "any agreement by the accused to plead guilty in return for the promise of some benefit." This definition perhaps fits well with the popular concept of the phenomenon of plea bargaining. However, the term is generally used in a much broader sense by those involved in criminal justice research. Indeed, as Verdun-Jones and Hatch (1985: 1) note, *plea bargaining is really a compendious term used to describe a wide diversity of behaviours that occur among actors in the court system.* The police, the Crown and defence counsel may engage in behaviours ranging from simple discussions through negotiations to agreements. Clearly, discussions and negotiations may not ultimately lead to any form of agreement between the parties; however, these behaviours have generally been considered by researchers as falling within the concept of plea bargaining (Cousineau and Verdun-Jones, 1979).

It is also important to point out that some researchers have questioned whether the terms *plea negotiations* and *plea bargains* are appropriate given the so-called realities of the criminal justice process. For example, Ericson and Baranek (1982) question whether the word *negotiate* is meaningful in light of the stark imbalance of power between the police and the Crown on the one hand, and the defendant on the other. Furthermore, they argue that it is more realistic to view the accused's decisions within the criminal justice system as being "coerced" or "manipulated" and that, therefore, any accommodation with the Crown will scarcely be perceived by the accused as a genuine "bargain." In addition, even where an agreement is actually reached, it is perhaps a little misleading to refer to it as a *plea bargain*, because, as we shall see, neither the Crown nor the defendant has any guarantee that such an agreement will ultimately be carried into effect by the sentencing judge, who is not bound by anything that has been agreed to by the parties concerned. In any event, we shall use the term *plea bargaining* in the following discussion because of its widespread use in the criminal justice research literature. Nevertheless, it is always necessary to bear in mind that the term covers a broad range of potential interactions that may occur between the Crown and the defence in Canada.

If plea bargaining is concerned with reaching an agreement to secure a concession from the Crown in return for the accused pleading guilty, what concessions may the defence seek from Crown counsel? Broadly speaking, these benefits may be considered to fall into three overlapping categories: namely, promises relating to the *charges* to be laid, promises relating to the ultimate *sentence* to be meted out by the court, and promises relating to the *facts* that the Crown is willing to bring to the attention of the court (assuming that the trial judge's knowledge of such facts will have a significant impact on the sentencing decision). Verdun-Jones and Hatch (1985: 3) have suggested the following list of potential benefits that might be promised by the Crown:

Charge Bargaining:
   (a) reduction of the charge to a lesser or included offence;
   (b) withdrawal or stay of other charges or the promise not to proceed on other possible charges; and
   (c) promise not to charge friends or family of the defendant.

Sentence Bargaining
   (a) promise to proceed summarily rather than by way of indictment;
   (b) promise that the Crown will make a particular recommendation in relation to sentence;
   (c) promise not to oppose defence counsel's sentence recommendation;
   (d) promise not to appeal against sentence imposed at trial;
   (e) promise not to apply for a more severe penalty (under section 665 of the *Criminal Code*);
   (f) promise not to apply for a period of preventive detention under section 753 of the *Code*;
   (g) promise to make a representation as to the place of imprisonment, type of treatment, etc.; and
   (h) promise to arrange sentencing before a particular judge.

Fact Bargaining
   (a) promise not to "volunteer" information detrimental to the accused (for example, not adducing evidence as to the defendant's previous convictions under section 255 of the *Code*); and
   (b) promise not to mention a circumstance of the offence that may be interpreted by the judge as an *aggravating* factor (and, therefore, deserving a greater degree of severity of punishment).

The Official Response to Plea Bargaining

While it has probably been practised for many years, plea bargaining was traditionally frowned upon and most individuals involved in the criminal justice system would not openly admit that it took place (Verdun-Jones and Cousineau, 1979). Until relatively recently, plea bargaining was held in such low regard that the Law Reform Commission of Canada (1975a: 14) contended that it was "something for which a decent criminal justice system has no place." However, such attitudes now appear to be undergoing a significant degree of change. Indeed, only a decade after its extremely negative comment on the practice, the Law Reform Commission (1984) refers to plea bargaining, in one of its working papers, almost as a routine part of the court process. A similar evolution of thought is apparent on the part of the judiciary, who were highly critical of the practice until fairly recently (Verdun-Jones and Cousineau, 1979); however, there now appears to be a greater degree of (at least tacit) tolerance of the practice (Verdun-Jones and Hatch, 1985: 24). Indeed, in a case decided in 1979, a Justice of the Supreme Court of Canada mentioned, without any apparent disapproval (and almost as an afterthought), that the guilty plea had been obtained as a result of a plea bargain.[55] Even professional bodies, such as the Canadian Bar Association, appear to have sanctioned certain forms of plea bargaining. For example, the *Code of Professional Conduct* of the Canadian Bar Association (1974) recognizes the legitimacy of a defence lawyer entering into a "tentative" plea agreement with the Crown and sets out ethical guidelines for the regulation of such conduct (Verdun-Jones and Hatch, 1985: 22–23).

While they have not openly endorsed the practice of plea bargaining, Canadian courts have nevertheless offered a subtle condonation, and even a certain degree of encouragement, of the practice by establishing an atmosphere that permits it to flourish unchecked (Verdun-Jones and Hatch, 1985: 29). In most cases, Canadian courts do not actively investigate the circumstances surrounding the entry of a guilty plea before they accept it. If the accused is represented by defence counsel, the trial judge will normally refrain from conducting a meticulous inquiry into the circumstances surrounding a guilty plea (Verdun-Jones and Cousineau, 1979). In these circumstances, it is unlikely that there will be any investigation into the nature of the inducements offered to an accused person to plead guilty or any inquiry into whether the accused fully understands the implications of any plea bargain into which he or she may have entered. Indeed, it may well be argued that the lack of a requirement under Canadian law that a judge ferret out the critical factors that may have led to the defendant's decision to plead guilty has effectively created an environment in which it is possible for Crown and defence counsel to enter into plea bargains behind the inscrutable veil of secrecy.

The courts may also give some tacit encouragement to the practice of plea bargaining as a consequence of the widespread belief that accused persons entering guilty pleas may legitimately expect to receive a more lenient sentence than they would have if their guilt had been determined by a trial. This form of "sentence discounting" has been referred to as *tacit plea bargaining*. A more lenient sentence may be justified on the basis that the guilty plea indicates remorse,[56] the community is spared the cost of a trial,[57] the victim does not have to undergo the trauma of testifying,[58] or the accused has cooperated with the police.[59] These justifications are necessary in order to avoid the impression that accused persons may be *penalized* for exercising their right to a trial. In one case, for example, the judge stated:

> It is a fundamental concept of our system of justice that a person accused of a crime is entitled to demand that the Crown prove his guilt by a fair and impartial trial. There is nothing that the court should ever do to whittle down or undercut that fundamental principle. At the same time, it would be unrealistic not to recognize that if everyone demanded a full and complete trial our system of justice would come to an abrupt halt. It is for that reason that those who are guilty, and wish to so plead, should be given special consideration when they appear before the court.[60]

By encouraging guilty pleas in this manner, the courts appear to be facilitating the practice of plea bargaining. However, there is, to date, little evidence to establish that those who plead guilty do, in fact, receive more lenient sentences than those who go to trial. Solomon's (1983) analysis of data taken from a study of "Robert County," Ontario, did not reveal any evidence to support the notion that there was a penalty imposed for pleading not guilty. Solomon (p. 39) notes that in only one of the seven cases in which there was a conviction after a fully contested trial did the offender receive a more severe punishment than that received by those who had pleaded guilty to the same offences. However, Solomon (p. 39) rightly notes that these data are "too scanty to be conclusive." Nevertheless, it appears that most of the defence lawyers in "Robert County" did genuinely believe that there was a discount for pleading guilty (Solomon, 1983: 41), and this belief may well have exerted a strong influence over their clients' decision whether or not to plead guilty. Indeed, lawyers interviewed by Ericson and Baranek (1982) noted that the promise of a more lenient sentence can be extremely persuasive in convincing a reluctant client to plead guilty.

The courts have also facilitated plea bargaining practices by encouraging the submission of sentence recommendations by the Crown and defence (Verdun-Jones and Hatch, 1985: 34). There is evidence that some Canadian courts are prepared to encourage *joint sentence recommendations* by the Crown and defence.[61] Since many Canadian courts appear to permit, and frequently accept, such sentencing recommendations, they thereby encourage plea bargaining by giving Crown counsel a valuable commodity to bargain with; in other words, a favourable sentence recommendation may be exchanged for a guilty plea. However, the courts have consistently emphasized that they have absolute discretion in sentencing matters and no particular recommendation, not even one made as part of a plea bargain, is binding on the sentencing judge.[62] However, as Ruby (1987: 74) points out, such sentencing recommendations are "customarily given considerable weight."[62a]

Empirical Research into Plea Bargaining in Canada

The empirical research conducted in Canada suggests that plea bargaining does occur at least in certain jurisdictions in this country. However, a number of these studies are affected by major methodological problems (Cousineau and Verdun-Jones, 1979). Research into plea bargaining in Canada has taken three forms: interviews, analysis of official documents, and observations of the practice itself.

Two of the pioneering studies of plea bargaining in Canada were based on interviews. Grosman (1969) drew both upon his own experience as a prosecutor and upon a series of interviews with 45 Crown attorneys in the County of York, Ontario. He suggested that plea bargaining occurred routinely as part of a well-established pattern of accommodations and concessions that were exchanged between prosecutors and certain "favoured" defence counsel. While the impact of Grosman's trail-blazing study should not be underestimated, it must nevertheless be noted that his analysis was based on impressions and hearsay rather than systematic observation of the actual practices associated with plea bargaining. It has also been pointed out that Grosman's findings, which related to a jurisdiction that contained the massive metropolitan area of Toronto, would not necessarily be applicable to other Canadian jurisdictions (Bowen-Coulthurst, 1970: 496).

Another fascinating study based on interviews was conducted by Klein (1979), who interviewed some 115 inmates in a maximum security federal penitentiary in 1972. Klein (1979: 132) focused upon the types of "deals" that the offenders had struck "in interaction with the agents in the criminal justice system to minimize the possible punitive consequences" of their illegal activities. Slightly more than half of the inmates claimed that they had been involved in deals with the police or prosecutors.

The Grosman and Klein studies were exploratory in nature and, as is the case with all research that relies upon interviews as the major source of data, there is a question about the accuracy with which they represent the phenomenon studied.

Another group of studies involved an examination of official court documents as an indication of the nature and extent of plea bargaining. The first of these quantitative studies was undertaken by Hartnagel and Wynne (1975) and Wynne and Hartnagel (1975)[63] in a prairie city during 1972 and 1973. The researchers examined the files of all those persons charged with

Criminal Code offences where they believed that there was "evidence" of plea bargaining between the Crown and defence counsel. The factors that they found to affect plea bargaining, as they defined it, were the existence of multiple charges against the accused and the specific nature of the offence(s) charged (for example, plea bargaining did not customarily occur in relation to summary conviction offences). The researchers found that those who were unrepresented did not share in the benefits of plea bargaining and that native Indians were less likely to gain any advantages from this process than were their white counterparts.

In a similar vein, Hagan (1975) studied the role played by legal, procedural and extra-legal factors in the sentencing process using data from court files and, incidentally, offered a number of significant observations in relation to the practice of plea bargaining. The study was conducted in the City of Edmonton and involved the examination of the files of some 1,018 offenders. The researcher concluded that the sentence imposed by a court was primarily a reflection of the seriousness of the initial charge and the defendant's prior record rather than of such procedural variables as charge alteration and initial plea (which may be closely related to the existence of plea bargaining). Hagan also found that plea bargaining is much more likely to occur where the Crown has laid multiple charges. However, he suggested that the accused's race did not appear to have any significant effect upon the incidence of plea bargaining.

Both these studies, based on court documents, provide valuable insights into the operation of the court process. However, they are not entirely satisfactory as studies of plea bargaining, since the researchers did not observe the phenomenon itself but rather *inferred* that plea bargaining had taken place on the basis of indicators identified in court files. For example, Hagan concluded that plea bargaining had occurred whenever the record indicated a reduction in the charge against the accused; however, charges may be reduced for many reasons and there is no reason to suppose that all charge reductions are in fact the consequence of plea bargaining. Hartnagel and Wynne, on the other hand, considered plea bargaining to have taken place only where there were, *inter alia*, written comments or correspondence in the file that indicated a deal had occurred; clearly, it is a somewhat doubtful assumption that all plea bargains will be recorded in writing in the official court files.

More recently, a group of researchers at the University of Toronto's Centre of Criminology conducted a major study of discretionary decision making in the criminal justice process, in the course of which a wealth of data based on a variety of research methods, including direct observation of the plea bargaining process, was uncovered. One hundred and one accused persons were tracked through the criminal justice system from arrest to sentence. The data from this study have been reported in several sources,[64] the most comprehensive of which is a book by Ericson and Baranek (1982). A number of different research techniques were employed in the collection of the data. Verbatim transcripts were kept of interviews with the accused and interviews with lawyers; recordings were also made of conversations in the Crown attorney's office. Researchers also observed the court appearances of the defendants in the sample. This study represents the first occasion when researchers have actually been able to document the dynamics involved in the process of plea bargaining.

In their book, Ericson and Baranek (1982: 117) employ the term *plea discussions* rather than *plea bargaining*, because the former expression renders it clear that discussions may be entered into without an agreement ever being reached. They concluded (p. 121) that "plea discussions were a widespread and integral part of the order out of court." In this respect, they found (pp. 117–18) that of the lawyers for 80 accused persons who were interviewed, lawyers for as many as 57 accused said that they had entered into plea discussions. Furthermore, they found (p. 121) that participation in plea discussions was not confined to Crown and defence counsel; indeed, the police were frequently involved at various stages in the plea discussion process.

Ericson and Baranek (1982) suggest that the existence of multiple charges appears to be a major element in the circumstances that lead to plea discussions taking place. Of the 23 accused whose lawyers did *not* engage in such discussions, 17 had only one charge laid against them (as compared with only 9 of the 57 accused whose lawyers were involved in pleas discussions). The authors suggest that this underlines the importance of multiple charging as a vital component of the plea discussion process in Canada; without the existence of multiple charges, the defence could not negotiate for the withdrawal of some charge(s) in return for the entry of a guilty plea to others. Lawyers who engaged in discussions with the Crown said that withdrawal of charges was the major topic of conversation (Ericson and Baranek, 1982: 119).

Given that there was widespread involvement in plea discussions, what was the outcome of such involvement? The striking finding made by Ericson and Baranek (1982: 143) was that although many of the lawyers engaged in plea discussions, only about a quarter of them stated that they had reached an agreement that could be considered a bargain. For this group of lawyers, the most frequently mentioned bargain was one that included a sentence concession. Of the remaining lawyers who entered plea discussions, 12% stated that they had not reached an agreement, while lawyers for the remaining 88% claimed that the agreement reached brought no real advantage for the accused. More than half of the lawyers (representing 23 accused) who thought that an agreement had brought no tangible benefit stated that the charges withdrawn or reduced in their cases did not represent a concession because such charges were merely the result of overcharging by the police in the first place (Ericson and Baranek, 1982: 145).

Solomon (1983) also analyzed the data gathered from the study conducted by the Centre of Criminology at the University of Toronto. He indicates that the data were collected in central Ontario and assigned the fictional title "Robert County" to the jurisdiction studied. Solomon (p. 37) contends that the data suggest that plea bargaining occurred more frequently in the provincial courts of "Robert County" than might have been expected from a reading of the Canadian literature on the topic.[65] However, as is the case with Ericson and Baranek, he contends that plea bargaining "did not result in important concessions for the accused." In the Provincial Court, almost 80% of criminal cases that were not withdrawn by the Crown terminated with guilty pleas, and 60% of these cases involved plea discussions. It appears that the discussions between defence counsel and the Crown and/or police usually focused on the charges to which the accused would plead guilty rather than the sentence (although there was some discussion of the approach that the Crown would adopt at the sentencing stage). Plea agreements resulted in the dropping of charges (which were often not justified in the first place) and at least a tacit agreement about the Crown's recommendation regarding sentence. However, Solomon (p. 37) points out that there was no clear relation between the charges to which the accused ultimately pleaded guilty and the sentence handed down by the court. Furthermore, the sentencing recommendations made by the Crown had no direct impact upon the sentence actually handed down by the court. In these circumstances, an accused person who entered into a plea arrangement with the Crown had no guarantee that his or her guilty plea would make any difference whatsoever to the ultimate outcome of the case!

If the defendant does not normally gain any special advantages from the plea discussion process, what is the rationale for the participation of so many defence counsel in the practice? In Solomon's view (1983: 43), the data from Robert County are consistent with the view that the "primary responsibility of defence counsel in plea bargaining ... consists not in seeking special advantages, but in assuring that the outcome of the case is no worse than the local norms dictate." He also contends (p. 48) that, from the point of view of the accused, plea bargaining may have some tangible benefits as an alternative means of disposing of his or her case. Although accused persons did not seem to gain more lenient sentences for themselves as a consequence of entering into a plea agreement, they did nevertheless derive a "procedural gain":

> More than anything else, plea bargaining offered the accused through his counsel a forum for presenting a defence of the case informally without the need to bear the costs (in money, time, and emotional strain) associated with contesting trial. From the defence counsel's presentation in plea discussions two tangible benefits did emerge. First, he could ensure that the interpretation of the evidence reflected in the final charges and the crown attorney's sentencing recommendation (if any) would be no worse than the local norm for that genre of case. Secondly, in some cases counsel could also obtain the prosecutor's agreement to consider, if not a lenient sentence, then suggesting a particular kind of sentence.

Conditions that Facilitate Plea Bargaining in Canada

There are many factors in the structure of the Canadian system of criminal justice that facilitate the practice of plea bargaining. Among the more significant of these are, as we have seen, the very broad discretionary powers enjoyed by the prosecution coupled with the essentially passive role adopted by the judiciary, who rely upon the Crown and the defence to present the relevant facts of the case instead of conducting their own inquiries into the facts (Feeley, 1982). By way of comparison, Feeley (1982: 347) points out that in Germany, where the prosecutor does not have such broad discretionary powers and where the judge plays an active role in the criminal trial, plea bargaining is virtually unknown.

Another major factor that facilitates plea bargaining is the close relationships that develop between the court actors (Brantingham, 1985; Grosman, 1969). The existence of salaried prosecutors and the availability of professional lawyers for the representation of the accused permits trusting relationships to develop between these professionals. Ericson and Baranek (1982: 13–14) note that this sense of trust also extends to the police. Individuals making "deals" have to be reasonably confident that the other party will honour his or her part of the bargain, and such trust can evolve during the course of a number of plea discussions. In this context, it appears that defendants who are not members of this "bargaining unit" are precluded from participating directly in pre-trial negotiations (Hartnagel and Wynne, 1975). Having a lawyer, therefore, appears to be a necessary condition for plea bargaining to occur (Verdun-Jones and Hatch, 1985: 41).[66]

Their relationship with the other court actors poses major problems for defence lawyers. As Ericson and Baranek (1982) point out, the various court actors have a vested interest in maintaining mutually beneficial relationships between themselves and other court actors, even if the latter are ostensibly on the "other side." Defence counsel are in a particularly precarious position because they are attempting to serve the best interests of their clients while simultaneously maintaining a harmonious relationship with the Crown. In the words of the researchers:

> The lawyer has a particularly complex set of stakes. These involve a balance between doing a job which appears competent to his client and maintaining the professional respect and collaboration of crime control officials. [P. 26]

It has been argued (e.g., Warner and Renner, 1981) that the existence of such a rapport between the court actors is contrary to the notion of the adversary system of justice. These researchers examined cases heard by three magistrate's courts and two county courts in Halifax. The authors found little evidence of the operation of a vigorous adversary system, based on a struggle by opposing advocates; rather, they suggested that the court

system operated as a bureaucracy that was geared primarily to the processing of criminal cases in the most *efficient* manner possible. The majority of
defendants were unrepresented. However, in those cases where the accused
were represented, there was evidence of a lack of adversariness. The judge
usually accepted the sentencing recommendation made by one of the
lawyers with the other usually manifesting tacit acceptance by remaining
silent, or else both the lawyers agreed and the judge concurred (Warner and
Renner, 1981: 91).

However, it has been questioned whether the rise of plea bargaining truly
represents a retreat from a golden past in which criminal cases were fought
out between aggressive adversaries in the crucible of a full trial of the issues.
Feeley (1982: 340), for example, strongly rejects the notion that plea bargaining is a cooperative practice that strikes at the heart of the adversarial
system of criminal justice:

> Plea bargaining is not a cooperative practice that undermines or compromises the
> adversary process; rather, the opportunity for adversariness has expanded in direct
> proportion to, and perhaps as a result of, the growth of plea bargaining. As the
> requirements of due process have expanded, as resources have become more accessible
> to both the prosecution and the criminally accused, as the substantive criminal law has
> developed, and as the availability and role of defence counsel have expanded, the
> opportunity for both adversariness and negotiations has increased.

According to Feeley, the adversary system has in fact become more
vigorous in recent years. Indeed, in his view (1982: 346), there never was a
"golden era" or "high noon" of the adversary process in the United States,
and one can perhaps extend the force of his comments to the Canadian
situation as well. Even in the distant past, when there was a greater reliance
upon the trial than on the guilty plea as a means of deciding criminal cases,
the trial process was generally very brief and perfunctory and the accused
was *unlikely to be represented by defence counsel*. In short, although there
may have been a greater proportion of "trials," these tended to be rushed
affairs with none of the adversarial protections that are claimed by defendants in the contemporary criminal trial process. In these circumstances,
Feeley suggests that the access of accused persons to defence counsel has
greatly enhanced the adversarial nature of the criminal justice process even
if much of the work of defence lawyers is concentrated upon the task of plea
bargaining. Indeed, Feeley (p. 352) suggests that the very presence of a
lawyer who can negotiate with the prosecution represents an increase in
adversariness.

Solomon is equally skeptical of the contention that the close relationships between Crown and defence counsel necessarily represent a
threat to the adversarial underpinnings of the criminal justice system. In
his view (1983: 42), "maintaining a working relationship with crown
attorneys did not call for abdication of defence responsibilities, but for
avoiding unreasonable and unproductive tactics." According to Solomon,

there was a "marked convergence of interest" between defence lawyer and client, and defence lawyers tended to reserve their main efforts for the process of plea discussions on behalf of their clients.

A vital element in facilitating the plea bargaining process is the power of the police to lay multiple charges in relation to the same basic incident. In addition, with a view to future bargaining, the police may lay a more serious charge than the facts really warrant. Ericson and Baranek (1982: 71) discovered some evidence for this proposition in their study:

> . . . the police decide to charge with an eye towards outcomes in court. They "frame" the limits to what is negotiable, and produce conviction and sentence outcomes, by "overcharging," "charging up," and laying highly questionable charges.

Solomon (1983: 45) draws the same conclusions from this data when he states that in "Robert County" overcharging was the normal practice of the police, who laid every conceivable charge on the assumption that some of the excess charges could be bargained away for a guilty plea. Since the extra charges do not appear to have an impact on the ultimate sentence handed down by the court, their abandonment did not inflict a particularly high "cost" upon the police.

There is little doubt that the ability of the police to lay more charges than may reasonably be expected to result in convictions is an important facilitating condition of plea bargaining. Indeed, Brannigan and Levy (1983: 404) state that:

> Such a looseness of fit between the police latitude in laying charges and limitations on the Crown's ability to secure convictions on them is probably the single most important source of charge reductions and one of the most important factors in so-called plea bargaining.

Unlike Ericson and Baranek and Solomon, however, Brannigan and Levy (1983: 403) are reluctant to characterize this process as "overcharging," since they state that the police do not make up facts to justify additional charges. Instead, they contend that the police "are being technical in their charging behaviour."

The Supreme Court of Canada has indirectly encouraged the laying of multiple charges by the police by ruling that while an individual cannot be *convicted* of more than one offence for exactly the same incident, he or she can still be *charged* with more than one offence.[67] In the *Kienapple* case, the accused had been convicted of both rape and unlawful sexual intercourse with a girl under the age of 14 years. The Supreme Court quashed the second conviction on the basis that the defendant could not be convicted more than once for the same crime. However, the Court also ruled that more than one charge can be laid in such circumstances and that these charges should be treated as alternative counts. In other words, the Supreme Court forbade multiple convictions for the same offence but did not prevent the police from laying more than one charge. As Brannigan (1984: 149) points out,

> ... the application of the Kienapple doctrine is frequently quite ambiguous. Typically the police will lay whatever charges seem appropriate, leaving the question of double jeopardy for the lawyers to sort out. This affects plea discussions quite directly.

One possible danger in such circumstances is that the defendant may be induced to plead guilty on the basis of the Crown dropping a charge in a situation where he or she could not have been convicted of more than one offence in any event. Such a plea agreement would be an "illusory" bargain since the accused has gained nothing from the decision to enter a plea of guilty (Verdun-Jones and Hatch, 1985: 20).[68]

A further facilitating factor for plea bargaining is the ability of the police, as well as the Crown and defence counsel, to control the information that is ultimately introduced to the court, thereby having some impact on the sentence meted out (for example, not mentioning an accused person's prior record during the sentencing hearing). This has been called fact bargaining and has been extensively documented by Ericson and Baranek (1982: 19– 23, 66, 120–21).

Regulating Plea Bargaining

At present, plea bargaining operates without any substantial controls to protect the interests of society, the victim and the offender. What should be done about this disturbing situation? At the outset, it should be recognized that plea bargaining appears to be so deeply entrenched in the fabric of the Canadian criminal justice system that it would appear that outright aboli- tion of the practice is not a viable option. Indeed, it is highly probable that any attempt to abolish plea bargaining would be fraught with insurmount- able difficulties (Cousineau and Verdun-Jones, 1979; Verdun-Jones and Cousineau, 1979; Verdun-Jones and Hatch, 1985 and 1987). Some Amer- ican studies suggest that attempting to abolish the practice does not eradi- cate it but rather changes its nature and/or displaces it to a different point in the criminal process (Church, 1976; McCoy, 1984). In this respect, Verdun- Jones and Hatch (1985: 14–15) note that research in the United States suggests that "plea bargaining is pervasive, tenacious and very adaptable." It would appear that some form of discretionary decision making is a necessary component of any criminal justice system. Indeed, as Verdun- Jones and Hatch (1985: 15) point out:

> Given the fact that criminal justice systems are characterised by attempts to achieve many *varied* and often *conflicting* goals, then it seems reasonable to assume that these systems will always *generate* and *perpetuate* discretionary decision-making processes as adaptations to these multiple ends. Plea bargaining appears to allow and facilitate the accommodation of these multiple purposes of criminal justice systems.

If outright abolition is not feasible, what steps can be taken to ensure that plea bargaining is not abused? Perhaps the first step is to accept the legitimacy of the practice and to establish formal controls to monitor the conduct of those involved in it. As the Canadian Sentencing Commission (1986: 415) states, ". . . it would be far more realistic to recommend methods of enhancing the visibility and accountability of plea bargaining decisions than to recommend the abolition of the practice."

To this end, the Commission (1986: 417) recommends that sentencing judges should inquire of defendants whether they fully understand the nature and implications of a plea agreement and that, if they do not, then judges should be granted the discretion to set aside the plea or sentence. The judiciary could, for example, take special care to ensure that defendants not plead guilty when there are doubts about their guilt. In this respect, it is significant that Ericson and Baranek (1982: 158) found that 16 of the 101 defendants whom they interviewed pleaded guilty despite claiming that they were innocent. The Commission (pp. 422–23) recommends that the appropriate federal and provincial authorities should devise, and attempt to enforce, guidelines concerning the ethics of plea bargaining and that the Crown should normally be required to "justify in open court a plea bargain agreement reached by the parties." The Commission (p. 425) also recommends that the judiciary not become involved in the plea negotiation process and that the *Criminal Code* be amended so as to provide that the court is not bound by any joint sentencing submission made by the Crown and the defence or any other arrangement by the parties concerning a particular charge or sentence.

The recommendations of the Canadian Sentencing Commission, to some extent, reflect developments in the United States, where there has been a strong trend towards recognizing the legitimacy of plea bargaining and establishing judicial supervision over the process (McDonald, 1987). For example, Rule 11 of the *Federal Rules of Procedure* provides that all plea agreements must be submitted to a judge, who may either ratify or reject the proposed agreement (Verdun-Jones and Cousineau, 1979: 259–60). The Rule embodies a number of requirements designed to ensure that the defendant is made fully aware of the implications of any proposed plea agreement. Similarly, the *Sentencing Reform Act, 1981* of Washington State provides for judicial supervision of the plea agreement process and even goes on to establish specific standards for the behaviour of prosecutors participating in the process (Verdun-Jones and Hatch, 1985: 104–109).

No matter what the ultimate outcome of the Canadian Sentencing Commission's recommendations may turn out to be, it should be noted that plea bargaining may well become more institutionalized as a consequence of an amendment to the *Criminal Code* that establishes *pre-hearing conferences* between the Crown, defence counsel and the trial judge in order to try and settle certain issues before they come to trial. Section 625.1 of the *Criminal Code*, which was enacted in 1985 but has not yet been proclaimed in force, makes such hearings mandatory in the case of jury trials and optional in other cases (provided the prosecutor and accused agree). The section envisages the pre-trial hearing as a method of promoting a "fair and expeditious" hearing or trial. Clearly, such hearings could well provide a forum for plea bargaining, with the judge ensuring that the outcome is fair from the points of view of the accused, the victim (if any) and society at large.

Even if the courts are given greater power to supervise the plea bargaining process, there is always a danger that the Crown and defence may fail to present the "full facts" of the case to the judge, thereby influencing whether or not a proposed plea agreement is accepted. One method by means of which the dangers of "fact bargaining" could be reduced would be to ensure that the sentencing judge is made aware of the impact of the offence upon the victim (if there is one). The use of victim impact statements (Clarke, 1986: 39–40) by the Crown may ensure that the facts presented to the court by the Crown and defence are not too far removed from the victim's perception of what actually took place.

Dubious behaviour on the part of lawyers involved in the plea bargaining process may also be controlled by the application of ethical principles by the various provincial Law Societies in the course of disciplinary proceedings. The Canadian Bar Association's *Code of Professional Conduct* (1974) already contains specific guidelines concerning plea agreements, and the Code has been adopted by most provincial Law Societies. Unethical conduct might well be found to have occurred, for example, where a lawyer has persuaded a client to plead guilty despite the latter's belief that he or she is not guilty.[69] In addition, the behaviour of Crown counsel is very likely to be controlled, at least to some extent, by principles established by the Attorney General, usually in written form.[70]

NOTES

1. Farris, C.J.B.C., in *R. v. Ewing and Kearney*, [1974] 5 W.W.R. 232 at 233, 18 C.C.C. (2d) 356.

2. *Joplin v. Chief Constable of the City of Vancouver* (1983), 2 C.C.C. (3d) 396, 4 C.R.R. 208, 144 D.L.R. (3d) 285 (B.C.S.C.); affirmed 19 C.C.C. (3d) 331, [1985] 4 W.W.R. 538, 20 D.L.R. (4th) 314 (B.C.C.A.).

3. Section 650(3). This particular section applies in the case of indictable offences. However, section 802(1) provides for a similar right to make a "full answer and defence" in the case of summary conviction offences. Section 802(2) also provides that the accused "may examine and cross-examine witnesses personally or by counsel or agent."

4. *R. v. Bowles and Danylak* (1985), 21 C.C.C. (3d) 540, 40 Alta. L.R. (2d) 1 (Alta. C.A.).

5. *Barrette v. The Queen* (1976), 29 C.C.C. (2d) 189, 68 D.L.R. (3d) 260, [1977] 2 S.C.R. 121.

6. *R. v. Huebschwerlen,* [1965] 3 C.C.C. 212 (Y.T.C.A.).

7. Section 684.

8. It should be noted that section 615(4) of the *Code* provides that where "there is sufficient reason to doubt that the accused is, on account of insanity, capable of conducting his defence," then the court *shall* assign counsel to act for him, if he is unrepresented.

9. *Re White and The Queen* (1976), 32 C.C.C. (2d) 478, 1 Alta. L.R. (2d) 292, 73 D.L.R. (3d) 275.

10. *R. v. Ewing and Kearney*, [1974] 5 W.W.R. 232, 18 C.C.C. (2d) 356. This ruling was followed in the Ontario case of *R. v. Ciglen* (1979), 10 C.R. (3d) 226 (Ont. H.C.).

11. *Deutsch v. Law Society of Upper Canada Legal Aid Fund et al.* (1985), 48 C.R. (3d) 166, 16 C.R.R. 349, 11 O.A.C. 30.

11a. An important issue that will probably be considered with increasing frequency under the *Charter* is the whole question of the *effectiveness* of defence counsel and whether the *incompetence* of counsel should be a ground for ordering a new trial where it is claimed that the accused was convicted as a consequence of such incompetence. After all, there is little point in the courts recognizing a right to counsel if they do not also ensure that defendants receive effective assistance from their counsel. However, it appears that there is considerable reluctance on the part of the courts to set aside a trial verdict on this basis. For example, in *R. v. Garofoli* (1988), 41 C.C.C. (3d) 97, 27 O.A.C. 1, 64 C.R. (3d) 193, the Ontario Court of Appeal rejected the accused's claim that his constitutional right to the effective assistance of counsel (under sections 7, 10(b) and 11(d) of the *Charter*) had been infringed. In the view of Justice Martin, the accused had not shown that his counsel's alleged errors had prejudiced his right to a fair trial:

> ... where the defendant alleges that the incompetence of counsel deprived him of the effective assistance of counsel, the defendant must show, in addition to the lack of competence of the part of defence counsel, that there is a reasonable probability that, but for counsel's unprofessional errors, the result of the trial would have been different. [41 C.C.C. (3d) at 151]

12. See, for example, the discussion in *Mountain v. Legal Services Society*, [1984] 2 W.W.R. 438, 9 C.C.C. (3d) 300, 5 D.L.R. (4th) 170 (B.C. C.A.).

13. Their average total assets were only $818.

14. However, in exceptional circumstances, lawyers may be retained from private firms to deal with legal aid cases.

15. In the staff system, the legal aid authority may also operate a number of community law offices or community legal aid clinics. For example, in British Columbia, community law offices are governed by community boards and contract annually for funds from the legal aid authority (Brantingham and Brantingham, 1984: 31).

16. Legal aid programs are peculiarly susceptible to cutbacks in government funding. By early 1982, there was a world economic recession, and both the federal and provincial governments announced policies of restraint. While the federal government did not reduce its overall commitment to the funding of legal aid, certain provincial governments made significant reductions in their contributions to their legal aid authorities. In British Columbia, for example, the Legal Services Society was forced to make significant cutbacks, resulting in the layoff of staff and a dramatic reduction in the availability of services (Brantingham and Brantingham, 1984: 47–53). During the period of the most severe restraint in British Columbia, during 1982–83, for example, the eligibility standards were reduced to the poverty line. For those who qualified, there was also a user fee of $10 for those on social assistance and $30 for everyone else. Even before the advent of the restraint program (in 1982), it appears that resources could not keep pace with the need for legal aid services (Brantingham and Brantingham, 1984: 247). This raises serious questions about the degree of "due process" that can be offered in a court process that does not provide an adequate level of legal representation to defendants in a criminal case. In the case of British Columbia, it is interesting to note that the British Columbia Court of Appeal ruled that the legal aid authority was in breach of the provincial legislation that had established it and ordered that services be provided to certain defendants who had been refused services because of cuts made by the provincial government: *Mountain v. Legal Services Society*, [1984] 2 W.W.R. 438, 9 C.C.C. (3d) 300, 5 D.L.R. (4th) 170. It will be interesting to see if courts will be prepared, in the future, to order the provision of legal aid services as part of the duty to provide a "fair trial" that is guaranteed by the *Charter*.

17. *R. v. Kalanj and Pion* (1986), 26 C.C.C. (3d) 136 (B.C.C.A.).

18. *Carter v. The Queen* (1986), 26 C.C.C. (3d) 572, 52 C.R. (3d) 100, 67 N.R. 375 (S.C.C.).

19. *Mills v. The Queen* (1986), 26 C.C.C. (3d) 481 at 542–43, 52 C.R. (3d) 1, [1986] 1 S.C.R. 863.

20. *Ibid.*, at 544.

21. *Ibid.*, at 546. In *Rahey v. The Queen* (1987), 33 C.C.C. (3d) 289, [1987] 1 S.C.R. 588, 57 C.R. (3d) 289; reversing 13 C.C.C. (3d) 297, 11 C.R.R. 272, 141 A.P.R. 275 (N.S.C.A.); reversing 9 C.C.C. (3d) 385, 61 N.S.R. (2d) 385, 133 A.P.R. 385 (N.S.T.D.), the Supreme Court of Canada held that when deciding whether there has been a waiver of the right to a speedy trial, a court must apply different principles where the delay is caused by the trial judge rather than the Crown. In this case, a stay of proceedings was entered because the Court held that an 11-month delay, during which the trial judge failed to rule on the accused's motion for a directed verdict of acquittal, was unreasonable and could not be justified. For example, Madam Justice Wilson said that

... in the context of judge-generated delay it is unfair to deem waiver on the basis of a consent to the presiding judge's adjournment of the case as opposed to a consent to a Crown request for an adjournment. [33 C.C.C. (3d) at 313]

In the *Rahey* case, the trial judge had asked for no less than 19 adjournments.

22. *Ibid.,* at 548.

23. *Ibid.,* at 555.

24. *R. v. Misra* (1986), 32 C.C.C. (3d) 97, 54 C.R. (3d) 305, 33 C.R.R. 245.

25. Criminal proceedings that have been stayed by a court cannot be recommenced by the prosecution (Stenning, 1986: 359).

26. (1986), 32 C.C.C. (3d) 97 at 121.

27. Sections 645(2) and 803(1) of the *Criminal Code.*

28. Where the adjournments are caused by the unjustified failure of defence counsel to show up at a trial, counsel could be found in contempt of court (Osborne, 1986).

29. For Mackaay (1976: 94), a particularly notorious example of a device that contributes to delay is the right of the accused to seek re-election (i.e., to change his or her choice as to the method of trial for an indictable offence).

30. This finding was later substantiated by a Royal Commission, headed by Mr. Justice Thomas Zuber of the Ontario Court of Appeal (Zuber, 1987).

31. For discussion of these problems, see *R. v. Jones,* [1978] 3 W.W.R. 271, 40 C.C.C. (2d) 173, 4 C.R. (3d) 76 (B.C.S.C.), and Hogarth (1979).

32. See *Attorney-General of Quebec et al. v. Lechasseur* (1981), 63 C.C.C. (2d) 301, [1981] 2 S.C.R. 253, 28 C.R. (3d) 44, and *Re Dowson and The Queen,* [1983] 2 S.C.R. 144, 35 C.R. (3d) 289, 7 C.C.C. (3d) 527.

33. In Saskatchewan, Quebec, Prince Edward Island, and Newfoundland, the chief law officer of the Crown is known as the Minister of Justice or the Minister of Justice *and* Attorney General. In other provinces, he or she is simply known as the Attorney General. In the Yukon and the Northwest Territories, prosecutions are the responsibility of the federal Department of Justice. See Stenning (1986: c. 9).

34. Criminal prosecution sections in the nine regional offices, as well as the Department of Justice Headquarters in Ottawa, employ some 100 lawyers. There are also about 500 private lawyers who are retained on a "standing agent" basis to conduct federal prosecutions in areas not served by the nine regional offices. Where there are no standing agents, private lawyers may be appointed to prosecute individual criminal cases. See Department of Justice, 1986: 35.

35. There have been a number of important cases concerning this constitutional issue that have been decided by the Supreme Court of Canada. However, there are still many matters that have not been resolved: see *R. v. Hauser*, [1979] 1 S.C.R. 984, [1979] 5 W.W.R. 1, 8 C.R. (3d) 89; *R. v. Aziz*, [1981] 1 S.C.R. 188, 19 C.R. (3d) 26, 57 C.C.C. (2d) 97; *A.-G. Can. v. Canadian National Transportation, Ltd. et al.*; *A.-G. Can. v. Canadian Pacific Transport Co. Ltd. et al.*, [1983] 2 S.C.R. 206, 7 C.C.C. (3d) 449, [1984] 1 W.W.R. 193; *R. v. Wetmore and A.-G. Ont. et. al.*, [1983] 2 S.C.R. 284, 7 C.C.C. (3d) 507, [1984] 1 W.W.R. 577.

36. In *Boucher v. The Queen*, [1955] S.C.R. 16 at 23–24, 110 C.C.C. 263, 20 C.R. 1. This passage was cited by the Ontario Court of Appeal in the case of *R. v. Logiacco* (1984), 11 C.C.C. (3d) 374, 2 O.A.C. 177. In *Logiacco*, the Court ordered a new trial because Crown counsel, in his cross-examination of the accused, was deemed to have been abusive and insulting and was considered to have raised irrelevant material. The Court emphasized that the prosecutor should be viewed as a symbol of fairness.

37. See, for example, *R. v. Smythe*, [1971] S.C.R. 680, 3 C.C.C. (2d) 366, 19 D.L.R. (3d) 480.

38. *R. v. Catagas* (1977), 38 C.C.C. (2d) 296, 81 D.L.R. (3d) 396, 2 C.R. (3d) 328 (Man. C.A.).

39. *Ibid.*, at 301.

40. Sections 579(1) and 795.

41. See *Re Dowson and The Queen*, [1983] 2 S.C.R. 144, 35 C.R. (3d) 289, 7 C.C.C. (3d) 527, and Morgan (1986: 29).

42. *R. v. Beaudry*, [1967] 1 C.C.C. 272, 50 C.R. 1, 57 W.W.R. 288.

43. Crown counsel immediately preferred a new indictment for a different offence, and the accused was ultimately convicted.

44. *Ibid.*, at 275. In a more recent case, Boilard, J., refused to review the decision of the Crown to stay a charge of murder laid by a private citizen (*Re Faber and The Queen* (1987), 38 C.C.C. (3d) 49 (Que. S.C.)). The Judge emphasized very strongly the view that the courts should not intervene to review the exercise of this sort of discretionary power by the Crown:

> It is not simply the existence of a crime which obliges the Attorney-General to lay charges. There are other considerations of equal importance, notably the public interest . . .
>
> . . .
>
> If a person contends that the Attorney-General acted badly in the execution of his functions, it is not for the courts to censure him, but rather for Parliament and ultimately for public opinion. [38 C.C.C. (3d) at 61, 62]

45. Section 579(2).

46. In this respect, Stenning (1986: 246) refers to a case before the Ontario High Court, in which Lieff, J., said:

> Once it is premised that the Attorney-General is under a duty to decide whether or not to prosecute in any given case and, if it is decided to prosecute, to carry out that task, it

must follow as a corollary thereof that, in the absence of special circumstances, he not only has the right, but is under a duty to withdraw a charge where, in his opinion, the decision to prosecute has, in the light of later factors, turned out to be ill-conceived.

See *R. v. Dick*, [1969] 1 C.C.C. 147 at 156, [1968] 2 O.R. 351, 4 C.R.N.S. 102.

47. *R. v. Karpinski*, [1957] S.C.R. 343, 117 C.C.C. 241, 25 C.R. 365.

48. See *R. v. Osborne* (1975), 25 C.C.C. (2d) 405, 33 C.R.N.S. 211 (N.B. C.A.).

49. In 1956, one federal Minister of Justice (Mr. Guy Favreau) did resign after questions were raised in the House of Commons and after a report was issued following a public inquiry, which strongly criticized the manner in which he had exercised his prosecutorial discretion. See Stenning (1986: 305).

50. *Vogel v. Canadian Broadcasting Corp. et al.*, [1982] 3 W.W.R. 97, 21 C.C.L.T. 105, 36 B.C.L.R. 7 (B.C.S.C.).

51. *Nelles v. The Queen in right of Ontario et al.* (1985), 46 C.R. (3d) 289, 16 C.R.R. 320, 21 D.L.R. (4th) 103.

52. *R. v. Jewitt* (1985), 21 C.C.C. (3d) 7, [1985] 2 S.C.R. 128, 47 C.R. (3d) 193.

53. *R. v. Young* (1984), 13 C.C.C. (3d) 1 at 31, 46 O.R. (2d) 520, 40 C.R. (3d) 289.

An example of a case where it was held that the community's sense of fair play demanded that a stay of proceedings be entered is *Re Parkin and The Queen* (1986), 28 C.C.C. (3d) 252, 14 O.A.C. 150. In this case, the Ontario Court of Appeal held that there had been an abuse of the court's process where the Crown had elected to proceed on a charge of sexual assault by way of summary conviction procedures and then obtained the permission of the trial court to withdraw the charge and lay a new information, which would be prosecuted by indictment. The reason for the Crown's action was that the alleged assault had occurred outside the six-month limitation period that applies to summary conviction cases and the second information was presented solely to get around this problem. The Court of Appeal noted that the defendant would have been exposed to a much more severe penalty, if convicted upon indictment, and that this was unfair in light of the fact that the Crown had originally taken the view that the alleged offence was not so serious as to require that the trial proceed by way of indictment.

53a. *Keyowski v. The Queen* (1988), 40 C.C.C. (3d) 481, [1988] 1 S.C.R. 657, 32 C.R.R. 269; affirming 28 C.C.C. (3d) 553, 53 C.R. (3d) 1, [1986] 5 W.W.R. 150 (Sask. C.A.); reversing 48 Sask. R. 4, [1986] 4 W.W.R. 140 (Sask. Q.B.).

54. *R. v. Young* (1984), 13 C.C.C. (3d) 1, 10 C.R.R. 307, 40 C.R. (3d) 289.

55. *R. v. Zelensky et al.* (1978), 41 C.C.C. (2d) 97 at 116, [1978] 2 S.C.R. 940, [1978] 3 W.W.R. 693, *per* Pigeon J.

56. *R. v. Ikalowjuak* (1980), 27 A.R. 492 (N.W.T.S.C.); *R. v. Beriault* (1982), 26 C.R. (3d) 396 (B.C.S.C.).

57. *R. v. Johnson and Tremayne*, [1970] 4 C.C.C. 64, [1970] 2 O.R. 780 (Ont. C.A.).

58. *R. v. Shanower* (1972), 8 C.C.C. (2d) 527 (Ont. C.A.); *R. v. Traux* (1979), 22 Crim. L.Q. 157 (Ont. C.A.); *R. v. Pineau* (1979), 24 A.R. 176 (Alta. S.C.).

59. *R. v. Bartlett; R. v. Cameron* (1961), 131 C.C.C. 119 (Man. C.A.).

60. *R. v. Layte* (1983), 38 C.R. (3d) 204 at 206 (Ont. Co. Ct.), *per* Salhany, Co. Ct. J.

61. *R. v. Greene* (1971), 20 C.R.N.S. 238 (Ont. Co. Ct.); *R. v. Simoneau* (1978), 40 C.C.C. (2d) 307 at 316, *per* Matas, J.A. (Man. C.A.).

The potential danger inherent in the process of joint sentencing submissions is well illustrated by the case of *R. v. Rubinstein* (1987), 41 C.C.C. (3d) 91, 24 O.A.C. 309. The accused had entered a plea of guilty to charges of "wash trading" and fraud, apparently after a plea bargain of some sort. Crown and defence counsel put forward a joint sentencing submission, which recommended a suspended sentence with probation and the making of restitution to two of the accused's victims in the sum of $85,000. The trial judge refused to accept this recommendation and sentenced the accused to five years' imprisonment. The Ontario Court of Appeal (although it reduced the sentence to a period of two years less a day) held that the trial judge had acted correctly in refusing to allow the accused to withdraw his guilty plea once he had discovered that the joint sentencing recommendation was going to be rejected. Justice Zuber said: "To permit an accused to withdraw his plea when the sentence does not suit him puts the court in the unseemly position of bargaining with the accused" (41 C.C.C. (3d) at 94–95).

62. *R. v. Mouffe* (1971), 16 C.R.N.S. 257 (Que. C.A.).

62a. This view was also expressed by the Ontario Court of Appeal in *R. v. Wood* (1988), 43 C.C.C. (3d) 570, 29 O.A.C. 99.

63. The data from this article were re-analyzed by Taylor (1982).

64. See, for example, Brannigan (1984); Brannigan and Levy (1983); Osborne (1983); Solomon (1983); Wilkins (1979).

65. Solomon (1983: 37–38) points out, however, that this pattern of plea bargaining might not be applicable to the higher courts.

66. However, note that both Ericson and Baranek (1982: c. 2) and Klein (1979) indicate that accused persons claimed to have bargained with the police. Klein reported that some inmates even claimed to have negotiated directly with Crown counsel.

67. *Kienapple v. The Queen* (1974), 15 C.C.C. (2d) 524, [1975] 1 S.C.R. 729, 26 C.R.N.S. 1.

68. Another form of "illusory bargaining" can occur if the Parole Board decides to compensate for the plea bargain by delaying release of an individual on parole (Shin, 1973). The bargain is illusory in such circumstances because any gain made during sentencing is lost at the parole stage of the criminal justice process.

69. The potential for abuse is evident in the light of Ericson and Baranek's finding (1982: 159–60) that the defence lawyer plays a critically important role in convincing an accused person to plead guilty.

70. For example, the B.C. *Provincial Crown Handbook* states that:

> The Crown is not to
> (a) compel a guilty plea to a reduced charge,
> (b) take a guilty plea on an offence which is banned at law and therefore cannot be prosecuted,
> (c) take a guilty plea to an offence when no *prima facie* case exists,
> (d) agree to a specific sentence,
> (e) speak to the judge in chambers without the defence.

See Verdun-Jones and Hatch (1985: 23–24).

REFERENCES

Anon. 1987. "Mediation: No Winners, No Losers." 13(1) *Liaison* 4–9.

Blomberg, T. G. 1977. "Diversion and Accelerated Social Control." 68 *Journal of Criminal Law and Criminology* 274–82.

Bowen-Coulthurst, T. G. 1970. "Book Review." 20 *University of Toronto Law Journal* 494–96.

Brannigan, A. 1984. *Crimes, Courts and Corrections: An Introduction to Crime and Social Control in Canada.* Toronto: Holt, Rinehart and Winston.

Brannigan, A., and J. C. Levy. 1983. "The Legal Framework of Plea Bargaining." 25 *Canadian Journal of Criminology* 399–419.

Brantingham, P. L. 1985. "Judicare Counsel and Public Defenders: Case Outcome Differences." 27 *Canadian Journal of Criminology* 67–81.

Brantingham, P. L., and P. J. Brantingham. 1984. *An Evaluation of Legal Aid in British Columbia.* Ottawa: Department of Justice.

Brantingham, P. L., and P. Burns. 1981. *The Burnaby, British Columbia Experimental Public Defender Project: An Evaluation.* Ottawa: Department of Justice.

Burns, P. 1975. "Private Prosecutions in Canada: The Law and a Proposal for Change." 21 *McGill Law Journal* 269–97.

———. 1986. "The Power to Prosecute." In *Criminal Procedure: Canadian Law and Practice,* edited by J. Atrens, P. Burns, and J. P. Taylor, V-1–V-43. Vancouver: Butterworths (Western Canada).

Burns, P., and R. S. Reid. 1981. "Delivery of Criminal Legal Aid Services in Canada: An Overview of the Continuing 'Judicare versus Public Defender' Debate." 15 *U.B.C. Law Review* 403–29.

Canadian Centre for Justice Statistics. 1986. *Legal Aid in Canada, 1985.* Ottawa: Supply and Services Canada.

Canadian Sentencing Commission. 1986. *Sentencing Reform: A Canadian Approach. Report of the Canadian Sentencing Commission.* Ottawa: Minister of Supply and Services.

Church, T. 1976. "Plea Bargains, Concessions and the Courts: Analysis of a Quasi-Experiment." 10 *Law and Society Review* 377–401.

Church, T., Jr. et al. 1978. *Justice Delayed: The Pace of Litigation in Urban Trial Courts.* Williamsburg, Va.: National Center for State Courts.

Clarke, P. 1986. "Is There a Place for the Victim in the Prosecution Process?" 8 *Canadian Criminology Forum* 31–44.

Cohen, S. A. 1977. *Due Process of Law: The Canadian System of Criminal Justice.* Toronto: Carswell.

Cousineau, F. D., and S. N. Verdun-Jones. 1979. "Evaluating Research into Plea Bargaining in Canada and the United States: Pitfalls Facing the Policy Makers." 21 *Canadian Journal of Criminology* 293–309.

Department of Justice. 1986. *Department of Justice: Annual Report 1985/1986.* Ottawa: Minister of Supply and Services.

Elton, T. 1980. "The Diversion Controversy." In *New Directions in Sentencing,* edited by B. Grosman, 194–212. Toronto: Butterworths.

Ericson, R. V., and P. M. Baranek. 1982. *The Ordering of Justice: A Study of Accused Persons as Dependants in the Criminal Process.* Toronto: University of Toronto Press.

Feeley, M. M. 1979. *The Process is the Punishment: Handling Cases in a Lower Criminal Court.* New York: Russell Sage.

——. 1982. "Plea Bargaining and the Structure of the Criminal Process." 7 *The Justice System Journal* 338–54.

Ferguson, G., and D. Roberts. 1974. "Plea Bargaining: Directions for Canadian Reform." 52 *Canadian Bar Review* 498–576.

Genova, L. R. 1981. "Plea Bargaining: In the End, Who Really Benefits?" 4 *Canadian Criminology Forum* 30–44.

Gourlie, W. C. 1982. "Role of the Prosecutor: Fair Minister of Justice with Firm Convictions." 12 *Manitoba Law Journal* 31–42.

Greenspan, E. L. 1985. "The Future Role of Defence Counsel." In *Perspectives in Criminal Law: Essays in Honour of John LL.J. Edwards,* edited by A. N. Doob and E. L. Greenspan, 204–25. Aurora, Ont.: Canada Law Book.

Griffiths, C. T., D. F. Cousineau, and S. N. Verdun-Jones. 1980. "Appearance without Counsel: Self-Representation in the Criminal Courts of the United States and Canada." 4 *International Journal of Comparative and Applied Criminal Justice* 213–31.

Grosman, B. A. 1969. *The Prosecutor.* Toronto: University of Toronto Press.

Hagan, J. 1975. "Parameters of Criminal Prosecution: An Application of

Path Analysis to a Problem of Criminal Justice." 65 *Journal of Criminal Law, Criminology and Police Science* 536-44

Hann, R. 1973. *Decision-Making in a Canadian Criminal Court System: A Systems Analysis.* 2 Vols. Toronto: Centre of Criminology, University of Toronto.

Hartnagel, T. H., and D. F. Wynne. 1975. "Plea Negotiations in Canada." 17 *Canadian Journal of Criminology and Corrections* 45-56.

Hogarth, J. 1979. "Tentative Policy Proposals on Diversion." In *Expeditious Justice: Papers of the Canadian Institute for the Administration of Justice*, Canadian Institute for the Administration of Justice, 159-85. Toronto: Carswell.

Klein, J. F. 1979. *Let's Make a Deal: Negotiating Justice.* Lexington, Mass.: Lexington Books.

Law Reform Commission of Canada. 1975a. *Fourth Annual Report.* Ottawa: Information Canada.

_____. 1975b. *Working Paper No. 15: Criminal Procedure; Control of the Process.* Ottawa: Information Canada.

_____. 1984. *Report No. 22. Disclosure by the Prosecution.* Ottawa: Minister of Supply and Services.

_____. 1986. *Working Paper No. 52: Private Prosecutions.* Ottawa: Law Reform Commission of Canada.

Mackaay, E. 1976. *The Paths of Justice: A Study of the Operation of the Criminal Courts in Montreal.* Montreal: Groupe de Recherche en Jurimetrie, Université de Montréal.

McCoy, C. 1984. "Determinate Sentencing, Plea Bargaining Bans, and Hydraulic Discretion in California." 9 *The Justice System Journal* 256-75.

McDonald, W. F. 1987. "Judicial Supervision of the Guilty Plea Process: A Study of Six Jurisdictions." 70 *Judicature* 203-15.

Miller, P. S., and C. Barr. 1979. "A Management Philosophy for the Canadian Courts." 17 *University of Western Ontario Law Review* 199-222.

Morgan, D. C. 1986. "Controlling Prosecutorial Powers — Judicial Review, Abuse of Process and Section 7 of the Charter." 29 *Criminal Law Quarterly* 15-65.

Nimmer, R. 1978. *The Nature of System Change: Reform Impact in the Criminal Courts.* Chicago: American Bar Foundation.

Osborne, J. A. 1980. *Delay in the Administration of Criminal Justice: Commonwealth Developments and Experience.* London: Commonwealth Secretariat Publications.

_____. 1983. "The Prosecutor's Discretion to Withdraw Criminal Cases in the Lower Courts." 25 *Canadian Journal of Criminology* 55-78.

_____. 1986. "Delay, Contempt of Court and the Right to Legal Representation." 28 *Canadian Journal of Criminology* 31-45.

Renner, K. E., and A. H. Warner. 1981. "The Standard of Social Justice Applied to an Evaluation of Criminal Cases Appearing before the Halifax Courts." 1 *The Windsor Yearbook of Access to Justice* 62–80.

Ruby, C. C. 1987. *Sentencing.* 3rd ed. Toronto: Butterworths.

Salhany, R. E. 1984. *Canadian Criminal Procedure.* 4th ed. Aurora, Ont.: Canada Law Book.

Shin, H. 1973. "Do Lesser Pleas Pay? Accommodations in the Sentencing and Parole Processes." 1 *Journal of Criminal Justice* 27–42.

Solomon, P. H., Jr. 1983. *Criminal Justice Policy, From Research to Reform.* Toronto: Butterworths.

Stenning, P. C. 1986. *Appearing for the Crown: A Legal and Historical Review of Criminal Prosecutorial Authority in Canada.* Cowansville, Que.: Brown Legal Publications 359.

Sun, C. 1974. "The Discretionary Power to Stay Criminal Proceedings." 1 *Dalhousie Law Journal* 482–525.

Taman, L. 1975. "The Adversary Process on Trial: Full Answer and Defence and the Right to Counsel." 2 *Osgoode Hall Law Jornal* 251–77.

Taylor, J. P. 1985. "Division of Responsibility between Crown and Judiciary: Abuse of Process." In *Criminal Procedure: Canadian Law and Practice*, edited by J. Atrens, P. Burns, and J. P. Taylor, VI-1–VI-42. Vancouver: Butterworths (Western Canada).

Taylor, K. W. 1982. "Multiple Analysis of Race and Plea Negotiations: The Wynne and Hartnagel Data." 7 *Canadian Journal of Sociology* 391–401.

Verdun-Jones, S. N., and F. D. Cousineau. 1979. "Cleansing the Augean Stables: A Critical Analysis of Recent Trends in the Plea Bargaining Debate in Canada." 17 *Osgoode Hall Law Journal* 227–60.

Verdun-Jones, S. N., and A. J. Hatch. 1985. *Plea Bargaining and Sentencing Guidelines.* Ottawa: Canadian Sentencing Commission.

———. 1987. "An Overview of Plea Bargaining in Canada: Cautionary Notes for Sentencing Reform." In *Sentencing*, edited by J. Dumont, 71–106. Cowansville, Que.: Yvon Blais Inc.

Walker, M. D. 1984. "Congestion and Delay in the Provincial Court (Criminal Division)." 42 *University of Toronto Faculty Law Review* 82–104.

Warner, A. H., and K. E. Renner. 1981. "The Bureaucratic and Adversary Models of the Criminal Courts: The Criminal Sentencing Process." 1 *The Windsor Yearbook of Access to Justice* 81–93.

Wilkins, J. 1979. *The Prosecution and the Courts.* Toronto: Centre of Criminology, University of Toronto.

Wilkins, J. L. 1975. *Legal Aid in the Criminal Courts.* Toronto: University of Toronto Press.

Wilson, D. 1987. "Delay in the Criminal Justice System." 8 *Canadian Criminology Forum* 116–30.

Wynne, D. F., and T. F. Hartnagel. 1975. "Race and Plea Negotiation: An Analysis of Some Canadian Data." 1 *Canadian Journal of Sociology* 147–55.

Zemans, F. H. 1986. "Recent Trends in the Organization of Legal Services." 11 *Queen's Law Journal* 26–89.

Ziskrout, J. D. 1985. "Right to Counsel." In *Criminal Procedure: Canadian Law and Practice*, edited by J. Atrens, P. Burns, and J. P. Taylor, XIX-i–XIX-33. Vancouver: Butterworths (Western Canada).

Zuber, T. 1987. *Ontario Royal Commission: Report of the Ontario Courts Inquiry*. Toronto: Queen's Printer.

LEGISLATION

Criminal Code, R.S.C. 1985, c. C-46
Food and Drugs Act, R.S.C. 1985, c. F-27
Narcotic Control Act, R.S.C. 1985, c. N-1
Provincial Offences Act, R.S.O. 1980, c. 400

8 SENTENCING OPTIONS IN CANADA

Introduction

According to the Canadian Sentencing Commission[1] (1987: 115), *sentencing* may be defined as "the judicial determination of a legal sanction to be imposed on a person found guilty of an offence."

It would be trite to say that the sentencing process is an extremely critical component of the criminal justice system because it single-handedly determines the flow of cases through the various correctional services offered by the federal and provincial governments in Canada. However, it should be strongly emphasized that it would be most misleading to examine the sentencing process in isolation from the other components of the criminal justice system. For example, plea bargaining exerts a major influence on the sentencing process, since cases may be presented to the courts in a manner that predetermines the maximum severity of the sanctions that may be imposed (C.S.C., 1987: 401*ff*.; Verdun-Jones and Cousineau, 1979; Verdun-Jones and Hatch, 1985). By way of illustration, consider the case where, as the result of a plea bargain, the Crown agrees to proceed summarily rather than by way of indictment in relation to a so-called mixed offence. Here, the decision to proceed summarily clearly limits the sentencing discretion of the court to the relatively minor sanctions that may be imposed for summary conviction offences, as opposed to the more substantial penalties that are available upon conviction of an offence tried by indictment. Similarly, insofar as the relations between sentencing and other components of the criminal justice system are concerned, it is relevant to suggest that it is highly probable that the sentencing process is affected by such matters as prison capacity (Blumstein, 1982; C.S.C., 1987: 132); it is equally important to bear in mind that the sentence imposed by the court may bear relatively little resemblance to the sentence that is actually served by an offender, since, for example, remission and parole may substantially reduce the ultimate length of a sentence of imprisonment.

The Canadian Sentencing Commission (1987: 105*ff*.) has emphasized the need to distinguish between *sentencing* and *punishment*. While punishment may be regarded as the actual "imposition of *severe* deprivation on a person found guilty of wrongdoing" (1987: 109), sentencing may be considered a "*statement* ordering the imposition of a sanction and determining what it should be" (1987: 111). After all, the very word, *sentencing*, is derived from the Latin, *sententia*, which may be translated as an "opinion" or the "expression of an opinion" (C.S.C., 1987: 111). In the Commission's view (p. 111), even if it is assumed that sentencing is a punitive process, it should still be viewed "above all" as the "subordination of punishment to fundamental justice." Furthermore, certain sentencing options (such as an absolute discharge) cannot be considered *punitive* in the normal sense of that word; therefore, it is important to distinguish between the concepts of *sentencing* and *punishment*.

As is the case with most criminal justice processes, sentencing is characterized by the exercise of a considerable degree of discretionary power (Cressey, 1980). Indeed, the very breadth of this discretionary power renders sentencing one of the most difficult tasks that confronts the judge in a criminal case (Blumstein, 1982: 307). In the specific case of sentencing, the courts exercise discretion in relation to at least three critical questions (C.S.C., 1987: 120*ff.*): (1) the general nature of the sanction to be imposed (whether it is to be custodial or community in nature), (2) the specific type of sanction to be imposed (what type of custody or community disposition), (3) the *quantum* of the sanction (the length of custody or the specific "amount" of the community disposition chosen).

What are the options available to the sentencing court? They are as follows: (1) fine, (2) suspended sentence and probation, (3) imprisonment, (4) declaration that the accused is a dangerous offender, (5) discharge (either absolute or conditional), (6) order for compensation, (7) prohibitions and forfeiture.

The Sentencing Options

The Fine

The fine is the most commonly imposed disposition in the sentencing armoury of the courts (C.S.C., 1987: 374*ff.*; Mitchell-Banks, 1983; Verdun-Jones and Mitchell-Banks, 1986). Unlike other sentencing options, the fine actually generates revenue for the public purse rather than inflicting extra expense upon the taxpayer. It is a simple, straightforward penalty that spares the offender from the harmful consequences of imprisonment and results in a considerably lesser degree of stigma than many other criminal sanctions (Ruby, 1987: 256). According to Nadin-Davis (1982: 425), a fine is generally imposed where a "deterrent or punitive" sentence is deemed to be necessary but either the offence itself is not sufficiently serious to warrant incarceration or the presence of mitigating factors militates against the imposition of imprisonment. It has been asserted (e.g., Ruby, 1987: 256) that one of the more significant uses of the fine is to prevent an offender from making a profit from his or her crime, and it is clear that it may well be the only feasible sanction where a corporation is the offender (Nadin-Davis, 1982: 425) or where the offence is victimless in nature (Ruby, 1987: 256).

In certain cases, the *Criminal Code* and related legislation set out minimum and/or maximum fines that may be imposed for specific offences. However, the *Criminal Code* also provides that a fine may be imposed in addition to or in lieu of any other punishment where the offender has been convicted of an indictable offence that is punishable with a maximum term of imprisonment of five years or less; however, where a minimum term of imprisonment has been prescribed by Parliament, a fine may be imposed only in addition to (*and not as a substitute for*) such a minimum term.[2] Similarly, if the offender has been convicted of an indictable offence punishable with imprisonment for more than five years, a fine may be imposed only *in addition to*, but not in lieu of, "any other punishment that is authorized."[3] In line with its emphasis on the need for the courts to make greater use of *community* sanctions, the Canadian Sentencing Commission has recommended (1987: 374) that the *Criminal Code* be amended so as to permit the imposition of a fine *alone*, even for those offences that are punishable by a term of imprisonment of more than five years.

It is significant that a sentencing court, when dealing with a conviction for an indictable offence, is not restricted with respect to the amount of the fine that may be imposed;[4] however, as Salhany (1984: 405) aptly points out, it is always presumed that the "amount imposed will be reasonable in relation to the offence committed." As far as summary conviction offences are concerned, the *Criminal Code* provides that a fine may be levied either alone or in addition to any term of imprisonment that the court may decide to impose.[5] The *Code* limits the amount of the fine to $2,000 in the case of an individual[6] and to $25,000 in the case of a corporation (except where otherwise provided by law).[7]

The major problem with the fine is that, if unpaid, it may ultimately turn into a sentence of imprisonment. The *Criminal Code*[8] provides that the sentencing court may, if it so wishes, impose a term of imprisonment in case the offender should default in payment of a fine.[9] It is clear that where a period of imprisonment is ordered in default of payment and the offender finds it impossible to come up with the money, then the sentence imposed is, in reality, a term of imprisonment (Jobson and Atkins, 1986; Ruby, 1987: 261). Indeed, considerable concern has been expressed that the device of imposing a term of imprisonment in default of payment of a fine may be perceived as being discriminatory against the poor and particularly against women (Status of Women, Canada, 1986: 132) and native Canadians. For example, Schmeiser (1974: 69) has written that

Imprisonment for non-payment of fines appears to be an inconsistent and negative technique in the criminal process. It does not rehabilitate the offender . . . . It destroys the deterrent value of prison. It is very expensive, being the most costly form of supervision, and actually penalizes society for the wrongs of the offender. It also gives the appearance of being discriminatory against the poor.

There is considerable evidence that at least some of Schmeiser's concern is well-founded. For example, it is clear that fine defaulters presently represent a significant proportion of the populations of provincial correctional institutions. In 1983, for example, fine defaulters constituted 14% of the prison population in British Columbia and as much as 32% and 48% in Ontario and Quebec, respectively (Verdun-Jones and Mitchell-Banks, 1986: 72). A somewhat disturbing study has suggested that as much as 69% of the fine default admissions in the Province of Quebec were for failing to pay fines originally imposed for traffic violations (Quebec, Ministère du Solliciteur Général, 1986). A study by Hagan (1974) of admissions to provincial institutions in Alberta (during a period in the spring of 1973) underscores the implications of the fine default provisions for native Canadians. It was revealed that incarceration resulting from default in fine payment was nearly twice as common for native persons as for non-natives (see also Hagan, 1976).

On the other hand, it must also be recognized that the courts have increasingly emphasized the principle that the *Criminal Code* does not provide for the "routine imprisonment" of those offenders who default in payment of their fines; indeed, it has been stressed that the sentencing court is under a clear duty to investigate the offender's ability to pay.[10] For this reason, Nadin-Davis (1982: 435) has made the comment that

> The default period is, perhaps, one of the most misunderstood devices in penal law. Its proper purpose, it is submitted, is to enable the court to give alternatives to an accused who has the means to pay a fine.

A court has the authority to require payment of a fine forthwith (at the time of the sentencing) if it is satisfied that the accused has the ability to do so. Alternatively, the court may grant the offender time to pay, and if it does so, the latter may always apply for further time.[11] An important provision of the *Criminal Code* states that where an offender between the ages of 16 and 21 has been granted time to pay, then the offender may not be imprisoned until the court has obtained and considered a report concerning his or her conduct and ability to pay.[12]

Where the sentencing court does decide to impose a term of imprisonment in default of payment, it is assumed that the length of such a term should not be out of proportion to the size of the fine (Salhany, 1984: 406–7). If the offender has managed to pay a part of his or her fine, the *Criminal Code* provides that the term of imprisonment shall be reduced proportionately.[13]

In a comprehensive study of the problem of fine default, Mitchell-Banks (1983) discovered that in the Province of British Columbia, there was a marked disparity between the periods of imprisonment imposed as an alternative to payment of a fine. For example, it was found that offenders convicted of impaired driving were serving "in default" prison terms at an average *per diem* rate of $22.90. However, among this group, some offenders were serving "in default" prison terms at a rate of less than $4 a day, while the highest rate was as much as $50 a day (Mitchell-Banks, 1983: 182). Not surprisingly, the author concludes:

> ... it is difficult to justify a twenty-four hour period of incarceration being served at a rate approximate to one hour's minimum wage regardless of the offender's means. Surely one day of liberty is worth more than this? One cannot help but wonder if the judiciary is aware of this kind of sentencing disparity ... [P. 206]

In order to eliminate this type of sentencing disparity, Verdun-Jones and Mitchell-Banks (1986: 9) recommended that the length of an "in-default" prison sentence be commensurate with the size of the fine imposed and that a formula of some kind be devised to reduce the significant variations in the *per diem* rates at which offenders are serving these sentences. The Canadian Sentencing Commission (1987: 386–87) subsequently recommended the adoption of a table for the calculation of default periods where incarceration is imposed for wilful non-payment of a fine.

Mitchell-Banks (1983: 194) also discovered that in British Columbia, during the period 1977–83, 17% of fine defaulters served sentences of one week or less, 33% two weeks or less, 16% three weeks or less, and 22% four weeks or less. These figures would prompt the conclusion that "fine default" periods of imprisonment are relatively brief in the jurisdiction studied. Another interesting finding of this study is that only a very small proportion of persons fined are actually imprisoned for default. Indeed, Mitchell-Banks (p. 179) estimated that in any given year within the Province of British Columbia, approximately 100,000 cases will result in fines. However, from these cases, only some 1,500 to 1,600 offenders will ultimately be imprisoned for non-payment of their fines. That the threat of imprisonment may well serve as a particularly effective technique of enforcing payment of a fine is illustrated by Mitchell-Banks' finding (p. 179) that the vast majority of people pay their fines in full when presented with a warrant for committal to prison. The author concludes:

> Many people, it would seem, will only fully pay their fines when directly confronted with the threat of immediate imprisonment; in which case, imprisonment for fine default may be a necessary evil. If such people can further pay off their fines on a few hours notice, it would suggest that the fines imposed by the courts were not disproportionate to these offenders' means and that the delay in payment was a consequence of something other than poverty.

The Canadian Sentencing Commission was particularly concerned to reduce the extent of imprisonment for fine default and it strongly recommended that this device be used only for the *wilful* failure to pay a fine (1987: 381). According to the Commission, other methods of attempting to collect payment of a defaulted fine should be tried before resorting to imprisonment; such methods might include attaching the offender's wages or salary, seizing his or her property, registering the offender in a fine option program (see below) or enrolling him or her in a community service program (1987: 384).

An innovative response to the problem of fine default is the establishment of *fine option* programs in such provinces as Alberta, New Brunswick, Quebec and Saskatchewan (Ekstedt and Jackson, 1986: 20; Mitchell-Banks, 1983: 18). These programs permit offenders to perform community service work instead of paying their fines. In addition to the benefits bestowed upon the community by the work undertaken, fine option programs spare the taxpayers the immense cost of incarcerating a fine defaulter. For example, in Saskatchewan during the fiscal year 1977–78, it was reported that some 4,909 offenders performed the equivalent of $400,000 worth of community services. On the other side of the ledger, 75,795 days of incarceration were avoided at an estimated savings of $2 million to the taxpayers (Mitchell-Banks, 1983: 120). In 1985, Parliament gave its unequivocal approval to fine option programs by enacting section 646.1 (now s. 718.1) of the *Criminal Code*, which established a legislative framework for the use of such programs. Under this amendment to the *Code*, an offender may earn credits for work performed toward discharging a fine, either in whole or part, for any period up to two years.

An inherent problem besetting the fine is the flagrant inequity arising from the differential impact of this disposition upon the rich and poor. While a fine of $200 may be regarded as "peanuts" by a wealthy person, it may well exert real hardship in the case of a poor citizen. One potential solution to this injustice is the introduction of a *day-fine system*. This system has been adopted in a number of countries, such as Denmark, Finland, Sweden, West Germany and Austria (Verdun-Jones and Mitchell-Banks, 1986: 42). The purpose of the day-fine system is to develop a method of imposing fines that ensures that the fines levied will exert a similar impact upon both the rich and the poor (Mitchell-Banks, 1983: 81). In a day-fine system, the amount of any particular fine is determined by the size of the offender's income. Instead of setting a dollar amount for a fine, the sentencing judge imposes a specific number of day-fines. For example, in Sweden, it appears that one day-fine is equivalent to 1/1000 of the yearly gross income of the offender (after certain deductions have been made). If an offender with an income of $10,000 were sentenced to 20 day-fines, then he or she would actually pay $200. On the other hand, a more wealthy offender with an income of $100,000 would be required to pay $2,000 (Thornstedt, 1975; Law Reform Commission of Canada, 1974a: 33–34, 43–48).

In 1976, the Law Reform Commission of Canada (1976b: 25) recommended that "any fine of $50 or more be stated in terms of a day-fine." More recently, the Canadian Sentencing Commission (1987: 378–89) suggested that the Swedish day-fine system be studied and that the various provinces be encouraged to institute pilot projects on the use of day-fines. The Commission was not prepared to recommend the use of the day-fine on a national basis before such a study of the device had been undertaken. In the Commission's view, there were certain aspects of the Swedish system that were significantly different from the Canadian situation (for example, the fact that information concerning the financial status of an offender is much more accessible in Sweden than it is in Canada).

Suspended Sentence and Probation

The suspended sentence and probation are, *par excellence*, dispositions that reflect a concern for what has been called the individualization of the sentencing process (Nadin-Davis, 1982: 440). The theory underlying probation is that offenders are given the opportunity to rehabilitate themselves under the supervision of a probation officer as well as the sentencing court. The option of probation cannot be regarded as merely an expression of judicial lenience, since offenders must observe a number of conditions (some of which may be quite onerous in nature) while they are on probation; if these conditions are not observed, then offenders are liable to conviction for the offence of wilful breach of probation and, perhaps, a sentence of imprisonment in relation to the offence for which they were originally placed on probation. However, as Ruby (1987: 232) has observed, perhaps "the principal virtue of probation lies not in probation itself, but in the contrast which it provides for the inflexibility of imprisonment, and the impersonal nature of the fine" (see also Boyd, 1978; Parker, 1976; Barnett, 1977).

It is important to note that a probation order may be imposed in a variety of situations. Foremost among these is the situation in which a probation order accompanies a suspended sentence. However, a probation order may also be imposed in connection with a conditional discharge or in addition to a fine, a sentence of imprisonment[14] or an intermittent sentence.

The *Criminal Code*[15] provides that a sentencing court has the power to suspend the passing of sentence and to direct that an offender be released upon the conditions prescribed in a probation order; however, this power may *not* be exercised in relation to an offence for which a minimum punishment has been prescribed by Parliament. It is critical to bear in mind that, in Canada, it is the *passing* of sentence that is suspended rather than the *execution* of a sentence that has already been imposed (Nadin-Davis, 1982: 441). In other words, unlike the situation in England and Wales, a

Canadian court does not have the power to impose a term of imprisonment and then suspend its execution; instead, it must suspend the very process of sentencing itself.[16]

In making a decision whether to impose a probation order, a court is likely to take into account a number of factors that bear upon the issue of whether an "individualized disposition" is appropriate. For example, where an offender is youthful and/or is being sentenced for his or her first offence, then the court will give very serious consideration to the possibility of making a probation order (Ruby, 1987: 232). On the other hand, the court may well feel that the offence is so serious in nature that it demands a term of imprisonment for the purposes of deterrence and/or denunciation.[17] Similarly, the offender's prior criminal record may disqualify him or her from receiving probation (Nadin-Davis, 1982: 441). A further consideration is the likelihood of an offender benefiting from probation. It is most probable that the court will request a pre-sentence report (from a probation officer) in order to assist it in making its decision (Salhany, 1984: 410).

The *Criminal Code*[18] provides that every probation order shall contain the following conditions:

> ". . . that the accused shall keep the peace and be of good behaviour and shall appear before the court when required to do so by the court."

However, the *Code* also states that the court may, in addition, impose one or more of the following conditions: (that the offender)

(a) report to and be under the supervision of a probation officer or other person designated by the court;

(b) provide for the support of his spouse or any other dependants whom he is liable to support;

(c) abstain from the consumption of alcohol either absolutely or on such terms as the court may specify;

(d) abstain from owning, possessing or carrying a weapon;

(e) make restitution or reparation to any person aggrieved or injured by the commission of the offence for the actual loss or damage sustained by that person as a result thereof;

(f) remain within the jurisdiction of the court and notify the court or the probation officer . . . of any change in his address or his employment or occupation;

(g) make reasonable efforts to find and maintain suitable employment; and

(h) comply with such other reasonable conditions as the Court considers desirable for securing the good conduct of the accused and for preventing a repetition by him of the same offence or the commission of other offences.

The last provision (paragraph (h)) grants the court broad discretionary power to devise conditions that are specifically tailored for the individual offender. For example, a not infrequent condition is that the offender participate in a treatment program for a psychiatric problem or drug dependency (Nadin-Davis, 1982: 465). Perhaps the most ingenious use of this discretionary power has been the imposition of so-called *community service orders* (see C.S.C., 1987: 351–52; Nadin-Davis, 1982: 458–62; Ruby, 1987: 251–52; Groves, 1976; Stortini, 1979). For example, in one celebrated case, involving the conviction of a rock star for possession of heroin, an Ontario court imposed the condition that the offender perform a free concert for the benefit of charity.[19] A final example of a condition that has been developed on the basis of this broad discretionary power is the requirement that an offender who has been convicted of an alcohol-related offence and subjected to a probation order attend an impaired driver's program (Vingilis, Adlaf, and Chung, 1981). Before leaving the issue of conditions that may be imposed in a probation order, it is important to bear in mind that excessively broad conditions are likely to be considered in breach of the *Canadian Charter of Rights and Freedoms.*[20]

Another significant development, in recent years, has been the establishment of several so-called *victim-offender reconciliation* projects — most notably in the Province of Ontario, although such projects have emerged in all provinces except Newfoundland, Prince Edward Island, Nova Scotia, New Brunswick, and Alberta (Ekstedt and Jackson, 1986). The precise nature of these programs varies considerably; however, one form of victim-offender reconciliation revolves around the inclusion of a condition, in a probation order, that an offender meet with the victim (under the auspices of the project staff) in order to make an agreement on the appropriate restitution.[21] At least in some jurisdictions, when such an agreement is completed, then the term of the probation order is also deemed to have been completed (Norquay and Weiler, 1981: 62–64).

The *Criminal Code*[22] permits a court, at any time, to vary or add to the conditions included in a probation order or to relieve the offender of any of the optional conditions specified in such an order. The court may also decrease the length of the period of probation.

What happens if an offender wilfully fails to fulfil the conditions of his or her probation? The *Code*[23] renders it a summary conviction offence wilfully to disobey the terms of a probation order. However, a conviction on this offence may well constitute only the beginning of the offender's troubles. The court that originally imposed the probation order may vary or add to the conditions of the order and may extend it for a period of up to 12 months.[24] More drastically, the court also has the power to revoke the probation order and "impose any sentence that could have been imposed if the passing of sentence had not been suspended."[25]

Imprisonment

In recent years, the courts have repeatedly emphasized that imprisonment is a sanction that is to be employed only as a "last resort" (Nadin-Davis, 1982: 388–89). Indeed, there seems to be an increasing degree of acceptance that imprisonment serves no rehabilitative functions and, on the contrary, may well achieve precisely the opposite results (Fattah, 1982a; Law Reform Commission of Canada, 1974b: 5; Ruby, 1987: 274). As one Canadian judge has suggested, the penitentiary "has often been described as a college offering a post-graduate course in crime" (cited in Ruby, 1987: 275). It is therefore a well-recognized principle of sentencing that, except in unusual circumstances, a sentence of imprisonment should normally not be imposed upon a first or youthful offender (Nadin-Davis, 1982: 388–89). Nevertheless, there are many cases in which Canadian courts decide that a term of imprisonment is an appropriate disposition given the necessity for deterrence, denunciation or incapacitation of the offender (Nadin-Davis, 1982: 387).

The *Criminal Code* makes provision for five categories of *maximum* terms of imprisonment for indictable offences; namely, life, 14 years, 10 years, 5 years and 2 years. Where the offender is convicted of a summary offence, then the maximum term of imprisonment may not exceed six months, unless otherwise provided by statute (Salhany, 1984: 393–94). As might be expected, it has been recognized by the courts that the maximum penalty fixed by Parliament is intended to be applied only to the "worst case" of the particular offence concerned; it has been noted that the words *worst case* refer not only to the offence but also to the offender, whose prior criminal record may well exert a strong influence in the direction of increased severity of sentence (Nadin-Davis, 1982: 44–45). It should be emphasized that, in Canada, with the exception of life sentences and the sentences of "preventive detention" imposed upon so-called dangerous offenders,[26] prison sentences are determinate (or of fixed length) although, as will be shown later,[27] such sentences may subsequently be reduced by the award of remission and the granting of parole to offenders.

In line with the general policy of allowing a broad range of sentencing discretion to the judiciary, the *Criminal Code* contains few examples of mandatory *minimum* prison sentences (viz., sentences that *must* be imposed regardless of the particular circumstances of the case). The most important offences in relation to which the courts are required to impose a minimum sentence of incarceration are high treason, first and second degree murder (life),[28] use of a firearm during the commission of an indictable offence (one year upon a first conviction and three years upon subsequent convictions, to be served consecutively to the sentence imposed for the main offence itself),[29] and driving while impaired or with more than 80 milligrams of alcohol in the blood or refusing to provide a breath or blood sample (14 days on a second conviction and 90 days for each subsequent conviction).[30] The *Narcotic Control Act* (section 5) provides for a seven-year minimum sentence upon conviction of importing or exporting a narcotic; however, the Supreme Court of Canada recently struck down this provision as being in violation of the *Charter*.[31] The Canadian Sentencing Commission (1987: 189) has recommended the abolition of all mandatory minimum periods of incarceration, except for the offences of murder and high treason. In the words of the Commission:

> If the punishment is to fit the crime, there can be no pre-determined sentences since criminal events are not themselves pre-determined. Although the offence should be the focus in determining the appropriate penalty, the circumstances of the offender must also have some weight. [P. 186]

The length of a prison sentence is of considerable significance to the offender, since the *Criminal Code*[32] provides that a sentence of imprisonment for two years or more, or a sentence of life imprisonment, must be served in a federal correctional institution (except in the Province of Newfoundland), whereas a sentence of less than two years must be served in a provincial correctional facility.

What is the situation where an offender is convicted of multiple offences and is sentenced to more than one term of imprisonment? The *Criminal Code*[33] provides that the court *may* order that the terms of imprisonment shall be served one after the other (viz., "consecutively"). Alternatively, the court may order that they be served at the same time (viz., "concurrently"). It is fair to say that it is comparatively rare for a court to impose consecutive sentences. However, it is interesting that one of the leading commentators upon sentencing in Canada (Nadin-Davis, 1982: 396) has written that

> Few matters in the whole of sentencing law have caused as much difficulty as defining precisely when consecutive or concurrent sentences should be imposed. Running through all such considerations is the overriding principle, referred to as the "totality principle", that the total of sentences imposed should not be excessive in relation to the offender's overall culpability.[34]

It seems that a court is likely to exercise its discretion to impose consecutive sentences where the offences concerned are unrelated to each other and occurred at different times and in different places. Conversely, a court is unlikely to impose consecutive sentences where the offences concerned were committed within a short period and can be perceived as constituting "in reality one transaction" (Salhany, 1984: 399).

A significant provision of the *Criminal Code*[35] grants courts the discretionary power to order that a term of imprisonment be served *intermittently* — provided that such a term does not exceed 90 days.[36] If it makes such an order, the court must specify the times at which the offender will serve the sentence (e.g., on consecutive weekends) and must direct the offender to comply with the terms of a probation order during those periods when he or she is not in custody. The great advantage of the intermittent prison sentence is that it permits the offender to retain his or her employment, which might well be lost if a conventional, "straight" term of imprisonment were to be imposed (Nadin-Davis, 1982: 423).

Similarly, it may be used in an effort to avoid a number of other harmful effects of continuous imprisonment. For example, an intermittent sentence may be imposed in order to enable a spouse to care for the offender's children or to permit continued attendance at an educational institution (Ruby, 1987: 284).

One problem that has arisen in relation to the intermittent term of imprisonment is that its frequent use may well result in the overcrowding of provincial correctional institutions at certain "peak periods" (Dombek and Chittra, 1984). Interestingly, a Bill was presented to Parliament, in 1978, that would have prevented the imposition of an intermittent sentence if no facilities were available (Chasse, 1980). However, the Bill was never passed, and it is significant that the Ontario Court of Appeal has ruled that the trial judge must not take into account the views of the provincial correctional authorities concerning the overloading of their facilities; in short, the judge must impose the sentence that he or she deems to be "fit and proper" in light of all the circumstances of the case.[37]

In an influential report, the Law Reform Commission of Canada (1976b: 26) advocated the adoption of sentencing guidelines that would further reduce the courts' use of imprisonment. The Commission contended that

> Imprisonment is an exceptional sanction that should be used only:
> (a) to protect society by separating offenders who are a serious threat to the lives and personal security of members of the community; or
> (b) to denounce behaviour that society considers to be highly reprehensible, and which constitutes a serious violation of basic values; or
> (c) to coerce offenders who wilfully refuse to submit to other sanctions.

The Commission also articulated the principle that imprisonment should be resorted to only when the sentencing court is "certain that a less severe sanction cannot achieve the objective set out by the legislator." Furthermore, the Commission expressed the view that rehabilitation *per se* should not be used to justify the imposition of imprisonment; in other words, while offenders should be entitled to receive the same social and health services as the ordinary citizen, the availability of "treatment" in the prison setting should never be the main justification for imposing a sentence of imprisonment. It is interesting to note that despite public opposition to what is *perceived* to be excessive judicial "lenience" (Fattah, 1982b), the Government of Canada apparently endorsed the gist of the Commission's proposals relating to the use of imprisonment and sought to embody them in amendments to the *Criminal Code* in 1984. Unfortunately, the Government's attempts did not reach fruition and Bill C-19 (February, 1984) was never enacted, owing to the dissolution of Parliament for the election of September 1984. Subsequently, the Canadian Sentencing Commission (1987: 366) also recommended that sentencing guidelines be adopted and that the thrust of the guidelines be to ensure a greater reliance upon community sanctions, as opposed to the penalty of imprisonment. In this respect, the Sentencing Commission articulated principles that are very similar to those espoused by the Law Reform Commission:

> a term of imprisonment should not be imposed, or its duration determined, solely for the purpose of rehabilitation;
> a term of imprisonment should be imposed only:
> (aa) to protect the public from crimes of violence,
> (bb) where any other sanction would not sufficiently reflect the gravity of the offence or the repetitive nature of the criminal conduct of an offender, or adequately protect the public or the integrity of the administration of justice,
> (cc) to penalize an offender for wilful non-compliance with the terms of any other sentence that has been imposed on the offender where no other sanction appears adequate to compel compliance. [C.S.C., 1987: 154]

Declaration That the Accused Is a Dangerous Offender

One of the sentencing options that has aroused an increasing degree of concern among commentators on the criminal justice system is the power of a court to declare a convicted person a *dangerous offender* and to impose a term of *indefinite incarceration* in a penitentiary in lieu of any other punishment that may have been inflicted for the offence(s) of which the offender was convicted (Grant, 1985).

The dangerous offender provisions in the *Criminal Code* have their roots in legislation enacted just after the Second World War; more specifically, in 1947 Parliament enacted legislation to deal with the habitual criminal, and in 1948, it followed with legislation directed toward the so-called *criminal sexual psychopath*, later replaced by the term, *dangerous sexual offender* (Greenland, 1984; Webster, Dickens, and Addario, 1985b: 3). In 1977, Parliament did away with the habitual criminal legislation altogether and replaced the category of "Dangerous Sex Offender" with a new category, known as "Dangerous Offender."

Crown counsel must make a formal application before the court may hold a hearing to determine whether the convicted offender should be designated a dangerous offender. The provincial Attorney General must give his or her consent to any such application, and furthermore, the offender must be given at least seven days' notice of the prosecution's request for such a hearing.[38] The *Criminal Code* provides that the offender must normally be present when the hearing is held[39] and that the trial of the issue is to be held before the judge sitting without a jury.[40] If an accused person is ultimately found to be a dangerous offender, then the court *may* decide to sentence him or her to an *indeterminate period of incarceration in a penitentiary* in lieu of any other sentence that might be imposed for the offence(s) of which the offender has been convicted.[41] The offender may be released *on parole* only by the National Parole Board, which examines the offender's case initially after a period of three years has elapsed since the offender was taken into custody and, thereafter, at intervals of two years.[42]

What are the criteria for "dangerous offender" status? The first requirement is that the offender must have been convicted of a *serious personal injury offence*. This is defined in the following way:[43]

(a) an indictable offence, other than high treason, treason, first degree murder or second degree murder, involving
  (i) the use or attempted use of violence against another person, or
  (ii) conduct endangering or likely to endanger the life or safety of another person or inflicting or likely to inflict severe psychological damage on another person, and for which the offender may be sentenced to imprisonment for ten years or more, or
(b) an offence or attempt to commit an offence mentioned in section 271 (sexual assault), 272 (sexual assault with a weapon, threats to a third party or causing bodily harm), or 273 (aggravated sexual assault).

Once it has been established that a "serious personal injury offence" has been committed, the Crown must go on to prove, insofar as category (a) "serious personal injury" offenders are concerned, that they constitute "a threat to the life, safety or physical or mental well-being of other persons."[44] Insofar as category (b) offenders are concerned, the *Code*[45] provides that the Crown must prove that

. . . the offender, by his conduct in any sexual matter including that involved in the commission of the offence for which he has been convicted, has shown a failure to control his sexual impulses and a likelihood of his causing injury, pain or other evil to other persons through failure in the future to control his sexual impulses . . .

Since these criteria require that predictions be made about the offender's *future* conduct, Parliament, rightly or wrongly, assumed that psychiatric evidence would be necessary before a determination could be made to the effect that an offender is a dangerous offender. The *Criminal Code*[46] therefore provides that the court may order the offender to attend an examination at a specific location or it may remand him or her in custody for observation. The *Code*[47] makes it mandatory for the court to hear the evidence of at least two psychiatrists (one for the Crown and one for the defence). The court may also hear other evidence from any "psychologist or criminologist," provided it considers such evidence to be relevant. In short, it is clear that the underlying assumption of the dangerous offender provisions is that predictions about the offender's future conduct should be clinical in nature.

In a comprehensive analysis of the Canadian dangerous offender provisions, Webster et al. (1985b) address some of the major problems surrounding the whole concept of sentencing individual offenders to indeterminate detention on the basis of *psychiatric* predictions about their *future* behaviour. Empirical research has not established that clinical predictions of dangerousness *in relation to specific individuals* can attain a respectable degree of accuracy (Webster, Ben-Aron, and Hucker, 1985a). Indeed, it appears that such prediction is never likely to reach much more than 40% accuracy (see also, Menzies, Webster, and Sepejak, 1985; Monahan, 1981). In other words, when psychiatrists make predictions about future dangerous conduct, there will always be a substantial number of so-called false positives (namely, offenders of whom it will be *wrongly* predicted that they will commit serious offences in the future). According to Webster et al. (1985b: xviii):

> Predicting violence at the level of the individual prisoner is practically impossible without an almost inconceivable degree of control over key environmental, treatment, and biomedical variables. It is imperative to recognize that the most any clinician or researcher can *ever* offer is a probability estimate of future violent behaviour.

Webster et al. (1985b: 38*ff.*) suggest that statements regarding the *probability* of an individual committing a serious crime in the future may be made in terms of a technique known as risk assessment. However, this is not a technique in relation to which psychiatrists have any particular expertise compared to other professionals, since at the heart of this technique is a consideration of such variables as age, number of previous convictions and degree of force used in the commission of the offence, rather than the variables customarily employed in the clinical assessments made by psychiatrists.

Given the fact that psychiatrists cannot predict, with any degree of certainty, whether a specific individual will commit a serious personal injury offence in the future, it is clear that the dangerous offender provisions in the *Criminal Code* are difficult to justify on a logical basis (Webster et al., 1985b: 142). Even if a well-informed judgment is made by an expert regarding the degree of probable risk that an offender may commit another serious personal injury offence if he or she is released, is Canadian society justified in sentencing that offender to a very lengthy period of indeterminate detention based on the mere *probability* that he or she may commit such an offence in the future? Such a question is clearly a moral and social policy issue of great gravity (Petrunik, 1982). The answer depends on the extent to which society is willing to deprive individuals of their liberty in the name of the protection of the community. No doubt, where there is a high degree of probability that an offender will commit a serious personal injury offence if released, then it might be considered justifiable to detain that individual for the protection of society. However, such a grave decision should only be taken in accordance with procedures that are seen to be as fair as possible in all the circumstances. Unfortunately, there is little doubt that there is a considerable degree of arbitrariness in the manner in which the existing dangerous offender provisions are applied and that the current use of them represents a severe challenge to the value that Canadians place on basic fairness in the system of criminal justice.

A federal study (Jakimiec et al., 1986) has shown that only some 60 persons were found to be dangerous offenders between October 1977 and December 1985. Seventy-eight per cent of those found to be dangerous offenders had committed sexual offences that led to the Crown applying for a dangerous offender hearing (Jakimiec et al., 1986: 11). However, it is disturbing to note that the dangerous offender provisions have been used most unevenly across Canada (Jakimiec et al., 1986: 9–10). While Ontario has successfully used the provisions most frequently (29 times), the Province of Quebec has not resorted to the provisions at all, despite its relatively large population. British Columbia has used the provisions successfully a total of 16 times, and Alberta a total of nine times. In other words, just three provinces were responsible for 90% of the successful applications. Unless one hypothesizes that there is a much greater number of dangerous people in these three provinces than in the rest of Canada, it is hard to resist the conclusion that those offenders who are selected for dangerous offender hearings are the hostages of such ephemeral factors as the attitudes of individual prosecutors and local community sentiment against sex offenders. However, the drastic consequences of a dangerous offender designation surely underscore the need to eliminate such arbitrariness. Significantly, as of 1986, not one of the offenders designated as dangerous offenders since 1977 has yet been granted any form of parole by the National Parole Board (Jakimiec et al., 1986: 12). Furthermore, it is important to bear in mind that the great majority of dangerous offenders are detained in protective custody in order to protect them from the other inmates in the prison population (Jakimiec et al., 1986: 14). Since most dangerous offenders have been convicted of sexual offences, they are inevitably stigmatized by the label of dangerous offender and become the target for the aggression of other inmates (Webster et al. (1985b: 143).

There are a number of other weighty criticisms that can be made of the dangerous offender provisions. Webster et al. (1985b: 142) point out that the very indeterminate nature of the sentence can be destructive of the rehabilitation of offenders, since the removal of hope can cause serious deterioration in their mental state. These authors (1985b: 145) also assert that the dangerous offender provisions give a false impression that treatment will be provided. However, such treatment is unlikely to be given until a number of years have elapsed in the indeterminate sentence. In a situation reminiscent of "Catch 22," prison authorities realize that the Parole Board is unlikely to release a "dangerous" individual early in his or her sentence regardless of any progress in treatment, and therefore the initiation of treatment is delayed until there is some prospect of release on parole.[48] On the other hand, the Parole Board is unlikely to consider releasing an offender who has not been "treated." In any event, Webster et al. (1985b: 146) suggest that it is "highly questionable whether any methods exist that have sizeable demonstrable effects on Dangerous Offenders, including sex offenders." In the view of the authors,

... if in fact there are many offenders who are not receiving treatment and many whom treatment will not help, then the Dangerous Offender provisions operate for purely punitive or protectionary purposes.

Another major problem with the dangerous offender provisions is the degree of discretionary power that they place in the hands of the prosecutor. Jakimiec et al. (1986: 17–18) suggest that dangerous offender legislation is most likely to be applied when there is some uncertainty about the offender's dangerousness. Where the offender commits a particularly brutal act, it is most likely that the court will impose a heavy, determinate sentence or, in particularly extreme cases, life imprisonment. However, according to these authors, where the "prosecutors sense themselves on insecure terrain they are apt to want psychiatric support in reaching decisions" and "it is well known that, generally, the courts find sex offenders to be hard to deal with." It has also been pointed out that the power to invoke the dangerous offender provisions places an excessive discretion in the hands of the prosecutor, since he or she may be in a position to induce a plea of guilty by threatening to make a dangerous offender application if the offender does not plead guilty (Klein, 1973; Verdun-Jones and Cousineau, 1979).

In light of the harshness of the dangerous offender provisions, it is not surprising that they have been the subject of a number of legal challenges under the provisions of the *Charter* (Gordon and Verdun-Jones, 1987: 192–93). However, the constitutionality of the provisions has been consistently upheld by the courts, despite the apparent recognition that psychiatric predictions about future dangerousness are highly speculative at best.[49] Significantly, this approach was recently endorsed by the Supreme Court of Canada.[50]

The Canadian Sentencing Commission (1987: 213) has recommended that the dangerous offender provisions of the *Criminal Code* be repealed. The Commission believed that these provisions offend against the basic principles of criminal law in two major respects: first, the indeterminate nature of the sentence, and second, the "primary focus on the offender rather than the offence." In place of these provisions, the Commission recommends that the courts be given the power to impose an "exceptional sentence" in the case of a particularly heinous crime (such as an unusually brutal attempted murder). The "extended sentence" would exceed the normal maximum for the offence of which the offender has been convicted by up to 50%. However, the Commission stated unequivocally that the "procedure for enhancement should be reserved for only the most heinous crimes which demand a longer period of incapacitation for security reasons" (p. 217). Of course, the Commission's proposal would abolish the indeterminacy that is such a controversial feature of the existing dangerous offender provisions.

Absolute and Conditional Discharge

In 1969, the Ouimet Report (1969: 194) advocated the introduction of provisions that would permit a sentencing court to "deal with first offenders charged with a minor offence in such a way that would avoid the damaging consequences of the existence of a criminal record." Hard on the heels of this recommendation, Parliament amended the *Criminal Code*,[51] and for the first time, courts were granted the power to impose an absolute or conditional discharge for certain offences (Greenspan, 1973; Nadin-Davis, 1982: 474–89; Ruby, 1987: 207–19; Salhany, 1984: 419–22; Wilkinson, 1977). Under the provisions of the *Criminal Code*,[52] instead of convicting an offender who has either pleaded guilty to or been found guilty of an offence, the sentencing court may order that he or she be discharged either absolutely or upon the conditions prescribed in a probation order. As Nadin-Davis (1982: 475) points out, these provisions create two quite different dispositions. Where an *absolute* discharge is imposed, then the offender "is removed thereby entirely from correctional authority, and has no further obligation to the penal system." On the other hand, "the recipient of a conditional discharge is made subject to a probation order." An offender who fails to fulfil the conditions of a probation order or who commits a subsequent offence may find that his or her conditional discharge is revoked. If this should happen, the court will convict the offender of the original offence, for which he or she was granted a discharge, and is then empowered to impose any sentence that could have been selected at the time of the discharge. Alternatively, the court may, instead of revoking the discharge, decide merely to change or add to the conditions specified in the probation order.[53]

The court's power to impose an absolute or conditional discharge is by no means unfettered. Indeed, a discharge may not be granted where the offence concerned is one for which the *Criminal Code* imposes a minimum punishment or which is punishable by a prison term of 14 years or life. Furthermore, the court, before making its decision whether or not to discharge an offender, must consider such a discharge to be "in the best interests of the accused and not contrary to the public interest."[54]

It is clear that the courts have a considerable degree of discretion in determining whether or not to impose a discharge. However, during the past decade or so, some general guidelines have emerged regarding the circumstances in which such a disposition will be deemed appropriate (Nadin-Davis, 1982: 479).

Perhaps, the most significant principle is that the discharge should be imposed with a certain degree of "frugality" and should never be employed "routinely" in relation to any particular offence.[55] For example, if a discharge were to be imposed in relation to *all* cases of possession of marijuana, then the courts would effectively be inviting citizens to break the law of the realm. Therefore, it has been emphasized that the courts must consider each case on an individual basis. As Ruby (1987: 208) points out, a sentencing court "must consider all the circumstances of the offence against the background of proper law enforcement in the community." Another general principle that has frequently been articulated by the judiciary is that discharges should not be confined merely to "trivial" cases.[56] Indeed, the courts have emphasized that there is a broad range of offences for which a discharge may be deemed to be an appropriate disposition — depending upon the individual circumstances of the particular case concerned.[57]

In addressing the criterion of the "best interests of the accused," one leading decision of the British Columbia Court of Appeal suggests that this requirement

> . . . would presuppose that the accused is a person of good character, without previous conviction, that it is not necessary to enter a conviction against him in order to deter him from future offences or to rehabilitate him, and that the entry of a conviction against him may have significant adverse repercussions.[58]

In making its decision, the court will pay particular attention to the issue of whether the entry of a conviction will result in repercussions that are out of all proportion to the guilt of the accused. For example, an important consideration in favour of granting a discharge is the possibility that a conviction will result in the loss of a job or the likelihood that the accused's criminal record will bar him or her from entering a profession.[59] Similarly, the possibility that a conviction will result in the deportation of a non-citizen has been considered a significant element in the equation.[60] As far as the criterion of "public interest" is concerned, the courts have emphasized that a discharge should not be imposed where there is a particular need to deter others from committing a similar offence.[61] For example, it may not be appropriate to grant a discharge for an offence (such as shoplifting) that happens to be particularly prevalent in an individual community.[62] Similarly, it is clear that the seriousness of an offence might well be a factor that militates against the granting of a discharge. Finally, it may well be the case that a court will refuse to grant a discharge where it believes that the accused's offence should be brought to the attention of his or her potential employers in the future (Nadin-Davis, 1982: 486). For example, such a policy might be followed where a bank official has committed an offence involving an abuse of his or her trust.[63]

What is the effect of a discharge? The *Criminal Code*[64] states that the recipient of a discharge "shall be deemed not to have been convicted of the offence," although it is clear that there must be a "determination of guilt" before a discharge may be imposed. Clearly, the policy underlying this provision is to shield the offender from the stigmatizing consequences of a criminal record. As Davis (1980a and 1980b) has demonstrated, the existence of such a record may have potentially devastating consequences in relation to such critical matters as employment, immigration and travel to other countries. The offender who has obtained a discharge may "truthfully say that he or she has never been convicted of a criminal offence" (Ruby, 1987: 208).

However, there is an element of "Catch-22" in all of this because the provisions of the *Criminal Records Act*,[65] make it clear that records of discharges are, in fact, kept by the authorities. Indeed, this Act prescribes a procedure for the recipient of a discharge to apply for removal of such a record in a similar manner to that provided for in the case of an application following a conviction (Swabey, 1972: 138). In light of these provisions, it has been seriously questioned (Ruby, 1987: 218; Greenspan, 1973: 67–68) whether there really is much difference between the records that are kept in relation to absolute and conditional discharges, and criminal records that are maintained after a conviction.[66] On the other hand, it may very well be argued that it is necessary to maintain some kind of record of a discharge so as to avoid the possibility that a sentencing court that is considering granting a discharge is unaware that the offender has already received such a disposition in the past. Indeed, the courts have held that the offender's receipt of a discharge in relation to a previous offence is a highly relevant factor in determining whether a subsequent discharge should be granted.

Although an offender given a discharge is "deemed not to have been convicted," he or she may still appeal from the determination of guilt "as if it were a conviction." Similarly the prosecution may appeal from the decision not to convict the offender as if this decision were an acquittal or a dismissal of the information against the offender.[67]

Compensation

It has already been noted that a probation order may include a condition relating to *restitution* or *reparation* for any actual loss or damage inflicted as a consequence of the commission of a criminal offence.[68] However, there are also a couple of specific provisions of the *Criminal Code* that are concerned with the *compensation* of a victim of a crime (see Ruby, 1987: 327*ff*.). Of considerable significance is the *Criminal Code* provision[69] that empowers a sentencing court to order an offender who has been convicted of an offence or who has been given an absolute or conditional discharge to pay the victim compensation for "loss of or damage to property" suffered by the latter as a consequence of the commission of the offence. However, it is important to bear in mind that the victim must personally make an application for such compensation; the sentencing court may not make a compensation order on its own initiative. According to Hagan (1983: 178), this provision has primarily been taken advantage of by "organization victims" (e.g., retail stores) rather than by private individuals.

The *Criminal Code*[70] also makes provision for the situation where an innocent person purchases property that has been obtained by the commission of an offence and has subsequently been returned to its rightful owner. In this situation, the court is empowered to order that the offender reimburse the innocent purchaser in an "amount not exceeding the amount paid by the purchaser for the property." Once again, the purchaser is required to make a specific application to the court in order to obtain this form of relief.

What is the situation where the police have discovered "hot" property in the hands of an accused person and that property is before the court at the time the accused is tried? The *Code*[71] provides that where the court determines that an offence has indeed been committed, then it is required to order the return of any property that has been obtained as the consequence of the commission of such an offence to the rightful owner or possessor of the property in question (assuming, of course, such a person can be ascertained).

It is important to recognize that the *Criminal Code* presently makes no provision for the compensation of a victim who has been subjected to *bodily* injury by an offender. In order to obtain such compensation, the victim of a violent crime must turn to the criminal injuries compensation schemes that currently exist in all provinces and territories (except Prince Edward Island). These schemes permit an administrative body to make compensatory payment to victims and are supported by cost-sharing agreements between the provinces and territories, on the one hand, and the Canadian Government, on the other (see Department of Justice, Canada, 1985: 3). The extent of compensation and the rules of eligibility vary considerably from jurisdiction to jurisdiction. However, in 1984–85, $21,505,323 was paid by way of criminal injuries compensation (Department of Justice, Canada, 1985: 26); this figure presents a striking contrast to its counterpart in 1975–76, which was a mere $4,412,067 (Statistics Canada, 1983: 76). The average award, across Canada, in 1984–85, was $3,101.18 (Department of Justice, Canada, 1985: 32).

At present, it appears that restitution and/or compensation orders are made in only a relatively small minority of cases (Hagan, 1983: 194; Chretien, 1982: 30). On the basis of a comprehensive empirical study, Hagan (1983: 194–95) has suggested that the "public remedies" (such as restitution orders) that are available to victims of crime,

> ... may be serving a symbolic more than an instrumental function. That is, the existence of these remedies symbolizes a concern on the part of the State for the plight of victims, but it is a concern that is infrequently translated into action.

A familiar problem relating to the efficacy of restitution is the impecunious circumstances of many offenders. However, the impact of this problem may well be mitigated somewhat by the possibility that the offender may perform services or work for the victim (Law Reform Commission of Canada, 1976a: 24). Along similar lines, the Law Reform Commission (1976b: 24–25) has recommended that, in certain circumstances (including where the offender lacks funds), the sentencing court should be empowered to order that the state pay compensation to a victim of crime. In its 1974 Working Paper (1974a: 23), the Commission suggested that a special compensation fund could be established on the basis that it would be maintained by the income from the fines levied by the courts upon offenders.

Over the past decade or so, an increasing degree of concern has been expressed about the plight of the victims of crime (see, e.g., Norquay and Weiler, 1981). In response to this concern, there has arisen a strong demand for a greater degree of emphasis to be placed upon restitution within the context of the sentencing process. For example, the Law Reform Commission of Canada has been an enthusiastic advocate of such a policy. In an early working paper (1974a: 6–7), the Commission boldly contended that

> Doubtless there are offences in respect of which reconciliation is useless and where the most rational sanction may be prolonged imprisonment. For the great majority of offences, however, restitution would appear to be appropriate. Restitution involves acceptance of the offender as a responsible person with the capacity to undertake constructive and socially approved acts. It challenges the offender to see the conflict in values between himself, the victim, and society. In particular, restitution invites the offender to see his conduct in terms of the damage it has done to the victim's rights and expectations. It contemplates that the offender has the capacity to accept his full or partial responsibility for the alleged offence and that he will in many cases be willing to discharge that responsibility by making amends.

Subsequently, in an influential report to Parliament, the Commission (1976b: 24–25) recommended that the sentencing court should give priority to restitution, where the offence concerned involves a victim and where "restitution as a provision of conditional discharge is not appropriate." The Commission suggests that restitution may be "in symbolic form, by apologies, or the payment of a sum of money, or work done for the benefit of the victim." During the 1980s, Canadian governments have started to ride the wave of public opinion in favour of victim-oriented sentencing options. In August 1982, for example, the Government of Canada issued a significant document that articulated the principles that, in its opinion, should guide the ongoing process of criminal law review. A major principle espoused by the Government (Chretien, 1982: 62) is that

> ... wherever possible and appropriate, the criminal law and the criminal justice system should also promote and provide for:
> (i) opportunities for the reconciliation of the victim, community and offender;
> (ii) redress or recompense for the harm done to the victim of the offense....

The influence of this principle was clearly evident in certain of the provisions contained in Bill C-19, which was introduced into Parliament during February 1984 (Thorvaldson, 1987). These provisions would have introduced many of the recommendations made by the Law Reform Commission of Canada in relation to restitution and compensation for victims. However, Bill C-19 was never enacted owing to the dissolution of Parliament for the general election in 1984. Nevertheless, in November 1987, the Conservative Government announced that it was introducing a Bill to amend the *Criminal Code* and that this Bill would implement a number of reforms that would enhance the status of the victim in the sentencing process (Hnatyshyn, 1987).

An important component of the proposed reforms is the abolition of the requirement that the victim of a crime make a specific application for restitution. Instead, the proposed amendments to the *Code* would require the court to consider restitution in all those cases that involve either damage, loss or destruction of property stemming from the commission of a criminal offence or pecuniary damages caused by bodily injury to the victim. Before making any order for restitution, the court would be required to inquire into the extent of the victim's loss, as well as the offender's ability to pay. Most significantly, the proposed package of reforms would implement one of the major recommendations of the Law Reform Commission by permitting the courts to impose a *fine surcharge* on those individuals convicted of any offence under the *Criminal Code*, Parts III or IV of the *Food and Drugs Act* and the *Narcotic Control Act*. The proceeds of the fine surcharge would be dedicated to the provision of victim assistance programs in the various provinces. Another major reform would ensure a major role for the victim in the sentencing process through the presentation to the court of a *victim impact statement*. More specifically, the proposed reform package would give the courts the power to consider a written statement by a victim of the harm to, or the loss suffered by, him or her as a consequence of the commission of the offence in question. Such a statement would probably be prepared by a probation officer. No doubt, this procedure would do much to reduce the sense of alienation shared by many victims, who feel that under the existing system of criminal justice, they are of only tangential interest to the sentencing court. Finally, the reform proposals would provide for a doubling of the Federal Government's contributions to provincial criminal injuries compensation programs, a victim assistance fund would be set up to establish a "broader range of victim services and programs," and funding would be provided for research and projects that will "enhance the development of innovative approaches for victims' programs." Overall, it appears that the Federal Government would allocate some $27.2 million over a three-year period to services and programs for the victims of crime (Hnatyshyn, 1987: 3).[71a]

Although there is clearly a strong wave of reform in the direction of establishing restitution as a key element in the sentencing process, there have nevertheless been some harsh critics of this approach.[72] For example, Klein (1978) has raised serious questions about the practicality of requiring restitution in a broad range of criminal cases. Klein (1978: 393) contends that criminal courts may balk at the prospect of becoming "debt collectors" and that, in any event, such courts do not always represent an appropriate forum for the settling of minor disputes relating to property: indeed, he suggests that the *civil* courts (particularly small claims courts) are better equipped to deal with such matters (pp. 394–96). The author also raises the thorny issue of the inherent dangers associated with appearing to "trade dollars for lenience." Finally, Klein (pp. 399–401) suggests that there is insufficient empirical evidence to support the claims of the proponents of restitution that this sentencing option contributes significantly to the rehabilitation of offenders.

Prohibitions and Forfeiture

In certain circumstances, the sentencing court is empowered to order that an offender, convicted of a particular offence, be prohibited from engaging in certain activities for a specified period (Ruby, 1987: 303*ff*.). For example, an offender may be prohibited from possessing a firearm,[73] from operating or navigating a car or boat,[74] or from owning or having the custody or control of an animal or bird.[75] These prohibitions may be imposed only in addition to some other sentence that may be authorized. The best known of these prohibitions, of course, is that which may be made after an offender has been convicted of an offence related to drunken driving.

It is also important to note that conviction of a criminal offence will, in certain instances, result in the forfeiture to the Crown of property that is involved in the case (MacFarlane, 1985). For example, the *Criminal Code* provides for the forfeiture of explosives,[76] obscene publications,[77] electronic "bugging" equipment,[78] money or other items seized in a gaming house or brothel,[79] as well as hate literature.[80] Perhaps, the most severe form of forfeiture may be imposed under the provisions of the *Narcotic Control Act*: section 16(2) of this Act provides that where a person has been convicted of either trafficking in or importing or exporting a narcotic, then if an aircraft, motor vehicle or vessel was used in connection with the offence, such a "conveyance" may be forfeited. In most cases, forfeiture is dependent upon the issuance of a judicial order; however, in some instances, the *Code* provides for automatic forfeiture upon the conviction of the offender concerned.[80a]

The Use of the Sentencing Options

As the Canadian Sentencing Commission (1987: 60) has pointed out, there is a dearth of systematic information about sentencing in Canada.

The most recent Canada-wide sentencing statistics date from 1973, and according to the Commission (p. 60), the relatively recent establishment of the Canadian Centre for Justice Statistics has not yet improved this troublesome situation. Indeed, the Commission asserted that there has been no "reliable indication" of when the Centre might produce nationwide, aggregate statistics from the courts in relation to sentencing in criminal cases. However, there are some statistics available that relate to sentencing practices in selected Canadian jurisdictions. For example, Hann et al. (1983) have analyzed sentencing data gleaned from several provincial jurisdictions. Similarly, Mitchell-Banks (1983) has gathered sentencing data relating solely to provincial courts in the Province of British Columbia. These sources of data will be tapped in order to present a general idea of the extent to which Canadian courts make use of the various sentencing options, discussed above.[81]

The sentencing data analyzed by Hann et al. (1983) are concerned exclusively with defendants convicted of offences under the *Criminal Code*. They therefore relate to the more serious criminal offences, since they do not include the many quasi-criminal offences arising under federal and provincial legislation; in particular, they exclude the numerous minor driving offences that are covered by the provincial motor vehicle Acts. Figures 8.1 and 8.2 show the overall proportions of convicted defendants, who were sentenced to four major forms of disposition; namely, discharge, fine, probation and custody. Figure 8.1 focuses on indictable offences alone, while Figure 8.2 turns the spotlight upon both indictable and summary offences combined.

It can readily be seen that custody is the most frequent form of sentence for indictable offences (from 43% to 55% of all cases), while the fine is the disposition most frequently resorted to when both indictable and summary offences are combined (from 40% to 55% of all cases).[82] Probation was chosen as the most serious sentence in 35% to 39% of indictable offences, and in only 15% to 21% of cases when summary and indictable offences are combined.

Mitchell-Banks (1983), on the other hand, analyzed the sentencing practices of British Columbia courts in relation to all criminal offences (including the various quasi-criminal offences and, in particular, the numerous driving offences arising under provincial legislation). Therefore, her analysis includes a considerably greater proportion of the less serious criminal offences than does the Hann et al. study, which was concerned solely with *Criminal Code* offences. Figure 8.3, which is based on Mitchell-Banks' study, clearly indicates the predominance of the fine as the disposition of choice, over the seven-year-period between 1976 and 1982.

According to Mitchell-Banks (1983: 152), in 1976 the fine was the most serious penalty[83] imposed by the British Columbia courts in 68.6% of all cases; however, by 1982 this percentage had fallen to 56.1%. Mitchell-Banks

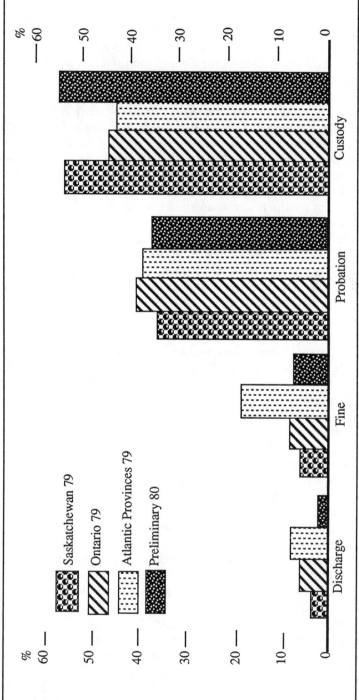

FIGURE 8.1

PERCENTAGE DISTRIBUTION BY SENTENCE TYPE OF CASES WHERE DEFENDANT WAS FOUND GUILTY OF SELECTED OFFENCES FOR JURISDICTIONS REPORTING INDICTABLE CASES ONLY

Source: R. G. Hann et al. *Sentencing Practices and Trends in Canada: A Summary of Statistical Information* (Ottawa: Department of Justice, Canada, 1983). Reproduced with permission of the Minister of Supply and Services Canada, 1989.

FIGURE 8.2

PERCENTAGE DISTRIBUTION BY SENTENCE TYPE OF CASES WHERE DEFENDANT WAS FOUND GUILTY OF SELECTED OFFENCES FOR JURISDICTIONS REPORTING INDICTABLE AND SUMMARY CASES COMBINED

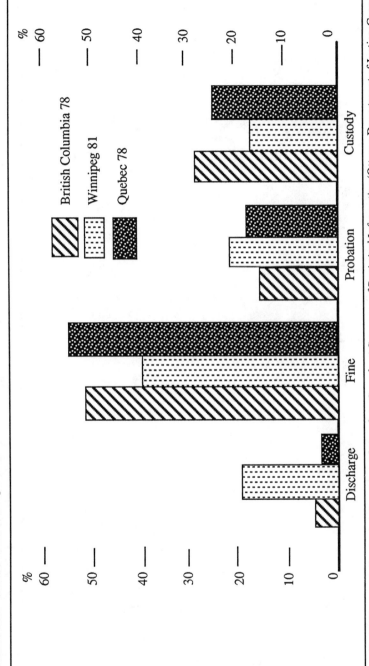

Source: R. G. Hann et al. *Sentencing Practices and Trends in Canada: A Summary of Statistical Information* (Ottawa: Department of Justice, Canada, 1983), p. 12. Reproduced with permission of the Minister of Supply and Services Canada, 1989.

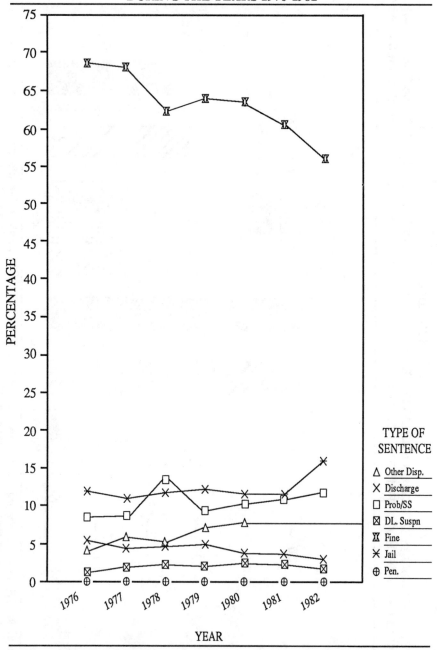

FIGURE 8.3
PERCENTAGE OF SENTENCES IMPOSED BY B.C. COURTS
DURING THE YEARS 1976-1982

Source: T. R. Mitchell-Banks. "The Fine: An Enigma." M.A. thesis (Burnaby, B.C.: School of Criminology, Simon Fraser University, 1983), p. 153.

points out (pp. 152–53) that the apparent decline in the use of the fine is largely a consequence of a significant shift toward the use of "other dispositions" in relation to traffic offences.[84] She discovered that as many as 52.5% of all cases resolved by the British Columbia courts were traffic offences, and when these offences were removed from her sample, it was revealed (pp. 155–56) that the use of the fine had remained fairly constant over the seven-year period (from 54.9% in 1976, to 50.4% in 1982). It is significant that there was a slight increase in the use of jail (custody for less than two years in a provincial facility) from 12% in 1976, to 16% in 1982. On the other hand, Figure 8.3 indicates that the percentage of sentences involving the incarceration of offenders in federal penitentiaries (sentences of two or more years) remained at a relatively low level (from 0.2% in 1976, to 0.06% in 1982). The rates of imposition of probation and suspended sentence rose from 85.% in 1976, to 11.7% in 1982, while the rates for discharge declined from 5.4% to 2.9% over the same period.

What conclusions can be drawn concerning the use of the various sentencing options by Canadian courts? The Canadian Sentencing Commission has argued that an analysis of Canadian sentencing practices reveals an over-reliance on imprisonment (1987: xxiii). Indeed, it has been pointed out that with an imprisonment rate of 108 per 100,000 inhabitants, Canada can be considered to have one of the *highest* rates of imprisonment among all Western countries (Correctional Service of Canada, 1986). As noted above, the Commission's response to this disturbing situation was to recommend that imprisonment be used only in very limited circumstances and that much greater emphasis be placed upon community sanctions. The Commission's opinion of the excessive use of imprisonment in current sentencing practice is well worth repeating (1987: 233):

> Besides the incalculable human costs to a person removed from society, there are easily calculable economic costs. Incarceration costs between 10 and 15 times as much as do alternative sanctions. . . . The average annual cost of keeping a prisoner in a maximum security penitentiary is $50,000. In medium or minimum security institutions the cost is $35,000. The cost per bed of building a new institution is now $200,000. One does not have to look far, then, for reasons to support the exercise of restraint in the use of incarceration.

NOTES

1. Hereinafter abbreviated as C.S.C. for the purpose of references.
2. Section 718(1).
3. Section 718(2).
4. Sections 717(2) and 719(a).
5. Section 787(1).
6. Section 787(1).
7. Section 719(b).

8. Section 718(3)(a) and (b).

9. The term is limited to five years if the offence is one for which a term of five years or more may be imposed, or two years where the maximum punishment for the offence is less than five years: section 718(3)(a) and (b).

10. *R. v. Natrall* (1972), 9 C.C.C. (2d) 390, 20 C.R.N.S. 265 (B.C.C.A.).

11. Sections 718(4), (5) and (11); 787(4) and (10).

12. Sections 718(10) and 787(9).

13. Section 722(1).

14. However, the court may impose a term of probation in addition to a sentence of imprisonment only where the period of imprisonment is "for a term not exceeding two years" (section 737(1)(b) of the *Code*): see *R. v. Amaralik* (1984), 16 C.C.C. (3d) 22, [1985] N.W.T.R. 39 (N.W.T. C.A.).

15. Section 737(1).

16. For example, the Ontario Court of Appeal has ruled that while a court has the power to impose a suspended sentence together with probation, it may not also impose a disposition such as a fine: *R. v. Polywjanyj* (1982), 1 C.C.C. (3d) 161. A suspended sentence necessarily implies that no sentence is imposed but, rather, that the trial judge suspends the passing of sentence altogether. The making of a probation order is not seen as the imposition of a "sentence."

17. For example, robbery is generally regarded as an offence in relation to which the courts have emphasized that the principle of deterrence must override the goal of individual rehabilitation: *R. v. Johnas et al.* (1982), 2 C.C.C. (3d) 490, 32 C.R. (3d) 1 (Alta. C.A.).

18. Section 737(2).

19. *R. v. Richards* (1979), 49 C.C.C. (2d) 517, 11 C.R. (3d) 193 (Ont. C.A.).

20. For example, in *Fields v. R.* (1984), 52 C.R. (3d) 398, 14 C.R.R. 77 (Ont. Co. Ct.), it was held that a condition prohibiting the accused from participating in any strike or lock-out, unless he was an employee of the premises concerned, should be struck down on the basis that it infringed the offender's right of freedom of peaceful assembly, guaranteed by section 2(c) of the *Charter*. The condition was varied so as to apply only to the particular strike concerned.

21. A recent study by Dittenhoffer and Ericson (1983) suggests that victim-offender reconciliation programs (VORPs) do not appear to be operating as an alternative to imprisonment (as they were apparently designed to do). The authors conclude (1983: 346) that

> ... on the whole VORP has contributed little to sparing offenders imprisonment. Instead of avoiding problems created by the use of the prison system, another sentencing option has been implemented which pulls a different set of offenders deeper into the system of social control and inevitably increased cost.

22. Section 738(3).
23. Section 740.
24. Section 738(4)(e).
25. Section 738(4)(d). It is significant that there is judicial authority to the effect that the power of the court, to revoke a probation order and impose a sentence, does not infringe the *Canadian Charter of Rights and Freedoms*: *R. v. Linklater* (1983), 9 C.C.C. (3d) 217, 7 C.R.R. 299 (Y.T.C.A.).
26. See *infra*.
27. See Chapter 11.
28. See sections 47 and 235.
29. See section 85. The maximum term that may be imposed is 14 years.
30. See section 255. The maximum terms that may be imposed are six months (if tried summarily) and five years (if tried on indictment).
31. *Smith v. R.* (1987), 34 C.C.C. (3d) 97, [1987] 1 S.C.R. 1045, 58 C.R. (3d) 193.
32. Section 731.
33. Section 717(4).
34. The application of this "totality principle" is illustrated in the case of *R. v. Johnas et al.* (1982), 2 C.C.C. (3d) 490, 32 C.R. (3d) 1 (Alta. C.A.). The Supreme Court of Canada has discussed some of the general principles, applicable to consecutive sentences, in *Paul v. R.* (1982), 67 C.C.C. (2d) 97, [1982] 1 S.C.R. 621, 27 C.R. (3d) 193.
35. Section 737(1).
36. It is important to recognize that a court has no power to impose consecutive 90-day prison terms to be served intermittently. Thus, an Appeal Court ruled that the imposition of two consecutive intermittent sentences, each of 90 days, constituted an illegal sentence: *R. v. Fletcher* (1982), 2 C.C.C. (3d) 221 (Ont. C.A.).
37. *Wortzman v. R.* (1979), 12 C.R. (3d) 115 (Ont. S.C.).
38. Section 754.
39. Section 758.
40. Section 754(2).
41. Section 753.
42. Section 761.
43. Section 752.
44. Section 753(a). That the offender is such a threat can be proved only on the basis of evidence establishing

(i) a pattern of repetitive behaviour by the offender, of which the offence for which he has been convicted forms a part, showing a failure to restrain his behaviour and a likelihood of his causing death or injury to other persons, or inflicting severe psychological damage on other persons, through failure in the future to restrain his behaviour,

(ii) a pattern of persistent aggressive behaviour by the offender, of which the offence for which he has been convicted forms a part, showing a substantial degree of indifference on the part of the offender respecting the reasonably foreseeable consequences to other persons of his behaviour, or

(iii) any behaviour by the offender, associated with the offence for which he has been convicted, that is of such a brutal nature as to compel the conclusion that his behaviour in the future is unlikely to be inhibited by normal standards of behavioural restraint.

45. Section 753(b).

46. Section 756.

47. Section 755.

48. For a discussion of the treatment programs available, see Borzecki and Wormith (1987); Wormith and Borzecki (1985).

49. *Re Moore and R.* (1984), 10 C.C.C. (3d) 306, 6 D.L.R. (4th) 294, 45 O.R. (2d) 3 (Ont. H.C.J.).

50. *R. v. Lyons* (1987), 37 C.C.C. (3d) 1, [1987] 2 S.C.R. 309, 44 D.L.R. (4th) 193.

51. S.C. 1972, c. 13, s. 57.

52. Section 736.

53. Section 736(4).

54. Section 736(1).

55. *R. v. Derksen* (1972), 9 C.C.C. (2d) 97 (B.C. Prov. Ct.).

56. *R. v. Vicente* (1975), 18 Crim. L.Q. 292 (Ont. C.A.).

57. *R. v. Webb* (1975), 28 C.C.C. (2d) 456 (P.E.I. C.A.).

58. *R. v. Fallofield* (1973), 13 C.C.C. (2d) 450 at 454–55, 22 C.R.N.S. 342 (B.C.C.A.). See, also, *R. v. Stewart (No. 2)* (1983), 11 C.C.C. (3d) 92, 45 O.R. (2d) 185, 8 D.L.R. (4th) 275 (Ont. H.C.J.).

59. *R. v. Meneses* (1974), 25 C.C.C. (2d) 115 (Ont. C.A.).

60. *R. v. Wing Shee Au Yeung* (1976), 19 Crim. L.Q. 22 (Alta. C.A.); *R. v. Melo* (1975), 30 C.R.N.S. 328 (Ont. C.A.).

61. *R. v. Macfarlane* (1976), 3 Alta. L.R. (2d) 341 (C.A.).

62. *R. v. Sanchez-pino* (1973), 11 C.C.C. (2d) 53, [1973] 2 O.R. 314, 29 C.R. (3d) 215 (Ont. C.A.).

63. Similarly, a court is unlikely to grant a discharge where a serious offence is committed by an official in whom a high degree of public trust has been placed. For example, a discharge was not granted to a police officer, who was convicted of assaulting a suspect: *R. v. Wigglesworth* (1983), 7 C.C.C. (3d) 170, 150 D.L.R. (3d) 748, 35 C.R. (3d) 44 (Sask. Q.B.); affirmed (1984), 11 C.C.C. (3d) 27, 9 C.R.R. 47, 38 C.R. (3d) 388 (Sask. C.A.); affirmed [1987] 2 S.C.R. 541, [1988] 1 W.W.R. 193, 32 C.R.R. 219.

64. Section 763(3).

65. R.S.C. 1985, c. C-47. See Nadin-Davis (1981).

66. In a Bill (C-19) presented to Parliament in February 1984, it was proposed that the *Code* provisions relating to discharges be overhauled (clause 206). Among the proposed changes was a requirement that application forms, relating to employment by anybody falling under the jurisdiction of the Parliament of Canada, not contain any questions designed to force an applicant to disclose that he or she has received a discharge. However, Bill C-19 was never enacted, owing to the dissolution of Parliament in July 1984.

67. Section 736(3).

68. Although it could be noted that a court has no power to order compensation for the victim's "pain and suffering" under the provisions of section 737(2)(e). For a discussion of some of the practical problems caused by the failure of an offender to fulfil such a condition of his or her probation, see Zapf and Cole (1985).

69. Section 725. It should be noted that the Supreme Court of Canada, in *R. v. Zelensky* (1978), 41 C.C.C. (2d) 97, [1978] 2 S.C.R. 940, [1978] 3 W.W.R. 693, ruled that compensation orders should be made with "restraint and caution." In particular, such an order should not be made where complicated issues of law or fact are involved; otherwise, the sentencing court would be usurping the civil law process, which falls under provincial jurisdiction. For a discussion of some of the factors relevant to the court's decision whether to make a compensation order, see *R. v. Scherer* (1984), 16 C.C.C. (3d) 30, 42 C.R. (3d) 376, 5 O.A.C. 297 (Ont. C.A.).

70. Section 726.

71. Section 491.1.

71a. These proposals were eventually enacted in 1988 (see sections 725 to 735 of the *Criminal Code*). However, only the provision concerning victim impact statements (section 735(1.1) to (1.4)) was immediately proclaimed in force on October 1, 1988.

72. For a discussion of the arguments *pro* and *contra* restitution, see Barnett (1982).

73. Section 100(1).

74. Section 259.

75. Section 446(5).

76. Section 492(1).

77. Section 164(4).

78. Section 192.

79. Section 199(3).

80. Section 320.

80a. In 1988, the *Criminal Code* was amended so as to facilitate the process of seizing the "proceeds of crime" (see sections 462.1 to 462.3). The new provisions, which were proclaimed in force on January 1, 1989, include making it an offence to "launder the proceeds of crime" (section 462.17) and requiring the sentencing court to order the forfeiture of any property that represents the proceeds of what the *Code* now calls an "enterprise crime offence." The court is also empowered to impose a fine where it is not possible to seize such property (because, for example, the offender has transferred it outside Canada); the fine would be in an amount equal to the value of the property that cannot be seized.

81. There are some more recent sentencing data that have been analyzed by Hann et al. (1987) and the Programs and Research Section, Department of Justice, Canada (1987). However, both of these studies deal only with custodial dispositions and probation and are not discussed here. The intent of this section is to give only a brief overview of the relative use of all the sanctions in the armoury of the courts in Canada.

82. It should be emphasized that Figures 8.1 and 8.2 provide an analysis of only the "most serious" disposition imposed. In many cases, a fine may be imposed in addition to imprisonment; however, since imprisonment is regarded as the "most serious" disposition, the fine would be ignored in the analysis undertaken in the two figures.

83. As is the case with the Hann et al. (1987) data, the analysis deals solely with the "most serious" disposition imposed by the British Columbia courts.

84. Mitchell-Banks indicates that it was not possible to ascertain precisely what forms of disposition are included in the category "other" (1983: 167).

REFERENCES

Barnett, C. C. 1977. "Probation Orders under the Criminal Code." 38 *Criminal Reports (New Series)* 165.

Barnett, R. E. 1982. "Restitution: A New Paradigm of Criminal Justice." In *The Canadian Criminal Justice System*, edited by C. L. Boydell and I. A. Connidis, 232–47. Toronto: Holt, Rinehart and Winston.

Blumstein, A. 1982. "Research on Sentencing." 7 *Justice System Journal* 307–30.

Borzecki, M., and J. S. Wormith. 1987. "A Survey of Treatment Programmes for Sex Offenders in North America." 28 *Canadian Psychology* 1–44.

Boyd, N. 1978. "An Examination of Probation." 20 *Criminal Law Quarterly* 355–82.

Canadian Sentencing Commission, Department of Justice. 1987. *Sentencing Reform: A Canadian Approach.* (Catalogue Number J2-67/1986E.) Ottawa: Supply and Services Canada. Reproduced with permission of the Minister of Supply and Services Canada, 1989.

Chasse, K. L. 1980. "Intermittent Sentences: A Question of Judicial Independence." 12 *Criminal Reports* (3d) 117–20.

Chretien, J. 1982. *The Criminal in Canadian Society.* Ottawa: Government of Canada.

Correctional Service of Canada. 1986. *Basic Facts about Corrections in Canada.* Ottawa: Supply and Services Canada.

Cressey, D. R. 1980. "Sentencing: Legislative Rule versus Judicial Discretion." In *New Directions in Sentencing*, edited by B. Grosman, 51–69. Toronto: Butterworths.

Davis, R. P. 1980a. "Employer Stigmatization of Ex-offenders and the Pardon under the Criminal Records Act." 22 *Canadian Journal of Criminology* 343–53.

—— .1980b. "The Mark of Cain: Some Subliminal Effects of Criminal Process." 44 *Saskatchewan Law Review* 219–60.

Department of Justice, Canada. 1985. *Criminal Injuries Compensation in Canada*. Ottawa: Department of Justice, Canada.

—— . 1987. *Sentencing Patterns in Canada: An Overview of the Correctional Services Project*. Ottawa: Programs and Research Section, Department of Justice, Canada.

Dittenhoffer, T., and R. V. Ericson. 1983. "The Victim/Offender Reconciliation Program: A Message to Correctional Reformers." 33 *University of Toronto Law Journal* 315–47.

Dombek, C. F., and M. W. Chittra. 1984. "The Intermittent Sentence in Canada — The Law and Its Problems." 26 *Canadian Journal of Criminology* 43–64.

Ekstedt, J. W., and M. A. Jackson. 1986. *A Profile of Canadian Alternative Sentencing Programmes: A National Review of Policy Issues*. Ottawa: Canadian Sentencing Commission.

Fattah, E. A. 1982a. "Making the Punishment Fit the Crime: The Case of Imprisonment. The Problems Inherent in the Use of Imprisonment as a Retributive Sanction." 24 *Canadian Journal of Criminology* 1–12.

—— . 1982b. "Public Opposition to Prison Alternatives and Community Corrections: A Strategy for Action." 24 *Canadian Journal of Criminology* 371–86.

Gordon, R. M., and S. N. Verdun-Jones. 1987. "The Impact of the Canadian Charter of Rights and Freedoms upon Canadian Mental Health Law: The Dawn of a New Era or Business as Usual?" 14 *Law, Medicine & Health Care* 190–97.

Grant, I. 1985. "Dangerous Offenders." 9 *Dalhousie Law Journal* 349–82.

Greenland, C. 1984. "Dangerous Sexual Offender Legislation in Canada, 1948–1977: An Experiment that Failed." 26 *Canadian Journal of Criminology* 1–12.

Greenspan, E. L. 1973. "Absolute and Conditional Discharge." In *Studies in Criminal Law and Procedure*, Canadian Bar Association, 65–76. Agincourt, Ont.: Canada Law Book Co.

Groves, P. 1976. "A Report on Community Service Treatment and Work Programs in British Columbia." In *Community Participation in Sentencing*, Law Reform Commission of Canada, 119–50. Ottawa: Supply and Services Canada.

Hagan, J. 1974. "Criminal Justice and Native People: A Study of Incarceration in a Canadian Province." (Special issue.) *Canadian Review of*

Sociology and Anthropology 220–36.

———. 1976. "Locking up the Indians: A Case for Law Reform." 55 *Canadian Forum* 16–18.

———. 1983. *Victims before the Law: The Organizational Dominance of the Criminal Law.* Toronto: Butterworths.

Hann, R. G., et al. 1983. *Sentencing Practices and Trends in Canada: A Summary of Statistical Information.* Ottawa: Department of Justice, Canada.

———. 1987. *Custodial and Probation Sentences (1984/85): Overview Report.* Ottawa: Department of Justice, Canada.

Hnatyshyn, R. 1987. *Notes for the Honourable Ray Hnatyshyn at a News Conference on November 5th, 1987.* Ottawa: Department of Justice, Canada.

Jakimiec, J., et al. 1986. *A Descriptive Study of Incarcerated Dangerous Offenders.* Ottawa: Solicitor General of Canada.

Jobson, K., and A. Atkins. 1986. "Imprisonment in Default and Fundamental Justice." 28 *Criminal Law Quarterly* 251–71.

Klein, J. F. 1973. "Habitual Offender Legislation and the Bargaining Process." 15 *Criminal Law Quarterly* 417–36.

———. 1978. "Revitalizing Restitution: Flogging a Horse that May Have Been Killed for Good Cause." 20 *Criminal Law Quarterly* 383–408.

Law Reform Commission of Canada. 1974a. *Restitution and Compensation and Fines (Working Papers 5 & 6).* Ottawa: Information Canada.

———. 1974b. *The Principles of Sentencing and Dispositions (Working Paper 3).* Ottawa: Information Canada.

———. 1976a. *Community Participation in Sentencing.* Ottawa: Supply and Services Canada.

———. 1976b. *A Report on Dispositions and Sentences in the Criminal Process: Guidelines.* Ottawa: Information Canada.

MacFarlane, B. A. 1985. "Confiscating the Fruits of Crime." 27 *Criminal Law Quarterly* 408–32.

Menzies, R. J., C. D. Webster, and D. S. Sepejak. 1985. "Hitting the Forensic Sound Barrier: Predictions of Dangerousness in a Pretrial Psychiatric Clinic." In *Dangerousness: Probability and Prediction, Psychiatry and Public Policy*, edited by C. D. Webster, M. H. Ben-Aron, and S. J. Hucker, 115–43. Cambridge: Cambridge University Press.

Mitchell-Banks, T. R. 1983. "The Fine: An Enigma." M.A. thesis. Burnaby, B.C.: School of Criminology, Simon Fraser University.

Monahan, J. 1981. *The Clinical Prediction of Violent Behavior.* Rockville, Md.: National Institute of Mental Health.

Nadin-Davis, R. P. 1981. "Canada's Criminal Records Act: Notes on How Not to Expunge Criminal Convictions." 45 *Saskatchewan Law Review* 221–57.

———. 1982. *Sentencing in Canada.* Toronto: Carswell.

Norquay, G., and R. Weiler. 1981. *Services to Victims and Witnesses of Crime in Canada.* Ottawa: Supply and Services Canada.

Ouimet, R. (Chairman). 1969. *Report of the Canadian Committee on Corrections. Toward Unity: Criminal Justice and Corrections.* (Catalogue No. JS52-1-1968.) Ottawa: Information Canada.

Parker, G. 1976. "The Law of Probation." In *Community Participation in Sentencing,* Law Reform Commission of Canada, 51–118. Ottawa: Supply and Services Canada.

Petrunik, M. 1982. "The Politics of Dangerousness." 2 *International Journal of Law and Psychiatry* 225–53.

Quebec, Ministère du Solliciteur Général. 1986. *Rapport du Comité d'étude sur les Solutions de Rechange a l'Incarcération.* Quebec: Ministère du Solliciteur Général.

Ruby, C. C. 1987. *Sentencing.* (3rd ed.) Toronto: Butterworths.

Salhany, R. E. 1984. *Canadian Criminal Procedure.* (4th ed.) Toronto: Canada Law Book.

Schmeiser, D. A. 1974. *The Native Offender and the Law.* Ottawa: Law Reform Commission of Canada.

Statistics Canada. 1983. *Criminal Injuries Compensation, 1983.* Ottawa: Supply and Services Canada.

Status of Women, Canada. 1986. *A Feminist Review of Criminal Law. Report.* Ottawa: Supply and Services Canada.

Stortini, R. 1979. "Community Service Orders." 21 *Criminal Law Quarterly* 503–507.

Swabey, T. R. 1972. "Absolute and Conditional Discharge under the Criminal Code." 20 *Criminal Reports (New Series)* 132.

Thornstedt, H. 1975. "The Day-Fine System in Sweden." (June) *Criminal Law Review* 307–12.

Thorvaldson, S. A. 1987. "Restitution by Offenders in Canada: Some Legislative Issues." 29 *Canadian Journal of Criminology* 1–16.

Verdun-Jones, S. N., and F. D. Cousineau. 1979. "Cleansing the Augean Stables: A Critical Analysis of Recent Trends in the Plea Bargaining Debate in Canada." 17 *Osgoode Hall Law Journal* 227–60.

Verdun-Jones, S. N., and A. J. Hatch. 1985. *Plea Bargaining and Sentencing Guidelines.* Ottawa: Canadian Sentencing Commission.

Verdun-Jones, S. N., and T. R. Mitchell-Banks. 1986. *The Fine as a Sentencing Option in Canada.* Ottawa: Canadian Sentencing Commission.

Vingilis, E., E. Adlaf, and L. Chung. 1981. "The Oshawa Impaired Drivers Programme: An Evaluation of a Rehabilitation Programme." 19 *Canadian Journal of Criminology* 93–102.

Webster, C. D., M. H. Ben-Aron, and S. J. Hucker. 1985a. *Dangerousness: Probability and Prediction, Psychiatry and Public Policy.* Cambridge: Cambridge University Press.

Webster, C. D., B. Dickens, and S. Addario. 1985b. *Constructing Dan-*

gerousness: Scientific, Legal and Policy Implications. Toronto: Centre of Criminology, University of Toronto.

Wilkinson, J. L. 1977. "Absolute and Conditional Discharge." 19 *Criminal Law Quarterly* 454–70.

Wormith, J. S., and M. Borzecki. 1985. *A Survey of Treatment Programs for Sexual Offenders in Canada.* Ottawa: Solicitor General of Canada.

Zapf, M. K., and B. Cole. 1985. "Yukon Restitution Study." 27 *Canadian Journal of Criminology* 477–90.

LEGISLATION

Criminal Code, R.S.C. 1985, c. C-46
Criminal Records Act, R.S.C. 1985, c. C-47
Food and Drugs Act, R.S.C. 1985, c. F-27
Narcotic Control Act, R.S.C. 1985, c. N-1

9 CRITICAL ISSUES IN SENTENCING

The Goals of Sentencing

As the Canadian Sentencing Commission (1987: 133) has aptly pointed out, it is important, when discussing the goals of sentencing, not to confuse the process of sentencing with the criminal law or with the entire criminal justice system. While it may be appropriate to ascribe the overall goal of "protection of the public" to the criminal law or to the criminal justice system, it would be an unjust burden to place on the shoulders of the judiciary if the same goal were to be assigned to the sentencing process. Indeed, as the Sentencing Commission (C.S.C., 1987: 119, 147), indicates the aims of sentencing must be limited by the fact that only a small fraction of offences reported to the police ever result in the imposition of a sentence on a specific offender.

The Commission (1987: 151) recommends the adoption of a fundamental goal that is appropriate to the specific functions of sentencing within the context of the overall criminal justice system:

> It is further recognized and declared that in a free and democratic society peace and security can only be enjoyed through the due application of the principles of fundamental justice. In furtherance of the overall purpose of the criminal law of maintaining a just, peaceful and safe society, the fundamental purpose of sentencing is to preserve the authority of and promote respect for the law through the imposition of just sanctions.

The Commission's approach is predicated on the notion that an offender who has been formally identified should not be seen by his or her fellow citizens to be "getting away scot-free." If this were to happen, then the very legitimacy of the rules, embodied in the criminal law, would be seriously undermined. According to the Commission, the average citizen should not be "demoralized" by the perception that those who break the law are not accountable for their culpable behaviour. In this sense, the Commission's recommended approach would ensure that the *just* imposition of sanctions in the sentencing process would promote general respect for the underlying community values embodied in the criminal law. It would also serve to strengthen the belief that individual citizens will be held to account for their criminal misconduct and that the perceived costs of indulging in such misconduct outweigh any benefit that may be apparently derived from it. In the Commission's view (1987: 152), their recommended goal is both realistic and achievable since "Sentencing is not committed to eradicate crime but to prevent it increasing beyond a threshold where freedom, peace and security can no more be enjoyed on the whole by a community."

It remains to be seen whether the Commission's fundamental goal will be formally adopted by the Canadian criminal justice system. In the meantime, it is necessary to refer briefly to the traditional goals ascribed to the sentencing process. These goals may be divided into two groups. The so-called utilitarian goals are deterrence (both individual and general), incapacitation and rehabilitation. Proponents of these goals contend that criminal sanctions may be justified by the social benefits that accrue from their imposition in the sentencing process. These benefits may be the deterrence of those who are convicted of offences, the deterrence of the general population, the incapacitation through imprisonment of those who would otherwise commit crimes, or the rehabilitation of offenders resulting in a cessation of their criminal activities. In this sense, the utilitarian approach looks to the future as a means of justifying the imposition of legal sanctions. On the other hand, the second group of sentencing goals looks primarily to the past, insofar as it focuses upon the blameworthiness of the offence committed rather than the future consequences of punishment. The central goal in this group is that of retribution, with which are associated the goal of denunciation and the philosophy of "just deserts." Of course, a major problem that becomes apparent immediately is that many of these goals relate primarily to punishment in general rather than to the sentencing process *per se*. Furthermore, these goals may well conflict and thus provide very little assistance to the decision maker in the sentencing process. For example, rehabilitation may require that an offender be given a community sanction, while deterrence may dictate that he or she be given a sentence of imprisonment. In this sense, therefore, these goals are really no more than considerations that the judge should take into account in determining a sentence in any particular case.

Deterrence

Much has been written about deterrence, although it is fair to say that very few solid conclusions can be drawn from the criminological literature on this subject. In theory, deterrence should be an important goal of sentencing, since, according to its proponents, the infliction of legal sanctions prevents the commission of crimes by rendering potential offenders fearful of the threat of punishment. Deterrence may be specific or general in nature. *Specific* deterrence occurs when a convicted offender is deterred from committing further offences as a consequence of his or her personal experience of punishment. *General* deterrence is achieved when the threat of legal sanctions prevents the commission of potential crimes by people *other than punished offenders*.

Although common sense would appear to indicate that punishment must have some effect in preventing crime (Miller and Anderson, 1986: 418), it is extremely difficult to conduct empirical research into the specific deterrent effects of legal sanctions (Hagan, 1982). Most research has focused upon general deterrence, and, as yet, the results are inconclusive.

After conducting an extensive review of the research literature, the Canadian Sentencing Commission (1987: 137) concludes with the rather enigmatic statement that "legal sanctions have an overall deterrent effect which is difficult to evaluate precisely." While the Commission believed that it is "plausible to argue" that legal sanctions have a general deterrent effect, it also doubted whether the literature supported the proposition that these sanctions could be used to achieve very specific results (such as deterring a particular category of offenders, such as impaired drivers).

A very important point made by the research literature revolves around the observation that it is the *certainty* rather than the *severity* of punishment that is most likely to exert a deterrent impact (Gibbons, 1982: 454). Indeed, according to Miller and Anderson (1986: 438), increasing the probability that an offender will be convicted and punished is likely to be more efficacious than lengthening the term of imprisonment under a system of punishment based on deterrence. A closely related issue concerns the whole question of the deterrent effect of the *swiftness* (or *celerity*) of punishment. Gibbons (1982: 454), in discussing the available research, notes that virtually nothing is known about this factor, although social learning theory would suggest that the more swiftly punishment follows the commission of a crime, the less likely it will be that this deviant act will be repeated in the future.

One factor that is frequently overlooked is that legal sanctions cannot exert any sort of deterrent impact unless they are widely known. After all, the person to be deterred must actually perceive that there is a significant threat of punishment should he or she break the law (Siegel, 1983: 99; Webb, 1980; Williams and Hawkins, 1986). Gibbons (1982: 455) notes that what evidence there is suggests that many people are relatively ignorant of the nature and severity of criminal penalties — a suggestion that is supported by the Canadian Sentencing Commission's research into Canadians' awareness of sentencing laws and practices (1987: 89*ff.*). This ignorance on the part of the general public may well explain why it has been difficult to furnish unequivocal evidence of the effectiveness of punishment in deterring others from committing offences.

The Canadian Sentencing Commission's research suggests that the media may well undercut the deterrent impact of the law by focusing on sentences that are lenient rather than severe and by publicizing the low clearance rates for many crimes (1987: 137). In this sense, the media contribute to public ignorance about the severity of legal sanctions and the likelihood that they will be applied. On the other hand, there is evidence that a widely publicized campaign warning the public of increased police enforcement of a law (such as that requiring the wearing of seat belts) can result in a substantial change in citizen's behaviour (Watson, 1986).

Of course, the impact of deterrence is likely to vary with the nature of the individual and the nature of the particular crime involved (Chambliss, 1967). Many crimes are committed by individuals who are affected by alcohol or other drugs or who are acting in a state of extreme emotion (such as anger or rage); clearly, these are persons who are not likely to be able to weigh calmly the potential benefits and drawbacks associated with the commission of a crime (Siegel, 1983: 101).[1] On the other hand, economically motivated offences may be much more amenable to the impact of deterrence. Miller and Anderson (1986: 438) suggest that the threat of punishment is a "central and multi-dimensional factor of information processed by individuals faced with perceived economically motivated crime opportunities" and recommend that, to be effective, crime control programs must "neutralize or discount the value of financial gain from crime." The differential amenability of individual offenders and types of crime to deterrence obviously renders the task of the judge an immensely difficult one if deterrence is a major aim of sentencing.

What about the question of specific deterrence? In the view of the Canadian Sentencing Commission (1987: 135), there is little evidence to suggest that deterrence has much impact upon those offenders who are convicted and sentenced to terms of imprisonment in the federal correctional system. Indeed, between 1975 and 1985, 60% of those offenders released on mandatory supervision from federal institutions were subsequently re-admitted to a penitentiary, while 49% of federal parolees were subsequently re-admitted to a federal institution. It has been suggested that imprisonment can actually *increase* the likelihood of subsequent re-offending, since offenders will be placed in an environment that is supportive of criminal activity (Bridges and Stone, 1986).

One recent study of the impact of punishment upon convicted offenders (Bridges and Stone, 1986: 230) found that

> . . . experiences with crime and criminal sanctions have few "eye-opening" effects. The effects are greatest among naive offenders, for whom punishment increases perceived threat. Among experienced offenders, the effects of punishment run counter to the prediction of specific deterrence. Punishment has no substantial direct effect on perceived threat and may actually lower perceived threat by increasing approval of criminal behavior.

In light of what little is known about deterrence, it is clear that sentencing courts adopting it as a goal should do so with extreme caution.

Incapacitation

The theory underlying the sentencing strategy of incapacitation rests on the premise that those offenders who are incarcerated are unable to commit crimes in the community and that therefore adoption of this strategy should result in the reduction of the level of crime. There are at least two major strategies of incapacitation (Cohen, 1983b). *Collective incapacitation* refers to a sentencing strategy that imposes a prison sentence on all those offenders convicted of a particular category of serious offence (e.g., all those offenders convicted of robbery would be sentenced to, say, five years' imprisonment). *Selective incapacitation*, on the other hand, refers to a strategy that would rely on individualized sentences based on predictions that particular offenders would commit serious offences at a high rate if they were not incarcerated.

One major problem with such strategies is that any incapacitative effect is significantly reduced by the extent to which the crimes that would have been committed by incarcerated offenders are replaced by those of other offenders (Blumstein, 1982). Crimes committed by a violent sex offender, for example, are not likely to be replaced by those of other offenders so that, for this category of crime, there is a strong incapacitative effect when such an offender is incarcerated. However, there are certain crimes that, as Blumstein (1982: 315) notes, are the "work of a criminal labor market," and these are very likely to be replaced. For example, the crimes of a convicted offender involved in the sale of illicit drugs will most likely be replaced, since his sales will be "picked up either by an increase in the activity of those still out or by recruitment of an additional seller to take his place."

Cohen (1983a) suggests that the research literature demonstrates that collective incapacitation strategies do not appear to achieve large reductions in crime. At most, the effect of such strategies is in the range of a 10 to 20% reduction. As Cohen points out, this is not insubstantial. However, she contends that "incapacitation does not make the dent in crime that might have been expected from a 'lock-em-up' strategy." More significantly, however, the research suggests that collective incapacitation strategies would result in a massive buildup in the prison population, thus rendering such strategies impractical.

The theory behind selective incapacitation is that a relatively small number of offenders commit a disproportionately large number of crimes (Blumstein, 1983; Cohen, 1983a). Locking up this group of offenders would result in a significant decrease in the crime rate, while, at the same time, avoiding overcrowding in the prisons. The strategy turns on the ability to identify such offenders early in their criminal careers and to imprison them for substantial periods. One major problem with this approach is that many people consider it unjust to give one individual a more severe sentence than another who has committed exactly the same offence, solely on the basis of a prediction about what he or she may do in the future (Von Hirsch, 1984). Punishment for what one *may do* in the future hardly seems fair. Furthermore, as Cohen (1983a) points out, past efforts at predicting future criminality have not been very successful (as our discussion of dangerous offenders concluded above). Without an adequate technique for making such predictions, Cohen contends that there is no sound basis for implementing selective incapacitation sentencing strategies. Even if reliable prediction techniques were to become available to the courts, a serious ethical problem would arise, because such techniques would most likely place some reliance on socio-economic variables and, by so doing, would discriminate against various minority groups (Blumstein, 1984: 135).

It has been suggested that an emerging, more sophisticated form of selective incapacitation may hold greater promise for the future. Cohen (1983a) has labelled this approach "criminal career incapacitation." It is based upon the identification of individual *criminal careers*, defined as the "pattern of offending engaged in by various categories of offenders" (Blumstein, 1984: 133). The object of this strategy is to use the information gathered about criminal careers in an attempt to identify those categories of offenders who, if released, would commit a large number of crimes. For example, it appears that robbery and burglary offenders commit these crimes at relatively high rates and yet have relatively short careers (Cohen, 1983a). Therefore, it would make sense to incarcerate such offenders for a relatively short period, and the result should be a significant reduction in the level of robberies and burglaries. Instead of locking up all those individuals who commit serious offences (collective incapacitation) or attempting to identify dangerous individuals on the basis of predictions about their future misconduct (selective incapacitation), the criminal career incapacitation strategy estimates, on the basis of information concerning the nature of criminal careers, the *probability* that certain categories of offenders will commit more crimes at a high rate of frequency. Using such estimates of probability the strategy would incarcerate such categories of convicted offenders for a period that is adequate to prevent them from re-offending. However, this approach is still at an early stage of development in the United States, and it seems reasonable to conclude that there is such uncertainty about the whole sentencing strategy of incapacitation that it would be unwise for Canadian courts to adopt the strategy as a major goal of sentencing in the foreseeable future.

Rehabilitation

During the last 15 years or so, the goal of rehabilitation has undergone a remarkable eclipse. The utilitarian notion that punishment can be justified by its rehabilitative effects has been overwhelmed by an increasing public clamour for punishment rather than treatment (Gibbons, 1982: 455) and by the belief that empirical research has failed to demonstrate that correctional programs are effective in reducing recidivism on the part of convicted offenders (Lipton, Martinson, and Wilks, 1975). Indeed, in the mid-1970s, Robert Martinson (1974) coined the phrase, "nothing works," which has had a major impact on criminal justice policy both in the United

States and in Canada. The problem is that most of the criticism of the goal of rehabilitation originally stemmed from the strong belief that imprisonment cannot, by any stretch of the imagination, be considered a strategy for reducing the rate of recidivism on the part of convicted offenders (Morris, 1974; Waller, 1974). Therefore, it has been accepted by Canadian courts that an offender should never be given a longer period of imprisonment than he or she would otherwise deserve, solely on the basis that such a term of imprisonment is allegedly necessary for the *treatment* or *rehabilitation* of the offender (Ruby, 1987: 26).

However, while few (if any) would argue that imprisonment has rehabilitative effects, it by no means follows that *community-based* correctional programs will not have any rehabilitative effects on at least some of those offenders who participate in them, despite the daunting methodological problems facing those evaluation researchers who seek to determine exactly what those effects might be (Gendreau and Ross, 1979).

If rehabilitation is a goal that a sentencing court *ought* to take into consideration, then it is clear that it may well conflict with other goals, such as deterrence. One leading Canadian commentator on sentencing (Nadin-Davis, 1982) has contended that the first step that is taken by judges in deciding upon an appropriate sentence is to resolve this conflict between goals. Nadin-Davis, therefore, suggests that sentencing courts are faced with a "primary decision" as to whether they should pursue the goal of deterrence and impose a sentence of imprisonment or a fine (according to the prevailing tariff) or whether they should impose an *individualized* sentence, which would consist of a disposition other than imprisonment or a fine. In the view of the Canadian Sentencing Commission (1987: 139), if a judge believes that a particular offender can be rehabilitated, then that offender should be given an individualized sentence that should be "neither a custodial sentence nor a fine."

Retribution

The doctrine of retribution has undergone considerable changes over the centuries. Historically, retribution was closely associated with simple revenge and was best encapsulated by the phrase "an eye for an eye and a tooth for a tooth," a doctrine that can be traced back to passages in the Bible and the Code of Hammurabai (Reid, 1982: 479). Under this doctrine, persons who transgressed the law were liable to be treated in the same fashion as they had treated their victims. Very few people would advocate this approach in the context of a modern criminal justice system, although some of those who advocate a return to the death penalty would be likely to use the approach as a means of justifying the imposition of this ultimate penalty for the ultimate crime of murder. However, it is an approach that can be applied only to homicide, since no one would seriously argue that we should burn down the houses of convicted offenders as a punishment for arson or mutilate those who have injured others in criminal assaults!

The notion of an "eye for an eye" is, therefore, only of historical interest rather than a current statement of the nature of the theory of retribution. Under this theory, punishment is imposed for its own sake, not because it is supposed to achieve any particular result such as deterrence or rehabilitation. Offenders are made to pay for their wrongdoing and to suffer by way of legal *retaliation* even if the punishment does not benefit either the offenders or others (Reid, 1982: 478). In other words, the focus of retribution is clearly upon the past, because it is not at all concerned with the *outcome* of punishment as a relevant issue in the sentencing process (C.S.C., 1987: 128).

Siegel (1983: 110) notes that it is an essential tenet of retribution that punishment is necessary in a "just society." In this perspective, punishment is viewed as a necessary method of maintaining the social equilibrium, which is disturbed when a crime is committed: "If a person acquires an unfair advantage by disobeying rules law-abiding citizens respect, then matters cannot be set straight until this advantage is erased."

Historically, retribution was advanced as a *justification* for the imposition of punishment because it emphasized the obligation placed upon society to punish those who committed crimes. However, as the Canadian Sentencing Commission has pointed out (1987: 141), retribution does not really provide a well-articulated rationale for imposing punishment, since the question "Why should a person be punished?" is answered by the rather lame statement that the offender has done something that *deserves* punishment — a classic example of circular reasoning!

In more recent years, proponents of retribution have advanced it as a reason for *limiting* the amount of punishment justified on other grounds such as deterrence or rehabilitation (Hart, 1968; Ruby, 1987: 12). In particular, it is contended that an offender should not be given a longer sentence of imprisonment than he or she "deserves" simply because such a sentence may have a deterrent value or because a lengthy period of incarceration is required in order to ensure rehabilitation. In other words, the "offender should not be treated as more (or less) *blameworthy* than is warranted by the character of his or her offence" (Siegel, 1983: 112). Most of the literature concerning this approach has originated in the United States, primarily because, until the mid-1970s, most American jurisdictions operated a system of indeterminate sentences, which placed great power in the hands of correctional authorities rather than the courts. It was strongly contended that such a system was basically unfair, since offenders who committed similar offences would be released at the end of vastly different periods purely on the basis of the parole board's predictions about their future behaviour (American Friends Service Committee, 1971; Kittrie, 1980; Reid, 1982: 481). In Canada, there are no indeterminate sentences (other than life sentences and the indeterminate detention of individuals who have been declared to be dangerous offenders), although the possibility of release on parole does lend an element of indeterminacy in the actual execution of a sentence handed down by a court. Although the American sentencing context is markedly different from that in Canada, the modern retributive approaches that have evolved south of the border are still of considerable significance to the evolution of criminal justice policy in Canada.

Just Deserts

The so-called just deserts perspective is the most influential of the attempts to use a form of retributivism as a means of limiting excessive punishment (C.S.C., 1987: 143; Siegel, 1983: 110). The most influential statement of this perspective was made in 1976 by Andrew Von Hirsch (1976). This scholar's main concern was not to justify the imposition of punishment but rather to limit the *quantum* of punishment meted out to the offender. For Von Hirsch, while sanctions must be justified by their preventive effects, those sanctions must nevertheless be commensurate with the degree of the offender's blameworthiness. In other words, punishment in an individual case should never exceed the level that is appropriate for the crime that has been committed. For example, suppose that two offenders have been convicted of offences of equal seriousness. It would be unjust, in light of the just deserts theory, to sentence one offender to a greater degree of punishment than the other simply because it is contended that a longer sentence of imprisonment will have a deterrent effect in the first case but not in the second. Similarly, it would be "unjust" to impose a significantly greater punishment than is "normal" simply because the court believes that such a sentence will have a strong deterrent effect in a particular local community that is experiencing a so-called crime wave.

It seems fair to suggest that the just deserts doctrine is beset by some major problems of a practical nature. While the general principle that punishment must be commensurate to the degree of blameworthiness of the offence is an attractive one in the abstract, applying it to specific cases is a complicated task. As Blumstein (1982: 310) notes,

> Offence seriousness is an extremely complex notion. At a minimum, it involves consideration of harm to the victim, malevolence of intent, degree of involvement, victim precipitation, prior relationship between the offender and the victim, premeditation, and many other factors associated with a combination of culpability and victim injury. Any demand for strict proportionality is thus far more difficult to implement than to articulate.

According to Blumstein (1982: 311–12), therefore, the just deserts principle can be applied only in a rather general sense, because it is clear that there is no *precisely calculable* sentence for any given crime. However, Blumstein (pp. 311–12) suggests that, for any specific offence, there is instead a "band of reasonable width to accommodate the variety of special circumstances associated with a particular offence and offender and any sentence within that band can reasonably be viewed as a 'just desert'." Therefore, the task of the sentencing process is to find the appropriate band so as to avoid imposing an "unjust desert."

The just deserts doctrine is not a goal of sentencing as much as it is a restraining principle that limits the *quantum* of punishment that may be imposed. The notion that the penalty imposed should be commensurate with the degree of the offender's blameworthiness clearly had a considerable influence upon the approach adopted by the Canadian Sentencing Commission, which in formulating its overall goal for the sentencing process noted that (1987: 152):

> If the fundamental purpose of sentencing is to preserve the authority of the law and to promote respect for it through the imposition of *just sanctions*, it follows that the principle of proportionality is given highest priority.

Denunciation

Denunciation has been identified as a goal of sentencing with increasing frequency; however, there are at least two quite different forms this goal has assumed. One form is based on the view that the sentencing process should serve an *educative function*. According to the Law Reform Commission of Canada (1974, 1976) the solemn imposition of a penalty in open court provides an undoubted opportunity for society to underline its basic values by strongly denouncing behaviour that is unacceptable. In this sense, it has been contended that the sentencing process has an educative effect that should consciously be taken advantage of by the courts. According to this view, therefore, the sentencing process can actually influence people's behaviour by indicating that unacceptable conduct will be punished.

The Canadian Sentencing Commission (1987: 142–43) has made the telling point that the denunciatory (or educative) aspect of sentencing can be effective only insofar as sentences are actually publicized. According to the Commission (p. 98), the evidence would appear to suggest that Canadians receive rather inadequate information about the nature of the sentencing process and, therefore, suffer from fundamental misconceptions about the nature of the process. The Commission also contends (pp. 142–43) that there is no empirical evidence to suggest that the degree of disapproval of any particular crime on the part of the public is either raised or lowered by information about sentencing. Indeed, the Commission suggests that public views about the seriousness of particular offences are moulded by other factors (such as the public's perception of the harm done or the offender's intent) than knowledge of the severity of the sentence imposed in court or the maximum penalty set by the *Criminal Code*.

Ruby (1987: 14) has contended that there is another form of the denunciation rationale that is beginning to influence Canadian courts and that is closely linked to the theory of retribution. This approach focuses on the need for sentences to express the abhorrence that society feels for certain types of serious crimes: as the Ontario Court of Appeal stated in one case:[2]

> The degree of repudiation to be expressed must itself be governed by the degree of disapproval which should be manifested by an average, high principled, intelligent citizen or, more accurately, by such a person's view of the gravity of the offence, not by what we judges as individuals with varying moral and religious opinions might reasonably consider proper.

As Ruby points out (1987: 14), the nature of the sentence meted out under this rationale is "inevitably harsh" because it is supposed to represent the revulsion of society in the face of what are, by definition, horrible crimes. However, it is very difficult for the courts to determine what the average, "high principled" Canadian really feels about any particular crime, and, furthermore, there is the very real danger that emotional public reaction, as expressed in the press and the electronic media at the time of a trial, may result in a much more severe sentence than would be imposed if a just deserts philosophy were being applied.

There is little doubt that none of the traditional justifications for punishing offenders can be converted into a single, overall goal of sentencing. To date, research into the deterrent, incapacitative and rehabilitative effects of punishment has been relatively inconclusive. Furthermore, there are serious doubts about the efficacy of the sentencing process as an educative or denunciatory device. Finally, the philosophy of retribution, as it has evolved in recent times, and the just deserts philosophy are not so much aims of sentencing as principles that limit the *quantum* of punishment meted out by the courts. One cannot fail to be attracted by the conclusion of the Canadian Sentencing Commission (1987: 145) that we know much more about what punishment *cannot do* than about what it *can actually achieve* and what should really justify its imposition. In these circumstances, the Commission strongly recommends that there is a great need for restraint in the use of punishment, since pain and deprivation are its direct consequence and society is uncertain about its benefits either to the offender or to society in general.

The Commission (1987: 145) raises the question of why such goals as deterrence, rehabilitation and incapacitation figure so prominently in most discussions about the justification for punishment, when it is increasingly clear that the sentencing process can have at best only a very limited capacity to prevent crime. The Commission suggests that punishment meets some deep-seated needs in our psychological make-up:

> Even if punishment cannot ultimately be justified, it apparently satisfies a strong desire, seated both in moral thinking and human emotions, and it cannot be re-

nounced. There is consequently a natural tendency to compensate for the limits of retributivism by attributing to penal sanctions an efficiency in preventing crime which they do not really possess.

Although there are major problems associated with the adoption of any of the traditional goals of sentencing and justifications for punishment, they continue to figure prominently both in the sentencing literature and in the opinions of the courts (Ruby, 1987: c. 1). It remains to be seen whether the Canadian Sentencing Commission's statement of the fundamental purpose of sentencing will be adopted in the future. In the meantime, the sentencing process will continue to be affected by conflicting goals and a lack of knowledge about the wisdom of pursuing such goals.

Public Opinion and Sentencing

In recent years, it has become almost axiomatic that Canadians consider the courts to be too lenient in their sentencing practices (Doob and Roberts, 1984). Indeed, on the basis of a nation-wide gallup poll, Doob and Roberts (1983: 1) found that 79.5% of Canadians believed that sentences in criminal courts were "too mild." The negative evaluation of the judiciary, in this respect, obviously creates a major problem for the public's overall confidence in the criminal justice system. The question clearly arises why there should be such a major discrepancy between the views of the judges and the views of those members of the public, who express an opinion on the appropriateness of judicial sentencing practices.

Doob and Roberts (1983) have demonstrated that this discrepancy is the result not so much of a basic philosophical difference between the public and the courts as of an "information deficit." On the basis of a number of empirical studies, these researchers concluded that when members of the public were furnished with background information concerning both offences and offenders, they were much more likely to recommend sentences that parallelled those imposed by the courts. In other words, there is a world of difference between answering a totally abstract question concerning whether the courts are dealing too leniently with offenders and being asked to consider an appropriate sentence while in possession of knowledge concerning the detailed circumstances surrounding the particular offence and the individual offender.

Doob and Roberts (1983: 11–12) suggest that the press plays an important role in shaping the public's perception that sentences are too lenient. As they point out, public opinion concerning sentencing is more likely to be moulded by what is reported in the media than by direct knowledge of what is actually happening in the courts. Unfortunately, it would appear that the media provide inadequate and selective information about sentencing. In particular, it is unlikely that the media will report run-of-the-mill cases, choosing instead to focus on those that are in some way exceptional or sensational (C.S.C., 1987: 96). Furthermore, the press and television tend to focus upon violent crime, thereby creating the impression that there is more violence in crime than there really is (C.S.C., 1987: 97). Indeed, a majority of Canadians in a gallup poll seriously overestimated the extent to which violence is involved in crime in Canada (Doob and Roberts, 1984: 271), and this preoccupation with violent crime probably influenced their perception that sentences were, in general, too lenient.

Doob and Roberts (1983: 19) emphasize that one's first "gut reaction" to a report of a serious criminal offence is almost certain to be one of moral outrage. However, this initial reaction would probably be modified once the various mitigating circumstances were made known. Unfortunately, media reports of sentencing practices are more likely to refer to the heinousness of a particular offence than to dwell on the mitigating factors that are usually present in most criminal cases. Doob and Roberts, therefore, urge that decision makers place relatively little weight on the public clamour for more harshness in sentencing:

> Those, then, who urge that the policy maker and the court follow the one-dimensional cry for judicial harshness in sentencing are not taking into account the willingness of Canadians to consider the complexity of each case on its own and the willingness of Canadians to temper their calls for harshness if the full facts of the case warrant it.
>
> Public opinion about the criminal justice system is important, but only the naive politician or judge would urge that a badly informed public be followed blindly.

It is clear that an important implication of this type of research is that there is a pressing need for more effective education of the public concerning this vital, albeit complex, process in the Canadian criminal justice system. The Canadian Sentencing Commission (1987: 98) points out, quite correctly, that media reports are only one of many reasons why the public has formed the view that sentencing practices in Canada are too lenient and it would be unfair to place all the blame for public misperceptions about sentencing upon the shoulders of reporters. However, the Commission concluded that

> . . . the analyses reported here do suggest that with little additional effort newspapers might present a more informative picture to their readers. In terms of public reactions to individual cases, the public might respond quite differently if it had reference points such as the maximum penalty and the average sentence.

The Commission also takes account of the fact that more systematic and adequate information has to be made available to reporters if they are to fulfil their responsibilities to the public. For example, it is still quite difficult to obtain information about average sentences, because there are no comprehensive, national statistics on sentencing. According to the

Commission, however, its recommendations for the reform of the sentencing process in Canada will render it much more understandable to both reporters and the public alike, thus contributing to the gradual elimination of some of the fundamental misconceptions that currently plague public attitudes to sentencing in Canada.

Sentencing Disparity and Discrimination

The problem of sentencing disparity has been identified as one of the major issues that should be addressed in any contemporary proposals for reform of the Canadian criminal justice system (Linden, 1986: 3), and this concern has been given new impetus by the advent of the *Charter*, which might well be interpreted in such a manner as to render excessive sentencing disparity unconstitutional (Jobson and Ferguson, 1987: 18).

Canada is a geographically immense country (with significant differences between the various provinces, territories and regions); since the *Criminal Code* generally leaves an enormous degree of discretion in the hands of the courts, it is scarcely surprising that it is often claimed that there is a considerable degree of sentencing disparity across the country. The maximum penalties in the *Criminal Code* provide little guidance to the courts, since they are set at a level that is generally far too high except for the most serious cases (C.S.C., 1987: 63*ff.*). Furthermore, the lack of guidance available to judges has been exacerbated by the complete absence of comprehensive court statistics gathered on a "national and continuing basis" (C.S.C., 1987: 61). Indeed, the last comprehensive, national sentencing data were released by Statistics Canada as long ago as 1978 (C.S.C., 1987: 60). As the Canadian Sentencing Commission (1987: 62) points out,

In the present system, where there are no formal "standards" against which to judge a sentence, the lack of systematic sentencing information accessible to judges in their determination of sentences almost ensures that there will be unwarranted variation in sentences.

Although both the Crown and the offender have the right to appeal against a sentence handed down by a trial judge, the system of appeal courts is not suited to establishing uniformity of sentencing on a *national* basis. While the Supreme Court of Canada has the power to hear appeals on all sentencing matters, its policy is to deal only with sentencing matters raising questions of law (C.S.C., 1987: 70). Therefore, the ten provincial Courts of Appeal effectively serve as the final tribunal on sentencing matters; this means that, instead of one court attempting to achieve sentencing uniformity on a national basis, there are ten different courts attempting to achieve such uniformity on a purely provincial basis. Furthermore, only a few of the Courts of Appeal have, to date, given trial courts specific guidance on the appropriate range of sentences that should be imposed in relation to different categories of offence (in other words, the Courts of Appeal have not shown a preference for the formulation of a sentencing tariff that gives concrete guidance on what the "going rate" is for specific offences) (C.S.C., 1987: 70).

Given this background, it is almost inevitable that there should be evidence of sentencing disparity across Canada. There are significant variations in the manner in which different offence categories are assigned sentences in the various provinces (Hann et al., 1983; Hann and Kopelman, 1986). Furthermore, there is clear evidence that there are significant sentencing variations within the various provinces themselves. For example, Murray and Erickson (1983) found widespread disparity in the sentencing of offenders charged with the possession of *cannabis* in five locations in Ontario. Similarly, in his classic study of magistrates' courts in Ontario, Hogarth (1971: 12) concluded that these courts varied "immensely" in terms of their sentencing practices:

> In the course of one year, one court used probation in nearly half of the cases coming before it, while another never used this form of disposition. Similarly, the use of suspended sentence without probation ranged from 0 to 34 per cent, fines from 2 to 39 per cent, short-term gaol sentences from 4 to 60 per cent, reformatory sentences from 1 to 37 per cent and long-term penitentiary sentences from 0 to 23 per cent. These differences appear to be too large to be explained solely in terms of differences in the types of cases appearing before courts in different areas.

Nevertheless, it is clear that a wide disparity in the sentencing of similar cases offends the basic notions of fairness held by most Canadians (Nadin-Davis, 1982: 8). As one Canadian Provincial Court Judge put it: "[T]he notion of uniformity of sentence . . . is an essential consideration in the fair and just administration and enforcement of the criminal law in any democratic society."[3] Indeed, it is primarily because of the need to control disparity in sentencing that, as we shall see, the Canadian Sentencing Commission (1987: 269*ff.*) has strongly recommended the introduction of a system of sentencing guidelines in Canada.

However, before discussing the research concerning unwarranted variations in sentencing practices, it is necessary to clarify the whole notion of disparity. In an excellent discussion of this issue, Forst (1982) emphasizes that the "essence of disparity is variation from some norm or standard" (1982: 24). However, in his view, the problem is that there are differing views on the exact nature of the norm or standard from which the alleged variation may be measured. Forst contends that there are two main approaches in this respect. The first views disparity as a variation from some norm of *proportionality*, while the second conceptualizes disparity in terms of variations from *statistical patterns* of sentencing. Suppose, for example, that a trial judge imposes a sentence of life imprisonment upon a first offender for a "simple" breaking and entering of a dwelling house. While this punishment is permitted by the *Criminal Code*,[4] most persons would regard it as disproportionate to the inherent seriousness of the offence; therefore, the sentence could be regarded as *disparate* in the first sense of the word. On the other hand, suppose that a researcher analyzed the dispositions of the court concerned and discovered that all first offenders, convicted of breaking and entering a dwelling house, were sentenced to life imprisonment. In these circumstances, although there is disparity in terms of there being a variation from a norm of proportionality, there is no deviation from the statistical patterns observed in the particular jurisdiction; therefore, there is no *disparity* in the second sense. In other words, as Forst (1982: 25) indicates, offenders in a certain offence category (such as breaking and entering) may well be treated uniformly but not with proportionality. Conversely, a judge could well impose a disposition that, while it clearly deviates from a statistical pattern, nevertheless does conform to a norm of proportionality. In the second sense of the word, the inherent justice or proportionality of a sentence is irrelevant; all that matters is whether or not it deviates from the statistical pattern.

Most researchers have adopted the second approach to the conceptualization of disparity. Within this approach, the focus is upon the issue of whether "similar" cases are treated *differently* by the courts. However, while there is considerable agreement that unjustified disparity occurs when similar cases are treated differently, there is remarkably little consensus regarding the criteria that should be employed in determining whether or not cases can be considered "similar" in the first place. Should the court consider only the nature of the offence committed or should it also take into account the prior record of the offender, the likelihood of the offender repeating the offence, his or her employment status, and so forth? While, in the United States, there has been an increasing desire to limit the scope of a sentencing court's deliberations to the seriousness of the offence and the prior record of the offender, in Canada the courts have continued to take a whole range of factors into account (Ruby, 1987: c. 6; Vining and Dean, 1980). Unfortunately for the researcher who attempts to investigate the issue of sentencing disparity, the greater the number of factors that may be taken into account, the more difficult it is to determine whether there has been dissimilar treatment of similar cases.

Nadin-Davis (1982) has contended that the sentencing process should be analyzed in terms of two distinct decision-making stages. The first decision is concerned with the *type* of sentence (e.g., imprisonment, fine, probation, etc.) that should be imposed. Nadin-Davis (1982: 3–6) suggests that this decision can be boiled down to a choice between a *tariff* disposition (such as imprisonment or a fine) and an *individualized* disposition (such as probation). The second decision-making stage is concerned, for example, with fixing the exact length of the prison term or probation order, or the precise amount of the fine. Where a tariff sentence is imposed, then according to Nadin-Davis (1982: 4), the sentencing court may turn for guidance to an appropriate "range of sentence" that has emerged in the evolution of the relevant case law. The precise placement of the particular case in the range for the offence concerned will be affected by certain aggravating or mitigating factors recognized in the case law (e.g., the presence of a lengthy prior record or the fact that the offender abused a position of trust may be regarded as aggravating factors, while the absence of a prior record, the youth or the mental illness of the offender may be considered mitigating factors). In Nadin-Davis's words (1982: 5):

> This choice between individualized and tariff sentencing may be phrased in a number of ways: treatment v. punishment, subjective sentencing v. objective sentencing, or sentencing the offender v. sentencing the offence.

In the view of Nadin-Davis (1982: 4), it is important to bear in mind that, while there is considerable uniformity in the length of prison terms or size of fines imposed in relation to a tariff sentence, such uniformity will necessarily be absent where the central focus is upon the individual offender rather than the offence (viz. in relation to an individualized sentence). However, Nadin-Davis (p. 14) contends that Canadian courts still apply certain clearly identifiable criteria in making the decision to impose an individualized sentence and do so in a *uniform* fashion. Unfortunately, Nadin-Davis has not yet provided empirical support for this analysis, although a study by Brantingham (1985) suggests that the analysis does bear some resemblance to the manner in which sentencing decisions are actually made.

What have researchers discovered in relation to the issue of sentencing disparity in Canada? There have been two major approaches that reflect, to some extent at least, both the methodological and theoretical predilections of the researchers. The first approach focuses upon the background characteristics of the judges themselves and suggests that the roots of disparity may best be sought in the social and psychological factors that impact upon the judicial decision makers. The second approach casts the spotlight upon the background characteristics of the cases and the offenders, and lends support to the notion that it is these factors that shape the outcome of the sentencing process.

The first approach is strongly represented by John Hogarth's classic work on sentencing in Canada (Hogarth, 1971). This researcher's basic premise was that sentencing must be regarded as a "human process" and is "subject to all the frailties of the human mind" (1971: 356). Hogarth studied the sentencing behaviour of 71 Ontario magistrates. He examined the background characteristics of magistrates, their penal philosophies, judicial attitudes, and socio-legal constraints on sentencing. Hogarth found that judicial attitudes and judicial perceptions of the facts of the cases accounted for a considerable proportion of the disparity in sentencing. Indeed, Hogarth (1971: 382) suggested that while only about 9% of the variation in sentencing practice could be accounted for by "objectively defined facts," more than 50% of this variation could be explained by "knowing certain pieces of information about the judge himself." In characterizing sentencing as a very human process, Hogarth (1971: 382), therefore, concluded that it is a

> ... dynamic process in which the facts of the cases, the constraints arising out of the law and the social system, and other features of the external world are interpreted, assimilated, and made sense of in ways compatible with the attitudes of the magistrates concerned.

Palys and Divorski (1984 and 1986) also concluded that judicial attitudes and perceptions are related to disparity in sentencing. Unlike Hogarth, who examined actual cases, these researchers applied the *simulated cases* approach, which involves presenting a group of judges with hypothetical cases and asking them to indicate what sentence they would impose (Palys and Divorski, 1984: 334). This approach permitted the researchers to employ a methodology in which the cases upon which the judges were asked to make judgments were held constant, thus permitting an "*unambiguous* demonstration of sentencing disparity" (Palys and Divorski, 1986: 349). It was found that there was a considerable degree of disparity among the sentences handed down by the judges, although the degree of disparity varied from case to case (Palys and Divorski, 1986: 353). In the case with the most marked degree of disparity — a case of assault causing bodily harm (involving the loss of sight in one eye) — sentences ranged from a $500 fine plus 6 months' probation to 5 years in a penitentiary. The researchers suggested that a major source of sentencing disparity could be found in the judges' differential subscription to legal objectives (e.g., rehabilitation, incapacitation, general deterrence), and the emphasis they placed on different case facts. The researchers suggested (1986: 358) that these two factors were closely related since "many, if not most judges perused case facts, chose salient ones, formulated legal objectives on this basis, and then proceeded to 'repackage' case facts in a manner which showed maximal harmony between legal objectives and case facts." This suggested to the researchers that the making of a sentencing decision and the justification of that decision are "two separate, sequential processes." In light of the finding by Hogarth and Palys and Divorski that the outcomes of sentencing decisions are strongly influenced by the particular sentencing philosophies of individual judges, the Canadian Sentencing Commission (1987: 77) suggests that the "primary difficulty with sentencing as it exists at the moment is that there is no consensus on how sentencing should be approached."

As noted earlier, there is a second type of research design that focuses upon the background characteristics of cases and offenders as a method of examining sentencing disparity (Brantingham, 1985). Quite often, such research is concerned with the issue of whether courts discriminate against certain groups of individuals, on the basis of socio-economic status, race, and so forth (Debicki, 1985; Renner and Warner, 1981).

Brantingham (1985) conducted a sophisticated statistical analysis of a large number of criminal cases decided in two Canadian courts during 1979 and 1980.[5] Brantingham found that the overall pattern of sentencing was one of "more consistency than inconsistency" in judicial decision making. The most important factors affecting decisions with respect to both the type of sentence to be imposed and the length of prison terms meted out were case facts (including, for example, the existence of aggravating factors, such as the use of weapons, and mitigating factors, such as provocation by the victim) and the prior record of the defendant. While there was some inconsistency on the part of individual judges, factors relating to judges were relatively unimportant in explaining sentencing outcomes as compared with the case facts and the prior record of the accused. While the study indicates that there was a certain degree of disparity in sentencing, the general conclusion appears to be that, overall, judges applied legalistic criteria fairly consistently in arriving at their decisions. Nevertheless, the study did find that, even with the numerous variables that Brantingham took into account, some 35% of sentencing outcomes were unpredictable and that "some proportion of these cases" probably reflected inconsistent sentencing patterns from case to case *even for the same judge.*

It has been strongly argued that while courts may apply legalistic criteria in a fairly consistent manner, the impact of their decisions, in fact, discriminates against certain disadvantaged groups within society. Mandel (1984) has noted that even if legalistic criteria are applied by the court in a consistent manner, the end result will still be discriminatory because the legal rules themselves are biased against those of low socio-economic status. For example, whether an offender is employed or unemployed may well affect the decision regarding the appropriate disposition made by the sentencing court. Those who would support such an approach may well argue that those who have steady employment have more to lose by being sentenced to imprisonment, while the fact of their employment demonstrates that they are a "better risk" to avoid re-offending. Furthermore, a court may feel that an unemployed person would not pay a fine, and therefore impose a sentence of imprisonment immediately. Thus, although the courts have applied legalistic criteria consistently, the result of this policy is discrimination against the poor.[6] There are two Canadian studies that suggest that this perspective is an appropriate one to apply to sentencing decisions in Canada.

Renner and Warner (1981) studied a number of cases heard by three magistrates' courts and two county courts in Halifax. The researchers found that even when the "legalistic" factors of nature of charge and prior record of the offender were controlled, unemployed persons were typically sentenced more severely than employed persons. Similarly, Debicki (1985) studied all 1,194 cases decided by the Winnipeg Provincial Court during a three-month period in 1983. He found (1985: 234) that there was evidence of differential sentencing on the basis of socio-economic status:

> Whether income, social status or type of job is used as a measure, similar results emerge. Those of lower socio-economic status are treated more harshly. The best measure has proved to be employment status. . . . The pattern is clear. Those who are employed pay for their crime with money, and those who are unemployed with a relatively short loss of freedom.

The research is inconclusive regarding whether there is a racial bias in Canadian sentencing practices. Renner and Warner (1981) found that sentencing patterns were significantly associated with the defendant's race; for example, white defendants who were first offenders convicted of summary charges were given discharges in 23% of cases, whereas black first offenders, in exactly the same circumstances, never received a discharge. On the other hand, Debicki (1985) did not find that there was a relation between sentencing severity and ethnicity insofar as the treatment of native Canadians was concerned. Much greater attention has been paid to this issue in the United States, where a consensus appears to be emerging to the effect that racial discrimination in sentencing is an extremely difficult phenomenon to measure because bias against certain racial groups may be very subtle in nature. For example, Zatz (1987: 86) contends that the most recent research has "consistently unearthed subtle, if not overt, bias." While race/ethnicity is not "*the* major determinant of sanctioning," it is nevertheless *a* "determinant of sanctioning and a potent one at that." In her view,

> . . . discrimination has not gone away. It has simply changed its form to become more acceptable. Increased formal rationality of the legal process has caused discrimination to undergo cosmetic surgery, with its new face deemed more appealing. The result is bias in a different form than it showed in the past. It is now subtle rather than overt. But, to borrow and twist an expression from Weber . . ., the "iron cage" still locks primarily minorities and lower class whites behind its bars.

In one study, for example, Zatz (1984) found that the offender's prior record, which many criminal justice commentators would consider to be a legitimate factor to take into account in the sentencing process, was, in fact, relied upon *differentially*, depending on whether or not the defendant was white, black or chicano.[7] This is a clear illustration of the subtle discrimination to which Zatz has referred. It has also been pointed out that until very recently, most research had ignored the effect of the *race of the victim* on sentencing practices; in this respect, it has been suggested that in the United States, harsher punishment appears to be imposed when the victim is white than when the victim is black (Hawkins, 1987; Farrell and Swigert, 1986). This represents another example of "masked" discrimination in the sentencing process. It is hoped that Canadian researchers will soon bring their attention to bear on some of the complicated issues raised by the American research literature dealing with sentencing discrimination.

Reform of the Sentencing Process: The Recommendations of the Canadian Sentencing Commission

We have already seen that the Canadian Sentencing Commission has recommended that a major objective of sentencing reform should be to reduce reliance on imprisonment as a disposition and to encourage a much greater use of community-based sentences as an alternative to imprisonment in all but the most serious cases. This critical recommendation, however, constitutes only one component of an ambitious blueprint for sentencing reform in Canada. What are the principles underlying the construction of this blueprint for sentencing reform?

First, the Commission (1987: 164) emphasized the need to bring clarity into the sentencing process: "To the greatest extent possible, this involves bridging the gap between the meaning of a sentence, as written in the law and as pronounced by the court, and its subsequent translation into practice." Second, the Commission (1987: 165) stressed the need for restraint in the imposition of punishment, particularly since there is little evidence to suggest that sentencing decisions can *per se* have much of an impact upon reducing the level of crime in society. Third, the sentencing process should be seen as both fair and equitable, and in order for this to be achieved, there must be some kind of structure that gives meaningful guidance to the courts regarding the factors that should be taken into account in imposing a sentence (p. 167). Such a structure (in the form of sentencing guidelines) is deemed to be the most practical way to reduce the problems caused by sentencing disparity. Fourth, the Commission (p. 167) emphasized that it was seeking to devise a blueprint for sentencing reform that was specifically appropriate to the unique nature of the Canadian context, including Canada's geographic and cultural diversity and the broad scope of Parliament's criminal law jurisdiction, which applies to the whole country.

It would be impossible to analyze the Commission's detailed proposals in any great depth in this textbook. However, the highlights of the proposals will be presented and, where appropriate, will be discussed. The Commission's own summary (1987: 170) of these highlights is as follows:

a) Elimination of all mandatory minimum penalties (other than for murder and high treason).
b) Replacement of the current penalty structure for all offences other than murder and

high treason with a structure of maximum penalties of 12 years, 9 years, 6 years, 3 years, 1 year, 6 months.

c) Elimination of full parole release for all sentences other than mandatory life sentences.

d) Provision for a reduction in time served for those inmates who display good behaviour while in prison.

e) Elimination of "automatic" imprisonment for fine default to reduce the likelihood that a person who cannot pay a fine will go to jail.

f) Establishment of presumptive guidelines that indicate whether a person convicted of a particular offence should normally be given a custodial or a community sanction. In appropriate cases the judge could depart from these guidelines.

g) Establishment of a "presumptive range" for each offence normally requiring incarceration. Again the judge could depart from the guidelines in appropriate cases.

h) Creation of a permanent sentencing commission to develop presumptive ranges for all offences, to collect and distribute information about current sentencing practice, and to review and, in appropriate cases, to recommend to Parliament the modification of the presumptive sentences in light of current practice or appellate decisions.

Perhaps the most striking aspect of the Commission's proposals is the extent to which they would require that a prison sentence handed down in court bear a close resemblance to the sentence that is actually served. Under the proposals, an offender would be able to earn a reduction of up to 25% of the custodial part of his or her sentence for "good behaviour" (remission). However, apart from this concession, the time that an offender would serve in prison would be the term actually imposed by the trial judge. This proposal would, of course, necessitate the abolition of parole, which at present is responsible for much of the uncertainty and unpredictability concerning the actual length of sentences served in prison. It would appear that the Commission's approach has been strongly influenced by the just deserts philosophy, which advocates that sentence length should be determined by the seriousness of the offence and not by predictions about the offender's future conduct. In the words of the Commission (1987: 237),

> At the present time in Canada, sentences of imprisonment are both unclear and unpredictable. The absence of clarity and predictability can only have deleterious effects upon the administration of justice and perceptions of sentencing by offenders, the public and criminal justice professionals. One of the aims of the Commission's proposals is to eliminate the confusion surrounding terms of imprisonment and to enhance equity, clarity and predictability in the process.

It is interesting to note that the Commission also recommends (1987: 259) that judges should have more say in determining the *nature of the custody* in which those sentenced to prison serve their time. Indeed, it recommends that where a court imposes a custodial sentence, the judge should be able to recommend that the sentence be served in open or closed custody. This recommendation is another reflection of the Commission's desire to shift discretionary power from the correctional authorities to the courts.

The Commission (1987: 195*ff*.) recommends that there be a new structure of maximum penalties for offences other than murder and high treason; namely, 12 years, 9 years, 6 years, 3 years, 1 year and 6 months. It is important to bear in mind that under the Commission's recommendations, an offender would serve a greater proportion of his or her prison sentence than is the case in the existing system (at least 75%). As noted above in our discussion of the existing dangerous offender provisions, the Commission (1987: 213) also recommended that courts should be empowered to impose an exceptional sentence, whereby the term of imprisonment may be increased by up to 50% "where the judge feels that in the interests of security, a custodial term longer than the maximum penalty period is necessary."

The central feature of the Commission's blueprint is the recommendation that Canada adopt a system of sentencing guidelines. According to the Commission (1987: 271):

> A complete set of guidelines has four components: a sentencing rationale; guidance on what type of sanction is viewed to be appropriate; numerical ranges for sanctions which involve a determination of *quantum* (e.g., for imprisonment and fines); and finally an indication of the degree of constraint implied by the guidelines.

We have already discussed the Commission's proposed rationale for sentencing in the form of a "Declaration of the Purpose and Principles of Sentencing." The second component of the guidelines is the provision of guidance on the *type of sentence* that should be imposed. The guidance is provided in the form of a *presumptive disposition*, viz. a disposition that should normally be imposed. The Commission recommends that the guidelines should fix a presumptive sentence for each criminal offence. There would be four of these presumptive sentences (1987: 309*ff*.):

(1) An unqualified presumption of custody
(2) An unqualified presumption of non-custody
(3) A qualified presumption of custody
(4) A qualified presumption of non-custody

Unless a trial judge decides to depart from the presumptive disposition, then, in the case of an *unqualified* presumption, the offender will be sentenced to either prison or a non-custodial disposition regardless of the particular circumstances of the individual case. On the other hand, where there is a *qualified* presumption, consideration must be given to all the circumstances of the case in order to determine whether that presumption should prevail. For example, in the case of theft over $1,000, the Commission (1987: 313) suggests that there should be a *qualified* presumption of non-custody. This means that the usual sentence will be non-custodial in nature. However, in a case where the theft was very serious in nature (for example, $10,000 was stolen) and the offender has a long record of prior property offences, then custody would become the appropriate disposition. In pursuit of its task of structuring judicial discretion, the Commission (1987: 315) assigned a presumptive disposition to every offence in the *Criminal Code, Narcotic Control Act,* and *Food and Drugs Act.*

The proposed system of guidelines would also provide *numerical* guidance to judges imposing a term of imprisonment. Briefly, a custodial range of years or months would be assigned to each offence (e.g., 2 to 4 years for certain kinds of robbery). The custodial ranges would be broad enough to permit the judge to take account of the particular circumstances of the case and would be proportionate to the seriousness of the offence. The Sentencing Commission (1987: 316) notes that these custodial ranges would be developed by the permanent sentencing commission (whose establishment is recommended in the Sentencing Commission's report). The Commission (p. 318) suggests that the use of the guidelines should result in an overall decrease in the use of incarceration and an eventual reduction in the prison population.

What is the degree of constraint implied by the guidelines? To what extent must judges apply the guidelines in a "slavish way"? The proposed guidelines permit a trial judge to depart from the indicated sentence in certain circumstances. However, if a judge wishes to impose a sentence that departs from the sentencing guidelines, then he or she must give written reasons (C.S.C., 1987: 303). The Commission (1987: 320) prepared a list of aggravating and mitigating factors that would justify a judge's departing from the guidelines. For example, among the aggravating factors are the existence of a prior criminal record and the use of excessive cruelty in the commission of an offence, while mitigating factors include the absence of previous convictions and the existence of mental impairment on the part of an offender. In giving reasons for departing from the guidelines, the judge would be required to identify the aggravating or mitigating factors that would justify such a departure. The Commission (p. 305) recommends that either the Crown or the defence should be able to appeal a sentence, whether or not it departs from the guidelines.

It is important to note that the Sentencing Commission (1987: 302) decided not to make the guidelines purely *advisory* in character, as was the case in those United States jurisdictions that were among the first to adopt a system of guidelines. The evidence from the United States indicates that voluntary compliance with purely advisory guidelines was disappointingly low (Blumstein, 1982; Cohen and Tonry, 1983; Rich et al., 1982). However, when guidelines have the force of law, it appears that there is a much greater degree of judicial compliance with them in the United States (Kramer and Lubitz, 1985). The Canadian Sentencing Commission (1987: 305) rejected the notion that the sentencing guidelines should be enacted as legislation. However, it did recommend (p. 308) that they be submitted to Parliament and come into effect within 90 days unless rejected by a negative resolution of the House of Commons. The guidelines would not be binding in the sense that a judge cannot depart from the presumptive sentences; however, if he or she does so, such a departure must be justified in writing and it is always open to review by a Court of Appeal. In this sense, although the proposed sentencing guidelines do not impose unbreakable fetters upon trial judges, they do require them to justify any departure from the indicated sentences, and this requirement is likely to ensure a high degree of compliance in Canada.

It is also important to recognize that the Commission decided not to follow the model set by the earliest sentencing guideline systems that were established in the United States, which merely *codified existing sentencing practice* (Wilkins et al., 1978). Instead, the Commission adopted the approach by such states as Minnesota (Minnesota Sentencing Guidelines Commission, 1981), whose sentencing guidelines went far beyond the mere codification of existing practice; indeed, under this approach, the Minnesota Sentencing Guidelines Commission formulated its "own schedule of sentences based on normative principles" (Blumstein, 1982: 322). The adoption of this normative approach by the Canadian Sentencing Commission is illustrated by its clearly articulated desire to change Canadian sentencing practice in the direction of reducing the use of the sanction of imprisonment and fostering a greater use of community sanctions.

An important element in the system of sentencing guidelines, proposed by the Commission (1987: 437*ff.*), is the creation of a permanent sentencing commission, the majority of whose members would be drawn from the judiciary. Among the commission's numerous functions would be the establishment and administration of a sentencing information system; the development and revision of the national guidelines for presumptive dispositions and the range of sentences; the making of recommendations to Parliament on matters such as the revision of maximum penalties for offences; and conducting research and providing information on sentencing. However, the Canadian Sentencing Commission (p. 328) wished to maintain a major policy-making role for the Courts of Appeal and recommended that they be granted the power to set policy governing the actual application of sentencing guidelines and, most significantly, to amend the presumptive custodial ranges for "substantial and compelling reasons." In this sense, the various provincial Courts of Appeal would not be totally excluded by the national sentencing commission from policy-making in sentencing matters. In a country as large and diverse as Canada, it clearly makes sense to encourage such a role for the provincial Courts of Appeal.

The proposal for a system for sentencing guidelines is not a revolutionary concept. Guidelines have been used for more than a decade in many United States jurisdictions, and other Canadian bodies, such as the Law Reform Commission of Canada, have recommended the establishment of systems similar to that proposed by the Canadian Sentencing Commission. Indeed, the Law Reform Commission of Canada, in a submission to the Canadian Sentencing Commission (1987: 288) also recommended a system for structuring judicial discretion in the sentencing process, both as a means of reducing sentencing disparity and as a means of reducing an over-reliance on imprisonment. The Law Reform Commission recommended the creation of a permanent sentencing commission and the establishment of a system of *benchmark sentences* (see, generally, Jobson and Ferguson, 1987). Under this scheme, offences would be placed into five broad categories of seriousness and a benchmark sentence would be assigned to each category. According to the President of the Law Reform Commission (Linden, 1986: 5), a "benchmark punishment would be an indication of the usual disposition of a case." Judges would be able to depart from the benchmark punishment; however, any such departure would be limited to a 10% or 15% variation, depending on the appropriate aggravating or mitigating circumstances (although a court could impose a greater or lesser punishment where a "clearly compelling reason" exists for going outside the 10% or 15% variation).

The Canadian Sentencing Commission (1987: 301) ultimately decided that the benchmark system was not "wholly satisfactory for the Canadian criminal justice system." The major problem with the benchmark system appears to be that it is too simplistic in its basic structure. The small number of categories of offences are, of necessity, very broad and include offences in relation to which present sentencing practice varies considerably. In the view of the Canadian Sentencing Commission (p. 300): ". . . the benchmark approach allows for too little differentiation between the classes of offences and it forces uniformity on a diversity of practices." The Sentencing Commission (p. 301) also rejected the Law Reform Commission's benchmark approach because it placed very little emphasis on the offender's prior record. In the view of the Sentencing Commission, such an approach would represent a major departure from present sentencing practice in Canada, which places considerable emphasis upon this factor. In any event, it is significant that both the Law Reform Commission and the Canadian Sentencing Commission have proposed similar solutions to the problems of sentencing disparity and excessive use of imprisonment.

Of course, there are many criticisms that may be made of the Sentencing Commission's proposals. Some critics of the sentencing guidelines approach (e.g., McIntyre, 1985: 217) have voiced the concern that the establishment of a separate sentencing commission will add an unnecessary "new bureaucracy" to "our already cumbersome criminal process." Such critics would prefer to rely on a system in which the appellate courts took more responsibility for articulating sentencing principles. Vining and Dean (1980: 147) suggest that an "extensive analysis of appellate sentencing decisions, in all provinces, will encourage the development of sentencing principles that are empirically grounded (that is, judges actually utilizing such factors) and are normatively sound." This criticism may have some validity, but it is important to recognize that the Commission's proposals *do* include a major role for the provincial Courts of Appeal. Furthermore, it might be contended that a national sentencing commission is particularly necessary in a large country such as Canada in which there is one *Criminal Code* that is applicable from west to east and north to south.

Palys (Palys and Divorski, 1986: 360) suggests that guidelines *will* be of some benefit to judges because they will point out the "going rates" for particular offences and, hence, reduce one potential source of sentencing disparity (namely, misperceptions regarding what sentencing standards are). However, he questions the assumption, implicit in the guidelines approach, that it is the *amount of discretion per se* that causes sentencing disparity. In fact, the Palys and Divorski study found that the amount of discretion that the judges had in relation to sentencing an offender for any particular offence had no effect on the degree of sentencing disparity that was evident in the various, hypothetical cases the researchers presented to their sample of judges. Indeed, they found that it was in the case where there was the greatest amount of discretion that the judges showed the least disparity! In Palys's view, it would be preferable to legislate sentencing objectives rather than to establish sentencing guidelines, because it is the judges' differential subscription to legal objectives that accounts for a considerable proportion of sentencing disparity. In addition, Palys rightly points out that a reduction in disparity does not necessarily equate with justice in any given case. As noted above, if the factors applied in the making of sentencing decisions are, in some way, biased against a particular group in society, the consistent application of those criteria will result in injustice even if there is no disparity (Griswold, 1985). However, in defence of the Canadian Sentencing Commission's proposals, it should be noted that the proposed list of aggravating and mitigating factors (C.S.C., 1987: 320) is strikingly free from the socio-economic variables that are likely to discriminate against those of lower socio-economic status.

It is always possible that any major reform of the sentencing process, along the lines recommended by the national Sentencing Commission, could be frustrated by the exercise of discretion elsewhere in the criminal justice system (MacMillan, 1984; Rothman, 1983). The possibility of the parole system defeating the purpose of the guidelines would be avoided if parole were abolished, as recommended by the Commission. However, if the abolition of parole were not implemented along with the remainder of the sentencing guidelines "package," then there is the very real possibility that the clarity and equity sought in the guidelines would be counteracted by the inherent uncertainty generated by parole decisions, which unlike the original sentencing decisions, place considerably less emphasis upon the seriousness of the offence committed.

The reduction of the degree of discretion exercised by judges could well increase the power of other actors in the system, such as the police or Crown counsel (Rothman, 1983). The major threat to any system of sentencing guidelines is that plea bargaining may defeat the underlying intent to bring about greater equity in the sentencing process (Verdun-

Jones and Hatch, 1985). By controlling the charge that may be laid, the prosecutor, to some extent at least, controls the ultimate sentence that may be imposed. Furthermore, plea bargaining can possibly result in the case facts presented to the court being highly selective, thus defeating the purpose of the guidelines, which depend on the availability of full case facts in order to establish the appropriate sentence. The Canadian Sentencing Commission (1987: 401*ff.*) clearly recognized this danger and recommended that there be much greater regulation of the processes of plea bargaining in Canada. For example, it recommended (p. 428) that the relevant federal and provincial authorities should formulate and attempt to enforce ethical guidelines in relation to plea bargaining and that they should establish guidelines restricting the power of the Crown to reduce charges in those cases where it has the means to prove a more serious charge. In addition, it recommended that a prosecutor should be required to justify a plea bargain agreement in open court (or in chambers if the public interest so requires). It may be suggested that the Commission's recommendations regarding the control of plea bargaining are vital to the ultimate success of the sentencing guidelines; if these recommendations are not implemented, then the goals of the sentencing guidelines are highly likely to be frustrated or thwarted.

It remains to be seen whether the Canadian Government as well as the provincial governments will be willing to adopt the recommendations of the Canadian Sentencing Commission. The sweeping nature of these recommendations means that it will be very difficult to implement them, given the inherent resistance of the criminal justice bureaucracy to fundamental change. The Commission's recommendations on this score clearly foreshadow a major change in the operation of the criminal justice system, with a significant degree of discretion being removed from correctional authorities and transferred to the courts. This proposed shift in the location of discretionary decision making, to some extent, reflects the fact that the majority of members serving on the Sentencing Commission were drawn from the ranks of the judiciary. However, one suspects that the Commission's proposal to abolish parole has strong popular support. It remains to be seen how the Commission's proposals fare in the political process that faces them in the future. There is no doubt that they will face strenuous opposition from some quarters. However, if they are ultimately implemented, they will effect the greatest change in the structure of sentencing in Canada since the *Criminal Code* was enacted almost a century ago.

NOTES

1. However, there is some evidence to suggest that even in such emotionally charged situations as domestic assaults, the use of arrest by the police is considerably more effective in reducing subsequent assaults than other, informal strategies (Sherman and Berk, 1984).

2. *R. v. Moore* (1979), 30 N.S.R. (2d) 638 at 652 (C.A.), cited in Ruby (1987: 14).

3. *Per* Reid P.C.J. in *R. v. McLean et al.* (1980), 26 Nfld. & P.E.I.R. 158 at 168; reversed 29 Nfld. & P.E.I.R. 194 (C.A.), cited in Nadin-Davis (1982: 8).

4. Section 348(1)(d).

5. The sample of cases was limited to those in which legal aid had been granted to the defendant.

6. Research conducted in the United States (Myers, 1987) suggests that socio-economic bias in sentencing practices is a complicated phenomenon and that its precise nature may well vary according to the nature of different communities, particularly the degree of economic inequality that may exist in any particular community.

7. Welch, Gruhl and Spohn (1984) also found an interaction between the variables of prior record and race. They contended that different types of prior record appeared to have different consequences for blacks as compared with whites (1984: 224).

REFERENCES

American Friends Service Committee. 1971. *Struggle for Justice.* New York: Hill and Wang.

Blumstein, A. 1982. "Research on Sentencing." 7 *Justice System Journal* 307–30.

——. 1983. "Selective Incapacitation as a Means of Crime Control." 27 *American Behavioral Scientist* 87–108.

——. 1984. "Sentencing Reforms: Impacts and Implications." 68 *Judicature* 129–39.

Brantingham, P. L. 1985. "Sentencing Disparity: An Analysis of Judicial Consistency." 3 *Journal of Quantitative Criminology* 281–305.

Bridges, G. S., and J. A. Stone. 1986. "Effects of Criminal Punishment on Perceived Threat of Punishment: Toward an Understanding of Specific Deterrence." 23 *Journal of Research in Crime and Delinquency* 207–39.

Canadian Sentencing Commission, Department of Justice. 1987. *Sentencing Reform: A Canadian Approach.* (Catalogue No. J2-67/1986E.) Ottawa: Supply and Services Canada. Reproduced with permission of the Minister of Supply and Services Canada, 1989.

Chambliss, W. J. 1967. "Types of Deviance and the Effectiveness of Legal Sanctions." 67 *Wisconsin Law Review* 703–19.

Cohen, J. 1983a. *Incapacitating Criminals: Recent Research Findings.* Washington, D.C.: National Institute of Justice.

——. 1983b. "Incapacitation as a Strategy for Crime Control: Possibilities and Pitfalls." In *Crime and Justice: An Annual Review of Research,* Vol. 5, edited by M. Tonry and N. Morris. Chicago: University of Chicago Press.

Cohen, J., and M. H. Tonry. 1983. "Sentencing Reforms and Their Impacts." In *Research on Sentencing: The Search for Reform*, Vol. 1, edited by A. Blumstein et al., 305–459. Washington, D.C.: National Academy Press.

Debicki, M. 1985. "Sentencing and Socio-Economic Status." In *Law in a Cynical Society: Opinion and Law in the 1980's*, edited by D. Gibson and J. K. Baldwin. Calgary: Carswell Legal Publications (Western Division).

Doob, A. N., and J. V. Roberts. 1983. *Sentencing: An Analysis of the Public's View of Sentencing*. Ottawa: Department of Justice, Canada.

———. 1984. "Social Psychology, Social Attitudes, and Attitudes toward Sentencing." 16 *Canadian Journal of Behavioural Science* 269–80.

Farrell, R. A., and V. L. Swigert. 1986. "Adjudication in Homicide: An Interpretive Analysis of the Effects of Defendant and Victim Social Characteristics." 23 *Journal of Research in Crime and Delinquency* 349–69.

Forst, M. L. 1982. "Sentencing Disparity: An Overview of Research and Issues." In *Sentencing Reform: Experiments in Reducing Disparity*, edited by M. L. Forst, 9–34. Beverly Hills, Calif.: Sage Publications.

Gendreau, P., and R. R. Ross. 1979. "Effective Correctional Treatment: Bibliotherapy for Cynics." 25 *Crime and Delinquency* 463–89.

Gibbons, D. C. 1982. *Society, Crime, and Criminal Behavior*. Englewood Cliffs, N.J.: Prentice-Hall, Inc.

Griswold, D. B. 1985. "Florida's Sentencing Guidelines: Progression or Regression?" 49 *Federal Probation* 25–32.

Hagan, J. 1982. *Deterrence Reconsidered: Methodological Innovations*. Beverley Hills, Calif.: Sage Publications.

Hann, R. G., et al. 1983. *Sentencing Practices and Trends in Canada: A Summary of Statistical Information*. Ottawa: Department of Justice, Canada.

Hann, R. G., and F. Kopelman. 1986. *Custodial and Probation Sentences Project: Overview Report and Individual Offence Reports*. Ottawa: Department of Justice.

Hart, H. L. A. 1968. *Punishment and Responsibility*. Oxford: Oxford University Press.

Hawkins, D. F. 1987. "Beyond Anomalies: Rethinking the Conflict Perspective on Race and Criminal Punishment." 65 *Social Forces* 719–45.

Hogarth, J. 1971. *Sentencing as a Human Process*. Toronto: University of Toronto Press.

Jobson, K., and Ferguson, G. 1987. "Toward a Revised Sentencing Structure for Canada." 66 *Canadian Bar Review* 1–48.

Kittrie, N. N. 1980. "The Dangers of the New Directions in American Sentencing." In *New Directions in Sentencing*, edited by B. A. Grosman, 32–50. Toronto: Butterworths.

Kramer, J. H., and R. L. Lubitz. 1985. "Pennsylvania's Sentencing Reform: The Impact of Commission-Established Guidelines." 31 *Crime & Delinquency* 481–500.

Law Reform Commission of Canada. 1974. *The Principles of Sentencing and Dispositions (Working Paper 3)*. Ottawa: Information Canada.

———. 1976. *A Report on Dispositions and Sentences in the Criminal Process: Guidelines*. Ottawa: Information Canada.

Linden, A. M. 1986. "A Fresh Approach to Sentencing in Canada." 48 *RCMP Gazette* 1–7.

Lipton, D., R. Martinson, and J. Wilks, 1975. *The Effectiveness of Correctional Treatment: A Survey of Treatment Evaluation Studies*. New York: Praeger Publishers.

MacMillan, A. I. 1984. "Equitable Sentencing: Alternatives in Reducing Disparity." 42 *University of Toronto Faculty Review* 184–93.

Mandel, M. 1984. "Democracy, Class and Canadian Sentencing Law." 21–22 *Crime and Social Justice* 163–81.

Martinson, R. 1974. "What Works?: Questions and Answers About Prison Reform." 35 *Public Interest* 22–54.

McIntyre, B. E. 1985. "Sentencing: The Need for Clear Standards." 27 *Criminal Law Quarterly* 212–25.

Miller, J. L., and A. B. Anderson. 1986. "Updating the Deterrence Doctrine." 77 *Journal of Criminal Law & Criminology* 418–38.

Minnesota Sentencing Guidelines Commission. 1981. *Minnesota Sentencing Guidelines and Commentary*, rev. ed. St. Paul, Minn.: Minnesota Sentencing Guidelines Commission.

Morris, N. 1974. *The Future of Imprisonment*. Chicago, Ill.: University of Chicago Press.

Murray, G. F., and P. G. Erickson. 1983. "Regional Variation in Criminal Justice System Practices: Cannabis Possession in Ontario." 26 *Criminal Law Quarterly* 74–96.

Myers, M. A. 1987. "Economic Inequality and Discrimination in Sentencing. 65 *Social Forces* 746–66.

Nadin-Davis, R. P. 1982. *Sentencing in Canada*. Toronto: Carswell.

Palys, T. S., and S. Divorski. 1984. "Judicial Decision-Making: An Examination of Sentencing Disparity Among Canadian Provincial Court Judges." In *Psychology and Law*, edited by D. J. Muller, D. E. Blackman and A. J. Chapman, 333–44. New York: Wiley.

———. 1986. "Explaining Sentence Disparity." 28 *Canadian Journal of Criminology* 347–62.

Reid, S. T. 1982. *Crime and Criminology*. 3rd ed. New York: CBS College Publishing.

Renner, K. E., and A. H. Warner. 1981. "The Standard of Social Justice Applied to an Evaluation of Criminal Cases Appearing before the Halifax Courts." 1 *Windsor Yearbook of Access to Justice* 62–80.

Rich, W. D. et al. 1982. *Sentencing by Mathematics: An Evaluation of the*

Early Attempts to Develop and Implement Sentencing Guidelines. Williamsburg: National Center for State Courts.

Rothman, D. J. 1983. "Sentencing Reforms in Historical Perspective." 29 *Crime & Delinquency* 631–47.

Ruby, C. C. 1987. *Sentencing.* 3rd ed. Toronto: Butterworths.

Sherman, L. W., and R. A. Berk. 1984. "The Specific Deterrent Effects of Arrest for Domestic Assault." 49 *American Sociological Review* 261–72.

Siegel, L. J. 1983. *Criminology.* St. Paul, Minn.: West Publishing Co.

Verdun-Jones, S. N., and A. J. Hatch. 1985. *Plea Bargaining and Sentencing Guidelines.* Ottawa: Canadian Sentencing Commission.

Vining, A. R., and C. Dean. 1980. "Towards Sentencing Uniformity: Integrating the Normative and the Empirical Orientation." In *New Directions in Sentencing,* edited by B. A. Grosman, 117–54. Toronto: Butterworths.

Von Hirsch, A. 1976. *Doing Justice: The Choice of Punishments.* New York: Hill and Wang.

———. 1984. "Selective Incapacitation: A Critique." 183 *NIJ Reports/SNI* 5–8.

Waller, I. 1974. *Men Released from Prison.* Toronto: University of Toronto Press.

Watson, R. E. L. 1986. "Research Note: The Effectiveness of Increased Police Enforcement as a General Deterrent." 20 *Law & Society Review* 293–99.

Webb, S. D. 1980. "Deterrence Theory: A Reconceptualization." 22 *Canadian Journal of Criminology* 23–35.

Welch, S., J. Gruhl, and C. Spohn. 1984. "Sentencing: The Influence of Alternative Measures of Prior Record." 22 *Criminology* 215–27.

Wilkins, L. T. et al. 1978. *Sentencing Guidelines: Structuring Judicial Discretion — Report on the Feasibility Study.* Washington, D.C.: U.S. Department of Justice.

Williams, K. R., and R. Hawkins. 1986. "Perceptual Research on General Deterrence: A Critical Review." 20 *Law & Society Review* 545–72.

Zapf, M. S. 1984. "Race, Ethnicity and Determinate Sentencing: A New Dimension to an Old Controversy." 22 *Criminology* 147–71.

———. 1987. "The Changing Forms of Racial/Ethnic Biases in Sentencing." 24 *Journal of Research in Crime and Delinquency* 69–92.

LEGISLATION

Criminal Code, R.S.C. 1985, c. C-46
Food and Drugs Act, R.S.C. 1985, c. F-27
Narcotic Control Act, R.S.C. 1985, c. N-1

10 THE STRUCTURE AND OPERATION OF CANADIAN CORRECTIONS

Any discussion of the structure and operation of corrections in Canada must consider the historical, social, and political context within which correctional systems developed. In the following discussion, we trace the historical response to crime and criminals in Canada and the emergence of the penitentiary as an instrument of punishment, control, and reform. We then examine the structure and operation of federal and provincial corrections today. Our discussion will reveal, among other things, that the use of prisons for punishment is a relatively recent development and that the term *corrections* is somewhat of a misnomer when applied to the ways in which Canadians have responded to criminal offenders throughout history and into contemporary times.[1]

Corrections in Early Canada

While the response to criminal offenders in Canada from early times to the present has been influenced by events in both England and the United States, Ekstedt and Griffiths (1988: 15) have argued that Canada has a unique correctional history, "one determined and influenced by the geography, political history, and governmental arrangements of the country as well as by economics, religion, and philosophical movements." These influences are evident in the sanctions used to respond to offenders in early Canada and in the decision to construct the first penitentiary in 1835.

Punishment in Early Canada

The nature and severity of the response to criminal offenders in the seventeenth and early eighteenth centuries reflected the adoption of the English criminal law in Lower and Upper Canada. The death penalty was inflicted on those offenders convicted of serious offences, while for less serious crimes, a wide variety of sanctions were utilized, including transportation, branding, fines, whipping, and confinement in the stocks or pillory. Punishment was progressive, Coles (1979: 1) noting that in Nova Scotia, "Murderers were hung while thieves were branded with the letter 'T' on first conviction and hung for a second offence." In 1640, a 16-year-old girl convicted of theft became the first person to be put to death in Canada (Cooper, 1987: 128).

Punishment was designed to shame and humiliate the offender, as well as to serve as a general deterrent for the community. As such, sanctions were often inflicted in public, and in many instances at the scene of the crime. Fox (1971: 146) describes the punishment of one Patrick Knowlan, convicted of stealing a bedspread from a store in St. John's, Newfoundland. After receiving 20 lashes,

> ... a halter was put around his neck and he was led to Mr. Prim's store where he received twenty lashes more on his bare back. Next, he was led to the Vice-Admiral's Beach and received another twenty lashes. In addition, all his goods and chattles were to be forfeited, he was to pay the charges of the court, and to depart the Island by the first vessel never to return on pain of having the same punishment repeated every Monday morning; and he was to be kept in prison until he went on board the ship.

Knafla and Chapman (1983: 258, 271) note that similar public punishments were administered in the Maritimes in an attempt to remind the public "of the dire consequences of crime." The stocks and the pillory were particularly suited for these purposes:

> The pillory stood in the centre of every market place and the men who were brought to it for punishment had an ear clipped off and nailed to the pillory, in addition to being whipped publicly ... When a prisoner was placed in the pillory, he faced the market where he was the recipient of thrown eggs and rotten vegetables.

Morel (1963: 28) reports the case of an offender, convicted of killing a Montreal merchant in 1692, who was condemned by a judge to have his right hand cut off and his limbs broken before being placed on a rack to die, all in front of the house of his victim. And Anderson (1982: 9) recounts the historical record, which indicates that 12 thieves, one of whom had stolen a bag of potatoes, were hanged in Halifax in 1795. In 1803, a 13-year-old boy was hanged in Montreal for stealing a cow, and in 1829, also in Montreal, three men were hanged for stealing an ox. The bodies of the hanged were often put on public display as a further deterrent to the citizenry.

Early Canadians also used banishment and transportation to rid themselves of troublesome citizens. Banishment was first used in Upper Canada in 1802, a convicted offender being ordered to "depart the province at his or her own expense and peril" (Edmison, 1976: 351). The use of transportation began in 1838, and until the practice was officially terminated in 1853, a large number of offenders were sent to England, Australia, and Bermuda.

Gaols in Early Canada

While Canadians utilized a wide variety of sanctions against offenders during the 1600s and 1700s, the use of incarceration as punishment for criminal offenders was not widespread. Municipal jails and lock-ups held individuals who were either awaiting trial or who had been convicted and were yet to be punished. A notable exception was in Nova Scotia, where a workhouse was constructed in 1754, patterned on the bridewell workhouses of England.

Prisoners in the workhouses were employed at a variety of tasks, including cutting granite and laying road bed. Coles (1979: 2) notes that by 1818 confinement in the workhouses had become the primary sanction in Nova Scotia. This system of workhouses, however, was to fail, an 1834 grand jury report stating that the facilities had deteriorated into a "miserable condition totally unfit to give shelter to Human Beings" (Coles, 1979: 7).

While legislation requiring the construction of houses of corrections was enacted in Upper and Lower Canada in the late 1700s, the historical record suggests that many municipalities did not construct such facilities (see Baehre, 1977; Splane, 1965). Canadians at this time took a very lenient approach toward criminal behaviour, largely because it was so rare. In the more unpopulated areas of the country such as the Maritimes and Rupert's Land in the west, authorities sent offenders to England for trial and punishment.

The houses of correction that were built were woefully inadequate, and conditions soon approximated those of their English counterparts. Baehre (1985: 12) describes the bridewell that opened in Halifax in 1790:

> It was a general house of confinement for criminals, delinquents, debtors, and other social problem types . . . no systematic classification of offenders was attempted. The building was often cold, damp, and unhealthy. Prisoners slept on straw; the quality of clothing, blankets, and food depended upon the prisoner's ability to pay. The poorest were sustained on a diet of molasses and tea. The jail keeper supplemented his meagre income by selling liquor to the prisoners.

The major problems were the lack of classification, the failure to separate juvenile and adult offenders, corrupt and brutal administrators, and the lack of employment within the institutions. The lack of adequate classification is evident in the criticisms of the local gaol by a grand jury in the York Assizes in 1850:

> "The unthinking boy, and the young girl, as yet unhackneyed in the ways of vice, untainted by the germ of immorality, incarcerated for the first time and perhaps for some reckless, freak, or trifling offence . . . are associated with the old, the profligate, the abandoned offender." [Cited in Beattie, 1977: 78–79]

Similar to their English counterparts, prisoners in these early Canadian gaols were subjected to considerable exploitation by their keepers. Coles

(1979: 2) notes that in Nova Scotia, where responsibility for operating the jails had been turned over to the municipalities in the late 1870s, prisoners "had to pay for meals and liquor as well as rent for themselves and upon release further handed the jailkeeper a fee for this service. Failure to make this payment could result in longer detention, though more commonly, a prisoner was allowed to beg in the streets for his jail fees." Despite various reform efforts, the poor conditions of confinement in municipal gaols and provincial institutions were to continue throughout the 1800s and into the early twentieth century.[2]

The Penitentiary in Canada: The Building of Kingston

One of the most significant developments in Canadian corrections was the building of the first penitentiary in Kingston, Ontario in 1835. The decision by Canadians to construct a penitentiary was influenced by social, political, and economic changes that were occurring in Canadian society in the early 1800s, as well as by events in the United States.

The use of penitentiaries for the long-term confinement of offenders had first appeared in the United States in the period between 1790 and 1830. Until the late 1700s, Americans had viewed crime as a natural part of society and of no great threat to community stability. The colonists believed that the best defences against crime were strong community relations built around the family and the church. Detention facilities held individuals awaiting trial or punishment, and there was no attempt to create programs or institutions to rehabilitate offenders. As in Canada, punishment was progressive, and repeat offenders who did not respond to fines and corporal punishment were put to death.

Toward the end of the 1700s, however, increasing urbanization and industrialization precipitated a shift in the perceptions of and response to criminal behaviour. A rise in population and increased social mobility led to a breakdown in the effectiveness of community-based mechanisms of social control. Previously viewed as an individual phenomenon, crime came to be seen as a consequence of family disorganization and community corruption. There was a need to create an environment in which the offender could be separated from the influences of a corrupt community and be reformed. The penitentiary would provide the training and discipline the individual had not received from the family, church, or community. The penitentiary also satisfied the criticisms of the Enlightenment writers and of religious groups such as the Quakers who argued for the development of alternatives to capital and corporal punishments.[3]

Two types of penitentiary systems emerged in the United States during the 1800s: the Pennsylvania, or "separate and silent," system in which prisoners were isolated from each other at all times in small cells, and the Auburn, or "congregate," system, which allowed prisoners to work and eat together during the day and then segregated them in individual cells at night. The Auburn system was operated under a strict "silent system" that forbade prisoners from communicating or even gesturing to one another, and was the model upon which most prisons in the United States and Canada were patterned.

The building of the Kingston Penitentiary was also the result of changes that occurred in Canadian society in the late 1700s and early 1800s. This was accompanied by a shift in the perceptions of crime. While historians disagree about whether there was an actual increase in the crime rate during the early 1800s (cf. Beattie, 1977; Bellomo, 1972), it is evident that Canadians became increasingly concerned with criminality, viewing it as "evidence of much deeper and more serious evils — evils that threatened the moral and social fabric of the society . . ." (Beattie, 1977: 2–3). Of considerable concern to Canadians were immigrants, particularly the Irish, and other individuals who "did not accept or had not been taught to accept the essential principles on which the social order rested" (Beattie, 1977: 2–3).

Canadians viewed crime as the consequence of "immorality, intemperance, lack of religious practices, idleness," and criminals comprised a "dangerous class" that was a clear threat to the stability of Canadian society (Bellomo, 1972: 11). In the view of legislators and others involved in design and construction, the penitentiary would provide an environment in which offenders could be educated and their ways corrected, and would serve as a model for both the offender and society (see Taylor, 1979). A similar function was assigned to the penitentiary constructed in Halifax in 1843 (see Baehre, 1985). As Ekstedt and Griffiths (1988: 30) note: "the prison would become the major weapon in the fight to insure order and stability, and the general principles upon which it would operate were the expiation of crime, the deterrence of potential crime, the protection of society, and the reformation of the convict." The building of the penitentiary was also facilitated by the overcrowded conditions in the local gaols and concern with the effectiveness of capital and corporal punishments.[4]

The Kingston Penitentiary opened in 1835. Unlike the local and district gaols, the penitentiary provided for the separation of offenders on the basis of sex and offence, and prisoners were given bedding, clothing, and adequate food. The cornerstones of the Kingston penitentiary were hard labour, silence, and strict adherence to prison regulations, all of which were designed to punish the offender as well as to reform him (Curtis et al., 1985). Prisoners were required to walk lock-step and were forbidden to "exchange looks, wink, laugh, nod, or gesticulate" (cited in Splane, 1965: 134). A similar regimen was imposed on the prisoners in the penitentiary in Halifax, completed in 1843, Baehre (1985: 18) noting the following regulations: "In passing to and from the cells, to and from the shops, and to and from their meals, the convicts must move in close single file with lock step, in perfect silence, and facing towards the officer in immediate charge of them . . ."

By the early 1940s, however, concerns were being voiced about the excessive use of corporal punishments within Kingston and the effectiveness of the prison regimen in reforming offenders. In 1848, a Royal Commission of Inquiry, chaired by the editor of the Toronto *Globe*, George Brown, was appointed to inquire into the operation of the Kingston Penitentiary and the activities of the warden, Henry Smith. In its first report, issued in 1848, the Brown Commission condemned the use of corporal punishment within the penitentiary and recommended the removal of the warden. While the Commission criticized the manner in which Kingston had been operated, it did not question the effectiveness of the structure of the institution and the regimen imposed upon the prisoners. Rather, the warden was blamed for failing to realize "the benefits to be derived from the silent system" (Beattie, 1977: 29).

In its second report a year later, the Commission proposed that the primary aim of the penitentiary should be the reformation of offenders. Although there is disagreement about the impact of the Brown Commission on correctional reform (cf. Baehre, 1977; Bellomo, 1972), the reports of the Commission do appear to have significantly influenced subsequent legislation. The *Penitentiary Act* of 1851, for example, established specific guidelines for the use of corporal punishments within the institution, specified that mentally ill offenders be moved to a separate institution, and provided for the appointment of two inspectors who would oversee the operation of the Kingston.[5]

At Confederation in 1867, the penitentiaries at Kingston, Halifax, and St. John, New Brunswick came under the legislative authority of Parliament, and with the passage of the *Penitentiary Act* in 1868, the federal penitentiary system was created. Additional penitentiaries were constructed in Montreal, Quebec (1873), Stony Mountain, Manitoba (1876), New Westminster, British Columbia (1878), and Prince Albert, Saskatchewan (1911). These institutions, many of which are still in operation in the 1980s, were the foundation of the federal correctional system in Canada (Zubrycki, 1980). Even with the expansion of federal and provincial systems of correction, it was not until the late 1930s that Canadian correctional policy incorporated the reformation and rehabilitation of the offender as an objective. However, as we shall see in our discussion of correctional treatment in Chapter 11, this model was to survive for only a relatively short period of time.

The Rise and Fall of Rehabilitation

In their examination of Canadian correctional history, Ekstedt and Griffiths (1988) identified several models of correctional practice. From the early 1700s until the late 1930s, punishment and penitence were the basis of correctional policy at the federal and provincial levels. It was not until the report of the Royal Commission on the Penal System of Canada (Archambault) issued in 1938 that the reformation of the offender was raised as an objective of the correctional system.

In the years following World War II, vocational training and education programs, as well as a wide variety of therapeutic techniques, were introduced into federal and provincial institutions. This was accompanied by the involvement of psychologists and psychiatrists in developing and operating correctional treatment programs. The increased emphasis on the rehabilitation of offenders received additional support from a Committee of Inquiry chaired by Mr. Justice Fauteux (1956). One of the more significant conclusions of the Committee was that individuals who violated the law had been somehow "damaged" in the process of growing up. This view of criminal offenders came to be known as the *medical model* and was a cornerstone of the myriad of correctional treatment programs that were developed during this time.

By the late 1960s, however, there was increasing concern with the effectiveness of correctional treatment programs in rehabilitating criminal offenders. In 1969, the Canadian Committee on Corrections (Ouimet) concluded that the reformation of offenders was more effectively pursued in the community than within correctional institutions. Imprisonment, the Committee argued, should be utilized only as a last resort.

A report of the Law Reform Commission (1975) and the report of the Parliamentary Sub-committee on the Penitentiary System in Canada (MacGuigan, 1977) further concluded that penal institutions should not be used for rehabilitative purposes. These reports precipitated the expansion of probation, parole and diversion programs and the development of community-based facilities and programs, particularly during the years 1970 to 1978, during what Ekstedt and Griffiths (1988) have labelled the *reintegration model* of correctional practice.

In 1977, a federal government task force proposed the adoption of the *program opportunities model*, whereby corrections would provide the programs for offenders, but it was the responsibility of the offender to take the initiative to participate in and benefit from them. No longer was criminal behaviour viewed as the symptom of some underlying disorder or sickness that required diagnosis and intervention. According to the Task Force (1977: 31), the program opportunities model was based on the principle that "the offender is ultimately responsible for his behaviour ... the offender is convicted and sentenced on the basis of his criminal behavior, not on the basis of some underlying personality disorder or deprived socioeconomic condition."

In adopting the opportunities model, corrections shifted total responsibility for reformation onto the offender and discarded previous claims of expertise in diagnosing and treating offenders. Cosman (1985: 13–14) has severely criticized the decision of federal corrections to implement the opportunties model:

This is as much an oversimplification as the deterministic view that preceded it. Many factors operate to influence human behaviour. Freedom of choice is not exercised in a vacuum. Man is not . . . completely master of his fate and captain of his soul. This so-called model is hardly a model at all. It is a design that is empty. It is based on nothing. It explains nothing. It says nothing about human development. And it says nothing about what rehabilitative activities should be carried out, in what ways, and why.

In its final report, the MacGuigan Sub-committee (1977: 160) declared that while an offender is responsible for his behaviour and for undertaking reformation, ". . . the penitentiary system must be structured to give positive support to his efforts by providing certain essential conditions: discipline, justice, work, academic and vocational training, and socialization." Our consideration of institutional treatment programs in Chapter 11 will suggest that while the responsibility for rehabilitation was shifted to offenders, in many instances the Correctional Service of Canada has not provided the environment of positive support deemed critical by the MacGuigan Sub-committee. Rather, during the late 1970s and into the early 1980s, Canadian corrections returned to the punishment objective based on the concept of reparation (see Ekstedt and Griffiths, 1988).[6] This shift is also noted in the report of the Canadian Sentencing Commission (1987).

Our brief review of the models of correctional practice indicates that since the 1700s, the rehabilitation and reformation of the offender in correctional institutions has been a formally stated objective for less than 20 years. In the next three chapters, we will explore further the issues surrounding the implementation and abandonment of the rehabilitation model, the expansion of community-based correctional programs, and the factors that appear to have influenced the return to punishment as a major objective of corrections.

Contemporary Canadian Corrections

In Canada, the responsibility for the provision of adult correctional services is shared between the federal, provincial, and municipal levels of government. The services and facilities can be divided into "custodial" and "non-custodial." Arrangements for the provision of correctional services for youths 18 years of age and under are quite different and will be discussed in Chapter 14.

Custodial facilities include RCMP/municipal lock-ups, provincial and federal institutions, and community-based facilities operated by the federal, provincial, and territorial governments and by the John Howard Society and the Elisabeth Fry Society on a contract basis (Figure 10.1). Within these facilities, a wide variety of programs and services are provided, including inmate employment and work programs and occupational/vocational training and counselling. Non-custodial programs and services include probation, parole, mandatory supervision and a variety of other programs that attempt to assist the offender within the community (Figure 10.2). In Chapter 11, we will explore further both custodial and non-custodial programs and services.

The basis for the split in correctional jurisdiction in Canada is the "two-year rule" that is embodied in section 731 of the *Criminal Code* of Canada. Those offenders who receive a sentence (or sentences) totalling two or more years fall under the jurisdiction of the federal corrections system, while those offenders receiving a sentence (or sentences) totalling less than two years are the responsibility of the provinces. The sole exception to this rule is in Newfoundland/Labrador, where the province maintains jurisdiction over federal offenders under an arrangement established when the province entered Confederation in 1949. Federal offenders in Newfoundland/Labrador can be transferred to federal facilities only with provincial consent.[7]

In 1987–88, the total average offender caseload for federal and provincial corrections (custodial and non-custodial) was 93,006. This represents a decrease of 15.3% from the previous year and a 13.8% decrease from 1982–83 (see Figure 10.3).

Federal Correctional Services

Federal correctional services for adult offenders are provided by two agencies — the Correctional Service of Canada (CSC) and the National Parole Board (NPB), both of which are part of the Federal Ministry of the Solicitor General. The CSC was created in 1979, when the Canadian Penitentiary Service and the National Parole Service were amalgamated, and is directed by a Commissioner of Corrections who is appointed by the Governor-in-Council under provisions of the *Penitentiary Act.*

The Correctional Service of Canada

The CSC is organized into three levels — national, regional, and institutional or district offices. The National Headquarters is in Ottawa, and there are five regional headquarters: Moncton, New Brunswick (Atlantic Region, including Newfoundland, Prince Edward Island, Nova Scotia, and New Brunswick), Laval, Quebec (Quebec Region), Kingston, Ontario (Ontario Region), Saskatoon, Saskatchewan (Prairie Region, comprising Manitoba, Saskatchewan, Alberta, and the Northwest Territories), and Abbotsford, British Columbia (Pacific Region, which includes British Columbia and the Yukon Territory) (Figure 10.4). These regional headquarters are responsible for administering the maximum, medium, and minimum security institutions, as well as the community correctional centres and forest work camps.

FIGURE 10.1
CUSTODIAL SERVICE IN CANADA

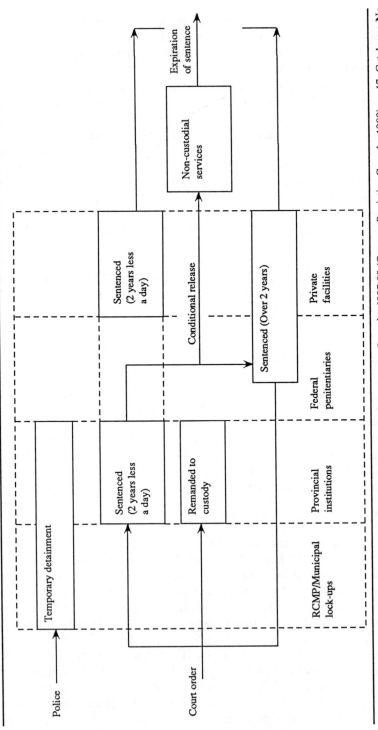

Source: Canadian Centre for Justice Statistics. *Adult Correctional Services in Canada, 1987-88* (Ottawa: Statistics Canada, 1989), p. 17. Catalogue No. 85-211. Reproduced with permission of the Minister of Supply and Services Canada, 1989.

In 1987–88, CSC was operating a total of 44 institutions: 2 high maximum security, 15 maximum security, 16 medium security, 11 minimum security facilities. In addition, CSC operated 14 community correctional centres (CCCs) (see Table 10.1). There are no federal institutions in Prince Edward Island, Newfoundland, the Yukon Territory, or the Northwest Territories. The CSC also operates 81 parole offices across the country and is responsible for the supervision of offenders on full parole, day parole, mandatory supervision, and temporary absences.

In 1987–88, approximately 11,079 persons were employed in federal corrections, providing custodial services (81%), administration and staff training (12%), and in parole offices (7%). These personnel were responsible for supervising, in custodial and non-custodial settings, approximately 19,304 offenders. These figures suggest that corrections is highly labour-intensive, which is one of the primary reasons for the escalating costs of corrections in Canada.

In fiscal year 1987–88, CSC spent approximately $781.1 million on custody (76%), administration for the CSC and the NPB (19%), and community supervision (5%). This represents a 2% decrease from 1986–87 and a 7% increase in expenditures from 1983–84. The average annual cost of maintaining an inmate during 1987–88 varied by the security level of the institution, from $22,000 per offender in community correctional centres to nearly $50,000 for a male offender in a maximum security facility. Even higher average annual costs are associated with incarcerating federal female offenders in Kingston Prison for Women — up to $60,000 per annum. In current dollars, the average daily cost for each federal offender in 1987–88 was $129. It is significant that while over 70% of all federal offenders were under some form of community supervision, only 5% of the expenditures were in this area, a further indication of the high costs of confinement.

The number of offenders incarcerated in federal facilities has shown a slight decrease since 1985–86 (see Figure 10.5).[8] During 1987–88, the average daily actual count of inmates in federal correctional facilities was 10,557, a 5% increase from 1986–87. This includes approximately 129 females confined in the Kingston Prison for Women, the only federal institution for female offenders in Canada. During the period 1983–84 to 1987–88, there was a 10% increase in average actual offender counts in Canadian institutions. Of the offenders admitted to federal facilities during 1987–88, 65% were serving sentences of less than four years, 37% were serving sentencs of two to three years and 22% were serving three to four year sentences. Four per cent of the admissions had been given sentences of ten years or more, and four per cent had been sentenced to either an indefinite sentence or life imprisonment.[9]

FIGURE 10.2
NON-CUSTODIAL SERVICES IN CANADA

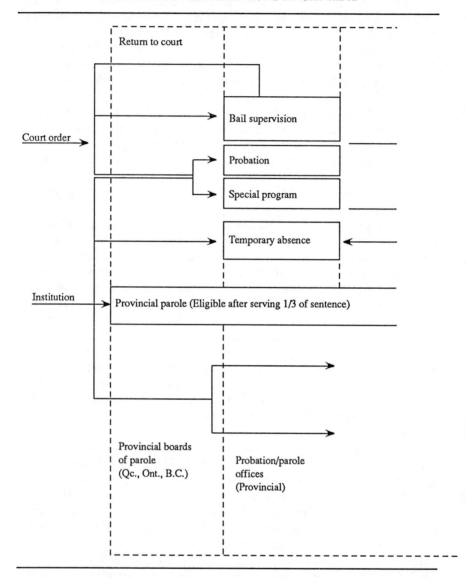

FIGURE 10.2
NON-CUSTODIAL SERVICES IN CANADA

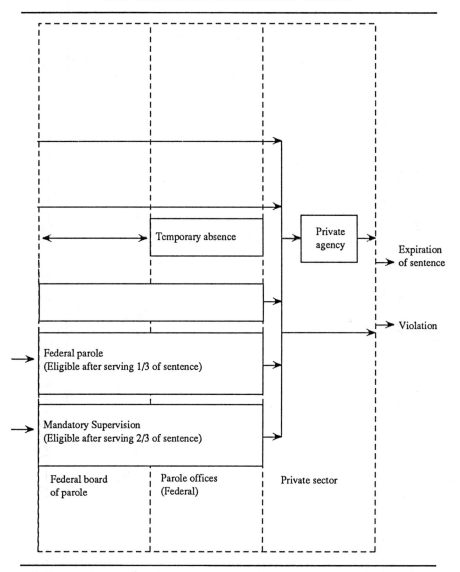

Source: Canadian Centre for Justice Statistics. *Adult Correctional Services in Canada, 1987-88* (Ottawa: Statistics Canada, 1989), p. 19. Catalogue No. 85-211. Reproduced with permission of the Minister of Supply and Services Canada, 1989.

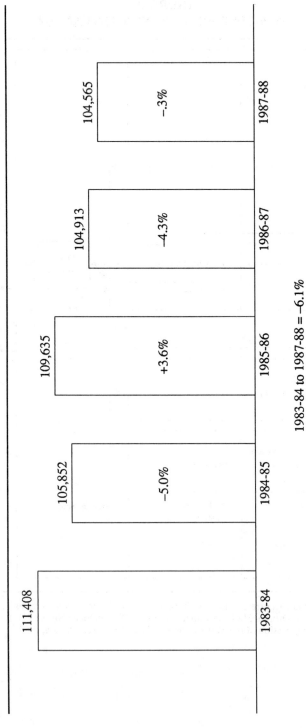

FIGURE 10.3

TOTAL AVERAGE OFFENDER CASELOAD, FEDERAL AND PROVINCIAL CORRECTIONS (CUSTODIAL AND NON-CUSTODIAL), 1983-84 TO 1987-88

111,408	105,852	109,635	104,913	104,565	
	–5.0%	+3.6%	–4.3%	–.3%	
1983-84	1984-85	1985-86	1986-87	1987-88	

1983-84 to 1987-88 = –6.1%

Source: Canadian Centre for Justice Statistics. *Adult Correctional Services in Canada, 1987-88* (Ottawa: Statistics Canada, 1989). p. 109. Catalogue No. 85-211. Reproduced with permission of the Minister of Supply and Services Canada, 1989.

The National Parole Board

The National Parole Board is an independent administrative agency in the Ministry of the Solicitor General. It has 36 full-time members, 18 of whom are distributed in five regional divisions: Atlantic, Quebec, Ontario, Prairie, and Pacific. The remainder of the members are located at the NPB headquarters in Ottawa (Figure 10.6). Each region also has Community Board Members and Temporary Board Members selected by the Solicitor General. During 1987–88, 43 Community Board Members were involved in reviewing all cases of inmates either serving life sentences or serving indeterminate sentences as dangerous offenders. In addition, Temporary Board Members, who numbered 46 in 1987–88, are often appointed for terms of up to one year to assist during periods of heavy caseloads. Parole Board members are appointed by the Governor-in-Council on the recommendation of the Solicitor General of Canada. There are no formal qualifications for being a member of the National Parole Board.

Under the *Parole Act*, the NPB has the authority to grant full and day parole to federal inmates and to provincial inmates who are confined in provinces where there is no provincial parole board; to grant temporary absences to federal inmates; and to terminate/revoke parole. The NPB also has authority to supervise and terminate/revoke mandatory supervision and to review applications for pardons under the *Criminal Records Act*. We will consider the activities of the NPB in greater detail in Chapter 12.

In 1987–88, there were 8,747 offenders supervised by the Correctional Service of Canada under full parole, day parole, or mandatory supervision (Figure 10.7). This figure includes provincial inmates from provinces that do not have their own parole board and represents a 5.8% increase from 1986–87 and a 20% increase since 1983–84.

Historically, the National Parole Board was not involved in the decision to release offenders on mandatory supervision from institutions. Offenders who had served two-thirds of their sentence and who had not been granted a parole were released automatically by the Correctional Service of Canada. In 1986, however, in response to public and political pressure and several highly publicized crimes involving offenders on mandatory supervision, amendments were made to the *Parole Act* and the *Penitentiary Act* empowering the National Parole Board to reject the applications for release on mandatory supervision of those offenders that it considers a clear danger to the community, forcing those offenders to serve their full sentence in confinement. Under the new legislative provisions, offenders who are released on mandatory supervision and are subsequently returned for a violation of conditions will not be eligible for a second release. While this legislation will result in many dangerous offenders serving longer periods of time in confinement, upon release they will receive no supervision whatsoever.

FIGURE 10.4
ORGANIZATION OF THE CORRECTIONAL SERVICE OF CANADA

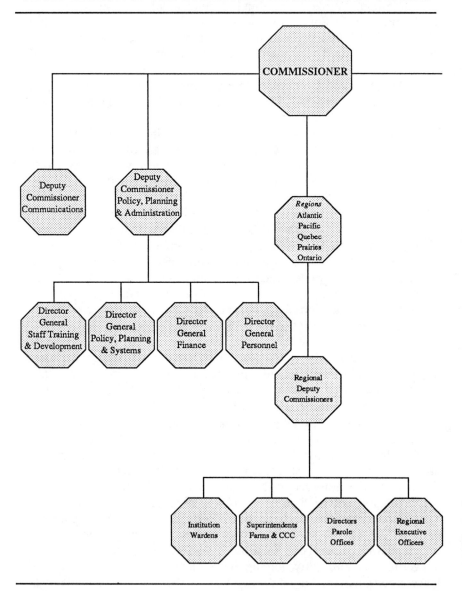

FIGURE 10.4
ORGANIZATION OF THE CORRECTIONAL SERVICE OF CANADA

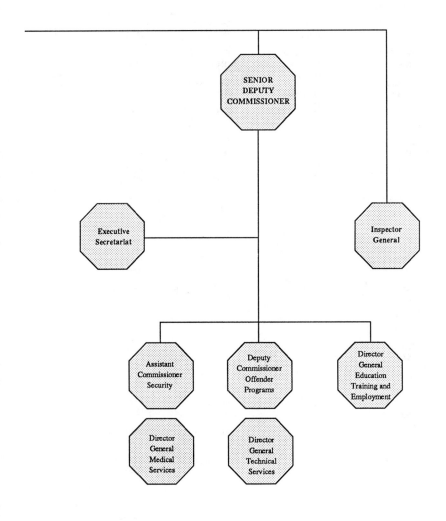

Source: Solicitor General of Canada. *Annual Report, 1986-87* (Ottawa: Supply and Services Canada, 1987), p. 50. Reproduced with permission of the Minister of Supply and Services Canada.

TABLE 10.1
FEDERAL CORRECTIONAL INSTITUTIONS
IN OPERATION, 1987–88; BY SECURITY LEVEL

Community Correctional Centre	Minimum	Medium	Maximum	High Maximum
Carlton (N.S.)	Westmorland Farm (N.B.)	Springhill (N.S.)	Atlantic (N.B.)	Regional Reception Centre (P.Q.)
Sand River (N.S.)	Montée-St. Francois (P.Q.)	Cowansville (P.Q.)	Dorchester (N.B.)	Sask. Pen. (Sask.)
Parrtown (N.B.)	Ste-Anne-des Plaines (P.Q.)	Drummond (P.Q.)	Archambault (P.Q.)	
Benoit XV (P.Q.)	Bath (Ont.)	Federal Trng. Centre (P.Q.)	Donnacona (P.Q.)	
Laferrière (P.Q.)	Beaver Creek (Ont.)	LaMacaza (P.Q.)	Laval (P.Q.)	
Martineau (P.Q.)	Frontenac (Ont.)	Leclerc (P.Q.)	Regional Reception Centre (P.Q.)	
Ogilvy (P.Q.)	Pittsburgh Farm (Ont.)	Collins Bay (Ont.)	Kingston Pen. (Ont.)	
Sherbrooke (P.Q.)	Rockwood (Man.)	Joyceville (Ont.)	Millhaven (Ont.)	
Keele St. (Ont.)	Sask. Farm (Sask.)	Warkworth (Ont.)	Prison for Women (Ont.)	
Portsmouth (Ont.)	Elbow Lake (B.C.)	Stony Mountain (Man.)	Regional Treatment Centre (Ont.)	
Osborne (Man.)	Ferndale (B.C.)	Bowden (Alta.)	Regional Psychiatric Centre (Sask.)	
Oskana (Sask.)		Drumheller (Alta.)	Sask. Pen. (Sask.)	
Robson[1] (B.C.)		Matsqui (B.C.)	Edmonton (Alta.)	
Sumas (B.C.)		Mission (B.C.)	Kent (B.C.)	
		Mountain (B.C.)	Regional Psychiatric Centre (B.C.)	
		William Head (B.C.)		

[1] Closed in 1988.

Source: Canadian Centre for Justice Statistics. *Adult Correctional Services in Canada, 1987-88* (Ottawa: Statistics Canada, 1989), p. 129. Catalogue No. 85-211. Reproduced with permission of the Minister of Supply and Services Canada, 1989.

FIGURE 10.5
AVERAGE NUMBER OF OFFENDERS IN FEDERAL CUSTODY (ACTUAL COUNT), 1983-84 TO 1987-88

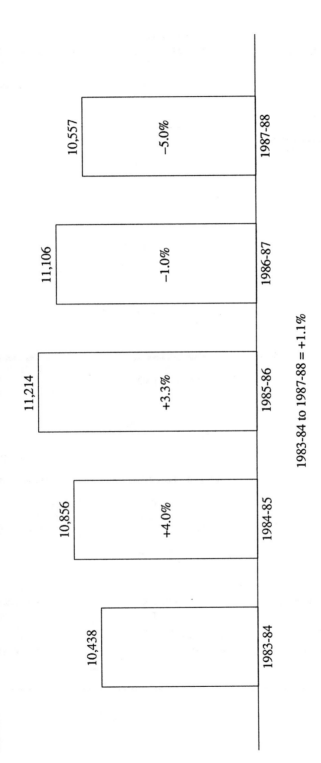

Source: Canadian Centre for Justice Statistics. *Adult Correctional Services in Canada, 1987-88* (Ottawa: Statistics Canada, 1989), pp. 90-91. Catalogue No. 85-211. Reproduced with permission of the Minister of Supply and Services Canada, 1989.

FIGURE 10.6
ORGANIZATION OF THE NATIONAL PAROLE BOARD

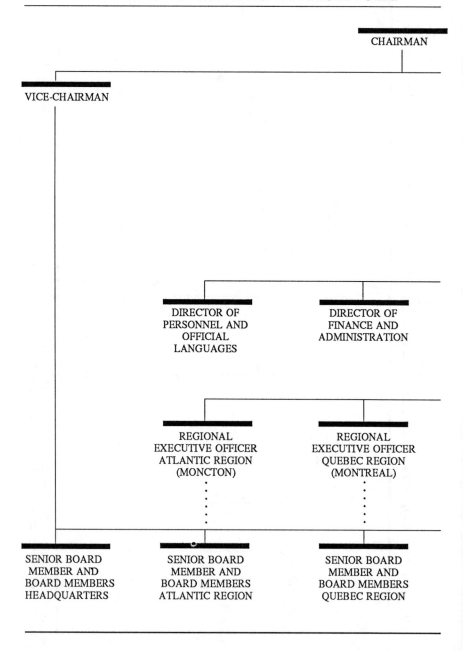

FIGURE 10.6
ORGANIZATION OF THE NATIONAL PAROLE BOARD

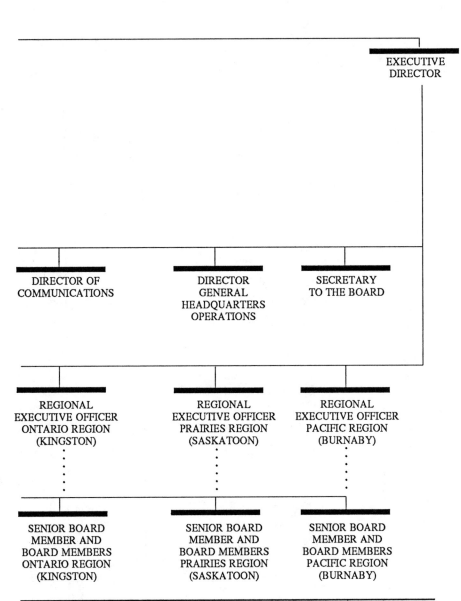

Source: Solicitor General of Canada. *Annual Report, 1986-87* (Ottawa: Solicitor General of Canada, 1987), p. 42.

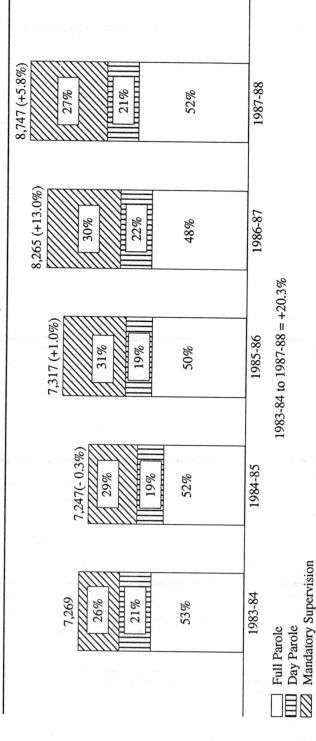

FIGURE 10.7

AVERAGE FEDERAL NON-CUSTODY CASELOAD: FULL PAROLE, DAY PAROLE, AND MANDATORY SUPERVISION, 1983-84 TO 1987-88 [1]

1987-88
8,747 (+5.8%)
27%
21%
52%

1986-87
8,265 (+13.0%)
30%
22%
48%

1985-86
7,317 (+1.0%)
31%
19%
50%

1984-85
7,247 (-0.3%)
29%
19%
52%

1983-84
7,269
26%
21%
53%

1983-84 to 1987-88 = +20.3%

Full Parole
Day Parole
Mandatory Supervision

[1] Includes inmates from provinces which do not operate their own parole boards.

Source: Canadian Centre for Justice Statistics. *Adult Correctional Services in Canada, 1987-88* (Ottawa: Statistics Canada, 1989), p. 98. Catalogue No. 85-211. Reproduced with permission of the Minister of Supply and Services Canada, 1989.

Provincial Correctional Services

The provincial governments are charged with the provision of correctional services for offenders receiving a sentence (or sentences) totalling less than two years. However, there is considerable variability in the provincial/territorial agency or ministry responsible for the delivery of correctional services (Table 10.2), in the specific types of program offered in provincial correctional facilities, and in the non-custodial services provided for adult offenders (Table 10.3).[10]

For example, while all the provinces/territories provide probation services, only British Columbia, Ontario, and Quebec have established provincial parole boards under the provisions of the *Parole Act*. In these provinces, probation officers serve as parole supervisors for offenders released by the provincial parole board. In the remaining provinces/territories, provincial cases are heard by the National Parole Board. Provincial probation officers across the country may also provide supervisory services for the National Parole Board where no CSC personnel are present. During 1987–88, there were a total of 5,731 inmates released by the three provincial parole boards, with Ontario accounting for 65% of the releases, and Quebec and British Columbia 21% and 14% respectively.

Provinces may also have responsibility for temporary lock-ups in which offenders are detained prior to their initial court appearance, although in Newfoundland and Labrador, New Brunswick, Saskatchewan, Alberta, British Columbia, the Yukon and the Northwest Territories such facilities are maintained on a shared basis between the municipalities and the province. Offenders under lock-up status are detained for short periods of time under provincial statutes, have not been sentenced, and are not considered to be on remand. Provincial institutions also hold offenders who are on remand. Under the provisions of the *Bail Reform Act*, the court may order an accused remanded into custody in order to ensure appearance in court or to protect the community. Also confined on remand status in provincial facilities are individuals who have been sentenced by the court but are awaiting the outcome of an appeal.[11]

During 1987–88, the provinces and territories spent $660 million on the provision of adult correctional services, broken down as follows: custodial services (82%); community supervision (i.e., probation and parole) (11%); administration (6%); and operation of the provincial parole boards (1%). Approximately 15,000 personnel were involved in the delivery of provincial correctional services.

In 1988, there were 125 "secure" institutions and 39 "open" facilities operated by the provinces/territories. The average offender count, sentenced and non-sentenced (lock-up and remand) in 1986–87 was 16,077, a 2% decrease from 1986–87 (Figure 10.8). The average number of offenders on probation and parole during 1987–88 was 69,184, a 1% decrease from 1986–87, and a 10% decrease from 1983–84 (Figure 10.9).

TABLE 10.2
PROVINCIAL/TERRITORIAL MINISTRIES AND DEPARTMENTS
RESPONSIBLE FOR ADULT CORRECTIONS

Government	Ministry/Department
Newfoundland	Adult Corrections Division, Department of Justice
Prince Edward Island	Corrections Division/Probation and Family Court Services Division, Department of Justice
Nova Scotia	Correctional Services Division, Department of the Solicitor General
New Brunswick	Correctional Services Division, Department of the Solicitor General
Quebec	Correctional Services Branch, Ministry of the Solicitor General
Ontario	Ministry of Correctional Services
Manitoba	Corrections Division, Department of Community Services
Saskatchewan	Corrections Division, Department of Justice
Alberta	Correctional Services Division, Department of the Solicitor General
British Columbia	Corrections Branch, Ministry of the Solicitor General
Yukon Territory	Institutional Services Branch/ Community Corrections Branch, Department of Justice
Northwest Territories	Department of Social Services

Source: Canadian Centre for Justice Statistics. *Adult Correctional Services in Canada, 1987-88* (Ottawa: Statistics Canada, 1989), pp. 35-52. Catalogue No. 85-211. Reproduced with permission of the Minister of Supply and Services Canada, 1989.

TABLE 10.3

COMMUNITY PROGRAMS FOR ADULTS

PROVIDED BY PROVINCIAL/TERRITORIAL CORRECTIONAL AGENCIES[1]

COMMUNITY SERVICES	NFLD	PEI	NS	NB	PQ	ONT	MAN	SASK	ALTA	BC	YK	NWT
Probation	x	x	x	x	x	x	x	x	x	x	x	x
Provincial Parole				x[2]	x	x				x		
Community Service Orders	x	x	x	x	x	x	x	x	x	x	x	x
Temporary Absence Program	x	x	x	x	x	x	x	x	x	x	x	x
Drinking/Driving Program	x		x	x	x	x	x	x		x	x	
Fine Option Program				x	x	x	x	x	x		x	x
Victim-Offender Reconciliation Program					x	x						
Victim-Witness Progam				x	x							
Bail Verification/ Supervision		x				x		x	x	x	x	
Restitution Program		x		x		x		x	x	x		
Community-Based/ Halfway House Program	x		x	x	x	x	x	x	x	x		x
Volunteer/Outside Agency Services	x	x	x	x	x	x	x	x	x	x	x	x

[1] In many jurisdictions, community services are operated by other criminal justice agencies. The Waterloo Region Victim Service Program, for example, is based in the Waterloo Regional Police Force.

[2] The New Brunswick Board of Parole has authority only over adults convicted of Provincial Statute violations and young offenders charged under the Young Offenders Act.

Source: Canadian Centre for Justice Statistics. *Adult Correctional Services in Canada, 1987-88* (Ottawa: Statistics Canada, 1989), pp. 35-52. Catalogue No. 85-211. Reproduced with permission of the Minister of Supply and Services Canada, 1989.

FIGURE 10.8
AVERAGE NUMBER OF OFFENDERS IN PROVINCIAL CUSTODY (ACTUAL COUNT), 1983-84 TO 1987-88

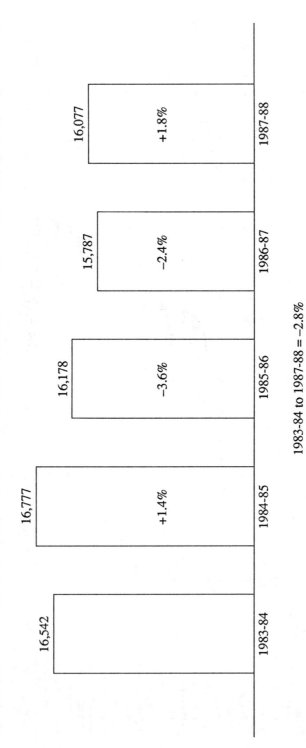

1983-84 to 1987-88 = –2.8%

Source: Canadian Centre for Justice Statistics. *Adult Correctional Services in Canada, 1987-88* (Ottawa: Statistics Statistics Canada, 1989), p. 117. Catalogue No. 85-211. Reproduced with permission of the Minister of Supply and Services Canada, 1989.

FIGURE 10.9
AVERAGE OFFENDER COUNT, PROVINCIAL PROBATION AND PAROLE, 1983-84 TO 1987-88

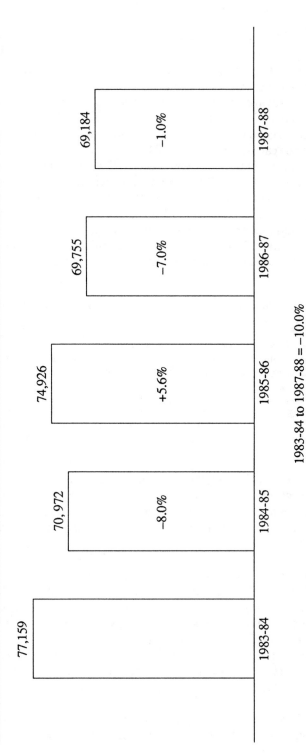

Source: Canadian Centre for Justice Statistics. *Adult Correctional Services in Canada, 1987-88* (Ottawa: Statistics Canada, 1989), p. 72. Catalogue No. 85-211. Reproduced with permission of the Minister of Supply and Services Canada, 1989.

The Split in Correctional Jurisdiction

The delivery of correctional services by both federal and provincial governments has led to increasing concerns with duplication of administrative structures and program services. Both levels of government operate correctional facilities and community-based programs, as well as providing supervision for offenders in the community. While the origins of the two-year rule can be traced to the 1840s, the specific reasons for the split in correctional jurisdiction are less clear (see Ekstedt and Griffiths, 1988).

A recent report by a federal study team investigating the improvement of justice delivery (Task Force on Program Review, 1985: 296) noted that the two-year rule was a "constitutional anomaly" and concluded that the current jurisdictional split impeded "effective service delivery and efficient administration." In fact, the two-year rule has been the subject of considerable debate and concern, as reflected in the following observations:

> The corrections field is further fragmented by the division of responsibility between federal and provincial governments . . . [Ouimet, 1969: 275]

> The division of responsibility creates a basic weakness inherent in Canadian corrections. . . The balkanization of the correctional process is the necessary result of the two year rule. [Ontario Ministry of Correctional Services, 1975: 3]

> . . . the federal-provincial division of responsibility . . . appears to have little rational basis. This has resulted in a duality in a number of areas of corrections, including institutions, paroling authority, community supervision and administrative and managerial practices. [Federal Government and the Government of British Columbia, 1976: 9]

In 1975, a Federal-Provincial Task Force was formed to examine the long-term objectives of Canadian corrections, including the issue of correctional jurisdiction. In its final report, released in 1976, the Task Force outlined 13 options, including the following four that were selected for further study:

1. retention of the present split based on the "two-year" rule;
2. a "six-month" jurisdictional split, under which offenders sentenced six months or less would fall under provincial jurisdiction, while those receiving sentences of six months or more would be the responsibility of the federal government;
3. administration of all correctional services by the provinces;
4. administration of all correctional services by the federal government.

While the Task Force on Program Review (1985: 297) reported widespread interest among the provinces in assuming full responsibility for correctional services (provided that financial support was forthcoming from the federal government), the two-year rule remains, and it is uncertain when and if any modifications to it will be made. Recently, through increased use of exchange-of-service agreements, the federal and provincial governments have attempted to increase the sharing of correctional resources (see Task Force on Program Review, 1985: 297).

The failure of the provincial and federal governments to resolve the long-standing issues surrounding the split in correctional jurisdiction appears to be due in large measure not to differences in correctional philosophy, but rather to financial considerations. Any alteration of existing arrangements, particularly if such changes involved provincial governments assuming a larger share of responsibility for correctional services, would require assurances of ongoing financial support from the federal government.[12]

Federal Correctional Investigator and Provincial Ombudspersons

Both the federal and provincial correctional systems, with the exception of Prince Edward Island, have established offices to investigate complaints by prison inmates and to inquire into various aspects of the operation of the correctional system. Such inquiries often involve complaints by prison inmates about their treatment in correctional institutions and specific policies and procedures of the correctional system. At the federal level, these activities are carried out by the office of the Correctional Investigator, and in the provinces by the ombudsperson offices, which may be involved in investigating other areas as well.

The office of the Correctional Investigator was created under the *Inquiries Act* largely as a result of criticisms of events that had occurred in Canadian federal penitentiaries. The Correctional Investigator acts as an ombudsperson for federal inmates and conducts investigations into specific allegations and events, on his or her own initiative, on the basis of complaints received by individual inmates, or in response to a directive from the Ministry of the Solicitor General. Recently, for example, the office of the Correctional Investigator was asked by the Solicitor General of Canada to conduct an investigation into allegations of mistreatment of inmates in Archambault penitentiary in Quebec, following a disturbance that occurred there in 1982 (see Stewart, 1984).

The annual report of the Correctional Investigator documents complaints received from inmates by category, institution, and month, as well as the institutional visits and interviews undertaken by the Investigator and the disposition of complaints. The annual report also contains the recommendations of the Correctional Investigator to the Solicitor General of Canada, and recent reports have addressed such issues as the involuntary transfer of inmates due to overcrowding, the need for a review of the procedures for transferring inmates of special handling units, amendments to provisions relating to privileged correspondence for inmates, the practice of double-bunking inmates in segregation cells, and the failure of institutional personnel to adhere to inmate grievance and appeal response time frames. The recommendations of the Correctional Investigator are not binding upon the Correctional Service of Canada, and in each annual report the Correctional Investigator notes those areas where no action has been taken.

Several concerns have been raised about the office of the Correctional Investigator, which has been called "A small response to a very large problem" (MacGuigan, 1977: 98). While the report of the Parliamentary Sub-committee on the Penitentiary System (MacGuigan, 1977) recommended that the role of the Correctional Investigator be reviewed every two years, no such review has taken place. It has also been suggested that improvements be made in the administrative remedies available to inmates before they resort to contacting the Correctional Investigator. Finally, the Task Force on Program Review (1985: 293) has recommended that a bill establishing the independence of the Correctional Investigator from government be tabled in Parliament.[13]

The Role of Corrections in Canadian Society

In our discussion of sentencing in Chapter 9, the justifications for imposing a criminal sanction on offenders were examined. These included the often conflicting objectives of rehabilitation, retribution, and deterrence. As the primary mechanism through which the sanctions imposed by the court are carried out, corrections has encountered difficulties in defining goals and objectives. As a federal government study team report on the Canadian justice system noted (Task Force on Program Review, 1985: 287): "The debate over the objectives of corrections has raged for decades and is likely never to be resolved, principally because corrections is asked, and likely always will be asked, to serve multiple and even conflicting aims which are inherent in sentencing and other factors."

The Working Group of the Correctional Law Review (1986: iii) stated that the purpose of Canadian corrections was "to contribute to the maintenance of a just, peaceful and safe society" by:

1. carrying out the sentence of the court
2. providing the degree of custody or control necessary to contain the risk presented by the offender
3. encouraging offenders to adopt acceptable behaviour patterns and to participate in education, training, social development and work experiences
4. providing a safe and healthful environment to incarcerated offenders which is conducive to their personal reformation.

These and other objectives are included in the *Manuals of Standards for Corrections* produced by the Canadian Criminal Justice Association (1985). The standards are set forth in a seven-volume series covering all areas of adult corrections, including probation services, prisons, paroling authorities, parole field services, community correctional centres, community residential centres and central administrative offices for corrections services. These are the most recent efforts to define the objectives for Canadian corrections, a task that has proved to be extremely elusive for the past 150 years.

In his classic book, *The Limits of the Criminal Sanction* (1968), Herbert Packer outlined two major purposes of punishment. One was "just deserts" — often referred to as retribution or revenge — which means that offenders deserve to suffer for the wrong they have committed. The other is the prevention of crime, which includes both utilitarian prevention through general and specific deterrence, and behavioural prevention, which attempts to rehabilitate the offenders and reintegrate them back into society. Galvin et al. (1977: 36) have illustrated the relation between the purpose of the sentence imposed by the presiding judge and the particular correctional option chosen (Table 10.4).

One of the major difficulties surrounding these justifications for punishment is a lack of reliable information on the effectiveness of criminal sanctions. This is evident in the ongoing debate over specific and general deterrence, which Morris and Hawkins (1969: 119) have characterized as a "boxing match between blind-folded contestants."[14] Specific deterrence focuses on the relation between the sanction imposed and the subsequent behaviour of the offender, once released from an institution or other correctional program.

It is extremely difficult to establish a direct relation between the sanction imposed and the subsequent behaviour of the offender. There are many reasons other than the specific sanction imposed that may contribute to an offender modifying his or her behaviour. It has proved equally difficult for social scientists to establish the extent to which sanctions imposed on individual offenders are successful in deterring members of the general population.

Contrary to the belief of many legislators and members of the general public, increasing the severity of penalties for criminal offences may not deter specific offenders or the general public. Rather, as Conklin (1986: 388) notes, there is a point of "diminishing returns [where] . . . the marginal deterrent effect of harsher penalties seems limited." The deterrent value of sanctions does appear to be strongly related to the certainty of punishment and the swiftness with which it is imposed. These relations were first noted by Beccaria (cited in Conklin, 1986: 389, 392–93) in his *Essay on Crime and Punishment* (1764):

The certainty of a punishment, even if it be moderate, will always make a stronger

TABLE 10.4

EFFECT OF PURPOSE ON CHOICE OF SENTENCE OPTION

OPTION(S) LIKELY TO BE FAVORED

Purpose of Sentence	Incarceration	Restitution	Fine	Community Service	Probation
Punishment	X		X		
Incapacitation	X				X^1
Reparation					
Victim-Oriented		X			
Community-Oriented			X	X	
Offender-Oriented		X^2		X	
Rehabilitation				X^3	X

[1] Probation with strict conditions and very close surveillance or some highly structured programs.

[2] Where more weight is placed on rehabilitative effects and the offender's ability to pay than full compensation for the victim.

[3] Some judges use community service as much because of assumed rehabilitative value as for purposes of reparations.

Source: John J. Galvin et al., *Issues and Programs in Brief.* Volume 1 of *Instead of Jail: Pre and Post Alternatives to Jail Incarceration* (Washington, D.C.: U.S. Government Printing Office, 1977), p. 36 (L.E.A.A.).

impression than the fear of another which is more terrible but combined with the hope of impunity... Promptness of punishments is more useful when the length of time that passes between the punishment and the misdeed is less, so much the stronger and more lasting in the human mind is the association of these two ideas, crime and punishment...

In the Canadian criminal justice system, however, there is often neither the certainty of punishment nor the prompt imposition of sanctions. Rather, there is a high rate of attrition of offenders, once detected, through the various stages of the criminal justice system from arrest to sentencing. Similarly, the legal provisions for offenders' rights and due process often act to slow the imposition of sanctions, even for those offenders convicted of offences. We will return to a consideration of the deterrent effect of sanctions in our discussion of capital punishment in Chapter 13.

Despite the varied objectives of the correctional system, research by Brillon, Louis-Guerin, and Lamarche (1984) suggests that the Canadian public has fairly specific ideas about the purpose of criminal sanctions. The most commonly stated objective of sanctions imposed by the criminal justice system on offenders was deterrence — "to discourage people from committing crimes and to protect the citizens against any attempt on their person or property." Respondents in the survey rarely mentioned punishment, rehabilitation, reparation or retribution as objectives of criminal justice. Rather, as the authors (1984: 261) state, the focus is on victimization and the consequences of the criminal act: "... punishment should reduce the threat of crime rather than simply punish offenders or reform and rehabilitate them."

A further finding was that the public knew very little about alternative sanctions, often confusing programs such as probation and parole. You will recall from Chapter 2 that the stereotypical and oversimplified views of crime and criminals held by Canadians were also due to a lack of knowledge of, and experience with, the criminal justice system. In Chapters 11 and 12 we will consider further the role that the public plays in corrections, both in relation to correctional institutions and community-based initiatives. It becomes clear that this lack of knowledge has severely hindered the potentially positive role that the public could play in the correctional process.[15]

NOTES

1. For detailed discussions of the historical response to crime and criminals, see Barnes (1972); Erikson (1976); Hay et al. (1975); Ignatieff (1978); Jacoby (1983); Newman (1978). See Ekstedt and Griffiths (1988) and Jackson (1983, c. 2) for discussions of the history of Canadian corrections.

2. See Baehre (1985) for an insightful analysis of the prison system in

Atlantic Canada prior to 1880; see also Fingard (1984). The report of the
Langmuir Commission (1891) provides valuable insights into the conditions of institutions in Ontario in the late 1800s, and Strange (1985)
provides a historical account of the establishment of the first prison for
women in Canada during the years 1874 to 1901.

   3. For a discussion of the factors contributing to the emergence of the
penitentiary in colonial America in the late 1700s, see Ekstedt and Griffiths
(1988); Rothman (1971); Scull (1977); Takagi (1975).

   4. Similar to the debate surrounding the "invention" of the penitentiary in the United States, there are several different interpretations offered
by Canadian scholars to explain the emergence of the penitentiary in
Canada. See Chunn (1981); Gosselin (1982).

   5. Investigations were also conducted into the alleged mismanagement of other penitentiaries. In 1984, a Royal Commission inquiry chaired
by Mr. Justice Drake of the British Columbia Supreme Court heard allegations against the warden and deputy warden of the British Columbia
Penitentiary, which included misappropriation of supplies, disregard for
prison regulations, and failure to supervise the prison guards adequately.
See Scott (1984).

   6. For a historical overview of the management of the Correctional
Service of Canada from 1960 to 1984, see Carson (1984).

   7. Exchange-of-service agreements between the federal government
and provincial governments have resulted in some flexibility in the two-
year rule. Federal offenders are generally held in provincial institutions
following sentencing for the 30-day appeal period prior to being sent to a
federal facility. In addition, transfer agreements exist between the federal
government and all provinces except Prince Edward Island and Ontario,
under which federal offenders may be detained in provincial facilities and
vice versa. Under an agreement reached between the federal government
and the Province of Quebec, all French-speaking female offenders whose
sentence(s) place them under federal jurisdiction serve their sentence in
Quebec.

   8. In 1985, the rate of imprisonment in Canada was 146 per 100,000
adult population and 108 per 100,000 total population. Several attempts
have been made to compare the rates of imprisonment in Canada with
those of other countries. Due to wide variations in the structure and
operation of criminal justice systems between countries, such comparisons
can only be made with extreme caution. The most recent data (Correctional Service of Canada, 1986: 9–10) indicate that in 1984–85, Canada had
an incarceration rate of 108 per 100,000 total population, which was higher
than the rate per 100,000 total population for Australia (67.6), New Zealand (91.1), the United Kingdom (96.5), West Germany (92), and France
(71.6) but lower than Austria (109), Fiji (112.7), and the United States

(286.8). For a comparative analysis of carceral trends in the United States and Canada, see Loman and Menzies (1986).

9. The average inmate count refers to the number of inmates actually present at the time the count is taken rather than on-register at the institution. The other measure that is used is the "average daily on-register" population, which includes those inmates actually in custody, those on day parole, temporary absence, hospitalized, and unlawfully at large. During 1987–88, for example, there were approximately 1,400 provincial and 1,700 federal inmates who were "on-register" but not in custody at the time of the count. In contrast to their United States counterparts, Canadian prisons are small, rarely holding more than 500 inmates. For an inquiry into the size of correctional institutions and its impact on program success, inmate behaviour, and recidivism rates, see Solicitor General of Canada (1979).

10. For a description of correctional services in the provinces/territories, see the annual report produced by the Canadian Centre for Justice Statistics entitled *Adult Correctional Services in Canada.*

11. A survey of the use of custodial remand in Canada (Canadian Centre for Justice Statistics, 1986) found that approximately seven per cent of persons charged with offences are remanded into custody and that one-third of the admissions to provincial/territorial facilities are under remand status. Despite the large number of individuals on remand status (Canadian Centre for Justice Statistics, 1986: viii), there was an information gap between the courts and correctional authorities regarding remanded persons, and the role of correctional authorities in the remand process was largely a "passive and uninformed" one. Further, since there is no classification of inmates on remand status, most are housed in maximum security quarters and are denied access to institutional programs and activities.

12. Financial issues have also played a major role in federal-provincial discussions and arrangements in other areas of the criminal justice system, including the provision of "contract" policing services to the provinces by the RCMP and the sharing of costs associated with the provision of justice services to youths under the *Young Offenders Act.*

13. For detailed information on the activities of the Correctional Investigator, see the *Annual Report of the Correctional Investigator,* available from the Minister of Supply and Services.

14. Important contributions to the deterrence debate have been made by Blumstein, Cohen, and Nagin (1978); Gibbs (1975); and Zimring and Hawkins (1973). See also Solicitor General of Canada (1981).

15. Flanagan and Caulfield (1984: 41) contend that the public's view of corrections and correctional reform is "diverse, multidimensional, and complex" and that correctional policy makers often misuse data from public opinion polls to support predetermined positions and initiatives.

REFERENCES

Anderson, F. W. 1982. *Hanging in Canada.* Surrey, B.C.: Frontier Books.

Archambault, J. (Chairman). 1938. *Report of the Royal Commission to Investigate the Prison System of Canada.* Ottawa: King's Printer.

Baehre, R. 1977. "Origins of the Penitentiary System in Upper Canada." 69 *Ontario History* 185–207.

____. 1985. *The Prison System in Atlantic Canada before 1880.* Ottawa: Solicitor General of Canada.

Barnes, H. E. 1972. *The Story of Punishment: A Record of Man's Inhumanity to Man.* Rev. ed. (originally published, 1930). Montclair, N.J.: Patterson-Smith.

Beattie, J. M. 1977. *Attitudes towards Crime and Punishment in Upper Canada, 1830–1850: A Documentary Study.* Toronto: Centre of Criminology, University of Toronto.

Bellomo, J. J. 1972. "Upper Canadians Attitudes towards Crime and Punishment, 1832–1851." 64 *Ontario History* 11–26.

Blumstein, A., J. Cohen, and D. Nagin. 1978. *Deterrence and Incapacitation: Estimating the Effects of Criminal Sanctions on Crime Rates.* Washington, D.C.: National Academy of Sciences.

Brillon, Y., C. Louis-Guerin, and M.-C. Lamarche. 1984. *Attitudes of the Canadian Public toward Crime Policies.* Montreal: International Centre for Comparative Criminology, University of Montreal.

Canadian Centre for Justice Statistics. 1986. *Custodial Remand in Canada — A National Survey.* Ottawa: Supply and Services Canada.

____. 1989. *Adult Correctional Services in Canada. 1987–88.* Ottawa: Supply and Services Canada.

Canadian Criminal Justice Association. 1985. *Manuals of Standards for Corrections.* Ottawa: Canadian Criminal Justice Association.

Canadian Sentencing Commission, Department of Justice. 1987. *Sentencing Reform: A Canadian Approach.* (Catalogue No. J2-67/1986E.) Ottawa: Supply and Services Canada.

Carson, J. J. (Chairman). 1984. *Report of the Advisory Committee to the Solicitor General of Canada on the Management of Correctional Institutions.* Ottawa: Supply and Services Canada.

Chunn, D. E. 1981. "Good Men Work Hard: Convict Labour in Kingston Penitentiary, 1835–1850." 4 *Canadian Criminology Forum* 13–22.

Coles, D. 1979. *Nova Scotia Corrections — An Historical Perspective.* Halifax: Communications Project in Criminal Justice, Correctional Services Division.

Conklin, J. E. 1986. *Criminology.* 2nd ed. New York: Macmillan Publishing Co.

Cooper, S. D. 1987. "The Evolution of the Federal Women's Prison." In *Too Few to Count: Canadian Women in Conflict with the Law,* edited by E. Adelberg and C. Currie, 127–44. Vancouver: Press Gang Publishers.

Correctional Service of Canada. 1986. *Basic Facts about Corrections in Canada, 1986.* Ottawa: Supply and Services Canada.

Cosman, J. W. 1985. "Education and Criminal Justice: Should Prisons be Federal or Provincial Responsibility?" Unpublished paper. Available from authors.

Curtis, D., A. Graham, L. Kelly, and A. Patterson. 1985. *Kingston Penitentiary: The First Hundred and Fifty Years, 1935–1985.* Ottawa: Supply and Services Canada.

Edmison, J. A. 1976. "Some Aspects of Nineteenth-Century Canadian Prisons." In *Crime and Its Treatment in Canada,* edited by W. T. McGrath, 347–69. 2nd ed. Toronto: Macmillan.

Ekstedt, J. W., and C. T. Griffiths. 1988. *Corrections in Canada: Policy and Practice.* 2nd ed. Toronto: Butterworths.

Eriksson, T. 1976. *The Reformers: An Historical Survey of Pioneer Experiments on the Treatment of Criminals.* New York: Elsevier.

Fauteux, G. (Chairman). 1956. *Report of a Committee Appointed to Inquire into the Principles and Procedures Followed in the Remission Service of the Department of Justice of Canada.* Ottawa: Queen's Printer.

Federal Government and the Government of British Columbia. 1976. *Bilateral Discussions on the Division of Correctional Responsibility — The Organization of Correctional Services in British Columbia: Report of the Federal-Provincial Task Force.* Victoria: Ministry of Attorney General.

Federal-Provincial Task Force on Long-Term Objectives in Corrections. 1976. *The Long-Term Objectives and Administration of Corrections in Canada.* Ottawa: Solicitor General of Canada.

Fingard, J. 1984. "Jailbirds in Mid-Victorian Halifax." 18 *Dalhousie Law Journal* 81–102.

Flanagan, T. J., and S. L. Caulfield. 1984. "Public Opinion and Prison Policy: A Review." 64 *The Prison Journal* 31–45.

Fox, A. 1971. *The Newfoundland Constabulary.* St. John's: Robinson Blackmore Printing and Publishing, Ltd.

Galvin, J. J., et al. 1977. *Issues and Programs in Brief.* Vol. 1. *Instead of Jail: Pre- and Post Alternatives to Jail Incarceration.* Washington, D.C.: U.S. Government Printing Office. (L.E.A.A.).

Gibbs, J. P. 1975. *Crime, Punishment, and Deterrence.* New York: Elsevier.

Gosselin, L. 1982. *Prisons in Canada.* Montreal: Black Rose Books.

Hay, D., P. Linebaugh, J. G. Rule, E. P. Thompson, and C. Winslow. 1975. *Albion's Fatal Tree.* New York: Pantheon.

Ignatieff, M. 1978. *A Just Measure of Pain: The Penitentiary in the Industrial Revolution 1705–1850.* New York: Pantheon.

Ives, G. 1970. *A History of Penal Methods.* (Originally published, 1914). Montclair, N.J.: Patterson-Smith.

Jackson, M. 1983. *Prisoners of Isolation: Solitary Confinement in Canada.* Toronto: University of Toronto Press.

Jacoby, S. 1983. *Wild Justice: The Evolution of Revenge.* New York: Harper and Row.

Knafla, L. A., and T. L. Chapman. 1983. "Criminal Justice in Canada: A Comparative Study of the Maritimes and Lower Canada 1760–1812." 21 *Osgoode Hall Law Journal* 245–74.

Langmuir, J. W. (Chairman). 1891. *Report of the Commissioners Appointed to Enquire into the Prison and Reformatory System of the Province of Ontario.* Toronto: Warwick and Sons.

Law Reform Commission of Canada. 1975. *Working Paper 11: Imprisonment and Release.* Ottawa: Information Canada.

Lowman, J., and R. J. Menzies. 1986. "Out of the Fiscal Shadow: Carceral Trends in Canada and the United States." 26 *Crime and Social Justice* 95–115.

MacGuigan, M. (Chairman). 1977. *Report to Parliament by the Sub-committee on the Penitentiary System in Canada.* Ottawa: Supply and Services Canada.

Morel, A. 1963. "La Justice Criminelle en Nouvelle-France." 14 *Cite Libre* 26–36.

Morris, N., and G. Hawkins. 1969. *The Honest Politicians Guide to Crime Control.* Chicago: University of Chicago Press.

National Parole Board. 1988. *A Guide to the Parole Act and Regulations.* Ottawa: Communications Division, National Parole Board.

Newman, G. 1978. *The Punishment Response.* New York: Lippincott.

Ontario Ministry of Correctional Services. 1975. "Preliminary Draft of a Discussion Paper — Ontario Ministry of Correctional Services." Federal-Provincial Conference on Corrections. Victoria, B.C. May 22–23.

Ouimet, R. (Chairman). 1969. *Report of the Canadian Committee on Corrections — Toward Unity: Criminal Justice and Corrections.* (Catalogue No. JS52-1-1968.) Ottawa: Information Canada.

Packer, H. 1968. *The Limits of the Criminal Sanction.* Stanford: Stanford University Press.

Rothman, D. J. 1971. *The Discovery of the Asylum.* Toronto: Little, Brown.

Scott, J. D. 1984. *Four Walls in the West — The Story of the British Columbia Penitentiary.* Vancouver: Retired Federal Prison Officer's Association of British Columbia.

Scull, A. T. 1977. *Decarceration: Community Treatment and the Deviant — A Radical View.* Englewood Cliffs, N.J.: Prentice-Hall.

Solicitor General of Canada. 1979. *Institutional Capacity. Maximum/ Medium Security: Recommendations.* Ottawa: Supply and Services Canada.

_____. 1981. *Solicitor General's Study of Conditional Release — Report of the Working Group*. Ottawa: Supply and Services Canada.

Splane, R. B. 1965. *Social Welfare in Ontario, 1791–1893. A Study of Public Welfare Administration*. Toronto: University of Toronto Press.

Stewart, R. L. (Chairman). 1984. *Report on Allegations of Mistreatment of Inmates at Archambault Institution following the events which occurred on July 25th, 1982*. Ottawa: The Correctional Investigator of Canada.

Strange, C. 1985. " 'The Criminal and Fallen of Their Sex': The Establishment of Canada's First Women's Prison, 1874–1901." 1 *Canadian Journal of Women and the Law* 79–92.

Takagi, P. 1975. "The Walnut Street Jail: A Penal Reform to Centralize the Powers of the State." 39 *Federal Probation* 18–26.

Task Force on Program Review. 1985. *Study Team Report — Improved Program Delivery: The Justice System*. Ottawa: Supply and Services Canada.

Task Force on the Creation of an Integrated Canadian Corrections Service. 1977. *The Role of Federal Corrections in Canada*. Ottawa: Supply and Services Canada.

Taylor, C. J. 1979. "The Kingston, Ontario Penitentiary and Moral Architecture." 12 *Social History* 385–408.

Working Group of the Correctional Law Review. 1986. *Working Paper No. 1. Correctional Philosophy*. Ottawa: Solicitor General of Canada.

Zimring, F. E., and G. J. Hawkins. 1973. *Deterrence: The Legal Threat in Crime Control*. Chicago: University of Chicago Press.

Zubrycki, R. M. 1980. *The Establishment of Canada's Penitentiary System: Federal Correctional Policy 1867–1900*. Toronto: Faculty of Social Work, University of Toronto.

LEGISLATION

Bail Reform Act, R.S.C. 1970 (2nd Supp.), c. 2; see now *Criminal Code*, Part XVI

Criminal Code, R.S.C. 1985, c. C-46

Criminal Records Act, R.S.C. 1985, c. C-47

Inquiries Act, R.S.C. 1985, c. I-11

Parole Act, R.S.C. 1985, c. P-2

Penitentiary Act, R.S.C. 1985, c. P-5

Young Offenders Act, R.S.C. 1985, c. Y-1

11 CANADIAN CORRECTIONAL INSTITUTIONS

Two of the major components of the Canadian correctional system are institutions and community-based programs. In this chapter, we examine the major issues surrounding the operation of correctional facilities, while in Chapter 12, community-based corrections programs for adult offenders in Canada are examined.[1]

It is important to note that there is a high rate of attrition of offenders throughout the various stages of the criminal justice process from detection and arrest to court. Only a very small proportion of offenders who are charged and found guilty of committing a criminal offence are ever sent to a correctional facility. However, since the time of the Brown Commission in 1848, correctional institutions have remained at the centre of controversy and have been the subject of numerous governmental and academic inquiries. As we consider the issues surrounding the operation of correctional facilities, we will experience considerable déjà vu, as many of the difficulties confronting Canadian correctional institutions are strikingly similar to those which first appeared in the decades following the opening of the Kingston Penitentiary in 1835.

While the widespread use of community-based corrections is a more recent development, concern has been raised regarding these techniques as well. Given the wide variability in institutional and community-based services at the provincial/territorial level, and the fact that offenders spend only a relatively short period of time in provincial/territorial facilities, our discussion will focus primarily on the federal level, although significant developments at the provincial level will be noted.

The Prison

Perhaps no one component of the correctional system has received more publicity or been the subject of more controversy than the prison (or penitentiary/correctional institution). Since the building of the first penitentiaries in Canada and the United States in the nineteenth century, a vast literature has developed documenting nearly every aspect of prison life from the perspectives of both keeper and kept. While an in-depth examination of all the critical issues surrounding the operation and management of correctional institutions is beyond the scope of this text, we will attempt to highlight some of the more important dimensions of the structure and operation of Canadian correctional institutions. In our consideration of the prison, it is useful to keep in mind Reid's (1982: 523) observation that the prison, unlike most other organizations, is a "human resource" organization: "Unlike the production of a manufacturing operation, administrative and treatment personnel in corrections are working with an intangible product — human behavior."

The Prison in Society

Similar to many other types of organizations, prisons are influenced by the larger societal context in which they exist. In characterizing the prison as a public and a political organization, Griffiths, Klein, and Verdun-Jones (1980: 212) note: "Social, political, and economic forces played a significant role in the development of the prison as a sanction and continue to determine to a large extent the goals of the prison and the extent to which they are achieved." There are several readily identifiable sources of influence on the prison and its operation that arise from the larger societal context within which it exists.

Politicians and legislatures, ever responsive to the concerns of their constituents, may enact legislation that results in more offenders being sent to prisons for longer periods of time. One legislative change that has had a significant impact on correctional institutions, particularly administrators, is Bill C-84 (the *Criminal Law Amendment Act (No. 2), 1976*, S.C. 1974-75-76, c. 105), passed in 1976. Under this law, offenders sentenced to life imprisonment for first-degree murder must serve a minimum of 25 years before being eligible for parole. In 1984, there were 275 individuals serving mandatory 25-year sentences, and by the year 2000 it is estimated that 800 offenders will be serving quarter-century terms.[2]

The courts have a direct impact on the operation of correctional institutions. The sentencing practices of the courts may result in overcrowding in correctional institutions, leading to increased violence and major disturbances. The courts may also be involved in issuing decisions against correctional institutions to reduce overcrowding. The courts have been particularly active in the United States, and many state institutions are currently under court-imposed deadlines to reduce the size of their inmate population. The Supreme Court of the United States has held in several cases that being confined in an overcrowded prison is a violation of an inmate's constitutional rights.

The entrenchment of a constitutional Charter of Rights and Freedoms increases the likelihood that the Canadian judiciary will be more involved in issues related to inmate civil rights, due process, and discipline within correctional institutions. Mandel (1986: 79–80) contends that the traditional "hands off" approach of the Canadian courts has changed and there is increased emphasis on procedural due process, although it is less certain that the power and broad discretion of corrections officials has been limited (see Jackson, 1986; Landau, 1984; Mandell and Mandell, 1985).

The media is the primary source of information about corrections for the majority of the public. Often, the media focuses on the more negative events in corrections, such as disturbances in institutions or crimes committed by offenders released from prison. The achievements of inmates inside or the successes of offenders released on parole or mandatory supervision in readjusting to a law-abiding life on the outside rarely receive media attention.

The general public has little opportunity to learn first-hand about prisons and the people who live and work within them. Kellough (1985: 243) noted that the community has little contact with prisons, and Brillon, Louis-Guerin, and Lamarche (1984: 211) reported that 72% of Canadians surveyed supported more severe sentences for offenders while at the same time indicating that they had little faith in the ability of prisons to rehabilitate. Brillon et al. (1984: 214) also found that citizens tend to have an image of prisons as either a "paradise-like prison-hotel" or a "nightmarish concentration camp." Those persons who ranked high in punitiveness (i.e., those who felt that sentences imposed by the courts were not harsh enough) tended to view prisons as "veritable hotels," minimize potentially negative consequences of confinement, and have the least confidence that criminals could be rehabilitated (see also Wanner and Caputo, 1987).

Once criminal offenders are sentenced by the court, for most of the general citizenry, they are "out of sight, out of mind." Throughout the history of corrections, from the time of the opposition of outside labour to the Nova Scotia workhouses in the mid-1750s and to teaching craft skills to the inmates of the Kingston Penitentiary in the 1850s, the role of the public in the operation of prisons has been primarily reactive. General community concern is raised when there are escapes and riots or when federal and provincial agencies announce plans to locate correctional institutions and facilities in neighbourhoods. Resistance to such initiatives may be organized by correctional interest groups who mobilize community opposition (see Tully et al., 1982).[3]

The Prison as a Total Institution

In his classic treatise *Asylums: Essays on the Social Situation of Mental Patients and Other Inmates,* Erving Goffman (1961) introduced the concept of the *total institution* to describe life inside hospitals, concentration camps, mental hospitals, and prisons. A total institution, according to Goffman (1961: 6) is "a place of residence and work where a large number of like-situated individuals, cut off from the wider society for an appreciable period of time, together lead an enclosed, formally administered round of life."

Goffman (1961: 6) outlined the structure of daily life in total institutions:

1. All aspects of life are conducted in the same place and under the same single authority.
2. Each phase of the member's daily activity is carried on in the immediate company of a large batch of others all of whom are treated alike and required to do the same thing together.
3. All phases of the day's activities are tightly scheduled, with one activity leading at a prearranged time into the next, the whole sequence of activities being imposed from above by a system of explicit formal rulings and a body of officials.
4. The various enforced activities are brought together into a single rational plan purportedly designed to fulfill the official aims of the institutions.

Another major characteristic identified by Goffman (1961: 7) is the split between the staff and the inmates. Orland (1975: 58) has described the impact of this split on each group: "Each sees the other in terms of stereotypes. Staff perceives inmates as secretive and untrustworthy; inmates view staff as condescending and mean. Staff feels superior and righteous, while inmates feel inferior, weak, and guilty." The discussion below, however, will reveal that the relations between the correctional staff and inmates are often complex and not always characterized by negative attitudes and behaviours.[4]

One of the most widely cited research investigations into the impact of total institutions on individuals who live and work in them was conducted by Haney and his colleagues at Stanford University during the 1970s. Commonly known as the Zimbardo study, after one of the research group's more prominent members, Philip Zimbardo, the project involved the creation of a "simulated prison" using student volunteers in the roles of guards and inmates. Within the first few days of the experiment, the volunteers assumed the attitudes and behaviours of inmates and correctional officers to such a degree that five of the "prisoners" were released from the study early due to traumatic reactions, while several of the guards displayed verbally and physically abusive behaviours toward the inmates.

Because of these unexpected difficulties, the researchers terminated the project after only six days, although it had been scheduled to run for two weeks. As Zimbardo (1972: 4) stated: "In less than a week the experience of imprisonment undid (temporarily) a lifetime of learning; human values were suspended, self-concepts were challenged and the ugliest, most base pathological side of human nature surfaced." The major conclusion from the Zimbardo experiment was that the environment of the prison has a detrimental effect on both the staff and the inmates. Despite the widespread acceptance of the findings of the experiment, Jones and Fowles (1984: 171–73) have criticized the design of the study, arguing that the use of college student volunteers (all but one of whom were white) resulted in an unrepresentative sample and, further, that the conditions created by the researchers in the simulated prison facilitated the development of both the stereotypes and the behaviours that emerged.

While all prisons can be properly labelled *total institutions*, they vary in such key attributes as the size of the inmate population, security level, and administration, all of which may significantly affect the patterns of interaction that occur within them.[5] Bowker (1982: 155) notes that "some prisons are more totalistic than others," and Thomas and Peterson (1977: 43) argue that these differences "have a major effect on the structure of the prison organization, the types of problems and pressures that confront the inmate population, the manner in which inmates respond to the conditions of confinement, and the consequences that these responses have for both the inmates and the movement of the organization toward the acquisition of its goal or goals."

It might be expected, for example, that maximum security institutions would evidence more severe conditions of confinement and patterns of interaction among the inmates and between the inmates and the staff than would occur at a minimum security work camp. Research studies have indicated that "prisons that are high on institutional totality — and that therefore are experienced by prisoners as being highly depriving — tend to be characterized by high levels of violence, punitiveness by correctional officers, strong antisocial sentiments among prisoners, tolerance of coercive homosexuality, and relatively poor social relations with both staff and peers" (Bowker, 1982: 155; see also Feld, 1978).

To reflect these differences, individual prisons can be located along a rough "continuum of correctional institutions," with institutions that are less "totalistic" at one end and those that are extremely "totalistic" at the other. While security level is a primary determinant of an institution's location on the continuum, Bowker (1982: 156) cautions that security level and degree of institutional totality are not the only determinants of the attitudes and behaviours that emerge in prisons: "Prisoners in a minimum security institution may feel subjectively more deprived than prisoners in a maximum security institution, even though the objective deprivations are greater in the maximum security facility." Such feelings may be precipitated by the actions of the correctional staff or the administration. The concept of a continuum of correctional institutions nevertheless provides important insights into the patterns of interaction that exist in prisons and cautions us against assuming that all prisons are the same.[6]

The Goals of Prisons

In 1969, the Ouimet Committee (1969: 311) identified the two objectives of correctional institutions as (1) to hold the inmate in custody and (2) to prepare the individual for release back into the community as a law-abiding citizen. The Stewart Committee (1984: 15) also listed the two primary functions of the Correctional Service of Canada (CSC) as the custody and control of offenders and rehabilitation. And the *Penitentiary Regulations* state that the mission of the CSC is "the custody, control, correctional training, and rehabilitation of persons committed to penitentiary" (cited in Stewart, 1984: 17). Cressey (1977) argued that it was possible to classify prisons on the basis of the extent to which they pursued either custody and control goals or treatment goals. The emphasis that a prison has will have a significant impact on the patterns of interaction that develop among and between the groups within the prison, as well as the patterns of communication and decision making.

In custody-oriented institutions, inmates have low status and there is restriction of communication among inmates. Correctional employees do not participate in organizational decision making, and authority is premised on rank. Communication flow is downward from the administration to the staff, who are often not aware of the overall objectives and goals of the administration. In the treatment-oriented institution, on the other hand, there is an emphasis on the rehabilitation of offenders. The correctional staff are encouraged to exercise discretion and are given considerable autonomy in carrying out tasks. Decision making is decentralized, and there is two-way communication between the administration and the staff. As we will see, correctional managers play a large role in determining the focus of the institution and the resulting patterns of interaction and communication that develop. Further, even in treatment-oriented institutions, numerous obstacles are encountered that may hinder the effectiveness of administrative policies and programs.

Several researchers have explored the relations between the orientation of the institution (custody/control or treatment) and the patterns of interaction that develop among and between the inmates, staff, and administration. In one of the earliest inquiries, Grusky (1959) found that inmates in a treatment-oriented facility held more positive attitudes toward the institution, the staff, and the programs than did their counterparts in a custody-oriented institution. This study was replicated by Berk (1966: 534), who reported similar findings:

> The goal of "custody", with its concomitant centralized- and formal-authority structure and increased deprivations for inmates, contributed significantly to the development of the hostile informal organization in the custodial prison. The disenfranchisement of inmates from positive rewards of the institution encouraged the development of negative attitudes and a hostile informal leadership.

More recently, several studies of the patterns of interaction in juvenile institutions have reaffirmed the relation between the orientation of staff and administration and the attitudes and behaviours of the inmates. In a study of several cottages in one juvenile facility, Feld (1978) found that in custody-oriented cottages, not only did the youths hold negative perceptions of the staff, but also there was a considerable amount of violence and exploitation among the residents. In those cottages in which the cottage parents were treatment oriented, the youths held favourable views of the staff and fellow residents and there was little or no conflict among the residents. From these findings, Feld (1978: 163) concluded that the differences in the orientation of the cottage parents had a significant impact on the relations that developed between the staff and the residents and on the patterns of interaction among the youths.

While the dual mandate of the prison is often viewed as a source of ongoing difficulties, and contributions by observers such as Cressey are valuable, it can be argued that the predominant purpose of the prison is the punishment of offenders. As a recent report of the Solicitor General (1981: 16) states: ". . . prisons are primarily places of punishment, though other activities may go on inside them. Punishment is an element in any decision to send an offender to a federal penitentiary, and punishment is what corrections does demonstrably best." In our discussion of correctional treatment, it will be argued that the requirements of custody and control hindered the potential effectiveness of many of the programs that were introduced.

There is no evidence that imprisonment acts as either a specific or general deterrent. From a review of the available research literature on crime rates and imprisonment rates, Blumstein, Cohen and Nagin (1978: 42) concluded that "no sound, empirically based conclusions can be drawn" about a relation between incarceration and deterrence. In its discussion of the effectiveness of incarceration and the need to develop alternatives to imprisonment in Canada, the MacGuigan Sub-committee (1977: 35) concluded:

Society has spent millions of dollars over the years to create and maintain the proven failure of prisons. Incarceration has failed in its two essential purposes — correcting the offender and providing permanent protection to society. The recidivist rate of up to 80 percent is the evidence of both.

Despite this, prisons continue to be employed for general and specific deterrence. As the Solicitor General's Working Group on Conditional Release states (1981: 16–17):

Valid measurement of the general deterrent effect of various sentences of imprisonment and accompanying release practices is not possible. However, "common sense" belief in the deterrent effect of punishment is as strong as the reasonable evidence of its existence is scarce ... Despite our lack of specific knowledge about the conditions under which it might work, general deterrence remains an actively pursued objective and a prominent consideration in the imprisonment and release process.

In addition to the objectives of incarceration, there may be differing (and often conflicting) goals pursued by the inmates, treatment staff, security personnel, and administration in the institution. Differences between the treatment staff and the security staff reflect the inherent conflict and tensions between control and rehabilitation. Further, while all inmates share the common goal of being released from the institution as soon as possible, their relations may be characterized by a considerable amount of violence and exploitation.

Doing Time: The World of the Inmate

Offenders who are sent to correctional institutions in Canada encounter a world unlike any other. According to Goffman (1961: 18–20) individuals who enter total institutions undergo a process of "mortification" that transforms them from citizens of the outside community to residents of the institution. Through a series of "status degradation ceremonies" (see Garfinkel, 1965), the offender is psychologically and materially stripped of possessions that identify him or her as a member of the "free" society. These are replaced by an identification number, prison issue clothing, and a list of institutional rules and regulations designed to control every aspect of the inmate's life inside the institution as well as contact with the outside world.[7]

In his classic work *The Prison Community*, Donald Clemmer (1940) coined the term *prisonization* to describe the process by which new inmates are socialized into the norms, values, and culture of the prison. These include the adoption of antisocial attitudes and behaviours and opposition to the authority of the institution. Bowker (1982: 144) has argued that prisonization also involves being "socialized into the official life of the prison by being indoctrinated in prison regulations and the many tacit understandings that are enforced by correctional officers and other staff members." And Williams and Fish (1974: 163) note: "Becoming a member of the prison community means thinking, acting, and feeling as the community thinks, acts, and feels; it means taking on the objectives, orientation, and codes of the system."

The degree to which offenders become prisonized may depend upon their individual personality, their pre-prison experiences, and the nature of the primary group relations they establish with other inmates in the prison. Research by Wheeler (1961) revealed that prisonization may follow a U-shaped pattern, with inmates being oriented toward conventional community norms and values during the first and last six months of confinement and the least oriented toward such values and norms during the middle phase of their confinement. Other research studies have found that the orientation of the particular institution in which the offender is confined and a variety of other factors may influence the nature and extent of prisonization among inmates (see Alpert, Noblit, and Wiokowski, 1977; Alpert, 1979).

The Inmate Social System

A universal characteristic of correctional institutions is the existence of a social system among the inmates. Despite administrative pronouncements to "do your own time," the conditions of confinement make it difficult for the inmate to remain isolated from and unaffected by the prison milieu. As Abdul-Mu'Min (1985: 152) notes: "Power and survival in a prison setting are best met through group affiliation." With the exception of those offenders housed in protective custody or special handling units, it is likely that all inmates have some affiliation with a group or clique in the prison. Such groups may be formed on the basis of racial identity, participation in religious or self-help groups, or pre-prison gang affiliations and friendships.

Since Clemmer's work in the 1940s, there have been attempts to understand the origins and functions of the inmate social system. In 1958, Gresham Sykes published *Society of Captives*, which was based on an in-depth examination of the lives of inmates in a United States maximum security prison. Sykes argued that incarcerated offenders experienced several "pains of imprisonment," including the loss of liberty, individual autonomy and personal security, as well as the lack of access to goods and services and heterosexual relations.

The lack of privacy is a major source of stress for prison inmates: "You can be sitting there, and you know you're not alone. Where I'm at, I've got twenty-five guys on the gallery I'm on. So I've got like guys laying there, guys defecating, guys coughing, and its close quarters . . ." (Toch, 1977: 31). Further difficulties are caused by the boredom of daily life inside and the deprivation of information from the outside world:

> Life is going on outside, but there ain't nothing happening inside . . . It's like another world. If they took that radio away and didn't let us have any magazines or newspapers, we wouldn't know there was anything out there . . . I can't even see over the wall. I haven't seen a car in I don't know how long. [Toch, 1977: 23]

Among the inmates interviewed by Zamble, Porporino, and Kalotay (1984: 68), the lack of contact with family and friends and the constraints on freedom imposed by being confined in an institution ranked highest among the problems encountered in prison. In what has become known as the *deprivation theory* of inmate subcultures, Sykes (1958) argued that the inmate social system functioned to mitigate these pains of imprisonment.

In 1961, John Irwin and Donald Cressey proposed an alternative explanation for the formation of the inmate social system, arguing that the criminal attitudes and behaviours that characterized the inmate social system were brought with offenders from their criminal careers on the outside. The importation "theory" of inmate social systems received initial empirical support from Jacobs (1974), although subsequent research by Akers, Hayner, and Gruninger (1977), Carroll (1977), Thomas (1977), and Thomas, Peterson, and Zingraff (1978) has suggested that both explanations are useful in attempting to understand the inmate social system.

The major components of the inmate social system include (1) a code of behaviour; (2) a hierarchy of power among the inmates; (3) an "informal" economic system, which provides illicit goods and services; and (4) a variety of social or "argot" roles assumed by prisoners.[8] The convict code is designed to increase inmate solidarity and implores prisoners not to exploit one another, to be strong in confronting the deprivations of confinement, and to assume an oppositional stance toward prison authorities. The social system is also characterized by differential status levels among the inmates. Some inmates hold high-status positions and wield considerable power, often on the basis of their criminal career or access to, and ability to control, illicit goods and services within the institution. Offenders confined for sexual offences, particularly against children, tend to have the lowest status and to be susceptible to attack by other inmates. Such a hierarchy of power and status was found by Mann (1967) in his study of the Guelph Reformatory.

There also appears to be a variety of social roles among the inmates, Bowker (1982: 149) noting that "there are social roles associated with group membership, sentence length, committing offense, degree of dedication to the traditional convict code, specific talents or deficiencies, demographic characteristics, sexual behavior, friendship relationships, and economic activities." Bowker (1982: 150) further notes that the following four social roles initially identified by Clarence Schrag (1961) have been repeatedly found in inmate social systems:

1. *square-John*: pro-social in attitudes and behaviour; not involved in inmate subculture; postive toward staff and administration;
2. *right guy*: anti-social; heavily involved in inmate social system and opposed to staff and administration;
3. *politician*: pseudo-social; manipulates both staff and inmates;
4. *outlaw*: asocial; use of violence to victimize both staff and inmates.

Toch (1977) and others have noted that there is considerable variability among inmates in their vulnerability to the pains of imprisonment and the strategies they employ to cope with them (see also Zamble et al., 1984). However, the efforts of inmates to adapt to and cope with the stresses of life inside are hindered by a lack of support mechanisms, Toch (1977: 180) pointing out that "it is generally not viewed as legitimate, by inmates as well as staff, for a stressed person to seek emotional support or to advertise his vulnerability in the hope of receiving recognition and assistance."

In a recently completed study of coping behaviour among inmates in ten federal institutions in the Province of Ontario, Zamble and Porporino (1988) found that correctional programming did little to assist offenders in altering inappropriate coping strategies and resulted in depression, stress, anger, and feelings of alienation. Offenders became concerned with survival in the prison environment and adjusting to the prison routine, rather than with developing coping strategies that would allow them to address their problems and make positive decisions about their future.

One of the major reasons why the prison may never be successful in deterring individuals from engaging in further criminal activity is that it is not possible to predict how the individual will respond to the incarceration experience and whether the prison experience will result in the development of pro-social or anti-social attitudes and behaviours both during confinement and upon release.[9]

The Inmate Subculture: Fact or Fiction?

While the concepts of prisonization and of the inmate subculture have proved valuable in increasing our understanding of correctional institutions, questions have been raised about their accuracy in describing life inside. Porporino and Zamble (1984: 406) have argued, for example, that the research on the process and effects of prisonization is methodologically flawed and has produced mixed findings: "... as a measure of how imprisonment affects individuals, prisonization is clearly too general and too crude a concept." These authors propose that the focus must be on the way in which "individual inmates perceive and react to specific events and conditions while they are imprisoned" (p. 409).

Questions have also been raised about the extent to which inmates in prison constitute an oppositional subculture. Research suggests that inmates exhibit considerable variability in the extent to which they participate in the social system and in the degree to which they adhere behaviourally to the tenets of the inmate code. In one early study of inmates' attitudes toward the code, Wheeler (1966) found a considerable amount of *pluralistic ignorance*: individual inmates misperceived the attitudes of fellow inmates toward the inmate code, assuming higher levels of adherence to it than actually existed. Similarly, Ramirez (1984: 451) found in a survey of correctional officers and inmate attitudes toward the severity of prohibited acts that "some groups of inmates exhibited more agreement with some groups of staff than they did with other groups of inmates."

These findings led Ramirez (1984) to conclude that the process of prisonization did not necessarily result in an "us versus them" split between the inmates and the correctional staff. Further, despite the existence of a code of conduct that includes among its basic tenets a pledge of solidarity and a prohibition against exploiting one another, there is considerable evidence that inmate relations are often characterized by psychological intimidation and physical force. We will encounter the concept of pluralistic ignorance again in our discussion on correctional officers.

Many observers have argued that the patterns of interaction among prison inmates have changed since the time of Clemmer (1940), Sykes (1958) and other early investigators and that life inside can now be best described as "a 'pluralistic prisoner community' with many inmate groups" (see also Fox, 1982; Stastny and Tyrnauer, 1982; Stojkovic, 1984). Irwin (1977: 32) has argued that inmates tend to confine their interaction to small groups of friends in a pattern of *ordered segmentation*. Rather than forming a solid block of opposition to prison authorities, such groups may find themselves in conflict with one another, either because of racial differences or due to power struggles.

While it can be anticipated that a social system will be present among inmates in all institutions, the "strength" and "form" of the system will vary depending upon the security level of the institution, the orientation of the prison administration, and the characteristics of the inmate population. It can be anticipated that the inmate social system will be more pronounced in institutions oriented toward custody and control and with a higher security level where the deprivations are greater than in facilities that are more treatment oriented and at a lower security level. Further, in Canadian provincial institutions, it is unlikely that inmate social systems become well established, given the relatively short period of time offenders are confined.

Abdul-Mu'Min (1985) argues that the inmate subculture can have a stabilizing, constructive influence in the prison and should be utilized more effectively by the correctional staff and the administration as an agent of positive change. However, it is unclear how this would be accomplished without creating situations that endanger both the inmates and the correctional staff. In our discussion of the relations that develop between the correctional officers and the inmates, we will see that the inmate "elites" are frequently used by correctional officers to maintain order and stability within the institution, often with negative consequences for both staff and inmates.

Life in Women's Prisons

The above discussion presents materials on the social systems in institutions for adult male offenders. There is a lack of published research on life inside institutions for female offenders in Canada, perhaps due to the relatively small number of women in provincial facilities and in the Kingston Prison for Women. Research conducted in the United States and England suggests that the patterns of interaction that develop among female inmates are considerably different from those of their male counterparts (see Bowker, 1981; Carlen et al., 1985; Dobash, Dobash, and Gutteridge, 1986; Foster, 1975; Giallombardo, 1966; Propper, 1981).

While the inmate social system in female institutions may include identifiable social roles, such as "snitches" (rats or squealers), "squares" (the accidental criminal who is pro-administration), and "jive bitches" (a troublemaker among the inmates), the different roles that males and females play in outside society appear to have a significant impact on the patterns of interaction that develop within the institution. As Shover (1979: 182) notes: ". . . male prisoners, both individually and collectively, respond to the pains of imprisonment in typically masculine ways while females respond to them in typically feminine ways." Among the differences identified by the research are the following:

1. patterns of interaction among female inmates are less violent and result in much lower rates of inmate victimization than do those that characterize male institutions;
2. the "pains of imprisonment" for female inmates include the loss of close, supportive family relationships and contribute to the development of pseudo-families that include "parents" and "relatives";
3. homosexual relationships, whether within a pseudo-family arrangement or involving two women, are entered into voluntarily and for emotional support rather than as an expression of physical dominance and aggression;
4. institutions for female offenders are characterized by less overt conflict between the inmates and the staff and administration than are male institutions;
5. the *sub rosa* economic system that provides illicit goods and services in male institutions is generally absent from female facilities, most likely due to the lack of pre-prison criminal career experiences among the women and the physical setting of female institutions, which is often less depriving than that of male facilities.

Wilson (1986: 402) suggests that the differences in the social systems between male and female institutions may be due, at least in part, to "organizational rules, staff training and attitudes, and staff expectations of inmates." From a survey of male and female inmates in a mixed (co-educational) provincial facility in Alberta, Wilson (1986) found no differences between the two genders in their stated level of commitment on several measures of the inmate code, including group solidarity and distrust of staff. This finding led Wilson to conclude that "the prison environment plays a significant role in the degree of commitment to the inmate code held by its charges" (p. 405).

Caution should be exercised in assuming that these attributes apply to female inmates in Canada. The short period of confinement of offenders in provincial institutions, for example, would seem to preclude the development of pseudo-families, while the confinement of all federal female offenders (except those who remain in provincial institutions under federal/provincial agreements) in the multi-level institution at Kingston may result in patterns of interaction unique to the Canadian context. We will return to a consideration of the female offender in Canada in Chapter 13.[10]

The Classification of Offenders

Classification is particularly important in any discussion of institutional programs. The initial classification decision following sentencing, and subsequent assessments by case management teams during the offender's term of confinement, will determine (1) the level and type of institution the offender will be confined in, and (2) the program opportunities available to the offender. In Canada, the classification of offenders assumes a critical role in the correctional process, as convicted offenders are not sentenced to a specific institution by the court, but rather to a specific length of time in confinement.

The Ouimet Committee (1969: 311) defined *classification* as "a continuous process through which diagnosis, treatment-planning and the execution of the treatment plan are coordinated to the end that the individual inmate may be rehabilitated." Federal classification policy is premised on two concepts: *direct penitentiary placement* and *cascading*. Following sentencing, those offenders whose sentence length (two years or more) places them under the jurisdiction of federal corrections are classified by a community case management officer, a parole officer of the Correctional Service of Canada, in the provincial institution to which they were remanded. The sole exception is in the Province of Quebec, where the classification decision is made at a Regional Reception Centre. Classification decisions for offenders under provincial jurisdiction (a sentence or sentences totalling two years less a day) are made by classification units in each province.[11]

The community case management officer identifies the initial security level for the offender based on the security and programming needs of the offender, considering such factors as the nature and seriousness of the offence and criminal history and the length of sentence received. Under the Direct Penitentiary Placement scheme, the offender is then sent directly to a specific institution. The classification process continues throughout the offender's confinement through cascading. On the basis of assessments by an institutional case management team, conducted at least once a year, inmates are transferred to progressively lower levels of security as their time remaining to be served decreases.

A primary consideration in all classification decisions is the security risk of the offender. The Correctional Service of Canada utilizes three broad levels of security:

1. maximum security: the inmate is likely to escape and, if successful, would be likely to cause serious harm in the community;
2. medium security: the inmate is likely to escape if given the opportunity, but should not cause serious harm in the community should such an escape occur;
3. minimum security: the inmate is not likely to escape and would not cause harm in the community if such an escape should occur.

Despite its pivotal role, the development and application of adequate classification systems has been an elusive goal. While considerable progress has been made since the 1800s, when little concern was given to the age, sex, or criminal history of offenders, as recently as 1977 the Mac-Guigan Sub-committee (1977: 130) found that "the classification process is disorganized and varies from region to region." Particular concern was expressed by the Sub-committee about "overclassification" — offenders confined at higher security levels than is warranted, often due to over-crowding and lack of adequate facilities. The Sub-committee (1977: 132) called for a major review of classification procedures and for the creation of Regional Reception Centres for classification in every CSC region. This recommendation was subsequently rejected by the Solicitor General, one of only seven of a total of 65 recommendations made by the MacGuigan Sub-committee that were rejected.

In calling for a review of federal classification policy in 1984, the Carson Committee (1984) raised several concerns about both direct penitentiary placement and cascading. In its inquiry, the Committee (pp. 40–41) found that in the direct penitentiary placement process, security concerns often took precedence over the program needs of the offender, with the result that "large numbers of offenders may be sent to institutions for which they are not suited." The Committee (p. 40) was also critical of cascading, noting that the procedure resulted in "excessive movement" of inmates, which interrupted program plans and hindered the efforts of correctional staff working with inmates. To illustrate its concern, the Committee (p. 39) noted that during 1983–84, there were 14,423 transfers between institutions, although the total inmate population in the federal correctional system was 11,031.

Similar to the MacGuigan Sub-committee (1977), the Carson Committee (1984: 40) recommended the creation of regional reception centres. The Committee (pp. 40–41) also called for a complete review of cascading and of the impact of transfers on the program needs of offenders. In an attempt to reduce the excessive use of regional transfers (transferring offenders from one region of the country to another), the Committee (p. 41) recommended that, with only certain specified exceptions, offenders remain in the region where they were sentenced.

The failure of the Correctional Service of Canada to act on the recommendations of the MacGuigan Sub-committee (1977) and the Carson Committee (1984) would suggest that reform of the classification process is not a high priority.[12]

Institutional Programs

The Correctional Service of Canada and the various provincial/territorial correctional agencies operate a wide variety of institutional programs for offenders. These include inmate employment and work programs; occupational and vocational training programs; educational programs; chaplaincy and religious services; athletic and recreational services; medical, dental and psychiatric services; and programs and services provided by volunteer and outside agencies. These programs attempt to meet the needs of an offender population recently described as follows: "40 percent are functionally illiterate; many have a drug or alcohol dependency; most have few marketable skills and a history of sporadic employment; many have learning disabilities, poor social skills, family problems, and low maturation. A few have severe mental disorders but cannot be accommodated by the mental health system" (Government of Canada, 1986: 287–88).

In 1938, the report of the Royal Commission on the Penal System of Canada, chaired by Mr. Justice Archambault, asserted that in addition to protecting the community, prisons should assume the task of reformation. In 1956, a Committee of Inquiry under the chairmanship of Mr. Justice Fauteux reaffirmed rehabilitation as the primary objective of corrections, and noted the failure of the correctional system to implement the recommendations of the Archambault Committee (1938) made nearly two decades earlier. Beginning in the late 1940s, a wide variety of educational, vocational training, and treatment programs were introduced in federal and provincial institutions, although the introduction of rehabilitative programs was slow and uneven.

A guiding principle of the rehabilitative approach was the *medical model*, which viewed offenders as "sick" and criminal behaviour as symptomatic of some underlying disorder in the emotional makeup or psyche of the offender. Proper diagnosis of the "illness," followed by appropriate therapeutic intervention, would promote reformation. The medical model assumed that "criminogenic factors are indigenous to the individual offender and that it is by doing 'something' for, to, or with him that rehabilitation can be affected" (MacNamara, 1977: 440). The strong clinical orientation of the medical model led to the increased involvement of psychologists and psychiatrists in designing and operating treatment programs. A wide variety of treatment modalities were introduced, including individual and group psychotherapy, reality therapy, transactional analysis, psychodrama, and behaviour modification.[13]

In an attempt to create an environment within correctional institutions conducive to the various programmatic and treatment initiatives, the Correctional Service of Canada developed the Living Unit Program in the early 1970s. The Living Unit Program was based on the idea of a "therapeutic community" within which close communication is established between staff and inmates to increase the likelihood of reformation and post-release success.

Under the Living Unit Program, each inmate is assigned to a residential unit within the institution and to a case management team that monitors his or her progress and ensures that the programmatic and security needs of the offender are being met. To facilitate the development of positive patterns of interaction between the staff and inmates, Living Unit Officers, attired in civilian clothes, replaced uniformed correctional officers and assumed the dual role of counselling inmates and ensuring adherence to institutional rules and regulations.

Education Programs

The regimen of strict discipline and hard labour in early Canadian institutions did not provide the opportunity for the development of education programs. The few literacy programs that were implemented in the 1800s were operated by prison chaplains and available to only a few selected inmates. The Archambault Committee (1938), in calling for an increased emphasis on the reformation of offenders in prison, was highly critical of federal corrections for failing to develop adequate educational programs and recommended a complete overhaul of the prison education system.

Subsequent reports by the Fauteux Committee (1956) and the Mac-Guigan Sub-committee (1977) documented the continuing failure of federal corrections to develop a viable curriculum, provide qualified teachers, and secure external accreditation. Cosman (1980: 46), in concluding that such criticisms were justified, contends that in Canada "penitentiary education has been mainly thought of either as a time-filling activity whose main purpose is to relieve boredom . . . or as a means of providing skill-training for the employment market."

From a review of the history of educational programming in federal institutions, McCarthy (1985: 444–45) concludes that the development of relevant educational courses is a low priority, noting that correctional officials rejected 89 of 106 recommendations made in a study of prison education by the Ontario Institute for Studies in Education (OISE) in 1979: "They reject the demands for increased funding and for part-time, adult, and continuing education . . . They disregard proposals for developing special programs, post-secondary courses, pay parity, and other significant issues." The OISE (cited in McCarthy, 1985: 451) had examined the structure and operation of education programs in federal institutions and concluded that the system of education "as a whole is patchy in operation, at times fumbling in implementation, and existing in an environment of half-hearted support." Annual expenditures by the Correctional Service of Canada for the education and training of inmates is generally less than one-fourth of that alloted to custody.

Through its Education and Training Division, the CSC offers courses in 26 institutions, including literacy and life skills programs, and elementary, secondary, and college and university-level certificate/diploma and degree programs, several of which utilize correspondence courses. One of the better-known post-secondary prison education programs is operated by Simon Fraser University. The program of university-level liberal arts courses was initiated by the University of Victoria in 1972 in the British Columbia Penitentiary and was subsequently extended to several federal institutions in the province. In 1984, the contract for operating the program was assumed by Simon Fraser University, which currently offers courses in five degree areas: Psychology, Anthropology, English, History, and Sociology (see Duguid, 1979; 1981; 1983; Duguid and Hoekema, 1985; Morin, 1981).

There is a lack of evaluative research on the impact of education programs on offenders, and many of the studies that have been conducted are methodologically flawed. Studies conducted in the United States have provided inconclusive results. Glaser (1964), for example, found that inmates who participated in prison education programs had higher than average rates of recidivism, hypothesizing that exposure to higher education only heightened the expectations of offenders, which were not subsequently met upon release. Waldo (1973), on the other hand, presents the results of several evaluations that reported that exposure to prison education programs did serve to increase the likelihood of success upon release (see also Glaser, 1973; Greenberg, 1977; Reker and Meissner, 1977).

Several research inquiries have attempted to assess the impact of the prison education program now operated by Simon Fraser University. Duguid (1981), for example, reports the results of an evaluation that found that only 15% of a group of 75 offenders who had participated in the program were reincarcerated during a three-year follow-up period, compared to a rate of 55 to 65% for those offenders who had not participated in the prison education program (see also Gendreau, Ross, and Izzo, 1985; Linden et al., 1984).

Vocational Training Programs

There have also been difficulties in establishing and operating vocational training programs for prison inmates. Early attempts to establish a system of workhouses and to teach inmates trade skills were successfully opposed by outside labour organizations, and convict labour was utilized primarily for the maintenance of the institution (see Palmer, 1980). In 1977, the MacGuigan Sub-committee reported that federal corrections suffered from (1) too few vocational training opportunities that would assist the offender upon release from the institution, (2) limited inmate participation in programs, (3) a lack of qualified instructors and up-to-date machinery, and (4) a lack of apprenticeship opportunities (see Griffin, 1978).

Currently, occupational and vocational training are provided in a number of areas, including autobody repair, carpentry, and welding. The specific training provided is dependent upon the inmate's security classification and the programs available in the institution, although there is considerable variability between institutions in the types of vocational training opportunities available. These training initiatives are often integrated into prison industry programs, although CORCAN, the federal prison industries corporation, had traditionally reported deficits, high production costs, and high inventory levels.

The primary obstacle to the expansion of prison industry programs is the provisions of the *Penitentiary Act* that specify that goods and services produced by inmates may be sold only to federal, provincial, and municipal governments or to charitable, religious, and non-profit organizations. This restriction, to which there have been only a few exceptions, is the legacy of the resistance by outside labour to allowing products produced in the prison to compete on the open market. The MacGuigan Sub-committee recommended that the *Penitentiary Act* be amended to allow inmate-produced goods to compete on the open market, and research by MacDonald (1982) in Canada and by several investigators in the United States suggests that community resistance to prison industries may be overestimated.

In a survey of a wide range of community groups, including business and labour, MacDonald (1982) found widespread support for paying inmates and allowing prison-produced goods to be sold on the open market, so long as such products were not subsidized or given any other unfair advantage. Similarly, in a review of research findings on public attitudes toward work in prison in the United States, Cullen and Travis (1984) concluded that while the public has hardened in its view of criminal offenders and feels that stringent criminal sanctions should be applied, there is widespread support for the notion that inmates should be provided with work opportunities, particularly if a portion of the monies earned by the inmate were paid to victims in the form of restitution. These authors (pp. 55–58) argue that prison industry programs would not constitute a major threat to most businesses in the corporate sector and, further, that prison industries could attract much of the labour-intensive work that is currently being done "offshore" in such countries as Taiwan and Hong Kong (see also Gandy and Hurl, 1987: Miller, Funke, and Grieser, 1983).

The Effectiveness of Prison Programs

While the rehabilitative approach to offenders and the accompanying medical model provided the basis for the development of a wide range of programs within federal and provincial institutions, in the mid-1960s the effectiveness of these programs came under increasing scrutiny. In the United States, Bailey (1966) concluded that "evidence supporting the efficacy of correctional treatment is slight, inconsistent, and of questionable reliability." This conclusion was echoed in reports by Greenberg (1977), Robison and Smith (1971) and van den Haag (1975), who asserted that "rehabilitation treatment has not been shown to be effective in reducing recidivism."[14]

Perhaps the most influential voice in the chorus of criticism was that of Robert Martinson (1974: 25), who concluded after examining over 200 evaluations of correctional treatment programs conducted between 1945 and 1967 that "with few and isolated exceptions, the rehabilitative efforts that have been reported so far have had no appreciable effect on recidivism." Although the methodology and findings of the Martinson study were severely criticized (Cousineau and Plecas, 1982; Palmer, 1975), the "nothing works" finding contributed to the shift away from rehabilitation programs in prisons.

Prior to his death, Martinson (1979: 201) undertook a re-evaluation of correctional treatment programs and, on the basis of his findings, qualified the "nothing works" conclusion, stating that "some treatment programs do have an appreciable effect on recidivism." More recently, Gendreau and Ross (1979: 488–89) concluded from a review of evaluations of treatment programs that several types of programs did have a positive impact on the offenders who participated in them and noted the consequences of abandoning treatment initiatives: "If we persist in the negative view of correctional treatment, we are encouraging the correctional system to escape its own responsibility. By labeling the offender as untreatable, we make it apparent to one and all that we cannot be held responsible for his improvement or his deterioration" (see Cullen and Gilbert, 1982).

In Canada, concerns about the effectiveness of prison programs were raised in the 1969 report of the Ouimet Committee and in subsequent reports of the Law Reform Commission (1975) and a federal Task Force report on corrections (1977). Ekstedt and Griffiths (1988) note that a major conclusion of these investigations was that the rehabilitation of offenders within prisons was an unrealistic and unattainable goal that should be abandoned in favour of an increased emphasis on community corrections. This conclusion was reached despite the fact that the vast majority of treatment programs that were developed in Canadian institutions were never subjected to controlled evaluation.

While many of the evaluative studies that attempted to measure program effectiveness suffered from severe methodological shortcomings, there were additional obstacles that have been identified by Griffiths et al. (1980) and Ekstedt and Griffiths (1988). These can be generally grouped under (1) the difficulties posed by the total institution environment of the prison, (2) the manner in which correctional treatment programs were implemented within the prison, and (3) how the effectiveness of programs was measured (in those instances in which evaluations were undertaken).

While correctional treatment programs were designed to develop self-confidence, the acceptance of responsibility, and independence of thought in inmates, the regimen of the prison required total obedience to institutional regulations governing every aspect of the offender's life.[15] This has led observers such as Conrad (1983) to argue that it is pointless to pursue rehabilitation within prisons. Further, within the institution, the opposition to treatment initiatives was often expressed by administrators, correctional officers, and even inmates. Administrators and correctional officers often viewed treatment initiatives within the institution as a threat to order and stability. Inmates often gave little legitimacy to institutional treatment initiatives due to adherence to the convict code, the perception that many treatment programs were imposed upon them in a coercive manner, or due to the fact that inmates had little, if any, input into the design and implementation of treatment programs. Further, programs were subject to manipulation by inmates who participated only to improve their chances of release.

There were also difficulties surrounding what Ekstedt and Griffiths (1988) have labelled the "integrity" of correctional treatment programs. More specifically, questions have been raised concerning the validity of the assumptions of the medical model, the discrepancy that often existed between how a treatment program was designed to operate and how it was actually implemented in the institution, and the degree to which treatment programs were matched with the needs of individual inmates. Ekstedt and Griffiths argue, for example, that a major difficulty with the medical model was "its failure to clearly define the objectives of treatment and to provide a body of empirical evidence which treatment specialists could utilize in designing and operating programs" (pp. 241–42).

In retrospect, it appears that the treatment professionals that became involved in institutional programs following World War II may have oversold their ability to diagnose and treat offenders. Gibbons (1965; 1980), Conrad (1981) and others have further argued that the development and operation of treatment programs were hindered by the failure of correctional authorities to define the terms *treatment* and *rehabilitation* clearly and to establish measurement indicators.

Measuring the effectiveness of treatment programs also proved to be an elusive objective. The majority of evaluations utilized recidivism rates to assess the impact of treatment programs on the offender. This involved determining the "rate of return" of released offenders back to institutions, either due to a technical violation of their parole or mandatory supervision conditions or the commission of a new offence. To ascertain the effectiveness of a particular treatment program, the recidivism rate of offenders who had participated in a treatment program was compared with that of offenders who not been involved in the program.

There is disagreement among correctional observers concerning the usefulness of recidivism rates as an accurate indicator of treatment effectiveness. Critics argue that recidivism rates are poor indicators of the effectiveness of correctional treatment because

1. by focusing on the violation of the law as a measure of success, they obscure improvements in the individual, such as an increased level of education or the acquisition of a vocational skill;
2. the individual may have returned to criminal activity, but not have been detected by the criminal justice system;
3. there are many factors, other than having participated in a program while confined, that contribute to an individual's success upon release back into the community, including a supportive family, stable employment, and the process of maturation, and
4. the fact that offenders who participated in a particular treatment program are returned to prison is not conclusive evidence that the program itself is ineffective.

Despite these arguments and suggestions that alternative measures for assessing the effectiveness of prison programs be developed (see Glaser, 1964; Warren, 1977), correctional systems continue to rely upon recidivism rates as the primary indicator of program success or failure.

Correctional Officers

In spite of their critical position within the prison, correctional officers have received little attention from correctional organizations and researchers. Traditionally, the occupation of correctional officer (or prison guard) has been characterized by low prestige, poor pay, inadequate training, and high turnover. In the last decade, research studies in the United States and Canada have provided important insights into the occupational perspectives of correctional officers and into the patterns of interaction that develop between officers and inmates, treatment staff, and prison administration, as well as among the officers themselves.

In the majority of state and federal prisons in the United States, correctional officers are uniformed security personnel distinct from the treatment staff, who are involved in classification, case management, and the operation of programs (see Fogel, 1975). A similar arrangement exists in most provincial correctional facilities in Canada. Similar distinctions existed between correctional officers and program personnel in federal institutions until the introduction of the Living Unit concept in the early 1970s. This resulted in uniformed security personnel being relegated to perimeter security functions and the creation of several new positions within the institution, including Living Unit Development Officer and Living Unit Officers. These personnel, who wear civilian clothes, are charged with counselling inmates and routine supervision within the "therapeutic milieu" of the prison.

Working Inside

The primary motivations for becoming a correctional officer appear to be job stability and fringe benefits, rather than a keen interest in working with offenders (see Jacobs, 1978; Willett, 1983). As a correctional officer in a United States state prison related to one of the co-authors of this text:

> I just got out of the Service. I didn't know a dang thing but the Service. I was starving to death and then a friend of mine told me about the prison. Higher pay, veteran's benefits, the possibility of going to school. It sounded pretty good.

For the majority of officers interviewed by Lombardo (1981: 21), ". . . it was not that prison work was attractive, rather, becoming a prison guard was an escape from the dirt and drudgery of their former occupations." Willett (1977) found similar motivations among a group of Canadian correctional officers. As a consequence of this, new officers often experience considerable uncertainty about their role in the institution, as evidenced by comments such as "I had no idea, I just didn't know" and "All I knew was that I was getting a job" (Lombardo, 1981: 23)

Once hired, correctional officers undergo a period of socialization into life inside the total institution (see Crouch and Marquart, 1980). Lombardo (1981: 111) notes that "guards, like inmates, must also learn to deal with the stress-laden prison environment if they are to pursue their careers successfully." Webb and Morris (1978: 20) describe this process as becoming "con-wise": ". . . he must come to have an understanding of the inmate culture, certain expectations of inmates, and a method of interacting with inmates that is common to guards."

Becoming "con-wise" does not preclude the officer from being manipulated by the inmates, but means that "the individual is aware of the frequency with which he is apt to be lied to, deceived, or manipulated" (Webb and Morris, 1978: 23). And, while officers tend to discard their pre-prison employment stereotypes of offenders as all alike, there is the continuing perception that inmates will manipulate and take advantage of the officers if the opportunity arises.

Many observers have argued that correctional officers constitute an occupational subculture similar to that which exists among police officers (see Chapter 3). Bowker (1982: 178) notes that the stigma attached to being a correctional officer by the larger community, the perceptions by officers that they cannot talk to "civilians" about their work, and the reliance of officers upon one another in an unpredictable, potentially dangerous environment contribute to solidarity among officers (see also Duffee, 1974; Jacobs and Retsky, 1975; Philliber, 1987).

Others, however, have argued that correctional officer solidarity and the extent to which officers constitute an occupational subculture has been overstated (see Klofas and Toch, 1982). There is evidence to suggest that, similar to the shared misperceptions that may exist among prison inmates in terms of their support for the inmate social system, a considerable amount of "pluralistic ignorance" may exist among correctional officers as well. Kauffman (1981: 387) reported, for example, that officers viewed one another as "more antagonistic to inmates and treatment than the reality of the individual officers' attitudes warrant." From his extensive research on correctional officers, Lombardo (1981: 163) concluded that "the 'regime of the custodians' appears to be a highly fragmented collectivity of individuals." And in a Canadian study, Willett (1983) found that correctional officers did not tend to socialize with one another during off-hours, although officers did experience considerable stress associated with their occupation, which often adversely affected their family relationships.

It might be expected that, similar to the inmate social system, the patterns of interaction that develop among correctional officers will be in part determined by the security level, social climate, and administrative policies of the institution. Duffee (1974) found that the management style of the prison administration directly influenced the perceptions of and support for the administration and its objectives among the correctional officers, as well as the patterns of interaction that developed between the officers and the inmates.

A little-studied component of the interaction that develops among officers within the institution system involves officers "snitching" on one another, usually to gain favour with supervisory staff. One of the co-authors of this text first encountered this phenomenon in a United States prison where he was teaching inmates and correctional officers (separately) in university-level courses. One correctional officer stated:

There is a lot of back-stabbing. People trying to gain brownie points. I've heard of several incidents now where guys are getting turned in. One of my classmates is getting turned for not having his hat on out on the wall.

Similarly, Willett (1977: 443) reported that there were " 'rats' among the guards who 'brown-nosed' — ingratiating themselves with keepers and passing information about the shortcomings of other men. These were the men who seemed to others to get the 'cushy' posts, leaving the 'joe-jobs' to the less favoured."

A long-standing concern of correctional administrators is the corruption of correctional officers, which may take one of the following forms: (1) theft, including stealing from inmate cells; (2) bringing contraband, such as drugs, money, alcohol, or weapons, into the prison; (3) misappropriating government property for private use; and (4) abusing authority for personal gain (see McCarthy, 1984). The extent of officer corruption in contemporary Canadian corrections is unknown. In recent years, the Correctional Service of Canada has increased the education and training requirements for institutional staff, shifting from a "keeper" role to a focus on communication. These and other developments will result in increased professionalism among correctional staff and reduce and perhaps eliminate many of the problems that have traditionally afflicted the occupation.

Correctional Officers and Inmates: Conflict and Accommodation

Our discussion of the inmate code indicated that inmates often do not adhere behaviourally to the tenets of the inmate code, and this is evident in the accommodative relations that develop between the inmates and correctional officers. While correctional officers may be referred to as "pigs," "the police," or "the man" by inmates, there are pressures on each group to accommodate the other — the inmates to reduce the pains of imprisonment and the correctional officers to ensure stability and order on a day-to-day basis. The specific patterns of interaction that develop between the correctional officers and the inmates will depend upon a variety of factors, including the size of the inmate population, the security level of the institution, and whether treatment or custody and control are the primary objectives of the prison administration.

As officers become familiar with the prison environment, stereotypical views of criminals are replaced by the realization that each inmate is an individual and that not all inmates are alike. Similar to police officers, correctional officers develop their own "style" of carrying out their tasks and of coping with the demands placed upon them by inmates and administration (see Crouch, 1980; Hommant, 1979). New officers must become acquainted with the informal accommodative relations that exist between the inmates and the correctional officers. Should an officer fail to display flexibility in decision making, he or she may be the subject of criticism from both the inmates and fellow officers.

There is a considerable amount of discretion employed by correctional officers in the day-to-day interpretation and enforcement of prison regulations. Most officers take a common-sense approach in applying regulations to specific situations, realizing that full enforcement of prison regulations would make life unbearable for both themselves and the inmates. In a study of correctional officer decision making in a United States prison, Hewitt, Poole, and Regoli (1984) found that in an attempt to maintain stability, the officers reported very few of the violations of prison rules that they observed. To maintain control, officers may employ a variety of "informal" sanctions against inmates, such as ignoring inmate requests and delaying the movement of an inmate from one area of the prison to another.

There is also some evidence to suggest that correctional officers and the prison administration may recruit inmate "elites" to assist in controlling the prison population (see Marquart and Crouch, 1984). Marquart and Roebuck (1985) found in a study of a prison in the United States that correctional officers coopted certain inmates to act as informants. Contrary to the traditional portrayal of inmate informants or "snitches" as weak and exploited, the inmates utilized by the correctional officers were among the most feared and aggressive. While the lack of research precludes even speculative statements regarding the use of inmates to maintain control in Canadian institutions, it is generally agreed that such practices are quite precarious, and violent disruptions may result should power shifts occur among the inmates (see Colvin, 1982).

While there are pressures for the inmates and the correctional staff to develop accommodative relations, Bowker (1982: 144) argues that fear among the staff of being taken advantage of or being "burnt" by the inmates mitigates against such relations being maintained over time. This fear of being "burnt" was mentioned to Webb and Morris (1978: 47) as the one aspect the officers most disliked about the inmates: "The fact that they can smile at you and stab you in the back."

The Officers and the Administration

While correctional officers are charged with enforcing the regulations of the prison and carrying out directives issued by the prison administration, the relations between these two groups may be characterized by suspicion and distrust. As Webb and Morris (1978: 42) note with respect to the manner in which officers regard the administration: "They are viewed as a necessary evil; something that in good times may support them and in bad times will blame them when things go wrong." Depending upon the particular "style" of management in the prison, administrators may be viewed as insensitive to the needs of officers, as far removed from the realities of daily life in the institution, and as having little understanding of inmates and the practical realities of implementing prison regulations and administrative directives.

Many of the officers interviewed by Lombardo (1981: 90) believed that the regulations they were asked to enforce were often unnecessary, and they blamed prison administrators for directives that increased tension and undermined their authority at the line level. Inmates are often aware of the estranged position of the correctional officers: "You can't blame the officers that much, because they're kept in the dark as much as we are a lot of the times. And it changes from one day to the other, they don't know what is happening either" (Toch, 1977: 83).

Treatment programs sponsored by the administration may be a particular source of resentment. Officers may express considerable frustration at the amount of attention given to inmate needs. The realization that the inmates may have opportunities for vocational and educational advancement and improvement not available to the officers may lead officers to resist the implementation of specific programs or to be less than enthusiastic in supporting them.

Recruitment, Training and Education of Correctional Officers

The MacGuigan Sub-committee (1977) found that many correctional officers in federal penitentiaries had received little or no formal training. In recent years the Correctional Service of Canada has strengthened its staff training and development program and now attempts to recruit only individuals who are graduates of universities or community colleges or of accredited correctional training programs (Ross and McKay, 1981). In addition, increased emphasis has been given to the recruitment of female correctional officers in both Canada and the United States (see Crouch, 1985). This has given rise to numerous legal issues, including the inmates' right to privacy where women are employed as correctional officers in institutions for male offenders (Horne, 1985; Parisi, 1984).

There are no national standards for the selection and training of correctional officers at the provincial level, and there is considerable variability across the various jurisdictions in selection criteria and training programs. In British Columbia, correctional officers are trained at the Justice Institute, which serves as a training facility for municipal police as well. In other provinces, training programs for correctional officers are offered through college and university programs (Wahler and Gendreau, 1985).

Many observers have argued that correctional officers constitute an underutilized resource in the correctional process and that, given their proximity to the inmates on a daily basis, the potential exists for officers to assume the role of agents of change. Johnson (1977), for example, has suggested that correctional officers should be incorporated into the treatment process and work with, rather than against, the efforts of the program staff (see also Johnson, 1979).

The introduction of the Living Unit concept in the early 1970s as part of the development of a "therapeutic community" within institutions, and the creation of the position of Living Unit Officers, charged with both security and counselling functions, were an attempt to transform correctional officers into agents of change. However, as our discussion of treatment in correctional institutions will reveal, Living Unit Officers have experienced considerable difficulty in carrying out these dual roles.

In 1986, the CSC undertook a major reorganization of the operational structure within federal institutions. This involved the replacement of the Living Unit concept with the concept of Functional Unit Management. Rather than the previous split between living unit officers (CXs) and the Living Unit Officers (LUs), all institutional personnel are hired in the position of correctional officer (CO). The entry position, CO1, is concerned primarily with the security function. Upon promotion to CO2, correctional officers will have more contact with inmates and be involved both in a security function and in a human relations approach in interacting with the inmates. The CO2 will be intimately involved in producing assessments of the inmates' activities and institutional progress. The CO1s and CO2s will report to the Unit Management Team, headed by a Unit Manager. This reorganization is designed to increase the interaction between correctional officers and inmates and to structure increased involvement of line-level personnel with offenders in the role of agents of change.

The increased education and training of correctional officers will produce positive results only if mechanisms are developed by which officers can function as agents of positive change in the correctional institution. There must also be increased attention to the environment in which correctional officers work and the impact of the stresses of the total institution on their attitudes and behaviours. The fact that there has traditionally been very little "carry-over" from training courses to the operational setting of the prison, however, has hindered any significant changes in the role of correctional officers (see Willett, 1983).

Managing Correctional Institutions

Despite the pivotal role of the warden in the operation of the prison, historically individuals occupying this position have often not been equal to the task. The focus of the Brown Commission inquiry in 1848 was the mismanagement of Kingston Penitentiary by its first warden, Henry Smith. Similar inquiries, such as the Royal Commission (Canada, 1895) inquiry into the activities of the warden of the British Columbia Penitentiary in 1894, also focused on allegations of misconduct. At the local level, the character and conduct of the individuals given responsibility for supervising gaols were often indistinguishable from those of their clients. Prior to the 1960s, the management of prisons was based on a paramilitary model, under which wardens had total, dictatorial control. Within the walls, the warden's word was "law," and absolute power over both the guards and the inmates was maintained by strict regimentation and harsh responses to those who violated the rigid rules: "Wardens mixed terror, incentives, and favoritism to keep their subjects fearful but not desperate, hopeful but always uncertain" (Bartollas, 1981: 266). Following World War II, correctional management systems were implemented and corrections became increasingly bureaucratized: "The czars who had rules as they pleased became field officers whose performance and recommendations were reviewed in the central office; the sovereigns, in effect, became the accountable bureaucrats" (Bartollas, 1981: 267).

The "Double-Bind," Management Style, and Institutional Climate

The prison warden of today is a professional manager charged with the almost impossible task of responding to demands from external publics and from the various groups within the institution. There are many "external" activities and decisions over which the wardens have no control, but which may have a significant impact on the operation of the institution, such as the sentencing patterns of the courts, the placement decisions of classification officers, and decisions regarding when offenders will be released from the institution. Within the institution, the warden is responsible for a wide range of administrative tasks, as well as for mediating the often conflicting interests of the inmates, security personnel, and treatment staff (see Fox, 1984). And it is the warden who will be held accountable for disruptions such as riots, suicides and escapes, all of which may be precipitated by overcrowding and inappropriate inmate transfers or other decisions over which the warden has no control.

Bowker (1982: 208) characterizes the position of the warden as the "double-bind" dilemma, which places administrators in "no win" situations where "middle-ground" decisions are "more likely to displease all groups than to satisfy any one of them." The decision to implement or expand a treatment program within the institution, for example, will have direct implications for the inmates, treatment staff, and correctional officers (see also Bowker, 1979). The comments of a former warden (cited in Bartollas, 1981: 284) illustrate the "double-bind": "When you get up in the morning, you have to decide who's going to belt you that day. Is it going to be the conservatives, the liberals, the inmates, the (guards) union, or some other group?" A failure to balance the custody and control mandate of the prison with that of providing opportunities for inmates to change may lead to disturbances among the inmates and low staff morale.

Duffee (1975) identified two "ideal types" of correctional management: the aggregate style and the integrative style. In the aggregate style of management, the activities of the warden centre around coordinating the separate divisions in the institution, such as custody and treatment. Rather than there being direct contact and problem solving between the different divisions, the supervisors report directly to the warden. Wardens adopting an integrative style of management, on the other hand, focus their energies on improving the interaction between the different divisions of the institution. The warden assumes the position of providing overall direction and ensuring that the supervisors of each division work in concert with one another.[16]

The management style of the warden will have a significant impact on the "climate" that develops in the institution. Duffee (1975: 156) defines the *institutional climate* as "the total effect of living and working within the organization." The institutional climate is an important determinant of the patterns of interaction that develop among the various groups within the institution, and institutions, even at the same security level, will have a distinctive "climate." However, the efforts of even the most enlightened warden may be severely hindered by overcrowding, a poor physical facility, and the resistance of correctional officers and/or security staff to specific programmatic initiatives.

Wardens: Agents of Change or Bureaucrats?

Many correctional observers have been critical of correctional management at the institutional level. Cohn (1976: 124–26) suggests that an undue concern with security and avoiding risks, the uncertainty among administrators regarding who their constituents are, and inadequate training are among the factors that have led to a "failure" of correctional management. Reid (1982: 532) argues that significant changes in correctional administration have been hindered by (1) the conflicting interests of the inmates, guards, and treatment staff; (2) the conflict between the custody and control goals and rehabilitation; (3) the lack of a sound body of information on the use of management techniques within the prison; and (4) limited financial resources, which have resulted in overcrowding, staff shortages, and program cutbacks (see also Cohn, 1979).[17]

One of the more serious difficulties confronting Canadian wardens is a consequence of the increasing bureaucratization of corrections noted earlier. A recent inquiry into the management of federal correctional institutions (Carson, 1984) identified the regional and national offices of the CSC as a major source of difficulty for wardens. More specifically, the Committee (1984: 20) found that many wardens had "little actual authority and no perceived authority to manage their institutions," but rather were bound by an ever larger number of directives that "increasingly prescribe not only what to do, but direct how to do it." One recommendation of the Committee (p. 21) was that institutional priorities should take precedence over external demands.

There was also often conflict between the operational requirements of the institution and the implementation of directives from regional and national headquarters. As one warden told the study team (Carson, 1984: App. B, p. 24): "What we need is one correctional service with autonomous institutions; unfortunately, what we have is management by centralized systems and functional directives. The latter are not working at the institutional level."

It was also found that wardens tend to be assessed on the extent of their compliance with directives rather than results obtained at the individual institutional level. The report (Carson, 1984: App. B, p. ii) argued that there was a need to recognize "the unique operational requirements of each institution" and to "shift away from measuring performance largely by compliance with national and standardized directives toward measuring results at a specific institution against objectives that are reasonable and attainable at that institution . . ."

Recent organizational changes suggest that the CSC is not heeding the recommendations of the Carson Committee (1984). Under the Functional Unit Management plan discussed earlier, wardens of institutions will be required to spend the majority of their time in a liaison role with regional headquarters, while deputy wardens will assume an increasing role in overseeing the operation of the institution on a daily basis. Given these developments, it is likely that wardens will continue to find themselves at the centre of the conflicting demands of the public, the inmates, the correctional staff, and the Correctional Service of Canada.[18]

NOTES

1. For a detailed examination of correctional institutions and community-based corrections in Canada, see Ekstedt and Griffiths (1988).

2. A growing concern among correctional administrators is the feelings of hopelessness and desperation that may develop among long-term offenders and the likelihood of increased violence within institutions (see Lemire, 1984; Mohr, 1985; Palmer, 1984; Wormith, 1985; Zubrycki, 1984a, 1984b). In 1982, two "lifers" committed suicide after instigating a major disturbance at Archambault Penitentiary, during which three correctional officers were killed. A major task confronting corrections is the development of meaningful program opportunities for the long-term offender.

3. While Conrad (1984: 48) has argued that it is not possible for corrections to develop a strong constituency because "corrections is unrelated to citizen's personal interests," other observers contend that the public is an underutilized resource and that, as the majority of offenders in

confinement will be returning to society, it *is* in the interest of both the community and the individual citizen to understand and have input into the operation of the correctional enterprise. Kellough (1985) has proposed a model for community participation in the correctional process, although Duffee (1984) has argued that there are distinct limitations to citizen involvement in correctional programs.

4. For a critical review of Goffman's writings on institutions, see Jones and Fowles (1984).

5. A major difference between Canadian and United States correctional institutions is size. While it is unusual for a Canadian penitentiary to have an inmate population of over 700, in the United States many state prisons have over 2,000 inmates. Also, in the United States there is considerable ethnic diversity in the populations of many state prisons, which has significant consequences for the operation of the institution and the types of problems that arise.

6. In *Ideas on Institutions*, Jones and Fowles (1984) present a comprehensive overview of various perspectives on institutions.

7. For insightful first-person accounts of life "inside," see Abbott (1983); Caron (1978; 1985).

8. For a description of various social roles in a United States state maximum security prison, see McCoy (1981).

9. The authors (Zamble et al., 1984: 133) have also questioned the often stated assertion that imprisonment has a negative impact on the emotional state of inmates, concluding from their investigation of inmates in Canadian penitentiaries that "for most subjects the initial traumatic effects of imprisonment were greatly alleviated over time." These findings suggest that inmates develop techniques to cope with the stresses associated with confinement, although these findings remain to be corroborated by additional research.

10. Perhaps the most insightful examination of life inside the Kingston Penitentiary for Women is provided by the film *P4W*, available from Pan Canadian Films, 214 King St. West, Toronto, Ontario. See also *C'est Pas Parce Que C'est un Chateau Qu'on est des Princesses (Castle/No Princess),* a documentary film on female inmates at the Maison Gomin in Quebec, available from Video Femmes, 56 St.-Pierre, #203, Quebec, G1K 4A1.

11. The Quebec Regional Reception Centre is all that remains of the network of federal Regional Reception Centres that previously existed across Canada.

12. In documenting the excessive use of regional transfers, the Carson Committee (1984: 41) reported that during 1983–84, 1,183 offenders had been transferred across regional boundaries. This included sending native offenders from the Prairie region to the Maritimes and anglophone offenders to Quebec. In the *Annual Report of the Correctional Investigator* (Government of Canada, 1987: 21–22), concerns are raised about the exercise of

fairness by the CSC in involuntary transfer decisions, despite court decisions and CSC policy directives that have addressed this problem.

13. For an in-depth consideration of issues surrounding the treatment
of offenders, see Bartollas (1985); Ekstedt and Griffiths (1988).

14. Similar arguments were made in relation to treatment programs
for youthful offenders. See Glaser (1979).

15. The conflict between custody and control and treatment is best
illustrated by the difficulties that Living Unit Officers have in fulfilling
both a custody role and a therapeutic function in the institution (Vigod,
1974). In 1977, the MacGuigan Sub-committee noted that the Living Unit
Program had not reached its objectives. Beginning in 1986, the Correctional Service of Canada modified the Living Unit Program.

16. In the book *Stateville — The Penitentiary in Mass Society*, James
B. Jacobs (1977) presents a historical analysis of the management of the
maximum security institution at Stateville, Illinois from the 1930s to the
1970s. See also Curtis et al. (1985).

17. With few exceptions, women are noticeably absent from both
policymaking and managerial levels of federal and provincial correctional
systems in Canada (Nicolai, 1981). In discussing a similar situation in the
United States, Bergen (1984: 112, 113) pointed out that the contributions of
women to the development of corrections are generally excluded from
published correctional histories and noted: "Today, as a rule, women are
excluded from the correctional arenas that facilitate policymaking. As a
result of the 'women's place' philosophy, women both as workers and as
clients have been delegated to the poor cousins' rank."

18. The extent to which the decision-making autonomy of the wardens at the institutional level has been eroded is illustrated by an example
conveyed to one of the text authors by a Living Unit Officer working in a
medium security institution in the Pacific region. This officer noted that
the institutional administration had, during 1986, received a memorandum from CSC headquarters in Ottawa specifying *how much tack board
space each inmate in the institution was allowed to have in his room.*

REFERENCES

Abbott, J. H. 1983. *In the Belly of the Beast — Letters from Prison.* New
York: Random House.

Abdul-Mu'Min, E. M. 1985. "Prisoner Power and Survival." In *Correctional Institutions*, edited by R. M. Carter, D. Glaser, and L. T.
Wilkins, 140–60. 3rd ed. New York: Harper and Row Publishers.

Akers, R. L., N. S. Hayner, and W. Gruninger. 1977. "Prisonization in Five
Countries: Type of Prison and Inmate Characteristics." 14 *Criminology* 527–54.

Alpert, G. P. 1979. "Patterns of Change in Prisonization: A Longitudinal Analysis." 6 *Criminal Justice and Behavior* 159–74.

Alpert, G. P., G. Noblit, and J. J. Wiokowski. 1977. "A Comparative Look at Prisonization: Sex and Prison Culture." 1 *Quarterly Journal of Corrections* 29–34.

Archambault, J. (Chairman). 1938. *Report of the Royal Commission to Investigate the Prison System of Canada.* Ottawa: King's Printer.

Bailey, W. C. 1966. "Correctional Outcome: An Evaluation of 100 Reports." 57 *Journal of Criminology, Criminal Law and Police Science* 153–60.

Bartollas, C. 1981. *Introduction to Corrections.* New York: Harper and Row.

———. 1985. *Correctional Treatment: Theory and Practice.* Englewood Cliffs, N.J.: Prentice-Hall.

Bergen, D. R. 1984. "Women Managers in Corrections." 64 *The Prison Journal* 111–19.

Berk, B. B. 1966. "Organizational Goals and Inmate Organization." 71 *American Journal of Sociology* 522–34.

Blumstein, A., J. Cohen, and D. Nagin. 1978. *Deterrence and Incapacitation: Estimating the Effects of Criminal Sanctions on Crime Rates.* Washington, D.C.: National Academy of Sciences.

Bowker, L. H. 1979. "The Warden: A Classic Case of the Double-Bind Dilemma." 23 *International Journal of Offender Therapy and Comparative Criminology* 159–63.

———. 1981. "Gender Differences in Prisoner Subcultures." In *Women and Crime in America*, edited by L. H. Bowker, 409–19. New York: Macmillan.

———. 1982. *Corrections — The Science and the Art.* New York: Macmillan.

Brillon, Y., C. Louis-Guerin, and M.-C. Lamarche. 1984. *Attitudes of the Canadian Public toward Crime Policies.* Montreal: International Centre for Comparative Criminology, University of Montreal.

Canada. Commission to Investigate the Administration and Affairs of New Westminster Penitentiary. 1895. *Report.* Ottawa: Debates of the Senate.

Canadian Centre for Justice Statistics. 1989. *Adult Correctional Services in Canada, 1987–88.* Ottawa: Supply and Services Canada.

Carlen, P., J. Hicks, J. O'Dwyer, D. Christina, and C. Tchaikovsky. 1985. *Criminal Women.* Cambridge: Polity Press.

Caron, R. 1978. *Go-Boy: Memoirs of a Life behind Bars.* Toronto: McGraw-Hill Ryerson.

———. 1985. *BINGO!* Toronto: Methuen.

Carroll, L. 1977. "Race and Three Forms of Prisoner Power: Confrontation, Censoriousness, and the Corruption of Authority." In *Contemporary Corrections: Social Control and Conflict*, edited by C. R. Huff, 40–53. Beverly Hills, Calif.: Sage.

Carson, J. J. (Chairman). 1984. *Report of the Advisory Committee to the Solicitor General of Canada on the Management of Correctional Institutions.* Ottawa: Supply and Services Canada.

Clemmer, D. 1940. *The Prison Community.* Boston: Christopher Publishing Co.

Cohn, A. W. 1976. "The Failure of Correctional Management." In *Corrections and Administration — Selected Readings*, edited by G. G. Killinger et al., 491–512. St. Paul, Minn.: West Publishing Co.

———. 1979. "The Failure of Correctional Management — Revisited." 45 *Federal Probation* 13–14.

Colvin, M. 1982. "The New Mexico Prison Riot." 29 *Social Problems* 449–63.

Conrad, J. P. 1981. "A Lost Ideal, A New Hope: The Way toward Effective Correctional Treatment." 72 *Journal of Criminal Law and Criminology* 1699–1734.

———. 1983. "What Prospects for Rehabilitation? A Dissent from Academic Wisdom." In *Corrections: An Issues Approach*, edited by L. F. Travis, M. D. Schwartz, and T. R. Clear, 216–26. 2nd ed. Cincinnati, Ohio: Anderson Publishing Co.

———. 1984. "Corrections and Its Constituencies." 64 *The Prison Journal* 47–55.

Cosman, J. W. 1980. "Penitentiary Education in Canada." 20 *Education Canada* 42–47.

Cousineau, F. D., and D. B. Plecas. 1982. "Justifying Criminal Justice Policy with Methodologically Inadequate Research." 24 *Canadian Journal of Criminology* 307–21.

Cressey, D. R. 1977. "Sources of Resistance to Innovation in Corrections." In *Correctional Institutions*, edited by R. M. Carter, D. Glaser, and L. T. Wilkins, 491–512. 2nd ed. New York: J. B. Lippincott.

Crouch, B. M. 1980. "The Book vs. The Boot: Two Styles of Guarding in a Southern Prison." In *The Keepers: Prison Guards and Contemporary Corrections*, edited by B. M. Crouch, 207–24. Springfield, Ill.: Charles C. Thomas Publishers.

———. 1985. "Pandora's Box: Women Guards in Men's Prisons." 13 *Journal of Criminal Justice* 535–48.

Crouch, B. M., and J. Marquart. 1980. "On Becoming a Prison Guard." In *The Keepers: Prison Guards and Contemporary Corrections*, edited by B. M. Crouch, 93–109. Springfield, Ill.: Charles C. Thomas Publishers.

Cullen, F. T., and K. E. Gilbert. 1982. *Reaffirming Rehabilitation.* Cincinnati, Ohio: Anderson Publishing Co.

Cullen, F. T., and L. F. Travis. 1984. "Work as an Avenue of Prison Reform." 10 *New England Journal of Criminal and Civil Confinement* 45–64.

Curtis, D., A. Graham, L. Kelly, and A. Patterson. 1985. *Kingston Penitentiary: The First Hundred and Fifty Years.* Ottawa: Supply and Services Canada.

Dobash, R. P., R. E. Dobash, and S. Gutteridge. 1986. *The Imprisonment of Women.* New York: Blackwell.

Duffee, D. E. 1974. "The Correction Officer Subculture and Organizational Change." 11 *Journal of Research in Crime and Delinquency* 155–72.

———. 1975. *Correctional Policy and Prison Organization.* New York: John Wiley and Sons.

———. 1984. "The Limits of Citizen Involvement in Correctional Programs." 64 *The Prison Journal* 56–76.

Duguid, S. 1979. "History and Moral Education in Prison Education." 4 *Canadian Journal of Education* 81–92.

———. 1981. "Moral Development, Justice and Democracy in the Prison." 23 *Canadian Journal of Criminology* 147–62.

———. 1983. "Origins and Development of University Education at Matsqui Institution." 25 *Canadian Journal of Criminology* 295–308.

Duguid, S., and H. Hoekema. 1985. *University Education in Prison — A Documentary Record of the Experience in British Columbia, 1974–1985.* Burnaby, B.C.: Continuing Studies, Simon Fraser University.

Ekstedt, J. W., and C. T. Griffiths. 1988. *Corrections in Canada: Policy and Practice.* 2nd ed. Toronto: Butterworths.

Fauteux, G. (Chairman). 1956. *Report of a Committee Appointed to Inquire into the Principles and Procedures Followed in the Remission Service of the Department of Justice of Canada.* Ottawa: Queen's Printer.

Feld, B. C. 1978. *Neutralizing Inmate Violence: Juvenile Offenders in Institutions.* Cambridge, Mass.: Ballinger.

Fogel, D. 1975. "*. . . We Are the Living Proof. . .*" — *The Justice Model for Corrections.* 2nd ed. Cincinnati, Ohio: Anderson Publishing Co.

Foster, T. W. 1975. "Make-believe Families — A Response of Women and Girls to the Deprivation of Imprisonment." 3 *International Journal of Criminology and Penology* 71–78.

Fox, J. 1982. *Organizational and Racial Conflict in Maximum Security Prisons.* Lexington, Mass.: D. C. Heath and Co.

Fox V. 1984. "The Politics of Prison Management." 64 *The Prison Journal* 97–112.

Gandy, J., and L. Hurl. 1987. "Private Sector Involvement in Prison Industries: Issues and Options." 29 *Canadian Journal of Criminology* 185–204.

Garfinkel, H. 1965. "Conditions of Successful Status Degradation Ceremonies." 61 *American Journal of Sociology* 420–24.

Gendreau, P., and B. Ross. 1979. "Effective Correctional Treatment: Bibliotherapy for Cynics." 25 *Crime and Delinquency* 463–89.

Gendreau, P., R. Ross, and R. Izzo. 1985. "Institutional Misconduct: The Effects of the UVIC Program at Matsqui Penitentiary." 27 *Canadian Journal of Criminology* 209–17.

Giallombardo, R. 1966. *Society of Women: A Study of a Women's Prison.* New York: John Wiley and Sons.

Gibbons, D. C. 1965. *Changing the Lawbreaker: The Treatment of Criminals and Victims.* Englewood Cliffs, N.J.: Prentice-Hall.

———. 1980. "Some Notes on Treatment Theory in Corrections." In *Corrections: Problems and Prospects*, edited by D. M. Peterson and C. W. Thomas. Englewood Cliffs, N.J.: Prentice-Hall.

Glaser, D. 1964. *The Effectiveness of a Prison and Parole System.* Indianapolis: Bobbs-Merrill.

———. 1973. "The Effectiveness of Correctional Education." In *Readings in Prison Education*, edited by A. R. Roberts, 351–63. Springfield, Ill.: Charles C. Thomas.

———. 1979. "Disillusion with Rehabilitation: Theoretical and Empirical Questions." In *The Future of Childhood and Juvenile Justice*, edited by L. T. Empey, 234–76. Charlottesville, Va.: University of Virginia Press.

Goffman, E. 1961. *Asylums: Essays on the Social Situation of Mental Patients and Other Inmates.* Garden City, N.Y.: Doubleday Books.

Government of Canada. 1986. *Study Team Report to the Task Force on Program Review. Improved Program Delivery: Justice System.* Ottawa: Supply and Services Canada.

———. 1987. *Annual Report of the Correctional Investigator, 1985–86.* Ottawa: Supply and Services Canada.

Greenberg, D. F. 1977. "The Correctional Effects of Corrections: A Survey of Evaluations." In *Corrections and Punishment*, edited by D. F. Greenberg, 111–48. Beverly Hills, Calif.: Sage Publications.

Griffin, D. K. 1978. *Ontario Institute for Studies in Education: Review of Penitentiary Education and Training, 1978-1979. Phase I: Report to Reviewers.* Ottawa: Education and Training Division, Canadian Penitentiary Service.

Griffiths, C. T., J. F. Klein, and S. N. Verdun-Jones. 1980. *Criminal Justice in Canada: An Introductory Text.* Toronto: Butterworths.

Grusky, O. 1959. "Organizational Goals and the Behavior of Informal Leaders." 65 *American Journal of Sociology* 59–67.

Haney, C., C. Banks, and P. Zimbardo. 1973. "Interpersonal Dynamics in a Simulated Prison." 1 *International Journal of Criminology and Penology* 69–97.

Hewitt, J. D., E. Poole, and R. M. Regoli. 1984. "Self-reported and Observed Rule-Breaking in Prison: A Look at Disciplinary Response." 1 *Justice Quarterly* 437–47.

Hommant, R. J. 1979. "Correlates of Satisfactory Relations between Correctional Officers and Prisoners." 4 *Journal of Offender Counseling Services and Rehabilitation* 53–62.

Horne, P. 1985. "Female Correction Officers: A Status Report." 49 *Federal Probation* 46–54.

Irwin, J. 1977. "The Changing Social Structure of Men's Prison." In *Corrections and Punishment*, edited by D. F. Greenberg, 21–40. Beverly Hills, Calif.: Sage Publications.

Irwin, J., and D. Cressey. 1961." Thieves, Convicts, and the Inmate Code." 10 *Social Problems* 142–55.

Jackson, M. 1986. "The Right to Counsel in Prison Disciplinary Hearings." 20 *U.B.C. Law Review* 221–83.

Jacobs, J. B. 1974. "Street Gangs behind Bars." 21 *Social Problems* 395–409.

———. 1977. *Stateville — The Penitentiary in Mass Society.* Chicago: University of Chicago Press.

———. 1978. "What Prison Guards Think: A Profile of the Illinois Force." 24 *Crime and Delinquency* 185–96.

Jacobs, J. B., and H. G. Retsky. 1975. "Prison Guard." 4 *Urban Life* 5–29.

Johnson, R. 1977. "Ameliorating Prison Stress: Some Helping Roles for Custodial Personnel." 5 *International Journal of Criminology and Penology* 263–73.

———. 1979. "Informal Helping Networks in Prison: The Shape of Grass-Roots Correctional Intervention." 7 *Journal of Criminal Justice* 53–70.

Jones, K., and A. J. Fowles. 1984. *Ideas on Institutions: Analysing the Literature on Long-term Care and Custody.* London: Routledge and Kegan Paul.

Kauffman, K. 1981. "Prison Officers' Attitudes and Perceptions of Attitudes: A Case of Pluralistic Ignorance." 18 *Journal of Research in Crime and Delinquency* 272–94.

Kellough, G. 1985. "The Community, Prison, and Politics." In *Law in a Cynical Society? Opinion and Law in the 1980's*, edited by D. Gibson and J. K. Baldwin. Calgary and Vancouver: Carswell Legal Publications, Western Division.

Klofas, J., and H. Toch. 1982. "The Guard Subculture Myth." 19 *Journal of Research in Crime and Delinquency* 238–54.

Landau, T. 1984. "Due Process, Legalism and Inmates' Rights: A Cautionary Note." 6 *Canadian Criminology Forum* 151–63.

Law Reform Commission of Canada. 1975. *Working Paper 11: Imprisonment and Release.* Ottawa: Information Canada.

Lemire, G. 1984. "La sentence mimale d'emprisonement de 25 ans: princise et pratique." 26 *Canadian Journal of Criminology* 459–66.

Linden, R., L. Perry, D. Ayers, and T. A. A. Parlett. 1984. "An Evaluation of a Prison Education Program." 26 *Canadian Journal of Criminology* 65–73.

Lombardo, L. X. 1981. *Guards Imprisoned — Correctional Officers at Work.* New York: Elsevier.

MacDonald, G. 1982. *Self-sustaining Prison Industries:* Vancouver:

Institute for Studies in Criminal Justice Policy, Simon Fraser University.

MacGuigan, M. (Chairman). 1977. *Report to Parliament by the Sub-committee on the Penitentiary System in Canada.* Ottawa: Supply and Services Canada.

MacNamara, D. E. J. 1977. "The Medical Model in Corrections: Requiescat in Pace." 14 *Criminology* 439–48.

Mandel, M. 1986. "The Legalization of Prison Discipline in Canada." 26 *Crime and Social Justice* 79–94.

Mandell, C. C., and A. L. Mandell. 1985. "Accountability in Canadian Penitentiaries: Disciplinary Procedures and Judicial Review." In *Accountability and Prisons: Opening Up a Closed World,* edited by M. Maguire, J. Vagg, and R. Morgan, 245–63. London: Tavistock Publications Ltd.

Mann, W. E. 1967. *Society behind Bars: A Sociological Scrutiny of Guelph Reformatory.* Toronto: Social Science Publishers.

Marquart, J. W., and B. M. Crouch. 1984. "Coopting the Kept: Using Inmates for Social Control in a Southern Prison." 1 *Justice Quarterly* 491–509.

Marquart, J. W., and J. B. Roebuck. 1985. "Prison Guards and 'Snitches' — Deviance within a Total Institution." 25 *British Journal of Criminology* 217–33.

Martinson, R. M. 1974. "What Works? Questions and Answers about Prison Reform." 35 *The Public Interest* 22–54.

——. 1979. "New Findings, New Views: A Note of Caution Regarding Sentencing Reform." 7 *Hofstra Law Review* 243–58.

McCarthy, B. J. 1984. "Keeping an Eye on the Keeper: Prison Corruption and Its Control." 64 *The Prison Journal* 113–25.

McCarthy, B. 1985. "The Nature of Education within Canadian Federal Prisons." 27 *Canadian Journal of Criminology* 441–53.

McCoy, J. 1981. *Concrete Mamma: Prison Profiles from Walla Walla.* Columbia, Mo.: University of Missouri Press.

Miller, N., G. S. Funke, and R. C. Grieser. 1983. "Prison Industries in Transition: Private Sector or Multistate Involvements." 47 *Federal Probation* 24–31.

Mohr, J. W. 1985. "Long-Term Incarceration." 27 *Canadian Journal of Criminology* 497–501.

Morin, L. 1981. *On Prison Education.* Ottawa: Supply and Services Canada.

Nicolai, S. 1981. "The Upward Mobility of Women in Corrections." In *Prison Guard/Correctional Officer — The Use and Abuse of the Human Resources of Prisons,* edited by R. R. Ross, 223–38. Toronto: Butterworths.

Ontario Institute for Studies in Education (OISE). 1979. *Report to the*

Solicitor General of Canada Concerning the Educational Program of the Canadian Correctional System: Phase II. Ottawa: Canadian Penitentiary Service.

Orland, L. 1975. *Prisons: Houses of Darkness.* New York: The Free Press.

Ouimet, R. (Chairman). 1969. *Report of the Canadian Committee on Corrections — Toward Unity: Criminal Justice and Corrections.* (Catalogue No. JS52-1-1968.) Ottawa: Information Canada.

Palmer, B. D. 1980. "Kingston Mechanics and the Rise of the Penitentiary, 1833-1836." 13 *Social History* 7-32.

Palmer, T. 1975. "Martinson Revisited." 12 *Journal of Research in Crime and Delinquency* 133-52.

Palmer, W. R. T. 1984. "Programming for Long-Term Inmates: A New Perspective." 26 *Canadian Journal of Criminology* 439-57.

Parisi, N. 1984. "The Female Correctional Officer: Her Progress toward and Prospects for Equality." 64 *The Prison Journal* 92-109.

Philliber, S. 1987. "Thy Brother's Keeper: A Review of the Literature on Correctional Officers." 4 *Criminal Justice Quarterly* 9-37.

Porporino, F. J., and E. Zamble. 1984. "Coping with Imprisonment." 26 *Canadian Journal of Criminology* 403-21.

Propper, A. 1981. *Prison Homosexuality: Myth and Reality.* Lexington, Mass. D. C. Heath.

Ramirez, J. R. 1984. "Prisonization, Staff, and Inmates: Is It Really about Us Versus Them?" 11 *Criminal Justice and Behavior* 423-60.

Reid, S. T. 1982. *Crime and Criminology.* 3rd ed. New York: Holt, Rinehart, and Winston.

Reker, G. T., and J. A. Meissner. 1977. "Life Skills in a Canadian Federal Penitentiary: An Experimental Evaluation." 19 *Canadian Journal of Criminology* 292-302.

Robison, J. O., and G. Smith. 1971. "The Effectiveness of Correctional Programs." 17 *Crime and Delinquency* 67-80.

Ross, R. R., and H. B. McKay. 1981. "The Correctional Officer: Selection through Training." In *Prison Guard/Correctional Officer — The Use and Abuse of the Human Resources of Prisons,* edited by R. R. Ross, 259-72. Toronto: Butterworths.

Schrag, C. 1961. "A Preliminary Criminal Typology." 4 *Pacific Sociological Review* 11-16.

Shover, N. 1979. *A Sociology of American Corrections.* Homewood, Ill.: Dorsey Press.

Solicitor General of Canada. 1981. *Solicitor General's Study of Conditional Release — Report of the Working Group.* Catalogue No. JS 42-8-1981. Ottawa: Supply and Services Canada.

Stastny, C., and G. Tyrnauer. 1982. *Who Rules the Joint: The Changing Political Culture of Maximum-Security Prisons in America.* Lexington, Mass.: D. C. Heath and Co.

Stewart, R. L. (Chairman). 1984. *Report on Allegations of Mistreatment of*

Inmates at Archambault Institution Following the Events Which Occurred on July 25th, 1982. Ottawa: Correctional Investigator of Canada.

Stojkovic, S. 1984. "Social Bases of Power and Control Mechanisms among Prisoners in a Prison Organization." 1 *Justice Quarterly* 511–28.

Sykes, G. M. 1958. *Society of Captives — A Study of a Maximum Security Institution.* Princeton, N.J.: Princeton University Press.

Task Force on the Creation of an Integrated Canadian Corrections Service. 1977. *The Role of Federal Corrections in Canada.* Ottawa: Supply and Services Canada.

Thomas, C. W. 1977. "Theoretical Perspectives on Prisonization: A Comparison of the Importation and Deprivation Models." 68 *Journal of Criminal Law and Criminology* 135–45.

Thomas, C. W., and D. M. Petersen. 1977. *Prison Organization and Inmate Subcultures.* Indianapolis, Ind.: Bobbs-Merrill.

Thomas, C. W., D. Petersen, and R. Zingraff. 1978. "Structural and Psychological Correlates of Prisonization." 16 *Criminology* 383–93.

Toch, H. 1977. *Living in Prison: The Ecology of Survival.* New York: The Free Press.

Tully, H. A., J. P. Winter, J. E. Wilson, and T. J. Scanlon. 1982. "Correctional Institution Impact and Host Community Resistance." 24 *Canadian Journal of Criminology* 133–39.

van den Haag, E. 1975. *Punishment: Concerning a Very Old and Painful Question.* New York: Basic Books.

Vigod, Z. L. 1974. "A Prison Therapeutic Community and Its Decision Making Structure." 16 *Canadian Journal of Criminology and Corrections* 411–20.

Wahler, C., and P. Gendreau. 1985. "Assessing Correctional Officers." 49 *Federal Probation* 70–74.

Waldo, G. P. 1973. "Research in Correctional Education." In *Readings in Prison Education*, edited by A. R. Roberts, 364–76. Springfield, Ill.: Charles C. Thomas.

Wanner, R. A., and T. C. Caputo. 1987. "Punitiveness, Fear of Crime, and Perceptions of Violence." 12 *Canadian Journal of Sociology* 331–44.

Warren, M. Q. 1977. "Correctional Treatment and Coercion: The Differential Effectiveness Perspective." 4 *Criminal Justice and Behavior* 335–76.

Webb, G. L., and D. G. Morris. 1978. *Prison Guards: The Culture and Perspective of an Occupational Group.* Houston, Tex.: Coker Books.

Wheeler, D. 1961. "Role Conflict in Correctional Communities." In *The Prison: Studies in Institutional Organization and Change*, edited by D. R. Cressey, 229–59. New York: Holt, Rinehart, and Winston.

Willett, T. C. 1977. "The 'Fish Screw' in the Canadian Penitentiary Service." 3 *Queen's Law Journal* 424–49.

_____. 1983. "Prison Guards in Private." 25 *Canadian Journal of Criminology* 1–17.

Williams, V. L., and M. Fish. 1974. *Convicts, Codes and Contraband: The Prison Life of Men and Women*. Cambridge, Mass.: Ballinger Publishing Co.

Wilson, T. W. 1986. "Gender Differences in the Inmate Code." 26 *Canadian Journal of Criminology* 397–405.

Wormith, J. S. 1985. "Long-Term Incarceration Data and Reason Meet Ideology and Rhetoric." 27 *Canadian Journal of Criminology* 349–57.

Zamble, E., F. Porporino, and J. Kalotay. 1984. *An Analysis of Coping Behaviour in Prison Inmates*. Ottawa: Solicitor General of Canada.

Zamble, E., and F. Porporino. 1988. *Coping, Behavior and Adaptation in Prison Inmates*. New York: Springer-Verlag.

Zimbardo, P. G. 1972. "Pathology of Imprisonment." 10 Society 4–8.

Zubrycki, R. M. 1984a. "Long-Term Incarceration in Canada." 26 *Canadian Journal of Criminology* 397–402.

_____. (Chairman). 1984b. *Long Term Imprisonment in Canada. Working Paper No. 1: An Overview of Long Term Prisoner Population and Suggested Directions for Further Research*. Ottawa: Solicitor General of Canada.

LEGISLATION

Penitentiary Act, R.S.C. 1985, c. P-5

12 COMMUNITY-BASED CORRECTIONS PROGRAMS

Community-based, non-custodial programs are operated by the Correctional Service of Canada and provincial/territorial correctional systems. Probation, diversion, fine-option, restitution, electronic monitoring, and community service orders are designed as alternatives to incarceration, although they may be utilized in conjunction with a sentence of incarceration. Parole and mandatory supervision are post-release programs providing supervision to assist offenders in reentry and readjustment in the community. In addition, there are pre-release programs, such as temporary absence and day parole, that provide the opportunity for inmates to participate in community-based programs.[1] Community-based programs also provide a means for maintaining control and surveillance over offenders.

The Correctional Service of Canada and the National Parole Board operate temporary absence and day parole programs, parole and mandatory supervision, and a variety of community-based residential facilities and programs. Community correctional centres (CCCs) are residential programs operated by the federal government, while community residential centres (CRCs) are residences run by private agencies under contract. The provincial/territorial governments offer alternatives to incarceration as well as release programs. These are listed in Table 10.3. In Canada, private, non-profit agencies, such as the John Howard Society and the Elizabeth Fry Society, play a major role in the provision of community corrections services under contract. It is through non-profit agencies and community-based groups and organizations that volunteers are playing an increasingly larger role in Canadian corrections.

The importance of community-based correctional programs was first identified by the report of the Ouimet Committee (1969), which concluded that the rehabilitation of offenders could best be accomplished in a community setting rather than in institutions. Three years later, a federal task force (Outerbridge, 1972: 28) added its support to the concept of community-based correctional programs, concluding that "most criminal conduct is spawned in the community, contributed to by the social, economic and political circumstances of the community . . . criminal behaviour is a function of both the offender and the community, and the solutions must be sought in both." The Outerbridge Report (1972: ix) established the following objectives for community corrections:

1. to divert persons entirely from the criminal justice system and incarceration,
2. to provide temporary relief from incarceration, and
3. to reduce the length of incarceration.

The Controversy over Community Corrections

Correctional observers disagree about the primary reason why corrections shifted its focus of attention to the development of community-based programs. Some explanations have focused on the perceived failure of institutional rehabilitation programs and increased humanitarian concerns with the negative consequences of confinement, although other observers such as Scull (1977) contend that the move was economically motivated — an attempt to reduce the costs of incarcerating ever-increasing numbers of offenders.

A review of the North American literature reveals several recurring justifications for the development and expansion of community-based programs, including the arguments that such programs are (1) instrumental in reducing the number of offenders involved in the criminal justice system, (2) more humane than incarceration, (3) less costly to operate than institutional programs, and (4) more effective in assisting offenders to readjust to society.

Extensive criticism has been directed toward all of these justifications (cf. Cohen, 1985).[2] Rather than functioning to reduce the numbers of offenders incarcerated or involved in the criminal justice system, there is considerable evidence that "net-widening" has occurred, resulting in more people being placed under some form of supervision or control (see Blomberg, 1987; Lowman and Menzies, 1986). Chan and Ericson (1981: 55), citing the increased numbers of offenders incarcerated in Canadian institutions and the growth of probation caseloads in recent years, argue that "people are not diverted from, but into and within the system." And Rothman (1980: 9) contends that "innovations that appeared to be substitutes for incarceration have become supplements to incarceration." Hylton (1983), for example, found that the rapid growth of community-based corrections programs in Saskatchewan between 1962 and 1979 was accompanied by an increase in institutional populations.

The cost-effectiveness and humanitarian concerns of community-based programs have also been challenged. Hylton (1982: 349) contends that such humanity is more often assumed than demonstrated and that the numerous behavioural restrictions placed on offenders under supervision in community-based residences may be as coercive as the conditions of confinement (see Cohen, 1979). In addressing the relative costs of community corrections versus confinement, Hylton (1982: 372) notes: "While many clients are channeled into services that are inexpensive to operate, the social control apparatus as a whole has expanded and the costs associated with the maintenance of social order have continued to increase. Savings have not accrued to the state by means of the creation and use of community programs." Hylton (p. 367) also contends that cost savings in community corrections programs are often achieved at the expense of providing adequate services.

Finally, serious questions have been raised regarding the effectiveness of community-based programs in assisting offenders to readjust successfully in the community. Greenberg (1975: 4) concluded from a review of the evaluative literature that no evidence exists to suggest that such programs are any more effective than institutionally based programs. Blomberg (1987) suggests that there may be adverse effects for individuals participating in community-based programs, including "increased jeopardy for clients and their families, unwanted family intrusions, family dissolutions, accelerated penetration into the criminal justice system, [and] increased behavioral difficulties." In a recent Canadian study, however, Holosko and Carlson (1986) reported that over two-thirds (67.4%) of a sample of offenders released from a community residential centre (CRC) had not been reconvicted of an offence during a two-year follow-up period.

Additional concerns have focused on the failure of correctional systems to define clearly what is meant by "community based corrections" other than the fact that a particular program is situated outside the prison setting. The role of the community in community corrections has been queried as well, many observers arguing that community corrections programs are "in" but not "of" the community and that the general public has little awareness of or involvement in most community corrections programs (Griffiths, 1988).

In the following discussion, we consider the various alternatives to incarceration, as well as the pre- and post-release programs operated by federal and provincial corrections.

Alternatives to Incarceration

Diversion

Diversion is a mechanism by which alleged offenders, usually charged with relatively minor offences and without a lengthy criminal record, are removed from the formal criminal justice process and referred to an appropriate program resource. According to a federal government report (Solicitor General of Canada, 1978: 10) diversion is "an alternative less formal than the court system which has the potential to reduce court backlog, provide compensation to the victims or the community, and present a mechanism to establish community support for many people in conflict with the law, while protecting the rights of the offender." Under most diversion schemes, the alleged offender is given the option of participating in a resource program or facing prosecution on the charge. Throughout the 1970s a variety of diversion programs were established with the support of police, prosecutorial, and correctional officials.

Since their inception, diversion programs have been surrounded by controversy, critics arguing that they have functioned to widen the net, placing under supervision first-time, minor offenders who would otherwise have been screened out of the criminal justice system. Further, concerns have been expressed about the coercive nature of diversion programs, the *alleged* offender being presented with the option of either participating in a diversion program or facing prosecution. Although diversion programs appear to provide a considerable cost-savings for the criminal justice system, there is no clear evidence of their effectiveness (see Roesch and Corrado, 1983).

Probation

Probation is a disposition of the court that places the offender under supervision in the community. It falls under the jurisdiction of the provinces/territories and is the only community corrections program that is imposed by direct court order. Probation has been variously viewed as a measure of leniency, a treatment method, and a legal disposition. Griffiths, Klein, and Verdun-Jones (1980: 254) argue that probation is most accurately viewed as a legal disposition "which allows offenders to retain most of their freedom while simultaneously placing them under the threat of punishment should they not adhere to the terms of their probation order." However, an equally persuasive argument could be made that probation is a measure of leniency, particularly given the serious problems surrounding the enforcement of probation orders, which will be discussed below.[3]

The historical basis of probation is the *Act to Permit the Conditional Release of First Offenders in Certain Cases*, which was passed in 1889. This legislation allowed judges to release offenders on "probation of good conduct" rather than impose a sentence. While this legislation was entered into the *Criminal Code* in 1892, it was not until 1921 that an amendment to the Act provided for supervision of probationers in the community (see Sheridan and Konrad, 1976). Between 1921 and 1967, the provinces/territories enacted legislation establishing probation services, which are now offered in all Canadian jurisdictions. A rapid, albeit uneven, expansion of probation services and offenders under supervision occurred during the 1960s.

An offender may be placed under probationary supervision for a period not to exceed three years. During 1987–88, there were approximately 66,000 offenders under probationary supervision in Canada, a 1% increase from 1986–87. The median probation-order length during 1987–88 was 11 months, but the range was from 24 months in Quebec to 9 months in British Columbia (Canadian Centre for Justice Statistics, 1989: 74–75). Probation orders may be accompanied by a conditional discharge, a suspended sentence, fine, or jail sentence. In addition to requiring the offender to report to a probation officer on a regular basis, there may be general or specific conditions attached to the probation order by the court. General conditions require the probationer to be of good behaviour and obey the law, while specific conditions may require the offender to participate in a designated program, such as a community service order program or attendance centre program, or pay restitution to the victim of the crime. An offender may be breached on probation for either a violation of the general or specific conditions of the probation order or for the commission of a new offence.

The decision of the judge to place an offender on probation is strongly influenced by the pre-sentence report (PSR). The PSR is generally prepared by a probation officer and includes socio-biographical information on the offender, as well as details relating to the current offence and prior record. In many cases, the probation officer will conclude the PSR with a recommendation regarding the suitability of the offender for probation, as well as suggestions regarding general or specific conditions to be attached to the order, should one be issued.

Concerns have been expressed about the operation of probation, centring on the role of the PSR in determining the suitability of offenders for probation, the supervision of offenders, and the effectiveness of probation as a rehabilitative technique. In a study of how PSRs were composed in one Canadian jurisdiction, MacDonald (1981) found that the content of PSRs was strongly influenced by the socio-biographical attributes of the offender, the organizational procedures of the probation office, and the personal orientation of the probation officer preparing the report. Other observers have argued that probation officers exert very little influence on the sentencing process and assume a secondary role to the judiciary and Crown attorneys (see Drass and Spencer, 1987; Hagan, Hewitt, and Alwin 1979; Rosecrance, 1985; Rush and Robertson, 1987; Walsh, 1985).

Probationary supervision has also come under scrutiny. Smith (1983–84: 190) has argued that probation does not provide adequate control over offenders in the community: "If obeyed, the routine requirement that an offender spend an hour a month, or an hour a week, in the presence of his supervising officer leaves an offender more than enough time to continue his criminal career without missing a step." Efforts to reduce the generally high supervisory caseloads of probation officers (which in many jurisdictions may be as high as 100 cases per officer) in order to facilitate intensive supervision have not resulted in higher success rates (Smith, 1983–84).

Part of the difficulty, Hatt (1985: 302) has noted, is the conflict between probation as a rehabilitative device and as a control mechanism and over whether probation officers should be case managers, functioning to make specialized community resources available to the probationer, or case workers, counselling probationers on a one-to-one basis.

Jackson et al. (1982) reported that the decision to revoke probation in one Canadian jurisdiction was influenced by the personal style and orientation of the probation officer, as well as by the probationer's lifestyle. In nearly 50% of the cases studied, probation was listed as successfully completed despite non-adherence to the conditions of the probation order. Officers were generally reluctant to intervene in those cases where the probationer had a stable domestic life and employment. Similar findings have been reported in the United States, Smith (1983–84: 178) citing a New York study that found that over 70% of the probationers had committed an average of 4.7 violations of their probation conditions. In an exhaustive study of the enforcement of probation conditions in British Columbia, Aasen (1985) found that under the current provisions of the *Criminal Code*, the breach of probationers for violation of conditions was virtually impossible and that it often took a long period of time to charge and convict an offender for breaching a probation order.

Despite its widespread use as a community corrections technique, the lack of methodologically sound research studies, particularly in Canada, precludes a definitive assessment of the effectiveness of probation.

Conditions of Probation: Community Service Orders, Restitution, and Attendance Programs

Offenders placed on probation may be required to participate in one of several community-based programs operated at the provincial level. Among these are community service order (CSO), restitution, and attendance centre programs. In some jurisdictions, victim-offender reconciliation programs (discussed in Chapter 2) may be a condition of probation. Community service orders, available in all jurisdictions except New Brunswick, are imposed as a condition of probation and require the offender to complete a specified number of hours of community service for non-profit agencies in the community in lieu of a period of confinement. Often, this work is performed for the victim of the offender's criminal behaviour. The philosophy behind the community service order programs is reparation — through the performance of services, the offender is "making amends" to the community and/or the victim of his or her offence — although several observers have noted that community service order programs satisfy a broad range of penal philosophies, including punishment, reformation, deterrence, and as an alternative to incarceration (see Menzies, 1986; see also Perrier and Pink, 1985).

Community service order programs are administered by provincial probation services in all provinces/territories, with the exception of Ontario and British Columbia, where private agencies under contract are involved in operating most of the programs. In a survey of issues and attitudes surrounding the operation of CSO programs in Prince Edward Island, Ontario, and British Columbia, Ekstedt and Jackson (1986a) found that criminal justice personnel, including judges and probation officers, held generally positive views toward CSOs, although there was a lack of consensus about the purpose of CSOs and in many instances judges were not utilizing CSOs as an alternative to confinement.[4] Additional difficulties that have surrounded the use of CSOs are the lack of an upper limit on the number of hours offenders may be required to perform and disparity between judges in the assignment of community service hours to various categories of offenders (Daubney, 1988).

As a condition of probation, the offender may be required to pay restitution to the victim of the crime, either in the form of a payment of compensation for harm done or through the performance of specified services for the victim. Restitution is premised on the philosophy of reparation, and programs are currently operating in five Canadian provinces and in the Yukon Territory. Ekstedt and Jackson (1986a: 27) note evaluations of restitution programs have revealed "considerable difference of opinion as to what the definition of restitution is and . . . few established principles governing its application." Other problems have included the enforcement of restitution orders and the difficulties in determining the categories of offenders most suitable and amenable to a restitution order (see Thorvaldson, 1987). Among the provisions of the recently enacted Bill C-89 (*An Act to amend the Criminal Code (Victims of Crime*, S.C. 1988, c. 30) are a requirement that judges impose a penalty of restitution in appropriate cases and the expansion of restitution to include loss due to bodily injury and property damage.

In an evaluation of the restitution program in the Yukon Territory, Zapf and Cole (1985: 486) found that full payment of court ordered restitution was not made in nearly 40% of the cases surveyed, a rate similar to restitution programs in other jurisdictions (see Bonta et al., 1983). In enforcing restitution orders, Zapf and Cole (p. 485) found that probation officers exercised considerable discretion in making informal arrangements with probationers for payment and that in 70% of the cases in which full restitution was not made, the probation officer did not file a breach of probation charge.

Ekstedt and Jackson (1986a: 29) report that considerably more positive results have been achieved by the restitution program in Saskatchewan, where special coordinators were hired to determine the offender's ability to pay, to supervise offenders in fulfilling restitution orders, and to maintain liaison with criminal justice agencies and officials and crime victims. Such an integrated program approach appears to have a higher likelihood of success. Success also appears to be higher with offenders convicted of minor property offences, with more serious offenders tending not to fulfil the conditions of restitution orders.

In a survey of criminal justice personnel in Prince Edward Island, Ekstedt and Jackson (1986b) found high levels of support for the concept of restitution. In Ontario, Bonta et al. (1983) evaluated the Rideau-Carelton Restitution Program and found high levels of victim satisfaction with the program and concluded that high risk offenders in half-way houses might be suitable for participation in restitution programs.[5]

As a condition of probation or on the recommendation of a supervising probation officer, offenders may be required to participate in an attendance centre program on a regular basis. Attendance centres may be residential or non-residential and may be utilized for offenders on temporary absences and parole, as well as probation. Among the attendance centre programs operated by provinces are impaired drivers courses, alcohol and drug treatment programs, counselling programs for shoplifters, and various therapy programs for specific categories of offenders, including assaultive males and sexual offenders.

Attendance centres may be operated under contract by non-profit agencies, such as the John Howard Society, the Elizabeth Fry Society and church-sponsored groups. In Charlottetown, Prince Edward Island, the Protestant and Catholic Family Service Bureau co-sponsors a program for assaultive men. The Elizabeth Fry Society operates counselling programs for shoplifters in Calgary and Vancouver, and in New Brunswick the John Howard Society sponsors a life skills program for probationers. In Manitoba, the Alcoholism Foundation operates a program for impaired drivers and a similar program is offered by the Saskatchewan Alcoholism Commission.

In their review of the operation of attendance programs across Canada, Ekstedt and Jackson (1986a) identified the following areas of difficulty: (1) lack of consistency in the use of the programs by the courts, (2) lack of availability of programs on a province-wide basis, (3) lack of exposure of attendance programs to both the court and the community, and (4) uneven patterns of referral to attendance programs by probation officers.

In concluding their review of the operation of sentencing programs across Canada, Ekstedt and Jackson (1986a: 182–85) identified several issues that require attention:

1. While the development and utilization of sentencing alternatives and programs have increased, so has the number of offenders being sent to institutions.
2. The offenders being referred to community-based programs are low-risk, minor offenders who would not generally be given a sentence of confinement; the programs are not operating as true alternatives to incarceration. (Conversely, in some jurisdictions,

concern is being expressed that the number of serious offenders involved in community-based programs has increased.)

3. The success of alternative programs often depends upon the individuals involved in setting up and operating the programs, resulting in a lack of continuity when personnel change.

4. The increasing trend toward "privatizing" alternative programs has raised questions about standards of operation and mechanisms for monitoring program operation.

On a more general level, Ekstedt and Jackson (1986a: 185–89) note that the purpose and objectives of alternative sentencing programs must be re-examined and clearly defined. Further, controlled evaluations of specific programmatic initiatives, such as community service orders, restitution, and attendance centre programs must be undertaken in an attempt to answer the question, What works?

Pre-release Programs: Temporary Absences and Day Parole

Temporary absences and day paroles allow the temporary release of offenders from institutions in order to participate in community-based programs. All provinces/territories operate temporary absence programs, and temporary absences (TAs) may be granted for educational, medical, humanitarian, employment, or family-related reasons, as well as for pre-parole planning. Offenders on TAs may reside either in the institution or in a residential facility situated in the community. TAs are granted for varying lengths of time, depending upon the situation of the individual offender, with the decision being made by an institutional Temporary Absence Committee (see Table 12.1).[6]

There have been few attempts to evaluate provincial temporary absence programs, although Ekstedt and Jackson (1986a: 91) note that the temporary absence program operated in Ontario appears to be successful in facilitating the payment of restitution to crime victims and assisting offenders to remain employed following discharge from supervision. In a survey of criminal justice personnel in British Columbia, Ekstedt and Jackson (1986b: 85–86) found that while there was general agreement regarding the value of temporary absences as a "reintegrative tool," there were concerns surrounding the administration of temporary absence programs by correctional officials and the extensive discretion exercised in making release decisions: "Some respondents felt that abuses of this process seriously diminished the authority of the court."

Federal inmates may be granted either escorted (ETA) or unescorted (UTA) temporary absences for medical, humanitarian, rehabilitative, or

TABLE 12.1
PAROLE ELIGIBILITY DATES FOR
FEDERAL AND PROVINCIAL OFFENDERS

Length of Sentence	Time to be Served Before Eligibility
	Temporary Absence
0 to 2 years less a day	N/A
2 to 5 years	If entered penitentiary before March 1/78, 6 months after entrance;
5 to 10 years	on or after March 1/78, 6 months after sentencing or 1/2 time before PED, whichever is longer.
10 years or more excluding life sentences	
Life as a maximum punishment (for crimes other than 1st or 2nd degree murder)	If entered penitentiary before March 1/78, 6 months after entrance: on or after March 1/78, 3 years before PED
Preventive detention (as a habitual or dangerous sexual offender)	1 year
Detention for an indeterminate period (since Oct. 15/77 as a dangerous offender)	3 years
Life for murder before Jan. 4/68	3 years after entered penitentiary
Life for murder, Jan. 4/68 to Jan. 1/74	
Life: death commuted before Jan. 1/74	
Life for murder, Jan. 1/74 to July 26/76	3 years before PED
Life: death commuted by Jan. 1/74 to July 26/76	
Life: death not commuted by July 26/76	
Life for 1st degree murder on or after July 26/76	
Life for 2nd degree murder on or after July 26/76	

TABLE 12.1
PAROLE ELIGIBILITY DATES FOR
FEDERAL AND PROVINCIAL OFFENDERS

Time to be Served Before Eligibility	
Day Parole	Full Parole
1/2 time before PED[1]	1/3 of sentence
For 2 to 12 year sentences, 6 mos. or 1/2 time to PED whichever is longer. For sentences of 12 years or more. 2 years before PED	1/3 of sentence or 7 years whichever is less except if violent conduct (described in the Parole Act and Regulations) is involved, then it is: 1/2 of sentence or 7 years whichever is less
5 years	7 years
1 year	1 year
3 years	3 years
3 years before PED	7 years
	10 years
	10–20 years: Judicial Review possible at 15 years
	25 years: Judicial Review possible at 15 years
	10– 25 years: Judicial Review possible at 15 years

[1] PED refers to full parole eligibility date. It is calculated from sentencing date except for lifers where it is calculated from date of arrest.

Source: National Parole Board. *The National Parole Board* (Ottawa: Supply and Services Canada, 1987), p. 20. Catalogue No. JS92–22/1987. Reproduced with permission of the Minister of Supply and Services.

administrative purposes, generally for a period of less than 15 days. The Correctional Service of Canada has authority to issue ETAs, while the National Parole Board has jurisdiction over UTAs, although, in practice, the CSC has been given the authority to make UTA decisions for inmates serving sentences of less than five years and in cases where an offender is applying for a second or subsequent UTA. Federal inmates must have served six months of their sentence or one-sixth of their sentence, whichever is longer, before being eligible for a UTA. Unescorted absences greater than 72 hours for other than humanitarian or medical purposes must be taken through day parole under the authority of the NPB (see Table 12.1).

During 1987–88, there was a 1% decrease in the number of ETAs granted by the NPB from the previous year, and a 32% decrease in the number of UTAs awarded. This may have been due to increased publicity surrounding heinous offences committed by offenders on TAs. However, it is important to note that the success rate for ETAs and UTAs is high — during 1987–88, only 31 of 46,861 ETAs and 94 of 8,709 UTAs were not successfully completed. For the five-year period from 1983–84 to 1987–88, there was a 99% success rate for ETAs and UTAs (Canadian Centre for Justice Statistics, 1989).

Day parole is a flexible form of release that provides an opportunity for correctional officials to employ gradual release to "test" the inmate in a community setting prior to making a decision on full parole, and allows the inmate the opportunity to participate in community-based programs and become readjusted to life outside the institution. Inmates are generally eligible for day parole after serving one-sixth of their sentence (one-half of the time required for full parole consideration) or after serving six months from the date of the sentence, whichever is longer (see Table 12.1). Day paroles are granted for a period of four months and are renewable up to one year. The majority of inmates on day parole reside in community-based facilities operated by the federal government or by private agencies.

During the five-year period from 1983–84 to 1987–88, the number of federal inmates applying for and receiving day parole has remained fairly constant. The grant rate has ranged from 62% to 69%, while the grant rate for provincial inmates for 1987–88 was 66%. During 1987–88, 28% of the day paroles issued were revoked, an increase of 20% from 1983–84. In a review of day parole, a recent federal report (Solicitor General of Canada, 1981a: 58–60; hereafter referred to as the Working Group) found that day parole was often used as a "prerequisite" to full parole and that inmates were often kept on day parole for lengthy periods of time. The Working Group (1981a: 60) concluded that there was a need to clarify the objectives of day parole and to address the regional disparities in the use of day paroles across the country.

Post-incarceration Release: Full Parole

Full parole is a program of conditional release that allows inmates to serve a portion of their sentence in the community under supervision. Inmates are generally eligible for full parole after serving one-third of their sentence or seven years, whichever period of time is shorter. Prior to 1898, offenders could obtain early release from confinement only by order of the Governor General of Canada under the *Royal Prerogative of Mercy*. Such releases were generally granted for humanitarian reasons (see Miller, 1976).

Parole as a release mechanism was established in 1899 with the enactment of the *Act to Provide for the Conditional Liberation of Penitentiary Convicts*, which became known as the *Ticket of Leave Act*. In the early 1900s, a Remission Service was created in the Department of Justice, and the Salvation Army, the John Howard Society and the Elizabeth Fry Society became increasingly involved in supervising offenders as well as in providing "after-care" services. In 1959, the *Parole Act* replaced the *Ticket of Leave Act*, the National Parole Board was created, and the Remission Service became the National Parole Service.

The NPB reviews the cases of all inmates who have served either one-third of their sentence or seven years, whichever period of time is shorter, and must provide such reviews every two years thereafter until parole is granted or until the offender is released on mandatory supervision (see Table 12.1). The NPB also has the authority to deny the release of offenders on mandatory supervision if the board believes that the release of the offender will threaten the safety and security of the community. These offenders may be required to serve the full term of their sentence in confinement.

The number of affirmative votes required for release on full parole varies by the length of the inmate's sentence. For example, while two affirmative votes are required for inmates serving single or aggregate terms of imprisonment of less than five years, five votes are required for inmates serving a single or aggregate term of ten years or more. In cases of tie votes, an additional vote is cast by either the chairman of the NPB or by another parole board member. An Internal Review Committee, created by the NPB in 1978 and comprised of three NPB members not familiar with the case under review, hears complaints filed by inmates who have been denied full parole or who have had their day parole, full parole, or mandatory supervision revoked. Complaints generally include allegations that the reasons given by the NPB for its decision do not support the decision, not all the available evidence was heard, or the NPB committed an error in fact or in law in reaching its final decision.

During 1987–88, 36% of the federal inmates applying for parole after completing one-third of their sentence in custody were released. This represents a 4% increase in the parole grant rate from 1983–84. Sixty per cent of the provincial offenders applying for parole were released, an increase of 13% from 1983–84 (Canadian Centre for Justice Statistics, 1989).

The qualifications of members of the NPB have become an issue of some concern. Currently, there are no specific educational or training qualifications for individuals who are appointed to the parole board, leading a Study Team Report (Government of Canada, 1986: 327) to assert: "It is widely believed that the overall calibre of the board has decreased in recent years because a number of less qualified, less knowledgeable, less well educated members have been appointed." Evidence presented to the Standing Committee on Justice and Solicitor General (Daubney, 1988: 168–69) indicated that there had been a drastic decline in the number of parole board members with criminal justice experience, from 85% in 1977 to 52.1% in 1986.

The federal Working Group (1981a) examining conditional release also expressed concerns about the appointment of parole board members as political patronage. Both study reports recommended the creation of a screening committee, composed of individuals from the public and private sectors, a suggestion that has not, to date, been acted upon. This was designed to end a selection process characterized by a witness before the Daubney Committee (1988: 168) as one in which parole board members were "anointed rather than appointed."

The Role of Earned Remission

The original *Ticket of Leave Act*, which was the forerunner of parole in Canada, was strongly influenced by several graduated release schemes that had been developed by prison administrators in Italy, Australia, and Ireland during the mid-1800s. Colonel Manuel Montesinos y Molina (Italy), Captain Alexander Maconochie (Norfolk Island, Australia), and Sir Walter Crofton (Ireland), all devised systems under which inmates could progress toward conditional release from the institution. Under Maconochie's "mark system," an inmate could earn "marks" by hard work and good conduct (as well as lose "marks" for misbehaviour) and progress through several stages, each accompanied by increased freedom and personal autonomy. When a pre-determined number of "marks" had been earned, inmates were granted a "ticket of leave" that allowed them to leave the institution and live in the community.

In Ireland, Sir Walter Crofton's system operated in a similar fashion, and through the accumulation of marks, offenders could reduce their time in confinement by one-fourth (Eriksson, 1976). Ross and Barker (1986: 5) note that the philosophy behind the development of these incentive or remission systems was that "prison was not just a place to contain offenders or to punish them, it was a place to modify their attitudes and behaviour. Since it was considered that inmates would like nothing better than early release from imprisonment, remission was conceived as a powerful incentive in the hands of its keepers."

In Canada, remission developed as a concept separate from parole. O'Connor (1985), notes that during the period 1883–1961, an inmate could earn a maximum of 72 days' remission in the first year of confinement and 120 days in subsequent years. In distinguishing remission from parole, O'Connor (1985: 341) states: "The inmate who earned remission rendered himself entitled to early release and,when released, was a free man and not subject to the conditions of parole. Remission was an incentive for good behaviour and also a means of control within the penitentiary system."

The structure and operation of remission came under close scrutiny by the Archambault Commission (1938), the Fauteux Committee (1956) and a number of other investigative bodies. Criticisms focused on how remission was earned and forfeited and the purposes for which it was used. In 1961, statutory remission and earned remission were created. Statutory remission was given to inmates upon admission to the institution and was equal to one-fourth of the inmate's sentence. It could be forfeited by the commission of an offence in the institution or by a breach of parole. Statutory remission was designed as a device to control inmates and could be taken away. Earned remission, on the other hand, could be accumulated at a rate of three days per month for positive performance in the institution and was not subject to forfeiture.[7]

In 1978, this system was replaced by a system of earned remission under which inmates confined in institutions or residing in community-based facilities on day parole may earn up to 15 days' remission each month (10 of which are given for program participation and 5 for good conduct) and reduce their time in confinement by one-third. The remaining one-third of the inmates' sentence is served under mandatory supervision in the community. Inmates serving life sentences are not eligible for remission.

The inmates' institutional performance is assessed monthly to determine the amount of remission earned. Over 90% of all inmates receive the maximum amount of remission each month. Inmates who commit minor institutional offences or who receive unsatisfactory performance notices may lose one or two days' remission time, while inmates committing serious infractions of institutional regulations may lose remission for the month in which the offence was committed or may forfeit remission previously earned. The determination of the number of days of remission to be forfeited for unsatisfactory performance in the institution is made by an earned remission board. In more serious cases where the loss of remission may be more than 30 days or more than 90 days, approval of the Deputy Commissioner of the region or of the Minister of the Solicitor General, respectively, is required.

The report of the federal Working Group (Solicitor General, 1981a: 85–87) found that there were differences in the rates of awarding and forfeiture of remission across the various Correctional Service of Canada (CSC) regions and between institutions, even those at the same security level. The report recommended that the CSC not use remission as a mechanism to encourage or evaluate program participation, but only as a device for punishing serious infractions of institutional regulations. Should the dual use of remission continue, the Working Group recommended that clear criteria for awarding and forfeiting remission be established and that inmates be given the right to appeal the loss of remission to the National Parole Board.

In noting that remission is used to control institutional populations, to encourage inmates to participate in programs, and as a means to control the behaviour of inmates within the institution, Ross and Barker (1986: 2) argue that the current system is a "curious hybrid of discordant philosophies" which lacks "a clear rationale or purpose." These authors (p. 58) argue that research is required on the efficiency and reliability of remissions systems, on the attitudes of correctional officers and inmates toward remission, and on the extent to which remission systems achieve the objectives assigned to them by the corrections system (see Badovinac et al., 1986; Solicitor General of Canada, 1985; Weir, 1985).

Parole Board Decision Making: Discretion and Disparity

Perhaps no one point of decision making in the correctional process has been the subject of more controversy than the decision to grant or deny parole. Concerns with the decision-making activities of the parole board, as well as with the effectiveness of parole as a reintegrative technique, have resulted in its abolition in several states in the United States. And, in Canada, the report of the Canadian Sentencing Commission (1987) recommended the elimination of full parole release for all offenders, with the exception of those serving sentences of life imprisonment. Our discussion in this section will focus primarily on the activities of the National Parole Board (NPB), as there are few published evaluations of the decision making of the provincial parole boards in British Columbia, Ontario and Quebec (see McLeod and Sallinen, 1987).

The ongoing debate surrounding parole board decision making has centred on the failure of the National Parole Board to establish clear and consistent criteria for release decisions and on the broad discretionary powers exercised by parole board members. The *Parole Act* states that the following criteria should govern the granting of full parole: (a) the inmate has derived maximum benefit from imprisonment, (b) the reform and rehabilitation of the inmate will be aided by a grant of parole, and (c) the release of the inmate on parole will not constitute an undue risk to society.

In addition, the *Policy and Procedures Manual* of the NPB (cited in Mandel, 1984–85: 167) includes as factors that may be considered by the board in its decision making the nature and gravity of the offence, prior history of criminal involvement, the inmate's total personality, efforts at self-improvement made by the inmate during imprisonment, release plans, and community reaction to the release. In 1988, the NPB adopted a pre-release policy that divides criminal offences into three categories for purposes of review for parole and standardizes a procedure for risk assessment.

In making the parole decision, NPB members have access to a large amount of information in the offender's case file and, similar to police officers and judges, exercise considerable autonomy and discretion in their decision making. Case files include information of a socio-biographical nature and documentation on the offender's prior criminal history and present offence, the results of diagnostic tests, institutional performance, and release plans, as well as reports by the inmate's institutional case management team and recommendations of the parole officer.

In their examination of Canadian parole service files, however, Carriere and Silverstone (1976: 40–64) found inconsistencies and contradictions in the material, errors of fact, and a lack of clarity in statements made by contributors to the file. These researchers (pp. 64–65) recommended that the CSC develop guidelines for the collection and recording of information in the offender's case file, and in recent years an attempt has been made to increase the reliability and clarity of case file material.

The failure of the NPB to establish clear criteria for parole decision making has been widely criticized. In 1973, the Task Force on the Release of Inmates (Hugessen, 1973: 32) concluded: "Neither inmates nor members of the Board are able to articulate with any certainty or precision what positive or negative factors enter into the parole decision." More recently, the federal Working Group (Solicitor General of Canada, 1981a: 63) stated that "the full parole function is not well defined, particularly in a way which is of any use to decision-makers in deciding about how and when to exercise their powers in individual cases. The three criteria for full parole in the *Parole Act* are ... either too vague ... or inappropriate and largely beyond assessment in individual cases."

Research by Demers (1978) and Nuffield (1982) suggests that the offence, prior criminal record, and the recommendation of the parole officer play a major role in the decision of the parole board, while Carriere and Silverstone (1976) reported that the release plans and institutional performance also influenced the decision to grant or deny parole. The role of socio-biographical attributes of the offender is less clear, although Nuffield (1982) and Demers (1978) reported that, all things being equal, younger and more highly educated offenders were more likely to be paroled than older offenders and those with lower levels of education.[8]

Mandel (1984–85: 167) argues that the primary concern of the NPB is with "individual prevention ... the extent to which the prospective parolee can be expected to offend against the law when released and ... when the parole is finished." The NPB uses the parole hearing to assess the offender's attitude and the extent to which the offender accepts responsibility for his or her criminal behaviour. An attempt is made to balance the needs of the offender with the demands for protection of the community, and this makes the parole board sensitive to criticisms of past decisions that resulted in highly publicized crimes being committed by parolees and to the risks involved in granting parole to certain categories of offenders. While there is a predictive element in the decisions of the board, the members do not have the use of risk assessment instruments that might assist them. There are also no feedback mechanisms in place to provide the board with information on the outcomes of its previous decisions (see also Shewan, 1985).[9]

In addition to these offender-related factors, there is some evidence to suggest that the broad discretionary powers of the NPB, in conjunction with the vagueness of the criteria for parole, combine to produce different decision making "styles" among parole board members. In a study of NPB members in Ontario and Quebec, Carriere and Silverstone (1976) found that individual board members assigned differing levels of importance to various items of information in the offender's file: "Members seemed to have individual parole philosophies to guide their deliberations with the result . . . that in many cases their decisions appeared to be made almost intuitively" (Carriere and Silverstone, 1976: 138).

This creates a situation in which "there are as many criteria as Board members" and decisions that are "highly unpredictable and inconsistent . . ." (Solicitor General of Canada, 1981a: C-9). Or, as Nuffield (1981) has stated: "There may be not so much a single parole policy which is disparately pursued but there may be dozens or scores of individual parole policies being pursued by dozens or scores of individual staff and Board members." It also results in disparity in parole granting rates across the five regional parole boards, differences that Nuffield (1981) argues "are not explained by variations in penitentiary populations, or recidivism rates, in the regions" (see Chitra, 1980; Hann and Palmer, 1980).[10]

While the NPB has been unable (or unwilling) to develop more specific criteria to guide parole decision making, in recent years the operational procedures of the board have undergone significant changes. As an administrative board, the NPB is not subject to the requirements of due process, and inmates were often denied basic procedural safeguards. Parole boards, for example, were not required to grant hearings to inmates or to provide reasons for decisions. Collins (1985) identifies several areas in which the operational procedures of the parole board have been affected by court decisions and the recommendations of investigative committees. Inmates now have the right to a hearing, to be represented by legal counsel, and to have access to information being used by the parole board in its decision making. Parole boards must provide to the inmate, in writing, notification of whether parole has been granted or denied and the reasons for the decision.

Despite the significant reform that has occurred in the procedures of parole decision making, Collins (1985: 120) notes that the problems created by the wide discretion exercised by parole board members and the vague criteria for parole decisions have not been addressed and the NPB has retained considerable autonomy (see also Mandel, 1986). It is likely, however, that the *Canadian Charter of Rights and Freedoms* will result in further changes in the policies and procedures of the NPB. From an extensive review of court decisions on issues involving parole practices, particularly in relation to parole hearings, O'Connor (1985: 389) concludes: "The impact of the Charter on parole practices has been significant" (see also Johnson, 1984). However, O'Connor cautions that there will be limitations to the influence of the *Charter:*

> It is unlikely that the *Charter* will, in the current context of Canadian society, be employed to guarantee one a gradual and expeditious transition from high security to minimum security, or from there to a half-way house; or even to establish that it is unfair to take away several years of one's freedom for suspicion of criminal activity ... The Parole Board's power will remain immense and its criteria necessarily will remain broad. The impact of the *Charter* to date ensures, however, that, though those powers are broad, they are not unrestricted and cannot be exercised entirely behind closed doors. [P. 391]

Supervision of Offenders in the Community

Inmates granted a full parole are placed under the supervision of a parole officer employed by the CSC and are required to adhere to the conditions of release imposed by the NPB. The standard general conditions for inmates released on full parole (as well as day parole and mandatory supervision) include the requirements that the inmate remain in designated areas and obtain the approval of, or inform, the supervising parole officer prior to changing address, incurring debts by borrowing money, or purchasing a weapon. The parolee is also obliged to obey the law and fulfil all legal and social responsibilities. In addition to these general conditions, specific conditions may be attached to the release, such as a requirement to abstain from the use of alcohol and drugs and from associating with specific individuals in the community.

The Task Force on the Release of Inmates (Hugessen, 1973: 37) concluded that the conditions of parole release are "too vague and general in application" and was particularly critical of the general requirement that the parolee fulfil all social responsibilities, arguing that this condition was "so vague that it could form the basis for revocation of virtually any parole." Similarly, the federal Working Group on conditional release (Solicitor General, 1981a: 78–79) referred to parole conditions as "intru-

sive" and "unenforceable," often functioning only to create resentment among
parolees. An additional area of concern is the wide discretionary powers
exercised by parole officers in supervising offenders and enforcing the
conditions of parole. Research in the United States has found that in
attempting to balance the dual role of "helper" and "enforcer," parole
officers develop different "styles," which may affect the decision to suspend the parolee (see Irwin, 1970; Prus and Stratton, 1976). Similar to the
supervision of offenders on probation, many officers adopted a case management approach — assuming the role of "broker" in matching parolee
needs with community services — while others followed the case worker,
one-on-one approach.

Failure to adhere to the general or specific conditions may result in the
suspension and revocation of parole. Under provisions of the *Parole Act*,
parole may be suspended where a breach of a parole condition has occurred, to prevent the breach of a parole condition, or in order to protect
society. Following the decision to suspend parole, a "Warrant of Apprehension and Suspension" is issued and the parolee is taken into
custody. Figure 12.1 illustrates the suspension and revocation process.
Court decisions and the *Canadian Charter of Rights and Freedoms* have
resulted in increased procedural safeguards for inmates during the suspension and revocation process, including the right to a hearing and the
requirement that the inmate be provided with the reasons for the parole
suspension. Considerable discretion, however, continues to be exercised
by parole officers and NPB members in the suspension and revocation
process.

In 1987–88, nearly 70% of the terminated paroles were due to expiry of
the parole period, while 24% of the paroles were revoked. At the provincial
level, only 16% of the full paroles were revoked during 1987–88, reflecting a
continuing trend of over 80% successful completion over the past five
years. Thus, despite increased media attention on heinous crimes committed by offenders on parole, figures from the NPB indicate that only a
small percentage of parolees commit another offence.

Further, while several newspapers in 1988 reported that 130 homicides
had been committed between 1975 and 1986 by individuals on parole or
mandatory supervision, a more in-depth analysis revealed that during this
same period of time, there were 52,484 conditional releases, resulting in a
homicide commission rate of 0.25% for offenders on conditional release
(Canadian Bar Association, 1988: 17).

Dittenhoffer, Leroux, and Cormier (1986) examined a random sample of
629 cases from across Canada in which suspension warrants had been
issued during 1983–84. Fifty per cent of the cases in which full parole, day
parole, and mandatory supervision were suspended involved either a
police charge or conviction for a new offence. Forty-six per cent were the
result of a violation of general or specific release conditions, while the

FIGURE 12.1

THE PAROLE SUSPENSION AND REVOCATION PROCESS

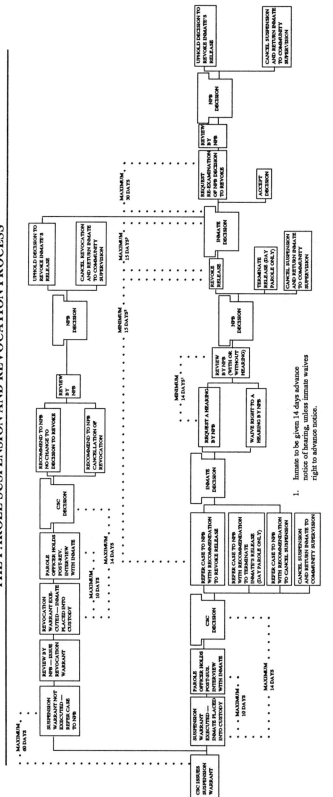

Source: Dittenhoffer, T., J.-P. Leroux and R.B. Cormier. *The Suspension and Revocation Process in Canada: A Study of How and Why Federal Inmates Under Conditional Release Are Returned to Imprisonment* (Ottawa: Solicitor General of Canada, 1986), pp. 5-6. Reproduced with permission.

remaining four per cent involved other reasons, including suspension in order to prevent an anticipated breach of conditions (see also Nicolas, 1976). While increased media attention on crimes committed by offenders on parole has resulted in the perception that parolees are responsible for a large number of heinous crimes, the data indicate that the offences committed by offenders on parole or mandatory supervision actually contribute very little to the Canadian crime rate.

Parole: The Pains of Reentry

While there is an emerging body of material on the decision-making activities of the parole board and on the supervision of inmates in the community, the difficulties encountered by inmates applying for parole and on reentry into the community have received considerably less attention. The lack of explicit parole guidelines creates among inmates uncertainty about what information to present during the hearing to indicate to the board a readiness to reenter society. This uncertainty is compounded by the fact that changes in board membership or pressure on the board from the community may result in different criteria being used in subsequent hearings (see Maslach and Garber, 1982).

Carriere and Silverstone (1976: 83) note that inmates experience difficulty in preparing for the parole hearing, which in Ontario averaged 35 minutes in length: "Rarely were inmates certain about the identity of Parole Board members presiding over the hearings, of what procedure would be followed, how long the hearing would last . . . even though such information is apparently a major topic of rumour and conversation in penitentiaries."

In addition to the "pains of imprisonment" that offenders may experience during confinement are the "pains of reentry" associated with release from the institution. Offenders who have experienced the status degradation ceremonies and the process of mortification, as well as the stresses of adapting to and coping with the daily routine of prison life, may be unprepared for release. While Canadian corrections appears to have perfected the mechanisms for removing individuals from society and transforming them from citizens into inmates, techniques for reestablishing the status of citizen and reintegrating offenders back into the community are less well developed. As over 90% of all inmates will, at some future date, return to society, this long-neglected area of corrections assumes even greater significance.

Among the initial impacts on the parolee are the overpowering pace of life in the community compared to the predictable daily routine in the prison and the loss of what Irwin (1970: 116) terms the "vast repertoire of taken-for granted, automatic responses and actions" that civilians use to handle day-to-day encounters and situations. In a study of parolees from federal institutions in Ontario, Waller (1974: 195) found that ex-prisoners experienced a variety of symptoms, including "depression, anxiety, difficulty getting used to things, loneliness, trouble talking to people, and feelings of looking like an ex-con."[11]

Despite these difficulties, the federal Working Group (1981a: C-10) found that increasing paperwork and administrative burdens, as well as a lack of direction and resources to provide community services for parolees, hindered the efforts of parole officers in providing adequate supervision to offenders. The Working Group (1981a: C-11) further reported that the majority of inmates interviewed stated that the supervision by parole officers was generally unhelpful. Further, while there are minimum standards that specify the amount of contact the parole officer is to have with the parolee, there is no direction concerning what the *nature* of the contact should be.

From its inquiry, the Working Group (1981a: 75–77) made several recommendations for improving the effectiveness of community supervision, including the increased use of after-care services provided by private agencies such as the John Howard Society and the Elizabeth Fry Society. In 1981, private agencies were involved in supervising 15% of the federal cases, a substantial decrease from the 70% level of 1968. There is also a need for further research to determine "what effect different parole officers will have in doing different things with different offenders." It is unlikely that parole is in danger of being abolished in Canada. However, the continuing difficulties experienced by offenders on reentry raise serious questions about the effectiveness of parole supervision as it is currently structured and the capacity of the CSC to undertake the reforms necessary to improve its efficacy.

Post-incarceration Release: Mandatory Supervision

Mandatory supervision (MS) was created by an amendment to the *Parole Act* in 1970, largely as a consequence of the Ouimet Committee (1969), which recommended that there be a mechanism to provide assistance and control during the offender's readjustment to life in the community. In contrast to parole, MS involves the release of offenders from the institution after serving two-thirds of their sentence, with the remaining one-third being served under supervision of the NPB in the community (see Figure 12.1). The decision to release offenders on MS is made by the CSC, based on an offender's earned remission. In 1987–88, 27% of the federal offenders under community supervision were on mandatory supervision.

Under 1986 amendments to the *Parole Act* and the *Penitentiary Act* (Bill C-67; see S.C. 1986, c. 42), however, the NPB has been given powers of review over MS decisions and the right to block the release of an inmate.

This is done if, in the opinion of the NPB, there is a likelihood that the inmate, if released, will commit another offence causing death or serious harm in the community prior to the expiry of the MS period. The NPB also has the authority to attach special conditions to a MS release, such as the requirement that the offender reside in a community-based facility. Another condition that may be imposed on the MS release is called "one-chance" mandatory supervision; should offenders fail on MS, they are ineligible for another release at a future point in time. In 1987, the Supreme Court affirmed the constitutionality of this legislation.

Inmates released under MS are supervised by parole officers and must abide by general and specific conditions set by the NPB. A violation of the conditions of MS can result in suspension and revocation and return to the institution where the offender must serve the remainder of his or her sentence. Inmates who are denied MS by the NPB on the grounds that they would constitute a threat to the community if released are required to serve the remainder of their sentence in the institution. Following completion of their sentence, however, these inmates are released into the community *without any supervision or assistance.* As a recent report of the Canadian Bar Association (1988: 13) noted, "The new legislation clearly does not resolve the problem of threat to public safety, it simply postpones its impact."

The implementation of MS was strenuously opposed by inmates, who argued that it violated the principle of earned remission. Rather than being unconditionally released after serving two-thirds of their sentence and achieving a reduction of one-third in confinement due to remission, they would serve the remaining one-third under supervision in the community.

The rates of success for offenders released on MS are much lower than those for offenders on full parole. During 1987–88, 44% of the MS releases were terminated through revocation. Given that the offenders released under MS have previously been denied parole, the higher rate of failure could be anticipated, although there are other factors that may contribute to this as well.

The offender released under MS will experience greater pains of reentry and require more intensive supervision and assistance in order to make a successful transition back into the community. The high rate of MS failures suggests that such assistance may not be available or effective in addressing the needs of the MS releasee. The Working Group on conditional release (1981a: 91–92) found evidence that MS inmates were treated differentially (more harshly) by parole officers, who had little interest in their needs and were more likely to violate MS inmates for technical reasons. There was also considerable resentment among MS inmates toward having to be under supervision, and among the inmates surveyed by the Working Group (1981a), there was unanimous support for the abolition of MS, which was viewed as an "opportunity to fail." The next few years may see an increase in the success rate of offenders released on MS, given the authority of the NPB to refuse to release on MS those offenders who constitute a clear danger to the community.

Concern with these and other issues prompted a thorough review of the operation of MS (Solicitor General of Canada, 1981b). On the basis of responses received from CSC and NPB staff and from inmates across the country, several options for changing MS were considered, including the abolition of MS (favoured by a majority of the inmates who responded) and a return to pre-1970, when inmates were released outright after completion of two-thirds of their sentence and earned remission; requiring supervision under MS to be voluntary on the part of the inmate; and increasing the level of supervision for MS cases. Subsequent to this report, it was decided to retain MS while providing the NPB with authority under Bill C-67 to prevent offenders considered dangerous to the community from being released until the completion of their sentence.[12]

NOTES

1. For an extensive discussion of community-based corrections in Canada, see Ekstedt and Griffiths (1988). Also, the Working Group of the Correctional Law Review (Solicitor General of Canada, 1987) has outlined the objectives and operation of conditional release in Canada.

2. For in-depth examinations of the effectiveness and impact of alternatives to incarceration, see Austin and Krisberg (1982); Doeren and Hageman (1982); Scull (1982); Smith (1983–84).

3. Several observers have argued that the use of probation by the courts has changed over the years. In discussing the evolution of probation in Canada during the late 1800s and early 1900s, Boyd (1978) argues that rather than being utilized as an alternative to incarceration, probation was a mechanism to place ever-increasing numbers of people under some form of control. See also Hatt (1985).

4. For discussions of the use of community service orders in various provincial jurisdictions across Canada, see Doyle and Gaudet (1984); Hackett (1980); Hermann and Carey (1985); Jackson (1982); Polonski (1981); Sandulak (1982).

5. For evaluations and discussions of several provincial restitution programs, see Mayne and Garrison (1979); Nasim and Spellisay (1985); Zapf (1984).

6. See Fox (1971) and McFarlane (1979) for materials on the development and operation of the temporary absence program in Ontario.

7. For discussions of the development of remission in Canada, see O'Connor (1985) and Ross and Baker (1986).

8. For particularly insightful examinations of parole board decision making in the United States that include issues relevant to parole in Canada, see Maslach and Garber (1982) and Talarico (1976).

9. Currently under discussion in the CSC is the development and implementation of risk assessment models that would be utilized in an attempt to predict the behaviour of the inmate upon release. Several different models are in use in the United States, the most notable being the Iowa Model, developed in the State of Iowa. This risk assessment model focuses on several key factors of the inmate's behaviour, including offence, prior record, drug or alcohol usage, and is completed by the case management team in the institution. Each of the factors is scored and the decision to grant or deny parole is based on this score. The Iowa Model has reported an 85% success rate in predicting behaviour upon release. Explicit parole guidelines have also been established in a number of states in the United States and by the U.S. Parole Commission, which is responsible for the parole process for federal offenders. The adoption of similar models in Canada would have profound implications for parole board decision making.

10. See Casey (1981) and Nuffield (1981) for discussions of the issues surrounding the development of parole guidelines in Canada.

11. Irwin's classic work *The Felon* (1970) contains perhaps the most valuable insights into the difficulties encountered by offenders upon reentry.

12. For a critique of mandatory supervision and arguments for its abolition, see Stewart (1983). In November 1986, the Supreme Court of Canada held that imposing conditions on offenders released on mandatory supervision did not violate the equality provisions of the *Canadian Charter of Rights and Freedoms*, even though it applies only to federal offenders and not to inmates under provincial jurisdiction. There are certain to be additional court challenges under the *Charter* to the operation of mandatory supervision.

REFERENCES

Aasen, J. N. 1985. *Enforcement of Probation in British Columbia.* Masters thesis. Burnaby, B.C.: School of Criminology, Simon Fraser University.

Archambault, J. (Chairman). 1938. *Report of the Royal Commission to Investigate the Penal System of Canada.* Ottawa: King's Printer.

Austin, J., and B. Krisberg. 1982. "The Unmet Promise of Alternatives to Incarceration." 28 *Crime and Delinquency* 374–409.

Badovinac, K., M. Harvey, S. Eastman, and R. Wormith. 1986. *Earned Remission: Analysis of Historical Trends and a Survey of Management Opinions.* Ottawa: Solicitor General of Canada.

Blomberg, T. G. 1987. "Criminal Justice Reform and Social Control: Are We Becoming a Minimum Security Society?" In *Transcarceration:*

Essays in the Sociology of Social Control, edited by J. Lowman, R. J. Menzies, and T. S. Palys, 218–26. Aldershot, England: Gower Publishers.

Bonta, J., J. Boyle, L. L. Motiuk, and P. Sonnichsen. 1983. "Restitution in Correctional Halfway Houses: Victim Satisfaction, Attitudes, and Recidivism." 25 *Canadian Journal of Criminology* 277–93.

Boyd, N. 1978. "An Examination of Probation." 20 *Criminal Law Quarterly* 355–82.

Canadian Bar Association. 1988. *Parole and Early Release*. Ottawa.

Canadian Centre for Justice Statistics. 1989. *Adult Correctional Services in Canada, 1987–88*. Ottawa: Supply and Services Canada.

Canadian Sentencing Commission. 1987. *Sentencing Reform: A Canadian Approach*. Ottawa: Supply and Sevices Canada.

Carriere, P., and S. Silverstone. 1976. *The Parole Process: A Study of the National Parole Board*. Ottawa: Supply and Services Canada.

Casey, M. 1981. "Parole Guidelines: Are They a Worthwhile Control on Discretion?" In *The National Parole Board Report on the Conference on Discretion in the Correctional System*. Ottawa: National Parole Board, Government of Canada.

Chan, J. B. L., and R. V. Ericson. 1981. *Decarceration and the Economy of Penal Reform*. Toronto: Centre of Criminology, University of Toronto.

Chitra, M. 1980. "Modern Trends in Parole Granting, 1957–1976." 5 *Queen's Law Journal* 46–72.

Cohen, S. 1979. "The Punitive City: Notes on the Dispersal of Social Control." 3 *Contemporary Crises* 339–63.

——. 1985. *Visions of Social Control*. Cambridge, U.K.: Polity Press.

Collins, O. O. 1985. *The Impact of the Rule of Law on the Operational Procedures and Policy-Making of the National Parole Board*. M.A. thesis. Burnaby, B.C.: School of Criminology, Simon Fraser University.

Daubney, D. (Chairman). 1988. *Taking Responsibility. Report of the Standing Committee on Justice and Solicitor General on Its Review of Sentencing, Conditional Release and Related Aspects of Corrections*. Ottawa: Solicitor General of Canada.

Demers, D. 1978. *Discretion, Disparity and the Parole Process*. Ph.D. dissertation. Edmonton: Department of Sociology, University of Alberta.

Dittenhoffer, T., J-P. Leroux, and R. B. Cormier. 1986. *The Suspension and Revocation Process in Canada: A Study of How and Why Federal Inmates under Conditional Release Are Returned to Imprisonment*. Executive summary. Ottawa: Supply and Services Canada.

Doeren, S. E., and M. J. Hageman. 1982. *Community Corrections*. Cincinnati, Ohio: Anderson Publishing.

Doyle, P., and M. Gaudet. 1984. *Community Service Orders: Justice in the Community — The Prince Edward Island Experience.* Charlottetown: Department of Justice.

Drass, K. A., and J. W. Spencer. 1987. "Accounting for Pre-sentencing Recommendations: Typologies and Probation Officer's Theory of Office." 34 *Social Problems* 277–93.

Ekstedt, J. W., and C. T. Griffiths. 1988. *Corrections in Canada: Policy and Practice.* 2nd ed. Toronto: Butterworths.

Ekstedt, J. W., and M. A. Jackson. 1986a. *A Profile of Canadian Alternative Sentencing Programmes: A National Review of Policy Issues.* Burnaby, B.C.: School of Criminology, Simon Fraser University.

———. 1986b. *Alternatives to Incarceration/Sentencing Option Programs: What Are the Alternatives?* Burnaby, B.C.: School of Criminology, Simon Fraser University.

Eriksson, T. 1976. *The Reformers: An Historical Survey of Pioneer Experiments in the Treatment of Criminals.* New York: Elsevier.

Fauteux, G. (Chairman). 1956. *Report of a Committee Appointed to Inquire into the Principles and Procedures Followed in the Remission Service of the Department of Justice of Canada.* Ottawa: Queen's Printer.

Fox, R. G. 1971. "Temporary Absence, Work-Release and Community Based Corrections in Ontario." 4 *Australian and New Zealand Journal of Criminology* 46–61.

Government of Canada. 1986. *Improved Program Delivery: Justice System. A Study Team Report to the Task Force on Program Review.* Ottawa: Supply and Services Canada.

Greenberg, D. F. 1975. "Problems in Community Corrections." 10 *Issues in Criminology* 1–33.

Griffiths, C. T. 1988. "Community Corrections for Young Offenders: Proposal for a 'Localized' Corrections." 12 *International Journal of Comparative and Applied Criminal Justice* 219–28.

Griffiths, C. T., J. F. Klein, and S. N. Verdun-Jones. 1980. *Criminal Justice in Canada: An Introductory Text.* Vancouver: Butterworths.

Hackett, C. 1980. *The Community Service Order Program in Newfoundland.* St. John's: Adult Corrections Division, Department of Justice.

Hagan, J., J. Hewitt, and D. Alwin. 1979. "Ceremonial Justice: Crime and Punishment in a Loosely Coupled System." 58 *Social Forces* 506–27.

Hann, R., and J. Palmer. 1980. *Determinants of Canadian Penitentiary and Prison Populations: Phase 1 Report.* Ottawa: Solicitor General of Canada.

Hatt, K. 1985. "Probation and Community Corrections in a Neo-Correctional Era." 27 *Canadian Journal of Criminology* 299–316.

Hermann, S., and C. Carey. 1985. *Alternative to Incarceration.* Toronto: Policy, Planning and Evaluation Branch, Ministry of Correctional Services.

Holosko, M. J., and T. M. Carlson. 1986. "Recidivism among Ex-offenders Residing at a CRC in St. John's, Newfoundland." 28 *Canadian Journal of Criminology* 385–96.

Hugessen, J. K. (Chairman). 1973. *Task Force on Release of Inmates.* Ottawa: Information Canada.

Hylton, J. H. 1982. "Rhetoric and Reality: A Critical Appraisal of Community Correctional Programs." 28 *Crime and Delinquency* 341–73.

———. 1983. "The Growth of Punishment: Imprisonment and Community Corrections in Canada." In *Deviant Designations: Crime, Law and Deviance in Canada,* edited by T. Fleming and L. Visano, 411–29. Toronto: Butterworths.

Irwin, J. 1970. *The Felon.* Englewood Cliffs, N.J.: Prentice-Hall.

Jackson, M. A. 1982. *Judicial Attitudes toward Community Sentencing Options.* Toronto: Ministry of Correctional Services.

Jackson, M. A., C. D. Webster, and J. Hagan. 1982. "Probation Outcome: Is It Necessary to Fulfill the Conditions?" 24 *Canadian Journal of Criminology* 267–77.

Johnson, H. R. 1984. "Procedural Safeguards and the National Parole Board." 26 *Canadian Journal of Criminology* 325–41.

Lowman, J., and R. J. Menzies. 1986. "Out of the Fiscal Shadow: Carceral Trends in Canada and the United States." 26 *Crime and Social Justice* 95–115.

MacDonald, K. D. 1981. *Information for the Court: An Analysis of the Adult Pre-sentence Report.* M.A. thesis. Burnaby, B.C.: School of Criminology, Simon Fraser University.

Mandel, M. 1984–85. "Democracy, Class and the National Parole Board." 27 *Criminal Law Quarterly* 159–81.

———. 1986. "The Legalization of Prison Discipline in Canada." 26 *Crime and Social Justice* 79–94.

Maslach, C., and R. M. Garber. 1982. "Decision-Making Processes in Parole Hearings." In *The Criminal Justice System — A Social-Psychological Analysis,* edited by V. J. Konecni and E. B. Ebbesen, 337–66. San Francisco: W. H. Freeman and Co.

Mayne, C., and G. Garrison. 1979. *Summary of the Study Report on Restitution.* Charlottetown: Probation and Family Court Services Division, Department of Justice.

McFarlane, G. G. 1979. "Ontario's Temporary Absence Programs: 'Phantom' or 'Phoenix'-like Phenomena?" 20 *Canadian Journal of Criminology* 310–37.

McLeod, S., and T. Sallinen. 1987. *British Columbia Board of Parole Decision Making Study.* Vancouver: British Columbia Board of Parole.

Menzies, K. 1986. "The Rapid Spread of Community Service Orders in Ontario." 28 *Canadian Journal of Criminology* 157–69.

Miller, F. P. 1976. "Parole." In *Crime and Its Treatment in Canada*, edited by W. T. McGrath, 439–48. 2nd ed. Toronto: Macmillan.

Nasim, S. A., and R. Spellisay. 1985. *An Evaluation of the Saskatchewan Restitution Program*. Regina: Policy, Planning, and Evaluation Branch, Department of Justice.

Nicolas, M. 1976. *La Suspension de la Liberation Conditionelle: Processus et Decision*. Montreal: Centre of Criminology, University of Montreal.

Nuffield, J. 1981. "Parole Guidelines: Are They a Worthwhile Control on Discretion?" In *The National Parole Board Report on the Conference on Discretion in the Correctional System*. Ottawa: National Parole Board.

———. 1982. *Parole Decision Making in Canada: Research toward Decision Guidelines*. Ottawa: Supply and Services Canada.

O'Connor, F. C. 1985. "The Impact of the Canadian Charter of Rights and Freedoms on Parole in Canada." 10 *Queen's Law Journal* 336–91.

Ouimet, R. (Chairman). 1969. *Report of the Canadian Committee on Corrections — Toward Unity: Criminal Justice and Corrections*. (Catalogue No. JS52-1-1968.) Ottawa: Information Canada.

Outerbridge, W. R. (Chairman). 1972. *Report of the Task Force on Community-Based Residential Centres*. Ottawa: Information Canada.

Perrier, D. C., and F. Steven Pink. 1985. "Community Service: All Things to All People." 49 *Federal Probation* 32–38.

Polonski, M. L. 1981. *The Community Service Order Program in Ontario: Summary*. Toronto: Ministry of Correctional Services.

Prus, R. C., and J. R. Stratton. 1976. "Parole Revocation Decision Making: Private Typings and Official Designations." 40 *Federal Probation* 48–53.

Roesch, R., and R. Corrado. 1983. "Criminal Justice System Interventions." In *Handbook of Social Intervention*, edited by E. Seidman, 385–407. Beverly Hills, Calif.: Sage.

Rosecrance, J. 1985. "The Probation Officers' Search for Credibility: Ball Park Recommendations." 31 *Crime and Delinquency* 539–54.

Ross, R. R., and T. G. Barker. 1986. *Incentives and Disincentives: A Review of Prison Remission Systems*. Ottawa: Solicitor General of Canada.

Rothman, D. 1980. *Conscience and Convenience: The Asylum and Its Alternatives in Progressive America*. Toronto: Little, Brown, and Co.

Rush, C., and J. Robertson. 1987. "Presentence Reports: The Utility of Information to the Sentencing Decision." 11 *Law and Behavior* 147–55.

Sandulak, S. D. 1982. *Community Service Order: Project Report*. Victoria: Corrections Branch, Ministry of the Attorney General.

Scull, A. T. 1977. *Decarceration: Community Treatment and the Deviant — A Radical View*. Englewood Cliffs, N.J.: Prentice-Hall.

Scull, A. 1983. "Community Corrections: Panacea, Progress or Pretense?" In *The Politics of Informal Justice*. Vol. 1: *The American Experience*, edited by R. L. Abel, 99–118. New York: Academic Press.

Sheridan, A. K. B., and J. Konrad. 1976. "Probation." In *Crime and Its Treatment in Canada*, edited by W. T. McGrath, 249–302. 2nd ed. Toronto: Macmillan.

Shewan, I. 1985. "The Decision to Parole: Balancing the Rehabilitation of the Offender with the Protection of the Public." 27 *Canadian Journal of Criminology* 327–39.

Smith, M. E. 1983–84. "Will the Real Alternatives Please Stand Up?" 12 *New York University Review of Law and Social Change* 171–97.

Solicitor General of Canada. 1978. *Diversion: A Canadian Concept and Practice*. Ottawa: Communication Division.

——. 1981a. *Solicitor General's Study of Conditional Release. Report of the Working Group*. Ottawa: Supply and Services Canada.

——. 1981b. *Mandatory Supervision: A Discussion Paper. Report of the Committee on Mandatory Supervision*. Ottawa: Communication Division.

——. 1985. *Remission*. Ottawa: Correctional Law Review, Solicitor General of Canada.

——. 1987. *Conditional Release. Correctional Law Review Working Paper No. 3*. Ottawa: Solicitor General of Canada.

Stewart, G. 1983. "Mandatory Supervision: Politics and People." 25 *Canadian Journal of Criminology* 95–104.

Talarico, S. M. 1976. "The Dilemma of Parole Decision Making." In *Criminal Justice — Law and Politics*, edited by G. F. Cole, 447–56. 2nd ed. North Scituate, Mass.: Duxbury Press.

Thorvaldson, S. A. 1987. "Restitution by Offenders in Canada: Some Legislative Issues." 29 *Canadian Journal of Criminology* 1–16.

Waller, I. 1974. *Men Released from Prison*. Toronto: University of Toronto Press.

Walsh, A. 1985. "The Role of the Probation Officer in the Sentencing Process: Independent Professional or Judicial Hack?" 12 *Criminal Justice and Behavior* 289–303.

Weir, D. 1985. *Earned Remission and Mandatory Supervision: Some Alternatives*. Ottawa: Solicitor General of Canada, Supply and Services.

Zapf, M. K. 1984. *Yukon Restitution Study*. Whitehorse: Department of Justice, Yukon Territory.

Zapf, M. K., and B. Cole. 1985. "Yukon Restitution Study." 27 *Canadian Journal of Criminology* 477–89.

LEGISLATION

Act to Permit the Conditional Release of First Offenders in Certain Cases,
   S.C. 1889, 52 Vic., c. 44
Act to Provide for the Conditional Liberation of Penitentiary Convicts, S.C.
   1899, 63–64 Vic., c. 49
Criminal Code, R.S.C. 1985, c. C-46
Parole Act, S.C. 1958, c. 38
Parole Act, R.S.C. 1985, c. P-2
Penitentiary Act, R.S.C. 1985, c. P-5

13 CRITICAL ISSUES IN CANADIAN CORRECTIONS

The Female Offender

Throughout the preceding chapters, our discussion centred primarily on adult male offenders in Canada. However, there are major issues surrounding the female offender, the majority of whom have been described as "poor, uneducated members of minority groups who are lacking in marketable skills, dependent on welfare, alcohol and men, and are single parents who are solely responsible for child-care" (Ross and Fabiano, 1985: 4; Johnson, 1986). The majority of *Criminal Code* offences committed by women involve theft or fraud and a large number of these are theft under $1,000 (primarily shoplifting).

Materials presented to the Daubney Committee (1988: 221–22) included a profile of female offenders admitted to the Pine Grove Correctional Centre in Prince Albert, Saskatchewan in 1985. Twenty-one per cent of the women were serving sentences for drinking and driving; 25% for property crimes, and 45% for non-payment of fines. Sixty per cent of the women were serving sentences of less than 30 days, consistent with data from other provinces that suggest that as many as 75% of women receive sentences of less than 30 days. Among the Pine Grove inmates, 83% were native Indian, 75% were under age 30; 78% had more than two children; most had been unemployed prior to admission and nearly three-fourths had a grade nine education or less. Fifty-five per cent had been victims of sexual abuse, and nearly 80% admitted to serious drug or alcohol addiction problems.

The primary concerns surrounding the incarcerated female offender in Canada include: (1) the lack of policies and programs that address the specific needs of female offenders, (2) the problems of inmate mothers and their children, (3) the native Indian female offender, and (4) the ongoing controversy over the Prison for Women at Kingston, Ontario.[1]

Policies and Programs

Berzins and Cooper (1982: 401) characterize the treatment received by female offenders historically as a "mixture of neglect, outright barbarism

469

and well-meaning paternalism." Until the construction of the Prison for Women (P4W) at Kingston in 1934, women federal offenders were often housed in temporary quarters in male prisons and had little or no access to programs and services. Such arrangements often gave rise to mistreatment, the Brown Commission noting in its reports in 1848–49 that women housed in the Kingston Penitentiary had been physically and sexually abused (Cooper, 1987).

Administratively and programmatically, the Correctional Service of Canada (CSC) has applied the same principles to both male and female offenders, even though the female inmates face unique problems not encountered by their male counterparts (see Hunter, 1984; Moyer, 1984). In documenting the lack of programs and services, Berzins and Cooper (1982: 405) argue that female offenders "have been given the left-overs and hand-me-downs of facilities and programs designed for men; and when nothing has been left over to hand down, a poor imitation of the model, an outmoded version, has been hastily provided, with inferior facilities, less space, fewer programs and at less cost." This applies to both institutional and community-based facilities and programs.

In 1981, the Canadian Human Rights Commission held that the CSC discriminates against female prisoners by not providing facilities and services equal to those afforded male inmates, including the lack of facilities for "cascading" female offenders, the lack of psychiatric facilities for women, and inferior programs. This decision, however, did not provide any specific direction on how programs and services for the female offender should be similar to or different from those for males.

It appears that the Canadian courts may also become involved in the issues surrounding the Prison for Women. In early 1987, a female inmate at Kingston initiated a legal suit against the Correctional Service of Canada, the Commissioner of Corrections, and the warden of Kingston alleging that the manner in which the institution is operated, including the lack of separate security levels and programs similar to those available for male inmates, violates the equality provisions of the *Canadian Charter of Rights and Freedoms.*

The lack of programs for female offenders is often attributed to the relatively small number of women in institutions and under supervision in the community. In 1987–88, female offenders constituted 7% of provincial/territorial sentenced admissions to custodial facilities. The percentage of females in provincial/territorial correctional institutions ranged from 4% in Newfoundland, Prince Edward Island, and Nova Scotia to 10% in Manitoba, Saskatchewan, and Alberta (Canadian Centre for Justice Statistics, 1989). In addition, there were 129 women in the Prison for Women in Kingston, Ontario, the only federal facility for women serving sentences of more than two years. Berzins (1977: 6) notes that while correctional officials often contend that the high numbers of male offenders hinder the development of program opportunities, a similar argument is used in explaining the lack of program initiatives for the small number of female offenders:

> We are always saying that if we only had fewer men, we could really do something. What an irony! Here we have a small number of women and instead of taking advantage of the situation, we use it as an excuse for not doing anything because the numbers don't justify the resources.

Historically, prison programs for female inmates have reflected traditional role-model activities such as hair dressing and sewing, although recent attempts have been made to make more educational and vocational opportunities available to the inmates of P4W. At the provincial level, there is wide variation in the nature and quality of custodial and community-based services available to female offenders.

From an extensive review of institutional and community-based programs and services for female offenders across North America, Ross and Fabiano (1985: 9–16) recommend that there be an emphasis on training programs that will assist the female offender to become economically independent and on the development of "social competence" through the teaching of survival skills in self-management, independent living, and parenting. In a similar review of programs and services available to female offenders in Nova Scotia, Manderson (1985: 45) recommended that planning should focus on the development of diversion programs and other alternatives to confinement and on improving job training programs, housing, and drug and alcohol counselling.

Female Inmates and Their Children

One area that has received relatively little attention is inmate mothers and their children. Estimates are that between 50 to 70% of female offenders have children, although MacLeod (1986: 6) notes that no information is collected on inmate mothers and their children at either the federal or provincial levels. From materials gathered from a variety of sources, MacLeod (1986: 11–12) estimates that in 1983, 4% of the women admitted to correctional institutions were pregnant, 50% had children, and 30% had been living with their children prior to incarceration. There are substantial costs associated with incarcerating women who are mothers, not only in terms of the costs of providing alternative child care arrangements, but also in terms of the social costs of separation for both the mother and the child(ren). Further, inmate mothers run the risk of being found "unfit" under provincial child welfare legislation and losing control of their children.

Isolated efforts have been made by federal and provincial corrections officials to address the special needs of inmate mothers. Inmates at the Prison for Women may record videotaped messages to their children, as well as qualify to use the Family Visiting Unit for periods up to 72 hours once every three months. Unlike their counterparts in many foreign countries, female inmates are not allowed to keep their children in prison with them. However, MacLeod (1986: 43–46) notes that the Twin Maples Correctional Centre for Women in British Columbia and the Portage Correctional Centre for Women in Manitoba have "live-in" programs that allow mothers to have their children with them, subject to certain specified conditions, including the suitability of the inmate and the age of child. At Twin Maples, for example, the child must not be older than two years at the time of the mother's release, and in Manitoba, the age limit is ten months.

It is at the community level that the greatest potential exists for programs for inmate mothers and their children. Across Canada, the Elizabeth Fry Society and the John Howard Society provide assistance to inmate mothers and their children by facilitating family contacts and by locating short- and long-term care for children. However, there are few community-based residence facilities that allow children to live with their mothers. MacLeod (1986: 59–64) has identified several areas requiring further research, including the collection of baseline information on the number of inmate mothers and their children, the impact of long- and short-term separation on mothers and their children, the development of community residential facilities for inmate mothers and their children, and the potential for the development of community-based resources and services.

The Native Female Offender

Our discussion in Chapter 15 will reveal that native Indians are overrepresented from arrest to incarceration in many Canadian jurisdictions. However, it is the native female offender who is most disproportionately represented in provincial and federal female prison populations, while receiving the least amount of attention from both researchers and correctional officials. This overrepresentation is particularly acute in the Prairie provinces and in the Territories. In 1982, native women constituted up to 40% of the admissions to provincial correctional facilities in Alberta and over 70% in institutions in the Northwest Territories, the Yukon, and Manitoba (see LaPrairie, 1984).

A recent report sponsored by the Canadian Association of Elizabeth Fry Societies (Adelberg, 1985: 17–18) notes that native women encounter particular types of problems in prison. These include difficulties in adjusting to white, urban culture and alienation from their home community and culture and the lack of specialized programs to address their needs. Even less attention has been given to the development of community-based programs and services for native female offenders in northern and rural areas of the country (see also Daubney, 1988).

P4W: An Enduring Legacy

There is perhaps no better illustration of the resistance of the Canadian correctional system to substantive reform than the ongoing debate over housing the federal female offender. Among the major difficulties of P4W are the limitations imposed by the physical facility (built in 1934), the long distances that families of inmates must travel, and the designation of P4W as a multi-level facility, which results in all levels of security being housed in the same institution. This undermines "cascading," which is one of the major techniques of the CSC. The great distances between the inmate's home community and Kingston also limit the ability to make release plans and to identify resources that might be utilized upon reentry.

Efforts to phase out the Prison for Women and regionalize accommodation for women under federal jurisdiction can be traced back over 70 years. In 1914, a report of the Royal Commission on Penitentiaries (Canada, 1914) recommended that female offenders be transferred to provincial institutions to serve their federal sentences. Despite this, the Prison for Women was opened in Kingston in 1934, although only four years later, the Archambault Commission (1938) severely criticized the operation of the P4W and recommended the transfer of inmates to provincial facilities.

Over the next 40 years, several major correctional inquiries, including the Fauteux Committee (1956), the Ouimet Committee (1969), the MacGuigan Sub-committee (1977), the Carson Committee (1984), three inquiries that specifically addressed the needs of the federal female offender (Solicitor General of Canada, 1978a; 1978b; 1978c) and numerous other reports recommended that the Kingston Prison for Women be closed and that services for female offenders be provided through provincial institutions. More recently, a report of the Canadian Bar Association and the Daubney Committee (1988) recommended that the Prison for Women be closed within five years and that alternative community and institutional accommodations be established across the country.

While female inmates under federal jurisdiction may be housed in provincial institutions close to their homes and families under federal-provincial exchange-of-service agreements, MacLeod (1986: 54–55) points out there is an uneven geographical distribution that puts women from certain parts of the country at a disadvantage. During the period 1975 to 1984, for example, 60% of the women serving their federal sentences in provincial institutions were in Quebec, one-third were in the Provinces of Alberta and British Columbia, and only 1% were in the Atlantic provinces. The CSC has also been unsuccessful in developing co-correctional prisons, where female offenders would be kept in facilities close to male institutions and thus have access to existing programs and services provided to male inmates. This was recommended in the *Report of the Joint Committee to Study Alternatives for the Housing of the Federal Female Offender* (Solicitor General of Canada, 1978a), but encountered stiff opposition from the designated institution and was never implemented.[2]

Electronic Monitoring of Offenders: High Technology in Corrections

In the future, one of the more unique and potentially controversial developments in Canadian corrections may be the electronic monitoring (EM) of offenders. The use of EM as a major correctional technique emerged in the United States during the early 1980s, and beginning in 1983, several provincial corrections agencies, as well as the Correctional Service of Canada, undertook feasibility studies and designed experimental programs for the use of EM.

In 1987, the Corrections Branch in British Columbia implemented a pilot program utilizing EM for offenders convicted of impaired driving who would otherwise have been sentenced to intermittent sentences. This project was completed in 1988 and was judged to have been successful, leading to plans to expand the program in 1989. While the Correctional Service of Canada announced in early 1987 that it was cancelling plans to implement EM on a trial basis, due to "threats of legal action from civil rights groups," this technique provides an illustration of how corrections may evolve in the next century and the legal and ethical issues that may arise with its use.

The rationale offered for the development of EM programs is similar to that used to justify the expansion of community-based correctional programs during the 1960s and 1970s. Proponents contend that EM is less costly than incarceration, provides a humane alternative to the negative consequences of confinement and, by allowing the offender to remain in the community and maintain family and employment ties, increases the likelihood that the offender will return to a law-abiding way of life. Further, it is argued, the widespread use of EM as an alternative to confinement would serve to lessen prison overcrowding and lower overall correctional expenditures.

The following discussion draws heavily on materials from EM programs in the United States, although the issues raised are relevant to any consideration of the use of EM in Canada.[3]

History of Electronic Monitoring

While the electronic monitoring of offenders is receiving an increasing amount of attention during the 1980s, the first proposals for its use appeared in the early 1960s. Schwitzgebel et al. (1964) developed a system of "electronic parole," which allowed authorities to locate parolees 24 hours a day via a portable transceiver worn by the parolee that relayed signals to a central station (see also Ingraham and Smith, 1972; Schwitzgebel, 1969; 1970). In the late 1960s, this system was used on an experimental basis with selected groups of mental patients and parolees, although the experiment was short-lived. Proposals were also put forth for systems that would provide supervision for large numbers of offenders on probation and parole. One such system involved transponders being worn by the offender, with receiver units being placed in buildings and on streets to allow for tracking. Signals indicating the location and movements of the offenders were to be transmitted through telephone lines to a central computer (Gable, 1986).

The first use of EM by a court in the United States occurred in the State of New Mexico in 1983. A state court judge, inspired by an episode of Spiderman in the comics section of the local newspaper that featured a locator bracelet, placed five offenders under EM as a condition of their probation. Two of the probationers had been convicted of impaired driving and the remaining three for violations of probation conditions.

How Electronic Monitoring Works

The most common application of EM is as a condition of probation in conjunction with house arrest or home incarceration. This requires that the offender remain in his or her residence, except for approved absences for employment and other activities. Many correctional observers have argued that house arrest may be a viable method for reducing overcrowding in institutions, a sentencing alternative for non-violent offenders, and a way to reduce escalating institutional costs (see Ball and Lilly, 1985; 1986a; 1986b; Corbett and Fersch, 1985).

Friel and Vaughn (1986: 4) identify the ways in which offenders under home incarceration can be monitored electronically:

1. by a telephone call to the offender's residence during specified curfew hours,
2. by a computer that automatically dials the offender's telephone and receives identification by the offender's voice or by an electronic signal, or
3. by a system that involves the offender wearing a transmitting device as a bracelet or anklet, which sends radio signals to a receiver attached to the offender's telephone, which then relays them to a central computer at the probation or parole office.

Internal electronic safeguards inform the central computer if any attempt is made by the offender to tamper with or remove the bracelet or anklet. Gable (1986: 173) notes that the usual arrangement is for two probation officers to supervise 25 probationers.

There are a number of EM systems operating in the United States, carrying such names as "The Supervisor" and "On Guard." GOSSlink, one of the most widely used monitoring systems, utilizes a transmitter that is attached to the ankle or wrist of the probationer. This transmitter emits a signal that is picked up by a receiver located in the residence and sent via telephone lines to a central computer. If the probationer is further than 200 feet from the transmitter, the signal is lost. The central computer, located at the probation office, is capable of recording the arrival and departure times of the probationer. Internal electronic safeguards inform the central computer if any attempt is made to tamper with the transmitter. Second-generation EM systems utilize cellular telephone systems and are capable of monitoring the offender's location on a continual basis (see Houk, 1984; Schmidt and Curtis, 1987).

Electronic Monitoring Programs

There is considerable variability in the number and types of offenders placed under EM in the United States. In some jurisdictions, both misdemeanour (minor) and felony (serious) offenders are eligible, while others restrict participation to less serious offenders. In the State of New Mexico, EM is used to supervise offenders convicted of impaired driving and white collar offences, while in Kentucky, individuals convicted of defaulting on child support payments have been placed under EM. Other potential applications of EM are for offenders on pre-trial release, work release, or other forms of temporary release (Gable, 1986).

Berry (1985) suggests that the most suitable candidates for EM are those offenders who have committed offences that could result in confinement, but are not of a personal, violent nature. In a survey of probation administrators, Friel and Vaughn (1986: 8) found strong support for the notion that EM should be utilized to divert offenders from confinement, rather than be applied to offenders who would otherwise be placed on probation. A preliminary discussion paper on the use of EM for community supervision by the Correctional Service of Canada (1986: 8) states that the two major criteria should be the degree of risk presented by the offender and the rehabilitative needs of the offender. There are no policy statements that would indicate, however, how EM programs would interface with existing corrections programs such as parole and mandatory supervision.

One of the more prominent United States programs is operated by Community Corrections in Clackamas County, Oregon. This program is designed to provide a sentencing alternative for the court, to act as a mechanism to reduce overcrowding in institutions, to generate revenue for the county, and to provide continuity in the probationers' family life and employment (Clackamas County, 1985). Currently, referrals to the program are received from the county residential centre, through direct placement by the sentencing court as a condition of probation or parole, from pre-trial diversion programs, and from courts and agencies outside the county.

There are several criteria for entry into the Clackamas Country EM program. The offender must be able to pay a daily participation fee of seven dollars (although the fee is waived in cases of financial hardship), must have stable employment, a suitable residence, a telephone, and have received a specified score on a Risk Assessment Scale.

Once the offender is placed under EM, there are a number of rules and regulations that must be followed. All participants must abstain from alcohol and drugs, maintain employment, attend a weekly group meeting, adhere to a pre-approved weekly schedule, and have signed a document giving informed consent. Offenders in the program must also wear an electronic bracelet. A central computer makes random telephone calls to the offender's residence, and the offender has 15 seconds to fit the bracelet into a monitor box attached to the telephone and recite the date, time, and his or her name.

A similar program is operated in Kenton County, Kentucky, and it has been proposed that EM should be available not only to probationers, but also to offenders who have been granted a parole or who are within six months of their parole eligibility date (Lilly and Wright, 1985; Lilly, Ball, and Wright, 1987). In West Palm Beach, Florida, EM is operated for the county by a private, non-profit corporation and is utilized for probationers and for offenders on work release from a minimum security facility. The probationers on EM are offenders who would otherwise have been incarcerated, and they are sentenced to three or four days of home confinement for each day they would have spent in confinement. Probationers and offenders on work release with financial means are required to pay a weekly fee ranging up to $65 to cover the cost of the transmitter anklet and the corporation's monitoring fee.

Electronic Monitoring: The Promise and the Peril

The infancy of EM programs and the lack of controlled evaluations precludes an assessment of the extent to which they are more cost-effective, humane, and effective in reducing recidivism than are more traditional correctional strategies (see Vaughn, 1987). A major concern is whether the courts and correctional agencies will use EM as an alternative to incarceration or merely as a condition for offenders placed on probation or parole. Those skeptical of EM recite the rationale offered for the expansion of community-based corrections in the 1960s and 1970s, noting that these initiatives often resulted in neither cost savings nor the reduction of institutional populations, often operating to "widen the net" of the criminal justice system. Berry (1985: 6) suggests that this may have already happened in EM programs in the United States: "Although the monitor has as one of its stated purposes the reduction of incarcerated offenders, it is possibly used for offenders who, in fact, would probably not be incarcerated."

From an exploratory analysis of the EM program in Kenton County, Kentucky, Lilly and Wright (1985) concluded that while the overall effectiveness of EM could not be determined, the program was more economical than institutional confinement and had not resulted in "net-widening." The EM program was functioning as a true alternative to confinement, although there was differential use of EM by judges due to variations in sentencing philosophies. Fifty-two per cent of the offenders sentenced to the EM program had maintained employment and only 3 of the 23 offenders in the program violated the conditions of the home incarceration. Sixty-five per cent of the offenders placed under EM were able to pay the fee required for participating in the program, which was based on 25% of their net weekly household income. The fees of those offenders with incomes of less than $100 per week were waived and paid by the county. In the West Palm Beach program, 98% of the offenders under EM were employed and financially able to pay the weekly fee (see also Lilly et al., 1987).

The major controversy over EM, however, is likely to centre on the legal and ethical concerns surrounding the increased use of high technology for surveillance and the fear of an emerging "Big Brother" as described by George Orwell in his novel 1984. Marx (1985: 47–48), in documenting the increased role of information technologies in surveillance and the dangers that such technologies pose for individual freedom and privacy, cautions that "today's surveillance technologies may be creating a climate of suspicion from which there is no escape. Proving innocence in such a society may become vastly more difficult than inferring guilt" (see Blomberg, Waldo, and Burcroff, 1987).

A contrasting view of the potential role of technology is provided by Alexander and Alexander (1985), who argue that technology "holds forth the possibility that the gravest threat to our civil liberties — crime, and the police, social, and political responses it has evoked — can be substantially eliminated with no real threat to our privacy and freedom." In discussing the potential benefits of EM, as well as citing concerns about its abuse, Berry (1985: 14) notes: "The new option of electronic monitoring provides the opportunity for less restrictive measures. At the same time, if used improperly, it can turn into an additional, more restrictive measure." The legal issues centre on whether the use of EM is a violation of citizens' rights under the *Canadian Charter of Rights and Freedoms* or of the U.S. Constitution. The developing case law in the United States may provide some indication of how the Canadian judiciary will view the issue.

In the United States concerns have been raised that EM violates first amendment rights of freedom of speech and association; fourth amendment rights, which protect against unreasonable searches; the fifth amendment, which protects citizens against self-incrimination; and the eighth amendment, which prohibits cruel and unusual punishment. Decisions by state and federal courts in the United States, as well as various legal opinions, have held that EM, if accompanied by legal safeguards such as informed consent on the part of the participant, does not violate citizen's rights under the U.S. Constitution. This position has also been adopted by the American Civil Liberties Union in many jurisdictions in the United States.

To date, the application of high technology in corrections has been largely restricted to efforts to improve administrative efficiency and there have been few applications of computer technology to programs and services for criminal offenders. The escalating costs of corrections and increase in the numbers of inmates beyond the rate of new prison-cell construction make EM an attractive alternative to correctional systems that are attempting to control costs while continuing the search for viable programmatic alternatives for criminal offenders. In the future, high technology will make possible even more accurate systems for monitoring the location of offenders outside the home and will have the capacity to control behaviour as well, either through implants or electronic signals. In the next century, it is likely that these developments will pose legal and ethical challenges not only for corrections but for Canadian society as well.

The Death Penalty: An Endless Debate

> The systematic and widespread application of the death penalty would preserve life. Its deterrent effect would be greater than that of any other punishment. By sparing the life of a murderer, we sacrifice the lives of the innocent. [Lehtinen, 1977: 251]

> The state has a duty to protect its citizens from crime. It should carry out this protective responsibility with a minimum of intervention in individual lives and the lowest net loss in human suffering. The use of the death penalty is inconsistent with this goal. [Smith, 1977: 259]

The above quotations are illustrative of the centuries-old debate over the death penalty, a highly emotional controversy involving conflicting religious and political views, arguments over morality, and disagreements over statistical data and the methods used to obtain them.

The use of the death penalty for a wide range of offences in early Canada was documented in Chapter 10 (see Greenland, 1987). Concerns about the harshness of the criminal law and the ideas of the writers of the Enlightenment led to a search for alternative punishments, one of which was the increased use of incarceration. Dissatisfaction with the use of capital punishment was one of the primary reasons for the construction of the Kingston Penitentiary in 1835, although the death penalty continued to be used in Canada until 1976, when it was abolished by an amendment to the *Criminal Code.*

In practice, the last execution in Canada occurred in 1962 and all death sentences received from 1967 to 1976 were commuted. Zubrycki (1984: 398) has traced the legislative history of the death penalty in Canada, and this information is reproduced in Table 13.1. During the 1980s, there has been increased political and community pressure on the federal government to reinstate the death penalty. In June 1987, a motion to reinstate capital punishment was defeated in Parliament, although this is not likely to resolve the issue.

The Arguments

There is an extensive body of literature in which the proponents and opponents of the death penalty argue their respective positions. Arguments in favour of the death penalty generally include the following assertions:

- The death penalty protects society and saves lives.
- There is no statistical evidence that the death penalty is not a deterrent to crime.
- The death penalty reinforces conformity to the law.
- Opinion polls consistently reveal that the majority of the general public support the death penalty.
- The failure to respond severely to persons who commit heinous crimes undermines community solidarity, heightens the fear of crime, and discredits the criminal justice system.
- The deterrent threat of punishment is reduced when there is less severe punishment than justice requires.
- There is no biblical prohibition against the use of the death penalty.

In response, the following arguments are generally offered in support of the position to abolish the death penalty:

- There is no statistical evidence to indicate that the death penalty deters crime.
- The deliberate taking of a human life is immoral and is harmful to the social order.
- The death penalty is administered in a discriminatory manner, with the poor and members of racial and ethnic minorities more likely to be subjected to it.
- Under the death penalty, innocent people have and will be executed for crimes they did not commit.

TABLE 13.1
CHRONOLOGY OF THE DEATH PENALTY IN CANADA

Date	Event	Offence	Penalty	Parole Eligibility
1961 and Prior		Murder (death occurring from an act known to be likely to cause death).	Death (often commuted)	Unrestricted
1961 (Sept.)	Legislative amendment, created Capital and Non-Capital Murder categories	Capital murder (planned and deliberate, police or prison officer)	Death (often commuted)	10 years (if commuted)
		Non-capital murder	Life Imprisonment	7 years
1962 (Dec. 29)	Last execution in Canada			
1967 (Dec. 29)	Legislative amendment, introduced a 5 year trial of restricted capital punishment	Capital murder (police, or prison officers, guard, or under "contract")	Death (all commuted)	10 years (if commuted)
		Non-capital murder	Life Imprisonment	10 years
1972 (Dec. 29)	1967 Legislation renewed, and Capital and Non-Capital Murder replaced by "Murder punishable by death" and "Murder punishable by Life imprisonment."	Murder punishable by death	Death (all commuted)	10 years (if commuted)
		Murder punishable by life imprisonment	Life Imprisonment	10 years
1974 (Jan. 1)	Legislative amendment, to allow court to set parole eligibility between 10 and 20 years.	Murder punishable by death	Death (all commuted)	10 to 20 years (if commuted), at discretion of court.
		Murder punishable by imprisonment for life	Life Imprisonment	10 to 20 years
1976 (July 26)	Legislative amendment, abolished the death penalty, created first and second-degree murder offences, and introduced judicial review of parole eligibility after 15 years, where applicable.	1st degree murder (police officer, prison staff, planned and deliberate, contract, death during kidnapping, hijacking or sexual offence, and any second murder)	Life Imprisonment	25 years
		2nd degree murder	Life Imprisonment	10 years minimum, up to 25 years at discretion of court.

Source: R.M. Zubrycki. "Long-Term Incarceration in Canada." Reprinted by permission from the *Canadian Journal of Criminology*, volume 26, no. 4, October 1984, pages 398–399. Copyright by the Canadian Criminal Justice Association.

- The use of the death penalty does not increase respect for the law — it undermines it by placing a low value on human life.
- The death penalty would violate the *Canadian Charter of Rights and Freedoms.*

Much of the controversy over the death penalty has focused on the concepts of deterrence and retribution (see Fattah, 1973). Research on the deterrent effect of the death penalty has involved statistical analysis that compares jurisdictions with and without the death penalty in terms of crime rates and homicide rates. Other studies have examined the homicide rates in jurisdictions before and after the abolition of the death penalty or prior to and following an execution.

One of the most widely cited (and controversial) studies of the deterrent effect of the death penalty was reported by Ehrlich (1975). From an analysis of nationwide data on crime rates and executions in the United States, Ehrlich concluded that each execution prevented seven or eight persons from being murdered. Although the methodology of Ehrlich's study has been severely criticized (see Bowers and Pierce, 1975), the findings are often used by supporters of the death penalty as evidence of the deterrent effect of the death penalty. From a review of research studies examining the deterrent effect of the death penalty, Blumstein, Cohen, and Nagin (1978: 62) concluded that "the current evidence on the deterrent effect of capital punishment is inadequate for drawing any substantial conclusions." The seemingly endless debates over statistical analyses of the deterrent effects of the death penalty have led Bowker (1982: 99) to conclude that "the same statistical data . . . can lead to very different conclusions depending upon the backgrounds and preconceptions of the individuals involved."

Despite the lack of evidence that the death penalty acts as a deterrent to serious criminal behaviour, a majority of the Canadian public continues to support its reinstatement. And, surveys in the United States have indicated that large numbers of people would continue to support the death penalty even if it were found to have no deterrent effect. These findings suggest that "public attitudes toward the death penalty seem to be based as much on ideas of retribution or just deserts as on ideas of deterrence" (Conklin, 1986: 405). *Retribution,* according to Conklin (1986: 412) "asserts that people who violate the law deserve punishment because they have intentionally hurt others . . . offenders deserve to be punished because they have gained an advantage over others by their crimes, and they must be punished in order to restore a balance among all citizens."

Canadian Attitudes toward the Death Penalty

Canadian public opinion polls have consistently revealed that the majority of Canadians favour reinstatement of the death penalty. From a survey of residents in the Provinces of Quebec, Ontario, and Manitoba, conducted as part of a larger study of Canadian attitudes toward crime policies, Brillon, Louis-Guerin, and Lamarche (1984: 196) reported the following responses to questions about the death penalty:

- opposed to the death penalty under any circumstances (15.8%);
- opposed to the death penalty except in a few cases where it may be appropriate (29.9%);
- generally in favour of the death penalty except in cases where it may not be appropriate (31.4%);
- strongly in favour of the death penalty as an appropriate measure (22.2%);
- don't know (0.7%).

These figures and the results of numerous Gallup Polls indicate that the majority of Canadians favour the use of capital punishment, at least in certain specified situations. Similar results have been obtained in surveys and opinion polls in the United States (see Ellsworth and Ross, 1983).

Brillon et al. (1984: 199, 202) also attempted to determine the factors that influence attitudes toward the death penalty. No relation was found between fear of crime and attitudes toward punishment and the use of the death penalty. Women, while more fearful of crime (and less victimized) than men, are not more punitive in their views of punishment, nor are persons who have been the victims of crime. The authors offer the following explanation for public attitudes toward punishment, which includes views on the use of the death penalty:

> People have become more punitive in latter years . . . because the increase in violent criminality has made their image of the delinquent correspond more to that of the dangerous criminal. Whether they have any fear or not, people have the same image of the offender, and it is in terms of this image and not of fear that their punitiveness is manifested. [P. 202]

The decision of Parliament in 1987 not to reinstate the death penalty will not end the ongoing controversy, and the reader is urged to become more acquainted with the materials on what is likely to remain a topic of debate in Canadian criminal justice (see Bedau, 1982; Berns, 1979; 1980; Fattah, 1972; Lempert, 1983; Seagrave, 1987; van den Haag, 1975; van den Haag and Conrad, 1983).

Violence and Victimization in Canadian Prisons

In Chapter 11, we noted that life inside the total institutional world of the prison is often characterized by psychological intimidation and physical violence. The nature and extent of such activities are often invisible to the outside world, although recent research, much of it Canadian, provides insights into the patterns of violence and the types of victimization experienced by inmates. Many of these investigations have also made recommendations designed to reduce the rates of violence and victimization. There are many different forms of violence and victimization involving inmates in prison. An inmate may be the victim of the actions of other inmates, of harassment and physical mistreatment by staff members, or of decisions by prison officials, including being placed in solitary confinement, a practice that many correctional observers argue constitutes cruel and unusual punishment. While inmates may suffer psychological and physical abuse from prison staff, far more common is inmate-to-inmate violence, despite the tenets of the inmate "code," which ostensibly includes a pledge of solidarity and a prohibition against inmates exploiting one another.

Bowker (1980) has identified three major types of inmate victimization:

1. Psychological: Inmates may be victimized by aggressive inmates who force them to provide sexual services, give up material goods, or submit to other demands. Such victimization may not involve physical violence, although many inmate suicides or incidents of self-injury can be traced to the impact of past or anticipated victimizations.
2. Economic: The deprivations within the institution may result in inmates being the victims of loansharking, fraudulent gambling activities, theft, robbery, or protection rackets.
3. Social: Inmates who are members of a racial, ethnic or religious group, or who have been convicted of a particular type of offence, are often at high risk within the general inmate population. Child molesters and rapists, for example, are often segregated in protective custody to ensure their safety.

These categories indicate that violence in prison can assume many different forms and have a significant impact on the rest of the inmate population, the correctional staff, and institutional administration.

Nature and Extent of Prison Violence and Victimization

The Preventive Security Division of the Correctional Service of Canada classifies as violent incidents the following: murder, attempted murder, assaults, inmate fights, hostage takings, major disturbances, suicide, attempted suicide, self-inflicted injury, arson, and damage to government property. Figures compiled by Porporino and Marton (1984: 5–6) suggest that the rates of violence in Canadian prisons have increased over the past 15 years. The most disturbing figures are those for inmate homicides and inmate suicides, which are comparable to the rates reported in state and federal prisons in the United States. The incidents of inmate homicide are 20 times, and of inmate suicides 3 times, those of comparable age groups in the Canadian public.

During 1987–88, there were 41 inmate deaths in provincial institutions, 24 of which were suicides. The Province of Quebec has consistently recorded high rates of inmate suicides. At the federal level, there were 36 inmate deaths, including 14 from suicide and 5 from murder (Canadian Centre for Justice Statistics, 1989).

The Causes of Prison Violence

Research by Canadian and American investigators suggests that the age of the offender population, overcrowding, and the extent of transiency of an institution's population are strongly correlated with levels of prison violence and victimization.[4] Young offenders are more likely than older offenders to be involved in homicides and collective violence, both as offenders and victims, and in acts of self-injury, as are inmates who are single, native Indian, Métis, or black and who have previous prison commitments (Burtch and Ericson, 1979; Campbell, Porporino, and Wevrick, 1985; Jayewardene and Doherty, 1985; Porporino and Marton, 1984). Many of the young perpetrators and victims of violence are in the first year of their sentence (Jayewardene and Doherty, 1985).

Overcrowding and "double-bunking" of inmates also appear to be related to increased levels of physical assaults between inmates, as well as to higher levels of inmate deaths, suicides, and disciplinary occurrences (McCain, Cox, and Paulus, 1985; Gaes and McGuire, 1985). During 1985–86, an average of 800 inmates were double-bunked, despite the continued recommendations of the Correctional Investigator that the CSC should discontinue this practice (Government of Canada, 1987: 21).

Larger prisons that are overcrowded and have a high proportion of young offenders evidence higher rates of violence, as do facilities that have high rates of transiency, resulting in greater anonymity among the inmates (see Farrington and Nuttall, 1980; Jan, 1980; Jayewardene and Doherty, 1985). Campbell et al. (1985) have also reported that inmates convicted of violent crimes were the most active in prison violence, although there is increasing involvement of property offenders. While concern has been expressed with the growing number of long-term offenders in Canadian institutions, Campbell et al. (1985) found that inmates serving life sentences were less involved in prison violence than were those serving shorter sentences and that they had a stabilizing influence on the prison community (see also Burtch and Ericson, 1979).[5]

Caution must be exercised, however, in generalizing these findings to specific institutions. In a study of violence in 24 maximum- and medium-security federal prisons in Canada, Porporino and Dudley (1984) found that the impact of overcrowding on rates of prison violence was not uniform. Further, the types of violence that existed when the overcrowding-incident relation was found varied as well. In some institutions, the violence was in the form of inmate-to-inmate assaults, while in others violence was manifested by assaults on prison staff. These findings led the authors to conclude that "overcrowding may have a differential effect, exacerbating particular kinds of violence depending on other characteristics of the institution, security measures and the nature of social control processes, and the type of inmate population" (p. 18).

The concept of a "continuum of correctional institutions," which was utilized to better understand the dynamics of life inside prisons in Chapter 10, may be a useful concept in understanding the levels of violence in Canadian prisons. There may be variations in the rates of violence not only between institutions at different security levels, but between prisons at the same security level as well. This is supported by a study of inmate homicides over the 15-year period 1967-1981, conducted by Jayewardene and Doherty (1985). Seventy per cent of the 59 homicides had occurred in maximum security institutions, while none had taken place in minimum security facilities. Thirty per cent of the homicides had occurred in two large maximum security prisons, Archambault (27%) and Millhaven (10%). The three medium security prisons of Matsqui (6.8%), Stoney Mountain (6.8%), and Drumheller (5%) also recorded a disproportionate number of inmate homicides. During 1983–84, 35% of all major incidents and 33% of all incidents of violence in the federal correctional system occurred in the Ontario region. This included 64% of all inmate murders and 45% of all serious assaults on inmates.

Inmate-Staff Victimization

The abuse of inmates by their keepers has a long history in Canadian corrections, dating back to the building of the local gaols and the first penitentiary at Kingston (see Chapter 10). The reader will recall that the reports of the Brown Commission, issued in 1848–49, documented the excessive use of corporal punishment by warden Henry Smith and his staff. The physical and mental abuse of inmates by prison staff and administration during the mid-nineteenth century can be ascribed, at least in part, to the near impossible task of maintaining order based on a strict "silent system" and to the low levels of education of prison staff. Concern with the physical and psychological abuse of inmates continues to the present time, although the lack of systematic inquiries into this issue precludes even speculative observations on its prevalence.

In one inquiry (Stewart, 1984), the Office of the Correctional Investigator was directed by the Solicitor General of Canada to examine the treatment of inmates by prison staff at Archambault Penitentiary during a major disruption in which three correctional officers were taken hostage and killed and five others injured. Two inmates involved in the disturbance committed suicide, and several others suffered injuries. Among the findings of the investigation (1984: 182–85) were that several inmates had been physically abused by correctional officers following the incident, officers violated directives and procedures by overusing tear gas, and inmates were subjected to psychological harassment, which included being prevented from sleeping, not receiving adequate bedding or clothing, and restricted access to health care. Throughout its investigation, however, the Committee (1984) experienced considerable difficulty in establishing the extent of such abuses, highlighting the closed nature of prisons and the low visibility of many of the activities that occur within them.

Correctional officers may also be vulnerable to victimization by both the inmates and other officers. Among the risks faced by line-level officers are riots, planned and spontaneous attacks by individual or groups of inmates, and being manipulated or "set up" by inmates. During the 14-year period from 1970 to 1983, there were a total of 12 staff homicides and 95 hostage takings, many of which involved staff members and ended in their deaths.

Reducing Prison Violence: An Elusive Goal

The increasing rates of violence in Canadian federal institutions have prompted major inquiries into inmate suicides, murders, and assaults. A study team (Botterell, 1984) investigating inmate suicides during 1983 in three penitentiaries in Atlantic Canada — Dorchester, Springhill, and Wesmorland — made 50 recommendations to the Correctional Service of Canada designed to reduce inmate suicides, including the development of policies and procedures for improving the identification of suicide-prone inmates and the reorganization of health care delivery services to better respond to inmates needs and to suicide attempts.

An inquiry (Vantour, 1984: 75–95) into inmate murders and serious assaults in institutions in the Ontario region — Millhaven, Collins Bay, and Frontenac — identified several factors in the institutional milieu that contributed to inmate-to-inmate violence. These included the lack of communication between management and staff and between staff and inmates, caused in part by the absence of a clearly defined correctional philosophy and mission within the Correctional Service of Canada.

To enhance communication, the report (Vantour, 1984) states that the CSC must clarify its basic mission and objectives and ensure that line-level staff participate in this process. Further, and in line with the recommendations of the Carson Committee (1984) report on correctional management, the managers of individual institutions must be given greater autonomy and more authority to run their own institutions. This would lessen the isolation between correctional managers and their staff and the inmates, as well as allow managers the discretion to take initiatives at the institutional level. Additional recommendations of the Vantour inquiry (1984) centred on the need to consider the impact of transferring inmates between institutions, to control the importation of drugs into institutions, and the adoption of other initiatives that would impose order on what the Committee (1984: 75) described as the major contributing factor in inmate-to-inmate violence — the "laissez-faire milieu" of many federal penitentiaries (see also Chocla, 1980).

Porporino and Marton (1984: 23–43) also proposed a number of measures to counteract prison violence, including an increased emphasis on design of the prison environment, training staff in conflict management and crisis intervention techniques, matching individual inmates to specific types of prison environments (i.e., some inmates function well in a structured setting, while others do not) and the development of behavioural intervention strategies, such as anger management, for inmates. One specific directive from these investigators (1984: 35) was that "correctional authorities should strive to avoid relatively large, crowded institutions, with populations that are highly transient, and that contain a high proportion of young rebellious inmates."

Solitary Confinement: Cruel and Unusual Punishment?

The use of solitary confinement is viewed by many observers as a major precipitator of violence and victimization and has been the subject of an ongoing debate in Canadian corrections (see Gendreau and Bonta, 1984; 1985; Mohr, 1985). The potentially detrimental effects of isolating prisoners were noted in the materials reviewed by the Langmuir Commission (1981: 189) in Ontario in the late 1800s: "When cellular imprisonment becomes absolute solitude, it is if unduly prolonged a serious evil, an unwarrantable cruelty, an outrage on humanity."

In his comprehensive treatise on the history and use of solitary confinement in Canadian prisons, Jackson (1983) describes in detail the case of *McCann et al. v. The Queen et al.*,[6] in which the court ruled that solitary confinement as practised in the now-abandoned British Columbia Penitentiary constituted "cruel and unusual punishment" under the terms of the *Canadian Bill of Rights*. Expert testimony for the plaintiffs focused on the negative consequences of solitary confinement, including anger, disorientation, and violence.

Similarly, a federal inquiry into the use of "dissociation" (solitary confinement) (Vantour, 1975: 24) reported that inmates in solitary confinement "expressed resentment, bitterness, considerable hatred and described deep depression, loneliness, concern about physical and mental well-being, and a feeling of hopelessness." Concerns about solitary confinement were also raised by Burtch and Ericson (1979: 45) who found that a disproportionate number of inmate suicides had occurred in solitary confinement areas.

In its report, the Vantour Committee (1975) made numerous recommendations relating to administrative procedures to be followed in utilizing solitary confinement and the conditions under which offenders are kept in segregation. Jackson (1983: 206–7) argues, however, that the Vantour report had little impact on the arbitrary use of solitary confinement and proposes the adoption of a Model Segregation Code that would protect the legitimate interests of both the inmates and the prison administration.

The position that solitary confinement is a major cause of violence and victimization in prison has been challenged by Suedfeld et al. (1982). In a survey of inmates in solitary confinement and in general prison populations in several United States and Canadian prisons, these authors (pp. 330–31) found no support for the assertion that solitary confinement creates emotional disturbances in inmates or that solitary confinement can be equated with "psychological torture." The major complaints of inmates interviewed by these researchers centred on physical mistreatment by certain correctional officers and missed program opportunities. Suedfeld et al. caution, however, that the experience of solitary confinement may be stressful and damaging for certain types of individuals, stating: ". . . it is the interaction between personality and environment that determines the final outcome, rather than the environmental factors by themselves" (p. 337).

With the enactment of the *Canadian Charter of Rights and Freedoms*, it is likely that the use of solitary confinement in Canadian prisons and its impact on inmates will continue to be the focus of controversy and the subject of court action. In fact, the Canadian judiciary appears to be altering its traditional "hands off" approach to issues relating to prison inmates and the administration of correctional institutions (see Landau, 1984; Mandell and Mandell, 1985; Solicitor General of Canada, 1986).

NOTES

1. For an overview discussion of the female offender in Canada, see Adelberg and Currie (1987); Daubney (1988); Hatch and Faith (1985); Johnson, 1986.

2. Co-correctional institutions are facilities in which male and female inmates share some or all programs and services, although the extent of the integration between the two groups varies considerably across institutions. As of 1984, there were three adult co-correctional institutions operated by the U.S. Federal Bureau of Prisons and there were ten state co-ed prisons (see Symkla, 1979; SchWeber, 1984). Also, the Province of Alberta operates co-correctional facilities for provincial male and female offenders.

3. Electronic monitoring is also referred to as electronic surveillance, electronic supervision, telemetrics, and telemonitoring.

4. In one of the more unique studies, Ganjavi et al. (1985) examined the effects of weather variables and population on rates of violence in six Canadian prisons. Among the findings were that the size of the prison population was consistently correlated with assaults on other inmates in medium security facilities during the summer months. There was also some evidence to suggest that temperature had a positive relation with minor offences during the summer months and a negative relation in winter.

5. The finding by Campbell et al. (1985) that federal prison inmates serving sentences of two years or less are more involved in violence than long-term offenders is somewhat misleading, as the "short-time" group may have a large number of inmates who have had either their parole or mandatory supervision release revoked and have been returned to the prison to serve the remainder of their sentence.

6. (1975), 29 C.C.C. (2d) 337, 68 D.L.R. (3d) 661, [1976] 1 F.C. 570.

REFERENCES

Adelberg, E. 1985. *A Forgotten Minority: Women in Conflict with the Law.* Ottawa: Canadian Association of Elizabeth Fry Societies.

Adelberg, E., and C. Currie. 1987. *Too Few to Count: Canadian Women in Conflict with the Law.* Vancouver: Press Gang Publishers.

Alexander, E., and L. Alexander. 1985. "Electronic Monitoring of Felons by Computer: Threat or Boon to Civil Liberties?" 11 *Social Theory and Practice* 89–95.

Archambault, J. (Chair). 1938. *Report of the Royal Commission to Investigate the Penal System of Canada.* Ottawa: King's Printer.

Ball, R. A., and J. R. Lilly. 1985. "Home Incarceration: An International Alternative to Institutional Incarceration." 9 *International Journal of Comparative and Applied Criminal Justice* 2–19.

——. 1986a. "The Potential Use of Home Incarceration for Drunken Drivers." 32 *Crime and Delinquency* 20–35.

——. 1986b. "A Theoretical Examination of Home Incarceration." 50 *Federal Probation* 24.

Bedau, H. A. 1982. *The Death Penalty in Amercia.* 3rd ed. New York: Oxford University Press.

Berns, W. 1979. *For Capital Punishment: Crime and the Morality of the Death Penalty.* New York: Basic Books.

——. 1980. "Defending the Death Penalty." 26 *Crime and Delinquency* 503–11.

Berry, B. 1985. "Electronic Jails: A New Criminal Justice Concern." 2 *Justice Quarterly* 1–24.

Berzins, L. 1977. "What Next for the Female Offender?" 3 *Liaison* 6–10.

Berzins, L., and S. Cooper. 1982. "The Political Economy of Correctional Planning for Women: The Case of the Bankrupt Bureaucracy." 24 *Canadian Journal of Criminology* 399–416.

Blomberg, T. G., G. P. Waldo, and L. C. Burcroff. 1987. "Home Confinement and Electronic Surveillance." In *Intermediate Punishments: Intensive Supervision, Home Confinement and Electronic Surveillance*, edited by B. R. McCarthy, 169–87. Monsey, N.Y.: Criminal Justice Press.

Blumstein, A., J. Cohen, and D. Nagin. 1978. *Deterrence and Incapacitation: Estimating the Effects of Criminal Sanctions on Crime Rates.* Washington, D.C.: National Academy of Sciences.

Botterell, E. H. (Chair). 1984. *Seven Suicides in the Atlantic Region: February 17 – August 25, 1983. Report of the Study Team.* Ottawa: Correctional Service of Canada.

Bowers, W. B., and G. Pierce. 1975. "The Illusion of Deterrence in Issac Ehrlich's Research on Capital Punishment." 85 *Yale Law Journal* 187–208.

Bowker, L. H. 1980. *Prison Victimization.* New York: Elsevier.

——. 1982. *Corrections: The Science and the Art.* New York: Macmillan.

Brillon, Y., C. Louis-Guerin, and M.-C. Lamarche. 1984. *Attitudes of the Canadian Public toward Crime Policies.* Montreal: Centre International de Criminologie Comparee, Université de Montréal.

Burtch, B. E., and R. V. Ericson. 1979. *The Silent System: An Inquiry into Prisoners Who Suicide/and Annotated Bibliography.* Toronto: Centre of Criminology, University of Toronto.

Campbell, G., F. J. Porporino, and L. Wevrick. 1985. *Characteristics of Inmates Involved in Prison Incidents.* Ottawa: Solicitor General of Canada.

Canada. 1914. *Report of the Royal Commission on Penitentiaries.* Ottawa: Government Printing Bureau.

Canadian Centre for Justice Statistics. 1989. *Adult Correctional Services in Canada, 1987-88.* Ottawa: Supply and Services Canada.

Carson, J. J. (Chair). 1984. *Report of the Advisory Committee to the Solicitor General of Canada on the Management of Correctional Institutions.* Ottawa: Supply and Services Canada.

Chocla, M. A. 1980. "Riots and Acts of Violence in the Penitentiaries: What Can We Learn?" 6 *Queen's Law Journal* 162–78.

Clackamas County. 1985. *Electronic Surveillance Program Manual.* Oregon City, Oreg.: Clackamas County Community Corrections.

Conklin, J. E. 1986. *Criminology.* 2nd ed. New York: Macmillan.

Cooper, S. D. 1987. "The Evolution of the Federal Women's Prison." In *Too Few to Count: Canadian Women in Conflict with the Law*, edited by E. Adelberg and C. Currie, 127–44. Vancouver: Press Gang Publishers.

Corbett, R. P., and E. A. L. Fersch. 1985. "Home as Prison: The Use of House Arrest." 49 *Federal Probation* 13–17.

Correctional Service of Canada. 1986. *Electronic Monitoring as a Tool for Community Supervision — A Discussion Paper on Its Potential Applications to Federal Corrections.* Ottawa.

Daubney, D. 1988. *Taking Responsibility. Report of the Standing Committee on Justice and Solicitor General on Its Review of Sentencing, Conditional Release and Related Aspects of Corrections.* Ottawa: Supply and Services Canada.

Ehrlich, I. 1975. "The Deterrent Effect of Capital Punishment: A Question of Life and Death." 65 *American Economic Review* 397–417.

Ellsworth, P., and L. Ross. 1983. "Public Opinion and Capital Punishment: A Close Examination of Views of Abolitionists and Retentionists." 29 *Crime and Delinquency* 116–69.

Farrington, D., and C. Nuttall. 1980. "Prison Size, Overcrowding, Prison Violence, and Recidivism." 8 *Journal of Criminal Justice* 221–31.

Fattah, E. A. 1972. *A Study of the Deterrent Effects of Capital Punishment with Special Reference to the Canadian Situation.* Ottawa: Information Canada.

Fauteux, G. (Chair). 1956. *Report of the Committee Appointed to Inquire into the Principles and Procedures Followed in the Remission Service in the Department of Justice.* Ottawa: Queen's Printer.

Friel, C. M., and J. B. Vaughn. 1986. "A Consumer's Guide to the Electronic Monitoring of Probationers." 50 *Federal Probation* 3–14.

Gable, R. K. 1986. "Applications of Personal Telemonitoring to Current Problems in Corrections." 14 *Journal of Criminal Justice* 167–76.

Gaes, G. G., and W. J. McGuire. 1985. "Prison Violence: The Contribution of Crowding Versus Other Determinants of Prison Assault Rates." 22 *Journal of Research in Crime and Delinquency* 41–65.

Ganjavi, O., B. Schell, J.-C. Cachon, and F. J. Porporino. 1985. *Geophysical Variables and Behaviour: Impact of Atmospheric Conditions on Occurrences of Individual Violence among Canadian Penitentiary Populations.* Ottawa: Solicitor General of Canada.

Gendreau, P., and J. Bonta. 1984. "Solitary Confinement Is Not Cruel and Unusual Punishment: People Sometimes Are!" 26 *Canadian Journal of Criminology* 467–78.

——. 1985. "The Cruel and Unusual Punishment of Solitary Confinement: A Challenge for Liberal Ideology." 27 *Canadian Journal of Criminology* 369–71.

Government of Canada. 1987. *Annual Report of the Correctional Investigator, 1986–87.* Ottawa: Supply and Services Canada.

Greenland, Cyril. 1987. "The Last Public Execution in Canada: Eight Skeletons in the Closet of the Canadian Justice System." 29 *Criminal Law Quarterly* 415–20.

Hatch, A. J., and K. Faith. 1985. "The Female Offender in Canada." Unpublished paper. Burnaby, B.C.: School of Criminology, Simon Fraser University.

Houk, J. M. 1984. "Electronic Monitoring of Probationers: A Step toward Big Brother?" 14 *Golden Gate Law Review* 431–46.

Hunter, S. M. 1984. "Issues and Challenges Facing Women's Prisons in the 1980's." 64 *The Prison Journal* 129–35.

Ingraham, B. L., and G. W. Smith. 1972. "Electronic Surveillance and Control of Behavior." 7 *Issues in Criminology* 35–53.

Jackson, M. 1983. *Prisoners of Isolation: Solitary Confinement in Canada.* Toronto: University of Toronto Press.

Jan, L. J. 1980. "Overcrowding and Inmate Behavior: Some Preliminary Findings." 7 *Criminal Justice and Behavior* 283–90.

Jayewardene, C. H. S., and P. Doherty. 1985. "Individual Violence in Canadian Penitentiaries." 27 *Canadian Journal of Criminology* 429–39.

Johnson, H. 1986. *Women and Crime in Canada.* Ottawa: Solicitor General of Canada.

Landau, T. 1984. "Due Process, Legalism and Inmates' Rights: A Cautionary Note." 6 *Canadian Criminology Forum* 151–63.

Langmuir, J. W. (Chair). 1891. *Report of the Commissioners Appointed to Enquire into the Prison and Reformatory System of Ontario.* Toronto: Warwick and Sons.

LaPrairie, C. P. 1984. "Selected Criminal Justice and Socio-demographic Data on Native Women." 26 *Canadian Journal of Criminology* 161–69.

Lehtinen, M. W. 1977. "The Value of Life — An Argument for the Death Penalty." 23 *Crime and Delinquency* 237–52.

Lempert, R. O. 1983. "Desert and Deterrence: An Assessment of the Moral Bases of the Case for Capital Punishment." 79 *Michigan Law Review* 1177–1231.

Lilly, J. R., R. A. Ball, and J. Wright. 1987. "Home Incarceration with Electronic Monitoring in Kenton County, Kentucky: An Evaluation." In *Intermediate Punishments: Intensive Supervision, Home Confinement and Electronic Surveillance,* edited by B. R. McCarthy, 189–203. Monsey, N.Y.: Criminal Justice Press.

Lilly, J. R., and J. Wright. 1985. *Home Incarceration with Electronic Monitoring in Kenton County, Kentucky: A Preliminary Report.* Frankfort, Ky.: Kentucky Department of Corrections.

MacGuigan, M. (Chair). 1977. *Report to Parliament by the Sub-committee on the Penitentiary System in Canada.* Ottawa: Supply and Services Canada.

MacLeod, L. 1986. *Sentenced to Separation: An Exploration of the Needs and Problems of Mothers Who Are Offenders and Their Children.*

Ottawa: Solicitor General of Canada.

Mandell, C. C., and A. L. Mandell. 1985. "Accountability in Canadian Penitentiaries: Disciplinary Procedures and Judicial Review." In *Accountability and Prisons: Opening Up a Closed World,* edited by M. Maguire et al., 245–63. London: Tavistock Publications.

Manderson, C. 1985. *The Female Offender in Nova Scotia: Community Programs and Services.* Ottawa: Solicitor General of Canada.

Marx, G. T. 1985. "The New Surveillance." 88 *Technology Review* 43–48.

McCain, G., V. C. Cox, and P. B. Paulus. 1985. "The Effect of Prison Overcrowding on Inmate Behavior." In *Correctional Institutions,* edited by R. M. Carter, D. Glaser, and L. T. Wilkins, 117–20. 3rd ed. New York: Harper and Row Publishers.

Mohr, G. T. 1985. "The Long-Term Incarceration Issue: The Banality of Evil and the Pornography of Power." 27 *Canadian Journal of Criminology* 103–112.

Moyer, I. L. 1984. "Deceptions and Realities of Life in Women's Prisons." 64 *The Prison Journal* 45–56.

Ouimet, R. (Chair). 1969. *Report of the Canadian Committee on Corrections. Toward Unity: Criminal Justice and Corrections.* (Catalogue No. JS52-1-1968.) Ottawa: Information Canada.

Porporino, F. J., and K. Dudley. 1984. *An Analysis of the Effects of Overcrowding in Canadian Penitentiaries.* Ottawa: Solicitor General of Canada.

Porporino, F. J., and J. P. Marton. 1984. *Strategies to Reduce Prison Violence.* Ottawa: Solicitor General of Canada.

Ross, R. R., and E. A. Fabiano. 1985. *Correctional Afterthoughts: Programs for Female Offenders.* Ottawa: Solicitor General of Canada.

Seagrave, J. 1987. "The Death Penalty: Will Canada Restore This Punishment?" 29 *Canadian Journal of Criminology* 405–19.

Schmidt, A. K., and C. E. Curtis. 1987. "Electronic Monitors." In *Intermediate Punishments: Intensive Supervision, Home Confinement and Electronic Surveillance,* edited by B. R. McCarthy, 137–52. Monsey, N.Y.: Criminal Justice Press.

SchWeber, C. 1984. "Beauty Marks and Blemishes: The Coed Prison as a Microcosm of Integrated Society." 64 *The Prison Journal* 3–14.

Schwitzgebel, R. K. 1969. "Issues in the Use of an Electronic Rehabilitation System with Chronic Recidivists." 3 *Law and Society Review* 597–611.

———. 1970. "Behavioral Electronics Could Empty the World's Prisons." 4 *The Futurist* 59–62.

Schwitzgebel, R. K., R. L. Schwitzgebel, W. N. Panke, and W. S. Hurd. 1964. "A Program of Research in Behavioral Electronics." 9 *Behavioral Science* 233–38.

Smith, G. W. 1977. "The Value of Life — Arguments against the Death Penalty: A Reply to Professor Lehtinen." 23 *Crime and Delinquency* 253–59.

Smykla, J. O. 1979. *Cocorrections: A Case Study of a Coed Federal Prison.* Rev. ed. Washington, D.C.: University Press of America.

Solicitor General of Canada. 1978a. *Report of the Joint Committee to Study Alternatives for the Housing of the Federal Female Offender.* Ottawa: Correctional Service of Canada.

_____. 1978b. *National Planning Committee on the Female Offender. Report.* Ottawa.

_____. 1978c. *National Advisory Committee on the Female Offender. Report.* Ottawa.

_____. 1986. *A Framework for the Correctional Law Review. Correctional Law Review Working Paper No. 2.* Ottawa: Ministry Secretariat.

Stewart, R. L. 1984. *Report on Allegations of Mistreatment of Inmates at Archambault Institution Following the Events Which Occurred on July 25th, 1982.* Ottawa: Office of the Correctional Investigator.

Suedfeld, P., C. Ramirez, J. Deaton, and G. Baker-Brown. 1982. "Reactions and Attributes of Prisoners in Solitary Confinement." 9 *Criminal Justice and Behavior* 303–40.

van den Haag, E. 1975. *Punishing Criminals: Concerning a Very Old and Painful Question.* New York: Basic Books.

van den Haag, E., and J. P. Conrad. 1983. *The Death Penalty: A Debate.* New York: Plenum Press.

Vantour, J. (Chair). 1975. *Report of the Study Group on Dissociation.* Ottawa: Solicitor General of Canada.

_____. (Chair). 1984. *Report of the Study Group on Murders and Assaults in the Ontario Region.* Ottawa: Correctional Service of Canada.

Vaughn, J. B. 1987. "Planning for Change: The Use of Electronic Monitoring as a Correctional Alternative." In *Intermediate Punishments: Intensive Supervision, Home Confinement and Electronic Surveillance,* edited by B. R. McCarthy, 153–68. Monsey, N.Y.: Criminal Justice Press.

Zubrycki, R. M. 1984. "Long-term Incarceration in Canada." 26 *Canadian Journal of Criminology* 397–402.

LEGISLATION

Criminal Code, R.S.C. 1985, c. C-46.

14 THE CANADIAN YOUTH JUSTICE SYSTEM*

*This chapter was co-authored with Alison Hatch-Cunningham.

In the preceding discussions we have focused primarily on the operation of the Canadian criminal justice system vis-à-vis adult offenders. In this chapter, an overview of the structure and operation of the youth justice system is provided, within the constraints imposed by space limitations. While the youth justice system in Canada has received far less attention from scholars than has its adult counterpart, the enactment of the *Young Offenders Act* (*YOA*) in 1984 signalled a profound shift in the philosophy of responding to youthful offenders and has far-reaching implications.

Given the significant changes introduced by the *YOA*, research materials produced prior to 1984 can be utilized only with considerable care. For this edition of the text, our discussion will focus primarily on the Act and its likely impact on the response to young offenders. In subsequent editions, the findings of Canadian researchers will be incorporated into our discussion. At this juncture, however, we can only speculate about the potential impact of the *YOA*.

Youth Crime in Canada

The sporadic nature and limited scope of the research conducted on juvenile and youth justice systems precludes a comprehensive discussion of the nature and extent of youth crime in Canada, not only on a national level, but also within the provinces and territories. In the absence of adequate primary research material, official government statistics provide the only available picture. Differences in methods of data collection allow comparison with neither adult statistics in Canada nor with youth crime patterns in the United States, despite the strong influence of that jurisdiction historically on Canadian youth justice policy and programs.

Official statistics on the nature and extent of youth crime in Canada must be viewed with caution because they are subject to the same influences as figures on adult criminality, as well as additional factors that are unique to the youth justice system (see Hackler and Paranjape, 1983). As with official statistics on adult crime, there may be a "dark figure" of youth crime that remains undetected or unreported, and crime rates for young offenders may be as much a function of the attributes of the youth justice

497

system in individual jurisdictions across the country, from the police to the youth court judge, as they are of actual youth misbehaviour. These factors may have an even more pronounced effect upon youth crime statistics than they have upon those for adults, given the greater likelihood of youths being handled informally, for example, when crimes are discovered but no charges are laid.[1]

Even interprovincial comparisons of youth misbehaviour are made difficult by variability in the age of juvenile court jurisdiction. While the *YOA* standardizes the age at which a young person is criminally liable at 12 to 17 years inclusive, under its predecessor, the *Juvenile Delinquents Act* (*JDA*), there was considerable variation among the provinces/territories in the age limits. In Quebec, the range was 14 to 17 inclusive; in Manitoba 7 to 17 inclusive; 7 to 16 years inclusive in Newfoundland and British Columbia; and 7 to 15 years in the remaining provinces and territories. Inconsistencies in reporting practices also hindered accurate measurement of youth crime over time.[2]

It is instructive to consider the general patterns of youth crime as reflected in official statistics for 1983, the last year for which such figures are available (Canadian Centre for Justice Statistics, 1984, 1985):

- In 1983, there were a total of 115,915 charges adjudicated, with the following breakdown: *Criminal Code* (74.9%); provincial statutes (20.6%); federal statutes (3.5%); and municipal by-laws (1.0%).
- There is wide interprovincial variation in the rate of youths charged per 1,000 population of all youths. For federal offences only, this ranged from 10.5 in New Brunswick to 67.6 in the Yukon. The national average is 30.
- In each province/territory, the highest charge rates occur among the oldest age groups. Less than two per cent of the total charges laid involved children under 12 years of age.
- Males account for nine of every ten charges adjudicated by the courts.
- Property offences constitute the vast majority of offences brought before the courts. The most prevalent charges are for breaking and entering and theft of property valued under $200.
- There is considerable variation between the provinces/territories in the rates of conviction, ranging from 91.8% in the Northwest Territories to 54.1% in Manitoba. The national average is 71.4%.
- Overall, the most frequently received disposition is probation supervision, followed by fines and suspension of final disposition. For federal offences only, committals to institutions are second to probation.

As previously noted, these findings are premised on data gathered prior to the enactment of the *YOA*. The collection and publication of data from 1984 onward will allow a general comparison of patterns of youth crime and response by the youth courts under the *JDA* and the *YOA* (see also Gomme, Morton, and West, 1984). Preliminary data for 1984/85 and 1985/86 (Canadian Centre for Justice Statistics, 1987) indicate that property offences, most notably break and enter and theft, constitute a high percentage of cases heard by youth courts. During 1984/85 and 1985/86, for example, break and enter cases represented 31% and 27% respectively of the cases heard, while youths charged with theft constituted 28% and 25% respectively of the total cases for these years.

Further insights into youth crime prior to the passage of the *YOA* are provided by self-report studies of delinquency. Youths, often high school students, are simply asked to report anonymously their criminal behaviour. This method overcomes many of the problems of official statistics, although it has other drawbacks, such as not "capturing" youths who are not in school and who may be extensively involved in misconduct.

The findings of self-report studies in Canada and the United States tend to confirm the picture of youth crime presented by official statistics. Generally, involvement in misbehaviour tends to increase with age, be very minor in nature, and be committed most often by boys (Gomme et al., 1984; LeBlanc, 1983; Linden and Filmore, 1980; Morton and West, 1983).

The one finding that is inconsistent with official statistics is that a large majority of youths engage in behaviour that could conceivably result in court processing. Those officially charged, therefore, represent only a fraction of all youths who are actually committing offences. Further, there are similarities between the offending patterns of youth in Canada and the United States (see Gomme et al., 1984; Linden and Filmore, 1980).

Other sources of information on the nature and extent of youth crime include in-depth studies conducted in specific settings. While some researchers have chosen to examine the court process (e.g., Bala and Corrado, 1985), others have focused upon the dynamics of youth crime. For example, LaPrairie and Griffiths (1981) compared patterns of delinquency between native and non-native youths in a northwestern Canadian community.

It can be expected that even with the enactment of the *YOA*, there will continue to be considerable diversity in the patterns of youth crime and court processing across Canada. The number of youths processed will increase in jurisdictions where the maximum age was raised from 15 or 16 to 17 (all provinces/territories except Quebec and Manitoba). To some extent, these increases may be offset by greater use of formal diversion programs (see below). Non-judicial handling of cases may also serve to screen out the less serious offences, meaning an overall increase in the severity of offences dealt with by the courts. In fact, as will be mentioned later in the chapter, an increase in custodial dispositions has already been noted in several jurisdictions across the country.

The Historical Response to Young Offenders

To understand fully the operation of the youth justice system in Canada today requires a review of the response to youthful offenders historically and of the shifts that have occurred in the dominant philosophy of youth justice. As with other segments of the Canadian criminal justice system, the response to children can be tied to events in the larger socio-political context. It is possible to identify key personalities and events that influenced the development of the youth justice system and contributed to the major shifts that have occurred in the identification of and response to youthful offenders.

It is important to recognize at the outset that a separate justice system for young persons is a relatively recent occurrence. Prior to the mid-nineteenth century, children were treated in much the same manner as adult offenders. This parallelled their position in society and the nature of family and social relations during the Middle Ages: ". . . lack of parental affection, physical and emotional remoteness, severe physical punishments and other discipline, rigid social class structure, and conflict, suspicion, hostility, and alienation among family groups all characterized child care . . ." (Siegel and Senna, 1988: 358).

There was, however, recognition of the reduced capacity of children to make moral and legal judgments. Under the English common law, persons below the age of seven years could not be convicted of committing an offence, as they were deemed incapable of forming the requisite criminal intent, or *mens rea*. Youths between the ages of 7 and 14 were subject to the doctrine of *doli incapax*, which involved a presumption of incapacity that could be contested by the Crown.[3] Beginning at age 14, children were considered as responsible as adults for their behaviour and were subject to the same penalties.

In early nineteenth century England, however, youths under the age of 14 often received harsh sentences for relatively minor offences, as illustrated by the following cases from the records of Stafford Prison (cited in Stubbs, 1972: 21):

- In 1834, George Saxon, aged 12 years, was sentenced to transportation for seven years for stealing a gold watch.
- In 1834, Thomas Tow, aged 10 years, was sentenced to transportation for seven years for stealing a donkey.
- In 1837, Matilda Seymour, aged 10 years, was sentenced to transportation for seven years for stealing one shawl and one petticoat.

Knell (1965) has documented cases of 103 children sentenced to death in the Old Bailey in London between 1801 and 1836, almost all for the crime of theft. These sentences were routinely commuted to a penalty of lesser severity, although records indicate that a 13-year-old boy was hanged for murder in 1831.

Changing Views of Children

During the early 1800s, several interrelated social changes occurred that were to have a tremendous impact upon the response to young offenders. The Industrial Revolution in Europe (1750–1825) had resulted in major changes in society. There was a mass exodus of people from the countryside to the cities to participate in the industrial labour force. The change from an agrarian to an industrial-based economy had implications for the nature of families. The nuclear family replaced the extended family, and traditional kinship patterns were weakened. In addition, "childhood" emerged as a separate status, and children were viewed as different from adults (Empey, 1979; 1982).

There emerged the view that human behaviour was influenced by the environment, and the family came to be seen as the primary mechanism by which children were shaped. Certain social characteristics came to be seen as "risk factors" for future delinquency. For example, in both Canada and the United States, there was great concern about immigrant children. The focus, therefore, shifted from what children did to who they were.

English penal reformers began to voice concerns about the confinement of children with adult offenders and the failure of authorities to separate offenders on the basis of age and severity of offence. A number of philanthropic societies, first in Britain and later in the United States, began lobbying for the creation of facilities solely for child offenders. As a consequence of these efforts, houses of refuge, or reformatories, were opened to house delinquent, dependent, and neglected youths. The first American reformatory was opened in New York in 1825, and by 1850, a large number of reformatories had been constructed. The facilities stressed education, vocational training, and religion and were designed to provide to youths what had been denied by inadequate parents and poor home environments.

In the United States, reformatories existed as a dispositional option for judges sentencing both child offenders and vagrant and destitute children. In practice, however, admission was restricted to petty offenders and those thought to be redeemable (Fox, 1970). Serious offenders continued to be processed and confined with adults. Within the reformatories, no distinction was made between youth who had committed crimes and those who, because of their dependent and neglected status, were believed to be potential offenders. Early intervention as prevention became, in practice, indistinguishable from the response to criminal behaviour. Reformatories were believed to prevent crime by taking children from crime-prone families, providing them with education and religious instruction, and ensuring they would not be confined with adult offenders.

Although an important step in the development of the juvenile court, reformatories soon waned in popularity in the United States. A major factor was the realization that reformatories were little more than prisons, replete with all the horrific conditions the reformers had sought to avoid. As Schlossman (1977: 35) notes: "It became increasingly clear . . . that many staff members were cruel, even sadistic, and were more concerned about maintaining order than about caring for inmates. Contrary to common belief, physical coercion was an instrument of first resort and was frequently as severe as in prisons."

Young Offenders in Early Canada

In early Canada, child offenders were subjected to the same penalties as adults and, when sentenced to terms of incarceration, were confined in local gaols. Children were confined in the Bridewell, which opened in Halifax in 1790 (Baehre, 1982: 12), and in 1864, 311 boys and girls under the age of 16 were admitted to the local gaols in Upper Canada (Hagarty, 1866: 4). Children were also confined in the Kingston Penitentiary, following its completion in 1835, without regard for their age, prior record, or severity of their crimes (Shoom, 1972).

The reformatory movement was much slower in gaining widespread acceptance in Canada. As late as 1888, children were being admitted to federal penitentiaries, as evidenced by the records from Dorchester Penitentiary in New Brunswick (cited in Sutherland, 1976: 102–103):

- – Herbert Smith, age 12: 5 years for breaking and entering
- – Enos Medley, age 13: 3 years for compound larceny
- – Edward Chambers, age 11: 2 years for burglary and larceny
- – Robert Welsh, age 14: 7 years for manslaughter.

In its investigation into the operation of the Kingston Penitentiary under Warden Henry Smith, the Brown Commission documented the excessive use of corporal punishment on child inmates. In the second of two reports issued in 1849, the Brown Commission criticized the practice of confining children in Kingston, noting:

It is distressing to think that no distinction is now made between the child who has strayed for the first time from the path of honesty, or who perhaps has never been taught the meaning of sin, and the hardened offender of mature years. All are consigned together to the unutterable contamination of the common gaol; and by the lessons there learnt, soon become inmates of the Penitentiary.

Among the recommendations of the Brown Commission were that houses of refuge, for the "reformation" of youth, be constructed.

There were additional factors that led Canadians to construct reformatories, including influences from the United States and the general social climate of mid-nineteenth century Ontario, in which education and schooling were seen as the primary defences against social problems such as juvenile delinquency. During the mid-1800s, there was the widespread perception that juvenile crime was increasing, although Houston (1982) and others note that whether an actual increase in crime was occurring is unclear. What is evident is that illiteracy and immorality and the apparent rise in juvenile crime were viewed as causally related and as threats to the order and stability of Canadian society.

Prentice (1977: 46) notes that, for Canadians of the time, institutionalization was considered a means of improving society by temporarily exposing children to an environment superior to that of their home: "[They] sought solutions to the social ills of their times by institution-building, in the creation of controlled environments which would contain, suppress, or avoid what they found unacceptable in wider society."

In 1857, two important pieces of legislation were enacted that responded to the concerns regarding the detention of children with adult offenders voiced by the Brown Commission nearly a decade earlier. The first, *An Act for the More Speedy Trial and Punishment of Juvenile Offenders*,[4] was primarily concerned with accelerating the processing of children's cases by the granting of bail to reduce the period of pre-trial detention for those under the age of 16. The second piece of legislation passed in 1857 was *An Act for Establishing Prisons for Young Offenders*,[5] which provided for the creation of two "reformatory prisons."

In 1859, two juvenile reformatories were opened — one on Isle aux Noix in Lower Canada and the other in Penetanguishene, Upper Canada — and the number of boys sentenced to these institutions steadily increased (see Shoom, 1972). Although these facilities were prisons, they responded to concerns for the classification and segregation of children from adults. Unlike their counterparts in the United States, initially at least, only children convicted of an offence could be sent to the juvenile reformatories.

As time passed, an increasingly larger group of children became subject to reformatory terms. Legislation enacted in 1875 allowed 16 year olds, who had previously been subjected to terms in adult penitentiaries, to be incarcerated in the reformatories. Reformatory terms were to be at least two years in length, but were not to exceed five years. If a term was to be greater than five years, the youth was sent to a penitentiary. Whenever possible, youths were to be placed in reformatories for pre-trial detention rather than in the local gaol. In 1879, one section of the Mercer Reformatory in Ontario was designated for girls under 14 years of age.

Another example of the expansion of jurisdiction of the emerging juvenile justice system was the gradual inclusion of pre-delinquents. It soon came to be realized that previous efforts had concentrated on those youths who were perhaps beyond redemption: "Thus, young people who were at least technically innocent of any law-breaking could be incarcerated and treated in exactly the same way as if they had been found guilty of an offence" (Sutherland, 1976: 99). As an example of this trend, beginning in 1880, "incorrigible" children in Ontario could be sent to a reformatory for up to five years upon the complaint of their parents.[6]

Industrial Schools and the Family Model

Disillusionment with the reformatories, first in the United States and then in Canada during the late 1800s, prompted the creation of industrial schools that stressed academic and vocational education. These facilities were to approximate as closely as possible a family atmosphere, as the family was now seen as both the cause of, and potential cure for, child crime. It was thought that institutions, particularly those designed along the cottage plan, could replicate all the benefits of a supportive and loving family. One way to accomplish this was by greater participation of women in the administration and daily management of the industrial schools (see Morrison, 1976).

Initially, the industrial schools were envisioned as facilities for neglected and dependent youth. Reformatories were still thought to be appropriate for delinquents. The Victoria Industrial School for Boys opened near Toronto in 1887, followed by the establishment of the Alexandria School, a similar institution for girls in 1891. From this time until the early 1900s, a number of industrial schools were constructed in the provinces.

Industrial schools were viewed as residential schools rather than as prisons and were designed to "be supplementary to the family which lacked adequate control" (Leon, 1977: 81). Parents could request that children be sent to an industrial school for an indeterminate period of time. These facilities soon replaced reformatories as the primary mechanism for controlling youth, except in those cases where a serious offence had been committed. Eventually, in Ontario youths under the age of 13 could be detained only in industrial schools.

In 1888, the *Child Protection Act*[7] was passed in Ontario, reaffirming the right of the government to place neglected children in industrial schools and creating the new option of children's homes. Another notable feature of this legislation was that provision was made for the creation of magistrates' courts for the separate trial of those under the age of 16 charged with provincial offences. The Act allowed for the appointment of a special "commissioner" to hear cases of those under 16 years of age, and where "practicable," the cases of those under the age of 21 were to be tried separately from adults. Although this idea was not immediately acted upon, the legislation was an important step toward the development of the juvenile court and further served to blur the distinction between the treatment of delinquent and dependent/neglected children.

An investigation of penal institutions for children and the response to juvenile delinquency was undertaken in 1890 by the Royal Commission on the Prison and Reformatory System in Ontario, chaired by J.W. Langmuir. Despite the provisions of the 1888 *Child Protection Act*, no separate courts for children had been established in Ontario, and in its final report, the Commission (Langmuir, 1891) was critical of the methods used to respond to child offenders, particularly the use of reformatories. Among the recommendations of the Commission were:

- the construction of industrial schools in each city and large town;
- the confinement of children in separate pre-trial detention facilities;
- the use of in-camera court proceedings for children under the age of 14;
- that confinement of children be used only as a last resort;
- the increased use of the dispositions of warning, suspended sentence, and probation;
- the use of industrial schools for confinement whenever possible;
- the use of indeterminate sentences for youths sent to reformatories; and
- the creation of a system of post-release apprenticeship or supervision.

The recommendations of the Langmuir Commission (1891) reflected a growing trend toward the deinstitutionalization of child care and the increased use of the child welfare system for delinquency-prone youths from poor home environments.[8]

In 1890, the Children's Aid Society was founded in Toronto, largely as the result of the work of one J. J. Kelso, a young journalist-cum-reformer who had co-authored the *Child Protection Act* of 1888. Kelso was heavily influenced by the growing deinstitutionalization movement in the United States and viewed the Children's Aid Society as a way to "deal with all matters affecting the moral and physical welfare of children, especially those who from lack of parental care or other causes are in danger of growing up to swell the criminal classes" (quoted in Jones and Rutman, 1981: 57). To accomplish this, it was necessary to enact legislation for neglected children and juvenile offenders, based on the motto: "It is wiser and less expensive to save children than to punish them" (Jones and Rutman, 1981: 58).[9]

Separate Justice for Children

The provisions of the 1888 *Child Protection Act*, which provided for separate trials for children, were put into effect in Toronto in 1890, although difficulties soon arose because the court was not empowered to hear cases involving contraventions of federal law. This was particularly problematic, as a large number of youths at the time were charged with larceny, which was a federal offence. Reform at the federal level was required, and in 1892, provisions allowing for separate and private hearings for children under 16 years of age "where it appears expedient and practicable" were included in Canada's first *Criminal Code.*[10] This legislation was complemented by an 1893 Ontario statute that provided for separate detention and trials for provincial offenders.[11]

Although these statutes authorized the operation of juvenile courts in the Province of Ontario, the matter was left to the discretion of the judges, and with isolated exceptions, children's courts were not created. Substantive legislative change was finally achieved in 1894, when the separate trial of young offenders was made mandatory and a children's court was opened in Toronto. Montreal was the second city to provide separate trial facilities for children, and a few other Canadian cities responded by conducting hearings in the judge's chambers, or in regular courtrooms when adult court was not in session (see Sutherland, 1976).

By the early 1900s, the idea of treating youths separately from adults was well entrenched. During this time, there was an increased emphasis on prevention with potential, as well as actual, offenders. There was increasing professionalization of what had previously been volunteer-based child welfare services, and the expanding network of children's aid societies had adopted delinquent youth as their responsibility, resulting in an overlap between the child welfare and juvenile justice systems (see Leon, 1977).

The move toward non-institutional, community-based responses to youthful misbehaviour included the use of foster home placements and the development of probation, first used in 1889.[12] Candians were becoming disillusioned, as had their neighbours in the United States, with the reformatories, which were increasingly viewed as little more than prisons for children, embodying all the negative attributes that reformers had sought to avoid by removing children from adult prisons in the mid-1800s. In 1904, the Ontario Reformatory for Boys in Penetanguishene was closed, following several years of declining admissions (Jones, 1978). While plans were made to replace the reformatory, the industrial school was fast becoming the preferred option. Indeed, the seeds for the creation of the *JDA* were all apparent by this time. What was needed was federal legislation that tied all these factors together and created statutory justification for current practice.

The *Juvenile Delinquents Act*: 1908

The *Juvenile Delinquents Act* (*JDA*) was principally drafted by W. L. Scott, president of the Children's Aid Society in Ottawa, and was passed by Parliament on July 8, 1908.[13] The provisions of the Act were modelled closely after the juvenile court statutes that were then in force in two dozen states in the United States. The underlying principles of the Act, as outlined by Scott (quoted in Kelso, 1907: 109) were:

> "1. That children are children even when they break the law and should be treated as such and not as adult criminals. As a child cannot deal with its property, so it should be held incapable of committing a crime, strictly so called;
>
> "2. That juvenile delinquents can be reformed through probation officers; and
>
> "3. That adults should be held criminally liable for bringing about delinquency in children."

Provisions of the *JDA*

Earlier attempts to create separate courts for children had required federal/provincial coordination. Under the provisions of the *Constitution Act, 1867*, the provinces were restricted from creating laws for the prosecution of violators of federal statutes, such as the *Criminal Code*.[14] Under this same legislation, the federal government was prohibited from enacting legislation concerning those areas that fell under provincial purview, such as contraventions of provincial statutes or matters of child welfare. The *JDA* addressed this problem by creating the federal offence of being a "juvenile delinquent," described in section 2(c) as:

> ... any child who violates any provision of the Criminal Code, any [federal] or provincial statute, or of any by-law or ordinance of any municipality, for which violation punishment by a fine or imprisonment may be awarded; or, who is liable by reasons of any other act to be committed to an industrial school or juvenile reformatory under the provisions of any [federal] or provincial statute.[15]

The definition of *juvenile delinquency* under the *JDA* was extremely broad and included any child who broke an existing law or was declared in need of protection under provincial child welfare legislation. The legislation represented the blending of the juvenile justice and child welfare systems. Children could qualify as juvenile delinquents without having committed a criminal offence, and children who did violate a law could be inducted into the child welfare system upon adjudication.

Among the notable features of the pre-adjudication process in the 1908 version of the *JDA* were the following:

–   All proceedings were to be governed by the procedures for summary trials.

- If a child over the age of 14 was charged with an indictable offence, he or she could be tried in the ordinary courts, if that course of action was deemed to be in the best interest of the child and demanded by the community.
- Parents were to be notified of proceedings against their children.
- Proceedings were to be held in private, away from areas where adults were tried, and were not to be reported upon in the press in such a manner as to identify the juvenile and his or her parents.
- Pre-court detention in a facility or gaol for adults was not allowed, except for children over the age of 14 who could only be safely detained or if such course of action was believed necessary to ensure the child's appearance in court.
- Bail provisions for adults applied to juveniles.
- Court proceedings were to be as informal as the circumstances would permit.

In cases where the child was adjudicated as a juvenile delinquent, several dispositional options were available to the presiding judge. The *JDA* provided for the imposition of a fine (not to exceed ten dollars), placement in a foster home, commitment to care of a children's aid society, or confinement in an industrial school.

The influence of anti-institutional forces was evident in the emphasis placed on probation as a dispositional option. Leon (1977: 81) has argued that one of the primary objectives of the *JDA* was to expand the use of probation as an alternative to reformatories and industrial schools. Upon adjudication, the *JDA* allowed the judge to

- commit the child to the care and custody of a probation officer;
- allow the child to remain at home, subject to the visitation of a probation officer, such child to report to the court or to the probation officer as often as may have been required; or,
- cause the child to be placed in a foster home, subject to the friendly supervision of a probation officer.

In addition to creating separate court proceedings for juveniles, the *JDA* created further distinctions between juveniles and adults. Juveniles were not charged with specific crimes; rather, they were *accused* of delinquencies. They did not plead guilty or not guilty; they admitted or denied the allegation. More important, in contrast to the adversarial nature of the adult system of justice, section 31 of the Act established the philosophy of *parens patriae* as the basis of the juvenile court: ". . . the care and custody and discipline of a juvenile delinquent shall approximate as nearly as may be that which would be given by its parents, and that as far as practicable every juvenile delinquent shall be treated, not as a criminal, but as a misdirected and misguided child, and one needing aid, encouragement, help and assistance."

Throughout the literature, there are competing views of the motives and achievements of reformers who lobbied for the creation of the juvenile court (see Houston, 1982; Leon, 1977; Sutherland, 1976). Part of the controversy surrounds the question of whether the juvenile court actually represented an improvement for child offenders. The arguments of the proponents of the juvenile court that children had "the right to the fatherly protection of the State" (Kelso, 1907: 110) have been challenged by scholars such as Platt (1969: 116), who contends that the "child savers" should not be considered humanitarians who created a new system of justice out of benevolent concern with youth, but "moral entrepreneurs" whose primary objective was to instil in the lower classes the values and ethics of the middle class. This view is reflected in the observations of Bartollas (1985: 439):

> ... the behaviors the child savers selected to be penalized, such as engaging in sex, roaming the streets, drinking, attending dance halls, and staying out late at night, were found primarily in lower-class children. Thus juvenile justice from its inception ... reflected class favoritism that resulted in the frequent processing of poor children through the system, while middle- and upper-class children were more likely to be excused.

Platt (1977: xix) later reassessed his views and turned his analysis to economic factors: "The child-saving reforms were part of a much larger movement to readjust institutions to conform to the requirements of the emerging system of corporate capitalism."

While it is beyond the scope of this book to explore the validity of these competing explanations, it is important to note that Canadian scholars have addressed these issues. The role of moral entrepreneurs and interest groups in juvenile justice has been examined by Hagan and Leon (1977), Houston (1972) and Leon (1977), and an argument involving economic factors and the role of the state has been advanced by West (1984). Readers are encouraged to review these and other materials.

Implementation of the *JDA*

While the *JDA* was "declared by experts to be the best [law] of its kind so far in the world" (Starr, 1913: 194), its adoption at the provincial level was uneven. The legislation had to be proclaimed in force in each municipality and province, separately, by federal order-in-council.[16] Proclamation was not made unless the jurisdiction had a temporary detention home, an industrial school (either locally or by agreement with another area), a juvenile court judge, probation staff, and a Juvenile Court Committee, as required by the *JDA*.[17]

Within the first few years of the passage of the *JDA*, juvenile courts were opened in the major urban areas from Halifax to Victoria, including Vancouver (1910), Toronto (1912) and Calgary (1912). In 1913, the *JDA* became operational province-wide for the first time in Alberta. When the authority of the *JDA* was extended to all areas of a province, provincial legislation was passed or amended empowering judges to hear cases under the *JDA*. In smaller towns and in the rural areas where there were no separate facilities for juveniles, court was held at a specially designated time in the judge's chambers or in the office of a police magistrate. Sutherland (1976: 129) notes that due to the lack of facilities and resources in many jurisdictions, the proclamation of the *JDA* made little actual difference in the handling of juveniles.

The uneven adoption of the *JDA* was also due to the fact that many provinces maintained control over delinquent youth by virtue of the definitions of "children in need of protection" by the state in their child welfare legislation. The *JDA* (s. 32) allowed provinces to continue to utilize provincial legislation in dealing with delinquent youth, except for offences classified as indictable under the *Criminal Code*, if it was deemed in the best interests of the juvenile.

Criticisms of the *JDA*

The *JDA* was slow to be implemented across Canada (MacGill, 1925), and it soon became apparent that the juvenile court was not the panacea originally envisioned. The rate of youth crime appeared to grow in the first half of the century (Watts, 1932; Brannigan, 1987). However, only minor amendments were made to the *JDA* in the years following its passage. In 1921, the upper age limit defining the court's jurisdiction was raised to 18 from 16.[18] Each province/territory could choose the age it desired. In 1929, the *JDA* was reorganized and consolidated into the form that it took until its repeal in 1984.[19]

The *JDA* remained substantially unchallenged until the 1960s. Prompted in part by the increased number of offenders expected with the maturation of the baby boom generation, the federal Department of Justice organized a Committee on Juvenile Delinquency (1965). By this time, attacks on the *JDA* were growing, with critics such as Lovekin (1961) and McGrath (1962) voicing the following concerns:

–   the financial penalties were not severe enough, being limited to a maximum of $25;
–   there should have been a uniform upper age limit, the provinces and territories having adopted 16, 17, and 18 years of age;
–   the informality of court procedures had led to widespread diver-

sity in practice across the country, including considerable disparity in sentencing;
- the language of the Act was stigmatizing;
- the *JDA* should have been in force nationwide; and
- there were no provisions for due process rights in the juvenile court process.

The Committee shared many of these concerns. Their greatest criticism was not of the Act itself, however, but of how it had been implemented. Support resources were lacking in many areas, and the spirit of the law was not being followed. In many jurisdictions, for example, children were being confined in facilities for adult offenders.

A major criticism of the *JDA* was its failure to provide a clear definition of *delinquency*. This lack of guidance left each province to devise its own policies and programs, resulting in inconsistent responses across the country. This situation, in conjunction with the variable upper age limit, led children committing the same crime in different provinces to be variously treated as juvenile delinquents, children in need of protection, or adult offenders. Further difficulties were caused by the wide range of behaviours being handled by the juvenile court, ranging from riding a bicycle on the sidewalk to murder. By 1960, there was a widespread view that the *JDA*, as a strategy to reduce juvenile delinquency, had failed and that replacement legislation was required. This opinion was shared by interested parties in other Commonwealth jurisdictions and in the United States.

The Evolution of the *Young Offenders Act*: 1965–82

The realization that juvenile court reform was necessary was not followed swiftly by change. Proposed drafts for a new Act were advanced in 1967, 1970, 1975 and 1977. Not until 1982 was an Act passed by Parliament. Disagreement among the groups having input into the drafting of the new legislation was a major reason for the delay. For example, there was intense debate over whether the new Act should be premised on a child welfare, or *parens patriae*, model; a crime control, or order maintenance, model; or a justice, or due process, model (see Catton, 1975–76).

Many groups and organizations argued for the retention of the *parens patriae*, or child welfare, philosophy of the *JDA*. This perspective views children as victims of their environment and as less responsible for their behaviour than adults. Other groups, including policing agenices, advocated a greater concern for order maintenance, while others argued that the new legislation should be based on a justice, or due process, model, extending to youths the procedural protections and rights accorded adults. Groups and organizations advocating all three perspectives lobbied those involved in drafting the new legislation (see Coflin, 1988).[20]

In its final form, the *YOA* begins with a section entitled "Declaration of Principle," which, while suggesting one overall philosophy, contains reference to all three (see Fox, 1985; Reid and Reitsma-Street, 1984; Bala, 1988). The statements that "young persons should not in all instances be held accountable in the same manner or suffer the same consequences for their behaviour as adults" and that "because of their state of dependency and level of development and maturity, they have special needs and require guidance and assistance" reflect the *parens patriae* orientation of the child welfare model. However, the final draft reflected a heavy emphasis on the justice, or due process, model, at the expense of rehabilitation and preventative intervention.

In addition to philosophical changes, the *YOA* introduced a number of other changes from the *JDA*:

- it raised the lower age of criminal responsibility to 12 years from 7;
- it dictated a uniform upper age limit of youth court jurisdiction of 18 years;
- it defined criteria and procedures for diversion from court;
- it mandated increased involvement of legal counsel;
- it permitted the youth court to issue only determinate dispostions;
- it eliminated status offences (e.g., sexual immorality).

The *Young Offenders Act*

The *Young Offenders Act* (*YOA*) received Royal Assent in 1982, but was not proclaimed in force until April 1984. This was to allow the provincial systems of juvenile justice time to adjust to the new requirements of the Act. In many jurisdictions, juvenile courts were functioning in a manner that necessitated little change; in other, mostly non-urban areas, courts were found to be operating in an informal, paternalistic style consistent with the *JDA* (Bala and Corrado, 1985). In either case, the proclamation of the *YOA* resulted in a period of confusion that, to some extent, has extended to the present.

Determining how the youth court is functioning under the *YOA* is difficult, given the complexity of the changes and the variation that still exists among the provinces/territories (see LeBlanc and Beaumont, 1988; Leschied and Jaffe, 1988; Mason, 1988; Ryant and Heinrich, 1988). The following discussion is, therefore, limited to a consideration of youth justice processing, as defined by the *YOA*. The reader is referred to Figure

14.1, which provides a general outline of the youth justice process under the *YOA*.

Among the highlights of the *YOA* are the following:

Youth Court Jurisdiction

The *YOA* grants youth courts jurisdiction over young persons, aged 12 to 18, who are suspected of violating any federal legislation, such as the *Criminal Code*, the *Food and Drugs Act*, and the *Narcotic Control Act*. Youth courts may also hear the cases of young persons accused of provincial offences (e.g., traffic violations) under the authority of provincial/ territorial young offenders legislation (e.g., *Young Offenders (British Columbia) Act*, S.B.C. 1984, c. 30), child welfare statutes (e.g., *Youth Protection Act*, R.S.Q. 1977, c. P-34.1), and modified versions of summary conviction Acts (e.g., *Provincial Offences Act*, R.S.O. 1980, c. 400).

Another notable feature of the *YOA* is the elimination of status offences, such as "sexual immorality." In keeping with the spirit of the federal Act, the provinces have repealed provincial legislation that made it a delinquency to be incorrigible, truant, and unmanageable.

Police Processing of Youths

The decisions that the police make upon the discovery of a young person suspected of committing an offence are very similar to those for adults described in Chapter 4. Under the *YOA*, all *Criminal Code* provisions governing arrest and bail apply to young persons. Youths must be informed of their rights by police officers when they are apprehended and/or arrested.

The options available to police officers under the *YOA* include informal handling and formal measures.

Informal Handling

Given the minor nature of the majority of youth offences, the police are able to exert a great deal of discretion once they have identified a suspect. A large, yet unknown, number of cases are handled informally and no further action is taken by the officer. Young persons may be reprimanded, warned of the consequences of future offences, and/or returned to their parent(s). The frequency of this practice will vary with the personal discretion of the officer and the policies of the individual police force.

In several provinces, informal handling is the course of action specified for dealing with children under the age of 12 who are suspected of behaviour that would be criminal if committed by an adult or a young person (e.g., in British Columbia, the *Family and Child Service Act*, S.B.C. 1980, c.

FIGURE 14.1
THE LEGAL PROCESS FOR YOUNG OFFENDERS

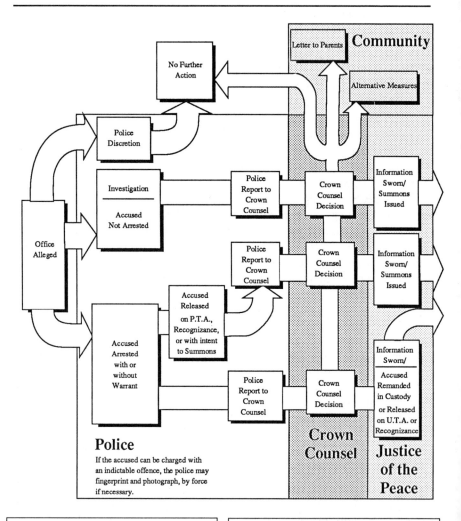

Right to Counsel

From the time of arrest or a request by the police for a statement, the accused has the right to consult a lawyer and/or parents or a suitable adult of the young person's choice.

This right to counsel is not an absolute right, i.e., the accused has a right to obtain a lawyer but the state has no obligation to provide one.

Absolute Right to Counsel

Before entering a plea or at any court hearing (including application to transfer to ordinary court, trial, appeal, and review of disposition), the accused has an absolute right to be represented by a lawyer. That is, if a lawyer has not been retained, the judge will appoint counsel on request to be paid for by the state.

FIGURE 14.1
THE LEGAL PROCESS FOR YOUNG OFFENDERS

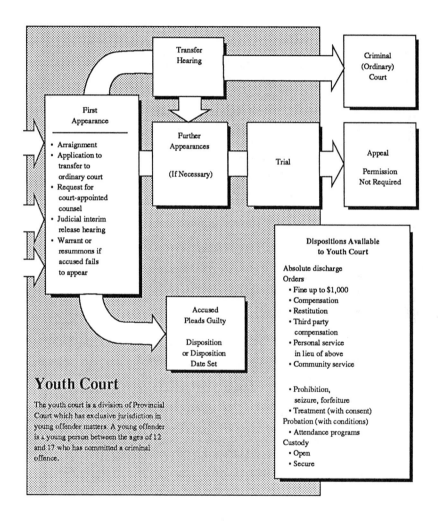

Source: Legal Services Society of British Columbia. Ministry of the Attorney-General of British Columbia. Reproduced with permission.

11, s. 22.1). The police are also encouraged to identify children under 12 who, as indicated by their "criminal" behaviour, may be in need of protective services of the State (e.g., in Alberta, the *Child Welfare Act*, S.A. 1984, c. C-8.1, ss. 4 and 5). In such cases, referral is made to the provincial child welfare authorities.

Formal Measures

If formal action is deemed necessary, the police will create a report recommending the laying of a charge. Who makes the final decision on the laying of an information varies across jurisdictions. In some areas, the police make this decision, while in others it is made by the Crown. In giving statements to the police, a young offender is entitled to be advised of the option of having a lawyer or a parent present. Those youths charged with an indictable offence may be photographed and fingerprinted.

In those cases in which there is cause to believe that a youth will not appear in court or presents a danger to him/herself or others, the youth may be detained, pending an appearance before a judge or a justice of the peace. Detainment is often used if the youth is apprehended after the issuance of a warrant. When this occurs, the parent(s) must be notified of the place of detention and the reason for arrest. While such detention should be in a place reserved exclusively for young persons, in many non-urban areas, such facilities do not exist.

The Role of Crown Counsel

As in the adult criminal justice process, the Crown counsel is responsible for reviewing the cases of youths referred by the police. Upon completion of this review, the Crown may drop the charges, refer the youth to an alternative measures program, or proceed to youth court.

In those cases in which a court appearance is selected as the most appropriate option, the attendance of the accused is sought with a Notice to Appear, served on both the young person and a parent. Youths detained in custody are generally not considered candidates for alternative measures programs, and in such cases, charges are routinely laid. After a first appearance, the young person may be released into the care of a responsible adult who will ensure his or her attendance at the court hearing. Young offenders are entitled to release on bail under the same *Criminal Code* provisions as adults.

Court Appearances

Under the provisions of the *YOA*, appearances in youth court resemble those in adult court, one notable exception being that cases are heard by a judge alone, with no provision for a jury. In most jurisdictions, legal counsel is accessible and the procedures followed are formal. Arraignment occurs when a youth is told of the accusation against him or her, and usually a plea is entered. In cases where the offence is admitted, the matter may move to the dispositional stage.

In those instances in which a plea of not guilty is entered, the hearing is adjourned for trial at a later date. Legal counsel is often sought at this point, if not before. In certain cases, the youth court judge may order the preparation of a psychological or medical assessment to aid in the determination of such issues as fitness to stand trial and insanity.

The *YOA* also provides for cases to be transferred to adult court. The youth must be at least 14 years of age and be accused of having committed a serious indictable offence. Generally, Crown counsel makes application for the transfer, although the youth court judge must make the final determination based on a complete review of all the information surrounding the case. This decision must be made prior to a determination of guilt or innocence and may be appealed by the youth.

Youth Court Dispositions

For youths who are subsequently found guilty by the youth court, there are a number of dispositional options under the *YOA*:

- – an absolute discharge;
- – a fine of up to $1,000;
- – a payment to the victim of the offence, in compensation for loss or damage to property, loss of income, or special damages that arose because of personal injury to the victim;
- – an order of compensation in-kind or by way of personal service to the victim of the offence;
- – a community service order, which would require the young offender to perform a specified amount of work for the community;
- – detainment for treatment in a hospital or other facility (as long as the offender agrees), if deemed warranted by a medical or psychological report;
- – probation for up to two years;
- – committal to intermittent or continuous custody for a specified period, generally not to exceed two years;
- – any conditions that the youth court judge considers in the best interests of the youth or the community;
- – any combination of the above, provided such dispositions do not exceed the general two year limit for supervision or custody.

(Solicitor General of Canada, 1986: 11)

The youth court may be aided in this decision by a pre-disposition report, which includes an assessment of the youth's family life, prior record, and a variety of other types of information. The report is designed to identify the youth's particular needs, as well as provide information on programs and facilities that may be available to address these needs.

The Right to Appeal and Provisions for Review

Both the young offender and the Crown counsel have the right to appeal the decisions of the youth court. The youth can appeal either the court's finding of guilt or the disposition rendered upon such a finding. There are also provisions for the review of custodial and non-custodial sentences of the youth court, upon application by any of the parties involved in the case.

The sentences of youths placed in custody are automatically reviewed after 12 months. During such reviews, youths have the option of being represented by legal counsel. Such reviews may result in confirmation or modification of the original disposition, although the severity of the sentence may not be increased without the consent of the youth.

Amendments to the *YOA*

In the fall of 1986, several amendments to the *YOA* were passed, including (1) the suspension of the three-year maximum sentence in those instances in which a youth commits a subsequent offence while under sentence for a previous offence; (2) provision for the publication of the identities of young persons who constitute a danger to the community, so as to allow the police to enlist the public's assistance in apprehending offenders; and (3) the inclusion of provisions to empower police to apprehend quickly youths who violate the conditions of their probation. Considerable controversy surrounded these changes, and it is unclear whether more substantial modifications of the Act will occur in the future (see Bennett, 1985).

Pre-court Programs for Young Offenders

There is a wide variety of pre-court programs for young offenders operated by both provincial/territorial ministries and non-profit groups and organizations. While many of the programs are designed specifically as alternative measures under section 4 of the *Young Offenders Act*, others are preventative in nature and attempt to attract youths who may be "at risk" but who have not been accused of a specific offence.

In the latter category are recreation, counselling and education/life skills programs. The rationale of these initiatives is that early intervention is superior to the reactive nature of youth court processing. Examples of such programs include the Preventive Intervention at the Pre-court Level Program in Sault Ste. Marie, Ontario and Project Intervention in Windsor, in which volunteers participate in one-to-one counselling with youths.

The Youth Assisting Youth program in Scarborough, Ontario, operates on a Big Brother model, with senior youths aged 16 to 18 conducting peer counselling with youths aged 6 through 12. This program is directed to children still too young to be charged with offences. Other programs focus upon specific groups. Fuchs and Bracken (1984) detail the structure and operation of Rossbrook House, a drop-in centre in Winnipeg that provides an alternative to involvement in street life and crime.

The Harbour Boys' Club Youth Services in Thunder Bay, Ontario, the O'Lokal program in Ste.-Hyacinthe, Quebec, and the Drop-In Centre Youth Recreation Program in Charlottetown, Prince Edward Island are examples of community-based programs that are designed to provide a variety of recreational activities for youth. Project Rediscovery in the Queen Charlotte Islands is an education and culture awareness program for native and non-native youths, conducted in a wilderness setting.

For youths suspected of, or charged with, a specific offence, the primary pre-trial intervention program is diversion. In most provinces, such programs are operated by police and probation agencies, as well as by private, non-profit groups such as the John Howard Society (see Rowe and Edelman, 1982). Diversion programs provide an opportunity for the youth to avoid the formal court process, while facilitating victim/offender reconciliation and/or the payment of compensation through performance of general community service or specific tasks for the victim (Pate and Peachey, 1988). In the Youth Alternative Society program in Halifax, volunteer mediators facilitate an agreement that addresses the youth's offence as well as the wishes of the victim (see Solicitor General of Canada, 1985).

Generally, diversion programs require that the offender have admitted responsibility for the offence and that the offender, the victim, and the offender's family give "informed consent" to participate in the program. Most programs restrict entry to first-time offenders and youths who have committed property-related crimes or summary offences. In Nanaimo, British Columbia, the Neighbourhood Accountabilty Board, operated by the John Howard Society, and comprised of adults and high school youth, receives referrals from the police and Crown counsel and identifies the needs of youth, arranges for restitution and refers youths to counselling.

The diversion program in Happy Valley–Goose Bay, Labrador is illustrative of the types of program being developed under the *YOA*. Established in 1980–81, the program has as its major objectives:

    1) to encourage community participation in managing conflicts of a minor criminal nature through an emphasis on conflict resolution and mediation outside of the judicial sphere;

2) to provide an opportunity for accused young persons to assume accountability for their criminal behaviour without recourse to the judicial process;
3) to clearly articulate and consistently apply legal safeguards and assurances of the participants in the conciliation process, i.e. victims and accused.
[Cited in RES Policy Research, Inc., 1985: 31–32]

Throughout the Province of Manitoba, youth justice committees have been established that facilitate community involvement in assisting youth in conflict with the law (Ryant and Heinrich, 1988). And in Nova Scotia, community volunteers work in conjunction with youth justice personnel to provide community-based services for youth.

The Use and Effectiveness of Alternative Measures Programs

While alternative measures programs are a primary component of the *YOA*, there are numerous difficulties that appear to be seriously undermining their potential effectiveness. These include the following:

The Implementation of Alternative Measures Programs

Under the provisions of the *YOA*, the development of alternative measures programs, such as diversion, is the responsibility of the provincial/ territorial governments. While one of the basic principles of the *YOA* is that it is sometimes appropriate to employ non-judicial intervention (section 3(1)(d)), in actual practice there appears to be wide disparity among jurisdictions in the alternatives that have been developed and the extent to which they are utilized.

As of 1987, for example, the Province of Ontario had made no provision for alternative measures programs. Indeed, the programs developed in that province are more closely allied with a correctional/custodial model of intervention (Faulkner, 1986). At the opposite extreme, British Columbia strongly emphasizes diversion, as part of a general policy of employing the least restrictive, community-based alternatives possible.

It is likely that, in many jurisdictions, pre-existing programs were merely continued after the enactment of the *YOA*. In Manitoba, for example, diversion had been employed since the late 1960s, and there has been only a slight increase in its use under the *YOA* (Province of Manitoba, 1986: 5–6). In those jurisdictions in which programs were created directly as a result of the *YOA*, the acceptance of diversion may be slower. Preliminary figures from Alberta (cited in Caputo and Goldenberg, 1986: 99) suggest that only a very small number of youths are being selected for the alternative measures programs that have been created in that province.

Community Awareness of, and Input into, Alternative Measures Programs

In those jurisdictions where alternative measures programs have been developed, the role that individual communities have played in the creation and implementation of such initiatives is unclear. Further, observers have noted that contrary to the original intent of diversion, many programs are created and staffed by members of the justice system (e.g., Lemert, 1981). An evaluation conducted by Morton and West (1983), for example, found that while the Frontenac Diversion Program in Kingston, Ontario was widely known throughout the justice community in Canada, the local community had little knowledge of the program and was only minimally affected by it.

Organizational Problems of Alternative Measures Programs

An ongoing problem with many community-based initiatives, particularly those operated by non-profit groups and organizations, is securing sufficient resources. Increasingly, diversion programs rely on volunteers, and they have often been unable to secure long-term funding support. It is unclear whether the trend toward privatization of alternative measures programs will resolve these and other organizational problems.

Widening the Net

Accompanying the expansion of diversion programs in the 1960s was the concern that such programs, rather than functioning to reduce the numbers of youths involved in the formal justice process, have served only to "widen the net," resulting in increased numbers of youths being placed under some form of supervision (see Austin and Krisberg, 1981). This factor also may serve to increase the costs of justice rather than reducing them, as had been originally anticipated.

Assessing the Effectiveness of Alternative Measures Programs

The objectives of initiatives such as youth diversion programs have included (a) a reduction in the number of cases coming before the youth court, (b) a decrease in the costs of the youth justice system, (c) a positive change in the attitude of young offenders, (d) increased victim/community satisfaction with the response to youth crime, and (e) a lowering of the rate of youth crime and recidivism among youth participants (see Kopelman and Moyer, 1985: 5–7).

Few evaluations, however, have been undertaken to assess whether diversion programs are achieving these objectives. There are only a few published evaluations on the cost reduction or cost-effectiveness of diversion programs that take into account the phenomenon of net widening (e.g., Blomberg, Heald, and Ezell, 1986). Nor is there any evidence that such programs have a positive impact on young offenders, as measured by either attitude change or reduced recidivism rates.

In one of the few Canadian attempts to measure the impact of diversion on the recidivism rates of young offenders and on the attitudes of youths and their parents who participated in a diversion program, Jaffe et al. (1985–86) compared matched samples of youths from London, Ontario, which had no diversion program, and youths who had participated in the diversion program in Windsor. The results of the study revealed no significant differences between the two groups of youths in terms of their recidivism rates or in terms of the attitudes of the youths and their parents toward experiences with the court or diversion process.

Similar findings were reported by Morton and West (1983) in a study of the Frontenac Diversion Program in Kingston, Ontario. The investigators found few differences between youths handled by the diversion committee and those sent to court, as measured by recidivism rates or the youths' sense of stigma as an offender. Somewhat more positive results, however, have been reported by Fischer and Jeune (1987) from a study of a diversion program in a western Canadian city. The diversion program did not function to widen the net, was delivered at a cost less than that of court processing, and was favourably viewed by the youths, their parents, and youth justice personnel.

It remains to be seen whether diversion programs developed within the framework of the *YOA* will be successful in avoiding the above-noted difficulties and achieve their stated objectives (see Moyer, 1980).[21]

The Youth Court

All existing materials on the operation of youth courts in Canada were produced prior to 1984, providing the basis for future comparative study between pre- and post-*YOA*, but limiting our ability to discuss the current operation of the courts. Consideration of any findings on the operation of the court reported prior to 1984 must be viewed with extreme caution. However, such studies are valuable as comparative data and for suggesting areas of court activity that should be the subject of further research.

Youth Court Decision Making

Research in the United States has attempted to determine the factors that influence the operation and decision making of juvenile courts. The most valuable insights into the operation of youth courts have been provided by studies that have examined the court from an organizational perspective, considering not only the impact of the socio-biographical attributes of the youth (i.e., age, sex, socio-economic status, family life, and offence-related information such as prior record and seriousness of the present offence), but also the influence of community pressure on the court, the police, and the personal and professional perspectives of the judges and probation officers (see Bortner, 1982; Griffiths, 1982; Hasenfeld, 1977).

The most extensive Canadian study to date, conducted prior to the enactment of the *YOA* in 1980–81, was the National Study on the Functioning of the Juvenile Court in Canada. This study involved observations of the court process and a survey of attitudes of personnel involved in the youth justice system in Vancouver, Edmonton, Winnipeg, Toronto, Montreal, and Halifax and several non-urban areas.

While a detailed consideration of the myriad of findings from this project is beyond the scope of this text (and of perhaps limited utility given the subsequent passage of the *YOA*), Bala and Corrado (1985: 146; 150) note that data from the six sites revealed "legislative, organizational and philosophical variations between courts." As well, the results suggested significant variations between the operation of the courts in rural and urban areas and "very substantial variation between different localities in terms of procedures, facilities and staff for dealing with juveniles who violated the law."

Similar inconsistencies in the decision making of the juvenile court were reported by Babe and Fernandes (1979) in a study of the use of probation by judges in Metropolitan Toronto. While probation was used more frequently for male youths over the age of 15 who were from broken homes, judges were highly individualistic in their dispositional practices and were influenced by recommendations made by various agencies involved with the youth. Again, these findings suggest that decision making in the youth court is characterized by considerable variability.[22]

In their examination of decision making in the Winnipeg Juvenile Court, Kueneman and Linden (1983) found that youths committing serious offences and those with prior records received the most severe dispositions in the court, while there was little relation between the socio-biographical attributes of age, socio-economic status, race, and family situation and the severity of the court's response. The strong influence of offence-related variables on the court, which was operating at the time under the provisions of the *JDA*, suggests that such factors may play an even more significant role under the *YOA*.

Additional insights into the operation of the youth court in northern and rural areas is provided by Kueneman, Linden, and Kosmick (1986), from a three-year study of 22 native and non-native communities in Manitoba, again prior to the enactment of the *YOA*. The focal point of the investigation was the travelling (or circuit) court and the manner in which services for young offenders were delivered in small communities. The study found consistency in court decision making at all of the sites, although there was no determination of the specific factors that influenced case outcomes. Perhaps the most important findings from this study were the issues raised regarding the circuit court, including the time constraints under which the court party operates, the lack of facilities in many communities, and the extent to which differences between communities were considered by the court. These issues will be considered in greater detail in Chapter 15 in our discussion of the role of the circuit court in delivering justice services to native communities in rural and northern areas of the country.

The finding of the National Study that considerable variability existed at all stages of the youth court process in the six cities is important, even though the majority of the research data were collected prior to the passage of the *YOA*. Similar legislation was enacted by state legislatures in the United States in the late 1960s and early 1970s. The experience, however, has been that although legislation may propose a shift in philosophy toward youthful offenders and create procedures for the processing of cases that are designed to safeguard the rights of youths while making them more responsible for their behaviour, many of the "human" dimensions of the court process cannot be legislated out or controlled (see Lefstein, Stapleton, and Teitelbaum, 1969; Sosin and Sarri, 1976).

Empey (1982: 349) notes that, in the United States, legislative attempts to change the youth court process "have been tempered by traditions favoring the informal treatment of children . . . it is likely that many juvenile courts today remain as much like the original juvenile court in their practices as the more formal court envisioned by the Supreme Court."

While, as Bala and Corrado (1985: 153) point out, the passage of the *YOA* will likely result in the creation of uniform policies for fingerprinting and photographing young offenders and for maintaining records, the legislation does little to limit the discretion exercised by police officers, probation officers, or judges in responding to youths. Nor does the *YOA* provide any assistance to decision makers in determining the specific type of intervention that will most appropriately address the needs of the offenders, the victim, and the community. A close reading of the *YOA* indicates that many of its provisions relate to the procedures to be followed in responding to youth, rather than to the way decisions are to be made. This is a critical distinction that ensures that the variability in the response to young offenders by youth justice personnel identified by Bala and Corrado (1985) will persist (see also Reid, 1986).

In concluding her extensive analysis of decision making in a youth court in the United States, a study which found vast discretion and inconsistency in decisions, Bortner (1982: 241–42) argues that more subjective considerations surrounding a case may outweigh objective factors:

> Court personnel . . . are charged with the awesome responsibility for evaluating a juvenile's entire life situation and offering a prognosis for the future. Court decisions are based on a multitude of considerations: the more identifiable factors such as alleged

offense, a child's age, or number of referrals to court; decision-maker's evaluation of the juvenile's individual character and family situation; and the decision-maker's personal propensities and professional orientations . . . Much of the research suggests that the more subjective considerations frequently outweigh the more objective factors.

Youth court personnel in Canada, operating under the provisions of the *YOA*, are no more restricted than those in the United States in their decision making involving youth in conflict with the law. Indeed, such variability may be required to ensure that the needs of individual young offenders and those of the community and victim are met through the decision making of the court.

Trends in Youth Court Decision Making

While the recency of the *YOA* and the lack of evaluative studies of the youth court in Canada preclude definitive statements about how youth courts are operating, several trends appear to be emerging that should be the subject of further inquiry. These are due in large measure to the shift from the *parens patriae*, rehabilitative approach that was predominant under the *JDA* to a "justice-as-fairness," correctional model under the *YOA* (see Caputo, 1987).

One of the more visible trends is the increase in the presence of legal counsel in the youth court and in the number of trials and the length of time required for completion of cases (see Felstiner, 1985; Gabor, Greene, and McCormick, 1986). Another is the apparent increase in the severity of sentences being given to youth by the courts. Leschied and Jaffe (1987) reported that for youths aged 12 to 15 in Ontario, there has been a 135% increase in sentences to closed-custody training schools and a 210% increase in sentence length for youths 12 to 15 sentenced to open-custody group homes. A follow-up study of youth court dispositions during 1985, the second year of operation of the *Young Offenders Act*, revealed that the trend toward increased severity of sentences was continuing (Leschied and Jaffe, 1987; Leschied and Gendreau, 1986).

This led the authors (Leschied and Jaffe, 1987: 425) to conclude that "deterrence through punishment as a means of crime control for young offenders has now become a popular concept." Under the *JDA*, the decision regarding length of sentence was made by provincial authorities; under the *YOA*, the judge alone decides sentence length. Data collected in Ontario by Leschied and Jaffe (1987) also revealed a decrease in the number of psychological assessments requested by the youth courts and an increase in the number of community service orders and victim reconciliation orders, all of which indicate that, at least in parts of Ontario, "the youth court has become more formal and restrictive with a greater orientation toward punishment" (Leschied and Jaffe, 1987: 429).

There does appear to be some variability in sentencing patterns emerging across the country. In some jurisdictions, judges have retained a treatment approach to youth crime (see Gabor et al., 1986), while in other jurisdictions, a more punitive approach is evident (see Kopyto and Codina, 1986). Wardell (1986) notes, however, that the rulings of the courts of appeal in several provinces have alleviated this trend to some extent, although he found "judicial disharmony at the Court of Appeal levels regarding the sentencing principles enumerated in the Y.O.A." (p. 146).

Similar findings have been reported by Krisberg et al. (1986) in a review of the consequences of attempts to reform the youth justice system in the United States during the period 1974–84. These authors found (pp. 11–23) that there had been (1) a decrease in the youth population and in arrest rates, (2) an increase in the number of youths referred to court, (3) an increase in the severity of youth court sanctions, (4) larger numbers of youths admitted to training schools for longer periods of detention, and (5) increased expenditures on youth justice (see also Erickson, 1979; Miller, 1979; Sarri, 1983).

However, until systematic evaluations of the youth justice system have been completed in Canada, extreme caution should be exercised in assessing the extent to which these trends characterize the decision making of individual youth courts in the various jurisdictions across the country.

Youth Corrections

For those youths who admit guilt or who are found guilty in the youth court, there are a variety of sentencing alternatives available under the *YOA*. For those youths not granted an absolute discharge by the court, the dispositions may be categorized generally as either community-based or custodial.

Community-Based Programs

The non-custodial dispositions available to the court include community service, a fine not to exceed $1,000, the payment of compensation or restitution, compensation by personal service, and probation. Probation is the most frequently used disposition and is designed to provide supervision for the youth in the community, while at the same time allowing the court to attach specific conditions to the probationary period. Such conditions may include the payment of restitution to the victim, the completion of a specified number of hours of community service, or participation in, and completion of, a specialized course such as a Wilderness Experience Program.

Probation

Siegel and Senna (1988: 496) note that probation was first used in England in the early 1800s, "when the magistrates of the Warwickshire quarter sessions adopted the practice of sentencing youthful criminals to prison terms of one day, then releasing them conditionally under the supervision of their parents or masters." In subsequent years, supervision of youths was undertaken by police officers, philanthropic organizations, and public agencies. In 1869, the State of Massachusetts became the first United States jurisdiction to enact legislation providing for the creation of juvenile probation. In Canada, probation emerged during the late 1800s (see Boyd, 1978).

A major role is played by probation officers who are involved in preparing social histories or pre-disposition reports for the youth court, and in providing supervision and counselling to youths placed on probation. To date in Canada there have been no published evaluations of youth probation, and the effectiveness of this particular youth court disposition in addressing the needs of the youth, the victim, and the community is unclear.[23]

Community Service and Restitution

One of the major conditions that is often attached to a probation order is the Community Service Order (CSO) requiring the youth to complete a number of hours of work in the community or for the victim. In a pre-*YOA* examination of the operation of the CSO program in the Durham, Ontario region, Doob and Macfarlane (1984) found that the probation officers involved in the program, the individuals supervising youths in the community, the youths, their parents, and the general public all had generally favourable views of the program. Further, the investigators found that participation in the CSO program tended to reduce the youths' subsequent involvement in misconduct and to have a positive impact on their attitudes.

The payment of restitution by the young offender may also be a condition of probation, and its use has expanded greatly in recent years. Restitution is designed to provide compensation for the victim, while at the same time making youths responsible for their actions (see Staples, 1986).

Wilderness Experience Programs

A popular alternative to confinement that is also often included as a condition of probation is Wilderness Experience Programs (WEPs). Many of these programs are based on the concept of Outward Bound, an experiential outdoor challenge program. In describing the application of the Outward Bound concept to WEP for young offenders, Winterdyk and Griffiths (1984: 36) note: "The various wilderness activities are designed to push the youth beyond their assumed capabilities, to help them break out of their adolescent identity crisis, and to develop in them a new awareness of their strengths and potential."

Despite the proliferation of these programs across Canada, many of which are operated under contract for provincial/territorial governments, research on the effectiveness of WEPs in altering the attitudes and behaviours of youths participating in the programs has produced mixed results. Some evaluations have reported a reduction in subsequent misconduct and an improvement in the youths' attitudes, while others have found no differences between youths who participated in WEPs and those who did not (see Callahan, 1985; Scott, 1985; Winterdyk and Roesch, 1982).[24]

As in adult corrections, there is an ongoing controversy over community-based programs for young offenders. Concerns have been raised regarding the extent of public involvement in such programs, and there is a lack of conclusive empirical evidence that community-based programs are more effective in reducing youthful misbehaviour than are institutionally based programs. Further concerns have been voiced about the "net-widening" tendencies of many community-based programs and about statistics that indicate that more youths than ever are becoming involved in the Canadian youth justice system.

Youth in Custody

The youth court may sentence a young offender to a maximum period of two years' confinement, or to a maximum of three years if the youth has committed a crime for which an adult offender would liable to life imprisonment or if the youth is being sentenced for two or more offences. The creation and operation of custodial or detention facilities for young offenders are the responsibility of the provincial/territorial governments, and there is wide variation across the country in the nature and types of facilities and the programs offered within them. Facilities may be designated as either "open" or "secure" custody. Open-custody facilities, such as group homes, may be operated by private, non-profit agencies under contract or by government ministries, while the secure facilities, often called Youth Detention Centres, are operated by the provincial/territorial governments (see Caputo and Bracken, 1988).

As noted earlier, preliminary findings suggest that since the enactment of the *YOA*, increasing numbers of youths are being incarcerated, although further research in provincial/territorial jurisdictions across the country is required. This trend raises concerns about not only the types of facilities within which youth are confined, but the dynamics of life inside detention facilities and the effectiveness of institutional programs and treatment strategies.

There are a number of "classic" studies of the social organization of institutions for young offenders, all of which were conducted in the United States.[25] While some of these studies are now over 20 years old, they provide insights into the world of confined youths and into the social systems and subcultures that develop in youth institutions (see Bartollas, Miller, and Dinitz, 1976; Feld, 1978; Giallombardo, 1974; Polsky, 1977; Propper, 1981).

From an analysis of institutional policies, staff behaviour, and the patterns of interaction among youth inmates, researchers have been able to identify the factors that contributed to or mitigated the amount of violence and victimization among the youth, as well as the conditions that led to the development of positive attitudes and behaviours. These investigations have also uncovered subcultures among male and female offenders in confinement and documented the patterns of exploitation and violence in these social systems (see Osgood et al., 1985; Reichel, 1985).[26]

Generally, the research suggests that, similar to adult offenders, the dynamics of institutions for young offenders are strongly influenced by the "pains of imprisonment" experienced by incarcerated youth and by the orientation of the institutional staff and administration. And, as in adult institutions, the social system among young inmates may be the source of considerable violence and exploitation. Feld (1978) found, for example, that in those cottages of a youth facility in which the goals of treatment were stressed, there were more positive attitudes and less violence among the youth than in cottages in which staff were more punishment oriented. Similarly, Sieverdes and Bartollas (1986), in a study of five co-educational youth institutions, found that group cohesion (the subculture) was more strongly developed in maximum security facilities (see also Leschied, Jaffe, and Stone, 1985).

As with inmate social systems among adult offenders, there appear to be differences in the patterns of interaction that develop in institutions for male and female youths. While little research has been conducted on Canadian youth facilities, findings from the United States suggest that institutions for females had fewer programs than their male counterparts and the programs that did exist tended to reinforce sex role stereotypes. Also, studies conducted in female institutions reported the tendency of girls to form "make-believe" families (see Foster, 1975).[27]

Treatment Initiatives and Their Effectiveness

There is a large body of literature, primarily from the United States, on the various treatment approaches that have been taken with young offenders in confinement. As with adult corrections, the treatment of young offenders has been the subject of considerable debate. A conclusive determination of the effectiveness of various treatment strategies has been hindered by conflicting research results and difficulties in measuring treatment "success." So too has youth corrections been afflicted with the tendency to seek treatment cure-alls or panaceas that will reverse a long history of frustration in attempting to alter the attitudes and behaviours of youth.[28]

The majority of treatment approaches applied to youths in custodial and community-based settings are psychological in orientation and include individual treatment methods, such as psychotherapy, reality therapy, vocational counselling, and behavioural contracts, as well as group treatment methods, such as group counselling, group psychotherapy, milieu therapy, and guided group interaction.[29]

In Canada, there are few published evaluations of the effectiveness of these various correctional techniques. Many of the issues surrounding correctional treatment for adult offenders, such as the failure to consider the impact of specific treatment techniques on individual offenders and the method in which treatment programs are delivered, are important to any discussion of youth corrections as well (see Gendreau and Ross, 1983). The importance of considering the concept of differential treatment effectiveness, for example, was noted by LeBlanc and Bosse (1980) in their longitudinal study of the effectiveness of the Boscoeville youth treatment centre in Quebec. Similary, Greenwood and Zimring (1985) have argued that a multi-faceted approach is required in developing treatment programs for young offenders.

"Scared Straight" and the Search for Treatment Panaceas

A major affliction of correctional treatment for youths has been the seemingly endless search for cure-alls or panaceas. As Finckenauer (1982: 4) has observed: "The highway of delinquency prevention history is paved with punctured panaceas." Perhaps no one initiative is more symbolic of the panacea phenomenon in youth corrections as the "Scared Straight" program. This approach originated with the Juvenile Awareness Project in the Rahway State Prison in New Jersey in 1976. It involved intensive confrontation or "shock confrontation" sessions between the inmates and youths, many of whom had been found delinquent by the court, as well as others who were only believed to be "at risk."

This program received widespread media attention and acclaim by politicians, prison administrators, and justice personnel, although subsequent analysis of the program by Finckenauer (1982) indicated that not only did participation in the Juvenile Awareness Project not reduce involvement of delinquent behaviour by youth participants, but that the behaviour of some youths deteriorated even further after attending the program (see also Heeren and Schichor, 1984).[30]

Despite the results of Finckenauer's analysis, "Scared Straight" programs proliferated in various forms across Canada and the United States and have become the focal point for intense debate (see Buckner and Chesney-Lind, 1983; Lewis, 1983; and Lundman, 1984). This has led Lundman (1984: 150, 152) to conclude:

> Intensive confrontation sessions sometimes increase involvement in delinquency. On other occasions they have no measurable impact. On still other occasions they apparently control delinquency. At best, scaring juveniles is not the panacea for the problem of delinquency. At worst, scaring juveniles invited more rather than less delinquency.

The search for effective treatment strategies for young offenders will continue, as will the debate over the effectiveness of the various initiatives. From an extensive survey of attempts to treat young offenders and control youth crime, Gibbons (1986: 196; 198–99) concluded:

> There seems to be some evidence upon which one can draw that seems to suggest that some kinds of treatment or preventive activities may have a payoff . . . although research has often failed to discover evidence that community treatment ventures are markedly more effective than is institutionalization of offenders, the other side of the coin is that the former have generally been shown to be at least as effective as is incarceration and at considerably less cost.

And, from his review of what "works" and what does not "work" in youth corrections, Lundman (1984: 223–35) made the following recommendations as the basis for future policy and programs:

1. Traditional delinquency-prevention efforts should be abandoned.
2. Diversion should be the first response of the youth justice system to minor offenders.
3. Routine probation should be retained as the first and most frequent sentencing option of youth court judges.
4. Efforts to scare youths straight should be abandoned.
5. Community treatment programs should be expanded to accommodate nearly all chronic offenders.
6. Institutionalization should be used only as a last resort for chronic offenders who commit serious crimes against persons.

The extent to which youth courts and corrections agencies in Canada will consider these types of recommendations and assess the effectiveness of the dispositions and treatment initiatives under the *YOA* is unclear. Similarly, the impact of much-needed research on the youth court and correctional process on policies and programs is also uncertain, but no less important.

NOTES

1. For example, police departments in British Columbia report that during the period 1977 to 1985, about one-third to one-half of all juveniles were treated informally (British Columbia Police Commission, 1985).

2. Problems in collecting data on crime rates are described in Canadian Centre for Justice Statistics (1984).

3. *Doli incapax* was available as a defence in Canada in section 13 of the *Criminal Code* until passage of the *YOA*, but was rarely used. See McLeod (1980).

4. S.C. 1857, 20 Vic., c. 29.

5. S.C. 1857, 20 Vic., c. 28. In the next consolidation of federal statutes, this was renamed *An Act Respecting the Trial and Punishment of Juvenile Offenders*, Cons. S.C. 1859, c. 106. It was eventually replaced by the *Juvenile Offenders Act*, S.C. 1869, 32 & 33 Vict., c. 33, which was itself incorporated into the first *Criminal Code* of 1892.

6. S.O. 1880, 43 Vic., c. 34.

7. *An Act for the Protection and Reformation of Neglected Children*, S.O. 1888, 51 Vict., c. 40.

8. For a detailed summary of the Commission's report, see Jones and Rutman (1981); Splane (1965); Sutherland (1976).

9. While Kelso had only an indirect impact on the passage of the *JDA*, he fancied himself at least partially responsible for the creation of the first juvenile court in the State of Illinois in 1899 (see Kelso, 1907). See also Jones and Rutman (1981) for a detailed account of Kelso's activities.

10. S.C. 1892, 55–56 Vict., c. 29, s. 550. Also incorporated into this statute were the provisions of the *Juvenile Offenders Act*, S.C. 1886, 49 Vict., c. 177, a consolidation of what had been *An Act for the More Speedy Trial and Punishment of Juvenile Offenders*.

11. *An Act for the Prevention of Cruelty to, and Better Protection of Children*, S.O. 1893, 56 Vict., c. 45.

12. *An Act to Permit the Conditional Release of First Offenders in Certain Cases*, S.C. 1889, 52 Vict., c. 44. Two criteria to be considered by the court in imposing a sentence of probation were the age of the offender and the seriousness of the offence. Young offenders charged with minor offences were the primary recipients of probation until 1900, when an amendment to the *Criminal Code* expanded the scope of those who qualified for probation (see Boyd, 1978).

13. *Juvenile Delinquents Act*, S.C. 1908, 7–8 Ed. VII, c. 40.

14. S.C. 1867, 30 & 31 Vict., c. 3, ss. 91 and 92.

15. This definition of *juvenile delinquency* remained substantially unchanged until the repeal of the *JDA* in 1984, with the exception that, in 1924, "sexual immorality or any similar form of vice" was added as a criterion in *An Act to Amend the Juvenile Delinquents Act, 1908*, S.C. 1924, 14 & 15 Geo. V, c. 53.

16. While the *JDA* came into effect in Alberta in 1913, for example, it was never in force in Newfoundland. Even following Newfoundland's joining of Confederation in 1949, juveniles were prosecuted under the provisions of the Newfoundland *Child Welfare Act.*

17. An example of an agreement between jurisdictions is provided by Klassen (1981), who notes that the few boys sent to industrial school by the Calgary juvenile court went to the Industrial School for Boys at Portage LaPrairie, Manitoba.

18. *An Act to Amend the Juvenile Delinquents Act,* S.C. 1921, 11 & 12 Geo. V, c. 37.

19. See Gagnon (1984) for a summary of the amendments made to the *JDA.*

20. During the 1970s, the juvenile court was shifting toward a due process model, prompted in part by a series of superior court decisions (cf. *R. v. Moore* (1974), 22 C.C.C. (2d) 189 (B.C.S.C.)) and moves by provincial governments to assume greater control over the juvenile justice system (Osborne, 1979). Despite this, in comparison to their counterparts in the United States, Canadian courts played a very small role in the events leading to the enactment of the *YOA.* In the United States, on the other hand, the major impetus for the shift from the *parens patriae* doctrine to a justice, due process model came from the United States Supreme Court in the landmark cases of *Kent v. U.S.* (1966), 383 U.S. 541, *In Re Gault* (1967), 387 U.S. 1, and *In re Winship* (1970), 397 U.S. 358.

21. For discussions of the major issues surrounding the creation and operation of diversion programs for young offenders, see Binder and Geis (1984); Blomberg (1983); Decker (1985); Lemert (1981); Polk (1984); Rausch and Logan (1983). O'Brien (1984) provides a review of the issues surrounding the operation of diversion under the *YOA* in the Atlantic provinces of Canada. And Pate and Peachey (1988) describe the use of victim–young offender reconciliation programs as a pre-trial alternative.

22. One of the more interesting findings of the Babe and Fernandes (1979) study was that judges assigned different dispositions to hypothetical cases presented to them by the researchers than they did to cases involving similar facts that appeared before them in the courtroom. This discrepancy between how the judges perceived they were responding and how they were actually making decisions in the court should be noted by investigators in future studies of youth court decision making.

23. Research on the effectiveness of probation carried out in the United States has produced mixed results. Several major inquiries have focused on the impact of probation officer caseload size on the effectiveness of probation and concluded that the numbers of youths being supervised by an officer is not significantly related to the youth's probability of success.

24. From their review of WEPs in North America, Winterdyk and Griffiths (1984) identified a number of problems related to both the design and implementation of WEPs and efforts to evaluate them. These authors outline a series of recommendations at the programmatic and evaluation levels to improve the effectiveness of WEPs.

25. For a historical analysis of the administration and operation of a boy's training school in Quebec, see Rains (1985).

26. Valuable insights into the dynamics of institutional life are provided by Menzies et al. (1987) in their study of disruptive and self-destructive behaviour among youth in a Canadian youth detention facility.

27. There is disagreement among observers over the extent to which "make-believe" families exist in institutions for girls, and it is unknown whether this phenomenon occurs in Canadian facilities. Many detention centres for youths in Canada are co-educational and house both boys and girls. The mixing of the sexes may have a significant impact on the social system that develops within the institutions.

28. For a debate over the relative effectiveness of institutionalization in reducing youth misconduct, see Lundman (1986) and Murray and Cox (1979).

29. For a thorough discussion of the various individual and group treatment strategies used with yound offenders, see Bartollas (1985); Siegel and Senna (1988); Trojanowicz and Morash (1983). For a description and analysis of a Canadian program that attempts to address the needs of "hard to serve" youth, see Leschied and Thomas (1985).

30. James Finckenauer's book *Scared Straight! and the Panacea Phenomenon in Corrections* is instructive not only for its analysis of the Juvenile Awareness Project at Rahway State Prison, but also for its insightful examination and discussion of the panacea phenomenon in youth corrections generally and the role that the media, individual personalities and events played in elevating the Scared Straight program to an international profile. The book is also a good case study of the impact (or lack thereof) of empirical research on co (or lack thereof) of empirical research on correctional policy.

REFERENCES

Austin, J., and B. Krisberg. 1981. "Wider, Stronger, and Different Nets: The Dialectics of Criminal Justice Reform." 18 *Journal of Research in Crime and Delinquency* 165–96.

Babe, J. E., and R. M. Fernandes. 1979. "Juvenile Probation in Metropolitan Toronto: An Empirical Study." 2 *Canadian Journal of Family Law* 160–87.

Baehre, R. 1982. *The Prison System in Atlantic Canada before 1880.* Ottawa: Solicitor General of Canada.

Bala, N. 1988. "The Young Offenders Act: A Legal Framework." In *Justice and the Young Offender in Canada,* edited by J. Hudson, J. P. Hornick, and B. A. Burrows, 11–35. Toronto: Wall and Thompson.

Bala, N., and R. Corrado. 1985. *Juvenile Justice in Canada: A Comparative Study.* Ottawa: Programs Branch, Solicitor General of Canada.

Bartollas, C. 1985. *Juvenile Delinquency.* New York: John Wiley and Sons.

Bartollas, C., S. J. Miller, and S. Dinitz. 1976. *Juvenile Victimization: The Institutional Paradox.* New York: John Wiley and Sons.

Bennett, J. F. 1985. "Concerns about the Young Offenders Act." 8 *Provincial Judges Journal* 17–18.

Binder, A., and G. Geis. 1984. "Ad Populum Argumentation in Criminology: Juvenile Diversion as Rhetoric." 30 *Criminology* 309–33.

Blomberg, T. G. 1983. "Diversion's Disparate Results and Unresolved Questions: An Integrative Evaluation Perspective." 20 *Journal of Research in Crime and Delinquency* 24–38.

Blomberg, T. G., G. R. Heald, and M. Ezell. 1986. "Diversion and Net Widening: A Cost Savings Assessment. 10 *Evaluation Review* 45–64.

Bortner, M. A. 1982. *Inside a Juvenile Court: The Tarnished Ideal of Individualized Justice.* New York: New York University Press.

Boyd, N. 1978. "An Examination of Probation." 20 *Criminal Law Quarterly* 355–81.

Brannigan, A. 1987. "Mystification of the Innocents: Comics and Delinquency in Canada." 8 *Criminal Justice History* 111–44.

British Columbia Police Commission. 1985. *Annual Report, 1984/85.* Vancouver.

Brown, G. (Chairman). 1849. *Second Report of the Commissioners Appointed to Investigate into the Conduct, Discipline and Management of the Provincial Penitentiary.* Toronto.

Buckner, J. C., and M. Chesney-Lind. 1983. "Dramatic Cures for Juvenile Crime: An Evaluation of a Prisoner-Run Delinquency Prevention Program." 10 *Criminal Justice and Behavior* 227–47.

Callahan, R. 1985. "Wilderness Probation: A Decade Later." 36 *Juvenile and Family Court Journal* 31–35.

Canadian Centre for Justice Statistics. 1984. *Juvenile Delinquents, 1983.* Ottawa: Supply and Services Canada.

———. 1985. *Juvenile Court Statistics, 1982 and 1983.* Ottawa: Supply and Services Canada.

———. 1987. *Youth Court Statistics: Preliminary Tables, 1984–85; 1985–86.* Ottawa: Statistics Canada.

Caputo, T. C. 1987. "The Young Offenders Act: Children's Rights, Children's Wrongs." 13 *Canadian Public Policy* 125–43.

Caputo, T., and D. C. Bracken. 1988. "Custodial Dispositions and the Young Offenders Act." In *Justice and the Young Offender in Canada,* edited by J. Hudson, J. P. Hornick, and B. A. Burrows, 123–43. Toronto: Wall and Thompson.

Caputo, T. C., and S. Goldenberg. 1986. "Young People and the Law: A Consideration of Luddite and Utopian Responses." In *The Administration of Justice*, edited by D. H. Currie and B. D. McLean, 92–111. Saskatoon: Department of Sociology, University of Saskatchewan.

Catton, K. 1975–76. "Models of Procedure and the Juvenile Courts." 18 *Criminal Law Quarterly* 181–201.

Coflin, J. 1988. "The Federal Government's Role in Implementing the Young Offender's Act." In *Justice and the Young Offender in Canada*, edited by J. Hudson, J. P. Hornick, and B. A. Burrows, 37–50. Toronto: Wall and Thompson.

Decker, S. H. 1985. "A Systematic Analysis of Diversion: Net Widening and Beyond." 13 *Journal of Criminal Justice* 207–16.

Department of Justice Committee on Juvenile Delinquency. 1965. *Juvenile Delinquency in Canada*. Ottawa: Queen's Printer.

Doob, A. N., and P. D. Macfarlane. 1984. *The Community Service Order for Youthful Offenders: Perceptions and Effects*. Toronto: Centre of Criminology, University of Toronto.

Empey, L. T. 1979. "The Progressive Legacy and the Concept of Childhood." In *Juvenile Justice: The Progressive Legacy and Current Reforms,* edited by L. T. Empey, 3–33. Charlotteville: University Press of Virginia.

———. 1982. *American Delinquency: Its Meaning and Construction*. Homewood, Ill.: Dorsey Press.

Erickson, M. L. 1979. "Some Empirical Questions Concerning the Current Revolution in Juvenile Justice." In *The Future of Childhood and Juvenile Justice*, edited by L. T. Empey, 277–309. Charlotteville, Va.: University Press of Virginia.

Faulkner, C. 1986. "More Problems Than Solutions?" 3 *Justice Report* 6–8.

Feld, B. C. 1978. *Neutralizing Inmate Violence: Juvenile Offenders in Institutions*. Cambridge, Mass.: Ballinger.

Felstiner, J. 1985. "Some Observations of Practice and Procedure under the Young Offenders Act." (Spring) *Ontario Association of Professional Social Workers Metro News* 19–23.

Finckenauer, J. 1982. *Scared Straight! And the Panacea Phenomenon in Corrections*. Englewood Cliffs, N.J.: Prentice Hall.

Fischer, D. G., and R. Jeune. 1987. "Juvenile Diversion: A Process Analysis." 28 *Canadian Psychology* 60–70.

Foster, T. W. 1975. "Make-believe Families: A Response of Women and Girls to the Deprivations of Imprisonment." 3 *International Journal of Criminology and Penology* 71–78.

Fox, R. G. 1985. "The Treatment of Juveniles in Canadian Law." In *Perspectives in Criminal Law,* edited by A. N. Doob and E. L. Greenspan, 149–85. Toronto: Canada Law Book.

Fox, S. 1970. "Juvenile Justice Reform: A Historical Analysis." 22 *Stanford Law Review* 1187-1239.

Fuchs, D., and S. C. Bracken. 1984. "Self-help Network and Community-Based Diversion." 26 *Canadian Journal of Criminology* 343–54.

Gabor, P., I. Greene, and P. McCormick. 1986. "The Young Offenders Act: The Alberta Youth Court Experience in the First Year." 5 *Canadian Journal of Family Law* 301–19.

Gagnon, D. 1984. *History of the Law for Juvenile Delinquents.* Ottawa: Solicitor General of Canada.

Gendreau, P., and R. Ross. 1983. "Success in Corrections: Programs and Principles." In *Current Issues in Juvenile Justice,* edited by R. R. Corrado, M. LeBlanc, and J. Trepanier, 335–43. Toronto: Butterworths.

Giallombardo, R. 1974. *The Social World of Imprisoned Girls: A Comparative Study of Institutions for Juvenile Delinquents.* New York: John Wiley and Sons.

Gibbons, D. C. 1986. "Juvenile Delinquency: Can Social Science Find a Cure?" 32 *Crime and Delinquency* 186–204.

Gomme, I. M., M. E. Morton, and W. G. West. 1984. "Rates, Types, and Patterns of Male and Female Delinquency in an Ontario County." 26 *Canadian Journal of Criminology* 313–23.

Greenwood, P. W., and F. E. Zimring. 1985. *One More Chance: The Pursuit of Promising Intervention Strategies for Chronic Juvenile Offenders.* Santa Monica, Calif.: Rand.

Griffiths, C. T. 1982. "Law Enforcement–Juvenile Court Relations: The Impact on Decision Making." 6 *Criminal Justice Review* 6–13.

Hackler, J., and W. Paranjape. 1983. "Juvenile Justice Statistics: Mythmaking or Measure of System Response?" 25 *Canadian Journal of Criminology* 209–26.

Hagan, J., and J. Leon. 1977. "Rediscovering Delinquency: Social History, Political Ideology and the Sociology of Law." 42 *American Sociological Review* 587–98.

Hagarty, J. 1866. "Vagrant Children in Our Cities." 19 *Upper Canada Journal of Education* 4–5.

Hasenfeld, Y. 1977. "The Juvenile Court and Its Environment." In *Introduction to Juvenile Delinquency: Text and Readings,* edited by P. F. Cromwell et al., 207–29. St. Paul, Minn.: West Publishing Co.

Heeren, J., and D. Schichor. 1984. "Mass Media and Delinquency Prevention: The Case of 'Scared Straight.' " 5 *Deviant Behavior* 375–86.

Houston, S. E. 1972. "Victorian Origins of Juvenile Delinquency: A Canadian Experience." 12 *History of Education Quarterly* 254–80.

———. 1982. "The 'Waifs and Strays' of a Late Victorian City: Juvenile Delinquents in Toronto." In *Childhood and Family in Canadian History,* edited by J. Parr, 129–42. Toronto: McClelland and Stewart.

Hudson, J., J. P. Hornick, and B. A. Burrows. 1988. *Justice and the Young Offender in Canada.* Toronto: Wall and Thompson.

Jaffe, P. G., and B. J. Kroeker, C. Hyatt, M. Miscevick, A. Telford, R.

Chandler, C. Shanahan, and B. Sokoloff. 1985–86. "Diversion in the Canadian Juvenile Justice System: A Tale of Two Cities." 37 *Juvenile and Family Court Journal* 59–66.

Jones, A. 1978. "Closing Penetanguishene Reformatory: An Attempt to Deinstitutionalize Treatment of Juvenile Offenders in Early Twentieth Century Ontario." 70 *Ontario History* 227–44.

Jones, A., and L. Rutman. 1981. *In the Children's Aid: J. J. Kelso and Child Welfare in Ontario.* Toronto: University of Toronto Press.

Kelso, J. J. 1907. "Delinquent Children: Some Improved Methods Whereby They May Be Prevented from Following a Criminal Career." 6 *Canadian Law Review* 106–10.

Klassen, H. C. 1981. "In Search of Neglected and Delinquent Children: The Calgary Children's Aid Society, 1909–1920." In *Town and City: Aspects of Western Canadian Urban Development,* edited by A. F. J. Artibise, 375–91. Regina: Canadian Plains Research Centre, University of Regina.

Knell, B. E. F. 1965. "Capital Punishment: Its Administration in Relation to Juvenile Offenders in the Nineteenth Century and Its Possible Administration in the Eighteenth." 5 *British Journal of Delinquency* 198–207.

Kopelman, F., and S. Moyer. 1985. *Juvenile Prevention and Diversion Programs in Canada.* Ottawa: Solicitor General of Canada.

Kopyto, H., and A. M. Codina. 1986. "Young Offenders Act Means More Frequent Custody Terms." 6 *Lawyers Weekly* 8.

Krisberg, B., I. M. Schwartz, P. Litsky, and J. Austin. 1986. "The Watershed of Juvenile Justice Reform." 32 *Crime and Delinquency* 5–38.

Kueneman, R., and R. Linden. 1983. "Factors Affecting Dispositions in the Winnipeg Juvenile Court." In *Current Issues in Juvenile Justice,* edited by R. R. Corrado, M. LeBlanc, and J. Trepanier, 219–35. Toronto: Butterworths.

Kueneman, R., R. Linden, and R. Kosmick. 1986. *A Study of Manitoba's Northern and Rural Juvenile Courts.* Ottawa: Programs Branch, Solicitor General of Canada.

Langmuir, J. W. (Chairman). 1891. *Commission Appointed to Enquire into the Prison and Reformatory System of Ontario. Report of the Commissioners.* Toronto: Warwick and Son.

LaPrairie, C. P., and C. T. Griffiths. 1981. *Native Indian Juvenile Delinquency in a Northwestern Canadian Community.* Unpublished paper. Burnaby, B.C.: School of Criminology, Simon Fraser University.

LeBlanc, M. 1983. "Delinquency as an Epiphenomenon of Adolescence." In *Current Issues in Juvenile Justice,* edited by R. R. Corrado, M. LeBlanc and J. Trepanier, 31–48. Toronto: Butterworths.

LeBlanc, M., and H. Beaumont. 1988. "The Quebec Perspective on the Young Offenders Act: Implementation before Adoption." In *Justice and the Young Offender in Canada*, edited by J. Hudson, J. P. Hornick, and B. A. Burrows, 81–92. Toronto: Wall and Thompson.

LeBlanc, M., and M. Bosse. 1980. *Boscoville: Evaluation of Its Effectiveness through the Psychological Development of Its Clients During Institutionalization and Its Follow-up*. Beverly Hills: Sage Publications.

Lefstein, N., V. Stapleton, and L. Teitelbaum. 1969. "In Search of Juvenile Justice: *Gault* and Its Implementation." 3 *Law and Society Review* 491–563.

Lemert, E. 1981. "Diversion in Juvenile Justice: What Hath Been Wrought." 18 *Journal of Research in Crime and Delinquency* 35–46.

Leon, J. 1977. "The Development of Canadian Juvenile Justice: A Background for Reform." 15 *Osgoode Hall Law Journal* 71–106.

Leschied, A. W., and P. Gendreau. 1986. "The Declining Role of Rehabilitation in Canadian Juvenile Justice: Implications of Underlying Theory in the Young Offender's Act." 28 *Canadian Journal of Criminology* 315–22.

Leschied, A. W., and P. G. Jaffe. 1987. "Impact of the Young Offenders Act on Court Dispositions: A Comparative Analysis." 29 *Canadian Journal of Criminology* 421–30.

——. 1988. "Implementing the Young Offenders Act in Ontario: Critical Issues and Challenges for the Future." In *Justice and the Young Offender in Canada*, edited by J. Hudson, J. P. Hornick, and B. A. Burrows, 65–79. Toronto: Wall and Thompson.

Leschied, A. W., P. G. Jaffe, and G. L. Stone. 1985." Differential Response to Juvenile Offenders to Two Detention Environments as a Function of Conceptual Level." 27 *Canadian Journal of Criminology* 467–76.

Leschied, A. W., and K. E. Thomas. 1985. "Effective Residential Programming for 'Hard to Serve' Delinquent Youth: A Description of the Craigwood Program." 27 *Canadian Journal of Criminology* 161–77.

Lewis, R. V. 1983. "Scared Straight — California Style: Evaluation of the San Quentin Squires Program." 10 *Criminal Justice and Behavior* 209–26.

Linden, R., and C. Filmore. 1980. "A Comparative Study of Delinquency Involvement." In *Crime in Canadian Society*, edited by R. A. Silverman and J. J. Teevan, 154–70. Toronto: Butterworths.

Lovekin, E. R. 1961. "Editorial: Truculent Juveniles." 2 *Criminal Law Quarterly* 413–14.

Lundman, R. J. 1984. *Prevention and Control of Juvenile Delinquency*. New York: Oxford University Press.

——. 1986. "*Beyond Probation*: Assessing the Generalizability of the Delinquency Supression Effect Measures Reported by Murray and Cox." 32 *Crime and Delinquency* 134–47.

MacGill, H. G. 1925. *The Juvenile Court in Canada: Origins, Principles, Governing Legislation and Practice*. Ottawa: Canadian Council on Child Welfare.

Manitoba. 1986. *Young Offenders Act — The Second Year, April 1985–May, 1986.* Winnipeg: Ministry of Community Services.

Mason, B. 1988. "Implementing the Young Offenders Act: An Alberta Perspective." In *Justice and the Young Offender in Canada*, edited by J. Hudson, J. P. Hornick, and B. A. Burrows, 51–63. Toronto: Wall and Thompson.

McGrath, W. T. 1962. "Some Suggested Amendments to Canada's Juvenile Delinquents Act." 4 *Criminal Law Quarterly* 259–64.

McLeod, J. L. 1980. "*Doli Incapax:* The Forgotten Presumption in Juvenile Court Trials." 3 *Canadian Journal of Family Law* 251–79.

Menzies, R. J., R. R. Corrado, W. Glackman, and K. Ryan. 1987. *A Seven-Year Survey of Disruptive and Self-injurious Conduct among Residents of a Youth Detention Centre.* Ottawa: Solicitor General of Canada.

Miller, J. G. 1979. "The Revolution in Juvenile Justice: From Reform to Rhetoric." In *The Future of Childhood and Juvenile Justice*, edited by L. T. Empey, 66–111. Charlotteville, Va.: University Press of Virginia.

Morrison, T. R. 1976. " 'Their Proper Sphere': Feminism, the Family, and Child-Centred Social Reform in Ontario, 1875–1900." 68 *Ontario History* 45–64.

Morton, M. E., and W. G. West. 1983. "An Experiment in Diversion by a Citizen Committee." In *Current Issues in Juvenile Justice*, edited by R. R. Corrado, M. LeBlanc, and J. Trepanier, 206–16. Toronto: Butterworths.

Moyer, S. 1980. *Diversion from the Juvenile Justice System and Its Impact on Children: A Review of the Literature.* Ottawa: Solicitor General of Canada.

Murray, C. A., and L. A. Cox. 1979. *Beyond Probation: Juvenile Corrections and the Chronic Delinquent.* Beverly Hills, Calif.: Sage Publications.

O'Brien, D. 1984. "Juvenile Diversion: An Issues Perspective from the Atlantic Provinces." 26 *Canadian Journal of Criminology* 217–30.

Osborne, J. S. 1979. "Juvenile Justice Policy in Canada: The Transfer of the Initiative." 2 *Canadian Journal of Family Law* 7–32.

Osgood, D. W., E. Gruber, M. A. Archer, and T. M. Newcomb. 1985. "Autonomy for Inmates: Counterculture or Cooptation?" 12 *Criminal Justice and Behavior* 71–89.

Pate, K. J., and D. E. Peachey. 1988. "Face-to-Face: Victim-Offender Mediation under the Young Offenders Act." In *Justice and the Young Offender in Canada*, edited by J. Hudson, J. P. Hornick, and B. A. Burrows, 105–21. Toronto: Wall and Thompson.

Platt, A. 1969. *The Child Savers: The Invention of Delinquency.* Chicago: University of Chicago Press.

———. 1977. *The Child Savers: The Invention of Delinquency.* 2nd ed. Chicago: University of Chicago Press.

Polk, K. 1984." Juvenile Diversion: A Look at the Record." 30 *Crime and Delinquency* 648–59.

Polsky, H. W. 1977. *Cottage Six: The Social System of Delinquent Boys in Residential Treatment*. Huntington, N.Y.: Krieger.

Prentice, A. 1977. *The School Promoters: Education and Social Class in Mid-Nineteenth Century Upper Canada*. Toronto: McClelland and Stewart.

Propper, A. 1981. *Prison Homosexuality: Myth and Reality*. Lexington, Mass. D. C. Heath.

Rains, P. 1985. "La Justice des mineurs et the Boy's Farm: 1909–1968." 18 *Criminologie* 103–27.

Rausch, S., and C. Logan. 1983. "Diversion from Juvenile Court: Panacea or Pandora's Box." In *Evaluating Juvenile Justice*, edited by J. Klugel, 19–30. Beverly Hills, Calif.: Sage.

Reichel, P. L. 1985. "Getting to Know You: Decision Making in an Institution for Juveniles." 36 *Juvenile and Family Court Journal* 5–15.

Reid, S. A. 1986. "The Juvenile Justice 'Revolution' in Canada: The Creation and Development of New Legislation for Young Offenders." 8 *Canadian Criminology Forum* 1–14.

Reid, S. A., and M. Reitsma-Street. 1984. "Assumptions and Implications of New Canadian Legislation for Young Offenders." 7 *Canadian Criminology Forum* 1–19.

RES Policy Research, Inc. 1985. *Needs of Native Young Offenders in Labrador in View of the Young Offenders Act*. Ottawa: Department of Justice.

Rowe, W., and S. Edelman. 1982. *A Systems Evaluation of Burnaby Youth Services: A Police-Based Youth and Family Counselling Program*. Vancouver: Ministry of the Attorney General, Province of British Columbia.

Ryant, J. C., and C. Heinrich. 1988. "Youth Court Committees in Manitoba." In *Justice and the Young Offender in Canada*, edited by J. Hudson, J. P. Hornick, and B. A. Burrows, 93–104. Toronto: Wall and Thompson.

Sarri, R. C. 1983. "The Use of Detention and Alternatives in the United States Since the Gault Decision." In *Current Issues in Juvenile Justice*, edited by R. R. Corrado, M. LeBlanc, and J. Trepanier, 315–34. Toronto: Butterworths.

Schlossman, S. L. 1977. *Love and the American Delinquent: The Theory and Practice of "Progressive" Juvenile Justice, 1825–1920*. Chicago: University of Chicago Press.

Scott, S. F. 1985. "Outward Bound — An Adjunct to the Treatment of Juvenile Delinquents: Florida's STEP Program." 11 *New England Journal of Criminal and Civil Confinement* 420–36.

Shoom, S. 1972. "The Upper Canada Reformatory, Penetanguishene: The

Dawn of Prison Reform in Canada." 14 *Canadian Journal of Criminology and Corrections* 260–67.

Siegel, L. J., and J. J. Senna. 1988. *Juvenile Delinquency: Theory, Practice, and Law.* 3rd ed. St. Paul, Minn.: West Publishing Co.

Sieverdes, C. M., and C. Bartollas. 1986. "Security Level and Adjustment Patterns in Juvenile Institutions." 14 *Journal of Criminal Justice* 135–45.

Solicitor General of Canada. 1985. *The Saint John Youth Project.* Ottawa: Supply and Services Canada.

———. 1986. *The Young Offenders Act: Highlights.* Ottawa: Supply and Services Canada.

Sosin, M., and R. Sarri. 1976. "Due Process — Reality or Myth?" In *Brought to Justice? Juveniles, the Court, and the Law,* edited by R. Sarri and Y. Hasenfeld, 176–206. Ann Arbor: National Assessment of Juvenile Corrections, University of Michigan.

Splane, R. 1965. *Social Welfare in Ontario, 1791–1893: A Study of Public Welfare Administration.* Toronto: University of Toronto Press.

Staples, W. G. 1986. "Restitution as a Sanction in the Juvenile Court." 32 *Crime and Delinquency* 177–85.

Starr, J. E. 1913. "First Annual Report of the Juvenile Court." 4 *Canadian Journal of Public Health* 194–205.

Stubbs, Roy. 1972. "The Young Offender." 5 *Manitoba Law Journal* 19–39.

Sutherland, N. 1976. *Children in English-Canadian Society: Framing the Twentieth Century Consensus.* Toronto: University of Toronto Press.

Trojanowicz, R. C., and M. Morash. 1983. *Juvenile Delinquency: Concepts and Control.* 3rd ed. Englewood Cliffs, N.J.: Prentice-Hall.

Wardell, B. 1986. "The Young Offenders Act: A Report Card 1984–1986." In *Administration of Justice,* edited by D. H. Currie and B. D. McLean, 128–56. Saskatoon: Department of Sociology, University of Saskatchewan.

Watts, R. E. 1932. "Trend of Crime in Canada." 39 *Queen's Quarterly* 402–13.

West, W. G. 1984. *Young Offenders and the State: A Canadian Perspective on Delinquency.* Toronto: Butterworths.

Winterdyk, J., and C. T. Griffiths. 1984. "Wilderness Experience Programs: Reforming Delinquents or Beating around the Bush?" 35 *Juvenile and Family Court Journal* 35–44.

Winterdyk, J., and R. Roesch. 1982. "A Wilderness Experiential Program As an Alternative for Probationers: An Evaluation." 24 *Canadian Journal of Criminology* 39-50.

LEGISLATION

Constitution Act, 1867, 1867 (U.K.), c. 3
Criminal Code, R.S.C. 1985, c. C-46
Food and Drugs Act, R.S.C. 1985, c. F-27
Juvenile Delinquents Act, R.S.C. 1970, c. J-3
Narcotic Control Act, R.S.C. 1985, c. N-1
Young Offenders Act, S.C. 1980-81-82-83, c. 110; now R.S.C. 1985, c. Y-1

15 NATIVE INDIANS AND THE CRIMINAL JUSTICE SYSTEM

In this chapter, we explore the major issues surrounding native Indians and the criminal justice system. This will include a consideration of the nature and extent of the involvement of native Indians with the law from arrest to incarceration, as well as the policies and programs that have been developed by governmental agencies and by native bands, communities, and organizations in an attempt to reduce native conflict with the law.[1]

Native Indians in Canadian Society

Approximately two per cent of the total population of Canada is native Indian and Inuit. They are, however, unevenly distributed across the country in terms of their percentage of territorial or provincial populations, ranging from 60% in the Northwest Territories and 20% in the Yukon, to 6% in Saskatchewan and Manitoba and 3% in Alberta and British Columbia. In the provinces east of Manitoba, only one person in 100 was identified in the 1981 Census as native Indian or Inuit (Statistics Canada, 1984). The highest numbers of native Indians are found in Ontario and British Columbia.[2]

Native peoples in Canada are distinguished by their cultural and linguistic attributes as well as their legal status (Morse, 1982a). Status Indians are native people who are registered under the *Indian Act*. Non-status Indians are those who identify themselves as native but who are not registered under the *Indian Act*. Métis are of mixed Indian and European ancestry, while the Inuit (Eskimo) are a distinct cultural group who reside in the Northwest Territories, Labrador, and Northern Quebec.

Statistics from the 1981 Census of Canada indicate that these groups are distributed as follows: Status Indians (59.9%); Métis (20.0%); non-status Indians (15.3%); and Inuit (5.2%). Throughout the chapter, the term *native Indian* is used to describe status and non-status Indians, Métis, and Inuit, although reference is made to specific groups where required.[3]

There is considerable diversity among the 573 recognized Indian bands in terms of their culture, social and political organization, and community resources. The majority of these bands, representing nearly 65% of the total registered Indian population, are situated in either rural or remote northern areas, compared to 25% of the national population (Department of Indian and Northern Affairs, 1980: 12). As we will see later in our discussion, this remoteness has significant implications for the delivery of justice services to native peoples.

Any discussion of native Indians and the criminal justice system must consider the political position and socio-economic condition of natives. Many observers argue that the subordinate political and economic position of native groups is a consequence of the colonization of natives by Europeans and of Canadian government policies that have exerted control over virtually every aspect of native life (Richardson, 1975; Tobias, 1976; 1983; Leslie and Maguire, 1978; Kellough, 1980; Ponting and Gibbons, 1980; Driben and Trudeau, 1983; Bostrom, 1984; Asch, 1984; Morrison and Wilson, 1986).

A major consequence of this minority status is "victimization" of native peoples, which is evidenced by pervasive poverty, high rates of unemployment and reliance upon public assistance, low levels of formal education, high death rates from accidents and violence, and increasing rates of family breakdown (see Siggner, 1979; Griffiths, Yerbury, and Weafer, 1987). Particularly vulnerable are native Indian youth, aged 15 to 24, who are most susceptible to violent and accidental death, suicide and alcohol and substance abuse.[4]

Siggner (1986) presents data on registered Indians that indicate that:

–   In 1984, 47% of native Indian housing was in poor physical condition, 36% was overcrowded, and 38% lacked running water, and/or indoor plumbing.
–   In 1981, the unemployment rate for native Indians was two and one-half times that for the Canadian workforce.
–   In 1980, the average annual income for native Indians was 60% that of the general population.
–   In 1981, 19% of native Indians had completed some post-secondary education, compared with 36% of the total Canadian population.

These socio-economic disparities extend to urban areas of the country. In Winnipeg, Clatworthy (1980) found that the unemployment rate among native Indians was four times higher than that for non-natives, while household income for native Indians was about one-half that of the total population. Among the native Indian population was a high percentage of single parent families, and native youths and women experienced particular hardships. Similar findings have been reported in Edmonton (Stanbury and Siegel, 1975; McCaskill, 1981; Native Counselling Services of Alberta and Native Affairs Secretariat, 1985).

In a recent discussion of the native "condition" in Canada, Siggner (1986) expressed cautious optimism, noting that over the past decade, there has been a decline in infant mortality rates, a rise in the average annual income of registered Indians, and increases in levels of educational achievement from primary school to post-secondary school. However, these data relate only to registered Indians, and it is unclear whether such trends are occurring among other native groups. For example, the 1981 Census revealed that Inuit and status Indians on reserves had lower levels of formal education than other native groups, while status Indians residing on reserves were less likely to be employed than were non-status Indians (Statistics Canada, 1984). Also, there are significant differences in the "condition" of native groups and individual bands and communities across the country.[5]

Native Indian Crime and Criminality

A discussion of patterns of crime and criminality among native peoples is hindered by a lack of published research (see May, 1982a). Official statistics generally include only status or registered Indians. Few data exist on the involvement of Métis, the Inuit, and non-status Indians in the criminal justice system, and little is known of the difficulties encountered by native Indian women, youth, and the elderly or the differences in crime patterns between bands and communities (LaPrairie, 1984a; 1984b; Hagan, 1985).[6]

To date, much of the research has been descriptive and anecdotal, revealing little beyond the fact that native Indians are overrepresented in the criminal justice process in many jurisdictions. There is some evidence to suggest that while native Indians commit less serious offences than whites, they are more frequently arrested, found guilty, and incarcerated. Such a generalization, however, should be viewed with extreme caution and does little to further our understanding of the reasons for this extensive involvement or to suggest alternatives that should be undertaken to reduce it.[7]

It is likely that the socio-economic condition of many native peoples plays a direct role in their involvement in criminal behaviour and with the criminal justice system. In an early study of native offenders in Manitoba, McCaskill (1970: 20) concluded: ". . . the problem of Native criminality is closely tied to the general socio-economic conditions which prevail in most Native communities and . . . any overall solution to the former situation entails a solution to the latter." Several years later, the Métis and Non-status Indian Crime and Justice Commission (1977: 127; 152) found in a survey of 316 native Indian inmates in 24 federal correctional institutions and two territorial correctional centres that

- over one-half of the inmates were from areas where more than 50% of the eligible work force was unemployed;
- the average size of the inmate's family was between 9 and 11 people;
- nearly 50% of the inmates had relatives who had been in jail when they were growing up;
- nearly 80% of the inmates had been in at least one foster home, reform school, residential school or Children's Aid Society home;
- 63% of the inmates had left home prior to age 16;
- 67% had been arrested by age 16;
- the first arrest for 57% of the inmates was for a property-related offence;
- only .07% of the inmates received any assistance when they came into conflict with the law, and social workers were the least likely to have been asked for help.

While these findings are nearly a decade old, similar socio-economic conditions and patterns of involvement with the law continue to exist in many areas of the country.

One factor that is clearly related to the involvement of native people in the criminal justice system is alcohol. Depew (1986: 18) notes that "there may be no other factor as pervasively and consistently related to the nature of Native crime and deviance and which separates the circumstances of Native from non-Native involvement in the criminal justice system as the excessive and hazardous use of alcohol" (cf. Birkenmayer and Jolly, 1981; Jolly, 1981; Finkler, 1982; Saddle Lake Tribal Justice Centre, 1985).[8]

The most in-depth examination of native Indian criminality undertaken to date in Canada is a longitudinal study of native offenders in Manitoba conducted by McCaskill (1985). This investigation involved comparison of data gathered from inmate and parolee files and from interviews with individuals in native organizations and communities, social service and criminal justice agencies in 1970 and in 1984. The findings of this study provide valuable insights into native criminality and suggest additional areas for research.

In comparing the socio-economic and offence profiles of inmates in 1970 with those in 1984, McCaskill (1970; 1985: 24) found that the backgrounds of native inmates and parolees in 1970 and 1984 were characterized by "serious social and personal disorganization" including family instability, alcohol abuse, and low levels of education and skill development. In 1984, native offenders had more serious social and personal problems than did the general native population in Manitoba, leading McCaskill (1985: 27) to conclude that "Native offenders do not appear to be sharing in the relative improvement in socio-economic status which is occurring in Native communities in Manitoba."

McCaskill (1985: 28–40) also compared the patterns of criminality among native offenders between 1970 and 1984. In 1970, the majority of offences were for either theft or assault, were unpremeditated and involved alcohol. In 1984, native inmates had committed a larger number of crimes, and there had been an increase in crimes of violence and sex-related offences. In comparison with non-native inmates in 1984, both provincial and federal native inmates were more frequently incarcerated for serious crimes against the person.

Similar findings were reported by Canfield and Drinnan (1981), who found in study of native and non-native admissions to federal correctional facilities during the years 1976–1981 that almost 50% of the native inmate admissions were for crimes against the person and that there had been an 87% increase in the number of native Indian inmates convicted of murder, as opposed to a 44% increase for non-natives. Similar increases in sex-related crimes were noted for native Indian offenders. High rates of violent crime among native Indians have also been reported in a study of offenders in Saskatchewan (Government of Canada et al., 1985), Manitoba (Singer and Moyer, 1981) and Quebec (Woods Gordon, 1982).

Data collected by McCaskill (1985) in 1970 and 1984 also revealed significant increases in crime among native Indians in urban areas and an overall decrease in the crime rate in native communities in rural areas of the province. The decrease was ascribed by the author (p. 48) to improvements in the individual native communities, which, in 1970, had contributed a disproportionate number of offenders to provincial and federal institutions. Among the changes that had functioned to reduce the crime rates in these communities were strong leadership, an increase in community awareness and participation in crime control and crime prevention, and a resurgence of traditional methods of social control. These changes were part of a growing movement through which natives assumed more control over their economic, political, and social affairs (McCaskill, 1985: 48).

In discussing the findings from the two surveys, McCaskill (1985: 61) concludes that native criminality has become more complex in the 1980s and that the "minority situation model," which "accounts for the causes of Native criminality by emphasizing the Native offender's responses to the social situation in which he finds himself," may not now be wholly applicable. Rather, McCaskill argues, native criminality must be considered in many instances to be the result of an individual pathology: "For some Native offenders being native may be almost irrelevant to their criminal activity" (p. 62).

There is a need for much more research on native Indian criminality, Verdun-Jones and Muirhead (1979/80: 18) noting that most of the published research is of a "book-keeping" nature and of limited focus:

Very few attempts have been made to develop any general theory capable of furnishing explanations for the nature of native criminality and the societal response to it ... What is required is a more comprehensive, multi-disciplinary and integrated focus which would draw together a number of perspectives.

Efforts to Reduce Native Overrepresentation

The issues surrounding native Indian involvement in the criminal justice system were first raised on a national level with the publication of *Indians and the Law* (Canadian Corrections Association, 1967). This report documented the socio-economic position of native peoples in Canadian society and noted the conflict between white and native societies in criminal justice (see also Schmeiser, 1974).

Over the past two decades, there have been an increasing number of initiatives taken by government and native Indian bands and communities to address the problems encountered by native peoples in the criminal justice system. These have included the development of the RCMP Native Special Constable program, the creation of native courtworker and communicator programs, and the implementation of band and reserve-based policing services.

The primary impetus for the creation of many of these programs was the National Conference on Native Peoples and the Criminal Justice System held in Edmonton in 1975. Among the conclusions and recommendations of the conference, which was attended by federal, provincial, and native leaders, were the following:

1. Native Indians in trouble with the law do not have equal access to most of the regular services provided to other suspects, convicted offenders, and ex-inmates;
2. Native persons should be closely involved in the planning and delivery of services associated with criminal justice and Native people;
3. Native communities should have greater responsibility for the delivery of justice services to their people;
4. Native communities must be given the resources to develop services for Native offenders which might (even should) look different from services offered to white offenders.

[Solicitor General of Canada, 1975: 38]

Despite the enthusiastic endorsement of these and other recommendations by white, native and Inuit leaders, many observers contend that, overall, there has been no reduction in the problems encountered by native peoples in the criminal justice system, nor any decrease in the high rates of arrests, convictions, and levels of incarceration found in many jurisdictions. This is due to the failure of the participants in the Edmonton conference to consider the causal factors related to native Indian involvement in the criminal justice system, including the role of the deprived socio-economic condition in which many native peoples live. Further, while the terms *justice* and *native-for-native services* were widely used during the conference, there was no attempt to define the precise meaning of these terms in relation to native peoples and the law.

In a survey conducted two years after the conference, Jolly, Peters, and Spiegel (1979) found that there had been little or no action taken on many of the recommendations by either the federal government or the Province of Ontario. Among the findings of the survey were that many senior federal civil servants had never read the recommendations and that there was widespread opposition at the federal level to the concept that "separate" or autonomous structures should be developed for the delivery of justice services to native peoples (see Keon-Cohen, 1982).

In the following discussion, we will present materials on the involvement of native peoples at the various stages of the criminal justice process, from policing to corrections. In addition, the various programs that have been developed in an attempt to address specific concerns at each stage will be considered.

The initiatives can be generally divided into (1) those developed within the framework of existing criminal justice agencies, for example, the Native Special Constable programs operated by the RCMP, and the Quebec and Ontario provincial police forces' Native Justice of the Peace programs; and (2) separate, "autonomous" justice structures created and operated by native Indian bands and communities, for example, the Dakota-Ojibway Tribal Police in Manitoba. These separate structures have generally been modelled after "white" criminal justice agencies, although efforts are being made by many native communities to re-establish traditional methods of social control or create new community-based mechanisms for addressing problems.

While the issues surrounding native Indian involvement in the Canadian criminal justice system are complex and defy simplistic solutions, there are numerous positive developments that may, in time, reduce native conflict with the law.

Native Indians and the Police

The high rates of native Indian arrests in many jurisdictions raise serious questions about native Indian-police relations. Initial concerns were raised in the report *Indians and the Law* (Canadian Corrections Association, 1967) and by the research findings of Bienvenue and Latif (1974) that native Indians in Winnipeg were arrested far more often than whites, due to their visibility in the city and to over-surveillance by the police.

In rural and remote areas of the country, police officers are often reluctant to respond, or unusually slow in responding, to calls for assistance on the reserves, particularly to calls involving domestic disputes (Alberta Board of Review, 1978; Government of Canada et al., 1984; Marrison,

1984). When officers do become involved with native Indians, there is frequently a reliance upon asserting authority and upon the *Criminal Code*. This led Depew (1986: 23) to express the concern that native Indians may be "overpoliced" in terms of the arrest and charging practices of police officers, and "underpoliced" in terms of their access to non-law enforcement policing services.

Relations between native Indians and the RCMP have been the focus of concern since the 1800s, Loree (1985: 1) noting that in early Canada "the R.C.M.P. were an important link between the government and Native peoples; enforcing the law of the land on the one hand and protecting the community on the other . . . the R.C.M.P., in particular, have long been among the most, if not *the* most, visible and obviously powerful manifestation of a dominant Euro-Canadian society, its institutions, customs and laws."[9]

The following discussion explores the major issues surrounding police–native Indian relations and examines the various native policing programs that have developed across Canada over the past 15 years. As a background to this section, the reader is encouraged to review materials on policing presented in Chapters 3 and 4, particularly those related to the history and role of the police in Canada and the factors that may influence police decision making.

Caution must be exercised in generalizing the findings from research studies carried out in specific jurisdictions at any one point in time. High rates of arrest alone cannot be taken as conclusive evidence of discriminatory treatment by police officers. Further, native Indian–police relations vary appreciably within and between urban and rural settings, and the quality of these relations, even within the same community or neighbourhood, may change over time.

The research findings discussed in this section should be taken only as illustrative of the types of difficulties that may afflict native–police relations. The reader should keep in mind that native Indians in Canada are policed by a variety of police forces in a great diversity of geographical and cultural settings.

Native Indian–Police Relations

Loree (1985: 8) describes the precarious nature of policing in native communities:

> The police officer working in a native community is frequently caught in the middle; as marginal in his role as are many Native people to the dominant society. Each exists and attempts to function in the grey area between the more traditional, non-European, norms, values and organizations of the Native community and laws, customs and structures of the larger society. The police officer is . . . a readily available and highly visible symbol of government failures, misunderstandings and broken promises.

The relations between the police and native Indians in many urban and rural areas are characterized by mutual hostility and distrust, increasing the likelihood of conflict and high arrest rates (Skoog, Roberts, and Boldt, 1980; Marrison, 1984; Depew, 1986). In interviews with RCMP officers, natives and resource personnel (probation officers, social workers, community officials, and nurses) in five Yukon communities, Parnell (1979: 6) found that while the officers in the communities tended to describe relations with the native Indians as "good" or "very good," native Indians tended to characterize relations with the police as "fair," and the resource persons depicted police–native Indian relations as "serious."

In a survey of regular RCMP members in Alberta, Saskatchewan and Manitoba, Loree (1985: 36) found that nearly 43% described the general state of native–non-native relations in their detachment area as "fair," while almost 34% defined them as "good," and only 3.7% as "very good." According to these officer, the greatest areas of difficulty in policing native communities were "Differences in Cultural Values and Outlook on Life," "Problems Linked to High Unemployment," and "Dealing with Young People" (Loree, 1985: 40).[10]

A primary determinant of the quality of native Indian–police relations appears to be the age, experience, and personal style of the individual police officer. Native Indians in the Yukon communities held more positive views of older, experienced police officers, who were regarded as using their discretion appropriately and who made a greater effort to become involved in community activities. There were problems, however, with younger RCMP officers, who "tended to be cocky and aggressive" in carrying out their tasks (Parnell, 1979: 21). The Alberta Board of Review (1978) also found that the abuses of police authority in dealing with native Indians were highest among young, inexperienced officers who had little understanding of the communities or the residents they were policing.[11]

A second factor is the knowledge (or lack thereof) that officers have of the communities and native peoples they are policing. Loree (1985) found that a significant proportion of his sample RCMP members described themselves as having only a "fair" level of general knowledge about native Indians. Officers reported the highest levels of general knowledge about the social and economic conditions of natives they policed, but had less information about the history, culture and traditions and the relations between native peoples and government. Most of the knowledge the officers did have was acquired *after* arriving in the community. Nearly 50% stated that receiving such information prior to their arrival would have been of little use.

There may be a similar lack of knowledge among native Indians, particularly in relation to their legal rights and the extent to which they understand the criminal justice process. In the Parnell study (1979), nearly 90% of the native Indians interviewed stated that they needed more information about the law, and 55% indicated they desired more information about their legal rights. The Alberta Board of Review (1978) also found that native Indians in northern Alberta had little or no understanding of their legal rights and were highly susceptible to pressures from officers to plead guilty to alleged offences prior to obtaining legal counsel.[12]

A third determinant of native Indian–police relations is the extent to which police officers go beyond the traditional crime-control model of policing and become involved in community life. Parnell (1979) found that a major complaint of native Indians in several Yukon communities concerned the crime control, enforcement orientation of police officers, which was viewed as inappropriate to the needs of the community and not conducive to the creation of positive relations. In the Yukon, police–native Indian relations had improved in those communities where officers had become involved in non-policing activities in the community and adopted more of a human relations approach.

From his findings, Parnell (1979: 42) concluded that a major change was required in the criteria for evaluating and promoting RCMP officers, particularly those policing in northern communities, and that the criteria "should involve more stress on qualities favouring educational and communication skills and the ability to develop positive working relationships with the public." This was hindered in part by the organizational policy of the RCMP, which requires that officers be transferred every two years.

The importance of adapting the orientation and delivery of policing services to the needs of native Indian communities has also been noted by Depew (1986: 23): "Many native community policing problems may be more closely related to issues of social disorder as opposed to more serious criminal activity." Parnell (1979: 18) came to a similar conclusion in his Yukon study, stating that "the police find themselves spending a very high proportion of their time dealing with problems which are essentially social in nature rather than legal." Among the officers surveyed in the Prairie provinces, Loree (1985: 16) found that alcohol-related incidents were by far the most common type of contacts, followed in frequency by "routine service calls."

Among the police officers surveyed by Loree (1985: 55), public relations programs and more active involvement in community social and sports activities were the most frequently mentioned ways by which relations with native communities could be improved. These same officers believed that the native community could improve its relations with the police by becoming more familiar with the law and the role of the police, by becoming more independent and responsible for dealing with community problems, and by addressing the problems associated with alcohol in the community.[13]

Perhaps Loree (1985: 80) has captured best the difficulties confronting RCMP officers policing native Indian communities:

... the police can often find themselves caught in a three jawed vice: between the political, economic and social realities of Native communities, an external society's conception of law and law enforcement, and the needs and demands of the police organization *per se*.

Native Policing Programs

Over the past two decades, there have been a number of initiatives by the RCMP and provincial police forces to improve police–native Indian relations and the quality of policing services delivered to native peoples and communities. During this time, several autonomous native Indian police forces have also been created.

Native policing programs can be generally divided into non-native-controlled and native-controlled programs. Non-native-controlled programs include the RCMP Indian Special Constable Program and the Indian policing programs operated by the provincial police in Quebec and Ontario. Native-controlled police programs are the separate, autonomous forces that exist on many reserves across the country, the largest of which are the Amerindian Police in Quebec and the Dakota-Ojibway Tribal Police in Manitoba. In addition, there are a large number of band constables who are involved in dealing with civil matters and enforcing band by-laws on individual reserves across the country. Band constables are responsible to the local band council but often suffer from inadequate training and supervision (see Depew, 1986: 66–67).

A brief review of the major native policing programs illustrates the range of initiatives that have been undertaken and the difficulties they have encountered. The findings of specific evaluative studies should be taken only as general indicators of the types of problem encountered by native- and non-native-controlled police forces. For further information on specific programs, the reader is urged to consult the cited literature.

Non-native-Controlled Police Programs

The development of native policing programs has been strongly influenced by the recommendations of several reports that reflect the federal government's reluctance to allow the development of autonomous native policing programs. The report *Indians and the Law* (Canadian Corrections Association, 1967), one of the first investigations of policing on native reserves, recommended that responsibility for policing native communities be assigned to a single police force assisted by native constables. Native policing programs were to be developed within existing policing arrangements under the authority of the RCMP rather than by native Indian bands.

Additional support for creating a native constable program was provided by a federal Task Force (1973) in a report entitled "Policing on

Reserves." Following a consideration of several options for policing Indian reserves, the report recommended the adoption of Option 3b, which provided for the creation of a native policing function within existing provincial police forces. Option 3a, which was rejected by the Task Force, provided for the development of separate, autonomous native Indian police forces that would have the status of a provincial police force on the reserve.[14]

Native policing programs are operated by the RCMP and the provincial police forces in Quebec and Ontario. The RCMP Indian Special Constable (ISC) program was established in 1973 "to enhance the quality of police services being provided to Native communities" (Solicitor General of Canada, 1987: 34). In 1985–86, there were 192 authorized ISC positions and ISCs were assigned to RCMP detachments in all provinces and territories except Quebec, Ontario, and New Brunswick. Special Constables have powers identical to those of regular provincial or federal police officers, whether they are on or off the reserve.

The RCMP is soley responsible for the recruitment, training, and supervision of ISCs. New recruits receive 16 weeks of training at the RCMP depot in Regina (nine weeks less than regular RCMP members) and are paid a lower salary than are regular members. There is a provision, however, for ISCs to transfer to regular member status via the normal application procedures.

Despite the continued expansion of the ISC program, evaluations of its impact on native Indian–police relations and on the crime rates on native reserves and in native communities have produced mixed results.[15] While improvements in native Indian–police relations have been reported in some investigations (see Penner, 1983), other inquiries have revealed "considerable tension, hostility and conflict in native communities affected by the program" (Depew, 1986: 43).

Among the major operational difficulties of the ISC program are (1) a lack of native community input into the recruitment and deployment of ISCs; (2) the failure of the RCMP clearly to identify the role of ISCs, resulting in confusion among ISCs concerning their role and wide discrepancies among individual detachments in how ISCs are utilized; and (3) a reluctance on the part of many natives to become ISCs due to the hostility and social isolation ISCs experience in many native communities (see Finkler, 1976; Bryant, Hawkes, and MacHan, 1978; Parnell, 1979; Native Counselling Services of Alberta, 1980; Van Dyke and Jamont, 1980; Depew, 1986).

The Ontario Provincial Police Indian Special Constable program began in 1975 "to improve the quality, quantity, and accessibility of policing services to Indian communities in Ontario" (Social Policy Research Associates/The Evaluation Group Incorporated, 1983a: 23). In 1982–83, there were 123 ISCs involved in policing on 56 Ontario reserves. The standards for recruitment of ISCs are less stringent than those for regular members, and unlike the RCMP program, there are no provisions for ISCs to transfer over to regular status. While the length of training for ISCs is the same as that provided for regular members, the native constables are required to attend, but not *pass*, the courses. While Ontario ISCs have full peace-officer powers, their legal authority is restricted to the reserve.

Evaluations of the Ontario ISC program suggest that native communities have generally positive views of the program and consider the presence of native constables an improvement over being policed by only regular OPP members (see Social Policy Research Associates/The Evaluation Group Incorporated, 1983a). In contrast to the RCMP program, native bands are extensively involved in the identification and selection of native constables. Ontario ISCs also expressed less confusion about their role, which is specifically defined by the OPP as one of acting as a liaison, rather than a replacement for regular OPP members (Ontario Provincial Police, 1982).

Native-Controlled Policing Programs

Despite the strong influence of the 1973 Task Force on policing and the adoption of Option 3b, there has been a slow but steady growth in separate, "autonomous" native Indian police forces (as proposed by Option 3a). These range in size from the Amerindian police in Quebec and the Dakota-Ojibway Tribal Police in Manitoba, each of which is involved in policing a number of reserves, to smaller, reserve-based police forces, such as those on the Kaknawake Mohawk reserve near Montreal, and the Blood, Louis Bull, and Saddle Lake Reserves in Alberta.[16]

The Amerindian Police

The Amerindian Police Program (APP) was established in Quebec in 1978 to improve policing services in native communities. Currently, there are nearly 100 officers who are involved in policing 26 reserves. The jurisdiction of APP officers is restricted to the reserves where they have full peace-officer status and authority. Unlike other native-controlled police programs, the Amerindian police operate their own training facility at Pointe Bleu, where new recruits receive a 20-week training course.

An evaluation of the APP revealed that while there were numerous administrative difficulties, native communities had a generally favourable impression of the program and made extensive use of the services of native officers (Woods Gordon, 1982). Further, the level of conflict between natives and the police due to misunderstandings and excessive use of force had declined appreciably. There was, however, dissatisfaction among band councils on the reserves concerning their lack of input into the recruitment and selection of APP officers and their general exclusion from decisions involving the administration of the program.

Dakota-Ojibway Tribal Council Police Program

The Dakota-Ojibway Tribal Council (DOTC) police program was established in 1978 to provide policing services to eight reserves in southwestern Manitoba. New recruits, the majority of whom are from one of the Tribal Council reserves, are trained via the 20-week ISC course at the RCMP Depot in Regina. The jurisdiction of officers is limited to the reserves policed, and the RCMP is generally called in to handle serious criminal matters (Singer and Moyer, 1981).

The DOTC program suffered a major setback in 1980 when the Chief of Police was fired and all the officers resigned. A major factor in the demise of the program was political interference on the part of many of the reserve chiefs at the administrative level (Singer and Moyer, 1981: 52). The DOTC program was reinstituted in 1981 and, since that time, has established a positive working relationship with the reserve communities (see Depew, 1986).

The Cree and Inuit Policing Program in Quebec

In 1980, on the basis of an agreement between the Quebec Provincial Police and the representative of the Cree and Inuit people in Quebec, a program was developed for the provision of policing services to 8 Cree reserves in the James Bay area and to 13 Inuit communities in northern Quebec. The agreement calls for the gradual transfer of management of the program from the Quebec Police Force (QPF) to the band councils involved in the program.

Officers are recruited from the communities and selected by a vote of the band council and representatives of the QPF. Training is provided at the Quebec Policy Institute and consists of four sessions, each of which is four weeks in length, the same as that given to regular QPF recruits. The Cree and Inuit constables have full peace-officer powers on the reserve and are responsible for policing services within their areas. Assistance is provided on a periodic basis by regular QPF members. In 1984, there were 20 native constables policing in the 8 Cree communities, and 18 Inuit constables in the 13 Inuit communities.

While no formal evaluation of this policing program is available, comments by the Native Policing Program Advisor (Bouchard, 1985) suggest that there has been a high turnover of officers in the Inuit program due to the isolation of the constables and to the pressures of policing within their home communities.[17]

Key Issues in Native Policing Programs

Our brief review of police–native Indian relations and of the major policing programs that have developed across Canada over the past two decades suggests several key issues that will require attention from governmental ministries and agencies and native bands and communities. These include the following:

The Impact of Native Policing on the Crime Rate in Native Communities

The lack of published evaluations precludes a determination of whether native and non-native controlled policing programs have resulted in a reduction in crime rates in native communities. In our discussion of police effectiveness in Chapter 5, it was noted that the police, *per se*, do not prevent crime, and therefore it may be inappropriate to assess the effectiveness of native policing programs by this criterion.

Of equal or greater significance, however, is the extent to which native communities are satisfied with the policing services they receive. There is substantial evidence that native-controlled policing programs have resulted in more positive relations between police and community and have provided the opportunity for communities to become more actively involved in addressing their needs and concerns.

Re-examining the RCMP Option 3b Policing Program

The development of the ISC by the RCMP was premised largely on the recommendations of a task force whose members were strongly influenced by the preferences of the RCMP for Option 3b. The Task Force (1973) failed to consider the complexity of the issues surrounding native policing and offered weak, unsubstantiated rationale for their final recommendation of Option 3b. This contributed to the major difficulties that have afflicted the 3b program and will require attention if the program is to achieve its stated objectives. As Van Dyke and Jamont (1980: 30) concluded from their study of ISCs: ". . . all programs must change or die of irrelevance."

The Diversity of Native Communities

The Native Counselling Services of Alberta (1980: 23) has cautioned that policing programs — both native and non-native controlled — must consider the needs of individual communities. The cultural diversity among native bands, their patterns of contact with white society, degree of community organization, and level of resources all affect the types of policing problems that exist (see Van Dyke and Jamont, 1980). Loree (1985: 98) recommends the adoption of a community policing model and increased community participation in the policing process: "It is increasingly recognized that it is unreasonable to expect communities alienated from the law, and policing, to be overly concerned with, or supportive of, processes they may feel are imposed upon them" (see also Hylton, 1982; Murphy and Muir, 1985).

Native Indians and the Police in Urban Areas

While the focus of our discussion has been primarily on policing in rural areas, the issues of native Indian police relations in urban areas are no less significant. These difficulties are compounded by the migration of native Indians into the urban areas, where the development of native-controlled police forces is precluded.

In an in-depth examination of the difficulties of recruiting native Indians for the police force in Regina, Cowley and Merasty (1982) found that a large number of native people in Regina had negative attitudes toward the police and had little input into decisions relating to policing native Indians, and that the police did not respond adequately to the needs of native Indians in the city. To improve the recruiting of native Indians for the Regina police, the report (Cowley and Merasty, 1982: 51, 53) recommended that the police department explore jointly with native people new approaches to policing, make it known that native recruits were desired on the force, and develop a strong cross-cultural training course for officers in the department.

In cities such as Winnipeg, Regina, and Vancouver, municipal police departments have given increasing attention to the special problems of policing natives in the urban environment. Heightened efforts have been made (with little success) to recruit native Indians into policing, and training courses now include a multicultural component.

There has been greater success in developing programs designed to improve relations with native Indians in urban areas. The Vancouver Police Department's Native/Police Liaison Community Program, for example, attempts to improve police–native community relations through cultural awareness training, workshops and seminars and to encourage native peoples to consider a career in policing.

Native Indians in the Criminal Courts

There has also been increased attention to the difficulties encountered by native Indians in the criminal courts. Observers have argued that native Indians often have little or no understanding of the legal proceedings and the language of the court, do not have access to adequate legal services and representation and, because of this, are more often found guilty and sentenced to custody than are white offenders (Wynne and Hartnagel, 1975; Morse, 1976; 1982a; McCarney, 1982).

The following discussion considers the major initiatives, native and non-native controlled, that have been developed to address the problems that native Indians encounter in the criminal court. These include the development of legal services for native peoples, the creation of native courtworker and Justice of the Peace programs, and public legal education programs.

Legal Services for Native Indians

In many areas of the country, native peoples do not have access to legal services, and where such services are available, they may not be utilized. As late as the mid-1970s, Morse (1976) noted that there were no reserve-based legal services programs and that multiple barriers of language, culture, and geographic isolation of many native communities hindered the effectiveness of existing urban-based programs staffed by white lawyers and volunteers. Morse (pp. 535–36) argued, however, that native Indians have needs different from those of other minority groups and that control over the development and operation of legal services programs should rest with the native community and its leadership rather than with provincial and federal ministries.

Efforts to develop legal services programs for natives in urban and rural areas have met with mixed success. The Regina Native Counsel Project was established in 1978 to provide legal services for native Indians and to open lines of communication between native organizations and criminal justice agencies in the city. The project's effectiveness was hindered by the failure to involve native people in the development and implementation of the program and by a lack of funding support from the provincial and federal governments (see Havemann, 1980).

The primary objective of the Thunder Bay District Legal Counselling Service was to increase the availability and accessibility of legal services to native Indians in the rural areas surrounding Thunder Bay, Ontario. The activities of the program focused on advocacy, mediation and negotiation, community education, community development, and law reform (Frewin and Maunula, 1980). Unlike the Regina project, native groups were involved in all phases of program development and operation. While successful in responding to the needs of native clients, poor administration, a high turnover among the board of directors and staff, and poor relations with the native courtworker program in the area impeded its overall effectiveness. The difficulties experienced by the Regina and Thunder Bay projects led Havemann et al. (1984: 60) to conclude that "an appropriate plan to provide legal representation to Indigenous peoples has yet to be designed and implemented successfully."[18]

Native Courtworker Programs

Native courtworker programs were developed to provide assistance to native accused in the criminal courts, or as the Native Counselling Services of Alberta (1982: 59) states, to "act as a bridge between the legal system and Native offenders." The first courtworker program in Canada was created in 1962 with a staff of one and was operated by the Canadian Native Friendship Centre. By the mid-1980s, courtworker programs were operating in all territories and provinces and were engaged in a wide range of activities designed to assist native clients, the court system, and native communities. In Saskatchewan and Ontario, native courtworker programs are operated by the Friendship Centres, although a decision by the Government of Saskatchewan in 1987 to cut off funding for the native courtworker program made its future in that province uncertain.

For native defendants, courtworkers provide information on legal rights and responsibilities and court procedure, assist the accused in making application for legal aid, appear in court with the defendant and assist with the needs of the accused's family. For the court, the courtworker may act as translator, provide information to increase cultural awareness among court officials, assist in the preparation of pre-sentence reports, and speak to sentence. At the general community level, courtworkers may be involved in public legal education, conducting workshops in the community and making school presentations.

The Native Courtworker and Counselling Association of British Columbia, for example, conducts cultural awareness workshops for police officers and assists native peoples with a variety of civil matters. In 1985, the Native Counselling Services of Alberta, with a staff of 156 (90% of whom were native Indian) was involved in criminal courtwork, family courtwork, and young offenders courtwork; operated a halfway house in Edmonton; provided adult probation and parole supervision; sponsored law awareness programs in Alberta schools, a suicide prevention program, and a family living skills program.[19]

Native courtworker programs have become an integral part of the criminal justice system and have generally received high marks from judges, lawyers, and other criminal justice personnel, as well as from native clients. Evaluations of native courtworker programs, however, have revealed several major areas of difficulty, many of which are similar to those afflicting the Indian Special Constable programs.

The dual mandate to serve both the client and the court has resulted in conflicting views of the role of the courtworker. In a review of the Ontario Native Courtworker Program, Obonsawin and Jolly (1980) found significant differences among courtworkers, police, social workers and probation officers in their perceptions of the role of courtworkers. While many viewed the courtworkers' role as one of providing a liaison between the native accused and the court, others believed the courtworker should act as an advocate for the native defendant. There was also considerable variability across the province in how courtworkers carried out their tasks. Similar findings were reported by Fearn and Kupfer (1981) in Alberta and by the Owen Consulting Group Limited (1983) in a review of the courtworker program in Saskatchewan.

Other problem areas that have hindered the effectiveness of the courtworker programs are a lack of formal training and on-the-job supervision, low salaries, and high turnover rates among the courtworkers. It has also been difficult to assess the impact of courtworker programs on either the conviction rates for native offenders or the rates of incarceration (see Hathaway, 1986).

Justice of the Peace Programs

Justice of the Peace (JP) programs are designed to make justice services more accessible to native communities, act as a buffer between natives and the police, increase the sensitivity of the courts to the needs of native defendants and communities, and increase community awareness of, and responsibility for, crime-related problems. In meeting these objectives, JP programs would contribute to reducing the numbers of native Indians in conflict with the law.

Traditionally, native Indians were appointed as lay magistrates (JPs) under section 107 of the *Indian Act*, although in recent times, appointments have been by an order-in-council under provincial legislation (Morse, 1982b). Justices of the Peace hear matters of a less serious nature, including violations of municipal or band by-laws, provincial and *Criminal Code* offences, conduct bail hearings, and issue arrest warrants, summonses, and licence suspensions.[20]

The development of JP programs, however, has been uneven, and their effectiveness has been considerably impeded by the now-familiar problems of lack of training and supervision, pressures on the justice of the peace from the community, low salaries, high turnover, too few sentencing alternatives, and a lack of jurisdiction and authority (Mewett, 1981; Weafer, 1986; Maracle, McCormick, and Jolly, 1982).

One particular difficulty is the underutilization of JPs. In a survey of JP programs in Ontario, Saskatchewan, Alberta, the Northwest Territories and the Yukon, Maracle et al. (1982) found that only a very small number of the appointed JPs were actually serving the hearing cases and, further, that only a small percentage of the JPs were native Indian. These difficulties contributed to the collapse of the Indian JP program in Saskatchewan after only two years of actual operation and continue to afflict programs in other jurisdictions (Government of Canada et al., 1985).

The Sentencing of Native Offenders

The overrepresentation of native Indians in many provincial, territorial, and federal correctional institutions has led researchers to focus on the sentencing stage of the criminal court process. In 1987–88, native Indians represented the following percentages of total inmate admissions to provincial institutions: Ontario, 9%; Manitoba, 55%; Saskatchewan, 66%; Alberta, 31%; British Columbia, 19%; the Yukon, 60%; and the Northwest Territories, 88%. These rates remained fairly constant over the previous five-year period. For federal correctional facilities, native Indians represented 11% of sentenced admissions (Canadian Centre for Justice Statistics, 1989: 122).

In certain jurisdictions within the province, there are extremely high rates of native admissions. Jolly (1982: 84) reported that in the Kenora area in northwestern Ontario, "natives accounted for 75 per cent of the total male admissions and 94 per cent of the total female admissions to the Kenora Jail" during 1980–81. In Saskatchewan, Hylton (1980: 24) found that "male Treaty Indians over fifteen were 37 times more likely to be incarcerated when compared with non-Natives, and Metis/non-Status were 12 times more likely." The rates of confinement for female natives were even higher, Hylton (1980: 24) noting that compared to non-native females, "female Treaty Indians were 118 times more likely to be incarcerated and female Metis/non-Status Indians were 25 times more likely to be incarcerated."

Among the findings of a recent study of native and non-native admissions to federal, provincial, and territorial correctional institutions (Moyer et al., 1985) were the following:

- Native Indians were heavily represented in admissions to custody in the Prairie provinces and in the Yukon and Northwest Territories and constituted a higher proportion of institutional populations than would be expected by their representation in the general population in these jurisdictions.
- In most jurisdictions, native and non-native admissions for provincial offences, *Criminal Code* and non–*Criminal Code* federal violations were similar, with the notable exception of Ontario, where nearly one-half of native admissions were for provincial offences relating to violations of provincial alcohol laws.
- Many of the native Indian admissions were for fine defaults, particularly in Saskatchewan.
- Native admissions to custody in Saskatchewan for non-payment of fines were twice that of non-native admissions, despite efforts to reduce the use of imprisonment through fine option programs.

- In Ontario, 16% of all native admissions were for non-payment of fines on provincial offences.

The sources of this overrepresentation are more difficult to determine. Concern has been expressed that, all other factors being equal, native Indians are more likely to receive a sentence involving custody than their white counterparts. Determining whether the criminal courts "discriminate" against native Indian defendants has proved a difficult task, due in large measure to the complexity of the sentencing process, the variations in available dispositional alternatives and sentencing patterns across jurisdictions, and the lack of controlled evaluations by Canadian researchers.

Probable causes that have been considered include the types of offences committed by native Indians, bias on the part of police officers, Crown counsel, probation officers, and judges, and the deprived socio-economic condition in which many native peoples live. The lack of research on the decision making of the criminal courts makes it difficult to determine the extent to which native defendants receive different dispositions than whites.

Early studies by Schmieser (1974) in Saskatchewan and Hartman and Muirhead (1975) in British Columbia reported that natives did receive different dispositions than whites, although caution must be exercised in generalizing the results of individual studies in individual jurisdictions to other areas of the country. The broad discretionary powers of judges, the variation in the settings (i.e., rural versus urban) in which court decisions are made, as well as the dispositional options available to the court may all influence the response to native Indians in the criminal court (Hogarth, 1971; Hagan, 1977a; Boldt et al., 1983; Jackson, 1982).

Hogarth (1971) found, for example, that the attitudes and perceptions of individual judges played a major role in their decision making, and Hagan (1977a: 609) discovered in an analysis of pre-sentence reports in Alberta that probation officers in rural areas treated native Indians more severely, "without the justification of correlated legal variables (i.e. prior record, offense seriousness, and number of charges)." Native Indians in the rural areas of the province were also more likely to be sent to jail for defaulting on fine payments than were those in the urban areas. These findings suggest the importance of considering the operation and decision making of the criminal court on a jurisdiction-by-jurisdiction basis.[21]

A particularly troublesome area is the high rates of native Indian admissions to custody for default of fines, which tend to be imposed upon conviction of minor crimes, such as liquor and vehicle-related offences. Schmeiser (1974) found that while native Indians committed less serious offences than non-natives, they were more likely to be incarcerated in Saskatchewan provincial institutions, due in large measure to non-payment of fines. Despite the enactment of legislation and the development of fine-option programs designed to alleviate the high rates of admissions for non-payment of fines, the problem continues to exist in many jurisdictions (see Jolly, 1981; Jolly and Seymour, 1983).

Community and Reserve-Based Alternatives to the Court

There has been an increasing interest in developing alternatives to the "formal" criminal court process to address more adequately the needs of native offenders, victims, and communities. Although native Indians do not have the authority to establish tribal courts, several bands and communities have created alternatives to the court that rely more heavily than the court on mediation and other techniques of community-based dispute resolution:

- The community of Povungnituk, Quebec has proposed (Novalinga and Tookalak, 1985) the creation of a local judiciary that would hear cases of a minor nature.
- The Saddle Lake Tribe (1985) has proposed a two-level system of tribal justice, which includes the position of Tribal Peacemaker and a Tribunal Tribe of Jurors that would be involved in mediating and resolving disputes on the reserve.
- Among the recommendations of a recent joint studies report (Government of Canada et al., 1985) is the creation of "peacemaker" courts on reserves in Saskatchewan, which would address community problems, resolve domestic matters, and hear cases of a minor nature.
- In many communities, local justice committees have been established to coordinate community response to crime problems and to act as a liaison with criminal justice officials.

The extent to which these and other proposals will be implemented and have a significant impact on crime problems remains to be determined.

Native Indians in the Correctional System

While native Indians represent a high percentage of the population of many provincial and federal correctional facilities, it is only recently that attention has been given to the development of policy and programs to address the special needs of native offenders during confinement and after release (Solicitor General of Canada, 1988a; 1988b). McCaskill (1985: 68) argues that there has been "little tangible change in the Correctional Service of Canada's policies or programmes" since the 1975 Edmonton Conference, and Havemann et al. (1984: 132) found that most of the published research on correctional programs for natives consisted of "the description of problems."

This lack of research precludes an assessment of the extent to which native inmates may be differentially treated by correctional authorities, parole boards, and probation and parole officers and the consequences of such treatment. There has been, however, increasing pressure upon provincial and federal correctional systems to recognize and address the special needs and requirements of native inmates. Native communities and organizations have become increasingly involved in developing alternatives to incarceration and programs to assist native inmates and parolees. Native prison liaison officers and native correctional workers provide assistance to native inmates and their families, and a number of wilderness camps for native offenders are operated by native organizations in collaboration with provincial correctional authorities. In addition, the Native Brotherhoods and Sisterhoods have become increasingly involved in assisting native inmates.

Since 1984, the Native Counselling Services of Alberta has operated a community residential centre, the Kochee Mena Apartments, which house native inmates released from federal and provincial institutions. A number of programs specifically designed for native Indians are offered at the facility, including a job placement program, an individual counselling program, and a family support program. The centre accepts inmates on day parole, full parole, mandatory supervision, and provincial temporary absence and is funded jointly by the Correctional Service of Canada and the Solicitor General of Alberta.

In the early 1980s, several reports outlined the need for the Correctional Service of Canada to examine federal correctional policy and practice vis-à-vis native Indians (see Newby, 1981; Couture, 1983; McCaskill, 1985). A major issue that emerged from these investigations is the extent to which policies and programs should be designed specifically for native inmates. From an analysis of native Indian inmates in Manitoba, McCaskill (1985: 75) concluded that for a majority of inmates "their 'Nativeness' is an important factor in their definition of themselves and should be recognized as a 'special' need in the development of correctional programmes."

Newby (1981: 111–12) noted, however, that the Correctional Service of Canada had not adequately confronted "the concept that equal (in the sense of the same) treatment for all offenders, when there is a minority group with different cultural backgrounds and needs, etc., may have an unintentionally discriminatory effect to the detriment of that group." Despite these arguments, there are few programs in federal and provincial institutions designed solely for native inmates.

In concluding her investigation, Newby (1981: 95) outlined a number of issues that required attention at the policy and program level, including the hiring of native Indians in the correctional system, the development of native correctional programs such as wilderness camps, the need to address the problems encountered by native Indians in applying for and returning to society under conditional release, and the need to strengthen institutional programs for native inmates. To better address the needs of native inmates, McCaskill (1985: 82) recommended the creation of small working groups at the national level and in those regions of the country where native Indians represent a significant proportion of institutional populations. These groups would oversee efforts to develop policies and programs for natives involved in the correctional system. Other recommendations included the development of cultural awareness training programs for correctional personnel and the need for increased involvement of native groups and organizations in providing programs for native inmates and parolees.

Native Youth and the Law

The consequences of the severe socio-economic condition of many native people in Canada are perhaps most evident in the difficulties encountered by native youth. In many areas of the country, native Indian youth are extensively involved in the youth justice and child care systems, evidence high rates of alcohol and solvent abuse and suicide, and experience considerable conflict in attempting to adapt to mainstream Canadian society while retaining traditional native customs and values (Jolly, 1983; Griffiths, 1987).

Native Youth and the Youth Justice System

Our discussion of native youth and the law is hindered by the lack of current, reliable figures on patterns of arrest, processing by the courts, and confinement in youth facilities. In a study of native youth involvement in the criminal justice system in a northwestern Canadian community, LaPrairie and Griffiths (1982) found that native youths were overrepresented at all stages of the youth justice system and became involved with the law at a much earlier age than did their non-native counterparts. There were, however, significant differences between the native and non-native youths as measured by such socio-economic indicators as education level, living arrangements, family income, and father's occupation. For example, over 70% of the native youths resided in families that were receiving social assistance and in which the father's occupation was listed as "unskilled." However, both the native and non-native youths in the sample were involved in the same types of offences, and the youth court responded in a similar fashion to both groups (see also LaPrairie, 1984a; Kueneman, Linden and Kosmick, 1986).[22]

Increasingly, concern has been voiced about the implications of the

Young Offenders Act (*YOA*) for native youth and about its implementation in native communities, particularly those in remote and rural areas (see Bissonnette, 1985; RES Policy Research, Inc., 1985). Specific concerns have been raised regarding the availability of legal counsel, ensuring separate detainment facilities for youth, and the development of alternative, community-based programs. Many observers have argued that the *YOA* is more relevant to the administration of youth justice in urban areas of the country than to native youths residing in northern and rural areas of the country and that the *YOA*'s emphasis on procedural formalities may actually hinder the development of more informal, community-based mechanisms to address the needs of youth (see Griffiths, 1987).

A survey of the needs of young offenders in Labrador (RES Policy Research, Inc., 1985) found that youths had limited access to legal representation and had difficulty applying for legal aid services. Further, there was a need to develop separate facilities for handling youth and for increased community involvement in responding to needs of youth in conflict with the law (see also Kueneman et al., 1986).

Programs for Native Youth

In recent years there has been a rapid expansion of programs for native youth in conflict with the law, a large number of which are sponsored by Friendship Centres, native communities and organizations and bands. In several jurisdictions, youth courtworker programs have been developed, as well as community-based forums for the resolution of disputes involving youth (see Loucks and Timothy, 1981; Ontario Ministry of the Attorney General, 1985).

The Native Counselling Service of Alberta, for example, operates a youth program that provides a wide range of social and cultural activities for youth, including sports, camping, meetings with elders and field trips (Kupfer and Kupfer, 1983). Across the country, there are numerous band and community-sponsored wilderness programs and youth caravans that expose youth to native culture, traditions, and skills. One of the better known programs is Project Rediscovery, a wilderness experience program in the Queen Charlotte Islands that teaches survival skills, self-confidence, and environmental awareness to native and non-native youths (Nelms-Matzke, 1982).

A major factor in the involvement of native youth with the justice system is alcohol and solvent abuse (Barnes, 1983). In an attempt to address this problem at a community level, the National Native Alcohol and Drug Abuse Program sponsors community projects and programs that are designed and delivered by native people. Many of these programs are directed toward youth and include social and cultural activities as well as education. The Labrador Inuit Alcohol and Drug Abuse Program, for example, sponsors preventive programs, sports tournaments, recreational events, and youth conferences.

While many of the community-based initiatives have suffered from organizational problems and a lack of stable funding, they nevertheless reveal the increased interest of native communities in assuming control over programs for youth.[23]

Taking Care of Their Own: Native Child Welfare Programs

Native youths are also overrepresented in child care systems in many parts of the country, due in part to the deterioration of native family life and the lack of alternative programs and resources at the community and band level. The delivery of child services to native reserves and communities has been impeded by jurisdictional disputes between the federal and provincial governments over the responsibility for the provision of such services and by conflict between the Euro-Canadian approach to child welfare and native values and traditions (Johnston, 1983; Carasco, 1986). This conflict between values and traditions is evident in disputes between native peoples and provincial authorities over the practice of traditional adoption, which is currently recognized only in the Northwest Territories and Quebec. Native groups have also expressed concern with the placement of native children with white families and, in some jurisdictions, the past practice of placing native youth in foster or adoptive homes in the United States.

These difficulties have provided the impetus for the development of native-controlled child and family services, including the Dakota-Ojibway Child and Family Services, which serves eight reserves in southern Manitoba, the Tikinigan Child and Family Services in Sioux Lookout, Ontario, and a child and family service program operated by the Champagne-Aishihik Indian Band in the Yukon (see also McDonald, 1983).

The Delivery of Justice Services in the Canadian North

The areas of northern Canada, comprising the Yukon and Northwest Territories, as well as the northern portions of the provinces, are generally invisible to the majority of Canadians who reside in "southern" urban areas. Few Canadians have had the opportunity to travel north of the 60th parallel or even into the northern-most reaches of their own province, most of which are accessible only by air. These factors have tended to obscure the issues surrounding the delivery of justice to native Indians and Inuit, many of which centre on the applicability and relevance of legislation, policies and programs conceived and delivered by "southerners." The introduction of the criminal law in the Canadian North, however, is a unique and integral part of any study of Canadian criminal justice (see Sissons, 1968; Moyles, 1979; Schuh, 1979).

Given the small size of communities in the North, the role of the police assumes even greater significance than in urban areas. The personal "style" of the police officer(s) in small detachments and the relations that exist between the police and the community will have a significant impact on the rates of arrest and charging, as well as on the success of any community-based initiatives designed to prevent or reduce crime. To be effective, police officers are required to adapt their role to fit the needs of the community in which they are policing.

While police officers are posted in northern communities, judicial services are provided via the circuit court (or "circuit circus," as it is called by many northerners), which has been the subject of increasing attention in recent years. Circuit court parties, comprised of the judge, court clerk, defence lawyer and Crown counsel, travel to communities, generally by air, on a regular basis to hold court. While many communities are served monthly, others are visited every three months, or more infrequently if there are no cases to be heard or if weather or mechanical problems with the court airplane prevent a scheduled visit. The most extensive circuit court systems are in the Northwest Territories, where territorial and supreme court justices travel on six circuits, and in northern Quebec, covering the James Bay and Ungava Bay regions of the province.

Recent years have seen increased concerns voiced about the circuit court system, including the problems of large court dockets that result from backlogs of cases; time constraints on the court party, which often preclude effective defence preparation and result in marathon court sessions, frequently lasting up to 12 hours; the lack of interpretative services for native and Inuit defendants who speak and/or understand little English; and the general difficulties caused by the cultural differences of Canadian law and its practitioners and native and Inuit defendants and the communities in which they reside (Lowe, 1985).

These concerns have led many observers to argue that neither defendants nor the residents of communities understand the function of the court, the role of the various members of the court party, or the court proceedings. Further, it is argued that the dispositions available under the *Criminal Code* do not address the unique needs of individual communities, offenders, and victims (Griffiths, 1985; Kueneman et al., 1986). A major problem confronting the court is whether to remove the offender from the community for a period of confinement or to utilize resources in the community, including native or Inuit elders. In the Northwest Territories, offenders receiving sentences of incarceration are sent either to the Baffin Correctional Centre in Iqualit or to the Yellowknife Correctional Centre.

There is evidence to suggest that the judiciary in the North is becoming more sensitive to the need to tailor dispositions to the offender and to the community in which the offender resides. Crawford (1985: 8–9) notes, for example, that in the Northwest Territories "in as much as cultural factors rarely make a difference in a determination of guilt or innocence, they are always relevant and always appear welcome in speaking to an appropriate sentence . . . the criminal law in the North has been prepared to adapt to the ways of the people who come before it."

While not a unanimous view, it does suggest that a concerted effort is being made to address many of the concerns surrounding the delivery of justice services to northern communities. There is also a trend toward the development of community-based mechanisms for dispute resolution and alternatives to incarceration (Bouchard and Pelletier, 1986).[24] Further evidence of change is found in the recommendation by the Northwest Territories Committee on Law Reform that the *Jury Act* be amended to allow citizens who speak and understand only an aboriginal language to serve as jurors (Northwest Territories, 1987).

Native Indians and Criminal Justice: Emerging Issues

Our discussion in this chapter has revealed the complexity of the issues surrounding native Indians in the Canadian criminal justice system and highlighted the extent to which native and white leaders underestimated the task of reducing native conflict with the law. It is likely that this area will continue to assume a high profile in the coming years. There are a number of major issues that will arise as native Indian bands and communities become more involved in the delivery of justice services:

The Role of Customary Law, Tradition and Native Communities in the Development of Alternative, Community-Based Justice Structures

Much attention has focused on the potential role of native customary law and tradition in creating native-controlled justice services. Considerable difficulties were encountered in attempting to document the principles of customary law in several native communities in Saskatchewan, and the researchers discovered considerable variability among the communities in the extent to which reference to and use of traditional mechanisms of social control existed (Government of Canada et al., 1985: 7–12).

While several recent proposals, such as that by the Saddle Lake Indian reserve in Alberta, incorporate specific elements on customary law and traditional methods of social control, many "autonomous" justice structures involve staffing "white" models, such as police services, with native Indians. There remains a considerable amount of uncertainty among many native peoples concerning how to implement traditional methods of social control and how such structures will interface with the *Criminal Code* and the provisions of the *Canadian Charter of Rights and Freedoms* (Boisvert, 1985; Hawkes and Peters, 1986; Morse, 1984).

The experience to date is that the most successful initiatives in justice delivery are those that originate in, and are fully supported by, the community (see Draper, 1987). Programs designed and implemented from the "outside" have a poor record of achievement. The involvement of the community appears to be a more significant factor in success than the specific reliance upon elements of custom and tradition.

Cultural Awareness Training for Criminal Justice Personnel

Among the recommendations of the 1975 Edmonton Conference was that judges, lawyers and other line-level criminal justice practitioners be required to undergo cultural awareness training to sensitize them to the culture and socio-economic position of the persons with whom they deal. However, the reluctance of the federal and provincial governments to follow through on this recommendation was highlighted by Jolly et al. (1979), who discovered that four years after the conference, little or no action had been taken by either the federal government or the Province of Ontario. More than a decade after the Edmonton Conference, a report from the Quebec Department of Justice (Bouchard and Pelletier, 1986: 82) recommended that ongoing training be provided to justice officials and personnel to sensitize them to "northern social and intercultural realities."

In addition to the cultural awareness training provided to RCMP recruits and other police officers, isolated efforts have been made to sensitize judges, lawyers, and other criminal justice personnel to native culture, traditions, and community life. In Ontario, "Judge's Northern Education Circuits" are sponsored by the Office of the Chief Judge of the Provincial Court. Provincial court judges travel to remote northern communities to meet face-to-face with native peoples and discuss justice-related issues (see Hayes and Jolly, 1986).

The actual impact and benefit of this training is difficult to assess. Loree (1985: 22) found that a majority of both regular members and Indian Special Constables surveyed in the Prairie provinces indicated that prior knowledge of native communities was either of marginal or no use to them in carrying out their tasks. This view is illustrated by the comments of one of the RCMP officers surveyed by Loree (1985: 26): "Basically knowledge of Natives is of no real use in police work. You treat all people the same. Whether they are Native or not. Why should we know more about Natives than Whites."

In a follow-up assessment of a native awareness training program for

Crown attorneys in Ontario, Auger et al. (1984) found that a high percentage of the attorneys stated that the sessions had done little to increase their understanding of native Indians, would likely not affect their charging and sentencing submission practices, and did not affect their basic view that native Indians and whites should be treated equally and individually, on the merits of the case rather than on the basis of race.

The Role of the Friendship Centres

Since the early 1970s, Friendship Centres have played a major role in the development and operation of justice programs in rural and urban areas of the country. Originally formed to assist native peoples who had migrated into urban areas, the number of Friendship Centres and the range of their activities have grown considerably. In 1986, there were 96 Friendship Centres funded by the federal Department of the Secretary of State. Across the country, Friendship Centres are involved in operating courtworker programs (Saskatchewan and Ontario), sponsoring public legal education programs, fund-raising, and initiating programs and services in response to community needs.

Among the activities at the Tree of Peace Friendship Centre in Yellowknife, Northwest Territories, for example, are an alcohol program, counselling, income tax services, camping and recreation programs and adult education programs. The Ma-Mow-We-Tak Friendship Centre in Thompson, Manitoba operates 32 programs, including referral and interpreter services, and the Ne-Chee Friendship Centre in Kenora, Ontario operates a Native Inmate Liaison Worker Program that assists native inmates and their families, a community service worker program, a program for urban native youth entitled "L'il Beavers," and a courtworker program. Increasingly, the Friendship Centres are being viewed by native communities as having a major role to play in the development of community-based programs.

The Needs of Native Victims

Only recently has attention focused on the needs of native victims. Concerns have been raised that victim-assistance programs developed in "southern," urban areas of the country may have limited usefulness and relevance to native Indians, particularly those residing in rural and remote communities. From a review of the major issues involved in providing effective assistance to native victims, G. S. Clark and Associates (1986) concluded that the Friendship Centres, native courtworker programs and other community-based organizations could play a major role in the development of victim services, which would also require the extensive involvement of native communities.

Native Women and the Law

Our discussion of the female offender in Chapter 13 established the overrepresentation of native women in federal and provincial/territorial institutions across the country. Despite this, there is a lack of empirical studies that examine patterns of criminality among native women, their involvement at various stages of the criminal justice process, and the policy and program issues raised when native women come into conflict with the law (see LaPrairie, 1984a; 1984b).

In the Northwest Territories, the Female Offender Study Committee (Martin, 1985) identified the need to develop programs to improve life management skills and increase economic self-sufficiency and to expand community-based programs. A study by Dubec (1982; cited in Havemann, 1984) found that native women inmates in Ontario provincial institutions were not participating in educational and vocational training programs and that there was a need to develop community-based programs and services. It is evident that a considerable amount of work — by researchers, policy makers and planners, and native bands and organizations — remains to be done in the area of native women and their involvement in the criminal justice system.

NOTES

1. No less important in the study of criminal justice in Canada is the involvement of other ethnic/religious minority groups with the law historically and in contemporary times. See Chan and Hagan (1982) and Chong (1985) for examinations of Chinese and the law. See Yerbury (1984) for a discussion of Doukhobors and the Canadian state.
2. For background reading on contemporary issues in Canadian native studies, see Steltzer (1982); Getty and Lussier (1983); Frideres (1983); Ponting (1986). Keon-Cohen (1982) provides a comparative analysis of native justice issues in Canada, Australia, and the United States, and the materials edited by Morse (1985) address issues related to the native Indian, Métis and Inuit rights in Canada. See also Michalis and Badcock (1979).
3. For research findings on the perceptions of native peoples held by non-natives, see Cooke (1984).
4. See Siggner (1979); Siggner and Locatelli (1981). The Department of Indian and Northern Affairs has published a series of overviews of the demographic, social and economic conditions among registered Indians in the provinces. Cf. Siggner and Locatelli (1981); Siggner et al. (1982b; 1983).
5. Perhaps the most insightful views of native Indian life in Canada are provided by community studies. See Braroe (1975), Condon (1987), Lithman (1978) and Shkilnyk (1985). See also Brody (1981).

6. Much of the material on native Indians and the criminal justice system is unpublished and has been inaccessible to students, researchers, government agencies, and native communities and organizations. Two of the more extensive collections of materials on native Indians and the criminal justice system are the Northern Justice Society Resource Centre at Simon Fraser University and the Native Law Centre at the University of Saskatchewan. Readers seeking additional information on issues discussed in this chapter should contact these resources.

7. For a discussion of the competing explanations for the overrepresentation of native Indians in the criminal justice system, see Havemann et al. (1984).

8. A discussion of the extensive literature on native Indian drinking is beyond the scope of this text. However, given its significance to any consideration of native Indians and the criminal justice system, the reader is urged to become familiar with the literature in this area. See Levy and Kunitz (1974); Leland (1976); May (1982b).

9. For an examination of the problems surrounding battered native women on reserves and the police, see Marrison (1984).

10. These same officers identified the two most serious problems in policing non-native communities as "Dealing with Young People" and "Mistrust of the Police," raising issues that should be examined by further research (Loree, 1985: 39). Loree's study is perhaps the most comprehensive analysis of policing in native communities conducted to date. See also Depew (1986) for a discussion of the major issues surrounding native policing.

11. The personal "style" of the police officer becomes extremely important in small detachments of one or two officers and can determine whether relations with the community are characterized by conflict and suspicion or cooperation and understanding. The officer's orientation toward the police task can also have a significant impact on the "official" crime rate in the community, depending upon whether a crime control or community policing orientation is taken.

12. In addition to providing sessions on native culture and native awareness training for recruits undergoing training at the Training Depot in Regina, the RCMP offers a course for instructors of multicultural education at the Canadian Police College in Ottawa. This course is open to members of police departments from across the country. Such training, however, may not replace the stereotypes of native peoples that officers develop, nor may it function to shift the focus of officers from a crime control/law enforcement orientation to include more community activities (Loree, 1985: 94).

13. In 1976, the RCMP established a Native Policing Branch at Headquarters in Ottawa, with Native Policing Coordinators assigned to each RCMP division across the country. The Native Policing Coordinator is charged with developing positive working relationships with native peoples, as well as with creating programs and services that meet the needs of native peoples and communities.

14. In examining the work of the Task Force and the rationale used for the adoption of Option 3b, Griffiths and Yerbury (1984: 18) argue that the members of the Task Force were strongly influenced by the preferences of the RCMP for Option 3b, citing a footnote early in the report that stated that close relations were established with the RCMP at an early stage and numerous meetings were held "to agree on the national acceptability of option 3(b)." Further, no evidence was presented by the Task Force to support the conclusion that there was a "widely shared Indian preference for option 3b."

15. Depew (1986: 41) contends that the lack of consensus on the viability of the Option 3b policing program is due at least in part to "the specific values and expectations held by program evaluators and their sponsors concerning such unresolved policy issues as separate, autonomous native police forces." A similar point was made by Havemann et al. (1984: 37): "Most studies done by or for Indigenous organizations approve of autonomous policing while those done by or for government agencies appear to prefer policing by special constables." These observers have raised a significant point that relates not only to the specific issue of the ISC program, but also to the evaluation of such programs and the potential bias of the agencies funding such inquiries.

16. Caution must be exercised in using the terms *native-controlled* and *autonomous* to describe native policing programs. As Depew (1968: 55) notes, such terms may merely connote the administrative and operational separation of a native police force from federal, provincial, or municipal forces, rather than the total control of such programs by native communities or bands. The majority of native-controlled police programs, for example, rely heavily upon funding from the federal and/or provincial government. Non-native representatives from these agencies often sit as members of the commissions or boards that oversee the operation of the police program.

17. There are several reports that present the major issues surrounding native policing programs and also include the findings of evaluation studies. See Native Counselling Services of Alberta (1980); Social Policy Research Associates/the Evaluation Group Incorporated (1983b); Havemann et al. (1984); and Depew (1986).

18. Programs have also been developed by the legal services societies and commissions across the country. The Legal Services Society of British Columbia, for example, has a Native Programs Department that operates Native Community Offices and sponsors various legal information projects.

19. The activities of courtworker programs vary considerably across the provinces and territories, particularly between programs operating in urban areas and those serving rural and remote communities. Readers are encouraged to become familiar with the activities of the native court-worker program in their area.

20. In contrast to native Indian tribes in the United States, Canadian natives do not have the authority to establish tribal or band courts (Keon-Cohen, 1982). For a discussion of the structure of tribal courts on reserves in the United States, as well as the major issues surrounding their operation, see Deloria and Lytle (1983) and Brakel (1978). See also Morse (1980) for an examination of the issues surrounding the creation of tribal courts in Canada.

21. One particularly difficult problem in studying native Indians in the criminal courts involves the issue of discrimination. While discrimination is generally seen to occur when the criminal court responds differently to native Indian and white defendants (all other case factors being equal), Hagan (1977b) argues that the equal treatment of unequal groups (i.e., native Indians and whites as measured by socio-economic indicators) constitutes discrimination. Equal penalties for a native Indian and a white defendant, such as imposing payment of a fine, may have unequal consequences for each, depending upon their ability to pay. As Verdun-Jones and Muirhead (1979/80: 17) point out, "the even-handed application of laws has very little (if anything) to do with the 'justice' of those laws."

22. In both the LaPrairie and Griffiths (1982) and the Kueneman et al. (1986) studies, concerns were raised about the equal treatment of native and non-native youths in the court. As Kueneman et al. note: ". . . it could be argued that such a uniform decision-making process is inadequate as it does not consider the individual circumstances and needs of the offender when arriving at a disposition" (p. 148). However, at the court stage, it is likely that such a consideration would only result in more severe dispositions being imposed on native youths, a consequence of equal concern.

23. For additional information on specific programs and services for native youth and discussions of the key issues surrounding native youth and the youth justice and child welfare systems, see Griffiths (1985; 1987).

24. Many of the issues associated with the operation of the circuit court and the role of traditional, community-based mechanisms of social control are presented in the film *Arctic Bay: A Community and the Court.* This film documents a sentencing hearing in an Inuit community on Baffin Island in which the presiding judge must decide whether to remove a young adult convicted of sexual assault from the community or give over supervision of the offender to the council of elders in the community. The film is available from Magic Lantern Films, 136 Cross Avenue, Oakville, Ontario, L6J 2W6. A documentary film has also been completed on the circuit court that services the Cree and Inuit communities in northern Quebec. The film is entitled *White Justice* and may be obtained from Parlimage Inc., 4398 boul. Saint-Laurent, Suite 103, Montreal, Quebec, H2W 1Z5.

REFERENCES

Alberta Board of Review. Provincial Courts. 1978. *Native People in the Administration of Justice in the Provincial Courts of Alberta.* Edmonton: Attorney General of Alberta.

Asch, M. 1984. *Home and Native Land: Aboriginal Rights and the Canadian Constitution.* Toronto: Methuen.

Auger, D., et al. 1984. *On the Path to Cultural Awareness.* Toronto: Ontario Native Council on Justice and Ontario Ministry of the Attorney General.

Barnes, G. E. 1983. *Northern Sniff: The Epidemiology of Drug Use among Indian, White and Métis Adolescents.* Ottawa: Health and Welfare Canada.

Bienvenue, R., and A. H. Latif. 1974. "Arrests, Dispositions, and Recidivism: A Comparison of Indians and Whites." 16 *Canadian Journal of Criminology and Corrections* 105–16.

Birkenmayer, A. C., and S. Jolly. 1981. *The Native Inmate in Ontario.* Toronto: Ontario Native Council on Justice.

Bissonnette, A. 1985. *Native Juveniles and Criminal Law. Preliminary Study of Needs and Services in Some Native Communities of Quebec.* Ottawa: Department of Justice.

Boisvert, D. A. 1985. *Forms of Aboriginal Self-government.* Kingston: Institute of Intergovernmental Relations, Queen's University.

Boldt, E. D., L. E. Hursh, S. D. Johnson, and K. W. Taylor. 1983. "Presentence Reports and the Incarceration of Natives." 25 *Canadian Journal of Criminology* 269–76.

Bostrom, H. 1984. "Recent Evolution of Canada's Indian Policy." In *The Dynamics of Government Programs for Urban Indians in the Prairie Provinces,* edited by R. Breton and G. Grant, 519–54. Montreal: Institute for Research on Public Policy.

Bouchard, G. 1985. "The Quebec Provincial Police Native Policing Program." In *Circuit and Rural Court Justice in the North,* edited by C. T. Griffiths, 2.19–2.20. Burnaby, B.C.: Northern Justice Society Resource Centre, Simon Fraser University.

Bouchard, S., and C. Pelletier. 1986. *Justice in Question — Evaluation of Projects to Create a Local Judiciary in Povungnituk (Northern Quebec).* Quebec City: Quebec Department of Justice.

Brakel, S. J. 1978. *American Indian Tribal Courts: The Costs of Separate Justice.* Chicago: American Bar Association.

Braroe, N. W. 1975. *Indian and White: Self-image and Interaction in a Canadian Plains Community.* Stanford: Stanford University Press.

Brody, H. 1981. *Maps and Dreams.* Vancouver: Douglas and McIntyre.

Bryant, V. M., F. J. Hawkes, and J. S. MacHan. 1978. *Evaluation of the R.C.M.P. Special Constable Program (Option 3b).* Ottawa: Department of Indian Affairs and Northern Development.

Canadian Corrections Association. 1967. *Indians and the Law. A Survey Prepared for the Honourable Arthur Laing.* Ottawa: Queen's Printer.

Canfield, C., and L. Drinnan. 1981. *Comparative Statistics — Native and Non-native Federal Inmates: A Five Year History.* Ottawa: Correctional Service of Canada.

Canadian Centre for Justice Statistics. 1989. *Adult Correctional Services in Canada, 1987–88.* Ottawa: Supply and Services Canada.

Carasco, E. F. 1986. "Canadian Native Children: Have Child Welfare Laws Broken the Circle?" 5 *Canadian Journal of Family Law* 111–38.

Chan, J., and J. Hagan. 1982. *Law and the Chinese in Canada: A Case Study in Ethnic Perceptions of the Law.* Toronto: Centre of Criminology, University of Toronto.

Chong, M. Y. L. 1985. "Conflict, Law and Social Control: A Descriptive Study of the Relationship between Chinese and the Legal System in British Columbia, 1858–1923." M.A. thesis. Burnaby, B.C.: School of Criminology, Simon Fraser University.

Clark, G. S., and Associates. 1986. *Native Victims in Canada: Issues in Providing Effective Assistance.* Ottawa: Solicitor General of Canada.

Clatworthy, S. J. 1980. *The Demographic Composition and Economic Circumstances of Winnipeg's Native Population.* Winnipeg: Institute of Urban Studies, University of Winnipeg.

Condon, R. G. 1987. *Inuit Youth: Growth and Change in the Canadian Arctic.* New Brunswick, N.J.: Rutgers University Press.

Cooke, K. 1984. *Images of Indians Held by Non-Indians: A Review of Current Canadian Research.* Ottawa: Department of Indian and Northern Affairs.

Couture, J. E. 1983. *Traditional Aboriginal Spirituality and Religious Practice in Federal Prisons. An Interim Statement on Policy and Procedures. Working Paper No. 1.* Edmonton: Correctional Service of Canada.

Cowley, D. C., and R. Merasty. 1982. *Native Recruitment Study.* Regina: Regina Police Service.

Crawford, A. 1985. "Outside Law and Traditional Communities in the Northwest Territories." Unpublished paper. Available from the Northern Justice Society Resource Centre, Simon Fraser University.

Deloria, V., and C. Lytle. 1983. *American Indians, American Justice.* Austin: University of Texas Press.

Department of Indian and Northern Affairs. 1980. *Indian Conditions: A Survey.* Ottawa: Supply and Services Canada.

Depew, R. 1986. *Native Policing in Canada: A Review of Current Issues.* Ottawa: Solicitor General of Canada.

Draper, C. 1987. "The Creation and Operation of Crisis Intervention Programs: The Case of Grassy Narrows, Ontario." In *Northern Youth in Crisis: A Challenge For Justice,* edited by C. T. Griffiths, 17–27.

Burnaby, B.C.: Northern Justice Society Resource Centre, Simon Fraser University.

Driben, P., and R. S. Trudeau. 1983. *When Freedom is Lost: The Dark Side of the Relationship between Government and the Fort Hope Band.* Toronto: University of Toronto Press.

Fearn, L., and G. Kupfer. 1981. *Criminal Courtworker: Native Counselling Services of Alberta. A Program Review and Evaluation Assessment.* Ottawa: Policy Planning and Development Branch, Department of Justice.

Finkler, H. 1976. *Inuit and the Administration of Criminal Justice in the Northwest Territories: The Case of Frobisher Bay.* Ottawa: Indian and Northern Affairs.

_____. 1982. "Corrections in the Northwest Territories 1967–1981, With a Focus on the Incarceration of Inuit Offenders." 5 *Canadian Legal Aid Bulletin* 27–38.

Frewin, C. C., and F. A. Maunula. 1980. *A Process Evaluation of the Thunder Bay Native Legal Counselling Service.* Thunder Bay, Ont.

Frideres, J. S. 1983. *Canada's Indians: Contemporary Conflicts.* 2nd ed. Scarborough: Prentice-Hall.

Getty, I. A., and A. S. Lussier, 1983. *As Long as the Sun Shines and Water Flows — A Reader in Canadian Native Studies.* Vancouver: University of British Columbia Press.

Government of Canada, Government of Saskatchewan, and the Federation of Saskatchewan Indian Nations. 1984. *Joint Canada-Saskatchewan-FSIN Studies of Certain Aspects of the Justice System as They Relate to Indians in Saskatchewan. A Report Prepared by the Working Group on "Law Enforcement."* Ottawa: Department of Justice.

_____. 1985. *Reflecting Indian Concerns and Values in the Justice System.* Ottawa: Solicitor General of Canada.

Griffiths, C. T. 1985. *Circuit and Rural Court Justice in the North.* Burnaby, B.C.: Northern Justice Society, Simon Fraser University.

_____. 1987. *Northern Youth in Crisis: A Challenge for Justice.* Burnaby, B.C.: Northern Justice Society, Simon Fraser University.

Griffiths, C. T., and J. C. Yerbury. 1984. "Natives and Criminal Justice Policy: The Case of Native Policing." 26 *Canadian Journal of Criminology* 147–60.

Griffiths, C. T., J. C. Yerbury, and L. F. Weafer. 1987. Canada's Natives: The Victims of Socio-Structural Deprivation?" 46 *Human Organization* 277–82.

Hagan, J. 1977a. "Criminal Justice in Rural and Urban Communities: A Study of the Bureaucratization of Justice." 55 *Social Forces* 597–611.

_____. 1977b. "Finding 'Discrimination': A Question of Meaning." 4 *Ethnicity* 177–87.

_____. 1985. "Toward a Structural Theory of Crime, Race and Gender." 31 *Crime and Delinquency* 129–46.

Hartman, D. M., and G. K. Muirhead. 1975. *Analysis of Native Indian Admissions to the B.C. Correctional System for 1974.* Victoria: Corrections Branch, Ministry of the Attorney General.

Hathaway, J. C. 1986. "Native Canadians and the Criminal Justice System: A Critical Examination of the Native Courtworker Program." 49 *Saskatchewan Law Review* 201–37.

Havemann, P. 1980. *The Regina Native Counselling Project: A Legal Service for Native Organizations, Groups and Societies in the City of Regina.* Regina: Prairie Justice Research Consortium, University of Regina.

Havemann, P., K. Crouse, L. Foster, and R. Matonovich. 1984. *Law and Order for Canada's Indigenous People.* Ottawa: Solicitor General of Canada.

Hawkes, D. C., and E. J. Peters. 1986. *Implementing Aboriginal Self-Government: Problems and Prospects.* Kingston: Institute of Intergovernmental Relations, Queen's University.

Hayes, Chief Judge F. C., and S. Jolly. 1986. *Ontario Native Justice of the Peace Program. Progress Report.* Toronto: Office of the Chief Judge, Provincial Court of Ontario.

Hogarth, J. 1971. *Sentencing as a Human Process.* Toronto: University of Toronto Press.

Hylton, J. H. 1980. *Admissions to Saskatchewan Correctional Centres: Projections to 1993.* Regina: Prairie Justice Research Consortium, University of Regina.

————. 1982. "The Native Offender in Saskatchewan: Some Implications for Crime Prevention Programming." 24 *Canadian Journal of Criminology* 121–31.

Jackson, M. A. 1982. *Judicial Attitudes towards Sentencing Options.* Toronto: Ministry of Correctional Services, Province of Ontario.

Johnston, P. 1983. *Native Children and the Child Welfare System.* Toronto: Canadian Council on Social Development and James Lorimer and Company.

Jolly, S. 1981. *Preliminary Report on a Survey of Fine Defaulters Incarcerated in the Kenora District Jail for Provincial Offences.* Toronto: Ontario Native Council on Justice.

————. 1982. "Natives in Conflict with the Law." 2 *Correctional Options* 83–84.

————. 1983. *The Kids Are Hurting — Fact Sheet on the Disproportionate Involvement of Indian Young People in the Juvenile Justice and Child Welfare Systems of Ontario, 1981–82.* Toronto: Ontario Native Council on Justice.

Jolly, S., C. Peters, and S. Spiegel. 1979. *Progress Report on Government Action Taken Since the 1975 Federal-Provincial Conference on Native Peoples and the Criminal Justice System.* Ottawa and Toronto: Solicitor General of Canada and Ontario Native Council on Justice.

Jolly, S., and J. P. Seymour. 1983. *Anicinabe Debtors' Prison: Final Report to the Ontario Native Council on Justice on a Survey of Fine Defaulters and Sentenced Offenders Incarcerated in the Kenora District Jail for Provincial Offences.* Toronto: Ontario Native Council on Justice.

Kellough, G. 1980. "From Colonialism to Imperialism: The Experience of Canadian Indians." In *Structured Inequality in Canada*, edited by J. Harp and J. R. Hofley, 343–77. Scarborough: Prentice-Hall.

Keon-Cohen, B. A. 1982. "Native Justice in Australia, Canada and the U.S.A.: A Comparative Analysis." 5 *Canadian Legal Aid Bulletin* 187–250.

Kueneman, R., R. Linden, and R. Kosmick. 1986. *A Study of Manitoba's Northern and Rural Juvenile Courts.* Ottawa: Solicitor General of Canada.

Kupfer, G., and L. Kupfer. 1983. *NEYUNAN Review. Native Counselling Services of Alberta's Native Youth Project.* Ottawa: Consultation Centre, Solicitor General of Canada.

LaPrairie, C. P. 1984a. "Native Juveniles in Court: Some Preliminary Observations." In *Deviant Designations: Crime, Law and Deviance in Canada*, edited by T. Fleming and L. A. Visano, 337–50. Toronto: Butterworths.

———. 1984b. "Selected Criminal Justice and Socio-Demographic Data on Native Women." 26 *Canadian Journal of Criminology* 161–69.

———. 1984c. "Native Women and Crime." 7 *Perception* 25–27.

LaPrairie, C. P., and C. T. Griffiths. 1982. "Native Indian Delinquency and the Juvenile Court: A Review of Recent Findings." 5 *Canadian Legal Aid Bulletin* 39–46.

Leland, J. 1976. *Firewater Myths: North American Indian Drinking and Alcohol Addiction.* New Brunswick, N.J.: Rutgers Center of Alcohol Studies, Rutgers University.

Leslie, J., and R. Maguire. 1978. *The Historical Development of the Indian Act.* Ottawa: Indian Affairs and Northern Development.

Levy, J. E., and S. J. Kunitz. 1974. *Indian Drinking: Navajo Practices and Anglo-American Theories.* New York: John Wiley and Sons.

Lithman, Y. G. 1978. *The Community Apart: A Case Study of a Canadian Indian Reserve Community.* Stockholm: Department of Anthropology, University of Stockholm.

Loree, D. J. 1985. *Policing Native Communities.* Ottawa: Canadian Police College.

Loucks, B., and A. Timothy. 1981. *Justice-Related Children and Family Services for Native People in Ontario: A Discussion Paper.* Toronto: Ontario Native Council on Justice.

Lowe, M. 1985. "Wrist-Watch Justice." *Canadian Lawyer*, June, 29–34.

Maracle, S., C. McCormick, and S. Jolly. 1982. *The Native Justice of the Peace: An Under-employed Natural Resource for the Criminal Justice System.* Toronto: Ontario Native Council on Justice.

Marrison, P. 1984. *Battered Native Women: A Review of Police Powers and Services Available to Reserves.* Ottawa: Indian and Inuit Affairs.

Martin, C. (Chair). 1985. *Female Offender Study Committee. Report to the Minister.* Yellowknife: Department of Health and Social Services, Corrections Division.

May, P. A. 1982a. "Contemporary Crime and the American Indian: A Survey and Analysis of the Literature." 27 *Plains Anthropologist* 225–38.

———. 1982b. "Substance Abuse and the American Indian: Prevalence and Susceptibility." 17 *International Journal of the Addictions* 1185–1209.

McCarney, R. A. 1982. *Legal Services for Native People in Canada.* Ottawa: Canadian Law Information Council.

McCaskill, D. 1970. *A Study of the Needs and Resources Related to Offenders of Native Origin in Manitoba.* Ottawa: Solicitor General of Canada.

———. 1981. "The Urbanization of Indians in Winnipeg, Toronto, Edmonton, and Vancouver: A Comparative Analysis." 1 *Culture* 82–89.

———. 1985. *Patterns of Criminality and Correction among Native Offenders in Manitoba: A Longitudinal Analysis.* Saskatoon: Prairie Region, Correctional Service of Canada.

McDonald, J. A. 1983. "The Spallumcheen Indian Band By-law and Its Potential Impact on Native Indian Child Welfare Policy in British Columbia." 4 *Canadian Journal of Family Law* 75–95.

Métis and Non-status Indian Crime and Justice Commission. 1977. *Report.* Ottawa: Supply and Services Canada.

Mewett, A. W. 1981. *Report to the Attorney General of Ontario on the Office and Function of Justices of the Peace in Ontario.* Toronto: Attorney General of Ontario.

Michalis, G., and W. T. Badcock. 1979. *Native People and Canada's Justice System: Programmes and Issues.* Vol. 2. Ottawa: Indian and Northern Affairs.

Morrison, R. B., and C. R. Wilson. 1986. *Native Peoples — The Canadian Experience.* Toronto: McClelland and Stewart.

Morse, B. W. 1976. "Native People and Legal Services in Canada." 22 *McGill Law Journal* 504–40.

———. 1980. *Indian Tribal Courts in the United States: A Model for Canada?* Saskatoon: Native Law Centre, University of Saskatchewan.

———. 1982a. "The Original Peoples of Canada." 5 *Canadian Legal Aid Bulletin* 1–16.

———. 1982b. "A Unique Court: S. 107 Indian Act Justices of the Peace." 5 *Canadian Legal Aid Bulletin* 131–50.

———. 1984. *Aboriginal Self-Government in Australia and Canada.* Kingston: Institute of Intergovernmental Relations, Queen's University.

———. 1985. *Aboriginal Peoples and the Law: Indian, Métis and Inuit Rights in Canada.* Ottawa: Carleton University Press.

Moyer, S., F. Kopelman, C. LaPrairie, and B. Billingsley. 1985. *Native and Non-native Admissions to Provincial and Territorial Correctional Institutions.* Ottawa: Solicitor General of Canada.

Moyles, R. G. 1979. *British Law and Arctic Men.* Saskatoon: Western Producer Prairie Books.

Murphy, C., and G. Muir. 1985. *Community-Based Policing: A Review of the Critical Issues.* Ottawa: Royal Canadian Mounted Police and Solicitor General of Canada.

Native Counselling Services of Alberta. 1980. *Policing on Reserves: A Review of Current Programs and Alternatives.* Edmonton.

——. 1982. "Native People in the Criminal Justice System: The Role of the Native Courtworker." 5 *Canadian Legal Aid Bulletin* 55–64.

Native Counselling Services of Alberta and Native Affairs Secretariat. 1985. *Demographic Characteristics of Natives in Edmonton.* Edmonton.

Nelms-Matzke, J. 1982. *Rediscovery Program: A Review.* Ottawa: Solicitor General of Canada.

Newby, L. 1981. *Native People of Canada and the Federal Corrections System — Development of a National Policy: Preliminary Issues Report.* Ottawa: Correctional Services of Canada.

Northwest Territories. 1987. *Committee on Law Reform. An Act to Amend the Jury Act. Working Paper No. 1.* Yellowknife.

Novalinga, R., and Q. Tookalak. 1985. *Proposal Made by the Inuit Community Council of Povungnituk Concerning Local Judiciary.* Ottawa: Department of Justice.

Obonsawin, R., and S. Jolly. 1980. *Review of the Ontario Native Courtworker Program: Final Report to the Ontario Native Council on Justice and the Ontario Federation of Indian Friendship Centres.* Toronto: Ontario Native Council on Justice.

Ontario Ministry of the Attorney General. 1985. *An Evaluation of the Lay Assessors Program on Christian Island.* Toronto: Research Services, Ministry of the Attorney General.

Ontario Provincial Police. 1982. *Indian Constable Program.* Toronto: Indian and Municipal Policing Section, Ministry of the Solicitor General.

Owen Consulting Group Limited. 1983. *The Native Courtworker Services of Saskatchewan Program Evaluation.* Ottawa: Department of Justice.

Parnell, T. 1979. *We Mean No Harm — Yukon Indian-Police Relations: A Preliminary Study of Attitudes.* Whitehorse: Yukon Association of Non-status Indians.

Penner, K. (Chairman). 1983. *Indian Self-government in Canada: Report of the Special Committee.* Ottawa: Supply and Services Canada.

Ponting, J. R. 1986. *Arduous Journey: Canadian Indians and Decolonization.* Toronto: McClelland and Stewart.

Ponting, J. R., and R. Gibbins. 1980. *Out of Irrelevance: A Socio-Political Introduction to Indian Affairs in Canada.* Toronto: Butterworths.

RES Policy Research, Inc. 1985. *Needs of Native Young Offenders in Labrador in View of the Young Offenders Act. Final Report.* Ottawa: Department of Justice.

Richardson, Boyce. 1975. *Strangers Devour the Land.* Toronto: Macmillan.

Saddle Lake Tribal Justice Centre. 1985. *A Proposed Tribal Justice Model for the Saddle Lake Tribe.* Saddle Lake, Alberta: Alberta Law Foundation.

Schmeiser, D. A. 1974. *The Native Offender and the Law.* Ottawa: Law Reform Commission of Canada.

Schuh, C. 1979. "Justice on the Northern Frontier: Early Murder Trials of Native Accused." 22 *Criminal Law Quarterly* 74–111.

Shkilnyk, A. 1985. *A Poison Stronger than Love.* New Haven: Yale University Press.

Siggner, A. J. 1979. *An Overview of Demographic, Social and Economic Conditions among Canada's Registered Indian Population.* Ottawa: Indian and Inuit Affairs Program.

———. 1986. "The Socio-Demographic Conditions of Registered Indians." (Winter.) *Canadian Social Trends* 2–9.

Siggner, A. J., and C. Locatelli. 1981. *An Overview of Demographic, Social and Economic Conditions among British Columbia's Registered Indian Population.* Ottawa: Department of Indian Affairs and Northern Development.

Siggner, A. J., D. Perley, D. Young, and P. Turcotte. 1982a. *Regional Comparisons of Data on Canada's Registered Indians.* Ottawa: Department of Indian and Northern Affairs.

Siggner, A. J., C. Locatelli, and G. Y. Laroque. 1982b. *An Overview of Demographic, Social and Economic Conditions among Quebec's Registered Indian Population.* Ottawa: Department of Indian Affairs and Northern Development.

Siggner, A. J., D. Perley, and D. Young. 1983. *An Overview of Demographic, Social and Economic Conditions among New Brunswick's Registered Indian Population.* Ottawa: Department of Indian and Northern Affairs.

Singer, C., and S. Moyer. 1981. *The Dakota-Ojibway Tribal Council Police Program: An Evaluation, 1979–1981.* Ottawa: Solicitor General of Canada.

Sissons, J. 1968. *Judge of the Far North — The Memoirs of Jack Sissons.* Toronto: McClelland and Stewart.

Skoog, D., L. W. Roberts, and E. D. Boldt. 1980. "Native Attitudes toward the Police." 22 *Canadian Journal of Criminology* 354–59.

Social Policy Research Associates/The Evaluation Group Incorporated.

1983a. *An Evaluation of the Ontario Indian Constable Program.* Ottawa: Indian Affairs and Northern Develoment.

——. 1983b. *National Evaluation Overview of Indian Policing.* Executive Summary and Main Report. Ottawa: Indian and Northern Affairs.

Solicitor General of Canada. 1975. *Report of the National Conference of Native People and the Criminal Justice System — Native Peoples and Justice.* Ottawa.

——. 1987. *Annual Report, 1985–86.* (Catalogue No. JS1-1986.) Ottawa: Supply and Services Canada.

——. 1988a. *Correctional Issues Affecting Native Peoples. Correctional Law Review Working Paper No. 7.* Ottawa: Solicitor General of Canada.

——. 1988b. *Final Report. Task Force on Aboriginal Peoples in Corrections.* Ottawa: Supply and Services Canada.

Stanbury, W. T., and T. H. Siegel. 1975. *Success and Failure: Indians in Urban Society.* Vancouver: University of British Columbia Press.

Statistics Canada. 1984. *Canada's Native People.* Ottawa: Minister of Supply and Services.

Steltzer, U. 1982. *Inuit: The North in Transition.* Vancouver: Douglas and McIntyre.

Task Force on Policing on Reserves. 1973. *Report.* Ottawa: Indian and Northern Affairs.

Tobias, J. L. 1976. "Protection, Civilization, Assimilation: An Outline History of Canada's Indian Policy." 6 *The Western Canadian Journal of Anthropology* 13–30.

——. 1983. "Canada's Subjugation of the Plains Cree, 1879–1885." 64 *Canadian Historical Review* 519–48.

Van Dyke, E. W., and K. C. Jamont. 1980. *Through Indian Eyes: Perspectives of Indian Special Constables on the 3b Program in "F" Division.* Regina: Royal Canadian Mounted Police.

Verdun-Jones, S. N., and G. K. Muirhead. 1979/80. "Natives in the Canadian Criminal Justice System: An Overview." 7/8 *Crime and/et Justice* 3–21.

Weafer, L. F. 1986. "The Development and Implementation of Community-Based Justice Programs for Native and Northern Communities: The Justice of the Peace Program in the Yukon Territory." M.A. thesis. Burnaby, B.C.: School of Criminology, Simon Fraser University.

Woods Gordon. 1982. *Amerindian Police Program Evaluation.* Ottawa: Department of Indian Affairs and Northern Development.

Wynne, D. F., and T. F. Hartnagel. 1975. "Race and Plea Negotiation: An Analysis of Some Canadian Data." 1 *Canadian Journal of Sociology* 147–55.

Yerbury, J. C. 1984. "Sons of Freedom Doukhobors and the Canadian State." 16 *Canadian Ethnic Studies* 47–70.

LEGISLATION

Criminal Code, R.S.C. 1985, c. C-46
Indian Act, R.S.C. 1985, c. I-6
Jury Act, R.S.N.W.T. 1974, c. J-2
Young Offenders Act, R.S.C. 1985, c. Y-1

16 LOOKING AHEAD: THE FUTURE OF CANADIAN CRIMINAL JUSTICE

The purpose of this text has been to provide an overview of the structure and operation of the Canadian criminal justice system and to identify the major issues surrounding the administration of justice in this country. Rather than attempting to summarize the vast amount of materials covered in the preceding chapters, we have identified a number of areas that are central to future discussions of Canadian criminal justice and are likely to receive the attention of politicians, criminal justice administrators, and researchers. This listing is by no means exhaustive, and instructors and students are encouraged to identify and explore additional areas and issues.

The Changing Patterns of Crime

In our introductory discussion in Chapter 1, it was noted that there is a clear link between the criminal justice system and the larger societal context and that both the form and administration of Canadian criminal justice have been, and continue to be, affected by social, political, economic, religious, and philosophical currents in Canadian society. There are several trends emerging during the late 1980s that will become even more pronounced as the century comes to a close and will pose new challenges to Canadian society and to the criminal justice system (Chappell, 1981; Stephens, 1982).

First, the predictions are that the crime rate in Canada will increase at a slower rate in the coming years, due primarily to the aging of the Canadian population and a corresponding decrease in the size of the crime-prone group of late teens to mid-twenties. The advancing average age of the Canadian population will also create a new group of elderly offenders, presenting unique challenges for the police, judiciary, and correctional authorities (see Goetting, 1984; Newman et al., 1984; Reed and Glamser, 1979).

Second, new types of crime are emerging, many of which pose a greater threat to communities and the country than do the more traditional types of offences (see Bennett, 1987). The Law Reform Commission (Canada, 1985) has proposed that the offence of "crime against the environment" be added to the *Criminal Code*. This would include acts that seriously harm or threaten the environment or pose a threat to human life or health. And Swaigen and Bunt (1985) have identified the need to develop a broader range of penalties and a wider range of sentencing options for environmental offences and offenders. In future editions of the text, we will broaden our consideration of the Canadian criminal justice system and examine the response to white-collar and corporate crime, as well as to other "less traditional" types of offences and offenders.

The recommendations of the Law Reform Commission have provided the basis for increased debate over the use of the criminal law to protect the environment (see Elder, 1984; Emond, 1984; Jeffrey, 1984; Wilson, 1986; see also Starr, 1986). The adoption of criminal sanctions would follow the lead of industrialized countries such as Japan, where environmental pollution that poses a threat to human health and the quality of life has been criminalized. Increased attention is also being given to corporate liability for workplace hazards and to the threat of terrorism against corporations, their employees and facilities (see Koprowicz, 1986).

Third, the spread of computers to nearly every segment of society has created a new category of computer crime, as well as offences involving the piracy of computer software, the use of "logic bombs" and other forms of sabotage designed to destroy computer systems (Makin, 1987). This, in turn, has necessitated the development of security measures to protect computer hardware (see Hertz, 1984; Milrad, 1985; 1986; Roach, 1986).

The Changing Legislative Framework

In Chapter 1, the legislative framework within which criminal justice is administered in Canada was outlined. There is little doubt that legislation has a significant influence on the procedures employed in the administration of justice, although it is less clear whether legislation is able to alter the decision making of criminal justice personnel or the development of criminal justice policy.

The most important process currently underway is the reform of the Canadian criminal law, which will lead, eventually, to a new Canadian Criminal Code. The present *Criminal Code*, virtually unaltered since the 1890s, has been described by one observer as "a patchwork — the product of haphazard accretion rather than systematic change . . . a depository of fossils of social conflicts long since spent" (Del Buono, 1985–86: 370). The formation of the Law Reform Commission in 1970, the work of the Criminal Law Review and the report of the Canadian Sentencing Commission (1987) have provided the basis for parliamentary discussions that will lead to a new Criminal Code.

The most recent piece of legislation is the *Young Offenders Act* (*YOA*), which replaced the *Juvenile Delinquents Act*. The *YOA* has significantly altered the procedures for processing youths through the justice system and includes provisions for the creation of a variety of alternative measures programs in communities. It is not clear, however, that the *YOA* has improved the ability of the youth justice system to respond to the needs of youth. The difficulties of implementing the provisions of the *Young Offenders Act* in northern and rural areas of the country suggest that this procedural framework may not be appropriate or relevant to the needs of communities, victims, or offenders in many jurisdictions.

While legislation may, therefore, determine the parameters within which the criminal justice process is carried out, it is likely to have only limited impact on the exercise of discretion by police officers and parole board members, and will neither reduce disparity in sentencing in the criminal courts, nor address the extensive involvement of native Indians in the criminal justice system. Over the next decade, it will be important to document the influence of the *Canadian Charter of Rights and Freedoms* on the administration of criminal justice in Canada. Observers such as Ericson (1983) have argued, for example, that the *Charter* will serve only to legitimate inequality and will have little direct impact in protecting the rights and freedoms of individuals.

The Fiscal Crisis of the Welfare State and the Impact of Monetarism

The 1960s and 1970s witnessed a rapid expansion of the criminal justice system and a concurrent increase in operating budgets and expenditures. Beginning in the mid-1970s, the federal and provincial governments experienced major financial crises, due in large measure to economic recession. This resulted in a major shortfall between government revenues and the financial resources required to sustain programs and services. Rather abruptly, governments were confronted with the need to curtail growth and this "crisis of the welfare state" led to an increased emphasis on fiscal accountability and restraint in the public sector areas of health care, education and social services (see Taylor, 1983; Lowman and Menzies, 1986).

While the criminal justice system initially continued to expand and appeared to be immune from cutbacks, a retraction of the system occurred during the early 1980s. Criminal justice agencies and organizations adopted the techniques of the private sector, including units of measurement such as "person-year" in the allocation and assessment of the performance of criminal justice personnel and the term *cost per bed* to assess the performance of individual correctional institutions. These and other fiscal terms common to the private business sector were unknown in the field of criminal justice prior to the 1980s.

The increased concern with the fiscal dimensions of criminal justice have created an ongoing tension between the provincial and federal governments over cost-sharing arrangements for the provision of criminal justice services. A major obstacle to the enactment of the *Young Offenders Act* was the dispute between the provincial governments and the federal government over the amount of increased funding the provinces would receive to accommodate the larger number of youths in the youth justice system, occasioned by standardizing the upper age limit at 18. Similarly, ongoing discussions (and disagreements) occur over the amount of monies to be contributed by the federal government in support of contract policing by the RCMP.

The move to private-sector measures of productivity and accountability in the public sector of criminal justice has had profound implications for resource allocation and program development. The era of finite resources and spiralling criminal justice costs have hastened the process of privatization, through which many services and programs are operated by non-profit and for-profit organizations (Genova and Genova, 1983; Pirie, 1985). In recent years, there has been an increase in the number of contracts between the federal and provincial governments and the John Howard Society, the Elizabeth Fry Society, the Salvation Army and other private, non-profit agencies for the delivery of programs and services, particularly in the supervision of adult offenders and in the provision of programs for youths in conflict with the law (see Gandy, 1985).

Concurrent with this has been the expanded involvement of the private, for-profit sector in bidding for contracts to provide justice-related services. In British Columbia, for example, many of the wilderness-experience programs for young offenders, previously operated by the Corrections Branch of the Ministry of the Attorney General, have been "privatized" and are operated on a contract, for-profit basis (see Harrison and Gosse, 1986). The increasing shift to privatization is also seen in the exponential growth of private-security police agencies, parallelling a similar development in the United States, where private police now outnumber their public service counterparts (see Shearing and Stenning, 1981; 1983; 1987).

The privatization of the administration of justice raises numerous questions about accountability, the role that the profit factor has in areas traditionally the responsibility of government, and whether privatization represents a true reform initiative in criminal justice. Ericson, McMahon, and Evans (1987) have argued, for example, that privatization will result in an expansion of control and serve to strengthen rather than decentralize the powers of the criminal justice system. And Ratner (1986) has pointed out that there has been little attention to the possible convergence of social control strategies in Canada with those in the United States due to the impending fiscal crisis.

Further, the limits of privatization must be explored. Is it acceptable, politically and morally, for correctional institutions to be operated under contract, for profit, by private companies, as is currently done in the United States, if such institutions can be built and operated at lower cost by private companies than by government agencies? Or, will the practice of privatizing merely serve to facilitate the expansion of criminal justice structures rather than to precipitate the search for more effective alternatives (Keating, 1985; Logan and Rausch, 1985; Mayer, 1986; Miller, 1986)? Few studies have examined the relative effectiveness, both fiscally and otherwise, of programs and services operated by non-profit and for-profit agencies and organizations as opposed to their governmental counterparts.

The Role of High Technology in the Criminal Justice System

In the coming years, the adoption of high technology may alter significantly the structure and operation of the criminal justice system in Canada while increasing the concerns about the abuse of power and authority of the State and the civil liberties of citizens. Although the criminal justice system has been slow (in comparison with other sectors of society) to utilize sophisticated electronic techniques, there are several areas of the criminal justice process where the introduction of technology is raising legal and ethical issues (see Abella and Rothman, 1985; McCamus, 1985; McDonald, 1985; U.S. Congress, 1985).

Among the police, there is increased reliance on electronic surveillance and videotaping in criminal investigations, although the legal limits of such use are often unclear (Miller, 1985; Canada Law Reform Commission, 1986; Grant, 1987). Concerns have been voiced about the collection and use of computerized police information systems (see Flaherty, 1986). The use of electronic monitoring for supervising offenders placed under house arrest, first in the United States and in 1987 on a pilot project basis in British Columbia, however, portends the adoption of technology in a wide range of areas. These developments may be only the tip of the technological iceberg.

Nevertheless, such strategies may serve only to extend the power of the criminal justice system without improving its effectiveness in addressing the needs of communities, victims, or offenders. If it is acknowledged that criminal justice agencies are largely "reactive" in nature and are able to respond only to the symptoms rather than the causes of crime, caution should be exercised in assuming that the adoption of more sophisticated technologies will solve the crime problem or increase the effectiveness and relevance of the criminal justice response. In the coming years, the application of high technology will raise numerous ethical and legal questions, but may also provide an opportunity to replace the nearly two-century-old techniques of parole, probation, and correctional institutions.

The Role of Communities and the Emergence of Participatory Justice

Our discussion of the history and development of the Canadian criminal justice system has revealed that, over time, community involvement in the administration of justice gradually decreased as the formal agents of control developed and expanded. In the 1980s, increased concern is being voiced about the rising costs and effectiveness of the police, the courts, and correctional systems, and this has been accompanied by the call for increased community involvement in the criminal justice system. This includes the development of community-based mediation and dispute resolution programs and other alternatives to the formal justice process, as well as increased community involvement in programs sponsored by criminal justice agencies.

Despite the initial optimism that accompanied discussions regarding increased community involvement, the results to date have been disappointing. Progress has been hindered by a lack of interest among the general public and a corresponding hesitancy of criminal justice agencies to solicit citizen participation. Citizen involvement is most extensive in crime prevention programs such as Neighbourhood Watch and Operation Identification, although research suggests that even in these programs, public participation is, at best, sporadic and, in most instances, minimal (Rosenbaum, 1987; Turk, 1987). In other areas, such as corrections, it is negligible (Griffiths, 1988). Within the current structure of the criminal justice system, there are few opportunities for community involvement on other than a peripheral level (see Duffee, 1987). At this juncture, it is unclear whether the necessary structural changes in the criminal justice process can be made to accommodate increased community involvement and participation.

The greatest potential for increased community involvement in the administration of justice appears to be in communities located in rural and remote areas of the country. In many native Indian and Inuit communities, for example, concerns about high rates of arrest and incarceration and about the relevance of Euro-Canadian concepts of justice have precipitated a resurgence of interest in traditional mechanisms of managing community life and have provided the foundation for the development of community-based alternatives to the formal criminal justice process.

A key lesson provided by these community-based initiatives is that programs must address the specific needs and requirements of the individual community and are less likely to be successful if imposed by outside governmental agencies (see Griffiths, 1987). The community and its residents must be the architects of programs and have the personal, community and monetary resources to initiate and sustain programs that address community concerns. This requires that the affected criminal justice agencies demonstrate understanding and flexibility in fulfilling their mandate while allowing communities the autonomy to identify and address their particular needs.

Perhaps it will be the rural and remote communities of Canada, traditionally subjected to criminal justice policy and programs formulated in the "southern" urban centres of the country, that will play a pivotal role in the move toward participatory justice. A participatory justice system, using dispute resolution techniques such as mediation and negotiation and having as a primary objective consensual agreements between parties and a restoration of order, has the potential to be less costly, more efficient, and more effective than the competitive and conflict-oriented approaches of the current adversarial model of criminal justice.

Stephens (1987) and others have argued that participatory justice is the most appropriate model for resolving a wide range of disputes and conflicts in an increasingly pluralistic world (see also Robinson, 1985; Lopez-Rey, 1986). Assuming a more critical perspective, Ericson et al. (1987) contend that communities will be used by the criminal justice system and by the State to legitimize policy and practice and to expand control.

Reform in the Criminal Justice System

Our consideration of the various components of the criminal justice process has illustrated the resistance of this system to substantive structural reform. The inability (or unwillingness) of legislators, politicians and criminal justice personnel to effect change is pervasive. Change, where it has occurred, has taken place at a glacial pace and concern has been expressed that efforts at reform have served only to expand the existing criminal justice system rather than to create alternatives and reduce the "net" of control.

Ericson and Baranek (1985) contend that reform is an essential mechanism of control that serves several functions for the State and criminal justice agencies. Reform initiatives, such as diversion and victim-offender reconciliation programs, have resulted in increased discretion for criminal justice personnel, an expansion of programs, and increased control over ever-increasing numbers of persons. These authors (1985: 262) state: "Reforms packaged and sold as real alternatives within the public culture turn out to really imply more doses of the same in the control culture." This cooptation may extend to reform initiatives emerging from the public section: ". . . when signs appear that citizens might be organizing for reform, state agents move in to monitor developments, participate in events, and ultimately bring the reform effort within their sphere of influ-' ence" (McMahon and Ericson, 1987: 38).

Kalinich and Banas (1984: 63) argue that national task forces and investigative committees, rather than being the source of substantive criminal justice reform, serve only to legitimate the existing system: "What, in effect, commissions affirm is that the existing institutions can solve the crisis at hand, with some modification of their structure, through the application of the collective wisdom of commissions." This is evident in the history of Canadian corrections, as one traces the findings and recommendations of the Brown Commission (1849), the Archambault Committee report (1938), the Fauteux report (1956) and the report of the Parliamentary Sub-committee to Investigate the Penitentiary System in Canada (MacGuigan, 1977). Kalinich and Banas (1984: 63) contend that such commissions and task forces are "conspicuous political symbols" that do little to promote system-wide change.

The continuing difficulties experienced by the federal female offender in Canada, the widely acknowledged failure of correctional institutions to protect the community or assist the criminal offender, and the traditional resistance of elected and appointed legislators and criminal justice policy makers to accept the recommendations of commissions of inquiry and task forces are indicative of the need to create mechanisms of accountability and change at all levels of the criminal justice process.

While reports documenting the existence of problem areas in the administration of criminal justice are numerous, specific initiatives to address these problem areas are few in number. Even the increased pressure on criminal justice agencies to be fiscally responsible may not serve to force such agencies to address these and other readily identifiable problems. An ongoing weakness of the criminal justice system, then, is the lack of mechanisms to ensure accountability and encourage innovation and experimentation. In concluding an insightful consideration of criminal law reform, Ericson and Baranek (1985: 271) pose several questions, including "where do reforms come from? how are they transmitted in governmental, scientific and mass media? how are they legitimated or rejected? what are their political, economic and socio-cultural functions?" These and other questions should provide the basis for more detailed analyses of reform initiatives in Canadian criminal justice (see also Ericson, 1987; Fattah, 1987).

The Role of Research in the Criminal Justice Process

The role of research in the formulation of criminal justice policies and the development of programs and services in the administration of justice is a complex one. There has traditionally been a split between academics and practitioners that has hindered the free flow of information and ideas, although there are other political and bureaucratic factors at work as well. Williams (1983: 3, 4) offers the following characterization of the prejudicial views that academics and practitioners hold of one another:

> The academic researcher is viewed by the practitioner and policymaker as an intellectual who is in pursuit of the trivial, who is slow moving, who lacks common sense, and is not in or of the "real" world. The academic researcher returns the compliment by viewing the practitioner and/or policymaker as being shallow thinkers, moving quickly, oversimplifying, being too political . . . and relying too much on common sense or "gut feelings". The researcher might describe this type as taking the "ready, fire, aim" approach to his work [and] the practitioner would surely counter that the researcher uses the SWAG method — Scientific Wild Ass Guess.

It is unclear to what extent the findings of research impact criminal justice policy and practice in Canada (Solomon, 1983). In discussing the political reaction to social science research in the United States, Newman and Griset (1983) note that research has had an impact in the areas of plea bargaining, the move toward determinate sentencing, and the development of guidelines for sentencing and parole. However, it has generally been ignored in discussions about capital punishment and the use of police discretion. A notable Canadian exception to this dictum was the very significant role played by the report *A Study of the Deterrent Effects of Capital Punishment with Special Reference to the Canadian Situation* (Fattah, 1973) in the debate over the death penalty in 1976/77.

Newman and Griset (1983: 18–20) content that the findings of social science research tend to be rejected when they dispute common sense or challenge cherished beliefs, run contrary to themes of law and order or threaten the entrenched interests of those in criminal justice agencies or organizations. The findings of rational and objective scholarly inquiries may not be welcomed by personnel in a criminal justice process heavily influenced by political demands and bureaucratic agendas. As these authors (1983: 20–21) point out:

> Resistance to change is pervasive. Empirical evidence may threaten economic hardship on personnel in programs that are operating but ineffective . . . as in all bureaucracies, there are entrenched interests in every criminal justice enterprise which are potentially threatened by research demonstrating ineffectiveness, inefficiency or both.

Perhaps the increased emphasis on fiscal accountability will provide the basis for an expansion in the use of evaluative research. Many areas of the Canadian criminal justice system remain unresearched, and numerous programs and services have not been subjected to evaluative inquiries. While many observers have argued that social science research has limited utility for personnel involved in the administration of criminal justice, others contend that the need to secure funding for research has resulted in research that is conceptually weak and largely descriptive. Robinson (1985: 110) describes the current state of criminal justice research as lacking strong theoretical underpinnings, having little historical depth, and being narrowly utilitarian so as to meet the organizational requirements of funding agencies. A critical weakness of criminal justice research, Robinson (1985: 110) argues, is its preference for examining "methodological or quantifiable subsidiary matters" rather than questions of power, so as not to challenge existing ideology or structural arrangements for the administration of justice (see also Alpert, 1984).

Robinson's (1985) observations may be particularly relevant to research on criminal justice in Canada, where the bulk of funding for criminal justice research is provided by the federal Department of Justice and the Ministry of the Solicitor General and provincial ministries and where there are few sources of non-governmental research monies. The extreme centralization of financial resources for criminal justice research may result in government agencies and ministries not only determining the research priorities but also being intimately involved in the conduct of research and in the manner in which the findings of research are disseminated and utilized.

Ericson and Baranek (1985: 267) have argued, for example, that "science sponsored by reformers — and here one would have to include the bulk of the criminological enterprise — . . . tends to make itself useful by conforming with the reformers' definition of the problem as it becomes intertwined with the desired solution." Sponsoring agencies may not only ignore the findings from empirical research, but have, on occasion, "reconstructed" the findings prior to the publication of the final research report and prohibited publication of research findings considered politically damaging (see Harding, 1982).

A discernible trend in criminal justice research in Canada is the increased use of private consultants to conduct criminal justice research on a contract basis, an arrangement that allows government agencies even greater control over the selection of research topics, the conceptual framework, methodology, and the final form of the conclusions and recommendations of the research. In commenting on the situation in the United States (no less applicable in Canada), Maines and Palenski (1986: 584) point out: "Federal guidelines . . . create schedules of requirements concerning contractor materials, services, and timetables which serve to cast the actual research process into bureaucratic moulds." Contract research firms have as an objective not only conducting research but staying in business, and this leads them to "reconstruct their activities in order to present themselves as capable of delivering a viable and useful product" (Maines and Palenski, 1986: 585). Such activities may seriously undermine the integrity of research designs and may significantly affect the final form of research reports.

Criminal Justice in a Multicultural Society

One of the predominant impacts on the administration of justice is the multicultural nature of Canadian society; yet this remains one of the most under-researched dimensions of Canadian criminal justice. The ethnic diversity of Canada may have a significant impact not only on the patterns of crime, but also on the difficulties in administering justice. The numerous ethnic groups in Canada's urban centres, including communities of recent immigrants, present unique challenges for all agencies of the criminal justice system, particularly in relation to groups and communities whose traditional views of justice systems are characterized by suspicion and distrust (Chan and Hagan, 1982; Cryderman and O'Toole, 1986). The religious beliefs of the Doukhobors, which often bring them into conflict with the legal system, present similar challenges (Yerbury, 1984).

Our discussion in Chapter 15 revealed the unique problems encountered in delivery of justice services to native Indian and Inuit communities. The diversity of languages, cultural perspectives, and values presents formidable challenges for a justice system operating under a national Criminal Code and raises numerous issues surrounding the equal application of the criminal law in a pluralistic society (Government of Canada et al., 1985). Despite the importance of the issues raised by the application of law in a multicultural society, too little attention has been given to this area by policy makers, practitioners, and researchers.

REFERENCES

Abella, R. A., and M. L. Rothman. 1985. *Justice Beyond Orwell.* Montreal: Editions Y. Blais.
Alpert, G. P. 1984. "The Needs of the Judiciary and Misapplications of Social Research." 22 *Criminology* 441–56.
Archambault, J. (Chairman). 1938. *Report of the Royal Commission to Investigate the Prison System of Canada.* Ottawa: King's Printer.
Bennett, G. 1987. *Crimewarps: The Future of Crime in America.* Garden City, N.Y.: Anchor Books.
Brown, G. (Chairman). 1849. *Second Report of the Commissioners Appointed to Investigate into the Conduct, Discipline, and Management*

of the Provincial Penitentiary. Toronto: Journals of the Legislative Assembly.

Canada. Law Reform Commission of Canada. 1985. *Crimes against the Environment. Working Paper 44.* Ottawa.

———. 1986. *Electronic Surveillance. Working Paper No. 47.* Ottawa.

Canadian Sentencing Commission. 1987. *Sentencing Reform: A Canadian Approach.* Ottawa: Supply and Services Canada.

Chan, J., and J. Hagan. 1982. *Law and the Chinese in Canada: A Case Study in Ethnic Perceptions of the Law.* Toronto: Centre of Criminology, University of Toronto.

Chappell, D. 1981. "Crime in the 21st Century." Unpublished paper. Burnaby, B.C.: School of Criminology, Simon Fraser University.

Cryderman, B. K., and C. N. O'Toole. 1986. *Police, Race and Ethnicity: A Guide for Law Enforcement Officers.* Toronto: Butterworths.

Del Buono, V. M. 1985–86. "Toward a New Criminal Code for Canada." 28 *Criminal Law Quarterly* 370–89.

Duffee, D. 1987. "The Limits of Community Involvement in Correctional Programs." 64 *The Prison Journal* 56–67.

Elder, P. S. 1984. "Legal Rights for Nature — The Wrong Answer to the Right(s) Question." 22 *Osgoode Hall Law Journal* 285–95.

Emond, D. P. 1984. "Co-operation in Nature: A New Foundation for Environmental Law." 22 *Osgoode Hall Law Journal* 323–48.

Ericson, R. V. 1983. *The Constitution of Legal Inequality.* Ottawa: Carleton University Information Services.

———. 1987. "The State and Criminal Justice Reform." In *State Control: Criminal Justice Politics in Canada,* edited by R. S. Ratner and J. L. McMullan, 21–37. Vancouver: University of British Columbia Press.

Ericson, R. V., and P. M. Baranek. 1985. "Criminal Law Reform and Two Realities of the Criminal Process." In *Perspectives in Criminal Law,* edited by A. N. Doob and E. L. Greenspan, 255–76. Aurora, Ont.: Canada Law Book.

Ericson, R. V., M. W. McMahon, and D. G. Evans. 1987. "Punishing for Profit: Reflections on the Revival of Privatization in Corrections." 29 *Canadian Journal of Criminology* 355–87.

Fattah, E. A. 1973. *A Study of the Deterrent Effects of Capital Punishment with Special Reference to the Canadian Situation.* Ottawa: Information Canada.

———. 1987. "Ideological Biases in the Evaluation of Criminal Justice Reform." In *State Control: Criminal Justice Politics in Canada,* edited by R. S. Ratner and J. L. McMullan, 69–82. Vancouver: University of British Columbia Press.

Fauteux, G. (Chairman). 1956. *Report of a Committee Appointed to Inquire into the Principles and Procedures Followed in the Remission Service of the Department of Justice in Canada.* Ottawa: Queen's Printer.

Flaherty, D. H. 1986. "Protecting Privacy in Police Information Systems: Data Protection in the Canadian Police Information Centre." 36 *University of Toronto Law Journal* 116–48.

Gandy, J. 1985. *Privatization of Correctional Services for Adults.* Ottawa: Solicitor General of Canada.

Genova, L. R., and V. Genova. 1983. "The Future of Policing: Private Security in Canada." 5 *Canadian Criminology Forum* 122–37.

Goetting, A. 1984. "The Elderly in Prison: A Profile." 9 *Criminal Justice Review* 14–24.

Government of Canada, Government of Saskatchewan, and the Federation of Saskatchewan Indian Nations. 1985. *Reflecting Indian Concerns and Values in the Justice System.* Ottawa: Solicitor General of Canada.

Grant, A. 1987. "Videotaping Police Questioning: A Canadian Experiment." (June) *Criminal Law Review* 375–83.

Griffiths, C. T. 1987. *Northern Youth in Crisis: A Challenge for Justice.* Burnaby, B.C.: Northern Justice Society, Simon Fraser University.

———. 1988. "Community-Based Corrections for Young Offenders: Proposal for a 'Localized' Corrections." 12 *International Journal of Comparative and Applied Criminal Justice* 218–28.

Harding, J. 1982. *A Comparison of a Final and Released Government Research Report on Prescribing to the Elderly in Saskatchewan.* Regina: School of Human Justice, University of Regina.

Harrison, E. W., and M. G. Gosse. 1986. "Privatization: A Restraint Initiative." 28 *Canadian Journal of Criminology* 185–93.

Hertz, A. Z. 1984. "Protecting Computer Systems with the Criminal Law." 1 *Computer Law* 61–62.

Jeffrey, M. I. 1984. "Environmental Enforcement and Regulation in the 1980s: *Regina v. Sault Ste. Marie.*" 10 *Queens Law Journal* 43–70.

Kalinich, D. B., and D. Banas. 1984. "System Maintenance and Legitimation: An Historical Illustration of the Impact of National Task Forces and Committees on Correction." 12 *Journal of Criminal Justice* 61–70.

Keating, J. M. 1985. *Seeking Profits in Punishment: The Private Management of Correctional Institutions.* Washington, D.C.: American Federation of State, County and Municipal Employees.

Koprowicz, K. M. 1986. "Corporate Criminal Liability for Workplace Hazards: A Viable Option for Enforcing Workplace Safety?" 52 *Brooklyn Law Review* 183–227.

Logan, C. H., and S. P. Rausch. 1985. "Punish and Profit: The Emergence of Private Enterprise Prisons." 2 *Justice Quarterly* 303–18.

Lopez-Rey, M. 1986. "The Dimensions of Crime." 50 *Federal Probation* 32–34.

Lowman, J., and R. J. Menzies. 1986. "Out of the Fiscal Shadow: Carceral

Trends in Canada and the United States." 26 *Crime and Social Justice* 95–115.

MacGuigan, M. (Chairman). 1977. *Report to Parliament by the Sub-committee on the Penitentiary System in Canada.* Ottawa: Minister of Supply and Services.

Maines, D. R., and J. Palenski. 1986. "Reconstructive Legitimacy in Final Reports of Contract Research." 15 *Contemporary Sociology* 573–89.

Makin, K. 1987. "Computer Systems Hit by Logic Bombs." *The Globe and Mail.* November 3.

Mayer, C. 1986. "Legal Issues Surrounding Private Operation of Prisons." 22 *Criminal Law Bulletin* 309–25.

McCamus, J. D. 1985. "The Protection of Privacy: The Judicial Role." In *Justice Beyond Orwell,* edited by R. A. Abella and M. L. Rothman, 163–87. Montreal: Editions Y. Blais.

McDonald, D. C. 1985. "Privacy and the Criminal Process." In *Justice Beyond Orwell,* edited by R. A. Abella and M. L. Rothman, 193–200. Montreal: Editions Y. Blais.

McMahon, M. W., and R. V. Ericson. 1987. "Reforming the Police and Policing Reform." In *State Control: Criminal Justice Politics in Canada,* edited by R. S. Ratner and J. L. McMullan, 38–68. Vancouver: University of British Columbia Press.

Miller, J. 1985. "The Victim Witness and Video Technology." 8 *Canadian Community Law Journal* 45–51.

Miller, J. G. 1986. "The Private Prison Industry: Dilemmas and Proposals." 2 *Notre Dame Journal of Law, Ethics and Public Policy* 465–78.

Milrad, L. H. 1985. "Computers and the Law: Criminal Code Combats Software Piracy." 2 *Business and the Law* 79–80.

_____. 1986. "Computers and the Law: Computer Crime and the Criminal Code." 3 *Business and the Law* 70–72.

Newman, D. J., and P. L. Griset. 1983. "Political Reaction to Social Science Research in Criminal Justice." In *Criminal Justice Administration: Linking Practice and Research,* edited by W. A. Jones, 1–29. New York: Marcel Dekker.

Newman, E., D. J. Newman, L. Gewirtz, and Associates. 1984. *Elderly Criminals.* Cambridge, Mass.: Oelgeschlager, Gunn and Hain.

Pirie, M. 1985. *Dismantling the State: The Theory and Practice of Privatization.* Dallas, Tex.: National Center for Policy Analysis.

Ratner, R. S. 1986. "Introduction to a Conjunctural Analysis of Social Control in Canada." 26 *Crime and Social Justice* 1–10.

Reed, M., and F. Glamser. 1979. "Aging in a Total Institution: The Case of Older Prisoners." 19 *The Gerontologist* 354–60.

Roach, J. Y. 1986. "Computer Crime Deterrence." 13 *American Journal of Criminal Law* 391–416.

Robinson, C. 1985. "Criminal Justice Research: Two Competing Futures." 23 *Crime and Social Justice* 101–28.

Rosenbaum, D. P. 1987. "The Theory and Research behind Neighborhood Watch: Is It a Sound Fear and Crime Reduction Strategy?" 35 *Crime and Delinquency* 103–34.

Shearing, C. D., and P. C. Stenning. 1981. "Private Security: Its Growth and Implications." In *Crime and Justice — An Annual Review of Research.* Vol. 3, edited by M. Tonry and N. Morris, 193–245. Chicago: University of Chicago Press.

————. 1983. "Private Security: Implications for Social Control." 30 *Social Problems* 493–506.

————. 1987. *Private Policing.* Beverly Hills, Calif.: Sage Publications.

Solomon, P. H. 1983. *Criminal Justice Policy, From Research to Reform.* Toronto: Butterworths.

Starr, J. W. 1986. "Countering Environmental Crimes." 13 *Boston College Environmental Affairs Law Review* 379–95.

Stephens, G. 1982. *The Future of Criminal Justice.* Cincinnati: Anderson Publishing Co.

————. 1987. "Crime and Punishment: Forces Shaping the Future." 21 *The Futurist* 18–26.

Swaigen, J., and G. Bunt. 1985. *Sentencing in Environmental Cases.* Ottawa: Canadian Law Reform Commission.

Taylor, I. 1983. *Crime, Capitalism and Community.* Toronto: Butterworths.

Turk, A. 1987. "Popular Justice in Toronto: A Pilot Study." Unpublished paper. Toronto: Department of Sociology, University of Toronto.

U.S. Congress. 1985. *Electronic Surveillance and Civil Liberties.* Washington, D.C.: Office of Technology Assessment.

Williams, J. R. 1983. "Researchers and Practitioners: Conflict or Consensus?" Unpublished paper. Research Triangle Park, N.C.: Center for Social Research and Policy Analysis, Research Triangle Institute.

Wilson, J. D. 1986. "Rethinking Penalties for Corporate Environmental Offenders: A View of the Law Reform Commission of Canada's Sentencing in Environmental Cases." 31 *McGill Law Journal* 313–32.

Yerbury, J. C. 1984. "Sons of Freedom Doukhobors and the Canadian State." 16 *Canadian Ethnic Studies* 47–70.

LEGISLATION

Criminal Code, R.S.C. 1985, c. C-46
Juvenile Delinquents Act, R.S.C. 1970, c. J-3
Young Offenders Act, R.S.C. 1985, c. Y-1

AUTHOR INDEX

SUBJECT INDEX